Adventure Guide to

Scotland

Martin Li

HUNTER

HUNTER PUBLISHING, INC,
130 Campus Drive, Edison, NJ 08818
☎ 732-225-1900; 800-255-0343; fax 732-417-1744
www.hunterpublishing.com

Ulysses Travel Publications
4176 Saint-Denis, Montréal, Québec
Canada H2W 2M5
☎ 514-843-9882, ext. 2232; fax 514-843-9448

Windsor Books
The Boundary, Wheatley Road, Garsington
Oxford, OX44 9EJ England
☎ 01865-361122; fax 01865-361133

ISBN 1-58843-406-0
© 2005 Hunter Publishing, Inc.

Manufactured in the United States of America

This and other Hunter travel guides are also available as e-books through Amazon.com, NetLibrary.com and other digital partners. For more information, e-mail us at comments@hunterpublishing.com.

Front cover: Castle Eilean Donan, MacRae stronghold,
Loch Duich, Highlands, © *Britstock*

Back cover, spine and interior color photos, © *Martin Li*

Maps by Toni Wheeler, © *2005 Hunter Publishing, Inc.*

4 3 2 1

About The Author

It was during a geology field trip to Arran as a Cambridge undergraduate that Martin Li first visited and fell in love with Scotland. A keen skier, horserider and trekker, he has always had a passion for exploring the adventure and culture of the world's great mountain regions and remote, hideaway destinations in the developed world. A not-brief-enough foray into accountancy and corporate finance hampered travels for several years, although his passion for Scotland's wilderness, mountains and islands remained undimmed. As a freelance writer, he has traveled extensively around the country, writing features on diverse subjects ranging from romantic hideaway hotels to exposing the truth behind the many Scottish stereotypes. Martin lives in London and is a fellow of the Royal Geographical Society.

Acknowledgements

This book would not have been possible without the generous and enthusiastic support of a great many people.

I would like to thank VisitScotland for providing information and help throughout the project. Many regional tourist boards provided invaluable assistance with local information and logistics during my research trips, particularly Caroline Gray (Glasgow), Sally Monro (Highlands), Grizelda Cowan (Fife) and Hugh Sim (Shetland). I would also like to thank Colin Simpson (Highlands) for his excellent advice on hiking, trekking and climbing.

I am indebted to the following for their generous help with transport to and within Scotland on some unforgettably scenic journeys: John Yellowlees (ScotRail); Andy Naylor (GNER); Allan McLean (Virgin Trains); Deborah Brown (Caledonian MacBrayne); and Elaine Tulloch (NorthLink Ferries).

Thanks to Barbara Fraser (Historic Scotland) and Françoise van Buuren (National Trust for Scotland) for providing background information and access to their many fascinating properties throughout Scotland.

I was blessed to be able to stay in some fabulous accommodation and experience numerous superb adventures during my research. I would like to thank my many hosts for their generous hospitality and for giving up their time to share their expertise and local knowledge with me. Above all, I would like to thank them for their wonderful company – many of my memories of chats late into the night beneath star-filled skies, sometimes over a few not-so-wee drams, will stay with me forever. There are too many people to mention individually, but I am sure they know who they are. I cannot wait until we next meet.

Contents

MAPS

Introduction

Perched on the outer rim of Europe and occupying the northern extreme of Great Britain, bonnie Scotland is as incomparably beautiful and alluring as anywhere on earth. Its spectacular topography is sculpted by intense glaciation and fiery geology, creating a breathtaking palette of mountains, lochs and glens, and a jagged coastline splashed with chains of wildly romantic islands. Numerous standing stone circles, burial cairns and forts dating back many thousands of years testify to prehistoric occupation of these unspoiled lands, which today sustain ancient cultures and lifestyles and preserve some of Europe's last surviving true wilderness.

A long and turbulent history ravaged by war and strife has left a legacy of proud castles – some now forlorn ruins, others retaining their full majesty – and poignant, whispering battlefields. Many monuments record Scotland's long history, ranging from Neolithic sites long predating Egypt's pyramids, to preserved medieval cities and fortresses, and magnificent Georgian and Victorian settlements.

A rich and varied culture manifests itself through colorful tartans, Highland Games, the Gaelic language, wide-reaching traditions such as Hogmanay and Burns Suppers, folk songs, fiddle and pipe music at *ceilidhs* (pronounced "kay-lees," these are informal gatherings with traditional music, dance and verse) and, of course, whisky – the water of life.

Romance courses deeply through Scotland. Who can fail to be moved by the poetry of Robert Burns or the haunting lament of a Gaelic ballad? Heroic but ultimately tragic figures such as William Wallace, Mary, Queen of Scots and Bonnie Prince Charlie retain a palpable presence. Their stirring tales of daring and crushed dreams continue to tug strongly at the heartstrings and even today tinge the land with nostalgia and sadness.

Scotland is rich in contrasts; landscapes can change dramatically within an hour's travel. This varied terrain and Scotland's wide, empty spaces offer boundless opportunities to enjoy the great outdoors, most notably hiking, climbing, cycling, sailing, shooting and fishing. Watchable wildlife ranges from eagles, deer, otters and Highland cattle, to seals, whales and basking sharks. And Scotland is the home of golf, with not just world-famous courses such as St Andrews, Muirfield, Carnoustie and Troon, but also a bewildering range of other beautiful and testing options.

Scotland's superb natural larder commands world-wide acclaim. Top chefs and gastronomes clamour for Angus and Highland beef, fish and shellfish to die for. Accommodation ranges from sophisticated city boutiques and stylish loft conversions, castles and grand country houses, to idyllic, romantic hideaways and converted crofts, mills, inns, and even railway carriages and lighthouses.

In so many ways Scotland threatens to overwhelm the senses. Yet, being relatively small and easy to travel around, visitors can readily experience its many wonders for themselves, and so understand the countless charms that make each visit to Scotland so beguiling and unforgettable, and so unlikely to be the last.

History

Prehistoric Settlers

 The earliest evidence of human settlement in Scotland dates from the **Mesolithic** period (8000-4000 BC), a time of hunter-fisher-gatherers that lasted from the end of the last Ice Age until the rise of farming.

During the **Neolithic** period (4000-2000 BC), the first farming communities were established. With the development of permanent settlements, people built communal tombs and monuments such as cairns and stone circles; examples of these are Knap of Howar in Papa Westray (Orkney), Skara Brae and Ring of Brodgar in Orkney, and the Callanish Standing Stones in Lewis.

The Bronze Age (2000-700 BC) began with the introduction of metalworking skills; during this era there was a shift from communal to single burials, marking the increased status of the individual over the collective.

During the **Iron Age** (700 BC-400 AD), in addition to the development of iron-working technology, was increased building of defensive settlements and enclosures such as *brochs* – circular, fortified dwelling towers – like Dun Carloway in Lewis and Mousa Broch in Shetland, and hill forts, such as Eildon Hill (Borders).

The Early Tribes

Scotland's population is a conglomeration of several immigrant and migrant peoples, languages and cultures.

Several barbarian tribes lived in northeast Scotland during the Iron Age, approximately 2,000 years ago. By the third century AD, these tribes had amalgamated to become the *Picti* (the Picts, or "painted people"), as they were named by the Romans in 297 AD. In their three periods of conquest and occupation, beginning in 79 AD, the Romans never conquered the north of Scotland and their hold on the south was precarious and brief. The Romans were initially driven back to their ambitious **Antonine Wall** (built 142-145 from the Firth of Forth to the Firth of Clyde), which they had abandoned by 161. They retreated farther south to their original barrier of **Hadrian's Wall** (built 118-122 from the Solway Firth to the mouth of the River Tyne) but abandoned this, too, by 400, and finally withdrew from Britain in 409.

The *Scotti* – Scots – were invaders who arrived in Kintyre from northern Ireland in the 6th century, and established the Gaelic-speaking **Dalriada** kingdom in what is now southern Argyll. In 563, **Columba**, an Irish missionary, came to Dalriada from northern Ireland and established a monastery on Iona. The **Vikings** launched a series of raids on Skye and Iona in the late eighth century, culminating in the slaughter of 68 Iona monks in 806. The Norsemen eventually settled in Caithness, Sutherland, Orkney, Shetland and the Western Isles.

The Unification of Scotland

The Picts and Dalriada tribes united against their common Norse enemy but suffered a setback in 839 when many Pictish nobles were killed in battles against the Vikings. **Kenneth mac Alpin** (MacAlpin) stepped in and claimed Pictavia. In 843, as king of both the Scots and Picts, MacAlpin founded a new kingdom – **Alba** or, as it came to be known, Scotland. Alba remains the Gaelic name for Scotland.

Stability didn't come easily to the new kingdom despite the efforts of the Christian church to introduce a civilizing and unifying influence. Three 10th-century kings were killed putting down revolts, and a fourth – **Duncan I** – was murdered by **Macbeth** (reigned 1040-57). Duncan's son **Malcolm Canmore** (Malcolm III) won back the throne in 1057 and ruled with his pious queen, Margaret (who in 1250 became Scotland's only royal saint).

English influence increased during the reign of Malcolm's youngest son **David I** (reigned 1124-53), who had spent time at the court of his brother-in-law, Henry I of England. David introduced coinage, established 15 Royal Burghs, including Dunfermline, Edinburgh, Perth and Stirling, and founded several famous abbeys in what is now the Borders region.

Relations with England

The Scottish kings made continuous attempts to extend their border southwards, aided by the political instability following the **Norman invasion** of England in 1066. David won Newcastle and Northumberland but his son **Malcolm IV** (reigned 1153-1165) was forced to relinquish them. His successor **William the Lion** (reigned 1165-1214) was captured attempting to regain Northumbria and was forced to accept the Treaty of Falaise in 1174, ceding Scotland to England as a feudal dependency.

The last of the Canmore kings – **Alexander III** (reigned 1249-1286) – defeated the Norwegian king **Haakon** in 1263 at Largs in Ayrshire and won the Western Isles for Scotland. His death in 1286 left as his successor a three-year-old grandchild, Margaret (the Maid of Norway), who died in Orkney on her way to Scotland in 1290. This left 13 claimants to the throne, known as the **Competitors** (chief of whom were **John Balliol** and **Robert**

Bruce), and the threat of civil war. Edward I of England seized the chance to adjudicate, choosing Balliol (a grandson of David I) but extorting recognition as overlord of Scotland.

The Wars of Independence

Edward's harsh and arrogant treatment of the Scots roused bitter resentment. Balliol finally turned on Edward and led a short-lived uprising that resulted in crushing defeat, Balliol's exile and military occupation by the English. Adding insult to injury, in 1296 Edward removed the Stone of Destiny, the ancient coronation stone of Scottish kings, from Scone and carted it off to London.

■ Wallace & Bruce

Acting in the name of the exiled king, Scottish patriot **William Wallace** led a guerrilla movement against the English and in 1297 won a major victory at the **Battle of Stirling Bridge**. A huge English army won a decisive victory at Falkirk the following year and recaptured Stirling Castle in 1304. In 1305, Wallace was betrayed to the English, convicted and executed.

After Wallace's death, **Robert Bruce** (grandson of the 1290 Competitor) assumed leadership of the resistance movement. He murdered his rival, the Earl of Comyn and, defying Edward I, was crowned **Robert I** in Scone in 1306. After suffering several reverses, he took advantage of the death of Edward I in 1307 to launch a devastating campaign into northern England. Edward II finally led his army north but the Bruce's much smaller force inflicted a shattering defeat on the English at **Bannockburn** in June 1314. In 1320, the Scots drew up a Declaration of Independence at **Arbroath Abbey**. The war finally ended in 1328 when the regents of the young Edward III approved the **Treaty of Northampton**, recognizing Scotland's independence.

The Bruce's son, **David II**, staged a series of raids into England, which was by that time involved in the Hundred Years' War with France and had abandoned most of its strongholds in Scotland. David was captured at Neville's Cross, near Durham, in 1346 and was not released until 1357 in return for a crushing ransom.

■ The Stewarts

On David II's death without heirs in 1371, his nephew, the son of Robert I's daughter Marjorie, became the first Stewart (later Stuart) king as **Robert II**. So began a 343-year dynasty of 14 monarchs, five of whom ruled on both sides of the border, beginning with James VI of Scotland (crowned James I of England in 1603 after the death of Queen Elizabeth) and ending with Queen Anne, who reigned from 1702 until her death in 1714. The Stewarts inherited a land struggling with its emerging nationhood and torn by powerful nobles. Over the next four centuries, they unified Scotland, brought it under central control, and guided it through the Renaissance, Reformation and finally union with England.

Robert II and his son **Robert III** were ineffective rulers. **James I** (reigned 1406-37) was captured by the English in 1406 and imprisoned in London until 1424. On his return from captivity, James tried to recover crown land and authority lost to the nobles in his absence but was assassinated by members of his household in 1437. **James II** (reigned 1437-60) and **James III** (reigned 1460-88) came to the throne as minors, which encouraged further strife between the nobles. Orkney and Shetland passed to Scotland in 1471 following the marriage of James III to Margaret of Denmark.

James IV (reigned 1488-1513) successfully reasserted royal authority over the nobles, improved justice and encouraged the arts. He married Margaret, daughter of **Henry VII of England**, in 1503. In support of the *auld alliance* with France, James invaded England, but his army was routed and he was killed at Flodden Field in 1513. But it was from his marriage to Margaret that, a century later, would spring the union of Scotland and England under James VI (I of England).

After a long minority, **James V** (reigned 1513-42) continued the French alliance and refused to break with the Pope as Henry VIII of England wanted. James sent an army to invade England but its defeat at Solway Moss in November 1542 contributed to his death shortly afterwards and left a six-day-old girl, Mary, as his successor, under the protection of her mother, **Mary of Guise**.

Mary, Queen of Scots
& The Reformation

Henry VIII wished to marry the young Queen Mary (reigned 1542-67) to his son Edward. When his wish was rebuffed, he devastated southern Scotland in the "rough wooing." After another English force defeated the Scots at Pinkie, the six-year-old Mary was sent to France for safety, where she remained for 13 years. She married the young Dauphin François (who a year later became **François II**) in 1558 and only returned to Scotland on his death in 1561.

Meanwhile, war with England came to an end in 1551 and Mary's mother, Mary of Guise, assumed the regency in 1554. Her government was thrown into turmoil as the Reformation reached Scotland in an extreme Calvinist form. John Knox, an uncompromising Protestant preacher, returned from exile to Scotland in May 1559 to head the reformers. However, it took open support from **Queen Elizabeth** of England, an English army, and the death of Mary of Guise to win ultimate victory for the Protestants. In August 1560, the Reformation Parliament adopted the Protestant *Confession of Faith*, repudiated the supremacy of the Pope and abolished the Catholic mass. The return to Scotland of the Catholic Mary threatened the success of the Reformation. Mary initially demonstrated adept statecraft, skilfully playing off the different factions against each other, but soon became embroiled in personal affairs. In 1565 she married **Henry Stuart, Lord Darnley**, and gave birth to the future James VI in 1566. In the same year, a Protestant conspiracy resulted in the murder of Mary's Italian secretary Rizzio. Worse still, Mary and the **Earl of Bothwell** were implicated in the mysterious murder of Darnley in 1567. Mary's hurried marriage to Bothwell lost her the favor of both Protestants and Catholics. She was imprisoned at Lochleven and forced to abdicate in favor of her infant son. Mary escaped the following year but after being defeated at Langside fled to England. Elizabeth, fearful both of aiding rebels against the sovereign and of Catholic conspiracies, imprisoned Mary for 19 years. In 1587 Mary was implicated in another Catholic plot, this time engineered by her page Anthony Babington. She was tried and executed.

Union of the Crowns

On the death of Elizabeth I in 1603, **James VI**, her nearest heir, inherited the Crown of England as **James I**. The religious struggle developed into one between episcopacy (defined as a heirarchical government of the church) and presbyterianism (government of the church by elders of equal standing). The **Covenanters** were devoted to maintaining Presbyterianism as Scotland's sole religion and helped establish the supremacy of Parliament over the monarch in both Scotland and England. James restored the bishops to the church and parliament, and **Charles I** went further, trying to change church doctrine and ritual. This provoked the signing of the National Covenant in 1638, resisting religious change, and later (in 1643) an alliance with English puritans.

Following **Cromwell's** victory over the royalists, the Scots refused to accept a republic and instead crowned **Charles II** in 1651, which resulted in another English invasion and occupation. After the restoration of Charles II in England in 1660, Covenanters were hunted down and shot. Charles II reigned until 1685, and was succeeded by his brother, **James VII** (II of England). James was deposed in the "Glorious Revolution" of 1688 in favor of his daughter Mary. She became **Mary II** and reigned with her husband **William III** (William of Orange), until her death in 1694. William died in 1702, and was succeeded by Mary's sister **Anne**.

In 1707, under the reign of Anne, the Scottish Parliament approved the **Act of Union**, which joined England and Scotland. Though cheered in London, the Union was far from popular in Scotland where unrest simmered and Jacobitism – support for the exiled James VII/II – refused to disappear.

The Jacobites

The first major **Jacobite Rising** in 1715 was not a rising of the Highlands but rather a protest by disillusioned Scots. Poorly led, the rising fizzled out long before the **Old Pretender** (James Edward, son of James VII), returned from France. The London government remained nervous, and General Wade, commander of the king's forces in Scotland, built a series of roads and fortresses across the Highlands in the 1730s for the use of British troops. This did little to deter the last and most spectacular Jacobite Rising in 1745. This time, **Bonnie Prince Charlie,** known as the Young Pretender, raised a largely Highland army. He reached Derby and could probably have taken London but, gaining little support from southern Jacobites, returned north. The Prince's army was crushed by the Duke of Cumberland's Government forces at Culloden in April 1746, so ending all hopes for a restoration of the Stewart monarchy.

The Clearances

In the savage backlash that followed Culloden, the Government sought to end the Jacobite threat once and for all. A raft of draconian legislation dismantled the Highland way of life, even banning tartan and bagpipes, and paved the way for the Highland Clearances.

The eviction of thousands of tenants from vast tracts of the Highlands remains a highly emotive issue even today. Landlords forced tenants from their crofts to free up land for sheep farming. Most notoriously, the Countess of Sutherland evicted some 700 families in 1819-21. Later clearances in the mid-19th century were mainly the result of famine caused by the failure of the potato crop. Although accurate numbers aren't known, hundreds of thousands of people left the Highlands (from Perthshire to Sutherland as well as Skye, the Western Isles and Shetland) between 1730 and 1880.

Industrialization & Urbanization

The first stage of industrialization took place between the 1770s and 1830s, mainly dominated by **textiles**. From the 1830s, a more skilled industrialization emerged with the rise of heavy industry – **shipbuilding**, **marine engineering** and **steel** – in Glasgow, whose population exploded from 147,000 in 1820 to over 760,000 by 1900. One in two Scots now lived in towns, whereas only a century and a half earlier it had been only one in five.

The 20th Century & Home Rule

Unlike the sister movements in Ireland and Wales, Scottish nationalism didn't emerge until the 1960s. Having its own press, banks and legal system, and the experience of the two World Wars, cemented the sense of being both Scottish and British. The discovery of **oil** in the North Sea in the early 1970s offered recovery from the post-war slump. It also provided Scottish nationalists with a new campaigning slogan, claiming that the oil revenue rightfully belonged to Scotland and not Britain.

Concessions by successive British governments culminated in a referendum in September 1997, in which Scots voted by nearly three to one for the creation of their own devolved parliament. On 6th May 1999, elections took place for the new **Scottish Parliament**, thus settling the issue of Home Rule and deferring any prospects for independence. The new Scottish Parliament, the first convened since 1707, sat for the first time on 12th May 1999.

Geography

 Scotland covers an area of over 30,000 square miles, including over 600 square miles of inland water. It is deeply indented by the **Moray Firth** and **Firth of Forth** in the east and by the firths of **Lorn** and **Clyde** in the west. Scotland's only land border – with England – runs 60 miles (96 km) along the line of the **Cheviot Hills**.

The terrain is predominantly mountainous and is divided into three main regions: the Southern Uplands, Central Lowlands, and Highlands and Islands. **The Southern Uplands** extend from the border and the Solway Firth to the firths of Clyde and Forth. Most of this area is covered by fertile plains, moorland plateaux and rounded hills rarely over 2,000 feet, with occasional mountainous outcrops.

The narrow **Central Lowlands** include the lower valleys of the Clyde, Forth and Tay rivers, traversed by several long but broken chains of hills, including the **Ochil** and **Sidlaw Hills**. Although only comprising a tenth of Scotland's land area, the Central Lowlands hold three-quarters of the country's population.

 The rugged **Highlands** consist of parallel chains of sandstone and granite mountains, trending generally southwest to northeast, broken by deep ravines and valleys. Common in this area are moorland plateaux, mountain and sea lochs, fast-flowing streams and dense thickets. The **Great Glen** bisects the Highlands from the southwest to northeast. To the northwest of the Great Glen rise heavily eroded peaks ranging around 2,000-3,000 feet. The topography southeast of the Great Glen is more diversified and is traversed by the **Grampian Mountains**, Scotland's principal mountain range. The northeast (Caithness and Aberdeenshire) is flatter and dominated by broad coastal plains. At 4,406 feet, **Ben Nevis** near Fort William is the highest point in Britain.

The **Highland Boundary Fault** traverses Scotland from the Isle of Arran in the west to Stonehaven in the east. In most places, the fault is only identifiable by a change in topography – from Highlands in the northwest to Lowlands in the southeast. **Loch Lomond** is one of the sites where the fault can be distinguished more clearly, in particular at **Conic Hill** and on several islands in the loch.

Of Scotland's 790 **islands**, 130 or so are inhabited. The major island groups are the **Inner** and **Outer Hebrides** off the west coast, and **Orkney** and **Shetland** to the northeast.

The **Tay** is Scotland's longest **river** (120 miles), although the **Clyde** (106 miles) is the principal commercial river. The other major rivers are the **Spey** (107 miles), **Tweed** (97 miles), **Dee** (85 miles) and **Don** (82 miles).

Loch Lomond (27.5 square miles) is Scotland's largest lake in surface area, but **Loch Ness** (21.8 square miles) is deeper.

Climate

Being surrounded by sea on three sides and enjoying the moderating influence of the **Gulf Stream** protects Scotland from the worst seasonal extremes of weather. Summers aren't too hot and winters relatively temperate, although overall the climate is very changeable and it can rain at any time. The weather can also vary significantly over small distances – even across neighboring glens.

May and June are usually drier than July and August. July and August are the warmest months, averaging 60-68°F (15-19°C). The east coast tends to be cool and dry; the west coast is milder and wetter (the western Highlands record the highest rainfall in Britain). Edinburgh receives only slightly more rainfall than London and some east coast towns are drier than Rome. Low winter temperatures and heavy snowfalls can occur, particularly in interior mountain regions.

AURORA BOREALIS

The Aurora Borealis (Northern Lights) is a gigantic natural light show that occurs when solar winds drive plasma (electrically charged solar particles) against the Earth. When the charged particles enter the Earth's upper atmosphere, they are drawn by magnetic fields down into the ionosphere at the polar regions. At the poles, they react with atmospheric gases and glow in colorful bands of red, green, blue and violet to create a beautiful aerial blaze. The Aurora is most visible at latitudes above 65 degrees north – the north mainland, Orkney and Shetland – on crisp, clear late autumn and winter evenings, although displays can be seen from all over the country, even in warmer months.

Wildlife

Birds

Scotland provides a home to over 300 species of birds, of which 200 are either residents or regular visitors. It lies at the junction of two major **migration flyways**: one from the high Arctic Canadian islands, across Greenland and Iceland; the other from the east, from north Russia across Scandinavia. This creates a great diversity of species during passage periods, with many Scottish habitats, especially wetlands, providing essential stopover points for these birds.

The **golden eagle** is a huge, magnificent bird of prey, with long, broad wings (spanning six to seven feet) with fingered ends, and a longish tail. They inhabit high, open moorland, mountains and remote glens and islands that offer plenty of open feeding ground. They generally avoid heavily forested areas. Eagles soar and glide on air currents, holding their wings in a shallow "V," and make occasional yelping calls. They have large territories and nesting places that may be used by generations, and are often seen in pairs. You will never forget the experience of seeing a golden eagle in the wild. Look for them throughout the Highlands and Islands.

The **white-tailed** or **sea eagle** is the largest UK bird of prey. It has brown body plumage, a lighter head (almost white in older birds) and distinctive white tailfeathers. In flight, it has massive long, broad wings with fingered ends. It is stockier than the golden eagle and has a short, wedge-shaped tail. The head and the beak are larger than that of the golden eagle. The eyes, beak and talons are bright yellow.

The white-tailed eagle was persecuted to extinction in the early 19th century; the present population was reintroduced beginning in 1975, using young birds from Norway. They prefer rocky coastlines and also live near rivers and large lakes, sometimes several hundred miles inland. Look for them on the west coast of Scotland.

 The **osprey** is a large bird of prey that catches fish near the surface of lochs, plunging in to grasp them with long hooked claws. The species became extinct in Scotland in 1916, and only returned to breed in 1953. Brown above and pale beneath, ospreys arrive in April to rebuild their nests, normally on top of high trees near water. The chicks are fed torn-up fish and taught how to fly, after which they set off at the end of August to winter in West Africa. Scotland is the only place in the UK where ospreys nest.

The **capercaillie** is a large woodland grouse, the large black male of the species being unmistakable. They spend a lot of time feeding on the ground, but may also be found in trees. The UK population has declined so rapidly that the capercaillie is at risk of extinction (for the second time). The species prefers mature Scots pine forests with an undergrowth of heather and berries, and is largely confined to Scotland's ancient Caledonian pine forests.

The endearing **puffin** is unmistakable with its black back and white front, distinctive black head with large pale cheeks and brightly colored bill. Its comical appearance is heightened by its red and black eye-markings, bright orange legs and constant worried expression. This clown among seabirds is one of the world's favorites. Puffins prefer offshore islands and high sea cliffs. They breed in colonies, nesting in burrows, under boulders or in cracks in cliffs. Good sites for puffin spotting are the breeding colonies on the Isle of May (Fife), Orkney and Shetland. Adults arrive back at the colonies in March and April and leave again in mid-August. Some winter in the North Sea; others fly south to the Bay of Biscay.

Mammals

Over 60 species of mammal live wild in and around Scotland, indigenous species including the red and roe deer, hare, rabbit, otter, pine marten and wildcat.

The indigenous **red deer** is Britain's largest mammal, standing up to five feet/1.5m at the shoulder. They have a reddish-brown coat, which changes in winter to brownish-grey, a creamy patch on their rump and a short, beige tail. The males (stags) carry antlers, which they lose between February and April and re-grow in August. Adult red deer come together for mating during the September/October "rut," at which time the roars of stags and the clash of their antlers often resound across the hills.

 The small **roe deer** (up to 30 inches/70 cm at the shoulder) have sandy to reddish-brown summer coats and grey-brown or black winter coats. They have a light patch on their rump, a black nose and white chin.

Highland cattle have a long and distinguished ancestry, and are one of Britain's oldest and most distinctive breeds, with their thick, shaggy coat of rich hair and outward-sweeping horns. The hardy breed is able to survive on poor grazing and thrives in areas of mountain land with high rainfall and bitter winds. The species originally had black hair, but most cattle nowadays have light, sometimes reddish, brown hair.

 The **red squirrel** has a bushy tail and ear tufts, and is only half the size of the introduced American grey squirrel. The red squirrel thrives in conifer woodland where it eats pine seeds, nuts, berries, shoots and fungi. The species has been declining throughout the last century, possibly because of the continuing spread of the grey squirrel.

The **otter** is a shy marine predator that is agile on land and highly adapted for swimming. It is found in or near water, and can often be seen where rivers spill into lochs or the sea. The northwest Highlands, Hebrides, Orkney and Shetland have the largest populations in Scotland. Early mornings and evenings are often said to be the best times to see otters, although they can be seen throughout the day, often fishing by day in less populated areas. Even in rural areas, it can take quiet, patient waiting to see otters, but there are times when you can see them at lunchtime crossing the main road outside the supermarket in Lerwick!

 Bottlenose dolphins are the acrobats of the animal kingdom and frequently jump clear of the water. They have grey backs and a lighter underside, a prominent dorsal fin and a short, well-developed snout. Dolphins travel in groups and constantly emit clicks and whistles. Dolphins cruise at around 20 mph, although they can reach 30 mph when hunting.

 Two species of seal live around Scotland's coasts. The larger **grey seal** (males reach eight feet/2.5m, weighing up to 550lb/250kg) comes ashore in autumn to breed on remote islands or isolated beaches. Scotland has over 110,000 grey seals, 40% of the world population. The smaller **common seal** (males reach six feet/1.8m, 260lb/120kg) is found more widely and breeds in summer on sandbanks, with their young swimming immediately. There are around 45,000 common seals in Scotland, some 10% of the European population.

Apart from the difference in size, the two species have different heads: grey seals have elongated snouts with parallel nostrils; common seals have stubby heads with shorter snouts and V-shaped nostrils. Seals are curious and will often approach (but not too closely) to investigate you.

Fish

 Atlantic salmon are widespread throughout Scottish rivers. Salmon hatch and spawn in fresh water, but spend much of their juvenile and adult lives at sea before returning to spawn.

Basking sharks can often be seen around the west coast of Scotland in summer when plankton is abundant. The basking shark is a huge fish – the second largest in the world – reaching 36 feet/11m in length and weighing up to seven tons. The shark is usually seen swimming slowly close to the surface, with the thick, triangular fin on its back (up to 6.5 feet/2m high) breaking the water, and a vertical tail fin sweeping from side to side. It swims with its gaping mouth wide open (with the snout often above the surface), allowing hundreds of gallons of seawater, equivalent to a swimming-pool-full an hour, to flow through its widely stretched gills, which trap the plankton it eats.

People & Culture

Scotland's population numbers just over five million and is declining. Like the rest of Britain, its people descend from various northern tribes, including the **Picts**, **Celts**, **Scandinavians** and, to a lesser extent, **Romans**.

Scottish, Scotch or Scots?

■ A Scottish person is called a **Scot**. Never describe a Scot as English or, at best, they'll never speak to you again. Scots are above all else Scottish. Similarly, don't refer to Britain (or worse, Scotland) as "England" and don't call a thistle a rose.

■ **Scottish** is the adjective used to describe something or someone that originates from Scotland, as in *"Scottish* castle."

■ **Scotch** describes certain Scottish products, for example *"Scotch* whisky" and *"Scotch* eggs."

■ **Scots** is used in limited contexts, for example to describe certain regiments, as in *"Scots* Guards."

Scots divide themselves into **Highlanders** and **Lowlanders**. In Orkney and Shetland, the Norse rather than Gaelic influence predominates. Jocular stereotypes of the Scotsman range from the dour, tight-fisted, heart-attack-waiting-to-happen, who eats deep-fried Mars bars, drinks (lots of) pints of heavy and supports any team playing against England – to the kilted bagpiper who eats haggis, neeps and tatties when he's not munching shortbread, and sips wee drams of whisky.

As ever, the truth lies nowhere near these extremes. Scots are friendly and generous. They are also proud of their roots and fiercely patriotic. They are first and foremost Scottish, before being either European or British. Some Scots still blame the English for the slaughter at Culloden and persecution that followed (even though more Scots fought against Bonnie Prince Charlie than for him at Culloden). While most Scots now tolerate their English neighbors, any competition between the two countries (football in particular) is likely to re-ignite the rivalry back to Bannockburn intensities.

Language

 Scotland has two recognized languages: **Gaelic**, spoken mainly in the Highlands and Western Isles, and **English**. Scots English has some marked regional accents but all are distinctively Scottish. There are dialectal variations of Scots: **Doric** in the northeast Grampians, and **Lallans** in the Lowlands.

Gaelic is the longest-standing language in Scotland and boasts one of the richest song and oral traditions in Europe. It is part of a family of Celtic languages that is spoken in six areas: Scotland, Ireland, the Isle of Man, Wales, Cornwall and Brittany. Scots Gaelic emerged from the Celtic society that once covered much of Europe. After arriving in Argyll in the 6th century, the Gaels spread their culture and language throughout the country. James IV (reigned 1488-1513) was the last Scottish monarch to speak Gaelic.

Urbanization and the emergence of Scots as the language of the 15th- and 16th-century royal court led to the decline of Gaelic, accelerated by the adoption of English as the official language following union with England in 1707. Gaelic further suffered severely in the 18th and 19th centuries as the government stamped out every aspect of Highland culture following Culloden, and because of the Clearances that destroyed many Gaelic-speaking communities.

The revival of Gaelic began in 1975 when the Western Isles Council started to use the language in its daily work and introduced bilingual education. The 1980s saw Gaelic playgroups set up to introduce the language to children and a new Gaelic development agency set up to promote the language and culture throughout Scotland. Much work remains to safeguard Gaelic. The 2001 census recorded 58,600 Gaelic speakers (down from 65,000 in 1991), mostly living in the Western Isles, Central belt and northern Highlands. A bill was introduced in the Scottish Parliament in 2003, which, if successful, will grant Gaelic full legal equality with English in public life and see it revitalized as a living entity.

Lews Castle College in Lewis (Stornoway, Isle of Lewis HS2 0XR, ☎ 1851-770 000, fax 1851-770 001, aofficele@lews.uhi.ac.uk, www.lews.uhi.ac.uk) offers short and full-time courses in Gaelic language, culture and music. **Sabhal Mòr Ostaig** in Skye (Sleat, Isle of Skye IV44 8RQ, ☎ 1471-888 000, sm.oifis@groupwise.uhi.ac.uk, www.smo.uhi.ac.uk) also offers short courses in Gaelic language and music, as well as full-time vocational courses taught in Gaelic in a Gaelic environment. You can also contact **Clì Gàidhlig** (North Tower, The Castle, Inverness IV2 3EU, ☎ 1463-226 710, cli@cli.org.uk, www.cli.org.uk), an organization for Gaelic learners and supporters.

DID YOU KNOW?

DID YOU KNOW? *The Gaelic alphabet has 18 letters (J, K, Q, V, W, X, Y and Z are not used). A stroke or "grave" above a vowel indicates that the sound of that vowel is lengthened, eg, à is sounded "ah" as in "father," and not short "a" as in "dad."*

Literature

Scotland has long fostered generations of world-class writers and poets, most notably **Robert Burns, Sir Walter Scott, Robert Louis Stevenson, Arthur Conan Doyle, Iain Banks, Sorley MacLean** and **Alasdair Gray**. More recently, **JK Rowling** created the *Harry Potter* phenomenon, writing from an Edinburgh café.

Robert Burns (1759-1796), Scotland's national bard, was born in Alloway, the son of a poor tenant farmer. An accomplished poet, songwriter and collector of traditional Scots songs, he became the darling of the Edinburgh literati, despite his often-satirical attacks on the establishment. His famous poems and songs include *Tam o'Shanter, John Anderson my Jo* and the universal Hogmanay (New Year's Eve) anthem, *Auld Lang Syne*. He later became an excise man in Dumfries where he died tragically at only 37 years of age. Burns' poetry carries common appeal and his reputation is truly international.

Despite being born into the famous lighthouse-engineering dynasty and called to the Scottish bar, **Robert Louis Stevenson's** (1850-1894) real love was literature. He penned magazine articles and a couple of travel accounts, but it is as a storyteller that he shone, producing classic novels and short stories, including *Treasure Island, Dr Jekyll and Mr Hyde* and *Kidnapped*. Stevenson was constantly dogged by ill health and traveled widely in search of a comfortable climate. He finally settled in Samoa where he died in the midst of creating *Weir of Hermiston*.

A lawyer by profession, **Walter Scott** (1771-1832) became the most important Scottish literary figure of the late 18th and early 19th centuries, establishing his reputation with a succession of ballads, including *Minstrelsy of the Scottish Border, Lay of the Last Minstrel* and *The Lady of the Lake*. From about 1814, Scott began writing the novels for which he is most famous, including *Waverley, The Antiquary, Rob Roy, The Bride of Lammermoor, Ivanhoe* and *The Talisman*. Scott suffered a financial crisis in later life and spent his latter days in unremitting labor to settle his debts, although much of the work from this period did nothing to enhance his reputation.

Harry Potter, the phenomenally successful boy-wizard creation of JK Rowling, has his roots firmly in Scotland. Although first conceived on a train between Manchester and London, it was in Edinburgh that Harry's magical world took form. Rowling arrived in Edinburgh in 1993 with her infant daughter. Unemployed and living on social security, she devoted her energies to looking after her daughter while snatching time to finish what was to become *Harry Potter and the Philosopher's Stone* (US title *Harry Potter and the Sorcerer's Stone*) in cafés that didn't object to her sitting there for hours having bought only one coffee. The book was finished in Nicolson's in the Old Town, then a café, now a bistro that draws in Potter-maniacs eager to sit in the same corner window seat where Harry's adventures took shape.

HAGGIS & THE BURNS SUPPER

Burns Night (January 25th, the poet's birthday) is celebrated the world over with Burns Suppers. These are often extravaganzas of tartan, kilts and sashes, but this isn't strictly necessary: Burns was a Lowlander and never wore a kilt.

Haggis (see page 54) is the culinary centerpiece of the Burns Supper. Burns Suppers have followed the poet's popularity around the globe and are found everywhere from Newfoundland to New Zealand.

They follow an established ritual. The chef delivers the steaming haggis to the table with due ceremony, ideally preceded by a kilted piper. The main speaker then ceremoniously stabs open the steaming haggis with a sharp knife while reciting, with appropriate theatricality and drama, *Address to a Haggis*, which begins with the immortal lines: "Fair fa' your honest, sonsie face, Great chieftain o' the puddin' race!"

The haggis is served with *bashed neeps* and *champit tatties* (mashed turnip and potato). Other dishes on the menu usually include Scotch broth or cock-a-leekie soup and a meat course, followed by biscuits and cheese – Scottish, of course. Various speeches and recitals follow the meal, including the *Immortal Memory of Robert Burns*, the *Toast to the Lassies* and their reply, followed by other favorite poems and songs, traditionally culminating with the great song of parting – *Auld Lang Syne*.

Religion

Scotland is a Christian country, the official denomination being **Presbyterianism**, represented by the **Church of Scotland**, although **Roman Catholicism** also maintains a strong following.

St Andrew is the patron saint of Scotland, a role he also plays in Greece, Russia and Romania. The brother of St Peter and one of the original Apostles, Andrew was reputedly martyred at Patras in Greece. Asking not to be crucified on the same shape cross as Christ, he was crucified on an X-shaped *Saltire*, which subsequently became his symbol.

St Andrew was probably Scotland's patron saint by 1000. St Andrew's Day is celebrated on 30th November, although it is not a public holiday in Scotland.

National Symbols

The Scottish national flag is the **Saltire** – a white diagonal cross on a blue background – that derives from the shape of the cross on which St Andrew was crucified. According to one legend, the flag was adopted as Scotland's national flag before a battle in 832 near the East Lothian village of Athelstaneford. A joint army of Picts and Scots under Angus mac Fergus, High King of Alba, was invading Lothian (at that time a Northumbrian territory) and faced a larger army of Angles and Saxons. Angus led prayers and believed he had received a divine sign when, above him in a clear blue sky, he saw a great white cross like that of St Andrew. The king vowed that if he gained victory, Andrew would thereafter be the patron saint of Scotland and his cross the flag of Scotland. Angus won the battle and the Saltire duly became Scotland's national flag.

Alongside the Saltire and tartan, the **thistle** is one of the most identifiable symbols of Scottishness. One legend tells how sleeping Scots warriors were saved from invading Vikings when one attacker trod on a wild thistle and his cries woke the Scots who duly defeated the Danes. The plant became known as the Guardian Thistle and was adopted in gratitude as the symbol of Scotland.

There are many species of thistle, including spear thistle, stemless thistle, cotton thistle, Our Lady's thistle, musk thistle and melancholy thistle. Despite uncertainties over origin and species, the thistle has remained an important Scottish symbol for more than five centuries. It appeared on 15th-century silver coins issued during the reign of James III. From the early 16th century, it was incorporated into the Royal Arms of Scotland. Members of Scotland's premier order of chivalry, **The Most Ancient and Noble Order of the Thistle** (established in 1687), wear a collar chain whose links are made of golden thistles and a breast star bearing the thistle emblem.

Music

Gaelic music is perhaps the most ancient form of traditional Scottish music. Despite its minority language status, Gaelic music thrives across the country, not just in its Highlands and Islands homeland. Lowland Scotland also boasts a rich musical heritage, characterized by a vibrant folk music scene. The fusion of traditional folk with modern folk-rock has spawned supergroups like **Capercaillie** and **Runrig**.

Instrumental music continues to be dominated by pipes, fiddles and accordions. Their rhythmic melodies accompany all forms of traditional dancing and also exist in their own right, as in massed pipe bands. Festivals, concerts and informal sessions throughout the year and across the country are ensuring Scotland's traditional music flourishes. Important music festivals include

Celtic Connections (Glasgow), Orkney Folk Festival, Hebridean Celtic Festival (Lewis) and the Skye Festival.

The **bagpipe** (specifically, the Highland bagpipe or *piob mhor)* is Scotland's national instrument. It is a reed instrument with a small cane blade or pair of blades inserted into the end of a pipe that vibrates under air pressure to produce the distinctive note. In the Highland bagpipe, the air comes from a bag inflated by the piper blowing through a pipe and pressed by the piper's arm. Three pipes, called **drones** (a bass and two tenors), sound a continuous fixed chord to accompany the melody played on a **chanter**, a pipe pierced with finger holes and played with both hands.

Bagpipes are not a Scottish invention. They were first recorded in Asia Minor in 1000 BC, and by the first century AD existed in many countries, including India, Spain, Egypt and France. It's not known whether the Romans or Irish first brought the instrument to Scotland, but the bagpipe became widespread in Europe in the 12th century and was probably being played in the Scottish Highlands by the 14th century. Pipes started to replace the harp, the traditional musical instrument of Gaelic society, in the 16th century.

There are two main musical styles played on the Highland pipes: the **march**, composed for military or social events; and the ***piobaireachd*** (pronounced "pee-broch"), the symphonic classical form of the pipes.

Clans

For centuries, in Scotland, the power of the state was strengthened by the competing political interests of great families or clans, a distinct Gaelic tribal culture. The Gaelic word "clan" means "children," and the original clan comprised simply the extended family.

Many of today's clans trace their origins to the 11th or 12th centuries and some are even older. Some clans have Norse connections, for instance the **MacLeods** of Skye and the **MacDougalls** of Lorn. Others are linked with ancient monastic houses: the **MacNabs** ("son of the abbot") descend from lay abbots of St Fillan on Loch Earn and the **MacLeans** in Morven come from Gillean, who descended from the abbots of Lismore, in Loch Linnhe. Others descended from Normans who intermarried with native Celtic families, for example the **Cummings** (Comyns), **Hays** (de la Haye), **Frasers** (de Friselle), **Sinclairs** (St Clair) and the **Bruces** (de Brus).

The clan system was well established in the Highlands by the 13th century and was completely separated by language, custom and geography from the south of the country. The clans lived off the land more or less self-sufficiently, with cattle as their main wealth. Cattle theft and territorial disputes were widespread. The most powerful clan chiefs kept expensive courts and retainers, commissioning bards, painters, musicians, architects and physicians (accounting for much of the region's artistic and intellectual community), and enjoyed virtual autonomy over matters of law and order within their territory.

In their 15th-century heyday, the clans threatened the authority of the Stewart monarchy itself.

The power of the clan descended through its male line. "Mac" in Gaelic means "son" and hence MacGregor means "son of Gregor." In later years, clans came to be based less on family associations and more on mutually beneficial arrangements of protection and loyalty. Ultimately, the power of the clan chief depended on the number of men he could order into battle.

The clan system changed completely from 1650 to 1800, particularly following the failed Jacobite Risings. Even before the shock of Culloden, when Highland chiefs ordered their men into battle for the last time, the traditional clan system was gradually being absorbed into a modern society. The bloody reprisals after Culloden systematically destroyed the power of the clans. Chiefs were stripped of their legal powers and became no more than commercial landlords. Clansmen became mere tenants over huge tracts of the Highlands, eventually to be disposed of through the Highland Clearances.

Tartan

 Tartan is a Scottish brand that is instantly recognizable around the world. The word tartan derives from an old French word *tiretaine*, which was a woolen cloth. What sets tartan apart from other checkered fabrics is the gallantry, romance, and stirring tales of Highland clans that seem to be woven into the very fabric.

Although many people through the ages, including the ancient Romans, have worn a form of the kilt, Scotland is now the only country where men wear such national dress as part of their daily lives. In the earliest times, Highlanders wore roughly woven plaid, colored with dyes made from local plants, mosses and berries and woven into distinctive striped or checked patterns. The weave of the cloth and the way it was worn reflected local customs rather than clan affiliations. The use of different patterns and colors of tartan to identify different families and clans dates only from the early 19th century.

WHICH TARTAN TO WEAR?

There are no firm rules or regulations governing which pattern to choose, although most people like to wear a tartan associated with their surname. To check whether you belong to a clan, contact the **Clan Tartan Centre** (Leith Mills, 70-74 Bangor Road, Leith, Edinburgh EH6 5JU, ☎ 131-553 5161, fax 131-553 4415, info@leithmills.co.uk), which has a computer database to research clan connections and provide clan information (other tartan shops have similar archives). Alternatively, wear the **Royal Stewart** tartan, which is regarded as being without family affiliation, or the **Black Watch** tartan, the universal military tartan.

The growth of clan tartans began with the standardizing of cloths worn by Highland regiments in the British army, during the years when its general wearing was prohibited (1747-82). The romantic novels of Sir Walter Scott, and the Royal patronage of George IV and, later, Queen Victoria, restored the status of the tartan.

Each clan and most surnames have their own tartan and, in most cases, variants on it: ancient muted "hunting" colors and brilliant "dress" colorings. Most surnames have established associations with particular clan tartans.

The Kilt & Highland Dress

Highland Dress has been worn by Scottish Highlanders since at least the 11th century. Today's skirt-like kilt evolved in the mid-18th century from the more commonly worn and functional "**big kilt**" (in Gaelic, *feileadh mor*). The big kilt was an untailored garment, some 18 feet long by six feet wide, worn gathered and belted at the waist to cover both upper and lower body. From the waist down, the "big kilt" resembled a modern kilt, while the remaining material was draped over the shoulder and pinned by a brooch on the left shoulder. The upper portion could be arranged in various forms to suit changing temperature or freedom of movement requirements. At the day's end, the kilt could be unbelted and transformed into a warm blanket (in Gaelic, *plaid* means blanket).

In the early 18th century, the big kilt was simplified by disposing of its top half, leaving the belt and knee-length skirt below, creating the "**little kilt**" (*feileadh beag*), reputedly at the behest of an English ironworks manager who felt his kilted employees needed greater freedom of movement to work. The kilt became a tailored garment with sewn-in pleats, making it neater and easier to wear. The upper half of the "big kilt" evolved into the separate plaid (sash) now worn at formal events. Other traditional elements include the *sporran*, a leather or fur purse, which hangs from the belt in front on a strap or chain; and a ***sghian dubh*** (dagger, pronounced "sgean doo"), worn in a sheath attached to the calf, under the top of the stocking.

Nowadays, kilts are mostly worn at formal celebrations, such as weddings, and at Highland Games. Although regarded as Highland dress, more kilts are now worn in Lowland cities than in the Highlands.

Other components of Highland Dress include *trews* (tartan trousers), traditionally worn by gentlemen on horseback, and the *tam o'shanter*, a cocked bonnet with ribbon streamers and sometimes a feather, brooch or both.

Highland Games

Highland Games are believed to derive from the trials of strength, speed, agility and skill that were commonplace at the various religious fairs, military musters and cattle fairs of medieval Scotland. These were often used by clan warriors to demonstrate their physical prowess.

The romanticization of Highland culture from the 1820s led to the formalization of Highland Games as annual events. The modern program of contests remains largely unchanged from the earliest recorded games: tossing the caber, throwing stones or hammers, tugs-of-war, lifting a heavy stone and running; and a variety of piping and dancing competitions. Happily, "twisting the four legs off a cow for which a fat sheep is offered as a prize" no longer features as an event.

There is a full schedule of Highland Games (*www.albagames.co.uk*) across Scotland throughout the summer, most famously at **Braemar**, traditionally attended by the Royal family; and at **Lonach** and **Cowal**.

Whisky

Uisge Beatha – the Water of Life

Scots should not take the credit for discovering whisky, but rather developing it. Distillation is believed to have originated in Asia around 800 BC, from where it eventually spread to Europe. To the ancient Celts, the potent distilled spirit was a gift from god: its power to revive weary bodies, keep out the cold and lift morale was magical – so they named it *uisge beatha* – pronounced "oosh-ga beay-huh," Gaelic for "water of life."

The first record of distilling in Scotland was in 1494, when an entry in the Scottish Exchequer Rolls listed "Eight bolls of malt to Friar John Cor wherewith to make *aquavitae* (water of life)." Production methods and spirit quality improved during the 16th and 17th centuries. Whisky consumption really grew in 1760 when an exorbitant tax on claret (red wine from Bordeaux, France) put it outside the reach of most tipplers. With its growing popularity, the Scottish Parliament introduced taxes on the malt and finished whisky. High taxes drove distillers underground and smuggling became rife, even among church ministers.

Many distillers operated from their homes, quiet bothies hidden in hills and glens, and caves. By 1777, there were eight "official" distilleries and around 400 illicit stills. Taxes were finally cut in 1823 and smuggling died out. That Excise Act laid the foundations of the modern whisky industry, sold to 200 countries and Scotland's leading export.

Scotch whisky can only be made in Scotland (the Scottish spirit is spelled *whisky*; the Irish/American equivalent is spelled *whiskey*). There have been many attempts to reproduce its unique flavor in different parts of the world, but with little success.

There are two kinds of Scotch whisky: **malt whisky**, made only from malted barley, and the lighter **grain whisky**, produced from a mixture of unmalted barley and other cereals mashed with malted barley.

A **single malt** is the product of a single Scottish distillery. A **blended whisky** is a blend of as many as 50 individual malt and grain whiskies (usually around 20% malt to 80% grain). Each blend's different flavor comes from the malt whisky that is added to the grain in differing quantities. Generally, the more expensive the blended whisky, the better are the malts used in its blending.

Blended whiskies dominate the market, but malts are more distinctive and prestigious. There are many, many single malts and variations thereon, including different ages and special editions, and each has its own characteristic taste. Single malts can vary enormously depending on the peating of the barley, distillation and casking used in their production. The stated age of a blended whisky is the age of the youngest whisky used in the blend. Many of the constituents could be much older.

■ Principal Whisky Regions

There are four main whisky regions: **Lowland** (produced below the Clyde-Tay line), **Highland**, **Speyside** (which contains over half of Scotland's distilleries) and **Island** (principally Islay, Skye and Orkney). Lowland malts are generally the softest and lightest of whiskies. Speyside malts tend to be mellow and fruity. Highland malts have a more rugged character and a wide range of flavors, from sweet and heathery to peaty. Island malts tend to have a sea-soaked, smoky, robust full flavor, with the Islay malts being distinctively peaty.

■ Making Malt Whisky

Malt whisky is made from three primary ingredients – barley, water and yeast – in five production stages: **malting**, **mashing**, **fermentation**, **distillation** and **maturation**.

Barley that has been steeped in water for around two days is spread over the floor of a malt barn and allowed to germinate for around a week. The barley is regularly turned to control the speed of germination. The grain starts to sprout and the insoluble starch in the barley begins to be converted to soluble sugar. Once the barley has reached the desired stage of germination, the "green malt" is kiln-dried to prevent it germinating further. The kilns are heated by peat fires, which impart a smoky flavor to the moist green malt.

The malted barley is crushed in a mill into "grist" and mixed with hot water ("mashed") in large vessels ("mash tuns"). The sugar dissolves into the solution and the sweet liquor, the "worts," is drained off, leaving a solid residue ("draff"), traditionally sold off as cattle food.

The worts is cooled and pumped into "washbacks" where yeast is added to convert the sugars into alcohol. During fermentation, which takes around two days, the sweet liquid is transformed into a sweet, smoky beer (known as the "wash," strength around 7% alcohol) ready for distillation.

Malt whisky is traditionally distilled twice, first in the wash still and then in the spirit still. The stills are heated and the spirit, which has a lower boiling point than water, is driven off as vapor and then condenses back as liquid in a condenser. The alcohol from the wash still ("low wines") is redistilled in the spirit still. It is here that the skill of the stillman is crucial. The first and last runs from the spirit still – the "foreshots" and "feints" – are held back for further distillation and only the middle cut – the "heart" – of the new spirit is collected for maturation.

A CONNOISSEUR'S WHISKY CABINET

Recommending a whisky selection can be a divisive and heavily subjective undertaking – so often the choice of the "perfect" Scotch depends on variables such as time of day, location, circumstances, company, etc. No single whisky will be perfect for all occasions. The following suggestions seek to balance superb quality against widespread availability and affordability, and exclude "silly money" malts. With the exception of Ardbeg 17-year-old, they're all the standard-aged offerings from the respective distilleries and are rarefied only in their outstanding quality.

LIGHTER, SMOOTHER MALTS

■ **Highland Park** 12-year-old (Orkney): Exceptionally drinkable and the nearest thing to the perfect all-rounder.

■ **Caol Ila** 12-year-old (Islay): A wonderful "undiscovered" malt that is very easy to drink and a delight on the palate.

■ **Bunnahabhain** 12-year-old (Islay): Difficult to pronounce, impossible to spell but very easy to drink.

■ **Glenmorangie** 10-year-old (Highland): Widespread availability doesn't detract from the quality or character of this excellent malt.

■ **Macallan** 10-year-old (Highland): Excellent, rich malt, ideal with a post-dinner coffee.

Mortlach 16-year-old (Speyside): Slightly rarer, but said to be the dram of choice of many distillery managers.

GRAND MALTS

For connoisseur moments (in excellent company, before a roaring fire, storm raging outside, etc):

■ **Ardbeg** 17-year-old (Islay): The standard 10-year-old is a superb malt but the 17-year-old is one of the best around.

■ **Talisker** 10-year-old (Skye): Hugely flavored and superbly drinkable, this is many people's favorite malt.

■ **Lagavulin** 16-year-old (Islay): Distinctive and powerfully flavored malt that evokes the Hebrides.

■ **Springbank** (Campbeltown): Always a great malt, particularly its longer-matured (16+ years) bottlings.

■ Drinking Malt Whisky

Does malt whisky improve with age in the bottle?

No. There is no further change in a whisky once it has been bottled and securely sealed. If you buy a bottle of 12-year-old Scotch in 2004, it will not be a 13-year-old spirit in 2005.

DID YOU KNOW?

DID YOU KNOW? *A new spirit (it can't be called Scotch whisky until it is at least three years old) is pumped into oak casks and stored in cool, dark warehouses where it breathes in the characteristics of its environment, eventually maturing and seeing daylight once more as a smooth and mellow malt whisky.*

What is the best way to drink Scotch whisky?

This depends entirely on your personal taste. Most distillers recommend adding a small dash of water to a single malt. This helps to release the aromas and flavors of the whisky.

Does the bouquet of Scotch whisky improve with slight warming?

No. The bouquet of Scotch whisky cannot be improved by warming. Warming only increases the rate of evaporation of the spirit, thus speeding up the release of the aroma but not improving it.

Are certain whiskies best drunk at certain times?

Broadly speaking, Lowland, Speyside and certain Highland malts are lighter, smoother, and best suited to beginners, as an aperitif or with food. Fuller, more robust Island malts would overpower food and are best enjoyed after dinner.

Planning Your Trip

Highlights of Scotland

Picturesque Villages

Plockton	Lochalsh
Tobermory	Isle of Mull
Culross	Fife
Glamis	Angus
Ballater	Royal Deeside
Crail	Fife
Drymen	Loch Lomond
St Margaret's Hope	Orkney
Fortingall	Perthshire

Mountains

The Cuillin. . . . . Isle of Skye
An Teallach . . . . Wester Ross
Buachaille Etive Mor . . . . Glen Coe
Paps of Jura. . . . . Isle of Jura
Beinn Eighe. . . . . Torridon

Lochs

Hourn . . . . Knoydart/Lochalsh
Coruisk. . . . . Isle of Skye
Maree . . . . Wester Ross
Loch an Eilein. . . . . Aviemore
Tummel. . . . . Perthshire
Etive . . . . Argyll

Glens

Affric . . . . Beauly
Etive . . . . Glen Coe
Nevis. . . . . Fort William
Clova. . . . . Angus
Lyon. . . . . Perthshire
Glenelg. . . . . Lochalsh

Castles & Palaces

Edinburgh
Stirling
Tioram. . . . . Ardnamurchan
Finlaggan. . . . . Isle of Islay
Duart. . . . . Isle of Mull
Crathes . . . . Royal Deeside
Blair . . . . Pitlochry
Eilean Donan . . . . Lochalsh
Dunnottar. . . . . Stonehaven
Corgarff. . . . . Donside
Holyroodhouse . . . . Edinburgh
Linlithgow . . . . West Lothian
Falkland. . . . . Fife

Religious Sites

Iona Abbey . . . . Isle of Iona
Arbroath Abbey . . . . Angus
Inchcolm Island . . . . Firth of Forth
Kildalton Cross . . . . Isle of Islay
Jedburgh Abbey . . . . Borders
Oronsay Cross. . . . . Isle of Oronsay

Rosslyn Chapel	Midlothian
St Magnus Cathedral	Orkney
Italian Chapel	Orkney

Prehistoric Monuments

Skara Brae	Orkney
Ring of Brodgar	Orkney
Callanish Standing Stones	Isle of Lewis
Mousa Broch	Shetland
Kilmartin Glen	Argyll

Whisky Distilleries

Ardbeg	Isle of Islay
Caol Ila	Isle of Islay
Edradour	Perthshire
Royal Lochnagar	Royal Deeside
Strathisla	Keith
Highland Park	Orkney
Talisker	Isle of Skye

DON'T MISS

 Dance at a *ceilidh* (informal gatherings with traditional music, dance and verse) and listen to live **Celtic folk music**.

Find solitude in a remote **glen** or beside a serene **loch**.

Take a **boat trip** to one of Scotland's many beautiful islands.

Wonder at the sight of **Neolithic monuments**, early **Christian crosses and abbeys**, and **medieval castles**.

Taste a dram of the finest **malt whisky** at the distillery where it was made.

Feast on delicious **seafood**, particularly west coast shellfish and east coast whitefish.

Watch the sun go down over the **Hebrides**.

Converse with born-and-bred **Glaswegians** (natives of Glasgow).

When to Go

 Although Scotland is a year-round destination, the main tourist season is **April to September**, with reduced services available in March and October. Most southern and city-based attractions open year-round but the farther north and west you travel, the more you will find that attractions and places to stay and eat close or operate reduced hours outside the main season. The Scottish calendar is full of **festivals**, and not just in Edinburgh. Festival considerations might dictate your timing and if you're interested in **Highland Games**, most take place in the summer and early autumn.

Midges inconveniently cause their maximum nuisance from May to September. Walkers will need to take into consideration **deerstalking** activities in the Highlands when planning itineraries from August to October. August is the best month to see **heather-clad hillsides** in the Highlands.

How Long to Stay

Scotland may look small on the map but that is deceptive. It has 6,200 miles (10,000 km) of indented **coastline** and hundreds of **islands** to explore. Traveling distances generally aren't large, although stunning scenery can make journeys surprisingly slow. Allow as much time as you can spare – in any event not less than a week.

Tourism Information

 Scotland's National Tourism Board is **VisitScotland**, PO Box 121, Livingston EH54 8AF; in the UK, ☎ 845-225 5121; outside UK, ☎ 1506-832 121; fax 1506-832 222, info@visitscotland.com, www.visitscotland.com. There is also a Scottish tourist office in London: VisitScotland Centre, 19 Cockspur Street, just off Trafalgar Square.

Scotland has a number of regional tourist boards and an excellent network of **Tourist Information Centres** (TICs). TICs provide information and accommodation booking, and sometimes other services such as foreign currency exchange and Internet, and are listed in the relevant regional chapters. Many TICs offer a walk-in service only. Others accept calls, although many calls are now diverted to a central **VisitScotland** call center. TIC offices are listed by region in each section of this book.

Most foreign diplomatic missions in the UK are in London, although Scotland has several **consulates**, most of which are based in Edinburgh.

■ **American Consulate General**: 3 Regent Terrace, Edinburgh EH7 5BW, ☎ 131-556 8315

■ **Australian Consulate**: 69 George Street, Edinburgh EH2 2JG, ☎ 131-624 3333

■ **Canadian Consulate**: Standard Life House, 30 Lothian Road, Edinburgh EH1 2DH, ☎ 131-220 4333

■ **Danish Consulate**: 48 Melville Street, Edinburgh EH3 7HF, ☎ 131-220 0300

■ **French Consulate General**: 11 Randolph Crescent, Edinburgh EH3 7TT, ☎ 131-225 7954

■ **German Consulate General**: 16 Eglinton Crescent, Edinburgh EH12 5DG, ☎ 131-337 2323

■ **Consulate General of Ireland**: 16 Randolph Crescent, Edinburgh EH3 7TT, ☎ 131-226 7711

- **Italian Consulate General**: 32 Melville Street, Edinburgh EH3 7HA, ☎ 131-226 3631
- **Japanese Consulate General**: 2 Melville Crescent, Edinburgh EH3 7HW, ☎ 131-225 4777
- **Netherlands Consulate**: Thistle Court, 1-2 Thistle Street, Edinburgh EH2 2HT, ☎ 131-220 3226
- **Royal Norwegian Consulate General**: 86 George Street, Edinburgh EH2 3BU, ☎ 131-226 5701
- **Spanish Consulate General**: 63 North Castle Street, Edinburgh EH2 3LJ, ☎ 131-220 1843
- **Swedish Consulate General**: 22 Hanover Street, Edinburgh EH2 2EP, ☎ 131-220 6050
- **Swiss Consulate General**: 66 Hanover Street, Edinburgh EH2 1HH, ☎ 131-226 5660

Specialized Organizations

Historic Scotland, Longmore House, Salisbury Place, Edinburgh EH9 1SH, ☎ 131-668 8600 general, ☎ 131-668 8800 property opening times, fax 131-668 8669, hs.explorer@scotland.gsi.gov.uk, www.historic-scotland.gov.uk. Historic Scotland manages more than 300 historic properties showcasing Scotland's architectural heritage, including Skara Brae Prehistoric Village, Callanish Standing Stones, Edinburgh, Stirling and Urquhart castles, Iona Abbey and St Andrew's Cathedral.

The **Explorer Pass** (available from the Historic Scotland web site and larger properties with an entry charge) provides free entry to more than 60 Historic Scotland properties. It is available for periods of three, seven or 10 days. Adult/concession/family: three days over a five-day period, £16/£12/£32; seven days over a 14-day period, £22/£16.50/£44; 10 days over a 30-day period, £25/£19/£50. Historic Scotland properties are indicated in this book by **HS** in their contact details.

AUTHOR'S NOTE: *Concession is a general term meaning a reduced rate, which in most cases applies to students and senior citizens (in those cases when a reduced rate for younger children differs from the "concession" rate we have quoted it separately). For the purpose of this guide the term indicates that reduced rates are available, and you should inquire when buying tickets or paying admission.*

National Trust for Scotland, Wemyss House, 28 Charlotte Square, Edinburgh EH2 4ET, ☎ 131-243 9300, fax 131-243 9301, information@nts.org.uk, www.nts.org.uk. The Trust manages Scotland's historic, architectural and natural heritage, including Culzean, Brodick and many Aberdeenshire castles, Glenfinnan, Culloden, Glen Coe and Torridon.

The **Discovery Ticket** (available from Trust properties and many Tourist Information Centres) provides free admission to Trust properties for periods of three, seven or 14 days. Adult/family: three days, £12/£25; seven days, £17/£35; 14 days, £22/£42. National Trust for Scotland properties are indicated by **NTS** in their contact details.

Forestry Commission, Silvan House, 231 Corstorphine Road, Edinburgh EH12 7AT, ☎ 131-334 0303/314 6156, fax 131-314 6152, fcscotland@forestry.gsi.gov.uk, www.forestry.gov.uk. The Forestry Commission is one of Scotland's largest landowners and maintains a vast network of excellent forest and woodland trails.

Scottish Natural Heritage, ☎ 1738-444 177, fax 1738-458 611, www.snh.org.uk. **SNH** maintains Scotland's National Nature Reserves such as Glen Affric, Beinn Eighe and the islands of Rum and St Kilda.

Scottish Wildlife Trust, Cramond House, Cramond Glebe Road, Edinburgh EH4 6NS, 131-312 7765, fax 131-312 8705, enquiries@swt.org.uk, www.swt.org.uk. **SWT** manages over 120 wildlife reserves and protects Scottish wildlife and habitats.

Royal Society for the Protection of Birds: RSPB Scotland, Dunedin House, 25 Ravelston Terrace, Edinburgh EH4 3TP, ☎ 131-311 6500, rspb.scotland@rspb.org.uk, www.rspb.org.uk. The RSPB maintains bird reserves that provide excellent opportunities to view and find out about birds and other wildlife.

Visas & Documents

Visitors to the UK need a valid **passport**, although EU visitors can travel on their **national identity cards**. Visitors from the USA, Canada, Australia, New Zealand and South Africa don't need entry visas, provided they are not planning to stay longer than six months and won't be working. EU citizens don't need entry visas and are free to live and work in the UK. Further information on UK entry requirements can be obtained from any **British Embassy**, **High Commission** or **Consulate**, or from the **Foreign & Commonwealth Office** (www.fco.gov.uk).

Money

■ Currency & Banknotes

 The British currency is the **pound sterling** (£), which is divided into 100 **pence** (*p*). The Bank of England and several Scottish banks issue banknotes. Scottish banknotes differ in design from English notes but are of equal value and legal tender throughout the UK (as are English notes), although some traders in remote areas might refuse to accept them. If you encounter any problems, change your Scottish notes for English ones at any bank. You're also advised to change any **Scottish £1 notes**, which aren't issued in the rest of the UK, for **£1 coins** before leaving Scotland. A small but growing number of establishments accept **euros**, the single European currency.

■ Banks

Banks are usually open Monday through Friday, 9am to 4 or 5pm (some are open Saturday mornings). Banks usually offer the best exchange rate for foreign currency, though you can also change money at airports, larger rail stations, travel agents and some large hotels (if you are a resident); there is usually a handling fee and commission. Most towns and cities have hole-in-the-wall cash machines (ATMs) where you can obtain cash with a check card, debit card or credit card.

■ Credit Cards

Most stores, hotels and restaurants, particularly in larger towns and cities, accept the major credit cards. Some establishments in remoter areas might only accept cash.

■ Tax Refunds

Value Added Tax (VAT) at 17.5% applies to goods and services. Non-EU visitors can reclaim VAT on goods on purchased from participating stores by using the **Foreign Exchange Tax Free Shopping** arrangements. Complete a Tax Free Shopping form from the shop (they may ask to see your passport to confirm that you reside outside the EU). When leaving the UK, show the goods to HM Customs & Excise at the port or airport. Customs will stamp the form to confirm that the items have left the EU. On returning home, mail the Customs-stamped form back to the shop, which will reimburse the VAT element of the purchase price.

■ Time

Time in Scotland follows **Greenwich Mean Time** (GMT) in winter, starting at 2am on the last Sunday in October (clocks go back, gaining an hour); and switches to **British Summer Time** (BST) at 2am on the last Sunday in March (clocks go forward, losing an hour).

■ Electricity

Voltage in Scotland is **240V/50Hz**, as in the rest of Britain. Plugs use three square-pin sockets and three-, five- or 13-amp fuses. North American appliances running on 110V will need a transformer.

■ Weights & Measures

Britain officially uses the **metric system** of weights and measures, although there remains a dogged reluctance to abandon certain well-loved **imperial** units such as the mile (1.609 km), pint (0.568 litres) and, to a lesser extent, the pound (0.454kg).

■ Health

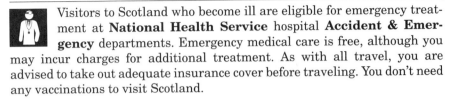 Visitors to Scotland who become ill are eligible for emergency treatment at **National Health Service** hospital **Accident & Emergency** departments. Emergency medical care is free, although you may incur charges for additional treatment. As with all travel, you are advised to take out adequate insurance cover before traveling. You don't need any vaccinations to visit Scotland.

■ Water

Scottish tap water is safe to drink. Water from hill streams is also generally safe, which is useful when you're out walking, but use common sense and look uphill to see if any herds of cattle or sheep are grazing near the stream.

■ Smoking

Smoking is restricted in most public buildings in Scotland, within airports and on most forms of public transport, although some may have designated smoking areas. Smoking is also restricted or banned in some restaurants and bars.

■ Emergencies

In an emergency dial **999** from any phone, ask for the relevant emergency service – police, ambulance, fire or coast guard – and be able to give your location.

Getting Here

■ By Air

Airports

 Scotland has four international airports: **Glasgow**, **Glasgow-Prestwick**, **Edinburgh** and **Aberdeen**. There are regional airports at Inverness and Dundee, other locations on the mainland and several islands of the Hebrides, Orkney and Shetland.

Glasgow (☎ 141-887 1111, www.baa.co.uk/glasgow) is eight miles from central Glasgow. Coach transfers leave every 15/30 minutes; taxis to the city are approximately £15.

Glasgow/Prestwick (☎ 1292-511 000, www.gpia.co.uk) is 32 miles from central Glasgow. Coach transfers leave every 30 minutes; taxis to the city are approximately £45.

Edinburgh (☎ 131-333 1000, www.baa.co.uk/edinburgh) is eight miles from central Edinburgh. Bus transfers leave every 10-15 minutes; taxis to the city are approximately £15.

Aberdeen (☎ 1224-722 331, www.baa.co.uk/aberdeen) is seven miles from central Aberdeen. Coach transfers are available (two an hour at peak times but the timetable is variable – call to check); taxis to the city are approximately £10.

Airlines

British Airways (☎ 870-850 9850, www.ba.com) flies to Edinburgh from London/Heathrow, London/Gatwick and Belfast; to Glasgow from Heathrow, Gatwick, Belfast and the Isle of Man; to Aberdeen from Heathrow and Gatwick; and to Inverness from Gatwick.

Flights are also available on British Airways to those cities from Birmingham, Bristol, Manchester, Southampton, Leeds/Bradford and Newcastle.

Flybe (☎ 871-700 0123, www.flybe.com) flies to Edinburgh from London City, Birmingham and Exeter; and to Glasgow from Birmingham and Exeter.

bmi (☎ 870-607 0555, www.flybmi.com) flies to Edinburgh from Heathrow and Manchester; to Glasgow from Heathrow and Manchester; to Aberdeen from Heathrow and Norwich; and to Stornoway from Heathrow.

easyJet (www.easyjet.com) flies to Edinburgh from Luton, Gatwick, Stansted and Belfast; to Glasgow from Luton and Stansted; to Aberdeen from Luton; and to Inverness from Gatwick and Luton.

Eastern Airways (☎ 1652-680 600, www.easternairways.com) flies to Aberdeen from Belfast, East Midlands, Humberside, Leeds/Bradford, Newcastle, Norwich, Southampton and Teeside; to Edinburgh from Norwich; and to Inverness from Birmingham and Manchester.

Ryanair (☎ 871-246 0000, www.ryanair.com) flies to Edinburgh and Aberdeen from Dublin; and to Glasgow/Prestwick from Stansted, Bournemouth, Dublin and several other European cities.

ScotAirways (☎ 870-606 0707, www.scotairways.com) flies to Edinburgh and Dundee from London City.

There are several direct flights to Scotland from North America:

Continental (www.continental.com) flies from the New York area (Newark) to Glasgow and Edinburgh (from June 2004).

American Airlines (www.aa.com) flies from Chicago to Glasgow (May-Oct).

US Airways (www.usairways.com) flies from Philadelphia to Glasgow (from May 2004).

Air Canada (www.aircanada.ca) flies from Toronto to Glasgow.

Air Transat (www.airtransat.com) flies from Toronto to Glasgow (April-Oct), Edinburgh (May-Oct) and Aberdeen (June-Sept). There are also flights to Glasgow from Calgary (May-Oct) and Vancouver (May-Oct).

Zoom Airlines (www.flyzoom.com) flies to Glasgow from Toronto, Calgary, Halifax, Ottawa and Vancouver (from May 2004).

Scotland also has good air links with European hubs, including Amsterdam, Paris and Frankfurt, which link to most North American cities.

■ By Rail

 There is excellent rail service to Scotland from England and Wales. Regular services operate throughout the day from London to Edinburgh (4½ hours) and Glasgow (5 hours). There are also direct services from London to Aberdeen and Inverness, and good links from other UK cities such as Birmingham and Manchester.

GNER (☎ 845-722 5225, www.gner.co.uk) operates inter-city services along Britain's east coast main line to Edinburgh and Glasgow and within Scotland as far north as Aberdeen and Inverness.

Virgin Trains (☎ 845-722 2333, www.virgintrains.co.uk) operates inter-city services along Britain's west coast main line to Glasgow and Edinburgh, and also runs some services to Scotland along the east coast and within Scotland as far north as Aberdeen. For general information on timetables and prices, contact National Rail Enquiries (☎ 845-748 4950).

ScotRail (☎ 845-755 0033, www.scotrail.co.uk) operates the overnight Caledonian Sleeper, with service (nightly except Saturday night) between London and Aberdeen, Edinburgh, Glasgow, Inverness and Fort William. Timings allow full days in London and Scotland before departure and on arrival. Single- and twin-berth sleeping cabins are available, with lower fares in seated coaches. Reasonably priced "Bargain Berths" are available from the web site.

 Scotland is a romantic country, and you can't beat the romance of arriving by train, particularly taking the overnight sleeper. Leave London late in the evening, enjoy a drink or late supper, retire to your cabin and wake up to breakfast against the spectacular backdrop of the Highlands rolling past your window (the scenery approaching Fort William is particularly stunning).

■ By Car

 The west coast via the **M1/M6/M74** provides the quickest driving route to Scotland from England, with options at Abington for Edinburgh or Glasgow.

Distances (miles) from London: Edinburgh 412; Glasgow 406; Aberdeen 549; Inverness 573; Fort William 514; Ullapool 635; Scrabster 690.

Distances (miles) from Birmingham: Edinburgh 290; Glasgow 286; Aberdeen 421; Inverness 446; Fort William 396; Ullapool 499; Scrabster 555.

■ By Coach & Bus

National Express (☎ 870-580 8080, www.nationalexpress.com) operates coach services to Scotland from all over the UK. The **National Express Discount Coachcard** is available to people aged 16-25, mature students and over-50s, and provides discounts of up to 30% on many fares. The cost is £10 and the cards are valid for a year.

■ By Ferry

 Stena Line (☎ 870-570 7070/400 6798, www.stenaline.com) sails from Belfast to Stranraer in Dumfries & Galloway (standard crossing 3¼ hours; fast ferry 1¾ hours).

SeaCat (☎ 870-552 3523, belfast.reservations@seacontainers.com, www.seacat.co.uk) sails from Belfast to Troon in Ayrshire (2½ hours).

P&O Irish Sea (☎ 870-242 4777, www.poirishsea.com) sails from Larne to Cairnryan in Dumfries & Galloway (standard crossing 1¾ hours; fast ferry one hour) and from Larne to Troon in Ayrshire (April-Sept; 1¾ hours by fast ferry).

There is a bus from Cairnryan to Stranraer (four miles), where there are rail and coach links to Ayr and Glasgow. Trains also link Troon with Glasgow (ScotRail, ☎ 845-755 0033, www.scotrail.co.uk).

Smyril Line (☎ 1595-690 845, www.smyril-line.com) operates a luxury cruise ferry between Norway, the Faroe Islands, Denmark and Iceland, which calls into Lerwick in Shetland on a regular basis.

From Belgium

Superfast Ferries (info.belgium@superfast.com, www.superfast.com) operates a service from Zeebrugge in Belgium to Rosyth in Fyfe (17½ hours).

Getting Around

■ By Air

 Loganair (Orkney, ☎ 1856-872 494/873 457; Shetland, 1595-840 246, www.loganair.co.uk) and **British Airways** (☎ 870-850 9850, www.ba.com) connect the islands and several regional airports to the main airports of Glasgow, Edinburgh, Aberdeen and Inverness.

Internal flights are fairly expensive and not great value unless you are short of time or want to experience the shell beach landing on Barra in the Outer Hebrides, or the world's shortest scheduled flight in Orkney (Westray-Papa Westray).

■ By Rail

Trains are an excellent way to travel within Scotland; they deliver you right to the heart of cities, and include steam services and some unimaginably scenic lines.

ScotRail (☎ 845-755 0033, www.scotrail.co.uk) operates a rail network that covers most major towns and cities, including four services per hour between Edinburgh and Glasgow (48 minutes), and other express services linking Edinburgh and Glasgow with Stirling, Perth, Dundee, Aberdeen and Inverness. Cycles are carried free on ScotRail services, although reservations are sometimes needed.

The **Freedom of Scotland Travelpass** (from ScotRail and railway stations) provides unlimited travel on all scheduled train services within Scotland, all Caledonian MacBrayne scheduled ferry services, and various bus services: any four out of eight consecutive days £89; any eight out of 15 consecutive days £119.

ScotRail also offers **Area Rovers** that provide discounted travel on a variety of services in the Highlands (unlimited train and bus travel and ferry reductions) and Central Scotland (unlimited train travel).

Scenic Lines & Steam Trains

 The railway lines from Inverness to Kyle of Lochalsh, Inverness to Wick and Thurso, Glasgow to Fort William and Fort William to Mallaig (where steam trains run in the summer – see below) provide unforgettable journeys through some of Scotland's finest scenery.

The **Kyle line** from **Inverness** to **Kyle of Lochalsh** is the most famous railway line in Scotland, although it's not the most continuously scenic. From Inverness, the landscape passes from pastoral to mountainous before reaching the beautiful coastal section from Strathcarron to Kyle of Lochalsh.

The **Fort William to Mallaig** line is rapidly gaining celebrity from its role in the *Harry Potter* films. This route is more eventful in its scenery than the Kyle line, with a succession of lochs (Eil, Eilt, nan Uamh), the superb view at Glenfinnan and the succession of tunnels and viaducts leading to the vistas over the Small Isles and Skye. The **Jacobite Steam Train** (West Highland Railway Company, ☎ 1463-239 026/1524-732 100, www.westcoastrailway-.co.uk) operates on this line from mid-June to September.

The **Strathspey Steam Railway** (Aviemore Station, Dalfaber Road, Aviemore PH22 1PY, ☎ 1479-810 725, fax 1479-812 220, information@strathspeyrailway.co.uk, www.strathspeyrailway.co.uk; open from the end of March through October) operates a steam service between **Aviemore**, **Boat of Garten** and **Broomhill** (better known as "Glenbogle" station in the popular TV series *Monarch of the Glen*).

■ By Car

 The primary road network covers most of the country, except for remoter areas, which are served by single-lane roads (see below). Many towns and cities are linked by motorways (designated "M") and dual carriageways. There are no tolls on Scottish roads, but four bridges levy charges: Forth, Tay, Erskine and Skye.

Renting a car can be the cheapest and most flexible way to explore Scotland, particularly if you are planning to visit remoter areas. You can rent ("hire") cars from the following national companies:

- **Arnold Clark** (☎ 845-607 4500, www.arnoldclark.com)
- **Avis** (☎ 870 010 0287, www.avis.co.uk)
- **Budget** (☎ 870-153 9170, www.budget.co.uk)
- **easyCar** (www.easycar.com) – rates are lower the earlier you book

- **Enterprise Rent-A-Car** (☎ 870-350 3000, www.enterprise.com)
- **Europcar** (☎ 870-607 5000, www.europcarscotland.co.uk)
- **Hertz** (☎ 870-844 8844, www.hertz.co.uk)
- **National Car Rental** (☎ 870-400 4552, www.nationalcar.co.uk)
- **Sixt Rent a Car** (☎ 1246-506 776, www.e-sixt.co.uk)

Most companies require drivers to be between 23 and 75, with a full current driving license held for at least a year. Foreign nationals are also required to show a passport. The rental contract usually includes third party liability, fire and theft insurance. Specify in advance if you prefer automatic transmission or need child seats. Don't forget to refuel the car if required at the end of the rental; it will be cheaper than letting the rental company do it.

Driving Regulations

Holders of overseas driving licenses can drive in Britain for up to a year. Visitors bringing their own cars from overseas require green-card insurance and the car's registration documents. Don't drink and drive, as the criminal penalties are severe. Above all else, don't forget to drive on the left!

Speed Limits

- **Motorway/Dual Carriageway**: 70 mph (112 kph)
- **Single Carriageway**: 60 mph (96 kph)
- **Built-up areas**: 30 mph (48 kph)

Seat Belts

It is compulsory to wear seat belts in both the front and rear of cars. Babies and small children must be restrained in carriers or child seats. The **Highway Code**, available from bookshops, newsagents and motoring organizations (AA and the RAC), sets out all the rules for driving in Britain.

Fuel

Four-star, unleaded, lead-replacement and diesel fuels are all available. Bear in mind that in remote areas, gas (petrol) stations can be quite some distance apart and their opening times limited. Fuel is generally more expensive the more remote you are, so fill your tank before you catch the ferry.

Single-Track Roads

 Many remote areas are served by single-track (one-lane) roads with intermittent passing places. The prospect of head-on collisions can be off-putting, but these roads are generally pretty safe and provide many of the most scenic drives in Scotland.

You'll see passing places on both sides of the road; when you stop to allow oncoming traffic and faster traffic behind you to pass, stay to the left, even if the passing place is on your right. The oncoming or passing vehicle will then be able to use the passing place to get around you.

AUTHOR'S NOTE: *Passing places can appear on either side of a single-track road. You must always stay on the left side of the road when letting other cars pass; they will go around you.*

■ By Coach & Bus

 Buses and coaches are a good – and often the cheapest – way to get around. **Scottish Citylink** (☎ 870-550 5050, www.citylink.co.uk) operates a modern coach fleet linking over 200 towns and cities across the country. Advance booking isn't usually required, but it is recommended for long journeys. **Explorer Passes** allow unlimited travel on Citylink services and start at £39 for three days.

The **Royal Mail Postbus** (☎ 845-774 0740; outside UK, ☎ 1752-387 112, www.royalmail.com/postbus) is a unique and charming way to travel through remote areas of the country. The service carries passengers on its mail delivery routes in rural areas where little or no other public transport is available. Postbuses are generally minibuses or sometimes just cars. Space is limited so you shouldn't rely on them if you have a strict schedule. You can hail a postbus anywhere along its (usually circuitous) route, but they don't run frequently and you're unlikely to encounter one unless you are specifically waiting for it.

■ By Ferry

 Scotland has 130 inhabited islands, and ferry travel is an integral part, and one of the most enjoyable aspects, of traveling around Scotland. The main island groups are the Inner and Outer Hebrides (Western Isles) off the west coast, and Orkney and Shetland off the northeast coast.

West Coast Islands

Caledonian MacBrayne (☎ 1475-650 100, fax 1475-637 607, reservations@calmac.co.uk, www.calmac.co.uk) sails to 24 islands off the west coast and in the Firth of Clyde. The summer season operates from Easter to mid-October with a reduced service in winter. Advance vehicle reservations are advised and often obligatory (☎ 870-565 0000, fax 1475-635 235).

Orkney & Shetland

NorthLink Ferries (☎ 845-600 0449, info@northlinkferries.co.uk, www.northlinkferries.co.uk) sails a modern fleet of luxury car ferries from Scrabster (north coast mainland) to Stromness (Orkney); and from Aberdeen (northeast mainland) to Lerwick (Shetland), with some sailings via Orkney. Comfortable cabins are available on early morning Orkney sailings and the overnight Shetland sailings. Advance bookings are advisable on sailings from Aberdeen to Lerwick.

John o'Groats Ferries (☎ 1955-611 353, fax 1955-611 301, office@jogferry.co.uk, www.jogferry.co.uk; sailings May-Sept) operates a passenger-only sailing from John o'Groats (northeast coast) to Burwick (Orkney).

Pentland Ferries (☎ 1856-831 226, www.pentlandferries.com) operates a car ferry from Gills Bay, near John o'Groats, to St Margaret's Hope (Orkney).

Orkney Ferries (☎ 1856-872 044, www.orkneyferries.co.uk) operates ferry services between the Orkney Islands.

Shetland Islands Council (www.shetland.gov.uk) operates ferry services linking the larger islands with the Shetland mainland.

Regional Ferry Lines

Local operators sail the following routes, details of which appear in the regional chapters as noted.

- Gourock (west of Glasgow) to Dunoon (Cowal): see *Argyll, Stirling & the Trossachs*, page 181.

- Isle of Islay to Isle of Jura: see *The Hebrides*, page 459.

- Corran (across Loch Linnhe, near Fort William): see *Highlands & Skye*, page 345.

- Glenelg (western Highlands)-Kylerhea (Skye): see *Highlands & Skye*, page 345.

- Mallaig to Inverie (across Loch Nevis, Knoydart): see *Highlands & Skye*, page 345.

Adventures

Scotland is a world-class adventure playground for numerous activities, including walking, climbing, cycling, riding, watersports, fishing and golf. Add to this the magnificent scenic backdrops and you're unlikely ever to forget your Scottish adventure.

Walking & Climbing

 Walking is one of the best ways to enjoy Scotland's wide, open landscapes and get up close to its spectacular flora and fauna. Most regions of Scotland offer a great choice of walking options, ranging from short strolls and waymarked paths to moderate hillwalking, multi-day treks and airy scrambling on remote mountain ridges. Although there are many existing trails, experienced walkers can also enjoy the thrill of wild, off-trail walking along untamed stretches of coastline, through steep-sided glens and over ancient drove roads.

We've included a number of walks but this doesn't even begin to scratch the surface of what is available. Many fine walking books are available, though the best advice is often to speak with local people about the best walks in their area; they often know about magical hidden trails that not even the best walking books have yet discovered. Tourist Information Centres also carry information on walks, local ranger services and guided nature walks.

■ Access & Rights of Way

Scotland has a long tradition of open access to its countryside, although it's a myth that there is no law of trespass. Simply walking onto someone's land is not a criminal offense, although the seldom-invoked **Trespass (Scotland) Act** of 1865 allows landlords to insist people leave their land if they are interfering with land management, lambing, etc.

The general right-of-access was recently formalized through the **Land Reform (Scotland) Act** 2003 (taking effect in 2004), which establishes statutory rights of access to land and water (which were already available in return for responsible use). The Act sets out statutory rights of non-motorised access (for walking, cycling, horse riding, canoeing, etc) to land and inland water for passage, recreation, education and commercial activities. Access rights must be exercised responsibly, as set out in the **Scottish Outdoor Access Code**, due to come into effect with the Act in 2004, and whose main points are expected to include:

- Guard against all fire risks
- Fasten all gates
- Keep dogs under close control
- Keep to public paths across farmland
- Use gates and stiles to cross fences, hedges and walls
- Leave livestock, crops and machinery alone
- Take all litter home
- Help to keep all water clean
- Protect wildlife, plants and trees
- Take special care on country roads
- Don't make unnecessary noise

■ Seasonal Restrictions

Stalking is the traditional way of managing Scotland's red deer herds. It is important in ensuring the long-term health of the wild deer population and provides valuable income for many estates. Although the stag stalking season runs from 1st July to 20th October, and the hind (female red deer) season from 21st October to 15th February, for the majority of estates the peak stalking time is from August to October. During this time, walkers should be prepared to accept alternative routes as requested by estates, so as to avoid disturbing stalking activities.

During stalking, check with the relevant estate (see *Hillphones*, below) to find out about stalking activities. Follow any advice on locally posted signs and keep to established tracks where possible. On hills, keep to ridges; avoid cutting through corries (hollows), particularly when descending, as this disturbs the deer. Keep to main routes through glens and principal watercourses when descending open hillsides.

Similar considerations apply during grouse shooting, which principally takes place from 12th August through October.

■ Hillphones

In some popular hillwalking areas, the Hillphones service provides daily messages about stalking activities and advice to hillwalkers on routes that are open and those to avoid. Don't forget that deerstalking also takes place in areas not covered by Hillphones.

- Grey Corries/Mamore: ☎ 1855-831 511
- Glen Dochart/Glen Lochay: ☎ 1567-820 886
- North Arran Hills: ☎ 1770-302 363
- South Glen Shiel: ☎ 1599-511 425
- Drumochter: ☎ 1528-522 200
- Glen Shee: ☎ 1250-885 288
- Callater & Clunie: ☎ 13397-41997
- Invercauld: ☎ 13397-41911
- Balmoral/Lochnagar: ☎ 13397-55532
- Glen Clova: ☎ 1575-550 335
- Paps of Jura: ☎ 1496-820 151
- Atholl & Lude: ☎ 1796-481 740
- Glen Fyne/Glen Falloch: ☎ 1499-600 137
- Balquhidder: ☎ 1877-384 724
- Corrour: ☎ 1397-732 343
- Fealar: ☎ 1796-481 731

■ Walking Safely

Adequate preparations and precautions are essential before and during longer walks, particularly when venturing onto high ground. Accidents and deaths are sadly not uncommon.

Planning

The Scottish **weather** is notoriously changeable – conditions can change at an alarming speed, particularly at altitude, and it can snow at any time in the hills and mountains. Obtain a weather forecast before setting out and carry adequate clothing to cover deteriorating conditions.

The **Meteorological Office** provides three-day online forecasts:

- **Northwest Scotland**: www.meto.gov.uk/weather/europe/uk/nw-scotland.html
- **Northeast Scotland**: www.meto.gov.uk/weather/europe/uk/ne scotland.html
- **Southwest Scotland**: www.meto.gov.uk/weather/europe/uk/sw-scotland.html

■ **Southeast Scotland**: www.meto.gov.uk/weather/europe/uk/sescotland.html

For mountain weather forecasts, you can also telephone **Climbline**:

■ **Western Highlands**: ☎ 891-333 198
■ **Eastern Highlands**: ☎ 891-333 197

Choose a walk appropriate to your experience, fitness, navigation skills and prevailing weather. Take **children** only on routes where there are safe and easy retreats and not on long walks. It's a good idea to **leave word** of where you are intending to walk and when you are expecting to return.

Scotland's **terrain** varies enormously, from heather and peat bog to rocky paths, and can slow your progress, as can rising (or impassable) rivers and burns. Ensure you consider these factors when planning the time your walk will take.

What to Take

Hillwalking boots are strongly recommended for all but the easiest strolls. In any case, footwear should provide good ankle support and have a firm sole and secure grip. Warm, wind and waterproof **clothing** is essential. This includes gloves, hat, waterproof and windproof jacket and trousers and spare clothing such as a warm sweater or fleece. Remember it gets colder and windier the higher you climb and, as with all mountain regions, summit conditions can be very different from those at the base of the mountain.

Always carry a **map** (Ordnance Survey maps scale 1:50,000 or 1:25,000) and **compass** and know how to use them. On longer walks, carry equipment for use in an **emergency** such as a flashlight (torch), whistle and first aid kit. The recognized emergency signal is six blasts on the whistle or six flashes with the torch. Carry ample **food and drink**, including reserve supplies. Simple, high-energy foods (eg chocolate, dried fruits, cheese and biscuits) are best, as are hot drinks in cold conditions.

MUNROS, CORBETTS & GRAHAMS

The 284 Scottish mountains higher than 3,000 feet (914 meters) are called Munros, named after **Sir Hugh Munro**, who first published a list of these peaks in 1891. Over 2,500 Munro "baggers" have claimed all 284 summits, although Sir Hugh himself still had two to climb at the time of his death. Hills from 2,500-3,000 feet (surrounded by a drop of at least 500 feet) are called Corbetts (219 are recorded) and those from 2,000-2,500 feet (surrounded by a drop of at least 500 feet) are called Grahams (224 are recorded).

On The Walk

Much of the attraction of walking in Scotland is the wilderness of its countryside, although this can obviously create navigational difficulties. Use your map and check your location constantly.

In an emergency, treat any injuries as best you can and calculate your exact map location. If possible, leave someone with the casualty and call the police (999) at the nearest telephone, reporting the grid reference where you left the casualty and details of the injuries.

Long-Distance Paths

 Scotland offers many opportunities for multi-day walks. Four routes have been designated **National Long Distance Routes** – the **Great Glen Way, Southern Upland Way, West Highland Way** and **Speyside Way**. All four have consistent signposting, maintained footpaths, good public transport links and reasonably spaced accommodation, and they pass some of Scotland's finest natural heritage along the way. Other long-distance walks range from signposted and maintained footpaths to less formal routes, some still being defined or even completely unmarked.

Great Glen Way (www.greatglenway.com), Scotland's newest long-distance path, connects Fort William in the west with Inverness in the east along a 73-mile (117-km) route passing famous Loch Ness. The route can be walked in four to six days, staying overnight in the various communities within the glen, and suits all levels of walker. For the less experienced, it is the perfect introduction to long-distance walking, being for the most part low-level and following mainly towpaths and woodland tracks. There are some challenging sections though, and the more experienced can tackle a few Munros or Corbetts within reach of the route. It can be walked in either direction, but by starting from Fort William you have the prevailing wind behind you, and you start with the easier sections of the path. The route is fully waymarked, and is managed by a dedicated ranger service.

Southern Upland Way (www.southernuplandway.com). Scotland's longest path is the 212-mile (340-km) route crossing southern Scotland from Portpatrick in the west to Cockburnspath in the east. The walk takes between 10 and 20 days and includes some very demanding stretches, with summits above 2,378 feet (725 m) and over 80 points above 2,000 feet (610 m). The Southern Upland Way is best walked from west to east. After leaving the west coast, the route heads through the heart of the Galloway hills, across the high moors of the Lowther Hills, past the Moffat Hills and St Mary's Loch to the River Tweed, from where it crosses the moors around Lauder before a gentler farmland section leads to the east coast. The route is fully waymarked and managed by a dedicated ranger service.

A variation on the Southern Upland Way is the **Sir Walter Scott Way** (www.sirwalterscottway.com), a 92-mile (148-km) route running from Moffat to Cockburnspath, that follows the eastern section of the Southern Upland Way. The route passes lowland valleys, lochs and reservoirs, alongside the River Tweed and its tributaries and over several Corbetts, and is steeped with numerous historical connections with Sir Walter Scott. The walk takes around six days.

West Highland Way (www.west-highland-way.co.uk). Scotland's original long-distance path is the superb 95-mile (152-km) route from Milngavie on the outskirts of Glasgow past Loch Lomond and across the wilds of Rannoch

Moor to finish in the Highlands at the foot of Ben Nevis, Britain's highest mountain. The route passes from the Lowlands, across the Highland Boundary Fault and into the Highlands, following ancient drove roads, military roads, coaching roads and disused railway lines. The walk usually takes six to seven days. This is a very popular walk and at busy times it is easier to find accommodation by avoiding a Saturday start. The route is fully waymarked and managed by a dedicated ranger service.

Speyside Way (www.speysideway.org). The Speyside Way runs 84 miles (135 km) from Buckie on the Moray Coast to Aviemore in the Highlands. Apart from a short section along the Moray coast, the path follows the valley of the River Spey from its mouth at Spey Bay to Aviemore at the foot of the Cairngorms. Allow five to seven days, more if you intend visiting many of the distilleries along the way. It's recommended to start from Buckie in the north, where the going is easiest, and make your way south toward the hills. The route is fully waymarked and managed by a dedicated ranger service.

Borders Abbeys Way (www.scot-borders.co.uk or www.visitscottishborders.com, click on "Walking" and follow the links). The Borders Abbeys Way is still being constructed but will eventually form a circular route of approximately 65 miles (104 km) connecting the four great Border Abbeys – Jedburgh, Dryburgh, Kelso and Melrose (also the start of St Cuthbert's Way; see below). The sections from Kelso to Jedburgh, Jedburgh to Hawick, and Hawick to Selkirk are now open (each is about 13 miles long). The path will continue from Selkirk to Melrose, Dryburgh and eventually back to Kelso; check the web site for updated information. The route is waymarked (AW for "Abbeys Way") in both directions.

Cateran Trail (www.caterantrail.com) Named after an ancient warlike tribe, this circular route from Blairgowrie into the beautiful Perthshire mountains measures 60 miles (96 km). The trail is based on historic drove roads used by the ancient Cateran hundreds of years ago and divides into five easily walked sections, which also make great day-walks.

The Fife Coastal Path (www.fifecoastalpath.com) When complete, the path will extend 78 miles, starting at the world famous Forth Bridges and finishing beyond the Tay Bridge. Currently the path stretches from North Queensferry in the west to Crail in the east, passing the beautiful coastline and picturesque fishing villages of the East Neuk. The currently open path measures 45 miles (72km), which takes three to four days to walk. Work is ongoing to complete the sections between Crail and Tay Bridge.

Isle of Arran Coastal Way (www.arrancoastalway.co.uk) This is a new circular walk around the Isle of Arran. The 65-mile (104-km) route takes six to seven days and generally follows the Arran coast, although it also includes two inland options.

Rob Roy Way (www.robroyway.com) This walk across the southern Highlands starts from the beautiful village of Drymen on the West Highland Way and travels northeast to the Perthshire town of Pitlochry, covering a distance of 79 miles (127 km) or 92 miles (148 km), depending on the route chosen, and taking up to seven days. The walk crosses scenic glens, rivers and streams and passes mountains and lochs as it follows tracks and paths used by the notorious outlaw Rob Roy MacGregor in the 17th and 18th centuries.

St Cuthbert's Way (www.scot-borders.co.uk/stcuthbertsway/index.htm) St Cuthbert's Way is a four-day, 62-mile (100-km) cross-border route connecting the border town of Melrose, where St Cuthbert is said to have started his ministry, and Holy Island (Lindisfarne) in England, with its superb priory and castle, where he ended his days. The route crosses varied terrain, including heather hills, woodland and coastal sections, and is fully waymarked in both directions with St Cuthbert's Cross.

For further information on walking and climbing contact **Ramblers' Association Scotland** (Kingfisher House, Auld Mart Business Park, Milnathort, Kinross KY13 9DA, ☎ 1577-861 222, fax 1577-861 333, enquiries@scotland.ramblers.org.uk, www.ramblers.org.uk/scotland); and **The Mountaineering Council of Scotland** (The Old Granary, West Mill Street, Perth PH1 5QP, ☎ 1738-638 227, fax 1738-442 095, info@mountaineering-scotland.org.uk, www.mountaineering-scotland.org.uk).

MIDGES

Tiny in stature they might be, but midges have been the bane of many a visit to Scotland and especially the Highlands. Midges are two-winged flies, similar to mosquitoes but smaller. They are most active between May and September, when the fierce evening feeding frenzies of females can cause maddening torment.

You can take steps to minimize the nuisance of midges:

1) Go out in bright sunlight. Midges dislike light and bite most vigorously toward long evening twilight, although they're active earlier in cloudy weather and in shade.

2) Time your activities when the weather is windy, which reduces midge attacks significantly.

3) Climb to higher ground. Away from shelter, midge activity diminishes with elevation. If pursued by midges, do as the red deer do and escape to higher ground.

4) Smoke them away. Smoke from a burning pipe or cigarette suppresses midges' ability to target their victims.

5) Use insect repellents, such as DEET-based formulas, although many swear that the most effective repellent is in fact a skin lotion – Avon Skin-So-Soft.

6) Wear light-colored clothing. Midges, like mosquitoes, are attracted to dark colors.

Cycling

 Cycling is a great way to explore many areas of rural Scotland. A wide network of cycle routes follows quiet roads and you can avoid traffic altogether by using canal towpaths, railway paths and waymarked forest trails throughout Scotland. Many forest routes and railway paths have been combined to create a 1,300-mile National Cycle Network. Long-distance, signposted routes run from Carlisle through Glasgow to Inverness, from the Firth of Clyde to the Firth of Forth and from Berwick-upon-Tweed to Edinburgh, Aberdeen and John o'Groats, and beyond to Orkney and Shetland.

You can obtain further information from **Cycling Scotland** (www.cycling-scotland.com) and **Sustrans** (☎ 845-113 0065, info@sustrans.org.uk, www.sustrans.org.uk), the sustainable-transport charity, which works to encourage people to cycle, walk and use public transport.

Sailing

 Scotland's pristine and uncrowded cruising waters are a pleasure to explore by boat. Sheltered coastal channels and sea lochs are ideal for novices to sail and there is no shortage of challenge for the ambitious yachtsman. Navigation is relatively straightforward, there is little shipping, and tides are no stronger than in the Solent, southern England's yachting playground. Inland from the coast, Scotland offers plenty of opportunities for sailing on canals (Caledonian, Crinan, Forth & Clyde and Union) and countless lochs.

Sailing lets you experience some of Scotland's finest scenery from a perspective few are lucky enough to enjoy. The Hebrides in particular, with the haunting beauty of their romantic islands, offer some of the finest and most scenic sailing waters in the world.

For further information on sailing and charter (skippered and bareboat) operators, contact **Sail Scotland** (PO Box 8363, Largs KA30 8YD, ☎ 1309-676 757, fax 1309-673 331, info@sailscotland.co.uk, www.sailscotland.co.uk).

Kayaking & Canoeing

 With its innumerable lochs, rivers and jagged coastline of sea lochs, islands and sheltered bays, Scotland is ideal for exploration by kayak or canoe. The inland and coastal waters offer excellent opportunities, from exhilarating plunges down steep cauldrons of white water to slow, gentle wanderings on canals, glassy lochs or sheltered bays.

For further information contact the **Scottish Canoe Association** (Caledonia House, South Gyle, Edinburgh EH12 9DQ, ☎ 131-317 7314, fax 131-317 7319, enquiry@scot-canoe.org, www.scotcanoe.org).

Diving

Scotland doesn't have the Red Sea or Great Barrier Reef, but its combination of clear waters, abundant sealife and a multitude of shipwrecks make it popular for scuba diving enthusiasts. Divers from around the world flock to renowned locations such as the Sound of Mull, the Summer Isles, St Kilda and the wreck divers' paradise – Scapa Flow. The water isn't as cold as you might imagine, typically varying from 14°C in September to 4°C in March. There are many wrecks to explore, including vessels from the German First World War fleet and a 300-year-old Cromwellian warship. There are opportunities to swim with seals, turtles, manta rays, dolphins, whales, and, if you're lucky, even 30-foot (10-meter) basking sharks.

For more information contact the **Scottish Sub Aqua Club** (The Cockburn Centre, 40 Bogmoor Place, Glasgow G51 4TQ, ☎/ fax 141-425 1021, ab@hqssac.demon.co.uk, www.scotsac.com).

Skiing & Snowsports

Scotland has five ski areas: **Glencoe** and **Nevis** in the west, and **Cairngorm**, **Glenshee** and **The Lecht** in the east. Glencoe, Nevis, Cairngorm and Glenshee each offer a fair range of skiing for all abilities with Cairngorm and Glenshee having the most extensive lift systems. The Lecht offers good skiing for beginners and early intermediates but is fairly limited for better skiers.

With their mountains covered more by heather than rocks, The Lecht and Glenshee (which are also the only Scottish centers with artificial snow-making facilities) are usually the best bet for early-season skiing. Once the deeper gullies of Glencoe and Cairngorm and the back bowl of Nevis fill with snow, they usually hold it well and can offer good skiing later into the season.

Scottish skiing in good conditions can be glorious but suffers a number of disadvantages compared with many resorts in continental Europe and North America. The steepest plunges in Scotland compare well with adrenaline-runs elsewhere, although Scotland lacks the length of run and continuous challenge provided by many other resorts.

The skiing in Scotland is relatively low and with low altitude comes an unpredictable snow record. Snow usually arrives in the Highlands in storms, ironically often blocking access roads when skiing conditions are perfect. However, when the snow will arrive, if it does arrive, is notoriously difficult to predict, even in the height of the season, from December to April. The Highland weather can also swing with dramatic fickleness, quickly melting and washing away thick blankets of snow. Historically, Scotland has often received its heaviest snowfalls a couple of weeks after heavy snowfalls over the east coast of North America, but this can't be relied on.

With uncertain snow conditions, it would take considerable bravery to pre-book a ski package trip significantly in advance. You would be much better advised to keep your timing and location options as flexible as possible.

Equipment rental, including ski suits, is available on-site at all five centers, so skiing can always be added on to a trip once local conditions are known. Lift passes aren't particularly cheap: £22-£25 per day or £16-£19 for a half-day.

High winds are another meteorological challenge faced by Scottish skiers. Exposed to the extremes of Atlantic weather, gales regularly blow away snow and close lifts. Only in Scotland have I pointed my skis straight down what was supposedly a run for reasonably competent skiers and been blown uphill!

Finally, you must dispel all notions of marching straight off the slopes and into a bar or your hotel. You won't find bars or accommodation within walking distance of any of the ski areas. With the exception of Nevis (with Fort William) and Cairngorm (with Aviemore), you might even have to travel 10 miles or more to reach your hotel.

Horseback Riding

 Horseback riding is a superb way to experience Scotland's wilderness and beautiful scenery, especially in areas where the terrain isn't suited to walking (for example thick bracken and boggy ground). Scotland's countryside offers acres of wide, open spaces, deserted beaches for exhilarating gallops and unspoiled trails over moorland and through pine forest.

Most riding stables offer pony trekking – relatively sedate half- or full-day rides, generally on sure-footed **Highland ponies**. More experienced riders can enjoy a number of organized trail rides. These offer the chance to negotiate varied terrain at all paces, and let you really get away from it all and see places walkers might not be able to reach.

For more information contact the **Trekking & Riding Society of Scotland** (☎ 1567-820 909, www.ridinginscotland.com).

Deerstalking

 Deerstalking, the annual cull of stags and hinds, is an age-old Scottish tradition that helps ensure adequate grazing for the deer herds and generates much-needed income for rural estates and their communities. Classic Scottish stalking is of **red deer stags** and **hinds** across the hills and glens of the Highlands (it's also possible to stalk **sika** or **roe deer** through the woodlands and forests of lower glens). Deer shot for "trophies" – the antlers kept as a souvenir – are carefully selected in accordance with herd-management plans.

Red deer generally inhabit remote hills away from roads and settlements. Just getting to the stalking grounds can be an exhilarating experience, particularly when the glens and deer forests resound to the roar of stags at the start of the rut (around mid-September).

The red stag stalking season runs from 1st July to 20th October, the peak stalking period being August-October for most estates. Hinds are culled from 21st October to 15th February, with most activity before Christmas. Roe stalking also takes place on forested estates. The roe buck stalking season runs from 1st April to 20th October and the doe stalking season from 21st October to 28th February, with June-August being the busiest months.

Fishing

 With Scotland enjoying so much pristine water, both inland and around its lengthy coastline, fishing is a popular and rewarding activity. You don't need a national rod license to fish in Scotland (as you do in England), although most fishing rights are privately owned and you need to buy permits locally.

■ Game Fishing

Scotland's game fishing – salmon, sea trout and brown trout – is world-class and provides thrilling sport and great eating. The salmon season generally runs from early February to late October, with slight regional variations. Salmon fishing on a Sunday is prohibited. The brown trout season runs from 15th March to 6th October. There is no closed season for rainbow trout (as they are not an indigenous species) and a number of commercial fisheries stay open throughout the year.

 AUTHOR'S NOTE: *Different sections (known as "beats") of rivers and lochs are owned by individuals, estates, fishing associations, etc., and you pay a fee to these owners for the right to fish on their property. Local hotels, fishing tackle shops and post offices are the best places to ask about buying permits and arranging ghillies, or guides.*

You can pay as much as you want to, particularly if you aspire to an exclusive salmon beat on one of the great rivers: **Tweed**, **Tay**, **Spey** and **Dee**. However, game fishing can also be great value, with hotels, tackle shops and post offices selling permits for as little as £5-£15 per day. Before paying for an expensive beat, check when the runs are and, if necessary, ask to see the five-year returns for the beat. Salmon and sea trout runs haven't been as prolific in recent years and many beats are enforcing or encouraging catch-and-release.

Salmon might be the "King of Fish" but, for a delightful wilderness experience, you can't beat fishing for feisty wild brown trout in one of the many remote lochs, rivers and streams spread throughout the country and the islands. If wilderness isn't your thing, you can fish for trout in The Water of Leith in Edinburgh and the Kelvin in Glasgow. Beautiful fisheries, such as the Lake of Menteith and Loch Leven, allow year-round fishing for rainbow trout.

■ Coarse Fishing

There are good opportunities to catch perch, roach and carp, but wild pike fishing provides the finest coarse fishing in Scotland. Lochs Lomond and Awe are legendary and Vennacher, Tummel and Lochy also provide good sport. There is no closed season for coarse fishing.

■ Sea Fishing

Cod and pollack are the mainstays of sea angling, although the remote northern and western waters offer three "big game" species: porbeagle sharks, huge common skate and sizeable halibut. There is no close season for sea angling and no permits are required.

For further information contact **Scottish Anglers National Association** (The National Game Angling Academy, The Pier, Loch Leven, Kinross KY13 8UF, ☎ 1577-861 116, fax 1577-864 769, admin@sana.org.uk, www.sana. org.uk).

Golf

Scotland is recognized as the home of golf. No other locale can match its golfing heritage, nurtured and developed over 600 years. The country boasts an overwhelming choice of superb courses, 540 in total, the highest number per capita in the world. These range from revered Open venues – **St Andrews**, **Muirfield**, **Royal Troon**, **Turnberry** and **Carnoustie** – and **Gleneagles**, setting for the 2014 Ryder Cup, to hidden gems like **Blairgowrie**, **Machrihanish**, **Boat of Garten** and **Gairloch**. Scotland's courses offer great diversity in challenge and scenery, most notably on its links (coastal) courses.

The season runs from April to mid-October, although – because of their generally drier coastal climate – links courses can usually be played throughout the year. It's best to book rounds in advance, particularly at popular courses such as St Andrews or Muirfield where you should lodge written applications at least 18 months in advance. Most clubs have dress codes and frown upon jeans, collarless shirts and trainers. In the most traditional clubs, men are asked to wear a jacket and tie in the main lounge.

Tours & Cruises

Scotland is easy to explore on your own, but excellent tours are available if you're short of time or want the thrill of visiting a remote area by unusual transport, such as a classic yacht, a luxury train or on horseback.

On Horseback

Argyll Trail Riding (Brenfield Farm, Ardrishaig, near Lochgilphead PA30 8ER, ☎ 1546-603 274, fax 1546-603 225, info@brenfield.co.uk, www.brenfield.co.uk; open April-early Oct). Explore the remote splendor of the West Highlands on horseback through a superb range of weeklong trail rides. The **Wild Boar** or **Castles Trail** is a fast and challenging trail for the competent rider and includes beach gallops, climbing mountains and swimming your horse in the sea! The **Rob Roy Trail** doesn't require such a high level of riding competence, although you must be fit as more hours are spent in the saddle – and you ride through magnificent Glen Coe. The **Loch & Forest Trail** is the easiest of the trails and involves day-rides, including a trip to Kilmartin Glen, and a beach gallop. There are also mini-breaks, pub/picnic rides, clinics and training in Le Trec (orienteering on horseback – in which David Hay-Thorburn, the son of owner Tove Gray-Stephens, is a former World Champion).

On the Water

Eda Frandsen (Doune, Knoydart, By Mallaig PH41 4PL, ☎ 1687-462 917, jamie@eda-frandsen.co.uk, www.eda-frandsen.co.uk; cruises April-Sept). Look no farther for the ultimate Scottish sailing experience. *Eda* is a beautiful traditional sailing cutter whose graceful lines, gleaming woodwork and huge rigging evoke the romantic days of sail and turn heads wherever she ventures. Jamie Robinson is an expert skipper who good-naturedly fuses his guests into a competent (barely so in the case of the author!) sailing unit. Learn the ropes, set the sails and steer. Unforgettable cruises from Mallaig take you to the Small Isles, Isle of Skye (the overnight mooring in Loch Scavaig beneath the towering Cuillin ridge is breathtaking), the Outer Hebrides and the remote outcrop of St Kilda. Themed trips include walking, photography, wildlife and whisky. Delicious meals (Knoydart lamb is a speciality) are somehow crafted from a galley the size of a telephone box, and Jamie provides great after dinner entertainment singing sea shanties. These are great trips. Book early!

Fingal of Caledonia (Caledonian Discovery, The Slipway, Corpach, By Fort William PH33 7NN, ☎ 1397-772 167, fax 1397-772 765, info@fingal-cruising.co.uk, www.fingal-cruising.co.uk; cruises mid-Apr to mid-Oct). Unforgettable cruises aboard a spacious holiday barge crammed with sailing boats, canoes, windsurfers, mountain bikes and fishing rods. As the barge makes its stately passage through the Caledonian Canal you face the impossible task of deciding which activities to choose – or maybe you just want to sit on deck or try your hand at piloting. To ease the stress of decision-making, many departures have fixed themes, including coast-to-coast walking or cycling on the Great Glen Way, art, photography, *ceilidh* (this cruise is very popular and you need to book well in advance), sea loch cruising, Great Glen heritage and wildlife. The only thing that's certain is that you won't have anywhere near enough time to try all the activities you will want to – be prepared to book another cruise.

Scottish Highlander (Go Barging, European Waterways, 35 Wharf Road, Wraysbury, Staines, Middlesex TW19 5JQ, ☎ 1784-482 439, US toll free 1-800-394 8630, fax 1784-483 072, sales@gobarging.com, www.gobarging.com; cruises from April to mid-Nov). Luxury cruising on the Caledonian Canal with day-trips by support Land Rover to Cawdor Castle, Culloden, Eilean Donan Castle, Urquhart Castle, Glen Coe and Ben Nevis Distillery. Unforgettable highlights include the overnight moorings at Urquhart Castle and Loch Oich and tea at Glengarry Castle Hotel on Loch Oich. An open bar, gourmet cuisine and all entrance fees are included. All the staterooms are air conditioned and have private facilities.

By Train

Royal Scotsman (46a Constitution Street, Edinburgh EH6 6RS, ☎ 131-555 1344, fax 131-555 1345, bookings@royalscotsman.co.uk, www.royalscotsman.com; tours mid-Apr to mid-Nov). Romantic tours aboard a luxury train through some of Scotland's finest scenery. Everything about Royal Scotsman oozes timeless glamour and style. Accommodation is in plush, wood-paneled state rooms. Watch the changing scenery from the relaxing **Edwardian Observation Car** with its open veranda. Visit castles, stately homes and other attractions. The dress dinners are an experience to savor.

On Foot

Walkabout Scotland (2 Rossie Place, Edinburgh EH7 5SG, ☎ 131-661 7168, fax 131-661 8162, tours@walkaboutscotland.com, www.walkaboutscotland.com). Guided hillwalking and musical festival tours from Edinburgh. The schedule of daily walks – including Ben Lawers, Ben Lomond and Buachaille Etive Mor – make excellent days out from the capital. Weekend (Glen Coe/Glen Nevis, Glen Affric, Arran) and week-long trips (northwest Highlands, Skye, etc) are also available, as are trips to music festivals in Orkney, Skye and elsewhere.

Wilderness Scotland (The Clockhouse, 72 Newhaven Road, Edinburgh EH6 5QG, ☎ 131-625 6635, fax 131-625 6636, info@wildernessscotland.com, www.wildernessscotland.com). Guided walking, classic yachting and wilderness expeditions to some of the remotest areas of the Highlands and Hebrides. Even the itineraries, to such locations as Glen Garry and Kintail, Knoydart, Glen Affric, Torridon, the Western Isles and Skye, are enough to set the blood racing. If you yearn for a true wilderness experience amid majestic scenery, this is where to find it.

Wild in Scotland (166 High Street, Royal Mile, Edinburgh EH1 1QS, ☎ 131-478 6500, fax 131-478 6501, mail@wildscots.com, www.wild-in-scotland.com). Lively, good-value minibus tours to the Highlands, Skye, Outer Hebrides and Orkney in the company of excellent, knowledgeable guides. Accommodation is in comfortable hostels and evening meals are either cooked by the group or eaten in local restaurants and pubs – some with live traditional music.

Holidays & Events

UK bank holidays are generally observed on **New Year's Day**, **Good Friday**, **Easter Monday**, first and last weekends in **May**, first weekend in **August**, **Christmas Day** and **Boxing Day**. The Glasgow Chamber of Commerce (30 George Square, Glasgow G2 1EQ, ☎ 141-204

2121) produces a booklet listing annual holidays observed in different areas of Scotland.

One of the unique attractions of visiting Scotland is the burgeoning calendar of special events and festivals, celebrating everything from history, culture, food and drink to sport and recreation. The major events and festivals are listed in each area chapter. Even if you're not interested in attending a festival you should note their dates as they may impact the availability (and price) of accommodation. The most notable example is Edinburgh around **Hogmanay** (end December) and **Festival** (August), when accommodation can be almost impossible to find or impossibly expensive.

Communications

Post Offices

Main post offices in cities and towns offer **international money transfer**, **postal order** and **bureau de change** services, in addition to selling **stamps** and sending **mail** and **parcels**. Rural post offices are often part of a general store or newsagent. Post offices are generally open Mon-Fri, 9am-5:30pm, Sat, 9am-12:30pm. Smaller offices often close for lunch. The Post Office sign has yellow lettering on a red background. Post boxes are red.

Telephone & Internet Connections

The country code for Scotland (and the UK as a whole) is **44**. To call a number listed in this book from outside the UK, dial the access code for the country you are dialing from, followed by 44, then the complete number as listed. From the US, for example, dial 011 44, then the local number with its **dialing code** (the part of the number before the hyphen).

If dialing from within the UK, dial "0" followed by the complete number. If dialing a local number, eg a Glasgow number from Glasgow, you can omit the dialing code.

Numbers starting with **08**, such as **0800** (called "freephone," similar to 1-800 numbers in the US), **0845** (local rate) and **0870** (national rate), generally can't be accessed from outside the UK. Beware when dialing numbers beginning with **090**. These are premium-rate calls and can be very expensive.

Telephoning from a hotel is generally expensive and it's much cheaper to use a public telephone. **Phone cards** are available from post offices, newsagents and Tourist Information Centres.

Internet cafés can be found in most major cities and towns, although not in huge numbers. **Tourist Information Centres** will be able to advise on where to find an Internet café locally. Many hotels have Internet facilities available to guests.

Scotland on Film

Scotland's pristine landscapes and historic buildings have long been popular backdrops for shooting films and television series.

At the Movies

Braveheart (1995; Mel Gibson) won five Oscars and was filmed in and around Glen Coe, Glen Nevis and the Mamore Mountains.

Chariots of Fire (1981; Ben Cross, Ian Charlson and Nigel Havers) won four Oscars and has scenes filmed at Sma' Glen near Perth, Edinburgh and St Andrews (including the famous beach training scenes).

Entrapment (1999; Sean Connery and Catherine Zeta-Jones) has scenes filmed at Duart Castle on the Isle of Mull.

Greystoke (1984; Christopher Lambert) used Floors Castle as the ancestral seat of Tarzan's Earls of Greystoke family.

Franco Zeffirelli's *Hamlet* (1990; Mel Gibson) filmed at Blackness and Dunnottar Castles.

The *Harry Potter* films have shot many scenes in Scotland. *Harry Potter and the Philosopher's Stone* (2001) used scenes from Glen Nevis and the Fort William-Mallaig Railway Line (Hogwarts Express). *Harry Potter and the Chamber of Secrets* (2002) again filmed at Glen Nevis and the Glenfinnan Viaduct. During filming for *Harry Potter and the Prisoner of Azkaban* (2004) above Glencoe village, sparks from the "Hogwarts Express" ignited a fire around Glenfinnan Viaduct during the dry, hot summer of that year.

Highlander (1986; Christopher Lambert and Sean Connery) has scenes shot at various locations in Scotland, including Eilean Donan Castle, Glen Coe, Glen Nevis, Loch Shiel, Torridon and Skye.

Kidnapped (1971; Michael Caine) has scenes shot at Seil Island and Stirling. The 1960 version (Peter Finch and Peter O'Toole) was filmed in Ardgour, Ballachulish and Glen Nevis.

Local Hero (1983; Burt Lancaster and Fulton MacKay) was mainly filmed on Moray's white sand beaches, with the Morar Hotel, Lochailort Inn and Ben Nevis Distillery featuring as well.

Loch Ness (1995; Ted Danson and Joely Richardson) has many scenes shot around Loch Torridon and Loch Ness, and the monster is sighted beneath Eilean Donan Castle rather than Castle Urquhart!

Monty Python and the Holy Grail (1975) has scenes filmed at Glen Coe, Loch Tay, Doune Castle and Castle Stalker.

Mrs Brown (1997; Judi Dench and Billy Connolly) has scenes filmed at Duns Castle (filling in for Balmoral) and on the Ardverikie Estate in Badenoch (now the set for the TV series *Monarch of the Glen*).

Rob Roy (1995; Liam Neeson and Jessica Lange) has scenes shot in Glen Coe, Glen Nevis, Castle Tioram, Drummond Castle, Morar, Loch Leven, Loch Arkaig and Rannoch Moor.

The 39 Steps (1935; Robert Donat and Madeleine Carroll) – Hitchcock's film was mainly shot in the studio but uses scenes shot at the Forth Rail Bridge and Glen Coe.

Whisky Galore (1949; Basil Radford and Gordon Jackson) was filmed on the island of Barra in the Outer Hebrides.

On Television

The delightful series *Monarch of the Glen* (from 1999) is filmed in and around Ardverikie House and Loch Laggan in Strathspey.

Hamish Macbeth (1995-1997) was filmed over a large area of the northwest Highlands.

The gritty police drama *Taggart* (from 1983) is filmed in Glasgow and its popularity has long survived the death of the actor who played the eponymous detective.

Accommodations

The diversity of accommodation is one of the greatest charms of visiting Scotland. With so much to choose from, we have tried to steer clear of merely functional establishments. Staying in a bland, modern hotel when an inviting, atmospheric inn is available nearby misses out one of the greatest delights of the Scottish experience.

The accommodation we highlight is notable above all for its character and romance: castles, country houses, island hideaways, crofts, farmhouses, mills and coaching inns. We also include delightful accommodation in luxury railway carriages, lighthouses and a converted church. Many of the establishments listed are centuries old, and have a long and fascinating history etched into their very fabric.

HOTEL PRICE CHART	
Per person, per night, based on double occupancy in high season. B&B rate includes breakfast; DB&B includes dinner and breakfast.	
£	Under £20
££	£21-£35
£££	£36-£50
££££	£51-£80
£££££	Over £80

The price chart is meant as a guide. Lower rates are often available, particularly at larger hotels, so it's worth asking about special deals. Off-season rates can be significantly lower; and discounts are often available for stays of two nights or longer. Single-room supplements may apply. Establishments are open year-round, unless otherwise stated.

Cuisine

DINING PRICE CHART	
Indicates the price per person for a full meal, excluding drinks. Generally three courses, though fixed menus of five or more courses may be available.	
£	Under £10
££	£11-£20
£££	£21-£30
££££	£31-£40

A common misconception, fortunately outdated, is that Scottish food is dour – haggis, black pudding, porridge and deep-fried Mars bars. Happily, the country's fine natural larder is now recognized as one of Scotland's great attractions, particularly when it offers the chance to enjoy the finest food at its source.

Scottish beef – Aberdeen Angus and the rarer but equally distinguished Highland beef – is some of the most sought-after in the world. **Wild venison** is plentiful and healthy, and there are numerous **game birds**, including pheasant, wild duck and grouse. About the only good to come out of the Highland Clearances has been the profusion of sheep that now provide some of the tenderest **lamb** you can eat.

Haggis is the most traditional of all Scottish dishes, comprising a large round sausage of chopped meat (lamb, mutton and/or beef), minced lamb or venison liver, possibly chopped sheep's heart, oatmeal, chopped onion, stock, seasoning and spices, conventionally boiled in a sheep's stomach. Neither the recipe nor its appearance is particularly appetizing, but the rich and peppery haggis is surprisingly tasty, particularly served to the sound of pipes, stabbed open with a traditional black stocking knife and accompanied by a glass of Scotch. **Macsween of Edinburgh** (page 128) is widely renowned for its haggis.

AUTHOR'S NOTE: *People from certain districts of Scottish cities, primarily Glasgow, have had a poor health record, resulting in Scotland being dubbed "heart attack capital of Europe." I am not aware of anyone outside Scotland eating deep-fried Mars bars – the iconic example of these bad eating habits; though less common nowadays, they are still sold in some fish-and-chip shops.*

Best of all is west coast seafood: melt-in-the-mouth **oysters** you can't stop eating; delicious **scallops** the size of pork pies; and succulent **mussels** you can pull off the beach, or even Skye Bridge. **Lobsters** and **prawns** (prawns cover all sizes, including langoustines) are also abundant. **Wild Scottish salmon**, particularly when pulled from the Tay, Tweed or Dee, is world-famous; **turbot** and **halibut** are the corresponding kings of North Sea white fish. Even fish and chips, a junk food in many parts of the UK, can be excellent, such is the freshness and high quality of the fish.

Restaurants are usually open from noon-2:30pm for lunch and 6-10pm for dinner, although outside large towns they are liable to close earlier. In the countryside, make sure you have ordered by 8:30pm at the latest to avoid missing the kitchen. Last orders are often taken 45 minutes before closing. Pubs generally open from 11am (later on Sundays) to 11pm or 1am. Most pubs serve coffee and snacks and many offer excellent bar and restaurant meals. Food festivals exist in many parts of the country for the serious gourmet. Fine food needn't be expensive in Scotland so don't hold back.Scotland's most famous drink is, of course, **whisky**, although several breweries produce excellent traditional **ales** (try Orkney Dark Island and Isle of Skye Red/Black Cuillin).

 DID YOU KNOW? *In contrast to commercial beers, **real ales** haven't been chill-filtered and pasteurised. Instead, they undergo a secondary fermentation in the cask after arriving at the pub, which generally provides greater flavor.*

Apart from alcoholic drinks, Scotland's other national beverage is **Irn-Bru**, a locally made soft fizzy drink that is so popular Scotland is the only developed country in the world where Coca-Cola is not the top-selling soft drink. Irn-Bru has a striking orange hue and a creamy, largely indescribable flavor, and is full of caffeine – making it a perfect hangover cure!

NOTE: *Licensing hours* are the times during which an establishment may serve alcohol. This generally coincides with opening hours, but not always.

Entertainment

Events, Festivals & Games

The Scottish calendar swells with notable events and festivals covering arts, whisky, food, traditional music, walking, horseback riding, real ales and fishing. We have listed the main annual events and festivals in each regional chapter. **Highland Games** and **Gatherings** are calendar highlights that mainly take place in the summer and early autumn. Selected Highland Games are listed in regional chapters.

Music

In addition to the major events and festivals, local performers throughout the country help maintain Scotland's music traditions. Many pubs present traditional music on a regular basis. Better still, if you play the guitar, fiddle, piano or accordion, you'll be encouraged to join in.

Every visitor should experience at least one *ceilidh* – informal gatherings with traditional music, dance and verse. Some venues hold them regularly, but by tradition they are not widely publicized. Look for notices at post offices and village halls, and ask locally.

Spectator Sports

Football (soccer) is played all over Scotland, with Premier League (the top division) football played as far north as Aberdeen. Scottish football is dominated by the two Glasgow clubs – **Celtic** and **Rangers**. Their clashes are intensely passionate but games against other teams are often very one-sided. **Rugby** is popular, particularly in the Borders. **Golf's** prestigious Open Championship is played on Scotland's great links courses (Troon in 2004 and St Andrews in 2005, www.randa.org). Scotland has five **horse racing** courses at Musselburgh, Kelso, Perth, Hamilton and Ayr.

Traditional Games

 **Shinty** (in Gaelic *"camanachd"*) is Scotland's oldest team sport and plays an important role in Gaelic tradition. The modern game is based primarily in the Highlands and, with its Irish cousin *hurling*, bears a superficial resemblance to field hockey. Teams are comprised of 12 players, each closely marked by an opponent. The stick, or *caman*, has two sloped faces, enabling players to hit the ball from either side, as in ice hockey. Players can swing the caman above the head and stop the ball with their feet, but only the goalkeeper may use his hands. (**Camanachd Association**, Queen Anne House, 111 High Street, Fort William PH33 6DG, ☎ 1397-703 903, www.shinty.com).

Curling involves sliding heavy circular stones down a sheet of ice and trying to stop them closest to the center of a set of rings (the house), aided by the frantic and slightly comical sweeping of the ice by team-mates. The stones are traditionally made of granite from Ailsa Craig off the Ayrshire coast. Describing the game as bowls on ice often annoys curlers, who regard the tactical intricacies of the game as closer to chess on ice. The game is known to be over 500 years old, although its origin is not certain. The Royal Caledonian Curling Club – the sport's mother club – was formed in 1838.

The game was originally played on frozen lochs, although most games are nowadays played on indoor ice. The GB (actually Scottish) women's team won a thrilling gold medal at the 2002 Salt Lake City Winter Olympics. (**Royal Caledonian Curling Club**, Cairnie House, Avenue K, Ingliston Showground, Newbridge EH28 8NB, ☎ 131-333 3003, fax 131-333 3323, www.royalcaledoniancurlingclub.org).

The South & Arran

Southern Scotland is a region of rich, rolling farmland, rugged coastland and the Clyde coast islands. The area is dotted with ancient abbeys, castles and historic houses, and boasts strong literary connections with both Robert Burns and Sir Walter Scott. The **Borders** region has a green, rolling landscape. Upland **Galloway** has forests and wild moors. **Ayrshire's** rich pastures are a vivid green, beyond which rise the steep mountains of the **Isle of Arran**.

DON'T MISS

■ Explore the atmospheric ruins of the southern **abbeys** – there are many, but notably **Jedburgh**, **Melrose** and **Sweetheart**.

■ Walk the **Eildon Hills**, laden with mystique and mythology and crowned by an ancient hill fort.

■ Walk in the **Moffat Valley** to Grey Mare's Tail waterfall, with magical Loch Skeen hidden above.

■ Visit the UK's smallest cathedral on **Great Cumbrae**.

■ Visit the **Alloway house** where Robert Burns was born, and drink a pint in the **Dumfries tavern** (Globe Inn) that was his local pub.

■ Sail to **Arran**, "Scotland in miniature," visit the standing stones at **Machrie Moor** and climb **Goat Fell**.

■ Best Freebie: **Scott's View**, near Melrose.

The Borders

Covering around 1,800 square miles, the Borders region stretches from rolling hills and moorland in the west, through gentler valleys to the rich agricultural plains of the east, and on to the rocky Berwickshire coastline with its secluded coves and picturesque fishing villages. Through its heart runs the silvery course of the **River Tweed**, which provides some of the finest game fishing in Scotland. Scattered around this peaceful countryside are attractive towns and castles, and the ruins of great **abbeys** that testify to the strife inflicted by the Wars of Independence fought with England in the late 13th and early 14th centuries. The Borders retains strong historical associations

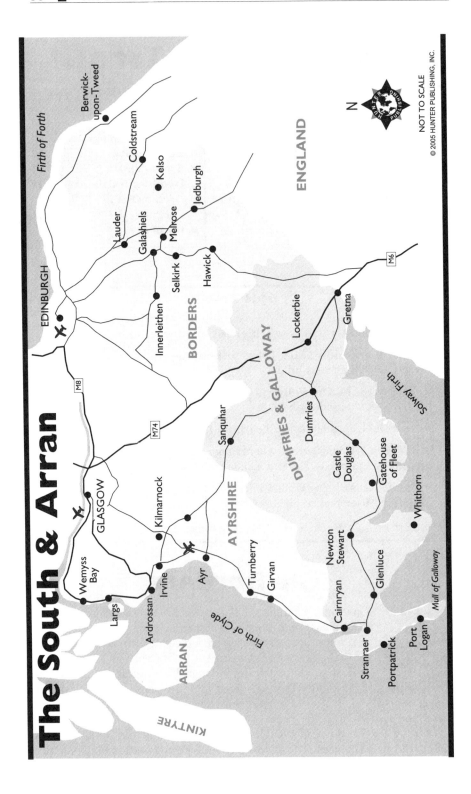

The South & Arran

NOT TO SCALE
© 2005 HUNTER PUBLISHING, INC.

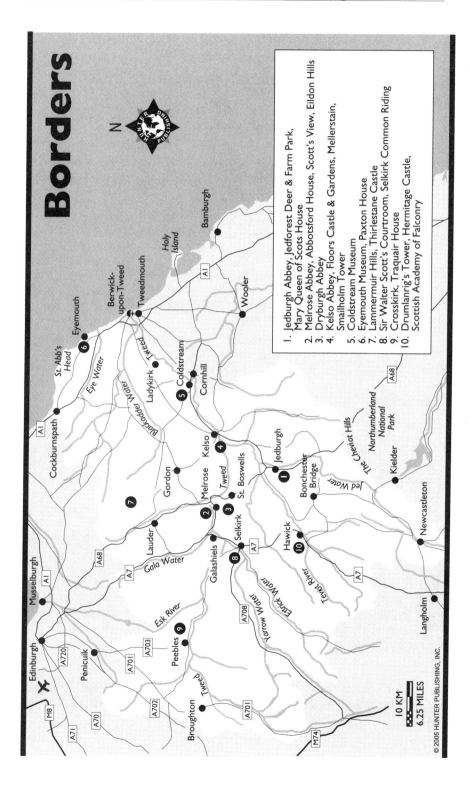

Borders

1. Jedburgh Abbey, Jedforest Deer & Farm Park, Mary Queen of Scots House
2. Melrose Abbey, Abbotsford House, Scott's View, Eildon Hills
3. Dryburgh Abbey
4. Kelso Abbey, Floors Castle & Gardens, Mellerstain, Smailholm Tower
5. Coldstream Museum
6. Eyemouth Museum, Paxton House
7. Lammermuir Hills, Thirlestane Castle
8. Sir Walter Scott's Courtroom, Selkirk Common Riding
9. Crosskirk, Traquair House
10. Drumlanrig's Tower, Hermitage Castle, Scottish Academy of Falconry

10 KM
6.25 MILES

© 2005 HUNTER PUBLISHING, INC.

with horseback riding, commemorated in the Common Ridings and other colorful local festivals.

 INFORMATION SOURCES: Scottish Borders Tourist Board is at Shepherd's Mill, Whinfield Road, Selkirk TD7 5DT, ☎ 870-608 0404, fax 1750-21886, info@scot-borders.co.uk, www.scot-borders.co.uk.

■ Special Events

Melrose Sevens (April; ☎ 1896-822 993, www.melrose7s.com). Traditional rugby competition.

Borders Festival of the Horse (May; ☎ 1835-863 020, festival@bhs-scotland.org.uk). Celebration of everything that makes the Borders Scotland's horse country.

Selkirk Common Riding (June; Tourist Board ☎ 870-608 0404, info@scot-borders.co.uk). One of the oldest and most impressive common ridings, involving bands at dawn, mounted processions through the town and riding to the boundaries (see next page).

Scottish Borders Festival of Walking (August; ☎ 1835-824 632, info@borderwalks.fsnet.co.uk). Based in Hawick, events include daily guided walks, receptions, ceilidhs and other evening entertainment.

■ Getting Here & Getting Around

By Air

Edinburgh, Glasgow and Newcastle airports are all within one to two hours' drive. There are no airports in the Borders region.

By Rail

Although the London-Edinburgh mail line runs along the Scottish Borders coast, there are no train stations in the Borders. The nearest are **Berwick-upon-Tweed** to the south and **Edinburgh** to the north. Buses are available from both stations to Borders destinations.

By Car

 Good roads connect northern England and central Scotland to the Borders. The **A68** (central Borders) and **A1** (eastern Borders) link the region with Edinburgh and Newcastle. The **A7** cuts through the central Borders from Edinburgh toward Carlisle in northwest England.

By Coach

National Express (☎ 870-580 8080, www.nationalexpress.com) links the Borders with many parts of the UK. Local buses link towns within the Borders.

■ Adventures

On Wheels

The Borders is excellent cycling country with lots of cycle routes along and around the River Tweed, including three major waymarked routes (guides available from regional Tourist Information Centres, see pages 60, 78, and 94).

The **Tweed Cycleway** is a waymarked 89-mile route running through the heart of the Borders. Starting at Biggar, the route avoids busy roads to take you through hills, forests and the attractive towns of Peebles, Melrose, Kelso and Coldstream, finishing on the coast at Berwick-upon-Tweed.

The **Borderloop** is a magnificent 250-mile waymarked circuit taking in the best of the Borders. The route links Peebles in the west with the coast at Eyemouth, along the way visiting Melrose, Kelso and other pretty towns and villages, and passing through a landscape of rolling hills, wild moorland, river valleys and meandering country lanes. Although the ride can be completed in a long weekend, most people take five to seven days. You're best off starting at Peebles and riding the circuit clockwise, thus leaving the toughest and most spectacular Hawick to Peebles section to last.

The **Four Abbeys Cycle Route** is a 55-mile circular route linking the abbeys at Melrose, Dryburgh, Kelso and Jedburgh. You'll save money by buying a Historic Scotland Three-Day Explorer Pass to gain entry to the abbeys.

You can rent cycles locally at **Hawick Cycle Centre** (previously known as Raleigh Cycle Centre, 45 North Bridge Street, Hawick TD9 9PX, ☎ 1450-373 352, fax 1450-377 531) and **Christopher Rainbow Bike and Tandem Hire** (Timpendean Cottages, Jedburgh TD8 6SS, ☎ 1835-830 326, fax 1835-830 327, christopher.rainbow@btinternet.com). Tandem and bike rental catering particularly to people tackling the Tweed Cycleway, Border Loop and Four Abbeys routes.

On Horseback

The history of the Borders is inextricably linked with horses through the tradition of **Common Ridings**. The area is rightly known as Scotland's horse country. There are more horses per capita here than anywhere else in Scotland. The old drove roads and tracks (once used by Border "reivers," or cattle raiders, for stealing cattle) today provide peaceful routes for exploring the rolling countryside on horseback.

The **Buccleuch Country Ride** is a waymarked 57-mile ride around Hawick and Selkirk through some of the most attractive Borders countryside. It generally caters to riders bringing their own horses, although some riding stables in the area do rent horses. It's best ridden between May and October when there are no distractions from lambing or shooting. Many local establishments provide facilities for horses, such as stabling and grazing.

The Borders

COMMON RIDINGS

Common Ridings date from lawless days when towns-people would ride their boundaries to protect their rights and common land. The unique traditions of the Common Ridings, some dating back to the 16th century, are celebrated each year in all major Border towns with magnificent ride-outs involving hundreds of horses, ridden with a passion worthy of the reivers (raiders) of old. **Selkirk Common Riding**, with over 400 riders taking part, is one of the oldest of the Borders festivals and dates from the Battle of Flodden in 1513.

On Water

The Borders region is a paradise for anglers with everything from the internationally renowned salmon fishing on the River Tweed, excellent sea trout fishing on its tributaries, rainbow trout in local lochs, wild brown trout in rivers, coarse fishing on lochs and the lower Tweed to sea fishing off the Berwickshire coast.

Salmon Fishing

The **River Tweed**, the second longest river in Scotland, is often called the "Queen of salmon rivers." It runs right through the heart of the Borders and attracts anglers from all over the world to its famous salmon pools such as Weetles, Galoshan and Carry Wiel. The salmon season runs from 1st February to 30th November and more salmon are caught on the fly here than in any other British river. The Tweed is most famous for its autumn run of large fish when some specimens approach 30 pounds.

The peak autumn months of October/November are expensive (around £600 per day) and heavily booked. Vacancies are occasionally available, particularly if booking at the last minute. These same beats can sometimes be fished at lower season times for as little as £30 per day.

Trout Fishing

The lower Tweed, River Till and Whiteadder provide the best **sea trout** fishing, with the largest fish running in the autumn. The sea trout season is also 1st February to 30th November.

Fish Tweed (Stichill House, Kelso TD5 7TB, ☎ 1573-470 322, fax 1573-470 259, info@fishtweed.co.uk, www.fishtweed.co.uk) can arm you with everything you need to know about salmon and sea trout fishing on the Tweed, including available beats, current conditions, recent catches and permits.

The **River Tweed** and its tributaries – the **Teviot**, **Ettrick**, **Leader** and **Whiteadder** – together with the **Meggett**, **Talla** and **Fruid** reservoirs, offer excellent **brown trout** fishing during the season from 15th March TO 6th October. During April and May daytime fishing is best, whereas from June-August dusk and evening fishing is better. Numerous local angling associations sell permits for their waters. Contact the **tourist board** (☎ 870-608 0404, info@scot-borders.co.uk) for details.

Cod, mackerel, coalfish, flounder, plaice, sole, haddock, whiting, catfish, ling and wrasse can all be caught from the shore or a boat, the latter giving larger fish. **Eyemouth Sea Angling Club** (20 Deanhead Drive, Eyemouth, ☎ 1890-751 718) can give further information.

There are several **fishing tackle** specialists in the area, providing all the equipment, clothing and permits you need, including **Tweedside Tackle** (36-38 Bridge Street, Kelso TD5 7JD, ☎ 1573-225 306, fax 1573-223 343), **Sanfords Country Sports** (6-8 Canongate, Jedburgh TD8 6AJ, ☎ 1835-863 019) and **R. Welsh & Son** (28 Castle Street, Duns, ☎/fax 1361-883 466).

School of Casting, Salmon & Trout Fishing (Station House, Station Yard, Clovenfords, near Galashiels TD1 3LT, ☎/fax 1896-850 293, fishingschool-@onetel.net.uk). Fly fishing courses on the River Tweed and neighboring lochs for all levels of angler, including equipment rental.

The Border Abbeys

Jedburgh, Melrose, Dryburgh and Kelso are four of the many religious centers established during the reign of **David I** (1124-1153). David grew up at the court of his brother-in-law, Henry I of England, where he experienced the newer, stricter religious orders blossoming across Europe. Although undoubtedly pious, David also appreciated that a well-organized church would help him control his unwieldy kingdom.

The four Border Abbeys were inextricably caught up in the continuing struggles between Scotland and England and suffered numerous attacks during the Wars of Independence, which began in 1296. Susceptible to the changing political climate, the abbeys at different times supported both Scotland and England. The attacks on the abbeys culminated in the "rough wooing" of 1544-45 when English King Henry VIII tried to "persuade" the Scots to marry their infant Queen Mary to her half-cousin Edward (Henry's son and future Edward VI).

■ The Religious Orders

Augustinian (Jedburgh)

Established in 1059 and known as the **Black Canons** on account of their black habits, the order was an example of ordained priests choosing to live the disciplined life of monks. The Augustinians helped develop gardening techniques and herbal medicines.

Cistercian (Melrose)

Formed in 1098 and known as the **White Monks** because of their undyed woolen habits, the order observed extremes of self-denial that significantly reduced the life expectancy of its monks. There was an emphasis on physical labor, although much of the daily work was carried out by illiterate lay brethren to free the monks for spiritual activities.

Tironensian (Kelso)

Also known as the **Grey Monks**, the order took its name from the abbey founded in Tiron near Chartres in 1109.

Premonstratensian (Dryburgh)

Also known as the **White Canons**, the order took its name from an abbey founded in Premontre, France in 1121, which developed its standards along Cistercian lines.

Coldstream

Coldstream lies on the **River Tweed** – the natural boundary between Scotland and England. Once a rival to Gretna as a destination for runaway marriages that could be held without prior public notice (this privilege was abolished in 1856, but not before at least two Lord Chancellors had taken advantage of this legal loophole!), the town is now best known as the birthplace of the **Coldstream Guards**, whose illustrious history is depicted in the local museum.

■ Attractions & Sights

Coldstream Museum (12 Market Square, Coldstream TD12 4BD, ☎ 1890-882 630, fax 1890-882 631; open April-Sept, Mon-Sat, 10am-4pm & Sun, 2pm-4pm, Oct, Mon-Sat, 1pm-4pm; admission free). Local history museum telling the story of the Coldstream Guards, with temporary exhibitions and a courtyard with fountain and picnic area.

■ Golf

 Hirsel Golf Course (18-hole parkland, 6,111 yards; Kelso Road, Coldstream TD12 4NJ, ☎ 1890-882 678, fax 1890-882 233, www.hirselgc.co.uk; green fees £20-£27). A challenging course of outstanding natural beauty.

■ Where To Stay & Eat

See the *Accommodation* and *Dining* price charts on pages 109 and 110.

 Fernyrig Farm (Birgham, By Coldstream TD12 4NB, ☎/fax 1890-830 251, fernyrig@btinternet.com; B&B £, dinner ££). B&B in a quiet, rural traditional stone cottage with rose garden and stables.

The Wheatsheaf at Swinton (Main Street, Swinton, By Coldstream TD11 3JJ, ☎ 1890-860 257, fax 1890-860 688, reception@wheatsheafswinton.co.uk, www.wheatsheafswinton.co.uk; B&B £££, lunch/dinner ££-£££). Family-run country inn with lots of character in the individually styled bedrooms. The inn has one of the best restaurants in the Borders, serving superb seafood and game.

Eyemouth

Eyemouth lies five miles north of the border, at a natural harbor with sandy beaches formed by the mouth of the **River Eye**. It has a strong fishing tradition dating back to the 13th century and the picturesque harbor still bustles with its colorful fleet. The new fish market has viewing areas for visitors.

 INFORMATION SOURCES: The tourism office is at Auld Kirk, Manse Road, Eyemouth TD14 5HE; open April through October.

■ Attractions & Sights

Eyemouth Museum (Auld Kirk, Manse Road, Eyemouth TD14 5JE, ☎ 1890-750 678; open Easter-Oct; adult/concession £2/£1.50, children free). Exhibits on farming, milling, blacksmiths and wheelwrights, based around the 15- by 4-foot tapestry woven to commemorate the great east coast fishing disaster of 1881 when 189 men lost their lives.

Paxton House (by Berwick-Upon-Tweed TD15 1SZ, ☎ 1289-386 291, fax 1289-386 660, info@paxtonhouse.com, www.paxtonhouse.com; open April-Oct, 11am-5pm; adult/child/family £6/£3/£16). One of Adam's finest 18th-century country houses, Paxton is set in 80 acres of estate on the banks of the River Tweed and contains the finest Chippendale furniture collection in Scotland. The large gallery is an outstation of the National Galleries of Scotland. There are also woodland trails, an adventure playground, Highland cattle, Shetland ponies and a red-squirrel hide.

■ Adventures

Ronnie Dale Off-road Driving School (Whiteburn Farm, Abbey St Bathans, Duns, near Eyemouth, TD9 0LF, ☎ 1361-840 244). Off-road adventure driving plus quad bike trekking for all ages.

 NOTE: *The vehicle referred to in this guide as a quad bike is what's more commonly known in the US as an ATV.*

Scoutscroft Dive Centre (Scoutscroft, Coldingham, near Eyemouth TD14 5NB, ☎ 1890-771 338, fax 1890-771 746, jhamilton@scoutscroftholidaycentre.fsnet.co.uk). Scuba diving, diving courses and a wide range of watersports.

New Ladykirk Stables (New Ladykirk Farm, Berwick-Upon-Tweed, near Eyemouth TD15 1XN, ☎ 1289-382 603, davisonros@aol.com). Hacking and trekking along the River Tweed for all abilities; lessons, show jumping and dressage.

■ Golf

 Eyemouth Golf Course (18-hole links, 6,520 yards; Gunsgreen Hill, Eyemouth TD14 5SF, ☎ 1890-750 004/750 551; green fees £20-£25). An enjoyable and challenging course featuring some of the most scenic and spectacular cliff-top holes in Scotland.

■ Where To Stay & Eat

See the *Accommodation* and *Dining* price charts on pages 109 and 110.

 Churches Hotel & Restaurant (Albert Road, Eyemouth TD14 5DB, ☎ 1890-750 401, fax 1890-750 747, admin@churcheshotel.co.uk, www.churcheshotel.co.uk; B&B £££, dinner £££). Former church manse converted into an elegant small hotel. Breakfast and lunch are served in a bright conservatory and the attractive restaurant serves excellent evening meals.

Dolphin Hotel (North Street, Eyemouth TO14 5ES, ☎ 1890-750 280; B&B ££). Small, family-run hotel on the Eyemouth beachfront.

Ship Hotel (Harbour Road, Eyemouth TD14 5HT, ☎ 1890-750 224; B&B ££). A reasonably priced inn and the only pub in Eyemouth, serving cask conditioned ales. Fishing and diving can be arranged.

Springbank Cottage B&B (The Harbour, St Abbs, By Eyemouth TD14 5PW, ☎ 1890-771 477, fax 1890-771 577; open Feb-Dec; B&B £-££). A fisherman's cottage with tea garden, close to the harbor's edge and nature reserve.

Lammermuir Hills

■ Attractions & Sights

 Thirlestane Castle (Lauder TD2 6RU, ☎ 1578-722 430, fax 1578-722 761, admin@thirlestanecastle.co.uk, www.thirlestane-castle.co.uk, open Easter & May-Sept, 10:30am-4:30pm, closed Sat; adult/concession/child/family £5.50/£5/£3/£15). Built originally as a defensive fort in the 13th century, the castle was rebuilt in the 16th century as the home of the Maitlands, subsequently enlarged and embellished, and remains the Maitland family home. There are many fine display rooms and ornate plasterwork ceilings, a woodland walk, adventure playground, tea room and gift shop.

■ Where To Stay & Eat

See the *Accommodation* and *Dining* price charts on pages 109 and 110.

The Lodge, Carfraemill (Oxton, Lauder TD2 6RA, ☎ 1578-750 750, fax 1578-750 751, enquiries@carfraemill.co.uk, www.carfraemill.co.uk; B&B ££). Traditional lodge with open fires and comfortable, stylish bedrooms. Dine on good country cooking in a choice of wood-paneled dining room, bistro or "Jo's Kitchen" – a cozy, themed restaurant with its own red Aga stove.

Kelso

The picturesque town of Kelso lies at the confluence of the rivers **Tweed** and **Teviot**. Its graceful five-arched bridge over the Tweed dates from 1803 and was a model for London's Waterloo Bridge. In parkland overlooking the Tweed stands **Floors Castle**, Scotland's largest inhabited house, while to the north of the town are the Adam mansion of **Mellerstain** and the 15th-century **Smailholm Tower**.

INFORMATION SOURCES: The tourism office is at Town House, The Square, Kelso TD5 7HF; open year-round.

■ Attractions & Sights

Kelso Abbey (HS; in Kelso; open at all times; admission free). Kelso was the earliest of David I's Border Abbeys and dates from 1128. The church was built in an unusual double-cross plan and was one of the most extraordinary Romanesque buildings in Scotland. Parts of the western transept and tower and the southwest corner of the nave still stand to their full height. Even in its fragmentary state, the abbey represents a superb work of architecture.

Floors Castle & Gardens (Roxburghe Estates, Kelso TD5 7SF, ☎ 1573-223 333, fax 1573-226 056, marketing@floorscastle.com, www.floorscastle.com; open April-Oct, 10am-4:30pm, last admission 4pm; adult/concession/child/family £5.75/£4.75/£3.25/£15). Floors Castle was the magnificent location of the Tarzan film Greystoke. It is the home of the Duke of Roxburghe and is the largest inhabited house in Scotland (it has 365 windows, one for every day of the year). It contains outstanding collections of paintings, furniture, porcelain and tapestries, and there are also walled gardens, an adventure playground and coffee shop.

Smailholm Tower (HS; near Smailholm village, six miles west of Kelso, ☎ 1573-460 365; open year-round, days and hours vary seasonally, so call ahead; adult/concession/child £2.20/£1.60/£0.75). Situated high on a rocky outcrop, Smailholm is a small rectangular tower set within a stone wall. The tower is associated with two noted Border families: the Pringles up until 1645 and thereafter the Scotts of Harden, ancestors of Sir Walter Scott. The Pringles built the tower around the middle of the 15th century. Family insolvency forced the sale of Smailholm to the Scotts, who built a new house in the courtyard and downgraded the tower house. The young Walter Scott was brought up on the nearby family farm of Sandyknowe. It was the sight of Smailholm that fired the young boy's imagination and in 1802 he published *Minstrelsy of the Scottish Border*, a collection of stories and ballads. The three upper stories of the tower now house an exhibition of costume figures and tapestries linking Sir Walter Scott to the area.

Mellerstain House (The Mellerstain Trust, Gordon TD3 6LG, ☎ 1573-410 225, fax 1573-410 636, enquiries@mellerstain.com, www.mellerstain.com;

open Easter & May-Sept, daily except Tues, 12:30pm-5pm, last admission 4:30pm; weekends only in Oct; admission £5.50, children under 16 free). Impressive Georgian house designed by William and Robert Adam, with beautiful plaster ceilings, exquisite interior décor, elegant period furniture and a large art collection. There is also a garden, shop and tearoom.

■ Golf

 Roxburghe Golf Course (18-hole parkland, 7,111 yards; Village of Heiton, Kelso TD5 8JZ, ☎ 1573-450 333, fax 1573-450 611, golf@roxburghe.net, www.roxburghe.net; green fees £50). Roxburghe is the first championship course in the Scottish Borders.

■ Shopping

Kelso Pottery (The Knowes, Kelso TD5 7BH, ☎ 1573-224 027). Specialists in "time tablets" (decorated local clays inlaid with historical and cultural images) and domestic stoneware.

■ Where To Stay & Eat

See the *Accommodation* and *Dining* price charts on pages 109 and 110.

 Roxburghe Hotel (Heiton, By Kelso TD5 8JZ, ☎ 1573-450 331, fax 1573-450 611, hotel@roxburghe.net, www.roxburghe.net; B&B ££££, dinner £££). Beautiful country house owned by the Duke of Roxburghe. There are log fires and a well-cooked, innovative menu using fresh seasonal produce from the estate.

Ednam House Hotel (Bridge Street, Kelso TD5 7HT, ☎ 1573-224 168, fax 1573-226 319, contact@ednamhouse.com, www.ednamhouse.com; B&B ££££, dinner ££). Imposing Georgian mansion dating from 1761, set in three acres of gardens overlooking the River Tweed. The attractive bedrooms are traditionally styled and the excellent restaurant combines classical techniques with innovative ingredients.

Lochside (by Kelso TD5 8PD, ☎ 1573-420 455, fax 1573-420 354, www.oldlochsidefarm.co.uk; B&B ££). Luxurious Victorian mansion set in attractive parkland overlooking Yetholm Loch Wildlife Reserve, with good home cooking, log fires and great views.

Whitehouse (St Boswells, By Kelso TD6 0ED, ☎ 1573-460 343, fax 1573-460 361, tyrer.whitehouse@lineone.net; B&B ££, dinner ££). Large house with spacious bedrooms and bathrooms, great views and a log fire in the drawing room. Dinners are available by arrangement.

Jedburgh

The historic town of Jedburgh lies 10 miles north of the border. Its beautiful red sandstone abbey was founded by David I around 1138 and sits above the banks of the **Jed Water**. In 1566 Mary, Queen of Scots stayed in Jedburgh in a house that now recounts the story of her turbulent life.

INFORMATION SOURCES: The tourism office is at Murray's Green, Jedburgh TD8 6BE; open year-round.

■ Attractions & Sights

Jedburgh Abbey (HS; Jedburgh, on the A68, ☎ 1835-863 925; open April-Sept, 9:30am-6:30pm; Oct-Mar, 9:30am-4:30pm; adult/concession/child £3.50/£2.50/£1.20). A splendid abbey founded by David I around 1138. The church is built in the Romanesque and early Gothic styles. Sections are remarkably complete, including the magnificent west door and remains of the cloister house, chapter house and ranges, but only foundations remain of the cloister and domestic quarters.

The abbey was settled by black-cloaked Augustinian canons from the abbey of St Quentin, near Beauvais in northern France. As the years passed, the enormous wealth of the house gradually corrupted successive generations of canons who lost the monastic vision and ideals of their predecessors. Like the other Border abbeys, Jedburgh was sacked repeatedly during the wars with England. The abbey was last attacked by Henry VIII in 1545 and the destruction he started was completed by John Knox and the Reformation.

Excavations of cloister buildings have uncovered interesting finds, including the 12th-century "Jedburgh comb," displayed in the excellent visitor center. An interesting video compares monastic life in12th-century Jedburgh with that today at Pluscarden Abbey (Aberdeenshire).

Jedforest Deer & Farm Park (Mervinslaw Estate, Jedburgh TD8 6PL, ☎ 1835-840 364, fax 1835-840 362, hopedale@globalnet.co.uk, www.aboutscotland.com/jedforest; open May-Aug, 10am-5:30pm; Sep-Oct, 11am-4:30pm; adult/child/family £4/£2.50/£12). Deer herds and rare breeds on a modern working farm, with nature trails, ranger-led activities and talks on farming and the environment. There is a hands-on interpretation barn and birds of prey displays with eagles, hawks and owls.

Mary, Queen of Scots House (Queen Street, Jedburgh TD8 6EN, ☎/fax 1835-863 331, open Mar-Nov, Mon-Sat, 10am-4:30pm & Sun, 11am-4:30pm; adult/concession £3/£2, children free). Mary visited the house in October 1566. She had come to preside at local courts but spent most of her four-week stay recovering after an arduous ride to visit her lover, the Earl of Bothwell, at Hermitage Castle. The house contains a popular museum presenting the compelling drama of her life.

■ Golf

Jedburgh Golf Course (9-hole parkland, 5,700 yards/18 holes; Dunion Road, Jedburgh TD8 6LA, ☎ 1835-863 587, fax 1835-862 360; green fees £16). An undulating moorland course set amid beautiful scenery.

■ Where To Stay & Eat

See the *Accommodation* and *Dining* price charts on pages 109 and 110.

 Jedforest Hotel (Camptown, Jedburgh TD8 6PJ, ☎ 1835-840 222, fax 1835-840 226, mail@jedforesthotel.freeserve.co.uk, www.jedforest-hotel.freeserve.co.uk; B&B £££, dinner £££). Refurbished hotel situated on 35 acres of grounds with attractive, well-furnished bedrooms and private fishing on the Jed Water. A team of French chefs expertly prepares haute cuisine and a brasserie-style bar menu is also available.

Glenfriars House (The Friars, Jedburgh TD8 6BN, ☎ 1835-862 000, fax 1835-862 112, glenfriars@edenroad.demon.co.uk, www.edenroad.demon.co.uk; B&B ££, dinner ££-£££). Elegant Georgian house in a quiet but central location in Jedburgh. Evening meals are available by arrangement.

Crailing Old School (Crailing, By Jedburgh TD8 6TL, ☎/fax 1835-850 382, info@crailingoldschool.co.uk, www.crailingoldschool.co.uk; B&B ££, dinner ££). Peaceful B&B accommodation in a former 19th-century school with great views and good food.

Meadhon House (48 Castlegate, Jedburgh TD8 6BB, ☎/fax 1835-862 504, meadhon@aol.com, www.meadhon.com; B&B £-££). 17th-century stone house with pleasant rooms and panoramic views over the abbey and castle.

The School House (Edgerston, Jedburgh TD8 6PW, ☎ 1835-840 627, fax 1835-840 683, a-robinson@supanet.com; open April-Dec; B&B ££, dinner ££). Refurbished 19th-century school and school house, with antique furnishings, minstrels' gallery and evening meals.

The Spinney (Langlee, Jedburgh TD8 6PB, ☎ 1835-863 525, fax 1835-864 883, thespinney@btinternet.com, www.thespinneyjedburgh.co.uk; open Mar-Nov; B&B ££). Spacious accommodation in an attractive house set in acres of mature gardens two miles south of Jedburgh.

Spread Eagle Hotel (High Street, Jedburgh TD8 6AG, ☎/fax 1835-862 870; B&B ££). Family-run hotel that claims to be Scotland's oldest continually inhabited hostelry.

The Caddy Man (Mounthooly, Jedburgh TD8 6TJ, ☎/fax 1835-850 78; lunch ££, dinner £££). Serves excellent light lunches and high-quality evening meals (evening meals during the week require minimum bookings – call to check).

Melrose & Galashiels

Melrose lies in the **Tweed Valley** at the foot of the triple peaks of the Eildon Hills. Robert the Bruce's heart is buried in its ruined abbey, which also marks the starting point for the 62-mile **St Cuthbert's Way**. Three miles west along the river is novelist Sir Walter Scott's romantic mansion of **Abbotsford**.

Nearby Galashiels lies in the narrow valley of the **Gala Water**, close to where it meets the Tweed. The town's prosperity was based on textiles and you can tour the cashmere and wool mill, which has supplied movie stars and famous designers, to watch the weaving process.

> **INFORMATION SOURCES:** The tourism office is at Abbey House, Abbey Street, Melrose TD6 9LG; open year-round.

■ Attractions & Sights

Melrose Abbey (HS; Melrose, off the A7 or A68, ☎ 1896-822 562; open April-Sept, 9:30am-6:30pm; Oct-Mar, 9:30am-4:30pm; adult/concession/child £3.50/£2.50/£1.20). One of Scotland's most famous ruins, the abbey was founded by David I in 1136 when he invited Cistercians from Rievaulx in Yorkshire to establish their first Scottish monastery. Melrose soon became one of the most prosperous religious houses in the country but suffered greatly in the wars with England. It was largely destroyed in 1385 by Richard II and, although rebuilding was begun, it was never completed. By the time of the Reformation, the abbey was already at a low spiritual ebb. The surviving remains are mostly 15th-century and include some fine medieval carvings, including humorous images of a bagpipe-playing pig and a cook with a ladle.

The heart of Robert the Bruce is believed to be buried at Melrose, as requested by the king just before his death in 1329. A mummified heart was uncovered during excavation of the Chapter House in 1996 and subsequently reburied. Unmarked, it cannot be certain it belonged to Robert the Bruce but it matches what is known about the burial. Objects found during excavations are on display and an audio guide is available.

Dryburgh Abbey (HS; eight miles southeast of Melrose on the B6404 near St Boswells, ☎ 1835-822 381; open April-Sept, 9:30am-6:30pm; Oct-Mar, 9:30am-4:30pm; adult/concession/child £3/£2.30/£1). Beautiful in location and design, the ruins of Dryburgh Abbey are remarkably complete. Much of what remains today dates from either the 13th century or the rebuilding in 1385. The finest reminder of its former grandeur is the north transept, and remains of the original finely painted decoration can be seen in the chapter house. After 1600, no canons remained at the abbey and distinguished local families appropriated the chapels for private burials, the most notable being Sir Walter Scott in 1832 and Field Marshal Haig in 1928.

Abbotsford House (By Melrose TD6 9BQ, ☎ 1896-752 043, fax 1896-752 916; open 3rd Mon in Mar-Oct, Mon-Sat, 9:30am-5pm & Sun: June-Sept, 9:30am-5pm, Mar-May & Oct, 2pm-5pm; adult/child £4/£2). Romantic house built and lived in by novelist Sir Walter Scott from 1812 until his death in 1832. See his study, library, drawing room, armouries and dining room overlooking the Tweed. There are extensive gardens and grounds, a woodland walk, a tearoom and a private chapel added after Scott's death.

Scott's View

Perhaps the most-photographed view in the Scottish Borders, this was Sir Walter Scott's favorite place for picnics and contemplation. When Scott's body was being carried to Dryburgh Abbey for burial, the horses bearing the carriage halted there automatically, so accustomed were they to stopping at this spot for Sir Walter. It was thus named "Scott's View."

Leave St Boswells by the B6404 northeastwards and in just over a mile cross the River Tweed. Turn left at the B6356 (signposted "Earlston"), bear left at Clintmains and turn right at the junction for Dryburgh. Climb uphill and in a mile bear left (signposted "Scott's View").

■ Adventures

On Foot

 The triple peaks of the **Eildon Hills** are the most distinctive single landmark in the Scottish Borders. North Eildon has a major Iron Age fort on its summit; it's the largest hillfort in Scotland, containing platforms for nearly 300 huts, and it was also used by the Romans as a signal station. The Romans also built a fort called **Trimontium** at nearby Newstead.

The walk starts and finishes in Melrose. Facing the abbey, turn right along Abbey Street to Market Square and beyond to Dingleton Road. Look for the **St Cuthbert's Way** sign. Walk under the road bypass, then left between houses on a footpath. A long flight of steps leads you up toward the hills (seats are provided for those who need them). At the top cross the stile and continue along the edge of fields, through three gates and onto the open hill.

The St Cuthbert's Way heads uphill to the right. Climb the lower slopes to the saddle between Mid Hill (on your right) and North Hill (to your left). Ascend Mid Hill, the highest, then to the fort and North Hill, continuing northeast. Follow Eildon Walk signs downhill to reach a quiet road, turn right then left down a lane between hedges. Walk under the bypass, then under the old railway bridge, skirting the pretty village of Newstead. Reach the houses at Priorswalk and continue back to the abbey and parking area (2 hours, easy).

On Wheels

Borders Experience (Galabank Mill, Wilderhaugh, Galashiels TD1 1PR, ☎ 1896-758 091, fax 1896-757 036, bmr@ringleader.co.uk). Quad bike through Borders forests and valleys with a guide.

Multi-Activity Operators

 Active Sports (Chain Bridge Cottage, Annay Road, Melrose TD9 9LP, ☎ 1896-822 452, info@activesports.freeserve.co.uk, www.activesports.freeserve.co.uk). A varied selection of outdoor activities on land, in water and in the air, including quad biking, kayaking, windsurfing, canoeing and hillwalking.

■ Golf

Galashiels Golf Course (18-hole parkland, 5,185 yards; off Ladhope Drive, Galashiels, near Melrose TD1 2DL, ☎ 1896-753 724, www.galagolfclub.co.uk;

green fees £16-£22). The course provides fantastic views of the Borders countryside and surrounding hills.

 St Boswells Golf Club (9-hole inland, 5,274 yards/18 holes; Brae-
heads, St Boswells, near Melrose TD6 0DE, ☎ 1835-823 527; green
fees £15). Scenic and peaceful course along the banks of the Tweed.

■ Shopping

Lochcarron Cashmere & Wool Centre (Waverley Mill, Huddersfield
Street, Galashiels TD1 3AY, ☎ 1896-751 100, fax 1896-758 833, enqui-
ries@lochcarron.com, www.lochcarron.com; open year-round, Mon-Sat,
9am-5pm, June-Sept, also Sun, noon-5pm; admission £2.50). Lochcarron has
produced kilts for movie stars Samuel L. Jackson and Ewan McGregor, and
has supplied fabrics to fashion designers Vivienne Westwood, Ralph Lauren
and Jean Paul Gaultier. There is a large factory shop, factory tours and local
museum.

■ Where To Stay & Eat

See the *Accommodation* and *Dining* price charts on pages 109 and 110.

 Burt's Hotel (Market Square, Melrose TD6 9PN, ☎ 1896-822 285,
fax 1896-822 870, reservations@burtshotel.co.uk, www.burtsho-
tel.co.uk; B&B £££, lunch/dinner £££). 18th-century family-run
townhouse hotel offering modern comfortable bedrooms and high-quality,
innovative bar and restaurant food that wins awards.

Buccleuch Arms Hotel (The Green, St Boswells, near Melrose TD6 0EW,
☎ 1835-822 243, fax 1835-823 965, bucchotel@aol.com; B&B £££, dinner ££).
Delightful family-run hotel that serves good food all day.

Dryburgh Abbey Hotel (St Boswells, near Melrose TD6 0RQ, ☎ 1835-822
261, fax 1835-823 945, enquiries@dryburgh.co.uk, www.dryburgh.co.uk; B&B
££££, dinner ££). Attractively furnished hotel with good-quality accommodation, an indoor swimming pool and the ruins of Dryburgh Abbey right on the
doorstep. There is also private trout fishing on the Tweed adjacent to the
hotel.

Greenside (St Boswells, near Melrose TD6 0AJ, ☎ 1835-822 140,
moira.steel@btinternet.com; B&B £). Victorian farmhouse B&B set on two
acres of grounds in a small village.

Old Abbey School (Waverley Road, Melrose TD6 9SH, ☎ 1896-823 432,
oneill@abbeyschool.fsnet.co.uk; open Mar-Nov; B&B £). Comfortable B&B in
a family home converted from a 150-year-old school close to the center of
Melrose.

Marmions Brasserie (Buccleuch Street, Melrose TD6 9LB, ☎ 1896-822 245;
££). Lively and elegant (almost) all-day dining in a distinctive, old oak-paneled interior.

Buckholmburn House (Edinburgh Road, Galashiels TD1 2EY, ☎ 1896-751 170, fax 1896-668 582, petersdickson@aol.com; B&B £). Familyrun B&B furnished with antiques. Special antique weekends are available.

Woodlands House Hotel (Windyknowe Road, Galashiels TD1 1RG, ☎ 1896-754 722, fax 1896-754 892, enquiries@scottishbordershotel.com, www.scottishbordershotel.com; B&B £££, dinner ££). Victorian gothic mansion hotel set in two acres of grounds, with paneled walls, open fireplaces and crystal chandeliers.

Selkirk

Selkirk stands high above the **Ettrick** and **Yarrow valleys**, which contain some of the finest scenery in the Borders. It was here that Sir Walter Scott served as Sheriff for 33 years, and his former courtroom features a presentation of the local Scott associations.

INFORMATION SOURCES: The tourism office is at Halliwells House, Selkirk TD7 4BL; open April-Oct.

■ Attractions & Sights

Sir Walter Scott's Courtroom (Market Place, Selkirk TD7 4BT, ☎ 1750-20096, fax 1750-23282, museums@scotborders.gov.uk; open April-Sept, Mon-Fri, 10am-4pm & Sat, 10am-2pm, May-Aug, also Sun, 10am-2pm, Oct, Mon-Sat, 1pm-4pm; admission free). Built in 1803 as the Sheriff Court, this is where the novelist Sir Walter Scott dispensed justice to the people of Selkirkshire. The courtroom museum explores Scott's life, his writings and his time as Sheriff.

■ Adventures

Dryden Riding Centre (Dryden, Ashkirk, Selkirk TD7 4NT, ☎ 1750-32208). Long-established family business providing riding for all ages and abilities, and lessons in indoor and outdoor schools.

■ Golf

Selkirk Golf Course (9-hole moorland, 5,575 yards/18 holes; Selkirk Hill, Selkirk TD7 4NW, ☎ 1750-20621; green fees £16). A delightful and challenging moorland course with stunning views.

■ Where To Stay & Eat

See the *Accommodation* and *Dining* price charts on pages 109 and 110.

Ettrickshaws Country House Hotel (Ettrickbridge, By Selkirk TD7 5HW, ☎/fax 1750-52229, jenny@ettrickshaws.co.uk, www.ettrickshaws.co.uk; B&B £££-££££, dinner £££). Nestling in 12 acres overlooking Ettrick Water, the hotel retains many original Victorian features and provides spacious, elegant accommodation and romantic candlelit dining. Private fishing, shooting and horseback riding are also available.

Gordon Arms Hotel (Yarrow Valley, By Selkirk TD7 5LE, ☎ 1750-82222, thegordonarms@aol.com; B&B ££, dinner ££). 200-year-old inn provides comfortable rooms, log fire, hearty local cuisine and real ale.

Peebles

Peebles is attractively set among hills on the banks of the **River Tweed**. Its wide High Street has an old **Mercat Cross**. The ruined **Cross Kirk**, high above Eddleston Water, was founded in 1261. To the east, surrounded by the hills and forest of the Tweed Valley, lies Innerleithen, home of **Traquair House**, the oldest inhabited house in Scotland.

INFORMATION SOURCES: The tourism office is at High Street, Peebles EH45 8AG; open year-round.

■ Attractions & Sights

Traquair House (Innerleithen EH44 6PW, ☎ 1896-830 323, fax 1896-830 639, enquiries@traquair.co.uk, www.traquair-.co.uk; open mid-April through Sept, noon-5pm; June-Aug, 10:30am-5:30pm; October, 11am-4pm; adult/concession/child/family £5.60/£5.30/£3.10/£16.50). The oldest continually inhabited house in Scotland was originally a 12th-century royal hunting lodge and has been a family home of the Stuarts since 1491. The house has played host to 27 monarchs, and was a refuge for Catholic priests in times of persecution. The Fifth Earl of Traquair closed the house's famous "Bear Gates" one autumn day in 1745 after wishing his guest, Prince Charles Edward Stuart, a safe onward journey, with a promise the gates would not be reopened until the Stuarts were restored to the throne. The gates have remained closed ever since. The house has craft workshops, an 18th-century working brewery, museum and restaurant.

■ Adventures

Manor Trekking (Castle Hill Farm, Manor Valley, By Peebles, ☎ 1721-740 250, fax 1721-740 353). Hacking and trekking, lessons, rides and rental horses for the Buccleuch Country Ride and Common Ridings.

Peebles Hydro Stables (Innerleithen Road, Peebles EH45 8BQ, ☎/fax 1721-721 325). Pony trekking and trail riding in Glentress Forest, with no road work.

■ Where To Stay & Eat

See the *Accommodation* and *Dining* price charts on pages 109 and 110.

 Castle Venlaw Hotel (Edinburgh Hotel, Peebles EH45 8QG, ☎ 1721-720 384, fax 1721-724 066, enquiries@venlaw.co.uk, www.venlaw.co.uk; B&B ££££, dinner ££). 18th-century baronial castle set in four acres of woodland overlooking Peebles. The hotel offers spacious, elegant bedrooms and fine food.

Cross Keys Hotel (Northgate, Peebles EH45 8RS, ☎ 1721-724 222, fax 1721-724 333; B&B ££, dinner ££). Haunted 17th-century coaching inn with brasserie, beer garden, good food and real ales.

Peebles Hotel Hydro (Innerleithen Road, Peebles EH45 8LX, ☎ 1721-720 602, fax 1721-722 999, info@peebleshotelhydro.co.uk, www.peebleshotelhydro.co.uk; DB&B £££££). Resort hotel with spacious, well-decorated rooms, excellent leisure facilities and walks within the grounds. The split-level **Lazels** restaurant serves a blend of international and traditional Scottish dishes.

Tontine Hotel (High Street, Peebles EH45 8AJ, ☎ 1721-720 892, fax 1721-729 732, info@tontinehotel.com, www.tontinehotel.com; B&B £££, dinner £££). Impressive family-run hotel overlooking the River Tweed, with open fires, cozy bar and top-quality food.

The Old Schoolhouse (Traquair, Innerleithen, near Peebles EH44 6PL, ☎/fax 1896-830 425; B&B £, dinner £). Overlooking the Tweed Valley, the B&B offers a friendly atmosphere, log fires, home cooking and animals to amuse the children.

Traquair Arms Hotel (Traquair Road, Innerleithen, near Peebles EH44 6PD, ☎ 1896-830 229, fax 1896-830 260, traquair.arms@scottishborders.com; B&B ££-£££, dinner ££). Charming country hotel with log fires, traditional cuisine and real ales.

The Old Bakehouse Restaurant (Main Street, West Linton, near Peebles EH46 7EA, ☎ 1968-660 830, theoldbakehouse@zetnet.co.uk; lunch ££, dinner ££-£££). Fresh, organic local produce, authentic Danish open sandwiches and tasty main meals served in the cozy atmosphere of an old bakehouse.

Hawick

Hawick is the largest of the Border towns and is famous for fashioning the fine knitwear sold in many factory outlets dotted around the town.

 INFORMATION SOURCES: The tourism office is at Drumlanrig's Tower, Tower Knowe, Hawick TD9 9EN; open April-Oct.

■ Attractions & Sights

Drumlanrig's Tower (1 Tower Knowe, High Street, Hawick, ☎ 1450-377 615, fax 1450-378 506; open Mon-Sat, 10 am-5 pm, April-June and Sept-Oct; 10 am-6 pm in July-Aug; Sun, 1-4 pm, April-June and Sept, and 1-5 pm, July-Aug; adult/concession £2.50/£1.50, children free). The 16th-century fortified tower was once a stronghold of cross-border warfare and has been beautifully restored to provide information on Hawick's turbulent history from medieval times. Audio tours are available.

Hermitage Castle (HS; six miles northeast of Newcastleton on the B6399, ☎ 1387-376 222; open April-Sept, 9:30am-6:30pm; adult/concession/child £2.20/£1.60/£0.75). A vast and eerie ruin dating from the 14th-15th centuries and occupying a lonely site surrounded by bleak moorland. It is associated with the de Soulis, Douglas and Bothwell families and was reputedly Sir Walter Scott's favorite castle. Mary, Queen of Scots once rode 50 miles in one day to visit her wounded lover, the Earl of Bothwell. The castle was partly restored in the 19th century. Nearby is the 14th-century **Hermitage Chapel**.

■ Adventures

Scottish Academy of Falconry (The Wigg, Bonchester Bridge, By Hawick TD9 9TB, ☎/fax 1450-860 666). For something historical and a little different try flying falcons and hawks, plus falconry on horseback. Residential and non-residential options are available.

Bailey Mill Trekking Centre (Bailey, near Newcastleton TD9 0TR, ☎ 1697-748 617, fax 1697-748 074, pam@baileymill.fsnet.co.uk). Trekking, lessons, own-a-pony days and full-board riding holidays through forest and quiet country lanes.

■ Where To Stay & Eat

See the *Accommodation* and *Dining* price charts on pages 109 and 110.

Mansfield House Hotel (Weensland Road, Hawick TD9 8LB, ☎ 1450-373 988/360 400, fax 1450-372 007, ian@mansfieldhouse.com, www.mansfieldhouse.com; B&B ££, dinner ££). Attractive Victorian country-house hotel standing in 10 acres of wooded grounds. The bedrooms are well furnished in traditional style and the plush dining room highlights fresh local produce.

Wiltonburn Farm (By Hawick TD9 7LL, ☎ 1450-372 414, fax 1450-378 098, shell@wiltonburnfarm.u-net.com, www.wiltonburnfarm.co.uk; B&B £-££). B&B in a traditional hill farm two miles from Hawick with a cashmere knitwear shop on site.

In nearby Denholm, midway between Hawick and Jedburgh, are **The Fox & Hounds Inn** (Main Street, Denholm TD9 8NU, ☎ 1450-870 247, vijstew@quista.net; £-££) and **Auld Cross Keys Inn** (Main Street, Denholm, By Hawick TD9 8NU, ☎ 1450-870 305, fax 1450-870 778, enquiries@crosskeysdenholm.co.uk, www.crosskeysdenholm.co.uk; £-££). Both are charming village inns that offer lots of character, home cooking, good beers and the chance to meet locals.

Dumfries & Galloway

Dumfries & Galloway, the forgotten southwest corner of Scotland, surprises many with its beautiful, unspoiled scenery, mild climate and fascinating attractions, including many strong links with Robert Burns. More than half the area comprises moorland, lochs and mountains. To the northwest lies the Galloway Forest Park where **Merrick**, the highest peak in southern Scotland, rises to a respectable 2,766 feet. Thanks to the warming Gulf Stream, Dumfries & Galloway enjoys the mildest climate in Scotland – the average winter temperature in the west is the same as that of Cornwall in southwest England.

 INFORMATION SOURCES: Dumfries & Galloway Tourist Board is at 64 Whitesands, Dumfries DG1 2RS, ☎ 1387-253 862, fax 1387-245 555, info@dgtb.visitscotland.com, www.visit-dumfries-and-galloway.co.uk.

■ Special Events

Dumfries & Galloway Arts Festival (May/Jun; ☎ 1387-260 447, www.dg-artsfestival.org.uk). Long-established arts festival celebrating its silver jubilee in 2004.

World Flounder Tramping Championship (July; ☎ 1556-600 284). Incredibly in its 30th year, barefooted contestants wade through low-tide mud catching flounders with their bare feet.

Gaelforce (Aug-Oct; ☎ 1387-260 335, www.gaelforcefestival.co.uk). Area-wide arts and entertainments program.

Scottish Book Town Festival (Sept; ☎ 1988-402 036). Literary festival celebrated in Wigtown, Scotland's book town.

Moffat Walking Festival (Oct; ☎ 1683-220 059). Guided walks, walking challenges and evening entertainment.

■ Getting Here & Getting Around

By Rail

 Dumfries lies on a branch line off the London-Glasgow main line. Traveling from the south (toward Glasgow) change at **Carlisle** for a train to **Stranraer**. From the north, regular service is available from **Glasgow**.

By Air

The area is served by **Edinburgh**, **Glasgow** and **Prestwick** airports, all within two-hours' drive.

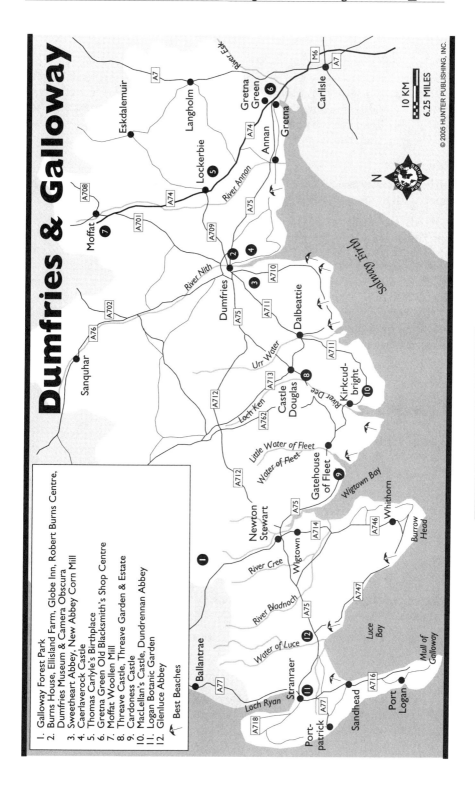

Dumfries & Galloway

1. Galloway Forest Park
2. Burns House, Ellisland Farm, Globe Inn, Robert Burns Centre, Dumfries Museum & Camera Obscura
3. Sweetheart Abbey, New Abbey Corn Mill
4. Caerlaverock Castle
5. Thomas Carlyle's Birthplace
6. Gretna Green Old Blacksmith's Shop Centre
7. Moffat Woollen Mill
8. Threave Castle, Threave Garden & Estate
9. Cardoness Castle
10. MacLellan's Castle, Dundrennan Abbey
11. Logan Botanic Garden
12. Glenluce Abbey

✦ Best Beaches

10 KM
6.25 MILES

© 2005 HUNTER PUBLISHING, INC.

N

Dumfries & Galloway

By Car

The Dumfries & Galloway region occupies the southwest corner of Scotland. The easiest access routes are the **M6** from the south, **M74** from Glasgow, **A701/A702** from Edinburgh, and **A75/A76** from the west coast, with ferry links to Ireland (see below). A scenic alternative is the **Galloway Tourist Route**. This links Gretna with Ayr, mainly along the **A713**, passing through many pretty villages.

By Coach

National Express (☎ 870-580 8080, www.nationalexpress.com) links the region with many parts of the UK.

Scottish Citylink (☎ 870-550 5050, www.citylink.com) operates services from Glasgow to **Dumfries** and **Stranraer**.

By Ferry

From **Northern Ireland**, ferries depart from Larne or Belfast. There are 20 crossings daily from Northern Ireland to Dumfries & Galloway. **Stena Line** (☎ 870-570 7070, www.stenaline.com) operates between **Belfast** and **Stranraer**. **P&O Irish Sea** (☎ 870-242 4777, www.poirishsea.com) operates between **Larne** and **Cairnryan**.

Adventures

■ On Water

Dumfries & Galloway has five major game fishing rivers – the **Border Esk**, the **Annan**, the **Nith**, the **Cree** and the **Bladnoch** – with the really big run of fish during October and into November depending on rainfall. Smaller rivers and lochs provide ample choice for rainbow and brown trout fishing and coarse fishing. There is little free fishing in the area – check locally with the TIC or at one of the following tackle shops for permits and season dates, which vary for different waters.

Galloway Angling Centre, The Manager's House, Bladnoch Bridge Estate, Bladnoch, Wigtown DG8 9AB, ☎ 1988-403 363.

Pattie's of Dumfries, 109 Queensberry Street, Dumfries DG1 1BH, ☎ 1387-252 891.

Galloway Angling Centre, 87 Queen Street, Newton Stewart DG8 6JR, ☎ 1671-401 333.

The Sports Shop, 86 George Street, Stranraer DG9 7JS, ☎ 1776-702 705.

Esk & Borders Guide Service (Netherknock, Bentpath, 11 miles north of Gretna Green, ☎ 1387-370 288, www.flyfishing.fsbusiness.co.uk). Fly fishing instruction and guiding for salmon, sea trout, trout, grayling and pike.

AUTHOR'S NOTE: *For sea anglers, the Flat Rock at Balcary is a popular place for catching large cod, and Luce Bay is excellent for tope.*

Dumfries

Dumfries, known as the "Queen of the South," is the region's largest town. It became a Royal Burgh (chartered city) as long ago as 1186, although little remains of that medieval town. Dumfries is a lively town with a large range of attractions and visitor facilities. Some of its houses are pleasantly painted in soft blue, cream, green or buff, contrasting with the largely red sandstone civic buildings.

A statue of Robert Burns overlooks the High Street, for it was in Dumfries that the poet spent the last five years of his life. Associations with the poet include the house where he lived, his local tavern and his tomb, as well as the splendid **Robert Burns Centre** in an old sandstone mill building by the river.

INFORMATION SOURCES: The tourism office is at 64 Whitesands, Dumfries DG1 2RS, ☎ 1387-253 862; open year-round.

■ Attractions & Sights

Robert Burns (1759-1796), Scotland's national bard, made his home in the Dumfries area. He farmed the land, scoured the coastline for smugglers and wrote some of his most popular works here. He left his mark all over the region, scratching impromptu works on the windows of local inns with a diamond ring, immortalizing local ladies in romantic verse and writing the world-wide Hogmanay anthem, *Auld Lang Syne*.

Burns House (Burns Street, Dumfries DG1 2PS, ☎ 1387-255 297; open April-Sept, Mon-Sat, 10am-5pm & Sun, 2-5pm; Oct-Mar, Tues-Sat, 10am-1pm & 2-5pm). The simple sandstone house in which Burns spent the last years of his life, until his untimely death in 1796 at the age of 37.

Ellisland Farm (Holywood Road, Auldgirth, By Dumfries DG2 0RP, ☎ 1387-740 426, www.ellislandfarm.co.uk; open April-Sept, Mon-Sat, 10am-1pm & 2-5pm, Sun, 2-5pm, Oct-Mar, Tues-Sat, 10am-5pm; adult/concession £2.50/£1, children free). This was Burns' home from 1788-1791, and its tranquil setting inspired some of his best nature poems and love songs, including *Auld Lang Syne* and *Tam o'Shanter*. The farmhouse and steading (farmstead) provide an intriguing insight into the poet's life, including Rabbie's original writings, possessions and a stroll along Burns' riverside walk.

Globe Inn (56 High Street, Dumfries DG1 2JA, ☎ 1387-252 335, mail@globeinndumfries.co.uk, www.globeinndumfries.co.uk). Enjoy a drink

Dumfries & Galloway

in this 1610 tavern, which Burns knew well and described as his *favourite howff* ("favorite house," or pub; his seat was on the right of the fireplace). Tours are available, with lunches and dinners by appointment.

Robert Burns Centre (Mill Road, Dumfries DG2 7BE, ☎ 1387-264 808; open April-Sept, Mon-Sat, 10am-8pm & Sun, 2-5pm, Oct-Mar, Tues-Sat, 10am-1pm & 2-5pm; admission free; fee for audiovisual presentation, adult/concession £1.50/£0.75). Situated in an 18th-century watermill, this award-winning exhibition tells the story of the last years of Robert Burns' life, which he spent in Dumfries. The exhibition is illuminated by many original manuscripts and personal belongings, together with a moving audiovisual presentation.

Dumfries Museum & Camera Obscura (The Observatory, Dumfries DG2 7SW, ☎ 1387-253 374, www.dumfriesmuseum.demon.co.uk; open April-Sept, Mon-Sat, 10am-5pm & Sun, 2-5pm, Oct-March, Museum only, Tues-Sat, 10am-1pm & 2-5pm; Museum admission free, Camera Obscura adult/concession £1.50/£0.75). Historical treasure house telling the story of the local land and people. Exhibits include fossil footprints left by prehistoric reptiles, wildlife, tools and weapons of the earliest people and stone carvings of Scotland's first Christians. The Camera Obscura was installed in 1836 on the top floor of the old windmill tower and provides panoramic views of Dumfries and the surrounding countryside.

Sweetheart Abbey (HS; New Abbey, seven miles south of Dumfries on the A710, ☎ 1387-850 397; open April-Sept, 9:30am-6:30pm; Oct-March, 9:30am-4:30pm; closed some days in winter; adult/concession/child £2/£1.50/£0.75; joint ticket with New Abbey Corn Mill is available, see below). The splendid ruin of a late 13th- to early 14th-century Cistercian abbey founded by Devorguilla, Lady of Galloway, in memory of her husband John Balliol, the founder of Balliol College, Oxford. Devorguilla is buried in the presbytery with a casket containing her husband's embalmed heart. The principal features are the abbey church and well-preserved wall enclosing the abbey precinct.

DID YOU KNOW?

DID YOU KNOW? *Sweetheart Abbey is the origin of the term "sweetheart." Lady Devorguilla so loved her husband John Balliol that when he died she carried his heart around in a casket and often talked to her "dulce cor" or sweetheart.*

New Abbey Corn Mill (HS; New Abbey, seven miles south of Dumfries on the A710, ☎ 1387-850 260; open April-Sept, 9:30am-6:30pm; Oct-Mar, 9:30am-4:30pm; closed some days in winter; adult/concession/child £3/£2.30/£1; joint ticket with Sweetheart Abbey is available). Carefully renovated water-powered oatmeal mill in full working order, with regular demonstrations at noon and 3pm in the summer.

Caerlaverock Castle (HS; by Glencaple, eight miles southeast of Dumfries on the B725, ☎ 1387-770 244; open April-Sept, 9:30am-6:30pm; Oct-Mar, 9:30am-4:30pm; adult/concession/child £4/£3/£1). Caerlaverock is the only triangular castle in Britain and one of the finest medieval fortresses in Scotland. The castle is notable for its twin-towered gatehouse and for the Nithsdale Lodging, a splendid Renaissance range dating from 1638. Edward I besieged and took the castle in 1300; Robert the Bruce re-captured it in 1312. There is a children's adventure park, replica siege engines and nature trail to the old castle.

Thomas Carlyle's Birthplace (NTS; Arched House, Ecclefechan, Lockerbie DG11 3DG, ☎ 1576-300 666; open May-Sept, Thurs-Mon, 1-5pm; adult/concession/family £2.50/£1.90/£7). Writer and historian Thomas Carlyle was one of the most powerful influences on 19th-century British thought. His father and uncle built the Arched House in which he was born on 4th December, 1795. The interior is furnished to reflect domestic life in Carlyle's time and includes a collection of portraits and his belongings.

■ Where To Stay & Eat

See the *Accommodation* and *Dining* price charts on pages 109 and 110.

Comlongon Castle (Clarencefield, near Dumfries DG1 4NA, ☎ 1387-870 283, fax 1387-870 266, reception@comlongon.co.uk, www.comlongon.co.uk; open Feb-Dec; B&B £££, dinner ££££). Family-run 14th-century castle and mansion set in 120 acres of secluded grounds. The restored medieval keep is a popular wedding venue and the castle has three bridal suites.

Friars Carse Country House Hotel (Auldgirth, near Dumfries DG2 0SA, ☎ 1387-740 388, fax 1387-740 550, enquiry@friarscarse.co.uk, www.friarscarse.co.uk; B&B £££, dinner £££). Impressive sandstone mansion set in 45 acres of woodlands, offering good-quality bedrooms, a magnificent oak-paneled hall, excellent dining and private salmon and sea trout fishing.

Mabie House Hotel (Mabie, near Dumfries DG2 8HB, ☎ 1387-263 188, fax 1387-249 696, niki@mabiehouse.co.uk; B&B ££). Elegant seclusion and tranquility in the Mabie Forest with charming rooms and good food.

Southpark House (Quarry Road, Locharbriggs, Dumfries DG1 1QG, ☎ 1387-711 188, fax 1387-711 155, ewan@southparkhouse.co.uk, www.southparkhouse.co.uk; B&B £). Popular country house on the edge of Dumfries with great views over the valleys.

Netherfield Farm (Lochanhead, Beeswing, near Dumfries DG2 8JE, ☎/fax 1387-730 217; B&B £). Organic farm in the Galloway hills serving good vegetarian meals. Massage, facials and oil bath therapies are available.

Benvenuto Pizzeria Trattoria (42 Eastfield Road, Dumfries, ☎ 1387-259 890; £-££). Seafood, steaks, pizza and pasta served around the log-fired oven, with "Happy Hour" discounts on pizza and pasta nightly from 5 to 6:30pm.

Courtyard Bistro (49 Lovers Walk, Dumfries, ☎ 1387-254 316; ££). Atmospheric bistro serving an imaginative menu and decent wine list.

The Globe Inn (56 High Street, Dumfries DG1 2JA, ☎ 1387-252 335, mail@globeinndumfries.co.uk, www.globeinndumfries.co.uk; lunch £). Meals (dinners by appointment only) is a 17th-century inn frequented by Robert Burns, which retains much of its original character and atmosphere.

Abbey Cottage (26 Main Street, New Abbey, Dumfries DG2 8BY, ☎ 1387-850 377, www.abbeycottagetearoom.co.uk; open Mar-Oct; lunch £). Friendly tearoom serving morning coffee, light lunches and afternoon teas baked and cooked on the premises with additional hot dishes at weekends.

Gretna & Gretna Green

Marriage and romance made Gretna Green famous, and the village blacksmith's shop became the focal point of the marriage trade. Several blacksmiths' houses survive from the days of droving, when cattle were shod at the border village on their long walk from Galloway through England. The modern village of Gretna, a short distance away from Gretna Green, is an interesting example of 20th-century town planning; it was built to house munitions workers during the First World War.

RUNAWAY MARRIAGES

Gretna Green will forever be associated with runaway marriages, and the village's **Old Blacksmith's Shop** lies at the heart of this fascinating tradition. Runaway marriages began in 1753 when Lord Harwicke's Marriage Act required parental consent to nuptials where both parties weren't at least 21. The Act didn't apply in Scotland where it was still possible to marry at 16, with or without parental consent. Many young couples fled from England to marry in Scotland, often pursued by irascible fathers or guardians.

Just inside the Scottish border, Gretna Green was the first village these elopers arrived at. The Blacksmith's Shop, the focal point of the village, also became the focal point of the marriage trade. The blacksmith's anvil became the symbol of runaway weddings – not only were metals joined together in the heat of the fire but couples were also joined in marriage, often in the heat of the moment.

INFORMATION SOURCES: The tourism office is at Old Headless Cross, Gretna Green, ☎ 1461-337 834; open April-Oct.

■ Attractions & Sights

Gretna Green Old Blacksmith's Shop Centre (Gretna Green DG16 5EA, ☎ 1461-338 441, fax 1461-338 442, info@gretnagreen.com, www.gretnagreen.com; open yearround from 9 am, closing times vary seasonally;

adult/concession £2/£1.50). The world-famous Old Blacksmith's Shop stands on the site where Gretna Green weddings were traditionally performed. Modern couples can marry or rekindle their vows over its famous anvil. Housed in the original shop and cottage, the exhibition recreates the blacksmith's living and working conditions, and an interactive display recreates an authentic Gretna Green wedding. There is also a rare collection of 19th-century coaches, typical of those in which runaways would have arrived. The shop sells clothing gifts and luxury foods, and there are two restaurants.

■ Where To Stay & Eat

See the *Accommodation* and *Dining* price charts on pages 109 and 110.

 Hunters Lodge Hotel (Annan Road, Gretna DG16 5DL, ☎ 1461-338 214, reception@hunterslodgehotel.co.uk, www.hunterslodgehotel.co.uk; B&B ££). The closest hotel to Gretna's registration office. A la carte and bar meals are available.

Gretna Hall Hotel (Gretna Green DG16 5DY, ☎ 1461-338 257, fax 1461-338 911, gretnahall@crerarhotels.com, www.british-trusthotels.com; B&B £££, dinner ££). An attractive hotel dating from 1710, set in 12 acres of landscaped grounds.

Moffat

Moffat was once a well-known spa town and retains the aura of its leisured past. The former baths and pump room now house the town hall. Northeast up Moffat Water on the A708 is Scotland's highest waterfall, **Grey Mares Tail**, where there is a superb walk, and the famous **Tibbie Shiels Inn** at the foot of St Mary's Loch. Northwest up the A701 is the **Devil's Beef Tub**, a huge natural depression in the wild hills where border thieves (*reivers*) would hide their stolen cattle.

INFORMATION SOURCES: The tourism office is at Ladyknowe, Moffat, ☎ 1683-220 620; open April to October.

■ Adventures

 **Grey Mare's Tail to White Coomb** is an outstanding walk over one of Scotland's highest waterfalls, cascading over 200 feet (61 m) from a hanging valley, with spectacular views into the churning abyss below. The area is rich in wildflowers and geological interest.

The walk starts from the Grey Mare's Tail parking area, 10 miles northeast of Moffat on the A708. A good path leads from here to the waterfall. Continue above the falls to a hidden glen, high above Moffatdale, formed by White Coomb (2,696 feet/821 m) and Lochcraig Head with Loch Skeen cradled between them. The route continues up over the tops around Loch Skeen. The surrounding hills are dramatic moorland, once a place of refuge for fugitive covenanters, and the stamping ground of Sir Walter Scott. In good visibility you can see the Lake District, 60 miles away in northwest England, the Eildons to the east and Criffel hill, overlooking the Solway firth. Feral goats can be seen on the hills. Don't stray from the path, as it can be dangerous and people have died here. A ranger service operates during July and August (4 hours, graded easy/moderate).

You can rent cycles locally from **Moffat Bike Hire** (Charlotte Place, Moffat, ☎ 1683-220 404).

■ Shopping

Moffat Woollen Mill (Ladyknowe, Moffat DG10 9EP, ☎ 1683-220 134, fax 1683-221 066). Weaving demos, clan tartans, bespoke (made-to-measure) Highland dress and the usual assortment of knitwear and Harris tweed, together with a whisky shop, coffee shop and restaurant.

■ Where To Stay & Eat

See the *Accommodation* and *Dining* price charts on pages 109 and 110.

 Star Hotel (44 High Street, Moffat DG10 9EF, ☎ 1683-220 156, fax 1683-221 524, tim@famousstarhotel.com, www.famousstarhotel-.com; B&B ££, dinner ££). Established, family-run hotel. At only 20 feet wide, the Star Hotel is famous for being officially Britain's narrowest hotel.

Moffat House Hotel (The Square, High Street, Moffat DG10 9HL, ☎ 1683-220 039, fax 1683-221 288, moffat@talk21.com, www.moffathouse.co.uk; B&B £££, dinner ££). A grand Adams building set in its own grounds yet central in the village, with an award-winning restaurant.

Auchen Castle Hotel & Restaurant (Beattock, By Moffat DG10 9SH, ☎ 1683-300 407, fax 1683-300 667, reception@auchencastle.com, www.auchencastle.com; B&B £££, dinner ££). Imposing 19th-century mansion set in 30 acres of gardens and woodland with high-quality accommodation, a private trout loch and great views over the Moffat hills. The restaurant is open to non-residents.

Rockhill Guest House (14 Beechgrove, Moffat DG10 9RS, ☎ 1683-220 283, fax 1683-220 822; B&B £-££, dinner £). Comfortable, flower-covered house close to the center of town that serves good home cooking.

Burnside (Well Road, Moffat DG10 9BW, ☎/fax 1683-221 900, kate.burnside@btinternet.com, www.burnsidemoffat.co.uk; open Mar-Nov; B&B ££). A beautiful house set in its own peaceful grounds in a residential area of the town. The breakfasts are delicious.

Ericstane (Moffat DG10 9LT, ☎/fax 1683-220 127; B&B ££). Traditional farmhouse B&B in secluded grounds in the upper reaches of Annan Water.

Well View Hotel (Ballplay Road, Moffat DG10 9JU, ☎ 1683-220 184, fax 1683-220 088, info@wellview.co.uk, www.wellview.co.uk; B&B £££, dinner £££). 19th-century house providing six individually decorated and furnished rooms. The excellent taster menu changes daily and features fresh local produce. Booking recommended.

Limetree Restaurant (High Street, Moffat DG10 9HG, ☎ 1683-221 654, fax 1683-221 721, www.limetree-restaurant.co.uk; dinner ££). This recently opened restaurant is fast gaining a reputation for its exciting, eclectic cooking served in relaxed surroundings.

Tibbie Shiels Inn (St Mary's Loch, Selkirk TD7 5LH between Selkirk and Moffat, ☎ 1750-42231; B&B ££). "Olde worlde" historic hostelry set in six lochside acres. Residents enjoy free fishing and the inn serves good, unpretentious cooking.

Castle Douglas to Kirkcudbright

Castle Douglas is a planned town founded in the late 18th century by Sir William Douglas. Although Sir William's plan to establish the cotton industry here failed, the town became an important market with cattle and horse fairs, and remains a thriving agricultural center. The town has a reputation for fine food and is a great place to sample regional produce.

Charming Kirkcudbright has historically been an important gateway to the sea, although today its picturesque harbor is largely a haven for small fishing boats. Much of the town has wide 18th-century streets and pastel-colored houses. The 1610 market cross still stands, as does the ancient *tolbooth* (town hall and jail) with its "jougs," iron manacles to which thieves and those suspected of heresy and witchcraft were attached for public beatings.

 INFORMATION SOURCES: There are TICs at Castle Douglas (Markethill Car Park, Castle Douglas, ☎ 1556-502 611; open April-Oct), Kirkcudbright (Harbour Square, Kirkcudbright, ☎ 1557-330 494; open April-Oct) and Gatehouse of Fleet (Car Park, Gatehouse of Fleet, ☎ 1557-814 212; open April-Oct).

■ Attractions & Sights

 **Threave Castle** (HS; three miles west of Castle Douglas on the A75, ☎ 7711-223 101; open April-Sept, 9:30am-6:30pm; adult/concession/child £2.50/£1.90/£0.75, including ferry crossing). A massive tower, situated on an island in the River Dee, built in the late 14th century by Archibald the Grim, Lord of Galloway. Around its base is an artillery fortification built before 1455 when James II besieged the castle. There is a quarter-mile (flat) walk to the castle. Ring the bell and the custodian will come to ferry you over.

Threave Garden and Estate (NTS; Castle Douglas DG7 1RX, ☎ 1556-502 575, fax 1556-502 683, threave@nts.org.uk; estate & garden open year-round from 9:30 am to sunset; hours vary for walled garden, glasshouses, country estate and visitor center. Admission to house & garden adult/concession/family £9/£6.50/£23; garden only £5/£3.75/£13.50). The 64-acre garden is best

Dumfries & Galloway

known for its nearly 200 varieties of springtime daffodils, although the herbaceous beds are colorful in summer and the trees and heather garden provide striking autumn tints. The interior of the Victorian Threave House has been restored to its 1930s appearance. The estate is a wildfowl refuge and sanctuary for breeding waders and wintering wildfowl and has marked trails and birdwatching hides.

Cardoness Castle (HS; one mile southwest of Gatehouse of Fleet on the A75, ☎ 1557-814 427; open year-round, days and hours vary seasonally; adult/concession/child £2.50/£1.90/£0.75). The well-preserved 15th-century ruins of a six-story tower house, ancient home of the McCullochs, standing on a rocky platform above the Water of Fleet. The architectural detail inside the tower is of high quality, particularly the fireplaces in the great and upper halls, and there are good views over Fleet Bay from the battlements.

MacLellan's Castle (HS; Kirkcudbright, ☎ 1557-331 856; open April-Sept, 9:30am-6:30pm; adult/concession/child £2.20/£1.60/£0.75). A fortified townhouse, built in 1577 by the then provost of Kirkcudbright, Thomas MacLellan, using stone from an adjoining ruined monastery. The house is complete except for its roof, and has some fine architectural details.

Dundrennan Abbey (HS; seven miles southeast of Kirkcudbright on the A711, ☎ 1557-500 262; open year-round, days and hours vary seasonally; adult/concession/child £2/£1.50/£0.75). These beautiful ruins of a **Cistercian abbey**, founded in 1142 by David I, lie in a peaceful setting in a small, secluded valley, its remoteness in keeping with the strict rules and observance of the order. The eastern end of the church and chapter house are particularly impressive. Mary, Queen of Scots spent her last night on Scottish soil here in May 1568.

■ Adventures

Galloway Cycling Holidays (Fineview, Abercromby Road, Castle Douglas DG7 1BB, ☎ 1556-502 979, mail@gallowaycycling.co.uk, www.gallowaycycling.co.uk, open May-Sept). Cycling breaks on quiet roads with places of interest along the way, with accommodation and luggage transfers arranged.

You can rent cycles locally from **St Ninians Bike Hire** (St Ninians House, Sandyhills, near Castle Douglas, ☎ 1387-780 274).

Galloway Sailing Centre (Parton, Loch Ken, Castle Douglas, ☎ 1644-420 626, www.lochken.co.uk). Watersports instruction and equipment rental for all abilities. There are also quad bikes, archery, a climbing wall, abseiling and mountain bike trails.

Longsheds Equestrian (Kelton, Castle Douglas, ☎ 1556-680 498, horses@longsheds.co.uk, www.longsheds.co.uk). Pony trekking and hacks

The magnificent ruin of Jedburgh Abbey

Above: Melrose Abbey

Below: Brodick, Isle of Arran, from Goat Fell

Above: Edinburgh Castle

Below: Edinburgh's medieval Old Town

Sir Walter Scott Monument, Edinburgh

from one hour to half-day through the Stewartry countryside, in addition to lessons in the all-weather arena.

Lochhill Equestrian Centre (Ringford, between Castle Douglas and Gatehouse of Fleet, ☎ 1557-820 225). Riding stable on the Galloway hills with plenty of woodland treks and faster rides for advanced riders.

Barend Riding Centre (Barend, Sandyhills, near Castle Douglas, ☎ 1387-780 533/780 632; open April-Oct). Riding lessons, hacks and treks through the forest for all ages.

Brighouse Bay Trekking Centre (Borgue, near Kirkcudbright, ☎ 1557-870 222, www.gillespie-leisure.co.uk; open April-Oct, closed Sat). Treks for complete beginners of all ages and hacks to the beach for experienced riders.

■ Shopping

Galloway Gemshop (130-132 King Street, Castle Douglas, ☎ 1556-503 254). Large supplier of art and craft materials, jewelry and gifts, together with a display of quality minerals and gemstones from around the world.

The Posthorn (26/30 St Andrew Street, Castle Douglas DG7 1DE, ☎ 1556-502 531, fax 1556-503 330, info@posthorn.co.uk, www.posthorn.co .uk). The leading supplier of **Border Fine Arts** sculpture and **Moorcroft** products in Scotland, specializing in collectable pieces of Border Fine Arts sculpture, with many limited edition pieces available. Not cheap, but stunning.

■ Where To Stay & Eat

See the *Accommodation* and *Dining* price charts on pages 109 and 110.

 Longacre Manor (Ernespie Road, Castle Douglas DG7 1LE, ☎ 1556-503 576, fax 1556-503 886, reception@longacremanor.co.uk; B&B £££). Small, elegant country-house hotel set in woodland gardens with oak paneling, antiques, luxury bedrooms and log fire.

Urr Valley Hotel (Ernespie Road, Castle Douglas DG7 3JG, ☎ 1556-502 188, fax 1556-504 055, info@urrvalleyhotel.co.uk; B&B ££, dinner ££). Lovely hotel set in 14 acres of pretty grounds, with log fires, a wide selection of whiskies and good local food.

Woodpark Farmhouse (Kirkpatrick Durham, Castle Douglas DG7 3HW, ☎ 1556-650 484, fax 1556-650 139, suzanne@gallowbreaks.co.uk, www.gallowaybreaks.co.uk; B&B ££, dinner ££). Good food and peaceful B&B accommodation in a 200-year-old renovated farmhouse set in 400 acres of Galloway pastureland.

Craigadam (near Castle Douglas DG7 3HU, ☎/fax 1556-650 233, inquiry@craigadam.com, www.craigadam.com; B&B ££-£££, dinner ££). Elegant country house on a sporting estate/working farm, with antique furnishings, log fires, billiard room and oak-paneled dining room serving excellent home cooking, specializing in venison, pheasant and salmon. Catch a trout on the private hill loch and have it for breakfast!

Balcary Bay Hotel (Auchencairn, By Castle Douglas DG7 1QZ, ☎ 1556-640 217, fax 1556-640 272, info@balcary-bay-hotel.co.uk, www.balcary-bay-hotel.co.uk; open Mar-Nov; B&B ££££, dinner £££). Family-run country-house hotel dating back to 1625, set on the shores of the bay. The dining room serves local delicacies such as Galloway beef and Balcary salmon and there are delightful conservatory lunches and afternoon teas in the drawing room.

Balcary Mews (Balcary Bay, Auchencairn, By Castle Douglas DG7 1QZ, ☎ 1556-640 276; B&B ££). Tranquil hideaway on the shores of Balcary Bay, offering good food and excellent views from every room.

Old School Tearoom (Ringford, near Castle Douglas, ☎ 1557-820 250; £). Tearoom-restaurant serving home-cooked meals and home baking in a converted school.

Mrs Marie McLaughlin (14 High Street, Kirkcudbright DG6 4JX, ☎/fax 1557-330 766, 14highstreet@kirkcudbright.co.uk; open April-Sept; B&B ££). Historic Georgian townhouse in the heart of the Old High Street with luxurious river-view rooms.

Selkirk Arms Hotel (High Street, Kirkcudbright DG6 4JG, ☎ 1557-330 402, fax 1557-331 639, reception@selkirkarmshotel.co.uk, www.selkirkarmshotel.co.uk; B&B £££, dinner £££). Small popular Georgian hotel with nicely decorated rooms. The renowned restaurant, bar and bistro serve top-quality local fare, such as succulent seafood and Galloway beef.

Auld Alliance Restaurant (5 Castle Street, Kirkcudbright, ☎ 1557-330 569; open Easter-Oct; ££-£££). Small, popular restaurant serving traditional and creative dishes (try the Solway scallops).

Cally Palace (Gatehouse of Fleet DG7 2DL, ☎ 1557-814 341, fax 1557-814 522, info@callypalace.co.uk, www.callypalace.co.uk; DB&B ££££). Grand Georgian hotel in grounds in the **Fleet Forest** with spacious bedrooms, 18-hole golf course, leisure center, swimming pool and spa.

Newton Stewart, Wigtown & Whithorn

Newton Stewart is a small market town picturesquely sited on the slopes above the **River Cree**. It has a good range of shops, hotels and restaurants. Wigtown was the medieval capital of the region, with a busy harbor, castle and priory, and remained an important harbor until the early 20th century when silt blocked many channels. Wigtown is famous for the many quaint bookshops that make it a haven for burrowing bibliophiles. Its annual September book festival attracts many eminent names from the literary world and the town holds several smaller events throughout the year. St Ninian founded the first Christian church in Scotland in Whithorn in the 5th or 6th century.

INFORMATION SOURCES: The tourism office is at Dashwood Square, Newton Stewart, ☎ 1671-402 431; open April-Oct.

■ Attractions & Sights

 **Whithorn** (church, visitor center and museum, 45-47 George Street, Whithorn, south of Wigtown, ☎ 1988-500 508, enquiries@whithorn.com, www.whithorn.com; open April-Oct, 10:30am-5pm; adult/concession/family £2.70/£1.50/£7.50). Whithorn was one of the earliest Christian sites, traditionally believed to have been founded by Ninian, Scotland's first saint, in the 5th or 6th century. A priory for Premonstratensian canons was built in the 12th century, later to become the cathedral church of Galloway. The museum houses a fine collection of early Christian carvings, including the Latinus stone, the earliest Christian memorial in Scotland. A richly colored exhibition of archaeological artifacts, including a magnificent 12th-century crosier, figures, models and replicas, guide you through the history of Whithorn, the church and the pilgrimage site from prehistoric times to the present day.

■ Adventures

 The **Galloway Forest Park** is the largest forest park in Britain, covering over 300 square miles of forest, moorland and lochs. You can walk anywhere in the park and there are a number of waymarked trails for all abilities.

The **Martyr's Tomb** at **Glen Trool** is one of many such tombs scattered among the hills and glens of Dumfries, Galloway and Ayrshire – a sad reminder of an age of religious cleansing that left 18,000 dead. Head north from Newton Stewart to Bargrennan where a minor road leads to Glen Trool. Continue through the village to the parking area by Caldons campsite at the western end of Loch Trool.

From the parking area follow the signs to visit the Martyr's Tomb. Retrace your steps and follow the road past the shop to the road on the left toward Loch Trool. Follow the Southern Upland Way through the forest, passing the site of Robert the Bruce's 1307 victory over the English. At the eastern end of the loch cross the bridge and turn left onto a track that leads to a road and waymarked path back to the campsite and parking area (2 hours; easy).

 West Drumrae Farm (Whithorn, south of Wigtown, ☎ 1988-700 518). Small riding stable offering accompanied treks over farmland and fell, riding and driving lessons and carriage rides.

■ Where To Stay & Eat

See the *Accommodation* and *Dining* price charts on pages 109 and 110.

Creebridge House Hotel (Newton Stewart DG8 6NP, ☎ 1671-402 121, fax 1671-403 258, info@creebridge.co.uk, www.creebridge.co.uk; B&B £££-££££, dinner £££). Listed country-house hotel set in beautiful gardens that offers comfortable accommodation and special golf and fishing breaks. The restaurant and brasserie serve modern Scottish menus using quality local produce.

Kirroughtree House (Newton Stewart DG8 6AN, ☎ 1671-402 141, fax 1671-402 425, info@kirroughtreehouse.co.uk, www.kirroughtreehouse.co.uk; open mid-Feb to Dec; B&B ££££, dinner ££). Splendid Georgian mansion set in eight acres of delightful gardens. The hotel serves gourmet cooking in two dining rooms reached from a wood-paneled lounge.

Black Sheep Inn (Nether Barr Steading, Nether Barr, Newton Stewart, ☎ 1671-404 326; ££). High-quality traditional Scottish and Irish dishes based on local produce.

Brig End Pantry (78 Victoria Street, Newton Stewart, ☎ 1671-402 003; £). Tearoom and licensed (to sell alcohol) restaurant serving all-day meals and takeaway fish and chips, ice cream and sandwiches.

Stranraer & Portpatrick

Stranraer, a busy harbor town, is the main terminal for ferries to Larne in Northern Ireland. Its shipping heritage dates from the 18th and 19th centuries, when it was also a center of the shipbuilding industry.

Portpatrick has a picturesque old harbor that bustles with small trawlers, yachts and boats. The round church tower probably served as a beacon for shipping in the 17th century. With the short crossing to Donaghadee, Portpatrick was for many years the main port for travelers to and from Ireland, and was the "Gretna Green" for Ireland, which had the same strict marriage laws as England. The town remains a favorite with holidaymakers and boasts several excellent seafood restaurants.

 INFORMATION SOURCES: The tourism office is at Harbour Street, Stranraer, ☎ 1776-702 595, fax 1776-889 156; open year-round.

■ Attractions & Sights

 **Logan Botanic Garden** (Port Logan, near Stranraer DG9 9ND, ☎ 1776-860 231, fax 1776-860 333, logan@rbge.org.uk, www.rbge.org.uk; open Mar-Oct, from 10am; closes at 5pm in Mar & Oct, 6pm April-Sept; Nov-Feb by arrangement; adult/concession/child/family £3/£2.50/£1/£7). Warmed by the Gulf Stream at the southwestern tip of Scotland, Logan is the country's most exotic garden, sustaining a remarkable collection of bizarre and beautiful plants, including groves of eucalyptus and brilliant blooms of southern hemisphere plants in the Walled Garden. Self-guided audio tours highlight interesting plants and features, and you can join the informative guided walks at 10:30am on the second Tuesday of each month (April-Sept) – walks included in the admission charge.

Glenluce Abbey (HS; two miles northwest of Glenluce village off the A75, ☎ 1581-300 541; open year-round, days and hours vary seasonally; adult/concession/child £2/£1.50/£0.75). The remains of a Cistercian abbey founded by Roland, Earl of Galloway around 1192, set in a lovely tranquil valley. An exhibition of objects found at the abbey is displayed at the site.

■ Wildlife Watching

Mull of Galloway RSPB Nature Reserve (five miles south of Drummore village, ☎ 1671-402 861; open at all times). The Mull of Galloway is the southernmost point in Scotland and offers excellent views over the **Solway Firth**. The cliffs are home to thousands of breeding birds, including razorbills, guillemots and a few **puffins**. Visit nesting birds from April to July and also see 2,000 pairs of gannets breeding on a small outcrop called **Scare Rocks**.

■ Where To Stay & Eat

See the *Accommodation* and *Dining* price charts on pages 109 and 110.

Stranraer

Corsewall Lighthouse Hotel (Corsewall Point, Kirkcolm, By Stranraer DG9 0QG, ☎ 1776-853 220, fax 1776-854 231, info@lighthousehotel.co.uk, www.lighthousehotel.co.uk; DB&B ££££). Its light still warns ships approaching the mouth of Loch Ryan, but the 1815 lighthouse now also provides unique, luxurious accommodation and fine dining – needless to say with fabulous sea views!

Inchparks Schoolhouse (Stranraer DG9 8RR, ☎ 1776-704 568, john36-@nimmoj.freeserve.co.uk; B&B ££, dinner ££). Comfortable B&B accommodation in a converted former school.

East Challoch Farmhouse (Dunragit, near Stranraer DG9 8PY, ☎ 1581-400 391; £, dinner ££). Spacious, high-quality farmhouse accommodation seven miles from Stranraer with excellent views over Luce Bay. Dinner is available on request.

L'Aperitif (London Road, Stranraer, ☎ 1776-702 991; ££). Established, recommended Italian restaurant run by the Lisi family.

Kelvin House Hotel (53 Main Street, Glenluce, By Stranraer DG8 0PP, ☎/fax 1581-300 303, kelvinhouse@lineone.net, www.kelvin-house.co.uk; B&B ££, dinner ££). Behind the unassuming façade of this 18th-century hotel are spacious rooms, a comfortable bar and restaurant serving good local produce.

Portpatrick

Fernhill Hotel (Portpatrick DG9 8TD, ☎ 1776-810 220, fax 1776-810 596, info@fernhillhotel.co.uk, www.fernhillhotel.co.uk; open Feb-Dec; B&B £££, dinner ££). The hotel is delightfully set in private gardens with great views over the harbor. Most rooms share the sea view and the superb conservatory restaurant specializes in locally caught lobster.

Dumfries & Galloway

Harbour House Hotel (Harbour Square, Portpatrick DG9 8JW, ☎ 1776- 810 456, fax 1776-810 488, enquiries@harbourhouse.co.uk, www.harbourhouse-.co.uk; B&B ££). Small, family-run hotel on the central seafront offering real ales and weekend live music.

Knockinaam Lodge Hotel (near Portpatrick DG9 9AD, ☎ 1776-810 471, fax 1776-810 435, reservations@knockinaamlodge.com; DB&B £££££). Country house attractively set on the water's edge with comfortable lounges, sea views and a huge whisky selection. The restaurant serves high-quality modern British and international cooking in luxurious surroundings.

Waterfront Hotel & Bistro (North Crescent, Portpatrick DG9 8SX, ☎ 1776-810 800, fax 1776-810 850, info@waterfronthotel.co.uk, www.waterfronthotel.co.uk; B&B £££, dinner ££). Situated next to the harbor in Portpatrick, the hotel offers high-quality rooms, sea views and fine dining in its attractive bistro.

Campbells Restaurant (1 South Crescent, Portpatrick, ☎ 1776-810 314; ££-£££). Local seafood, steaks and good wines served in a splendid location overlooking the bay.

Ayrshire

Ayrshire became part of Scotland during the 11th century and, two centuries later, the invading Vikings were defeated here at the **Battle of Largs**. Robert the Bruce was born at **Turnberry** and held the very first Scottish Parliament in Ayr after his victory at Bannockburn. Ayrshire is possibly best known as the birthplace of its other famous son – poet Robert Burns – who was born in **Alloway** in 1759.

St Andrews might be the home of golf but Ayrshire lays claim to have spawned Open Golf. The area's golfing history traces back to the 16th century and, more recently, the first **British Open** was held at Prestwick in 1860. Ayrshire boasts two flagship Open Championship courses at **Royal Troon** and **Turnberry**.

 INFORMATION SOURCES: Ayrshire & Arran Tourist Board, 15A Skye Road, Prestwick KA9 2TA, ☎ 1292-678 100, fax 1292-471 832, info@ayrshire-arran.com, www.ayrshire-arran.com.

■ Special Events

 Burns an' a' That (April/May; ☎ 1292-678 100, fax 1292-471 832, info@burnsfestival.com, www.burnsfestival.com). Rapidly becoming a major arts event, the festival showcases contemporary and traditional Scottish culture in celebration of the life and work of Robert Burns.

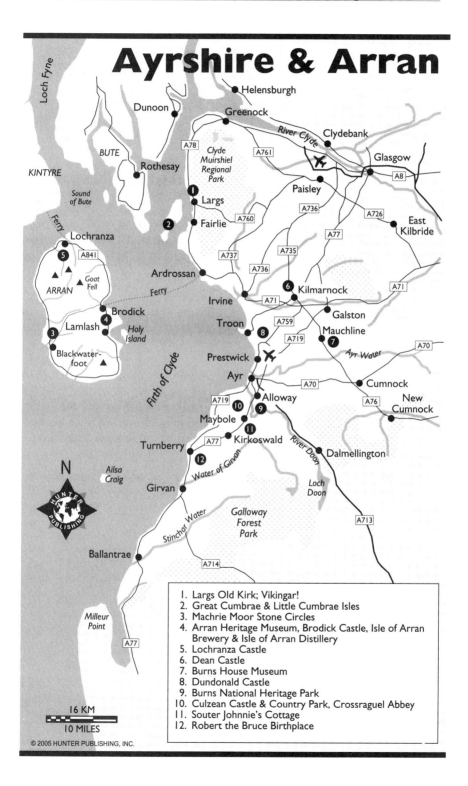

Ayrshire & Arran

1. Largs Old Kirk; Vikingar!
2. Great Cumbrae & Little Cumbrae Isles
3. Machrie Moor Stone Circles
4. Arran Heritage Museum, Brodick Castle, Isle of Arran Brewery & Isle of Arran Distillery
5. Lochranza Castle
6. Dean Castle
7. Burns House Museum
8. Dundonald Castle
9. Burns National Heritage Park
10. Culzean Castle & Country Park, Crossraguel Abbey
11. Souter Johnnie's Cottage
12. Robert the Bruce Birthplace

16 KM
10 MILES

© 2005 HUNTER PUBLISHING, INC.

Ayrshire

■ Getting Here

By Air

Prestwick Airport (☎ 871-223 0700, www.gpia.co.uk) has flight links to the UK, Ireland and mainland Europe. **Ryanair** (☎ 871-246 0000, www.ryanair.co.uk) operates budget services to Prestwick from London Stansted, Dublin and a number of other European cities.

By Rail

Rail service runs from Glasgow to **Troon, Prestwick, Ayr** and **Stranraer**.

By Car

The main road from the south is the **A75/A76** from Gretna Green and Dumfries. The **Galloway Tourist Route** is a scenic alternative linking Gretna with Ayr along the **A713**. From the north, take the **M77/A77** from Glasgow.

By Bus

National Express (☎ 870-580 8080, www.nationalexpress.com) links Ayrshire with many parts of the UK. **Scottish Citylink** (☎ 870-550 5050, www.citylink.co.uk) operates a service from Glasgow to Ayr and Stranraer.

By Ferry

 SeaCat (☎ 870-552 3523, www.seacat.co.uk) operates fast seacat services from Belfast to Troon. Stena Line (☎ 870-570 7070/400 6798, www.stenaline.com) operates ferries between Belfast and Stranraer, and **P&O Irish Sea** (☎ 870-242 4777, www.poirishsea.com) operates between Larne and Cairnryan, near Stranraer. From Stranraer you can travel up the scenic coast road into Ayrshire.

Caledonian MacBrayne (☎ 1475-650 100, www.calmac.co.uk) operates regular car ferries between Ardrossan and Brodick on the **Isle of Arran**, and from Largs to the **Isle of Cumbrae** (which connect to a frequent bus service to Millport, Cumbrae's main town).

Ayr

A settlement has existed on the site of Ayr since the 8th century. The town became a Royal Burgh in 1202 and was an important medieval port. Ayr is now a market town and popular resort and has a well-known racecourse. It is also a seaport and retains some fishing activity. Poet Robert Burns was born in the nearby village of **Alloway**.

> **INFORMATION SOURCES:** The tourism office is at 22 Sandgate, Ayr KA7 1BW; open year-round.

■ Attractions & Sights

Robert Burns is celebrated all over Ayrshire, particularly in Alloway, his birthplace, and the village of Mauchline with its Burns Museum.

Bachelors' Club (NTS; Sandgate Street, Tarbolton, South Ayrshire KA5 5RB, ☎ 1292-541 940; open April-Sept, Fri-Tues, 1pm-5pm; adult/concession/family £2.50/£1.90/£7). In 1780, Robert Burns and six friends formed themselves into a literary and debating society, calling themselves the Bachelors' Club. They met in this 17th-century thatched house, still decorated with period furnishings. It was here that Burns attended dance lessons, and was initiated into Freemasonry in 1781.

Burns National Heritage Park (Murdoch's Lone, Alloway KA7 4PQ, ☎ 1292-443 700, fax 1292-441 750, info@burnsheritagepark.com, www.burnsheritagepark.com; open April-Sept, 9:30am-5:30pm; Oct-Mar, 10am-5pm; adult/concession/family £3/£1.50/£9). Burns Cottage, where the bard was born on 25th January 1759, forms the heart of the park and brings to life his birthplace through modern technology, authentic locations and artifacts. The museum houses an important Robert Burns collection. Walk in the footsteps of **Tam o'Shanter** and across auld **Brig o'Doon**, where Tam's mare, Meg, had her narrow escape from the witches. Experience Burns's best-loved tale for yourself through laser disc technology and theatrical effects in the Tam o'Shanter Experience. The **National Burns Memorial Tower** (open April-Sept, 9:30am-5pm; Oct-Mar, 10am-4pm; admission £1) provides panoramic views over Ayrshire.

Burns House Museum (Castle Street, Mauchline, ☎ 1290-550 045; open mid-Apr to mid-Oct, Tues-Sat, 10am-5pm). The house that Burns lived in after his marriage now displays a collection of artifacts closely associated with the poet and the village of Mauchline.

■ Adventures

Ayrshire Equitation Centre (South Mains, Corton Road, Ayr KA6 6BY, ☎ 1292-266 267, fax 1292-610 323, kevin@ayrequitation.co.uk, www.ayrequitation.co.uk). Rides, hacks, group and private lessons. There is also a cross-country course and tack shop.

Ayr Sea Angling Centre (South Harbour Street, Ayr KA7 1YD, ☎ 1292-285 297). Sea angling trips for beginners and experienced anglers, equipment rental and evening cruises to Lady Isle to view the seal colony.

■ Golf

Prestwick Golf Course (18-hole links, 6,544 yards; Links Road, Prestwick, By Ayr KA9 1QG, ☎ 1292-671 020, fax 1292-447 255, secretary@prestwickgc.co.uk, www.prestwickgc.co.uk; green fees £95-£115). This historic course hosted the first Open Championship in 1860.

Royal Troon (18-hole links, 7,150 yards; Craigend Road, Troon, By Ayr KA10 6EP, ☎ 1292-311 555, fax 1292-318 204, bookings@royaltroon.com, www.royaltroon.com; green fees £100-£185, for two rounds, morning coffee and lunch). One of Scotland's great links courses and venue for the 2004 Open, Troon provides a stiff challenge and requires accurate shot making, particularly on the back nine.

■ Where To Stay & Eat

See the *Accommodation* and *Dining* price charts on pages 109 and 110.

 Abbotsford Hotel (14 Corsehill Road, Ayr KA7 2ST, ☎/fax 1292-261 506, info@abbotsfordhotel.co.uk, www.abbotsfordhotel.co.uk; B&B £££, dinner ££). Family-owned hotel converted from a 19th-century house, with open fires and restaurant serving local produce.

Brig o'Doon Hotel (Alloway, By Ayr KA7 4PQ, ☎ 1292-442 466, fax 1292-441 999, brigodoon@costleyhotels.co.uk; B&B £££, dinner ££). Impressive small hotel in pretty gardens bordering the River Doon. The hotel has two restaurants, a small bar and tearoom.

Old Manse House (3C Doonholm Road, Alloway, By Ayr KA7 4QQ, ☎ 1292-443 196, raypatjackson@aol.com; B&B ££). Comfortable B&B in a former Scottish manse situated opposite Burns's Cottage.

Pickwick Hotel (19 Racecourse Road, Ayr KA7 2TD, ☎ 1292-260 111, fax 1292-285 348, info@pickwickhotel.co.uk; B&B £££). 18th-century villa with a Charles Dickens theme throughout.

Savoy Park Hotel (16 Racecourse Road, Ayr KA7 2UT, ☎ 1292-266 112, fax 1292-611 488, mail@savoypark.com, www.savoypark.com; B&B £££). Classic small hotel with spacious, stylish bedrooms and a strikingly designed dining room.

Kirkton Inn & Studios (1 Main Street, Dalrymple, near Ayr KA6 6DF, ☎ 1292-560 241, fax 1292-560 835, kirkton@cqm.co.uk, www.kirktoninn.co.uk; B&B ££, dinner ££). Old coaching inn in a quiet conservation village 10 minutes from Ayr. There is a restaurant and three bars. Studios with kitchens are also available.

Nether Culzean Farm (Maybole, near Ayr KA19 7JQ, ☎ 1655-882 269, laura.blythe@ic24.net; B&B £-££). Pretty 18th-century farmhouse near Culzean Castle that serves home-baked bread at breakfast and fresh garden vegetables at supper.

Fouters Bistro (2A Academy Street, Ayr KA7 1HS, ☎ 1292-261 391; ££). Laurie and Fran Black are famous for their excellent steaks, seafood and game, as well as a wide selection of wines, malts and liqueurs.

Tudor Restaurant (8 Beresford Terrace, Ayr KA7 2EG, ☎ 1292-261 404; £-££). Long-established restaurant serving traditional Scottish cuisine, including fine steaks and fresh local seafood.

Blueberrys Coffee Shop (3 South Beach, Troon KA10 6EF, ☎ 1292-316 171, fax 1292-317 294; £). A popular, relaxed coffee shop offering a good choice, from light snacks and home baking to main courses.

Wheatsheaf Inn (3 Main Street, Symington, near Troon KA1 5QB, ☎ 1563-830 307; ££). Superb food served in a charming 17th-century inn in the picturesque village of Symington.

South Ayrshire

South Ayrshire is fertile and relatively low-lying. **Girvan** is a seaside town and fishing port; 10 miles off the coast lies the island of **Ailsa Craig**, a volcanic plug rising over 1,000 feet from the Firth of Clyde. Once famous as a source of granite for the manufacture of curling stones, the island is now more famous for its seabird colonies.

 INFORMATION SOURCES: The tourism office is on Bridge Street, Girvan KA26 9HH; open Easter-Oct.

■ Attractions & Sights

Culzean Castle & Country Park (NTS; Maybole, South Ayrshire KA19 8LE, ☎ 1655-884 455, fax 1655-884 503, culzean@nts.org.uk, www.culzeancastle.net; country park ☎ 1655-884 400, fax 1655-884 522; visitor center & country park open year-round, castle open April-Oct; days and hours vary seasonally; castle & country park adult/concession/family £9/£6.50/£23; country park only £5/£3.75/£13.50). Robert Adam's romantic 18th-century Italianate castle perches dramatically on a cliff high above the **Firth of Clyde**. From 1777-92, Adam converted a rather ordinary fortified tower house into an elegant residence for David Kennedy, 10th Earl of Cassillis, also adding a "Roman" viaduct and Ruined Arch for effect. The castle houses fine collections of paintings, furniture and arms, and the Oval Staircase is a design masterpiece. In 1945, the top floor was gifted to **General Eisenhower** in thanks for his role during World War II. His apartment is now a small country-house hotel and an exhibition tells the story of Ike and his visits to Culzean. There are tours, a shop, coffee house and visitor center. The 563-acre country park was Scotland's first, and provides miles of woodland walks, a cliff walk, gardens and an adventure playground.

 **Crossraguel Abbey** (HS; two miles south of Maybole on the A77, ☎ 1655-883 113; open April-Sept, 9:30am-6:30pm; adult/concession/child £2.20/£1.60/£0.75). Founded in the early 13th century by the Earl of Carrick, the abbey was much modified during the next three centuries. The remains are remarkably complete and include the church, cloister, chapter house and much of the domestic range. An exhibition in the sacristy describes medieval building techniques.

Souter Johnnie's Cottage (NTS; Main Road, Kirkoswald, South Ayrshire KA19 8HY, ☎ 1655-760 603; open April-Sept, Fri-Tues, 11:30am-5pm; adult/concession/family £2.50/£1.90/£7). A "souter" was a shoemaker, and the village souter who lived in this house at the end of the 18th century – John Davidson – was the original Souter Johnnie immortalised by Robert Burns in his poem *Tam o'Shanter*. The thatched cottage contains period furniture, Burns relics and a reconstructed souter's workshop; the ale-house in the cottage garden contains life-sized stone figures of the souter, Tam, the innkeeper and his wife.

■ Adventures

Shanter Riding Centre (Maidens, By Girvan KA26 9NQ, ☎ 1655-331 636). One-hour beach rides for all levels, with longer rides also exploring Culzean Country Park. Basic lessons, as well as instruction in dressage and show-jumping, are available.

■ Golf

 Turnberry Ailsa Course (18-hole links, 6,976 yards; Westin Turnberry Resort, Turnberry KA26 9LT, ☎ 1655-331 000, fax 1655-331 706, turnberry@westin.com, www.turnberry.co.uk; green fees £130-£175; less for residents). The Ailsa course is an Open venue and widely acknowledged as one of the finest golf courses in the world. The trademark hole is the ninth: a remote tee on a rocky premonitory at the edge of the sea, driving across the corner of the bay with a glimpse of the site of Robert the Bruce's castle.

Mark McCrindle Boat Trips (7 Harbour Street, Girvan KA26 9AJ, ☎ 1465-713 219). Boat trips to view Ailsa Craig birdlife and fishing trips.

■ Where To Stay & Eat

See the *Accommodation* and *Dining* price charts on pages 109 and 110.

 Dunduff Farm (Dunure, near Ayr KA7 4LH, ☎ 1292-500 225, fax 1292-500 222, gemmelldunduff@aol.com, www.gemmelldunduff.co.uk; open Feb-Nov; B&B ££). A striking 15th-century country house set on a 600-acre beef and sheep farm with comfortable accommodation overlooking the Firth of Forth to Arran and the Mull of Kintyre. Locally smoked kippers are a great choice for breakfast.

Glengennet Farm (Barr, Girvan, Ayrshire KA26 9TY, ☎/fax 1465-861 220, vsd@glengennet.fsnet.co.uk, www.glengennet.co.uk; open April-Oct; B&B ££). This former shooting lodge dates from the 1890s and is now part of a 500-acre sheep farm. The house retains many original features and provides comfortable accommodation with unspoiled views from its elevated position.

Irvine

Irvine was chartered as a Royal Burgh by Robert II in 1372 and became a major seaport, growing into Ayrshire's largest town in the 18th century.

> **INFORMATION SOURCES:** The tourism office is on New Street, Irvine KA12 8BB; open from Easter through October.

■ Attractions & Sights

Dundonald Castle (HS; Dundonald village, 12 miles north of Ayr on the A71, ☎ 1563-851 489; open April-Sept, 10am-5pm; adult/concession £2.20/£1.10). Large stone castle overlooking the village. The castle was built for Robert II, the first of the Stewart kings, in the 1370s. Many original features survive, including two great feasting halls, one above the other, with great vaults beneath. The remains of an earlier grand 13th-century Stewart castle can also be seen. Excavations show that the site was previously occupied by a large fort dating from before 1000 AD, and before that a prehistoric hill fort.

Dean Castle (Dean Road, Kilmarnock KA3 1XB, ☎ 1563-522 702, www.deancastle.com; open April-Oct, noon-5pm; guided tours only, Nov-Mar, Sat-Sun, noon-4pm; admission free). The 14th-century castle was formerly the home of the Boyd Earls of Kilmarnock and houses collections of arms, armour, tapestries and musical instruments.

■ Adventures

ATV Adventure Xtreme (Blackshaw Farm, Dalry Road, West Kilbride KA23 9PG, ☎ 1294-823 014, sales@atvxtreme.com, www.atvxtreme.com). Cross-country quad bike treks and rides on a 30-acre competition track.

Mucky Wheels Off-Road Experience (Lugtonridge Farm, Lochlibo Road, Bumhouse, Beith, ☎ 1560-484 820). 4X4 off-road driving course.

ASW Fishing & Diving Charters (22 Templand Road, Dalry KA4 5EU, ☎ 1294-833 724, wass@templandrd.freeserve.co.uk). Fishing and diving charters on the Firth of Clyde aboard the Rachael Clare in the Girvan area, Largs, Ailsa Craig, and Arran. Dive to visit wrecked ships from both world wars or explore the reefs off Arran.

■ Golf

Western Gailes Golf Course (18-hole links, 6,714 yards; Gailes, Irvine KA11 5AE, ☎ 1294-311 649, fax 1294-312 312, enquiries@westerngailes.com, www.westerngailes.com; green fees £90, including lunch except on Sundays). An excellent, undulating test of links golf.

■ Where To Stay & Eat

See the *Accommodation* and *Dining* price charts on pages 109 and 110.

Lochwood Farm Steading (Lochwood Farm, Saltcoats, near Ardrossan KA21 6NG, ☎ 1294-552 529, fax 1294-553 315, info@lochwoodfarm.co.uk, www.lochwoodfarm.co.uk; B&B ££, dinner ££). Superb, award-winning B&B on a family-run dairy farm. There is tea and home baking on arrival, delightful rooms, candlelit farmhouse suppers and an outdoor hot tub.

Lochgreen House Hotel (Monktonhill Road, Southwood, Troon KA10 7EN, ☎ 1292-313 343, fax 1292-318 661, lochgreen@costleyhotels.co.uk, www.lochgreenhouse.co.uk; B&B ££££, dinner £££). Traditionally furnished (log fires, antiques and paintings) country-house hotel set in 30 acres of woodland in the heart of Ayrshire's famous links (Royal Troon is two minutes away). Shooting, fishing, horseriding, sailing and art lessons are available.

Piersland House Hotel (15 Craigend Road, Troon KA10 6HD, ☎ 1292-314 747, fax 1292-315 613, reservations@piersland.co.uk, www.piersland.co.uk; B&B ££££, dinner ££). Elegant listed house built in 1899 for Sir Alexander Walker, grandson of **Johnnie Walker** (of whisky fame). Appropriately, the Walker Lounge, with its oak paneling and original woodcarvings and fireplaces, offers 200 malt whiskies. The hotel is opposite Royal Troon's Championship golf course.

Westin Turnberry Resort (Turnberry KA26 9LT, ☎ 1655-331 000, fax 1655-331 706, turnberry@westin.com, www.westin.com/turnberry; B&B £££££+, dinner ££££+). Plush bedrooms, luxurious lodges, cottages and delicious cuisine close to the famous golf courses, teaching and practice facilities. The resort offers a wide choice of outdoor activities in addition to golf.

Largs

Largs, on the **Firth of Clyde**, is the site of the 1263 battle in which Alexander III of Scotland defeated the Viking King Haakon. Ten minutes away by ferry is the charming island of **Great Cumbrae**, which boasts Europe's smallest cathedral and the site of Britain's narrowest house.

 INFORMATION SOURCES: The tourism office is at the Railway Station, Largs KA30 8BQ; open Easter-Oct. There is also a TIC in Millport (28a Stuart Street, Millport, Isle of Cumbrae KA28 0AJ; open Easter-Sept).

■ Attractions & Sights

Largs Old Kirk (Largs, signposted from High Street; open late May to early Sept, 2-5pm; admission free; collect key from Largs Museum, ☎ 1475-672 450). This monument was erected in 1636 for Sir Robert Montgomerie of Skelmorlie and contains an elaborate carved stone tomb in Renaissance style and a painted timber ceiling depicting lively scenes of the seasons.

Vikingar! (Barrfields, Greenock Road, Largs KA30 8QL, ☎ 1475-689 777, fax 1475-689 444, info@vikingar.co.uk, www.vikingar.co.uk; open year-round, opening hours vary seasonally; adult/concession/child/family £3.75/£2.75 /£2.85/£10.50). Multimedia presentations trace 500 years of Viking history from their earliest raids on the Western Isles to their defeat at the Battle of Largs in 1263. Visit a Viking homestead and meet the Gods and Valkyries in Valhalla – the Hall of the Gods. There is also a swimming pool, cinema, fitness suite and café; check the web site for additional fees and special events.

Isle of Great Cumbrae (Caledonian MacBrayne, ☎ 1475-650 100, runs ferries from Largs pier, off Largs Main Street, every 15 minutes in summer, less frequently in winter; a bus meets every ferry for transport to Millport, the island's only town). Great Cumbrae, along with Arran and Bute, became part of Scotland in 1263. The island preserves its Victorian charm and boasts sandy beaches, the UK's smallest cathedral (Cathedral of The Isles) and Britain's narrowest house. There are shops, cafés, pubs and two museums.

■ Adventures

 Flamingo Yacht Charter (23 Main Road, Fairlie, By Largs KA29 0DW, ☎ 1475-568 526). Bareboat yacht charter on the Firth of Clyde and west coast, offering weekly, daily and weekend rentals.

Flying Eagle Charters (14 Dykesmains Road, Saltcoats KA30 8DZ, ☎ 1294-469 294, flyingeagle@jteevan.freeserve.co.uk, www.flying-eagle.co.uk). Skippered charter boat for diving, fishing or cruise trips from Largs Yacht Haven.

■ Where To Stay & Eat

See the *Accommodation* and *Dining* price charts on pages 109 and 110.

 Morvern Cottage (1 Boathouse Road, Largs KA30 8PN, ☎ 1475-675 718, morvern@supaworld.com; B&B ££). Delightful cottage B&B close to a quiet beach, with an extensive breakfast menu.

Moorings Hotel (2 May Street, Largs KA30 8EB, ☎ 1475-672 672, fax 1475-670 050, themooringshotel@btconnect.com, www.mooringshotel.co.uk; B&B ££-£££). Family-run hotel on the Largs seafront with pretty bedrooms and a restaurant overlooking the Firth of Clyde.

Fins Seafood Restaurant (Fencefoot, Fairlie, near Largs KA29 0EG, ☎ 1475-568 989; closed Mon). Specializing in locally caught fish and shellfish. Open for lunch and dinner, Tuesday through Saturday; lunch only on Sunday.

Nardini's (The Esplanade, Largs KA30 8NF, ☎ 1475-674 555; £). Fine coffee, baked goods and ice cream and an array of Italian dishes in striking Art Deco surroundings. Open daily for lunch and dinner.

College of the Holy Spirit (College Street, Millport, Isle of Cumbrae KA28 0HE, ☎ 1475-530 353, fax 1475-530 204, tccumbrae@argyll.anglican.org, www.scotland.anglican.org/retreats; B&B £-££). Guest/retreat house attached to the Cathedral of the Isles on Great Cumbrae, Britain's smallest cathedral.

Isle of Arran

Arran is often called "Scotland in Miniature" on account of the lochs and mountains in the north and gently rolling hills and meadows in the south, all encompassed by a beautiful, sometimes dramatic, coastline. Ancient standing stones, castles, a distillery, brewery, museums, local crafts and high-quality local produce complete the likeness. The hills and glens in the north of the island provide superb walking. The quiet circular road and "The String," the road running east-to-west across the center of the island, are great for cycling. Arran is one of the most accessible of the Scottish islands, which makes it popular with visitors. Arran is also the most geologically complex island in Britain – divided by the Highland Boundary Fault – and its exceptional outcrops attract many geology undergraduates here for their first fieldtrips (including the author).

 INFORMATION SOURCES: The tourism office is at The Pier, Brodick, Isle of Arran KA278AU; open year-round.

■ Special Events

Brodick Highland Games (Aug; ☎ 1770-302 290). Traditional Highland Games.

■ Getting Here

 Caledonian MacBrayne (☎ 1475-650 100, www.calmac.co.uk) operates two car-ferry routes to Arran: one goes to Brodick from Ardrossan in Ayr, the other to Lochranza from Claonaig in Kintyre, with regular daily sailings on both routes.

Holy Isle Ferry (Old Pier, Lamlash KA27 8NH, ☎ 1770-600 998/600 349). Daily ferry service to Holy Isle, April-Oct, 10am-5pm; Nov-Mar, limited service.

■ Attractions & Sights

 **Arran Heritage Museum** (Rosaburn, Brodick, Isle of Arran KA27 8DP, ☎ 1770-302 636, info@arranmuseum.co.uk, www.arranmuseum.co.uk; open April-Oct, 10:30am-4:30pm). Housed on the site of a small school, the museum's buildings comprise a croft (small farmstead) and smiddy (blacksmith), and include a farmhouse, cottage, bothy (hut), milk house, laundry, stable, coach house and harness room. Exhibits reflect the social history, archaeology and geology of the island.

 **Brodick Castle** (NTS; Brodick, Isle of Arran KA27 8HY, general information ☎ 1770-302 202, walks and events ☎ 1770-302 462, fax 1770-302 312, brodickcastle @nts.org.uk; country park open year-round, 9:30am-sunset; castle open April-Oct, 11am-4:30pm, until 3:30 in Oct; reception centre, shop and walled garden, April-Oct from 10am; restaurant, April-Oct until 5pm; full admission adult/concession/family £7/£5.25/£19, reduced for just garden & country park). An ancient seat of the Dukes of Hamilton, the castle houses impressive collections of silver, porcelain, paintings and trophies, and was occupied by the Duchess of Montrose until 1957 when it was sold to pay death duties. The oldest part dates back to the 13th century with subsequent medieval, Cromwellian and Victorian additions. Following the standard route through the castle, you enter the Victorian chambers first and travel steadily back in time.

The 16th-century dining room, with its decorative Elizabethan paneling, is particularly fine. In the Red Gallery outside, the footmen's chairs have been so designed that anyone falling asleep will slide off onto the floor! The below-stairs rooms, especially the kitchen and scullery, are as fascinating as the upstairs state rooms. Near the kitchen, the late 13th-century prison and stocks are the oldest surviving parts of the castle. There once existed a secret passage from here to the shore, although its whereabouts have now been lost.

Outside in the Country Park, the woodland garden, begun in 1923, is now home to an acclaimed rhododendron collection. The 18th-century walled garden has been restored as a Victorian garden. The Country Park has over 10 miles of waymarked trails (including the start of the path to Goat Fell), and peaceful, fern-covered woodlands hiding waterfalls and sandstone gorges. There are also pastures grazed by Highland cattle and a wildlife garden full of native plants.

Isle of Arran Brewery (Cladach, Brodick, Isle of Arran KA27 8DE, ☎ 1770-302 353, fax 1770-302 653, info@arranbrewery.co.uk, www.arran-brewery.co.uk; open April-Oct, Mon-Sat, 10am-5pm & Sun, 12:30pm-5pm; tours any time, last 4pm; admission £1 includes a taster). Set beside the pedestrian entrance to Brodick Country Park, the new, high-tech microbrewery maintains the art of traditional brewing using island water and natural ingredients free of artificial additives and preservatives to produce Dark, Blonde and Light ales. Tours let you "walk through" the brewing process via the viewing gallery and observation windows.

Isle of Arran Distillery (Lochranza, Isle of Arran KA27 8HJ, ☎ 1770-830 264, fax 1770-830 364, visitorcentre@arranwhisky.com, www.arran-whisky.com; April-Oct, 10am-5pm, shop 10am-6pm, restaurant 10am-6:30pm, winter hours vary; adult/concession £3.50/£2.50). Scotland's newest working distillery revives the traditions of whisky distilling on Arran that had been lost for 150 years. The new malt combines characteristics from the Highland and island styles and has a toffee and vanilla finish. There is a modern visitor center and an excellent restaurant.

Machrie Moor Stone Circles (four miles north of Blackwaterfoot, on the A841, just a short distance north of the King's Cave parking area – a sign marks the one-mile path to the stone circles – park across the road). This area of Arran is rich in Neolithic and Bronze age remains dating back 5,500 to 3,000 years, including ancient houses, burial cairns, field systems and, most visibly, standing stones. Machrie Moor has always attracted settlers because it boasts some of the most fertile land on the island. The six stone circles currently visible represent the later phases of human activity; most earlier remains have been sealed by peat. Although other late Neolithic and early Bronze Age ceremonial monuments in Scotland were constructed to align with solar and lunar events, no such significance has been observed here.

Lochranza Castle (Lochranza; when locked the key is available from the nearby Post Office/local shop; admission free). Outwardly just the ruins of a typical 16th-century Scottish towerhouse, closer inspection shows that the castle was built on a much earlier medieval hallhouse. The original hallhouse comprised a two-story building with the lord's lodging (hall and chamber) on the first floor above an undercroft used for storage. The later tower house is typical of many L-plan towers built during the reign of James VI. A new entrance replaced the two smaller entrances of the hallhouse and the addition of two new floors substantially increased accommodation. Lochranza was used as a hunting lodge by Scottish kings, but from 1315 was a property of the Campbells. James IV used it as a base to attack the MacDonald Lords of the Isles and Cromwell garrisoned the castle in the 1650s. A violent storm destroyed the northeastern corner in 1897 but the castle had already long been abandoned.

■ Adventures

On Foot

 Providing an impressive backdrop to Brodick Bay, **Goat Fell** (from the Norse Gast Bheinn, meaning "windy hill") is Arran's highest peak (2,866 feet/874 m) and was formed by glaciers scouring the hard underlying granite bedrock during the last ice age. The climb is popular and the route generally well defined, although the path gets rather lost among large boulders just below the summit (3-4 hours; moderate).

Most people climb from the parking area at Cladach (at the pedestrian entrance to Brodick Castle), but you can also start from outside the Rangers' office in the castle grounds. The track enters Forestry Commission land and winds up through plantations that have been severely invaded by an Asian rhododendron. The path soon emerges from the dense rhododendron to follow the Cnocan Burn ("stream of the little hill"). Cross the deer fence (which runs across the entire island to keep the majority of deer in the north, away from the south's farms and forestry). Below the deer fence the track passes through birch, alder and rowan, remnants of Arran's ancient woodlands; above, the landscape is open heather moorland.

The path skirts northward around the mountain and joins a broad ridge where it becomes rockier and climbs more steeply. Take care toward the top where the route passes some large rocks and loose stones. A triangulation point marks the summit, where there are spectacular views of some daunting nearby peaks, notably Cir Mhor (2,618 feet), Caisteal Abhail (2,817 feet) and, some 35 miles away, the Paps of Jura.

King's Cave is one of a number of sea caves found on Arran's unspoiled and rocky west coast, formed by the action of the sea on the sandstone cliffs over thousands of years. In places the sea has penetrated the soft stone to depths of over 100 feet. The caves are linked to early Christian voyages. Carvings of early Christian and Pictish origin can be found in the King's Cave. These caves are also reported to have been the hiding place of Robert the Bruce when he began his campaign for the Scottish crown, although there is no evidence that the famous spider episode (where the future king was inspired by the determination of a small spider) occurred here (1-2 hours; easy).

The signposted path starts at a parking area four miles north of Blackwaterfoot on the coastal road. The route passes the site of numerous hut circles, the remains of houses from the late Neolithic or early Bronze Age. The path then strikes off through the forest and westwards toward the coast. The path leads high above the Machrie Basin before descending toward the coast. Follow the cliff-top southwards from where there are expansive views across Kilbrannan Sound to Kintyre before the path descends through a narrow gorge to the beach and the caves.

Arran Coastal Way, a new long-distance walking route, offers spectacular mountain and coastal scenery, diverse wildlife and fascinating geological sites along the way. The 65-mile route crosses forestry tracks, fields, beaches and boulder fields, and can be completed in five to seven days. Around a third of the route is on quiet roads.

On Wheels

Arran Quad Centre (The Balmichael Visitor Centre, Shiskine, Isle of Arran KA27 8DT, ☎ 1770-860 526, www.thebalmichaelcentre.co-.uk). Circuit quads and fully guided cross-country quad bike treks, including a two-day overnight safari. Individual instruction and guiding are also available.

In the Air

Flying Fever (2 Coastguard House, Kildonan, Isle of Arran KA27 8SD, ☎ 1770-820 292, email@flyingfever.net, www.flyingfever.net). Paragliding flights and instruction, including fledgling hops on gentle slopes and soaring flights.

On Horseback

Cairnhouse Riding Centre (The Stables, Blackwaterfoot, Isle of Arran KA27 8EU, ☎/fax 1770-860 466, cairnhouse@stables70.freeserve.co.uk). Hacking and trekking for novice and experienced riders over private farm tracks, hills and sandy beaches.

North Sannox Pony Trekking (Sannox, Isle of Arran KA27 8JD, ☎ 1770-810 222). Pony trekking for all standards of rider, mainly to remote country with little riding on main roads.

In & On the Water

Port-Na-Lochan Fishery (Kilpatrick, Blackwaterfoot, Isle of Arran KA27 8EY, ☎ 1770-860 276, bannatyne@lineone.net). Two stocked trout lochans for fly and bait fishing, with tackle rental and lessons available.

Holy Isle Ferry/Boat Hire (Old Pier, Lamlash KA27 8NH, ☎ 1770-600 998/600 349). In addition to taking passengers to Holy Isle, the ferry also runs chartered trips, mackerel fishing trips (including tackle rental) and has self-drive motor boats for rent.

Arran Adventure Company (Ormidale Park, Brodick, Isle of Arran KA27 8DA, ☎ 1770-302 244, fax 1770-303 907, info@arranadventure.com, www.arranadventure.com). Arran is a one-stop-shop for adventure activities, including gorge-walking, kayaking, RIB (Rigid Inflatable Boat) trips, climbing and abseiling, mountain biking and walking and trekking. Survival skills

Ayrshire

courses, orienteering, falconry and sailing trips around the Clyde and west coast are also available. Approximate cost £25-£45 per session.

■ Shopping

Arran Aromatics (The Home Farm, Brodick, Isle of Arran KA27 8DD, ☎ 1770-302 595, fax 1770-302 599, info@arranaromatics.com, www.arranaromatics.com). Excellent reviving essential oils, bath foams, oils and shower gels, soothing body lotions, scented candles, vegetable soaps and a wide range of other gifts, all made on-site using natural materials and without testing on animals. A viewing window lets you see into the factory. Discounts are available on Internet purchases.

Arran Chocolate Factory (Invercloy, Brodick, Isle of Arran KA27 8AJ, ☎/fax 1770-302 873). Based at the James of Arran shop, a viewing window lets you watch the production of hand-made chocolates. A mail-order service is available.

Balmichael Visitor Centre (Shiskine, Isle of Arran KA27 8DT, ☎/fax 1770-860 430, www.thebalmichaelcentre.co.uk). Converted mill complex offering a wide range of shops, including Arran Ceramics, specializing in hand-thrown functional stoneware; Stable Antiques; Trareoch Crafts, which sells local designs such as tapestries, jewelry and art; and Island Treasure, with a large selection of fine silver jewelry, perfumed candles, mirrors and locally turned wood.

The Island Cheese Co (Home Farm, Brodick, Isle of Arran KA27 8DD, ☎/fax 1770-302 788). Taste and watch the production of fine Scottish, farmhouse and continental cheeses. Wines, Scotch ales, pottery and other gifts are also available.

Ailsa McNicol Jewellery (Arran Craft Gallery & Jewellery Studio, Brodick, Isle of Arran KA27 8AJ, ☎ 1770-302 680). Locally-made jewelry, woodwork, pottery, silks and fabrics.

Old Byre Showroom (Auchencar Farm, Machrie, Isle of Arran KA27 8EB, ☎/fax 1770-840 227, lorna@oldbyre.co.uk, www.oldbyre.co.uk). Extensive range of hand-knitted Aran sweaters and cardigans, designer knitwear, sheepskins, travel rugs and children's wear.

Torrylinn Creamery (Kilmory, Isle of Arran, ☎ 1770-870 240). Maker of Scottish island cheeses, including Arran Dunlop Cheddar. You can watch traditional cheese making from the viewing gallery.

■ Where To Stay

Hotels

 Auchrannie Country House Hotel (Auchrannie Road, Brodick, Isle of Arran KA27 8BZ, ☎ 1770-302 234, fax 1770-302 812, hotel@auchrannie.co.uk, www.auchrannie.co.uk; B&B ££££, lunch £, dinner £££). Traditional hotel offering spacious rooms, fine cuisine and brasserie dining, swimming pool and leisure facilities, massage and body treatments.

Glenartney Hotel (Brodick, Isle of Arran KA27 8BX, ☎ 1770-302 220, fax 1770-302 452; open Mar-Oct; B&B ££). Small, informal hotel with a quiet location in Brodick, good views and a cozy guest lounge.

Kilmichael Country House Hotel (Glen Cloy, By Brodick, Isle of Arran KA27 8BY, ☎ 1770-302 219, fax 1770-302 068, enquiries@kilmichael.com, www.kilmichael.com; B&B ££££, dinner £££-££££). Country-house hotel in private grounds, with attractively decorated rooms, some with Jacuzzi baths and private entrances from the garden.

Corrie Hotel (Corrie, KA27 8JB, ☎ 1770-810 273, corriehotel@btinternet.com; B&B ££, dinner ££). Small hotel nestling beneath Goat Fell, five miles north of Brodick, serving lunches, teas, dinners and bar meals.

Kinloch Hotel (Blackwaterfoot, Isle of Arran KA27 8ET, ☎ 1770-860 444, fax 1770-860 447, kinloch@cqm.co.uk, www.kinloch-arran.com; B&B £££, dinner ££). Large, modern hotel by the shore at Blackwaterfoot. Extensive leisure facilities include an indoor pool, sauna, solarium, squash courts and gym.

Guest Houses & B&Bs

Belvedere Guest House (Alma Road, Brodick, Isle of Arran KA27 8AZ, ☎ 1770-302 397, fax 1770-302 088, belvedere@vision-unlimited.co.uk, www.vision-unlimited.co.uk; B&B ££, dinner £££). Comfortable guest house enjoying excellent views over Brodick Bay to the castle and Goat Fell beyond. The hearty, home-cooked evening meal is a convivial dinner party (free aperitifs and wine included) in which the friendly hosts Chris and Jan join guests at table. Vision Unlimited, which offers stress reduction and personal development courses, is based at Belvedere and clinical aromatherapy, reflexology, and reiki are also available in-house. There is also a two-person chalet with kitchen.

Carrick Lodge (Brodick, Isle of Arran KA27 8BH, ☎/fax 1770-302 550; open Feb-Oct; B&B ££). Lovely sandstone manse with great views from the garden.

Glen Cloy Farmhouse (Glen Cloy Road, Brodick, Isle of Arran KA27 8DA, ☎ 1770-302 351, mvpglencloy@compuserve.com; B&B ££). Set peacefully near Brodick, the rooms are comfortable and there is a large drawing room, extensive library and bright dining room.

Lochside Guest House (Kilpatrick, Blackwaterfoot, Isle of Arran KA27 8EY, ☎ 1770-860 276, bannatyne@lineone.net; B&B ££, dinner £). Tranquil accommodation in a specially built guest house beside a pair of trout lochans (owned by the pro-

HOTEL PRICE CHART	
Per person, per night, based on double occupancy in high season. B&B rate includes breakfast; DB&B includes dinner and breakfast.	
£	Under £20
££	£21-£35
£££	£36-£50
££££	£51-£80
£££££	Over £80

prietors – guests receive discounts) with views beyond to the Mull of Kintyre and Northern Ireland. Breakfasts are excellent and there is a hearty dinner followed by cakes, cheese and biscuits. Marjorie is an exceptional host and the warmth of her hospitality commands extraordinary guest loyalty – some return year after year over several decades! Get in early as it books up quickly.

Blackwaterfoot Lodge (Blackwaterfoot, Isle of Arran KA27 8EU, ☎ 1770-860 202, fax 1770-860 570, info@blackwater-foot-lodge.co.uk, www.blackwaterfootlodge.co.uk; open Easter-Sept; B&B ££, dinner £-££). Small hotel with a conservatory and bistro-restaurant that serves an ever-changing menu. Bar meals are also available.

Apple Lodge (Lochranza, Isle of Arran KA27 8HJ, ☎/fax 1770-830 229; B&B ££, dinner ££). At one time the village manse, this country house has plush bedrooms, antiques, original paintings, embroidery and excellent views. The food is superb too, although you need to bring your own wine and drinks.

■ Where To Eat

Creelers Restaurant (The Home Farm, Brodick, Isle of Arran KA27 8DD, ☎ 1770-302 810; open Easter-Oct; ££-£££) Creelers specializes in locally sourced fish and shellfish – the proprietor was a full-time fisherman and still creels for crabs, lobsters and langoustines. Meat and vegetarian dishes are also featured, and tapas-style starters are available at lunchtime.

Old Pier Tearoom (Lamlash KA27 8JN, ☎ 1770-600 249; £). Freshly prepared light snacks, main meals and home baking at Lamlash pier.

DINING PRICE CHART	
Indicates the price per person for a full meal, excluding drinks. Generally three courses, though fixed menus of five or more courses may be available.	
£	Under £10
££	£11-£20
£££	£21-£30
££££	£31-£40

Stalkers Eating House (Brodick, ☎ 1770-302 579; closed Sun; £-££). Good home cooking; open fromApril to October, lunch and dinner daily.

Trafalgar Restaurant (Whiting Bay, ☎ 1770-700 396; restricted winter opening; ££-£££). Long-established restaurant serving à la carte evening meals. Reservations essential.

Edinburgh & The Lothians

City of Edinburgh

Edinburgh, Scotland's glorious capital, exudes grace and grandeur of a quality that few who set eyes upon it will ever forget. Dominated by a historic castle sitting majestically atop a dark volcanic rock, the city's elegant buildings, with their neo-classical inspiration and checkerboard stonework, are interspersed by towering spires, creating a dramatic skyline befitting one of the world's most beautiful and elegant cities. Edinburgh's **Old Town** and **New Town** are UNESCO World Heritage Sites.

Lying between the **Pentland hills** to the south and the **Firth of Forth** to the north, the city's famous Castle Rock was formed by violent volcanic activity 350 million years ago. Mighty glaciers from a series of ice ages ground away the softer stone leaving only the hard basalt core of the rock, and a crag and sloping tail formation of the debris that forms today's Castle Rock and Royal Mile.

Castle Rock was the site of some very early settlements but, for the first 700 years of its existence, Edinburgh remained an unremarkable small town and didn't acquire any real significance until the 11th century. Medieval Edinburgh developed east of Castle Rock and was protected by a defensive stone wall – the *murus regius* (King's Wall) – and the waters of the **Nor' Loch** (an artificial lake). Despite being twice captured and repeatedly burned by English armies, Edinburgh continued to develop and in 1329 received a new charter from Robert I (the Bruce) making it the nation's chief burgh. By the end of the 15th century, Edinburgh was established as Scotland's permanent capital.

The **Royal Mile**, Edinburgh's oldest street, runs down the sloping tail of Castle Rock. As one of the original town's few open spaces, the area was used for markets, as a public meeting place and the site of public executions. People lived in darkened, narrow closes branching off the main street at regular intervals, giving the Old Town a herringbone layout.

Edinburgh's population had reached almost 22,000 by the 1690s and was still growing as people flocked to the capital. Constrained by the castle to the west, the burgh of Canongate to the east, the defensive Flodden Wall to the south and the Nor' Loch to the north, Edinburgh grew higher and higher. Housing in the city was primarily in tall, narrow tenement buildings called "lands," some of which reached 12 stories high. The city's overcrowding led Daniel

1. Edinburgh Castle
2. Gladstone's Land, Camera Obscura
3. Museum Of Scotland
4. Royal Museum of Scotland
5. St. Giles' Cathedral, Greyfriars Pub
6. Museum of Childhood
7. Tolbooth, People's Story Museum
8. Dynamic Earth
9. Palace of Holyroodhouse
10. Holyrood Park, Arthur's Seat
11. City Art Centre; Edinburgh Dungeon
12. National Gallery of Scotland
13. Royal Scottish Academy
14. Princes Street Gardens
15. The Exchange
16. St Mary's Episcopal Cathedral
17. Scottish National Gallery of Modern Art
18. Dean Gallery
19. Dean Village
20. Ainslie Place
21. Moray Place
22. Royal Circus
23. Royal Botanic Garden
24. Scottish National Portrait Gallery

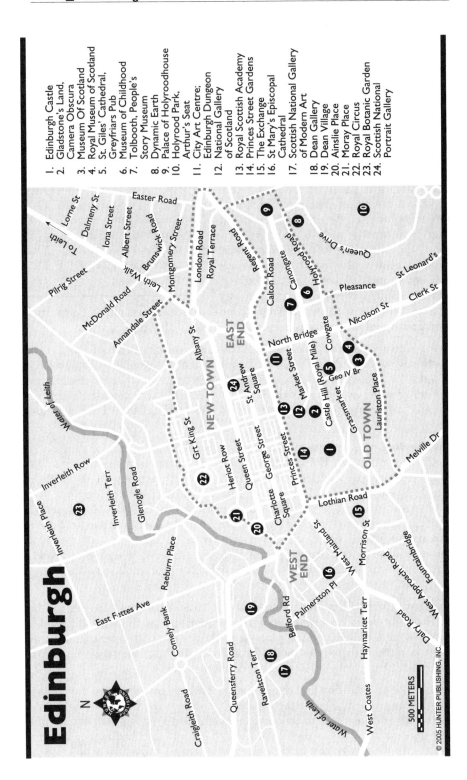

© 2005 HUNTER PUBLISHING, INC.

500 METERS

Defoe to remark in 1726: "in no city in the world do so many people live in so little room as in Edinburgh." In such cramped and unhygienic living conditions, outbreaks of disease and plague were common.

Relief from overcrowding came with the building of the **North Bridge** in 1772 and the draining of the Nor' Loch (the filled in hollow is now occupied by **Princes Street Gardens**). This opened the land to the north and led to the creation of the elegant, symmetrically designed Georgian New Town, built largely from 1767 to 1820. In sharp contrast to the narrow winding streets of the Old Town, the New Town contains light, spacious houses and wide, straight streets, crescents and circuses. The New Town soon attracted wealthier residents, such as landowners and professionals, who could afford to escape the crowds and squalor of the Old Town. Charlotte Square in the New Town, the last commission of influential architect Robert Adam (1728-1792), is one of the finest Georgian squares in Britain.

In time the city expanded north over the surrounding ridges and hollows right up to the **Firth of Forth** (present-day **Leith**). It also spread south and west, eventually surrounding its open spaces, most notably **Holyrood Park** (which contains Arthur's Seat, a famous vantage point rising 823 feet high) to the southeast and the **Meadows** to the south.

Apart from being a university city, the home of many well-known schools and the seat of Scottish government, Edinburgh is an important commercial center with substantial banking and insurance interests.

Following political union with England in 1707, Edinburgh diminished in importance, only to enjoy a revival at the end of the 18th century as a literary and cultural center. Since 1947, Edinburgh has hosted an annual festival of music, drama and other arts – the **Edinburgh Festival** – which has grown into the largest arts festival in the world.

DON'T MISS

■ Explore the fascinating, darkened closes of the **Royal Mile**.

■ Soak up the medieval atmosphere of **Gladstone's Land**, the high-rise tenement building typical of the Old Town.

■ Visit the **Palace of Holyroodhouse**, the Queen's Scottish residence.

■ Stroll the leafy banks of the **Water of Leith**.

■ Climb the **Salisbury Crags** (Arthur's Seat) or **Calton Hill** for a great view of the Edinburgh skyline.

■ Explore the magnificent, romantic ruin of **Linlithgow Palace**, birthplace of Mary, Queen of Scots.

■ Marvel at the mysterious, intricate carvings at **Rosslyn Chapel**.

■ Best Freebie: **The Royal Botanic Garden**.

■ Special Events

 Edinburgh offers a packed calendar of events and festivals through-out the year that keeps the city buzzing no matter when you visit. A web site (www.eventfuledinburgh.com) provides details of the events taking place, including the precise dates each year of the annual events listed below.

Edinburgh International Science Festival (Apr; ☎ 131-558 7666, www.sciencefestival.co.uk). Festival devoted to the celebration of science and technology.

Imaginate (Scottish International Children's Festival, May-June; ☎ 131-225 8050, www.imaginate.org.uk). Britain's biggest performing arts festival for children, providing entertainment to capture the imagination of young people.

Royal Highland Show (Jun; ☎ 131-335 6200, info@rhass.org.uk, www-.rhass.org.uk). The four-day show is a highlight of the country calendar and includes livestock, a huge exhibition of Scottish food and drink, and one of the largest flower shows in Scotland.

Edinburgh International Jazz & Blues Festival (July/Aug; ☎ 131-553 4000, www.jazzmusic.co.uk). Top-quality jazz over a 10-day period featuring jazz legends and upcoming new stars.

Edinburgh Military Tattoo (Aug; ☎ 870-7555 1188, fax 131-225 8627, edintattoo@edintattoo.co.uk, www.edintattoo.co.uk). An outdoor military spectacular set in the esplanade in front of Edinburgh Castle.

Edinburgh International Festival (Aug; ☎ 131-473 2001, fax 131-473 2003, boxoffice@eif.co.uk, www.eif.co.uk). One of the world's foremost arts festivals celebrates diverse areas of opera, theater, music, dance and drama.

Edinburgh Festival Fringe (Aug; ☎ 131-226 5257/226 0026, fax 131-220 4205, admin@edfringe.com, www.edfringe.com). Originally the informal part of the International Festival, the Fringe has now grown into the largest arts festival in the world, with 16,000 performers in nearly 200 venues showcasing every art form, including comedy, theater, music and magic.

Edinburgh International Film Festival (Aug; ☎ 131-228 4051, fax 131-229 5501, info@edfilmfest.org.uk, www.edfilmfest.org.uk). Established in 1947, the festival presents some of cinema's greatest and brightest moments from both established directors and newcomers.

Edinburgh International Book Festival (Aug; ☎ 131-228 5444, fax 131-228 4333, admin@edbookfest.co.uk, www.edbookfest.co.uk). The world's largest book event celebrates the written word with hundreds of authors at hundreds of lively events.

Hogmanay (Dec; ☎ 131-473 2000, www.edinburghshogmanay.org). The city's world-famous New Year celebrations take place over four days at various venues, culminating in a massive street party, concerts and fantastic fireworks displays. Entry is by ticket only, available at the Hub and seasonal ticket offices.

■ Getting Around

Walking is the best way to explore Edinburgh, particularly the Old Town's closes and wynds. If you'd rather not walk there are taxi ranks all along the Royal Mile. Private vehicles are restricted on the upper section of the Royal Mile; there are parking areas on Castle Terrace and New Street. If driving, pay particular attention to parking regulations – the city's blackjacketed traffic wardens come with a fearsome reputation!

It's fairly easy to find your bearings around Edinburgh. The city is centerd on its oldest street, the **Royal Mile**, which runs downhill from **Edinburgh Castle** in the west to the **Palace of Holyroodhouse** in the east. The Royal Mile is actually just over a mile and changes name several times during its course (**Castlehill**, **Lawnmarket**, **High Street** and **Canongate**).

To the north of the Royal Mile is **Princes Street**, Edinburgh's principal shopping street, which also marks the demarcation between the Old and New Towns. North of Princes Street is the **Georgian New Town** with its elegant houses and streets. South of Princes Street is the **Old Town**, the original medieval city, with its narrow closes and *wynds* (pronounced as in "wind your watch," these are alleys or narrow streets) spilling down from the Royal Mile.

INFORMATION SOURCES: Edinburgh & Lothians Tourist Board (and the Edinburgh & Scotland Tourist Information Centre) is at 3 Princes Street, Edinburgh EH2 2QP, UK ☎ 845-225 5121; outside UK ☎ 1506-832 121; fax 1506-832 222; www.edinburgh.org; open year-round. There are maps and brochures, accommodation booking, foreign exchange and Internet facilities. There is also a TIC at Edinburgh Airport.

■ Attractions & Sights

Castles, Palaces & Churches

Edinburgh Castle (HS; Castlehill, Royal Mile, Edinburgh, ☎ 131-225 9846; open April-Oct, 9:30am-6pm, Nov-Mar, 9:30am-5pm, last admission 45 minutes before closing; adult/concession/child £9.50/£7/£2) is a dramatic highlight of the Edinburgh skyline and its easily defendable hilltop position (three sides of Castle Rock are nearly vertical) is the very reason for Edinburgh's location. This site has been fortified since 1100 and the castle has played its full part in Scottish history, both as a royal residence and military garrison.

Edward I ("Hammer of the Scots") captured the castle in 1296 but **Sir Thomas Randolph**, nephew of Robert the Bruce, re-took it in 1314 in a daring night attack with just 30 men. Following the death of Robert the Bruce, the English once again captured the castle in 1335. **Oliver Cromwell** turned the castle into a garrison fortress following his invasion of Scotland in 1650 and much of its appearance today relates from this period onwards.

The approach to the castle is by a large parade ground, the **Esplanade**, which serves as a parking area offering great views to both north and south. The Esplanade is also the venue for the annual Edinburgh Military Tattoo.

> **DID YOU KNOW?** The Esplanade in front of Edinburgh Castle is legally owned by Nova Scotia, dating from a deal concluded by Charles I and never revoked.

The early-12th-century **St. Margaret's Chapel**, the tiny chapel that crowns the castle complex, is the oldest building in Edinburgh. It's also the smallest chapel in Scotland, measuring just 16½ x 10½ feet. The chapel was built by David I in honour of his Saxon mother, Queen Margaret (who was canonized in 1250). The battlements outside the chapel provide excellent views north over the New Town and beyond to the Firth of Forth and Fife.

Beside the chapel lies **Mons Meg**, one of a pair of gigantic Flemish-built cannons gifted to James II by the Duke of Burgundy in 1457. The cannon would have required more than 100 men to haul it into battle, and remains the finest example in Britain of the heaviest 15th-century "bombard" artillery.

 The castle's **One o'Clock Gun** has fired every day (except Sundays) since 1861 and is a great way to tell visitors from locals: visitors jump in fright whereas locals check their watches. The gun was originally a time signal for shipping in the Port of Leith and is also fired to mark the New Year at Edinburgh's world-famous Hogmanay celebrations.

The highlights of the complex cluster around **Crown Square** at the summit of Castle Rock. The hushed solemnity of the **Scottish National War Memorial** pays tribute to Scotland's regiments, individually remembered through a series of pillars and bays, beyond which is the shrine containing the original rolls of honour.

The **Great Hall** was built in the 16th century for James IV. It served as the main banqueting chamber and is still used for government receptions. An original hammer-beam roof dominates the hall, its principal trusses decorated with ornate carvings, some bearing James IV's monogram. A minstrels' gallery overlooks the entrance and on the opposite wall an iron-barred peephole window allowed spying on suspicious visitors.

The **Royal Palace** takes visitors through a series of vivid recreations to the **Crown Room** housing the **Honours of Scotland** (the Scottish Crown Jewels). The honours are the oldest British regalia and include the crown made for James V in 1540 (made of gold from Robert the Bruce's original gold circlet), and the Sword of State and Sceptre, presented by Popes Julius II and Alexander VI to James IV. The honours were sealed up in the Crown Room in 1707 after union with England and remained hidden until Sir Walter Scott instigated their re-discovery in 1818.

The **Stone of Destiny**, on which Scottish monarchs were crowned for over 400 years, is also displayed in the Crown Room. Edward I removed the stone to London's Westminster Abbey in 1296, where English and later British monarchs were crowned. The stone was symbolically restored to Scotland on St Andrew's Day (30th November) 1996.

The **Royal Apartments** include the bedchamber where Mary, Queen of Scots gave birth in 1566 to her son James, who in time united the crowns of Scotland and England as James VI of Scotland and James I of England. The **Laich Hall** and **King's Dining Room** were created in 1617 for James's return to his home country.

Edinburgh Castle is one of the UK's top 10 visitor attractions and Scotland's number-one tourist venue. Get there early if you're planning a weekend visit; the castle will be heaving by lunchtime, even outside high season. There are guided tours and an excellent audio guide available in several languages.

The National War Museum (Edinburgh Castle, Edinburgh, ☎ 131-225 7534, fax 131-225 3848, info@nms.ac.uk, www.nms.ac.uk/war; open April-Oct, 9:45am-5:45pm, Nov-Mar, 9:45am-4:45pm; admission included in castle ticket) recounts Scotland's history of war and military service over the last 400 years.

Holyroodhouse (Canongate, Royal Mile, Edinburgh, ☎ 131-556 5100, information@royalcollection.org.uk, www.royal.gov.uk; open April-Oct, 9:30am-6pm; Nov-Mar, 9:30am-4:30pm; last admission 45 minutes before closing; adult/concession/child/family £8/£6.50/£4/£20) is the Queen's official Scottish residence and is used for state occasions; the palace is closed during these visits. The royal apartments, renowned for their fine plasterwork ceilings and Brussels tapestries, are decorated with works of art from the Royal Collection. The Baroque palace is closely associated with several turbulent episodes from Scottish history. It briefly served as Bonnie Prince Charlie's headquarters during the 1745 Jacobite Rising and is perhaps best known as the former home of Mary, Queen of Scots (whose bedchamber, with its intimate supper room, is the highlight of the royal apartments), and scene of the brutal murder of Rizzio, her secretary. The ruins of a 12th-century abbey add further to the charm and atmosphere of the palace. There is an excellent audio guide.

St Giles' Cathedral (High Street, Royal Mile, Edinburgh, ☎ 131-225 9442, fax 131-225 9576, info@stgiles.net, www.stgiles.net; open May-Sept, Mon-Fri, 9am-7pm; Sat, 9am-5pm; Sun, 1-5pm; and Oct-Apr, Mon-Sat, 9am-5pm; Sun, 1-5pm; donations requested), the High Kirk of Edinburgh, was the focus of the Scottish Reformation and is built around four massive central pillars, dating from around 1120. In 1385 the church was burned by an English army and rebuilt soon afterwards. Around 1460 the roof was raised and the church extended eastward. The distinctive crown spire was completed in 1495. During the Reformation in 1560 many internal furnishings were removed and the walls whitewashed. The church suffered a lot of restoration work in the 1880s and only the crown steeple remains unspoiled.

The fascinating **Thistle Chapel** was added in 1911 and, while part of the cathedral, is the private domain of **The Most Ancient and Most Noble Order of the Thistle**, Scotland's order of chivalry. The Order, dating back to 1687, has the Queen as its head with 16 knights in attendance; the original Knights of the Thistle are commemorated with beautifully carved stalls around the tiny chapel, each with the knight's crest above.

St Mary's Episcopal Cathedral (Palmerston Place, Edinburgh, ☎ 131-225 6293, fax 131-225 3181, office@cathedral.net, www.cathedral.net; admission free) is a magnificent Victorian neo-Gothic cathedral designed by George Gilbert Scott, located in the West End. There are daily services, and the cathedral is particularly noted for its music.

Museums & Galleries

Museum of Scotland (Chambers Street, Edinburgh EH1 1JF, ☎ 131-247 4422, fax 131-220 4819, info@nms.ac.uk, www.nms.ac.uk; open Mon-Sat, 10am-5pm; Tues, 10am-8pm; Sun, noon-5pm; admission free except for special exhibitions). Housed in a stunning modern building, the Museum of Scotland opened in 1998 and recounts the history of Scotland, its land, people and their achievements through galleries of rich national collections. Starting with Scotland's geological formation and earliest people, exhibits lead right up to the 20th century. There are free highlights, themed guided tours and audio guides.

Royal Museum (Chambers Street, Edinburgh EH1 1JF, ☎ 131-247 4219, fax 131-220 4819, info@nms.ac.uk, www.nms.ac.uk; open Mon-Sat, 10am-5pm; Tues, 10am-8pm; Sun, noon-5pm; admission free except for special exhibitions). Unlike the ultra-modern Museum of Scotland with which it connects, the Royal Museum occupies a splendid Victorian building with elegant balconies overlooking an expansive Main Hall. Gallery after gallery opens up before you housing wide-ranging international collections of decorative arts, science, industry, archaeology and the natural world. Highlights include a blue whale skeleton and an ever-fascinating Ancient Egyptian gallery. Free highlights and themed guided tours are available.

National Gallery of Scotland (The Mound, Edinburgh EH2 2EL, ☎ 131-624 6200, fax 131-623 7126, nginfo@nationalgalleries.org, www.nationalgalleries.org; open 10am-5pm; Thurs, 10am-7pm; admission free except for special exhibitions). The gallery houses masterpieces from the Renaissance to Post-Impressionism, including works by Raphael, Rembrandt, Turner and Van Gogh.

Scottish National Portrait Gallery (1 Queen Street, Edinburgh EH2 1JD, ☎ 131-624 6200, fax 131-623 7126, pginfo@nationalgalleries.org, www.nationalgalleries.org; open 10am-5pm; Thurs, 10am-7pm; admission free except for special exhibitions). An ornate Gothic building displaying portraits and sculptures of the men and women who shaped Scottish history, including familiar portraits of Robert Burns by his friend Alexander Nasmyth; Bonnie Prince Charlie by Antonio David; and Mary, Queen of Scots by an unknown artist. Less well known but equally stunning is a huge painting of Queen Anne, the last Stewart monarch to occupy the British throne, by

Willem Wissing and Jan van der Vaardt. Murals on the beautiful balcony overlooking the main hall depict the battles of Bannockburn and Largs. The changing displays in the ground floor galleries can be very impressive.

Scottish National Gallery of Modern Art (75 Belford Road, Edinburgh EH4 3DR, ☎ 131-624 6200, fax 131-623 7126, gmainfo@nationalgalleries.org, www.nationalgalleries.org; open 10am-5pm; Thurs to 7pm; admission free except for special exhibitions). The gallery houses Scotland's finest collection of 20th/21st-century art, including works by Picasso, Moore and Hirst.

The Dean Gallery (73 Belford Road, Edinburgh EH4 3DS, ☎ 131-624 6200, fax 131-623 7126, deaninfo@nationalgalleries.org. www.national-galleries.org; open 10am-5pm; Thurs, 10am-7pm; admission free except for special exhibitions). The palatial, neo-classical building was originally a hospital for orphans. It was converted into a gallery to house works by Paolozzi (an Edinburgh-born sculptor), a wide collection of Dada and Surrealist art (including works by Dalí, Ernst, Miró, Tanguy and Picasso), and exhibitions of modern and contemporary art.

Museum of Edinburgh (142 Canongate, Royal Mile, Edinburgh, ☎ 131-529 4143, www.cac.org.uk; open Mon-Sat, 10am-5pm; during the Edinburgh Festival, Sun 2pm-5pm; admission free). An intriguing and surprisingly large museum of Edinburgh history housed in a fine 16th-century townhouse. Diverse collections cover the development of the city, law and order, water supply (including original wooden water pipes), the visit of George IV, recreations of period rooms, silver and glass collections and the famous story of Greyfriars Bobby.

GREYFRIARS BOBBY

Greyfriars Bobby is the Skye Terrier immortalized by his 14-year vigil beside the grave of his master John Gray, an Edinburgh police constable who died in February 1858. Bobby remained beside the grave in **Greyfriars Kirkyard** until his own death on 14th January 1872. A bronze statue to Bobby was commissioned by Baroness Burdett-Coutts as "A tribute to the Affectionate Fidelity of Greyfriars Bobby," and unveiled in 1873. The statue stands on a granite fountain outside the gates of Greyfriars Kirkyard (on George IV Bridge, opposite the Greyfriars Bobby pub) and a copy is housed in the Museum of Edinburgh. Bobby's story has been made popular through various books and films and his web site (www.greyfriarsbobby.co.uk) continues to attract hundreds of visitors each day.

Writers' Museum (Lady Stair's House, Lawnmarket, Royal Mile, Edinburgh, ☎ 131-529 4901, enquiries@writersmuseum.demon.co.uk, www.cac.org.uk; open Mon-Sat, 10am-5pm; also Sun during the Edinburgh Festival, 2pm-5pm; admission free). Located within the 17th-century Lady Stair's House, the museum contains collections from Scotland's illustrious writing sons, most notably Robert Burns (1759-1796), Sir Walter Scott

(1771-1832) and Robert Louis Stevenson (1850-1894), in addition to exhibitions featuring other writers. The museum houses rich collections of manuscripts, first editions, portraits and personal exhibits, including Burns' writing desk and Scott's chessboard. The adjacent Makars' Court ("Makar" is Scots for poet) contains commemorative engraved flagstones celebrating Scottish writers from the 14th century onwards.

The People's Story Museum (Canongate Tolbooth, Canongate, Royal Mile, Edinburgh, ☎ 131-529 4057, www.cac.org.uk; open Mon-Sat, 10am-5pm; also Sun during the Edinburgh Festival, 2-5pm). Housed in the original Canongate Tolbooth, which dates from 1591, the museum tells the story of the ordinary people of Edinburgh from the late 18th century onwards.

ROBERT LOUIS STEVENSON

Robert Louis Stevenson lived at **17 Heriot Row** in Edinburgh New Town. His poem *Leary the Lamplighter* was about the local lamplighter, whom Stevenson could see from his window. Other famous landmarks with RLS connections include the **Jeckyll & Hyde pub**, **Deacon Brodie's Tavern** and **The Hawes Inn** in South Queensferry, which features in *Kidnapped*.

28 Charlotte Square (NTS; 28 Charlotte Square, Edinburgh EH2 4ET, ☎ 131-243 9300, fax 131-243 9301; open Mon-Fri, 11am-3pm; admission free). 28 Charlotte Square contains a gallery exhibiting 20th-century Scottish paintings in a domestic setting and Regency furniture recreating an 1820s drawing room.

City Art Centre (2 Market Street, Edinburgh, ☎ 131-529 3993, cac.admin@edinburgh.gov.uk, www.cac.org.uk; open Mon-Sat, 10am-5pm; also Sun during the Edinburgh Festival, noon-5pm; admission free except special exhibitions). The gallery is home to Edinburgh's collection of Scottish art and houses many temporary exhibitions, from rare Egyptian antiquities to innovative contemporary art, and from Michelangelo's drawings to Star Trek.

Monuments & Civic Sites

Camera Obscura & World of Illusions (Castlehill, Royal Mile, Edinburgh EH1 2ND, ☎ 131-226 3709, fax 131-225 4239, info@camera-obscura.co.uk, www.camera-obscura.co.uk; open April-Jun & Sep-Oct, 9:30am-6pm; July-Aug, 9:30am-7:30pm; Nov-Mar, 10am-5pm; adult/concession/child £5.95/£4.60/£3.70). Take a fascinating guided city tour from inside a darkened room ("camera obscura" is Latin for "darkened room"). This intriguing Victorian "webcam" provides live 360° panoramas collected by a periscope camera mounted on the roof of the building and projected onto a circular table inside a darkened room. There are also excellent rooftop views, free telescopes and displays of holograms, interactive illusions and visions of Edinburgh through the ages.

Gladstone's Land (NTS; 477B Lawnmarket, Royal Mile, Edinburgh EH1 2NT, ☎ 131-226 5856, fax 131-226 4851; open April-Oct, Mon-Sat, 10am-5pm & Sun, 2-5pm; adult/concession/family £3.50/£2.60/£9.50). Atmospheric 17th-century tenement building typical of those that grew up in the overcrowded Old Town along the ridge of the Royal Mile. Dating to 1620, the six-story building presents a vivid image of the living conditions in old Edinburgh and contains remarkable original painted ceilings. The site and extent of accommodation in this building attest to the prestige of its owner.

EDINBURGH'S MEDIEVAL HIGH-RISES

With no room to expand to the sides, Edinburgh's growing population was housed in increasingly tall, narrow tenement buildings called "lands," built within the safety of the city walls. These lands could be as high as 12 stories. Each story comprised a separate house and each land had a steep communal staircase leading to the street below. The narrow alleyways between the lands were called closes.

People of all classes lived in lands. The cramped dwellings on the very top stories housed the city's poor. Professionals and aristocrats preferred the middle stories, away from the filth and stench of the streets below. Tradespeople lived below them and the ground floors were used as shops or taverns. None of the houses had running water or toilets; each evening those who lived on the upper stories would throw rubbish and human waste from their windows into the closes below. It was customary to shout "Gardyloo!" (from the French *gardez l'eau* – watch the water) to warn those below, although this was often done as an afterthought!

The Real Mary King's Close (2 Warriston's Close, High Street, Royal Mile, Edinburgh EH1 1PG, ☎ 870-243 0160, www.realmarykingsclose.com; tours every 20 minutes from 10am to 9pm, April-Oct; 10am to 4pm, Nov-Mar; reservations recommended for evening tours); adult/concession/child/family £7/£6/£5/£21). Beneath the City Chambers on the Royal Mile lies a fascinating warren of hidden streets dating back to the 17th-19th centuries. These underground closes were originally very narrow walkways with houses on either side stretching up to seven stories high. Part of the lower sections were kept as foundations for the construction of the **Royal Exchange** (now the City Chambers), leaving a number of dark and mysterious underground closes and ancient dwellings. Step back in time into the home of a gravedigger's family stricken with plague, or into a grand 16th-century townhouse, or a small "laigh" or low poor house, and even see an urban cowshed! Subtle lighting and audio effects bring to life the story of how these people lived, worked and died. The "Shrine Room," said to be haunted by the ghost of a young girl, is one of the best surviving 17th-century houses in Scotland. Costumed actors playing characters from the close's past excellently lead the guided tours. Staircases, uneven ground and dim lighting may cause difficulties for people with certain disabilities. Children under five are not admitted.

John Knox House (43 High Street, Royal Mile, Edinburgh EH1 1SR, ☎ 131-556 9579). Atmospheric, medieval house is the former home of James Mossman (1530-1573), goldsmith to Mary, Queen of Scots, and contains a memorial to John Knox (1513-1572), Scotland's religious reformer. The exhibition closed for refurbishment in 2003 and is expected to re-open in 2005. Check the status with the Tourist Board.

Our Dynamic Earth (Holyrood Road, Edinburgh EH8 8AS, ☎ 131-550 7800, fax 131-550 7801, enquiries@dynamicearth.co.uk, www.dynamicearth.co.uk; open April-Aug, 10am-6pm; Sep-Oct, 10am-5pm; Nov-Mar, Wed-Sun, 10am-5pm; adult/senior or child/student/family £8.95/£5.45/ £6.50/£24.50). Don't be deterred by the more than passing resemblance this white-tented structure bears to London's ill-fated Millennium Dome. Our Dynamic Earth contains an enthralling series of interactive galleries and educational multimedia displays, backed by powerful soundtracks, highlighting the history of our planet and its wide-ranging environments. Highlights include awe-inspiring images of space taken from the Hubble Space Telescope, a ground-shaking volcano eruption, a flight over a glacier and a rainforest storm. It's guaranteed to fascinate visitors of all ages – allow around two hours for the visit.

Scotch Whisky Heritage Centre (354 Castlehill, Royal Mile, Edinburgh EH1 2NE, ☎ 131-220 0441, fax 131-220 6288, info@whisky-heritage.co.uk, www.whisky-heritage.co.uk; open May-Sept, 9:30am-6:30pm; Oct-Apr, 10am-5pm; last tour one hour before closing; adult/concession/child/family £7.95/£5.95/£4.25/£18). Innovative and well-thought-out displays help you see, smell and taste your way toward expertise in Scotland's most famous product. Discover the secrets of malts and grain, distilling and blending. Best of all is the "whisky barrel ride," which brings 300 years of whisky history to life through fascinating, life-like recreations. Included is a free tasting for adults and commentaries are available in eight languages and Braille. There is also a good restaurant, bar and shop.

Tartan Weaving Mill & Exhibition (555 Castlehill, Royal Mile, Edinburgh EH1 2ND, ☎ 131-226 1555, fax 131-225 4846, castlehill@geoffreykilts.co.uk, www.tartanweavingmill.co.uk; open April-Oct, Mon-Sat, 9am-6:30pm; Sun, 10am-6:30pm; winter closing 5:30; adult/concession/child £4.50/£3.50/£2.50). See the tartan-weaving process close-up at this working mill, and follow the tartan story from sheep to kilt. Try your hand at weaving, and be photographed wearing ancient Scottish tartans. There is a colorful shop, and the Clans and Tartans Bureau can provide full information on tartans, clan histories and tartan designs.

Calton Hill, at the eastern end of Princes Street (☎ 131-556 2716), provides one of the best views over Edinburgh. The grandest of its several attractions is the **National Monument**, a memorial to Scots killed during the Napoleonic Wars. Intended to be a replica of the Parthenon in Athens, money ran out when the monument was less than half-completed, with only 12 columns, and tagged with the nickname "Edinburgh's disgrace."

Nelson's Monument (Calton Hill, Edinburgh, www.cac.org.uk; open Mon-Sat year-round, hours vary seasonally; admission £2.50). Erected in 1807 to celebrate the life of Lord Nelson, hero of Trafalgar, the monument was designed like an upturned telescope, inside which it's possible to climb the 143 steps for an even higher vantage point. In 1852, a large time ball was introduced, which is lowered as the One o'Clock Gun is fired from Edinburgh Castle each day.

The **City Observatory** and **Monument to Dugold Stewart** complete the Calton Hill complex.

Scott Monument (East Princes Street Gardens, Edinburgh, ☎ 131-529 4068, www.cac.org.uk; open year-round, hours vary seasonally; admission £2.50). The towering monument to Sir Walter Scott is an internationally recognized Edinburgh landmark and was funded by public subscription in the author's memory. You can climb the 200-foot statue to gain commanding views of the city, and view a display on Scott's life and statuettes of his characters.

The Georgian House (NTS; 7 Charlotte Square, Edinburgh EH2 4DR, ☎ 131-225 2160, fax 131-226 3318, thegeorgianhouse@nts.org.uk; open April-Oct, 10am-5pm; Mar & Nov-Dec, 11am-3pm; adult/concession/family £5/£3.75/£13.50). Part of a Robert Adam masterpiece of urban design, the Georgian House dates from 1796 when Edinburgh's wealthier residents began to escape the cramped and often squalid conditions of the city's Old Town for the fashionable and elegant New Town. Period china, shining silver, paintings and furniture recreate the domestic surroundings and social conditions of the times. There is a video and touch-screen program providing a virtual tour.

Royal Botanic Garden (20A Inverleith Row, Edinburgh EH3 5LR, ☎ 131-552 7171, fax 131-248 2901, info@rbge.org.uk, www.rbge.org.uk; open year-round from 10am, closing time varies seasonally; admission free, donations welcome). Scotland's premier garden covers 28 acres of beautiful, tranquil grounds, including the famous Rock Garden, a Chinese Hillside and 11 glasshouses. A Victorian palm house (the tallest in Britain) houses a massive 200-year-old cabbage palm. There is a shop, café, exhibitions and guided tours (April-Sept).

Edinburgh Dungeon (31 Market Street, Edinburgh EH1 1QB, ☎ 131-240 1000, fax 131-240 1002, www.thedungeons.com; open year-round, times vary seasonally; adult/concession/child £8.95/£7.95/£6.95). Discover Scotland's bloody past at the atmospheric dungeon, which includes the Rogues' Gallery, live shows and dramatic *Witchfynder* boat ride.

The Hub, Edinburgh's Festival Centre (Castlehill, Royal Mile, Edinburgh EH1 2NE, ☎ 131-473 2000, boxoffice@eif.co.uk, www.eif.co.uk/thehub; open 9:30am-5pm; admission free). The imposing former church (Highland Tolbooth Kirk) boasts Edinburgh's tallest spire (236 feet/72 m) and dates from 1842-45. Along with the Tron, St Giles' Cathedral and the Castle, the Hub forms part of Edinburgh's stunning skyline. The Hub's refurbished interior now houses the Edinburgh Festival ticket office and information bureau, as well as a pleasant café.

Holyrood Park is a respectably sized historic wilderness area whose dramatic crags and hills contribute greatly to Edinburgh's distinctive skyline. Believed to have been a royal park since the 12th century, Holyrood Park encloses a wealth of history and archaeology spanning thousands of years and has a surprisingly diverse landscape of parkland, moor and lofty crags.

You can drive or cycle around the park's perimeter along **Queen's Drive**, or hike via the long crest of **Salisbury Crags** to the summit of **Arthur's Seat** for a big-picture view of the city. Arthur's Seat is one of four hill forts dating back about 2,000 years, and sits on an extinct volcano. From Holyrood the climb to the 823-foot (250-m) summit takes close to an hour. The walk is not difficult, but the final climb to the summit is a little steep and in some places rocky and uneven. The summit provides clear views over the city and the Forth of Clyde but is so high you can't make out the relief of the city or the profiles of its many spires. The Salisbury Crags (half-way to Arthur's Seat) provide better views of the city and can be reached in 20-30 minutes from Holyrood.

Scottish Parliament Building (Royal Mile). The new Scottish Parliament Building at the bottom of the Royal Mile recently opened, badly behind schedule and greatly over budget. Hours are daily, year-round, 10am-4pm; til 6pm Mon-Fri from April to October. See www.scottish.parliament.uk for information.

■ Tours, Walks & Day-trips

In Edinburgh

Auld Reekie Tours (45 Niddry Street, Edinburgh, ☎/fax 131-557 4700, auldreekietours@blueyonder.co.uk, www.auldreekietours.co.uk; evening tours adult/concession/child £6/£5/£4, afternoon tours £5). Daily tours from the Tron Church (Royal Mile), including the underground city, haunted vault, pagan temple and medieval torture exhibition.

Edinburgh Literary Pub Tour (97b West Bow, Edinburgh EH1 2JP, ☎/fax 131-226 6665, info@scot-lit-tour.co.uk, www.edinburghliterarypubtour.co.uk; tours run year-round, and begin at 7:30pm at the Beehive Inn in the Grassmarket; daily in summer, check web site for winter schedule; adult/concession £8/£6). Highly acclaimed, witty frolic through the wynds, courtyards and pubs of Edinburgh to experience 300 years of vibrant literature and colorful characters. The tour involves entering several pubs so is not recommended for children.

Mercat Tours (Mercat House, Niddry Street South, Edinburgh EH1 1NS, ☎/fax 131-557 6464, info@mercattours.com, www.mercattours.com; adult/concession/child £6/£5/£4, higher for tours with refreshments; from the Mercat Cross, High Street). Discover Edinburgh's history, including its dark and sinister secrets, through a number of award-winning walking tours. There are daytime history tours and night-time ghost tours, including visits to the eerie and atmospheric underground vaults. Vivid stories bring the city's long history to life with factual accuracy and great theater. Genuinely scary.

The **Water of Leith Walkway** runs 12 miles from Balerno to Leith and passes near central Edinburgh. You can join and leave the path at lots of places up and down the river. A lovely section runs from the Gallery of Modern Art toward Stockbridge, passing wooded banks, Dean Village, weirs, bridges and historic mills. The walk takes under an hour.

City Sightseeing Edinburgh (departs Waverley Bridge, Edinburgh, ☎ 131-555 6363, info@edinburghtour.com, www.edinburghtour.com; adult/concession/child/family £8.50/£7.50/£2.50/£19.50). Regular daily departures of multilingual hop-on/hop-off city tours by open-top bus.

Mactours (departs Waverley Bridge, Edinburgh, ☎ 131-220 0770, enquiries@mactours.com, www.edinburghtour.com; adult/concession/child/family £8.50/£7.50/£2.50/£19.50). Guided tours of Edinburgh by open-top vintage bus.

In Leith

Royal Yacht *Britannia* (Ocean Terminal, Leith, Edinburgh, ☎ 131-555 5566, enquiries@tryb.co.uk, www.royalyachtbritannia.co.uk; open-year-round, hours vary seasonally; adult/senior/child/family £8/£6/£4/£20). The *Britannia* served the Royal family for over 40 years before being decommissioned in 1997. Since then she has been berthed in Leith and open to the public. After an introduction, a self-led audio tour takes you around five decks of the yacht to provide an insight into life aboard for the Royal family, officers and yachtsmen. Highlights include exhibits from the Royal Collection, the State Dining and Drawing Rooms and the pristine engine room.

Scotch Malt Whisky Society (The Vaults, 87 Giles Street, Leith, Edinburgh EH6 6BZ, ☎ 131-554 3451, fax 131-553 1003, enquiries@smws.com, www.smws.com). SMWS pioneered the commercial bottling of cask-quality single malts and is ideal for anyone wanting to share their interest in fine Scotch malts. The Society offers members special and rare bottlings, exclusive tastings and other whisky events in Edinburgh, London and elsewhere in the UK. The Edinburgh clubhouse has a spacious but very homely members' lounge and four apartments with kitchens.

Clan Tartan Centre at Leith Mills (70-74 Bangor Road, Leith, Edinburgh EH6 5JU, ☎ 131-553 5161, fax 131-553 4415, info@leithmills.co.uk). Find out if your name is linked to a Scottish clan or tartan by searching the database of 50,000 names and afterwards take home a printed clan certificate. You can of course also browse through a wide selection of knitwear, tartan, gifts and souvenirs.

Outside Edinburgh

Craigmillar Castle (HS; three miles southeast of Edinburgh off the A7, ☎ 131-661 4445; April-Sept, 9:30am6:30pm; Oct-Mar, 9:30am-4:30pm, closed certain days so call ahead; adult/concession/child £2.50/£1.90/£0.75). Built around a 15th-century L-plan tower house, the castle was much expanded in the late 15th and early 16th centuries. The castle is a handsome ruin and includes a number of private rooms linked to the hall of the old tower. Mary, Queen of Scots came here after the murder of her secretary, Rizzio.

Edinburgh Zoo (Murrayfield, Edinburgh EH12 6TS, ☎ 131-334 9171, fax 131-314 0382, marketing@rzss.org.uk, www.edinburghzoo.org.uk; open April-Sept, 9am-6pm; Oct & Mar, 9am-5pm; Nov-Feb, 9am-4:30pm; adult/concession/child/family £8/£6/£5/£24). This zoo in the west of Edinburgh displays over a thousand animals and boasts the world's largest penguin pool. There is a daily program of events, feeding and talks.

Royal Observatory Visitor Centre (Blackford Hill, Edinburgh EH9 3HJ, ☎ 131-668 8404, fax 131-668 8429, vis@roe.ac.uk, www.roe.ac.uk). The Visitor Centre is no longer open to casual visitors on a daily basis, although the observatory still operates a winter program (Oct-Mar) of evening talks and public observing. Call to check details.

■ Golf

Edinburgh's municipal courses provide all the traditions of Scottish golf and outstanding value for money.

Braid Hills Golf Club (18-hole inland, 5,390 yards; 22 Braid Hills Approach, Edinburgh EH10 6JY, ☎ 131-447 6666; green fees £13-£15). Challenging course with superb views over Edinburgh. Advance booking recommended.

Bruntsfield Links (18-hole parkland, 6,407 yards; 32 Barnton Avenue, Edinburgh EH4 6JH, ☎ 131-336 2006, fax 131-336 5538, secretary@bruntsfield.sol.co.uk; green fees £42-£48). A beautifully maintained, mature parkland championship course with magnificent views to the Fife coast.

Silverknowes Golf Club (18-hole parkland, 6,097 yards; Silverknowes Parkway, Silverknowes, Edinburgh EH4 5ET, ☎ 131-336 3843; green fees £11-£13.50). Gently sloping course with beautiful views over the Firth of Forth. Advance booking recommended.

■ Entertainment

Edinburgh has several theaters, concert halls and cinemas. Many pubs provide live entertainment, including traditional music, jazz and rock. The best guide to entertainment in Edinburgh (and Glasgow) is *The List* (www.list.co.uk), a magazine listing and reviewing films, music, theater, dance, art, clubs, sport and other events, published every other week and available from newsagents (£2.20).

Jamies Scottish Evening (Thistle Edinburgh Hotel, 107 Leith Street, Edinburgh EH1 3SW, ☎ 131-556 0111, fax 131-557 5333, edinburgh@thistle.co.uk, www.thistlehotels.com/edinburgh; April-Oct, 6:45-10:15pm; £42 for dinner, wine and show, £26 show only). Long-running show incorporating a Scottish banquet with unlimited wine, followed by music, dancing and songs.

St Giles' Cathedral (High Street, Royal Mile, Edinburgh, ☎ 131-225 9442). The cathedral holds a regular program of classical music, including popular lunchtime and evening concerts and recitals.

Usher Hall (Lothian Road, Edinburgh EH1 2EA, 131-228 1155, fax 131-228 8848, admin@usherhall.co.uk, www.usherhall.co.uk). Usher Hall is the Edinburgh home of the **Royal Scottish National Orchestra** and is the key venue for the **International Festival**. The attractive Beaux-Arts listed building is also popular for major rock, pop, folk and jazz events.

The Stand Comedy Club (5 York Place, Edinburgh EH1 3EB, ☎ 131-558 7272, fax 131-556 7091, admin@thestand.co.uk, www.thestand.co.uk). Scotland's only specially-built comedy club provides a constantly changing program of quality entertainment at low prices every night, with a free Sunday show 1pm-3pm. Booking essential.

■ Shopping

Princes Street is Edinburgh's principal shopping street and enjoys the magnificent vista of its gardens and the castle to one side. The shopping itself is less inspiring. Apart from **Jenners**, the world's oldest independent department store, most of Princes Street's shops are standard high-street outlets and fast food joints.

North of and parallel to Princes Street is **George Street**, a much better bet for quality shopping. Beneath the multifarious domes that crown many of the elegant buildings on this street are quality, individual stores and boutiques offering exclusive and specialist goods.

On and south of the **Royal Mile**, there are a number of attractive and varied shops, pubs and restaurants. **Victoria Street** boasts a fascinating array, including **Robert Cresser Brushmaker**, a unique specialist brush shop, which stands next to a cheese shop and sophisticated fabric and fashion boutiques. This sloping, curved terrace leads from **George IV Bridge** down to **Grassmarket**, which, with its attractive shops, bars and bistros huddled beneath the towering castle, is one of Edinburgh's most charming streets.

Clothing & Highland Dress

Canongate Jerseys & Crafts (164-166 Canongate, Royal Mile, Edinburgh EH8 8DD, ☎ 131-557 2967, www.canongatejerseysandcrafts.co.uk). A lovely little shop selling exclusively designed knitwear based on Celtic, Pictish and other traditional patterns, hand-woven shawls, Harris tweeds, jewelry, wall hangings, carved stones and other crafts, all sourced from Scottish designers.

The Cashmere Store (2 St Giles' Street, Edinburgh EH1 1PT & 67 George Street, Edinburgh EH2 2JG, ☎ 131-226 1577, fax 131-226 3324, info@scottish-cashmere.com, www.scottish-cashmere.com). A wide range of cashmere knitwear, coats, jackets, scarves, gloves and accessories, in classic and contemporary designs.

Designs on Cashmere (28 High Street, Royal Mile, Edinburgh EH1 1TB, ☎/fax 131-556 6394, cashmere.info@scotwebshops.com, www.designsoncashmere.com). Specialist in unusual and classic cashmere styles; also offers a mail-order service.

Geoffrey (Tailor) Kiltmakers (57-59 High Street, Royal Mile, Edinburgh EH1 1SR, ☎ 131-557 0256, fax 131-556 0615, enquiries@geoffreykilts.co.uk, www.geoffreykilts.co.uk). A large selection of Highland dress, tartan, ladies' kilts, kilted skirts and Scottish gifts.

Hawick Cashmere (71-81 Grassmarket, Edinburgh, ☎ 131-225 8634). Cashmere and other fine fabrics for men and women, direct from its mill in the Scottish Borders.

Hector Russell (95 Princes Street, Edinburgh EH2 2ER, ☎ 131-225 3315, fax 131-226 3923 & 137-141 High Street, Royal Mile, Edinburgh EH1 1SG, ☎ 131 558 1254, www.hector-russell.com). Maker of bespoke (made-to-measure) kilts, with shops across Scotland.

Ragamuffin (Canongate, Royal Mile, Edinburgh EH8 8AA, ☎ 131-557 6007, ragamuffin@madasafish.com, www.ragamuffinonline.co.uk). A long-established producer of colorful designer knitwear and clothing, with a sister outlet in Skye.

Food & Drink

Au Gourmand (1 Brandon Terrace, Edinburgh., ☎ 131-624 4666). A beautifully refurbished deli specializing in well-sourced provincial French food such as wonderful cheeses, charcuterie and freshly baked bread. People queue around the block to shop here. At the back is a small café that serves delicious soup.

Macsween of Edinburgh (Dryden Road, Bilston Glen, Loanhead, Edinburgh EH20 9LZ, ☎ 131-440 2555, fax 131-440 2674, haggis@macsween.co.uk, www.macsween.co.uk). The renowned haggis specialist, which sells through Edinburgh shops in addition to directly from its factory.

Royal Mile Whiskies (379 High Street, Royal Mile, Edinburgh EH1 1PW, ☎ 131-225 3383, fax 131-226 2772, info@royalmilewhiskies.com, www.royalmilewhiskies.com). A selection of hundreds of whiskies dating back to 1897, with enthusiasts on hand to help narrow down the choice.

Valvona & Crolla (19 Elm Row, Edinburgh EH7 4AA, ☎ 131-556 6066, fax 131-556 1668, sales@valvonacrolla.co.uk, www.valvonacrolla.co.uk). Legendary family-run deli with an almost cult following. Customers come from far and wide to buy pasta, cheese, wine, olive oil, vinegar and bread, and attend tastings and demonstrations. There is also a café-bar to the rear of the shop.

Scottish Goods & Specialty Gifts

The Edinburgh Bear Company (46 High Street, Royal Mile, Edinburgh, ☎ 131-557 9564). Charming shop full of collectors' teddy bears and bear lovers' gifts, many handmade in Scotland.

Kilberry Bagpipes (38 Lochrin Buildings, Gilmore Place, Edinburgh EH3 9ND, ☎ 131-221 9925, fax 131-228 1060, info@kilberry.com, www.kilberry-.com). Makers of Highland and Scottish smallpipes and stockists of learning kits and piping accessories.

Mr Wood's Fossils (5 Cowgatehead, Grassmarket, Edinburgh EH1 1JY, ☎ 131-220 1344, mwfossils@blueyonder.co.uk, www.mrwoodsfossils.co.uk). Unique shop with an international reputation for quality fossils and minerals from Scotland and abroad.

Rabbie's Gift Shop (207 High Street, Royal Mile, Edinburgh EH1 1PE, ☎ 131-226 3133, gifts@scottishmemories.com, www.scottishmemories.com). Handcrafted Celtic gifts, books and CDs.

Ye Olde Christmas Shoppe (145 Canongate, Royal Mile, Edinburgh EH8 8BN, ☎ 131-557 9220, fax 131-664 8092, enquiries@scottishchristmas.com, www.scottishchristmas.com). Scotland's original dedicated Christmas shop, with an exclusive range of locally crafted festive gifts and souvenirs. Tax-free and worldwide shipping services are available.

Jewelers

Argentium (105 Rose Street, Edinburgh, ☎ 131-225 8057, argentiumrosest@yahoo.com). Designer silver and gold jewelry, specializing in Celtic silver and gold wedding bands.

Scottish Gems (24 High Street, Royal Mile, Edinburgh, ☎ 131-557 5731, info@scottish-gems.co.uk). Wide selection of Scottish jewelry with a mailorder service available.

The Tappit Hen (89 High Street, Royal Mile, Edinburgh, ☎ 131-557 1852). Specialists in Celtic wedding rings, Scottish jewelry, Mackintosh inspirations, pewter tankards and flasks.

■ Where To Stay

Old Town

Apex City (61 Grassmarket, Edinburgh EH1 2JF, ☎ 131-243 3456, fax 131-225 6346, city@apexhotels.co.uk, www.apexhotels.co.uk; B&B ££££). Stylish, contemporary hotel set in the attractive Grassmarket district beneath Castle Rock, close to many restaurants and bars. Rooms have excellent castle views and good-value room service. Nearby is their sister hotel, Apex International (31-35 Grassmarket, Edinburgh EH1 2HS, ☎ 131-300 3456, fax 131-220 5345, international@apexhotels.co.uk; B&B ££££).

Jurys Inn (43 Jeffrey Street, Edinburgh EH1 1DG, ☎ 131-200 3300, fax 131-200

HOTEL PRICE CHART	
Per person, per night, based on double occupancy in high season. B&B rate includes breakfast; DB&B includes dinner and breakfast.	
£	Under £20
££	£21-£35
£££	£36-£50
££££	£51-£80
£££££	Over £80

0400, jurysinnedinburgh@jurysdoyle.com, www.jurysdoyle.com, www.book-ajurysinn.com; B&B £££). Good, mid-range hotel just a short distance from Princes Street and the Royal Mile, providing efficient, unfussy service with a welcoming Irish smile. There are great views of Calton Hill and the North Bridge from the higher rooms and the restaurant is reasonably priced.

The Scotsman (20 North Bridge, Edinburgh EH1 1YT, ☎ 131-556 5565, fax 131-652 3652, reservations@thescotsmanhotelgroup.co.uk, www.thescotsman-hotel.co.uk; B&B £££££). Luxurious five-star hotel occupying the baronial former offices of Scotland's leading newspaper of the same name. Preserving many original features, plush contemporary styling is complemented by lovely touches such as bathrooms set within turrets, rooms furnished in individual tweeds, private serving hatches and a battery of bathroom lotions and gels.

The Witchery by the Castle (352 Castlehill, Royal Mile, Edinburgh EH1 2NF, ☎ 131-225 5613, fax 131-220 4392, mail@thewitchery.com, www.the-witchery.com; B&B £££££). Lavishly indulgent, antique-filled suites hidden in a 16th-century building close to the castle offer the most romantic accommodation in Edinburgh.

Holyrood ApartHotel (1 Nether Bakehouse, Holyrood, Edinburgh EH8 8PE, ☎ 131-524 3200, fax 131-524 3210, enquiries@holyroodaparthotel.com, www.holyroodaparthotel.com; B&B £££££). An attractive alternative to hotel accommodation in the form of modern, spacious and well-equipped apartments. Its charming address of Nether Bakehouse is not easy to find, tucked away in a quiet court off the lower end of the Royal Mile, but is very peaceful and within easy walking distance of the Old Town center. The breakfast hampers are excellent.

New Town & West End

 Afton Town House (6 Grosvenor Crescent, Edinburgh EH12 5EP, ☎ 131-225 7033, fax 131-225 7044, e-mail@aftontownhouse.co.uk, www.aftontownhouse.co.uk; B&B £££). An elegant townhouse hotel set on a quiet crescent in the shadow of St Mary's Cathedral. The cathedral's musical tradition seems to have rubbed off on the hotel, which numbers several musicians among its many regular guests. There are friendly staff, bright, spacious rooms and excellent breakfasts. Proprietor Richard MacDonald has kindly offered a 10% discount to anyone showing a copy of this book on arrival.

The Bonham (35 Drumsheugh Gardens, Edinburgh EH3 7RN, ☎ 131-226 6050, fax 131-226 6080; reservations ☎ 131-623 6060, reserve@thebonham-.com, www.thebonham.com; B&B ££££-£££££). An excellent hotel housed within three elegant Victorian townhouses. The individually styled rooms use contemporary furniture, modern art, bold colors and bright fabrics to add a modern twist to their luxurious, slightly minimalist traditional feel. The service is efficient and personal without being in any way fussy. The stunning restaurant is highly fashionable and deserves its fine reputation.

Caledonian Hilton (Princes Street, Edinburgh EH1 2AB, ☎ 131-222 8888, fax 131-222 8889, ednchhirm@hilton.com, www.hilton.com; B&B ££££). The red-brick "Caley," as the hotel is affectionately known, celebrated its centenary in 2003. Built by the Caledonian Railway Company adjacent to its Princes Street station, the hotel remains a major city landmark and is an institution held in warm regard by residents and visitors alike. Some of the finest castle views can be enjoyed from Caley rooms. A slightly fading, "lived in" grandeur adds a charm often missing from newer hotels.

FESTIVAL ACCOMMODATION

The availability of Edinburgh accommodation varies significantly through the year with the city's packed schedule of cultural festivals and sports and music events. The population of 460,000 swells to well over a million in August when festivals are in full swing, and the city also bursts at the seams at Hogmanay, during rugby international weekends and when music stars are playing in the city. Book accommodation at least six months in advance if you're looking to visit during the Festival or Hogmanay and check with the Tourist Board regarding other busy dates if you prefer to avoid crowds.

Dunstane House Hotel (4 West Coates, Haymarket, Edinburgh EH12 5JQ, ☎ 131-337 6169, fax 131-337 6060, info@dunstane-hotel-edinburgh.co.uk, www.dunstane-hotel-edinburgh.co.uk; B&B ££££). This grand Victorian house in the West End was designed by Edinburgh architect William Playfair, who also designed the magnificent nearby Donaldson's College. It's comfortably furnished in warm, inviting shades, including the generous use of wood paneling and ornate cornicing; fourposter beds are available. The owners celebrate their Orkney roots by filling the menu with Orkney seafood, beef and lamb together with the islands' malt whiskies and beers. Orkney and other theme evenings are held on a regular basis.

The Howard (34 Great King Street, Edinburgh EH3 6QH, ☎ 131-557 3500, fax 131-557 6515; reservations, ☎ 131-623 9303, reserve@thehoward.com, www.thehoward.com; B&B £££££-£££££+). Three elegant Georgian townhouses provide gracious accommodation and discreet pampering, with a butler to attend to your every wish (such as unpacking, valeting, collecting shopping, serving drinks and dinner, and arranging social events). Bedrooms burst with period furniture and opulent furnishings, and the luxurious baths and huge Jacuzzi (in one of the suites) tempt inactivity.

Inverleith Hotel (5 Inverleith Terrace, Edinburgh EH3 5NS, ☎ 131-556 2745, fax 131-557 0433, info@inverleithhotel.co.uk, www.inverleithhotel-.co.uk; B&B £££). A friendly, family-run hotel set in a Victorian townhouse opposite the Royal Botanic Garden. Author Robert Louis Stevenson was once a neighbor. There are cozy rooms, one with a four-poster bed, and a bright and airy breakfast room. Free on-street parking is an added bonus.

Davenport House (58 Great King Street, Edinburgh EH3 6QY, ☎ 131-558 8495, fax 131-558 8496, enquiries@davenport-house.com, www.davenport-house.com; B&B £££). Elegant Georgian townhouse offering stylish accommodation in beautifully decorated bedrooms (especially the Deluxe Room available at higher cost).

Castle View Guest House (30 Castle Street, Edinburgh EH2 3HT, ☎ 131-226 5784, fax 131-226 1603, castleview@blueyonder.co.uk, www.castleviewgh.co.uk; B&B £££). Spacious Georgian apartment with castle views from the guests' lounge, dining room and some of the pleasant bedrooms. Kenneth Grahame (1859-1932), author of *The Wind in the Willows*, was born here.

Ashlyn Guest House (42 Inverleith Row, Edinburgh EH3 5PY, ☎/fax 131-552 2954, reservations@ashlyn-edinburgh.com; B&B £££). Elegant Georgian townhouse close to the Botanic Garden with attractive lounge, period dining room and comfortable bedrooms.

■ Where To Eat

Old Town

 The Doric Tavern (15-16 Market Street, Edinburgh EH1 1DE, ☎ 131-225 1084, fax 131-220 0894, www.thedoric.co.uk; ££). Cozy traditional tavern with a wide-ranging menu and wine list.

Gordons Trattoria (231 High Street, Royal Mile, Edinburgh, ☎ 131-225 7992). Popular Old Town Italian eatery serving pizzas, pastas and steaks.

Grain Store Restaurant (30 Victoria Street, Edinburgh EH1 2JN, ☎ 131-225 7635, fax 131-622 7313, contact@grainstore-restaurant.co.uk, www.grainstore-restaurant.co.uk; lunch ££, dinner £££). Delicious, freshly prepared food served in an intimate setting of alcoves and adjoining rooms with bare stone walls, wood floors and superb arched windows.

Jacksons (209 High Street, Royal Mile, Edinburgh EH1 1PE, ☎ 131-225 1793, fax 131-220 0620, www.jacksons-restaurant.co.uk; lunch ££, dinner £££). Superb Scottish cooking served in an attractive restaurant oozing Celtic charm. There is a reasonably priced business lunch.

Pancho Villa's (240 Canongate, Royal Mile, Edinburgh, ☎ 131-557 4416; lunch £, dinner ££). Tasty, authentic Mexican food served by Latin American staff. Booking recommended in the evening.

DINING PRICE CHART	
Indicates the price, per person, of a full meal, excluding drinks. Generally three courses.	
£	Under £10
££	£11-£20
£££	£21-£30
££££	£31-£40

Petit Paris (38-40 Grassmarket, Edinburgh EH1 2JU, ☎ 131-226 2442, www.petitparis-restaurant.co.uk; lunch £, dinner ££). Cozy, atmospheric bistro-café that serves authentic Gallic cooking. A plat du jour with coffee is an excellent value at just £5 (noon-3pm and 5pm-7pm). There aren't many tables so book or arrive early.

Reform Restaurant (267 Canongate, Royal Mile, Edinburgh EH8 8BQ, ☎ 131-558 9992, www.reformrestaurant.com; £££). Stylish, minimalist restaurant serving contemporary fusion menus with a good wine list.

La Garrigue (31 Jeffrey Street, Edinburgh, ☎ 131-557 3032; ££). Traditional French cooking from the Languedoc region.

Le Sept (7 Old Fishmarket Close, Edinburgh, ☎ 131-225 5428; ££). Established French bistro off the Royal Mile with an informal atmosphere, reasonably priced menu and terrace for sunny days.

Stac Polly (8-10 Grindlay Street, Edinburgh EH3 9AS, ☎ 131-229 5405, www.stacpolly.co.uk; lunch ££, dinner £££). Named after a well-known Highland mountain, the Scottish menu reflects both traditional and modern styles and is particularly famous for its steaks.

Suruchi (14a Nicolson Street, Edinburgh EH8 9DH, ☎ 131-556 6583, fax 131-622 7227; ££). Award-winning Indian cooking with a distinctly Scottish flavor, including innovative dishes such as haggis fritters and curried salmon. There are regular food festivals and live jazz Wednesday-Friday. Suruchi is the only restaurant with a menu written in Scots, describing the house specialty Nirvana dish as "A beezer o a curry wi flavors ye cannae beat." Enough said. A second Suruchi restaurant recently opened in Leith (121 Constitution Street, Leith, Edinburgh EH6 7AE, ☎ 131-554 3268, fax 131-467 7239).

Tower Restaurant (Chambers Street, Edinburgh EH1 1JF, ☎ 131-225 3003, fax 131-220 4392, mail@tower-restaurant.com, www.tower-restaurant.com; lunch/early supper – noon to 6pm – £, dinner £££). Enjoy stunning views over the Edinburgh skyline while dining on superb modern Scottish cooking at the top of the Museum of Scotland.

Viva Mexico (41 Cockburn Street, Edinburgh EH1 1BS, ☎ 131-226 5145, fax 131-449 4735, www.viva-mexico.co.uk; ££). A cozy Mexican-owned and -run restaurant, serving the standard Mexicana of margaritas, Mex beers, enchiladas and tacos.

The Witchery by the Castle (352 Castlehill, Royal Mile, Edinburgh EH1 2NF, ☎ 131-225 5613, fax 131-220 4392, mail@thewitchery.com, www.the-witchery.com; light lunch/theater supper £, served noon to 4pm, 5:30-6:30pm & 10:30-11:30pm; dinner ££££). The award-winning modern Scottish menu is complemented by sensational, candlelit décor of tapestries, 17th-century wood paneling, gilded screens and opulent upholstery. The light lunches and theater suppers are excellent value.

DID YOU KNOW? *Author JK Rowling wrote her first novel,* Harry Potter and the Philosopher's Stone, *in Nicolson's, an Edinburgh café.*

New Town & West End

Bar Napoli (75 Hanover Street, Edinburgh, ☎ 131-225 2600; £-££). Genuine Italian restaurant with quick, purposeful service and a range of authentic Italian dishes and seafood.

Bouzy Rouge (1 Alva Street, Edinburgh EH2 4PH, ☎ 131-225 9594, fax 131-225 9593, www.bouzy-rouge.com; ££). Stylish West End basement restaurant offering high-quality modern Scottish cooking to suit both the gourmet and casual diner.

Café Marlayne (76 Thistle Street, Edinburgh, ☎ 131-226 2230; ££). A tiny and usually packed French bistro serving delicious homemade food and an impressive wine list. Prices are reasonable and the service is friendly and efficient.

Café St Honoré (34 North West Thistle Street Lane, Edinburgh EH2 1EA just off Frederick Street, ☎ 131-226 2211, www.cafesthonore.com; ££-£££). A charming Gallic bistro-restaurant serving top-notch Scottish food cooked with a French influence. Game and fish are the focus of the daily changing menu.

The Dome (14 George Street, Edinburgh EH2 2PF, ☎ 131-624 8624, fax 131-624 8649, sales@thedomeedinburgh.com, www.thedomeedinburgh.com; lunch ££, dinner £££). A bank-turned-restaurant-bar like no other, housed in a magnificently decorated 19th-century building (not to be confused with the brasserie chain of the same name!). In addition to the Grill Room restaurant-bar housed beneath the dome, there is a separate cocktail bar, al fresco dining in the garden café and a nightclub in a former vault. The food blends the freshest local ingredients with the flavors of Europe and the Far East.

Harvey Nichols Forth Floor (30-34 St Andrew Square, Edinburgh EH2 2AD, evening access via Multrees Walk, ☎ 131-524 8350, fax 131-524 8351, forthfloor.reservations@harveynichols.com, www.harveynichols.com; lunch ££, dinner £££). A complete food experience in a stylish, new building, crowned by excellent views of the castle and Firth of Forth. The restaurant offers lunches (daily) and dinners (Tues-Sat). An informal brasserie opens during store hours and for evening fixed-price "Tempted!" menus (Tues-Sat). The scallop dishes and salmon fishcakes are excellent.

Howies Stockbridge (4-6 Glanville Place, Stockbridge, Edinburgh, ☎ 131-225 5553, www.howies.uk.com; lunch £, dinner ££). Lively, trendy bar-restaurant famous for its eggs Benedict. This is an excellent place for a leisurely brunch with the Sunday paper.

Juniper (117/121 Hanover Street, Edinburgh, ☎ 131-225 1552; ££). Licensed restaurant-coffee shop renowned for its hot soups and stews to go, although there are also two dining rooms to the rear.

La Lanterna (83 Hanover Street, Edinburgh, ☎ 131-226 3090; closed Sun; ££-£££). Cozy Italian basement restaurant serving freshly prepared food cooked by the proprietor.

No 27 (National Trust for Scotland, 27 Charlotte Square, Edinburgh EH2 4ET, ☎ 131-243 9339; closed Sun-Mon; lunch £, dinner ££). The coffee shop serves light lunches and cakes all day, and the fine Georgian rooms provide formal evening dining.

La Pompadour (Princes Street, Edinburgh EH1 2AB, ☎ 131-459 9988/222 8888, fax 131-225 6632; lunch Thurs-Fri, dinner Tues-Sat; lunch ££, dinner

£££). Elegant restaurant in the famous Caledonian Hilton, combining superb modern cooking with great views over the castle. ´

Loon Fung (2 Warriston Place, Edinburgh EH3 5LE, ☎ 131-556 1781; £-££). Authentic Chinese cooking in bright and pleasant surroundings close to the Botanic Garden. The menu includes delicious hot and sour soup and tender beef with ginger sauce. Seafood is also a specialty.

Mussel Inn (61-65 Rose Street, Edinburgh EH2 2NH, ☎ 131-225 5979, info@mussel-inn.com, www.mussel-inn.com; ££). The fact this restaurant is owned by west coast shellfish farmers says it all. The steaming pots of mussels, platters of scallops and delicious sauces are excellent.

A Room in the Town (18 Howe Street, Edinburgh EH3 6TG, ☎/fax 131-225 8204; lunch £, dinner £££). A busy, informal bistro serving reasonably priced modern Scottish cooking.

Stac Polly (29-33 Dublin Street, Edinburgh EH3 6NL, ☎ 131-556 2231, fax 131-557 9779, www.stacpolly.co.uk; lunch ££, dinner £££). Sister establishment of the Grindlay Street (Old Town) restaurant of the same name.

Pubs & Bars

Edinburgh overflows with historic pubs and bars, ranging from contemporary café-bars to historic real-ale taverns, many of which serve good food and have live entertainment. Hours vary; many establishments are open from the morning until 11pm or 1am, with extended hours during the Edinburgh Festival and at Christmas/New Year.

Music Bars

Fingers Piano Bar (61a Fredrick Street, Edinburgh, ☎ 131-225 3026). Unique piano bar that features guest performances.

Finnegans Wake (9b Victoria Street, Edinburgh, ☎ 131-226 3816). Irish bar playing folk and Irish music.

Guildford Arms (1-5 West Register Street, Edinburgh, ☎ 131-556 4312). Attractive Edwardian décor with a famous ceiling and 12 real ales.

Traditional Bars

The Conan Doyle (71-73 York Place, Edinburgh, ☎ 131-524 0031). Delightful heart-of-the-city Victorian tavern near the birthplace of the celebrated author.

Barony Bar (81-85 Broughton Street, ☎ 131-557 0546). A very popular, down-to-earth bar serving good food and good beer.

Deacon Brodie's Tavern (435 Lawnmarket, Royal Mile, Edinburgh, ☎ 131-225 6531). This 1806 tavern commemorates Deacon Brodie – a real-life 18th-century Jekyll-and-Hyde figure – who was respectable by day, dark and dangerous by night!

Greyfriars Bobby (34 Candlemaker Row, Edinburgh, ☎ 131-225 8300). Named after the faithful hound, whose statue sits outside the pub, immortalized in books and films.

Jenny Ha's (65 Canongate, Royal Mile, Edinburgh, ☎ 131-556 2101). Traditional tavern on the lower Royal Mile.

Scott's (202 Rose Street, Edinburgh, ☎ 131-225 7401). Charming Victorian pub.

Tolbooth Tavern (167 Canongate, Edinburgh, ☎ 131-556 5348). Part of the original 1591 tolbooth, the tavern retains lots of olde worlde charm and gives you a chance to drink with locals.

Ye Olde Golf Tavern (30-31 Wright's Houses, Edinburgh, ☎ 131-229 3235). The city's oldest tavern and supposedly Bonnie Prince Charlie's "local," or favorite pub.

Specialty

The Canny Man's (237 Morningside Road, ☎ 131-447 1484). A family-run pub and gentlemen's club whose owners don't let you in if they don't like the look of you! The Bloody Marys here are legendary and the food includes oysters, prawns, beautiful beef and massive smorgasbords, accompanied by an excellent wine list. Great value and very popular – booking recommended.

Frankenstein Pub (26 George IV Bridge, Edinburgh, ☎ 131-622 1818, fax 131-622 1111, info@frankenstein-pub.co.uk, www.frankenstein-pub.co.uk). Joking claims that it was established in 1818 (the year that Mary Shelley's *Frankenstein* was published) belie the fact this stylish bar is very much 21st century. There are three floors of fiendishly styled décor in a converted vaulted church, and hilariously themed cocktails ("The Generator," "Hell Raiser," "Blood Clot," etc). The all-day food includes excellent fajitas.

Milne's Bar (35 Hanover Street, Edinburgh, ☎ 131-225 6738). The Scottish literati used to meet at this tavern.

Rose Street Brewery (55-59 Rose Street, Edinburgh, ☎ 131-220 1227). "Auld Reekie" ales and brewery tours.

The Lothians

East Lothian

East of Edinburgh, beyond the former mining towns of Musselburgh and Dalkeith, lies East Lothian, a region of peaceful coastal scenery, charming villages and the birthplace of Scotland's national flag. East Lothian also boasts a high concentration of excellent **links golf courses**, including Muirfield and Musselburgh.

Above: Palace of Holyroodhouse, Edinburgh

Below: Linlithgow Palace

Darkened Close off Edinburgh's Royal Mile

Canongate Tolbooth, Edinburgh

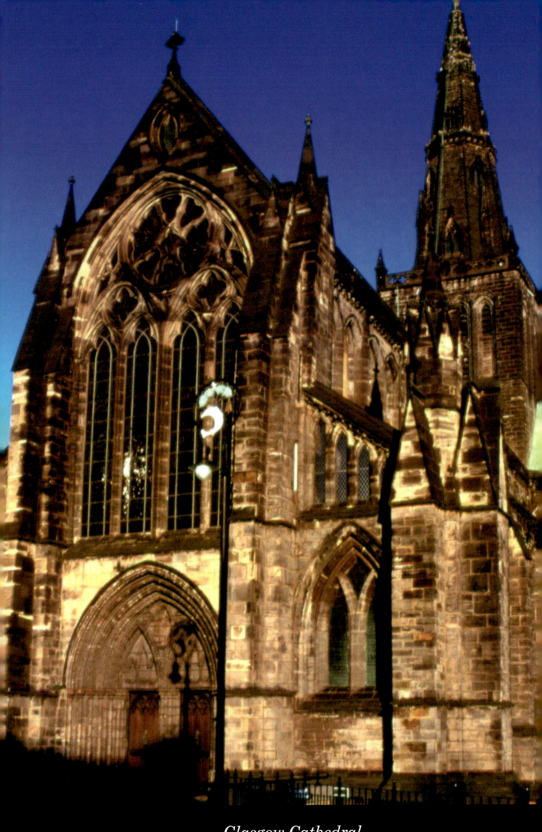

Glasgow Cathedral

■ Attractions & Sights

Dirleton Castle (HS; Dirleton, three miles west of North Berwick on the A198, ☎ 1620-850 330; open April-Sept, 9:30am-6:30pm; Oct-Mar, 9:30am-4:30pm; adult/concession/child £3/£2.30/£1). Romantic castle with an impressive drawbridge. The oldest part dates from the 13th century; it was partly rebuilt in the 14th century and modified in the 16th century. The castle's gardens also date from the 16th century and include the world's longest herbaceous border, an early-20th-century "Arts and Crafts" garden and restored Victorian garden.

Tantallon Castle (HS; three miles east of North Berwick off the A198, ☎ 1620-892 727; April-Sept, open 9:30am-6:30pm; Oct-Mar, hours and days vary, check schedule prior to visiting; adult/concession/child £3/£2.30/£1). A formidable cliff-top fortification that has had a stormy history due to its strategic position. The Red Douglasses built the castle on a promontory with views of Bass Rock, with earthwork defenses and a massive 14th-century curtain wall. The castle was strengthened to resist artillery during the 16th century, with a forework added to protect the central tower.

Scottish Seabird Centre (The Harbour, North Berwick EH39 4SS, ☎ 1620-890 202, fax 1620-890 222, info@seabird.org, www.seabird.org; open April-Oct, 10am-6pm; winter schedule varies; adult/concession/child/family £4.95/£3.50/£3.50/£13.50). Remote-controlled cameras zoom in to bring you close-up views of Scottish wildlife, including the east coast's largest grey seal colony on the **Isle of May**; 100,000 nesting gannets on **Bass Rock**; thousands of puffins and other seabirds; and regular sightings of bottlenose dolphins.

Museum of Flight (East Fortune Airfield, East Lothian EH39 5LF, ☎ 1620-880 308, fax 1620-880 355, www.nms.ac.uk/flight; open April-Oct, 10am-5pm; limited hours in winter, call for opening times; adult/concession/child £3/£1.50/free). The museum displays over 50 civilian, military and recreational aircraft, including the Concorde, and holds a regular program of events and flying displays.

Lennoxlove House (Haddington, East Lothian, ☎ 1620-823 720, enquiries@lennoxlove.com, www.lennoxlove.org; open Easter-Oct, Wed, Thurs & Sun; guided tours half-hourly, 2pm-4:30pm; adult/child £4.25/£2.25). Set among East Lothian woodlands with a fine outlook to the Lammermuir Hills, the house is architecturally interesting, boasts a long association with the Royal dynasty and contains fine contents, especially paintings and Mary, Queen of Scots memorabilia. The earliest parts of the house date from well before 1400, although it has been extensively refurbished and redecorated. The 14th Duke of Hamilton acquired the house in 1946 and, though the present Duke and Duchess don't live here, the house retains a comfortable and homely atmosphere.

National Flag Heritage Centre (Main Street, Athelstaneford, ☎ 1368-863 239; open April-Oct, 10am-6pm; also open St Andrew's Day/30 Nov; admis-

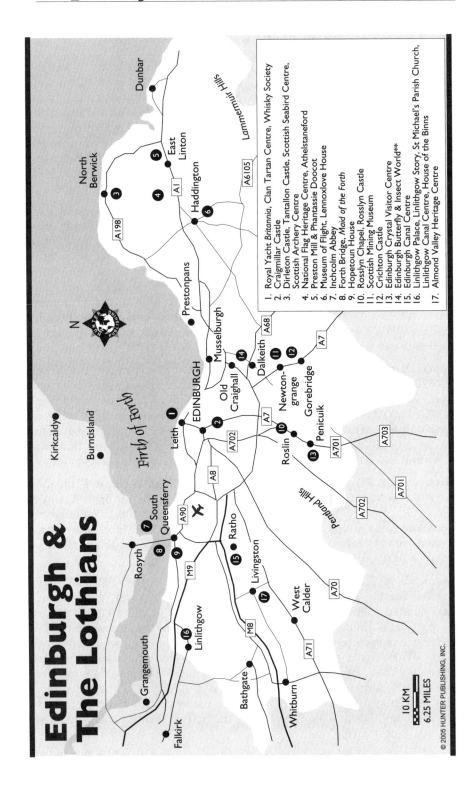

Edinburgh & The Lothians

1. Royal Yacht *Britannia*, Clan Tartan Centre, Whisky Society
2. Craigmillar Castle
3. Dirleton Castle, Tantallon Castle, Scottish Seabird Centre, Scottish Archery Centre
4. National Flag Heritage Centre, Athelstaneford
5. Preston Mill & Phantassie Doocot
6. Museum of Flight, Lennoxlove House
7. Inchcolm Abbey
8. Forth Bridge, *Maid of the Forth*
9. Hopetoun House
10. Rosslyn Chapel, Rosslyn Castle
11. Scottish Mining Museum
12. Crichton Castle
13. Edinburgh Crystal Visitor Centre
14. Edinburgh Butterfly & Insect World**
15. Edinburgh Canal Centre
16. Linlithgow Palace, Linlithgow Story, St Michael's Parish Church, Linlithgow Canal Centre, House of the Binns
17. Almond Valley Heritage Centre

10 KM

6.25 MILES

© 2005 HUNTER PUBLISHING, INC.

sion free). The village of Athelstaneford claims to have given birth to the Scottish national flag – the Saltire – before a 9th-century battle in which local warriors under Angus mac Fergus defeated a larger army of Angles and Saxons. According to legend, a coalition of Picts and Scots united beneath a vision of the Saltire in the sky before prevailing in the battle. The Heritage Centre has a Saltire Memorial and audiovisual dramatization of the battle.

Preston Mill & Phantassie Doocot (NTS; East Linton, East Lothian EH40 3DS, ☎ 1620-860 426; open April-Sept, Thurs-Mon, noon-5pm; Sun, 1pm-5pm; adult/concession/family £3.50/£2.60/£9.50). Picturesque 18th-century mill with working mechanisms (water wheel and milling machinery are relatively modern, though), conical-roofed kiln and attractive red-pantiled buildings, with a nearby millpond complete with resident ducks and geese. There are displays on milling and the history and people of Preston Mill. The *Doocot* (dovecote), or pigeon house, once held 500 birds.

> *i* **INFORMATION SOURCES:** There are tourism offices at Dunbar (143 High Street, Dunbar EH42 1ES, ☎ 1368-863 353), Musselburgh (Old Craighall Junction off the A1, ☎ 131-653 6172) and North Berwick (1 Quality Street, North Berwick EH39 4HJ, ☎ 1620-892 197), all of which are open year-round.

■ Adventures

Scottish Archery Centre (Fenton Barns, North Berwick, East Lothian EH39 5BW, ☎/fax 1620-850 401, eric@scottisharcherycentre.co.uk, www.scottisharcherycentre.co.uk; closed Thursday). Try modern-day archery, crossbow and air-rifle shooting under supervision. Coaching and practice facilities are also available.

■ Golf

 East Lothian is one of Scotland's finest golf areas. It boasts more links courses in close proximity than anywhere else in the world, including testing championship courses such as Muirfield (venue for the 2002 Open), Musselburgh Links (venue for six Opens), Gullane No 1 (qualifying course for the British Open), and others more suited to average players.

Gullane No 1 Course (18-hole links, 6,466 yards; West Links Road, Gullane, East Lothian EH31 2BB, ☎ 1620-842 255, fax 1620-842 327, bookings@gullanegolfclub.com, www.gullanegolfclub.com; green fees £75-£90). Superb links course used for Open qualification, with spectacular views over the Firth of Forth.

Muirfield Golf Course (18-hole links, 6,601 yards; Muirfield, Gullane, East Lothian EH31 2EG, ☎ 1620-842 123, fax 1620-842 977; visitors Tues & Thurs only; green fees £110). This was the venue for the 2002 Open Championship.

Musselburgh Golf Course (18-hole parkland, 6,725 yards; Monktonhall, Musselburgh, East Lothian EH21 6SA, ☎ 131-665 2005, secretary@themusselburghgolfclub.com, www.themusselburghgolfclub.com; green fees £25-£40). A demanding parkland course, lavishly bunkered with tree-lined fairways and large greens.

Musselburgh Links Old Course (9-hole links, 5,748 yards); Balcarras Road, Musselburgh, East Lothian EH21 7SB, ☎/fax 131-665 5438, info@musselburgholdlinks.co.uk, www.musselburgholdlinks.co.uk; see web site for fees). The world's oldest golf course, and venue for six Open Championships.

Royal Musselburgh Golf Course (18-hole inland, 6,237 yards; Prestongrange House, Prestonpans, East Lothian EH32 9RP, ☎/fax 1875-810 276, enquiries@royalmusselburgh.co.uk, www.royalmusselburgh.co.uk; green fees £22-£35). Engaging parkland course with wonderful views over Edinburgh and the Firth of Forth.

Winterfield Golf Course (18-hole links, 5,155 yards; North Road, Dunbar, East Lothian EH42 1AU, ☎/fax 1368-863 562, www.winterfieldgolfclub.net; green fees £15-£17). Superb links course with stunning sea views of the Firth of Forth, Bass Rock and the Isle of May, and the Lammermuir Hills as a backdrop.

Midlothian

 INFORMATION SOURCES: There are tourism offices at Newtongrange (Scottish Mining Museum, Newtongrange EH22 4QN, ☎ 131-663 4262; open April-Sept) and Penicuik (Edinburgh Crystal Visitor Centre, Penicuik EH26 8HB, ☎ 1968-673 846; open April-Sept).

■ Attractions & Sights

Only a few miles south of Edinburgh lies Midlothian, a long-established county with peaceful, scenic countryside and a wide range of outdoor activities.

 **Inchcolm Abbey** (HS; Inchcolm Island, in the Firth of Forth, ☎ 1383-823 332, reached by ferry from South Queensferry or North Queensferry; open April-Sept, 9:30am-6:30pm; adult/concession/child £3/£2.30/£1). Described as the "Iona of the East," Inchcolm Abbey is the best-preserved group of monastic buildings in Scotland. Founded around 1123, the abbey includes an impressive 13th-century octagonal chapter house. The island is home to seals and puffins, and dolphins swim in the waters around it.

 Rosslyn Chapel (Roslin, Midlothian EH25 9PU, ☎ 131-440 2159, fax 131-440 1979, rosslynch@aol.com, www.rosslyn-chapel.com; open Mon-Sat, 10am-5pm & Sun, noon-4:45pm, earlier closing in winter; adult/concession £4/£3.50). Magical Rosslyn Chapel was built in 1446 by William St Clair, the third and last Prince of Orkney. It is Scotland's most striking Gothic church and famous for the unique beauty and mystery of its intricate stone carvings. Conforming neither to tradition nor fashion, the chapel is richly ornate and its carvings – including the famous Apprentice Pillar – are varied and full of symbolic links to the Knights Templar and Freemasonry.

> **ROSSLYN CHAPEL** will be of special interest to readers of Dan Brown's novel *The DaVinci Code*, in which the chapel and its Masonic and Templar symbolism play an important role.

Maid of the Forth (Hawes Pier, under the Forth Rail Bridge, ☎ 131-331 4857, www.maidoftheforth.co.uk; almost-daily sailings to Inchcolm in July-Aug; weekends only in spring/autumn; adult/concession/child/family £11/£9/£4.50/£27). An onboard commentary tells the history of Edinburgh's seaway and describes various features you pass on your cruise. The trip gives you the chance to view seals, puffins and dolphins and climb to the island's viewpoint. Allow three hours, of which half is spent on the island. There are also evening jazz and ceilidh cruises.

Crichton Castle (HS; three miles southwest of Pathhead off the A68, ☎ 1875-320 017; open April-Sept, 9:30am-6:30pm; adult/concession/child £2.20/£1.60/£0.75). A large, sophisticated castle with a spectacular, Italian Renaissance-style faceted stonework façade erected by the Earl of Bothwell in 1581-91.

Scottish Mining Museum (Lady Victoria Colliery, Newtongrange, Midlothian EH22 4QN, ☎ 131-663 7519, fax 131-654 1618, enquiries@scottishmining-museum.com, www.scottishminingmuseum.com; open 10am-5pm, to 4pm in winter; adult/concession/family £4/£2.20/£10). The museum is in one of the finest Victorian collieries still surviving in Europe; it tells the story of the Scottish mining industry from early days to the present. The ex-miner guides couldn't be more qualified to show you around and you can see a recreated underground roadway, a coal face and the pithead where miners descended underground.

Edinburgh Crystal Visitor Centre (Eastfield Industrial Estate, Penicuik, Midlothian, ☎ 1968-675 128, fax 1968-674 847, visitorcentre@edinburgh-crystal.co.uk, www.edinburgh-crystal.com; open Mon-Sat, 10am-5pm & Sun, 11am-5pm; admission to the glasshouse adult/concession/family £3.50/£2.50/£9.50). Displays and demonstrations show how Edinburgh Crystal is made, and there is also a café and shop.

Edinburgh Butterfly & Insect World (Dobbies Garden World, Lasswade, Midlothian EH18 1AZ, ☎ 131-663 4932, fax 131-654 2774, info@edinburgh-butterfly-world.co.uk, www.edinburgh-butterflyworld.co.uk; open summer, 9:30am-5:30pm & winter, 10am-5pm, closed 25-26 Dec & 1-2 Jan; adult/concession/family £4.70/£3.60/£15). This is a chance to explore the world of exotic and colorful butterflies and insects in a rainforest setting of tropical plants, waterfalls and pools. Daily "Meet the Beasties" sessions let you handle a range of creepy crawlies, bugs and beasties – should you wish to.

Edinburgh Canal Centre (The Bridge Inn, 27 Baird Road, Ratho, Midlothian EH28 8RA, ☎ 131-333 1320, fax 131-333 3480, info@bridge-inn.com, www.bridgeinn.com). Various cruises throughout the year on the *Pride of the Union* and *Pride of Belhaven*, including summer sightseeing, dinner cruises and murder mystery sailings. The cruises are popular, and booking is recommended.

■ Adventures & Wildlife Watching

Dalkeith Country Park (☎ 131-654 1666; open April-Oct). The large wooded estate surrounding Dalkeith Palace (designed in 1701 for the Dukes of Buccleuch) has riverside walks, a woodland playground and farm park, as well as summer wildlife walks organized by the Ranger Service.

Pentland Hills Regional Park (near Penicuik, ☎ 131-445 5969). The unspoiled Pentland Hills spread out south of Edinburgh and offer signed walking tracks and a number of cycle paths. The best access to the park is from the Visitor Information Centre at Flotterstone on the A702, from where rangers organize regular walks and history tours.

Pentland Hills Icelandics (Windy Gowl Farm, Carlops, Penicuik, Midlothian EH26 9NL, ☎/fax 1968-661 095, jnoble-@phicelandics.co.uk, www.phicelandics.co.uk). Ride high into the Pentland Hills on a mount from the UK's largest herd of Icelandic horses.

Vogrie Country Park (near Gorebridge, ☎ 1875-821 990). The park covers over 280 acres of woods and Victorian parkland, and has woodland walks, nature trails, ponds and streams. The Ranger Service organizes regular events, including water divining, wildlife photography and the annual **Vogrie Festival** held in August.

Roslin Glen Country Park (Roslin, ☎ 1875-821 990). Rosslyn Chapel stands on the edge of the steep and richly wooded Esk Valley, the narrow rocky gorge below with its fast-flowing water giving Rosslyn its name. The Country Park has several peaceful woodland walks, including easy trails passing the ruined gunpowder mills and 15th-century **Rosslyn Castle** in addition to the famous chapel.

One such walk is a 2.5-hour circuit from the parking area in Roslin close to the castle (from the A720 take the A701 and then B7003 to Rosewell, parking below the z-bends). Follow the path to the footbridge over the River North Esk and then the steep, stepped path up to Rosslyn Castle. From here, a lane leads to Rosslyn Chapel and the village. Turn first right past the animal research center and continue past woodland to a stile, beyond which the route descends a narrow ridge between Roslin and Bilston glens. Loop back and follow the river to the stepped path to the castle.

In the south of Midlothian, the neighboring reservoirs at **Edgelaw**, **Rosebery** and **Gladhouse** provide a mix of trout and coarse angling, while **Glencorse** (which stocks brook trout normally found in North America) and **Loganlea** in the west specialize in trout. Both the **North** and **South Esk** rivers also provide fishing. Local tourism offices can give details of season dates and permits.

■ Golf

 Glencorse Golf Course (18-hole inland, 5,217 yards; Milton Bridge, Penicuik, Midlothian EH26 0RD, ☎ 1968-677 189, fax 1968-674 399; green fees £20-£26). Parkland course with a stream in play at 10 holes.

Kings Acre Golf Course (18-hole inland, 5,935 yards; Lasswade, Midlothian EH18 1AU, ☎ 131-663 3456, fax 131-663 7076, info@kingsacregolf.com, www.kings-acregolf.com; green fees £17-£24). Pay-and-play course with a state-of-the-art practice facility.

West Lothian

West Lothian lies between Edinburgh and Glasgow and is often traversed but less often visited. Its greatest claim to fame is as the birthplace of Mary, Queen of Scots, who was born at Linlithgow Palace in 1542.

 INFORMATION SOURCES: There are tourism offices at Linlithgow (Burgh Halls, The Cross, Linlithgow EH49 7AH, ☎ 1506-844 600) and Livingston (McArthurGlen Designer Outlet, Livingston, ☎ 1506-418 416), both of which are open April-Sept.

■ Attractions & Sights

 **Linlithgow Palace** (HS; Linlithgow, off the M9 at Junction 3 northbound or Junction 4 southbound, ☎ 1506-842 896; open April-Sept, 9:30am-6:30pm; Oct-Mar, 9:30am-4:30pm; adult/concession/child £3/£2.30/£1). The magnificent and romantic ruin of a great royal palace set in its own park beside Linlithgow Loch. Linlithgow was a favored residence of Stewart kings and queens from James I (reigned 1406-37) onwards and was the birthplace of James V (1512) and his daughter, Mary, Queen of Scots (1542). Built and adapted from 1424, the building retains many of the architectural features of its majestic past. The east range is the earliest surviving part of the palace and contains the great hall and main gateway, dating from the later part of the reign of James I. Throughout the palace is a labyrinth of atmospheric chambers and galleries it's possible to explore and stairwells it's possible to climb. The remains of the great hall and chapel are particularly fine and look as if only a little restoration would make them once again habitable.

The Linlithgow Story (Annet House, 143 High Street, Linlithgow EH49 7EJ, ☎ 1506-670 677, www.linlithgowstory.org.uk; open Easter-Oct, 10am-5pm; closes 4pm Sun; adult/child/family £1/£0.60/£2, free on Sun). The small museum and garden celebrate the Stewart monarchs and townspeople of Linlithgow.

The Lothians

St Michael's Parish Church (Church Peel, Linlithgow, ☎ 1506-842 188, www.stmichaels-parish.org.uk). Located beside the palace, this 13th-century church boasts interesting stained glass and is closely associated with many Scottish monarchs, including Mary, Queen of Scots. The distinctive timber and metal "crown" was added in 1964.

Linlithgow Canal Centre (Manse Road Basin, Linlithgow, ☎ 1506-671 215, info@lucs.org.uk, www.lucs.org.uk; open Easter to mid-Oct, Sat-Sun, 2-5pm; daily in July-Aug). Two-hour Union Canal cruises over the Avon Aqueduct depart at 2pm, adult/concession/family £6/£3/£15; shorter trips aboard a replica Victorian steam packet boat depart every half-hour after 2pm, adult/concession £2.50/£1.50; a canal museum housed in a former stable row (admission free); and a pleasant tearoom.

Hopetoun House (South Queensferry, West Lothian, ☎ 131-331 2451, fax 131-319 1885, enquiries@hopetounhouse.com, www.hopetounhouse.com; open April-Sept, 10am-5:30pm, last entry 4:30pm; adult/concession/child/family £6.50/£5.50/£3.50/£18). One of Scotland's finest stately homes, and residence of the Marquess of Linlithgow, Hopetoun was built in 1699-1702 and is a gem of European architectural heritage. Much of the original 18th-century furniture and wall coverings survive; in the **State Apartments** are collections of tapestries, Meissen ornaments and several famous paintings. The house sits in 100 acres of parkland with woodland walks, nature trails and a red-deer park.

House of the Binns (NTS; Linlithgow EH49 7NA, ☎ 1506-834 255, houseofthebinns@nts.org.uk; ranger, ☎ 131-665 1546; house open June-Sept, Sat-Thurs, 2pm-5pm; grounds open year-round, hours vary seasonally; adult/concession/family £5/£3.75/£13.50). Historic home of the Dalyell family for over 350 years, the house reflects the early-17th-century transition in Scottish architecture from fortified stronghold to more spacious mansion. Displays include collections of period furniture, porcelain and family portraits. The extensive grounds include towers erected in 1681 to mark the raising of the Royal Scots Greys regiments by General Tam Dalyell and a woodland walk to a panoramic viewpoint over the Firth of Forth.

Almond Valley Heritage Centre (Millfield, Livingston, West Lothian EH54 7AR, ☎ 1506-414 957, info@almondvalley.co.uk, www.almondvalley.co.uk; open 10am-5pm; adult/child/family £3/2/10). Displays, events and activities involving a watermill, museum and farmyard animals help you learn about West Lothian.

■ Adventures

Adventure Centre – Ratho (South Platt Hill, Ratho, Newbridge, Edinburgh EH28 8AA, ☎ 131-333 6333, info@adventurescotland.com, www.adventurescotland.com; day-entry adult/child £7/£5.50; course fees vary). The center boasts the world's largest indoor climbing arena (2,880 square yards of artificial wall surfaces, including over 480 square yards of bouldering and training), 6,000 square yards of outdoor rock cliffs; SkyRide, the UK's first – and world's largest – indoor suspended air-adventure course;

mountain bike skills courses and cycle ways; running and walking trails; scuba diving; and a gym, health spa and sauna.

■ Golf

Linlithgow Golf Course (18-hole inland, 5,729 yards; Braehead, Linlithgow, West Lothian EH49 6QF, ☎ 1506-671 044, fax 1506-842 764, info@linlithgowgolf.co.uk, www.linlithgowgolf.co.uk; green fees £20-£25). Undulating course with panoramic views of the Forth Valley and Linlithgow Palace.

■ Wildlife Watching

Almondell & Calderwood Country Park (access from Broxburn, Mid Calder and East Calder, ☎ 1506-882 254). The park encompasses 269 acres of natural woodlands along the River Almond. Its visitor center has an aquarium showing river, pond and canal life and the Ranger Service organizes a wide range of activities.

Beecraigs (near Linlithgow, West Lothian EH49 6PL, ☎ 1506-844 516, mail@beecraigs.com, www.beecraigs.com). West Lothian's largest country park is set in the Bathgate Hills close to Linlithgow and is inhabited by over 90 species of birds and animals. Feed trout in the fishery and watch red deer from a viewing platform in the deer farm. Archery, canoeing, climbing, fishing and mountain biking are also available.

■ Shopping

McArthurGlen Designer Outlet (Almondvale Avenue, Livinston, West Lothian EH54 6QX, ☎ 1506-423 600, www.mcarthurglen.com). Scotland's largest designer outlet has over 90 top brand stores under one roof.

■ Where To Stay & Eat

See *Accommodation* and *Dining* price charts on pages 129 and 132.

East Lothian

Kiloran House (Drylaw Terrace, East Linton EH40 3AY, ☎ 1620-860 410, kiloran@btinternet.com; B&B ££). Comfortable B&B accommodation in a detached Victorian house with a large garden.

Woodside (13 North Street, Belhaven, Dunbar EH42 1NU, ☎/fax 1368-862 384, packwood@dunbarwoodside.co.uk, www.dunbarwoodside.co.uk; open April-Sept; B&B ££). High-quality B&B with views and walks across Belhaven Bay toward Bass Rock. There are pleasant bedrooms and a guest lounge with large picture windows overlooking the garden and sea. The breakfast menu includes sliced haggis, "tattie" scones, local Eyemouth smoked haddock with a poached egg and smoked Eyemouth kipper fillets.

Midlothian

Ivory House (14 Vogrie Road, Gorebridge, Midlothian EH23 4HH, ☎ 1875-820 755, fax 1875-823 345, barbara@ivory-house.co.uk, www.ivory-house.co.uk; B&B ££). Elegant, well-furnished guest house accommodation in a peaceful Victorian house. There is also a converted cottage with its own private garden and rockery.

The Bridge Inn (27 Baird Road, Ratho, Midlothian EH28 8RA, ☎ 131-333 1320, fax 131-333 3480, info@bridgeinn.com, www.bridgeinn.com; ££-£££). Award-winning canalside pub-restaurant serving good food all day.

West Lothian

Thornton (Edinburgh Road, Linlithgow EH49 6AA, ☎ 1506-844 693, fax 1506-844 876, www.thornton-scotland.co.uk; open Feb-Nov; B&B ££). Stone Victorian house dating from the 1870s with two comfortable bedrooms, original features, spacious lounge and traditional dining room. The excellent breakfast menu includes homemade jams and fresh fruit compote, Arbroath smokies (smoked small haddock) and trout. No children under 14.

Newmills Cottage (472 Lanark Road West, Balerno, West Lothian EH14 5AE, ☎/fax 131-449 4300, info@newmillscottage.co.uk, www.newmillscottage.co.uk; B&B ££). Farmhouse-style accommodation with lovely, spacious gardens set in peaceful surroundings.

Glasgow &
The Clyde Valley

Glasgow and the Clyde Valley cover an area of more than 1,000 square miles, stretching from the **Clyde Coast** in the west to the **Campsie Hills** in the north and **Lowther Hills** in the south. At its heart is Glasgow, Scotland's largest city.

To the west of Glasgow lie the counties of **Renfrewshire** and **Inverclyde**, hub of the area's rich industrial and maritime heritage, which culminated in the region becoming one of the world's greatest shipbuilding centers. Bordering Glasgow to the south and east is **Lanarkshire**. North Lanarkshire is characterized by museums that pay homage to the area's industrial heritage. South Lanarkshire drives deep into the heart of the rural lowlands.

The **River Clyde** threads the area, leading from its source in rural Lanarkshire, past quiet market towns, villages and Glasgow City before flowing through Renfrewshire and finally reaching the sea at Inverclyde.

City of Glasgow

With a population of around 680,000, Glasgow is not only Scotland's largest city but also the fourth largest in Britain. Its history can be traced back to the 6th century, when St Mungo established a small religious settlement on the ground where the cathedral now stands. Old Glasgow grew up around the cathedral before expanding west into the Merchant City.

Glasgow's population exploded during the 19th century, growing from 77,000 in 1801 to 762,000 in 1901 due to the industrial revolution. It became a rich, industrial city known as the "Workshop of the Empire." The roots of this prosperity lie in the 18th century and the "Tobacco Lords" who made their fortunes trading tobacco with the Americas. Some re-invested in new developments, first West Indian sugar and later cotton. The **Tall Ship at Glasgow Harbour** stands as a symbol of Glasgow's former life as a great trading port.

With the growth of iron and steel production, shipbuilding and engineering, Glasgow traded goods all over the world, aided by rich local supplies of raw materials, an endless supply of workers and the trading network of the British Empire. The legacy of this 19th-century prosperity remains in the form of some of Britain's finest Victorian architecture, built to house the thousands of workers needed to sustain production. By 1921, Glasgow's population exceeded a million.

Glasgow's early industrialization proved to be its downfall. From the 1870s, Britain faced severe competition from America, Germany and, in later years, Japan. The city's dependence on exporting ships and engineering products and its slowness to modernize working methods made Glasgow's industries vulnerable to economic downturns.

The two world wars temporarily boosted Glasgow's economy with demand for battleships, armor plate and shells, but only disguised the decline of many of the city's industries. Glasgow was badly affected by the post-World War II economic downturn, and unfortunately became best known for unemployment, violence and a lifestyle that left it dubbed the "heart attack capital of Europe." The demise of its heavy industry remains the most poignant reminder of Glasgow's former greatness. Where the banks of the Clyde once teemed with forests of shipbuilding cranes, launching huge vessels into the river every week, only ghosts remain of this once world-beating industry.

Fortunately, Glasgow's greatest asset is its people who, perhaps because of their rollercoaster economic fortunes, have learned to look on the bright side of every situation and look out for each other as a matter of course. Glaswegians are the friendliest and most open, spontaneous and witty people you could hope to meet. You can ask one Glaswegian a question and receive answers from all directions from people you didn't even realize were within earshot. A total stranger once paid part of my bus fare when I was struggling with the city's "no change given" buses armed with only a £2 coin. And all the while Glaswegian humor shines through – so much so that local comedians like Billy Connolly aren't considered noticeably funnier than people you might meet any night in a pub.

The good news is that Glasgow's fortunes are once more on the upswing. In recent years the city has made great efforts to reinvent itself as a thriving new economy based on tourism, culture and services, and is cleaning up the grime left by a century and a half of heavy industry.

Its status as **1990 European City of Culture** sparked an urban regeneration that continues to spawn trendy boutiques, bars and restaurants. New investment is allowing the redevelopment of grim 1960s tenement blocks and is turning the city's redundant warehouses into desirable loft-style apartments. As in its Victorian glory days, not everyone is benefiting from this new prosperity. Poverty and depressed areas remain, but the city is making great strides in the right direction.

Today Glasgow is recognized as one of the liveliest and most cosmopolitan cities in Europe. Live performances, events and festivals take place throughout the year against a backdrop of galleries, award-winning, free museums, stylish eateries and a vibrant nightlife. Glasgow built on its City of Culture award by putting together a sustained city-wide **Festival of Architecture and Design** in 1996, the largest ever of its kind, and it won the accolade of **UK City of Architecture and Design** in 1999. One can only hope that the born-again Glasgow will retain the unique character of its people, expressed most vibrantly through their wonderfully amusing "patter."

GLASGOW PATTER

Glaswegians have a genius for uninhibited forthrightness, quick wit, sharp humor and spontaneous friendship. Combining natural irony and entertaining "craic" (pronounced "crack," meaning chat and banter, often drink-fueled) tempered by a warm Celtic friendliness, Glaswegian dialogue is uncompromising, unpretentious, very clever and effortlessly funny. Pop into any traditional pub and listen. Join in and you'll be there all night – Glaswegians love to play to an audience. To them, it's "nae bother ataw!"

 INFORMATION SOURCES: The **Greater Glasgow & Clyde Valley Tourist Board** is at 11 George Square, Glasgow G2 1DY, ☎ 141-204 4480, fax 141-566 4073, enquiries@seeglasgow.com, www.seeglasgow.com.

The **Glasgow Tourist Information Centre** (TIC) is also at 11 George Square, ☎ 141-204 4400, fax 141 221 3524, enquiries@seeglasgow.com, and there are TICs at Glasgow Airport (International Arrivals, Glasgow International Airport, ☎ 141-848 4440, fax 141-849 1444, airport@seeglasgow.com) and Paisley (9A Gilmour Street, Paisley PA1 1DD, ☎ 141-889 0711, fax 141-848 1363, paisley@seeglasgow.com). All three tourism offices are open year-round.

■ Special Events

Celtic Connections (January; Glasgow Royal Concert Hall, 2 Sauchiehall Street, Glasgow G2 3NY, ☎ 141-353 8000, www.celticconnections.co.uk). This is the world's largest winter festival of Celtic music, with big name performers from around the world and three weeks of modern Celtic rock, dance, traditional pipe bands, workshops and ceilidhs.

Glasgow International Comedy Festival (March; ☎ 141-339 6208/552 2070, info@glasgowcomedyfestival.com, www.glasgowcomedyfestival.com). Action-packed program of all aspects of comedy, including stand-up, cabaret and theater with some of the best live comics performing.

West End Festival (June; ☎ 141-341 0844, www.westendfestival.co.uk). A mix of theater, music, exhibitions, film, markets and the highlight Midsummer Carnival, when tens of thousands dance their way on to Byres Road.

RSNO Proms (June; Glasgow Royal Concert Hall, ☎ 141-353 8000, www.grch.com). Popular series of Royal Scottish National Orchestra's summer promenade concerts.

Bard in the Botanics (June/July; ☎ 141-334 3995, www.glasgowrep.org). Glasgow Repertory Company's summer Shakespeare festival of open air performances has become a runaway success – book early.

Glasgow Jazz Festival (July; ☎ 141-552 3552, www.jazzfest.co.uk). Annual jazz and blues festival that attracts famous performers.

World Pipe Band Championships (August; Royal Scottish Pipe Band Association, 45 Washington Street, Glasgow G3 8AZ, ☎ 141-221 5414, fax 141-221 1561, www.rspba.org). Massive tartan spectacular as over 200 bands from around the world compete for the coveted top prize.

■ Getting Here

By Air

Glasgow Airport (☎ 141-887 1111, www.baa.co.uk/glasgow) is eight miles from central Glasgow. Coach transfers leave every 15/30 minutes; taxis to the city are approximately £15.

By Rail

Glasgow has two main railway stations: **Central Station** on Argyll Street for West Coast Services from Stranraer, Ayr and Dumfries, and services from London and the south via Carlyle; and **Queen Street Station** in George Square for East Coast Services from Edinburgh, Stirling, Perth, Dundee and Inverness, as well as travel up the West Coast to Oban, Fort William and Mallaig. The stations are 10 minutes' walk from each other.

By Car

Coming from the south, Glasgow is reached via the M74; from Edinburgh by the M8, and from the north by the M9, M80 and A80.

■ Getting Around

Glasgow is built on a grid system with **George Square** at the center. **Queen Street Station** is on George Square and **Central Station** lies a few blocks to the west. **Buchanan Street Bus Station** is a few blocks north of George Square. Unusually, **Glasgow cathedral** is in the east rather than the heart of the city. The historic **Merchant City** lies to the east and south of George Square. To the west of George Square is Glasgow's main **shopping district**, beyond which is the **West End** with the university and a wide range of bars and restaurants.

AUTHOR'S TIP: *Unlike compact Edinburgh, which is a great city to explore on foot, Glasgow's attractions are spread over a large area. A great way to get around is to take one of the hop-on, hop-off sightseeing buses that not only take you to all the main attractions but also provide you with an excellent commentary en route.*

By Rail

Glasgow has an extensive suburban train network and a circular underground (subway) line.

Travel Passes

Roundabout Glasgow Ticket allows unlimited travel for one day on all local rail services within about 10 miles of the city center and on the **Strathclyde Passenger Transport (SPT) Underground**. Holders also receive a £1.50 discount on a Glasgow City bus tour. Valid after 9am on weekdays and all day on weekends. Adult/child £4/£2. Available from railway stations and SPT Travel Centres.

Discovery Ticket allows unlimited Underground travel for one day, valid after 9:30am, Mon-Sat and all day Sun. Ticket price £1.70; available from any Underground station.

Daytripper Ticket allows unlimited travel for one day by train, Underground, most buses and some ferries, and is an ideal way for families to travel around Glasgow. Valid after 9am, weekdays and all day on weekends. £14 for two adults and up to four children (five-15 years) and £8 for one adult and up to two children. Available at railway stations and SPT Travel Centres.

FirstDay Tourist Ticket provides unlimited travel 9:30am-12 midnight on First's bus services throughout Glasgow for £3. You also get a pocket-sized map, postcards and discounts to many tourist attractions. Available at SPT Travel Centres and tourism offices.

DON'T MISS

Discover Glasgow's fascinating past at the **People's Palace** museum.

Transport yourself back to the early 20th century in the atmospheric **Tenement House**.

Tour the interior splendor of **Glasgow City Chambers**.

Walk the **Merchant City Trail** and follow in the footsteps of tobacco lords and other merchants that made the city great.

Discover or re-discover the magic of science and the natural world at the wonderful **Glasgow Science Centre**.

Explore the meteoric rise and poignant demise of Glasgow's shipbuilding industry at **Clydebuilt**.

Visit **New Lanark Mill** and try to imagine what life was like in less "enlightened" mills.

Meet and talk to some real **Glaswegians**.

Best Freebie: **The Burrell Collection**.

■ Attractions & Sights

Glasgow Cathedral (Cathedral Square, Glasgow G4 0QZ, ☎ 141-552 6891, fax 552 0988, www.glasgowcathedral.org.uk; open April-Sept, Mon-Sat, 9:30am-6pm & Sun, 1pm-5pm; Oct-Mar, Mon-Sat, 9:30am-4pm & Sun, 1pm-4pm; Sunday services 11am & 6:30pm). A magnificent building and the only medieval cathedral on the Scottish mainland to survive the Reformation intact (except for its western towers). The cathedral was built in the 13th through 15th centuries and stands over the supposed burial site of **St Kentigern** (or **Mungo**, as he is more popularly known), Patron Saint of Glasgow.

St Mungo is believed to have established a Christian community on this site in the 6th century. The first stone cathedral was consecrated here in 1136 in the presence of King David I. This was destroyed by fire and rebuilt in 1197. Painted stones from the rebuilt church were discovered in the present foundations during 1993 excavations.

Visitors enter the cathedral by way of a side door to the Nave, the impressive western entrance. The open timber roof is of late medieval design and much of the timber is believed to date from the 14th century. The Quire is the center of the cathedral's religious worship and is where it holds its two Sunday services. Look for the Royal Pew, bearing the discreet monograms of the Queen and Duke of Edinburgh.

 The highlight of the cathedral is the **Lower Church**, a magnificent example of 13th-century Gothic architecture. The cluster of columns and vaults surrounds a raised stone platform where St Mungo was originally buried and where his shrine now stands. Thousands of pilgrims made their way here in medieval times and in, 1451, the Pope decreed it should be as meritorious to make a pilgrimage to Glasgow as to Rome itself.

Adjacent to the cathedral is the astonishing silhouette of **Glasgow Necropolis** ("City of the Dead," ☎ 141-287 3961, fax 141-287 3960; open dawn-dusk), rising above a hill known as **Fir Park**. The spine-tingling cemetery dates from the 1830s and was carefully planned to prevent the spread of disease. The graveyard contains many beautiful and impressive tombs and monuments of prominent Glaswegians, mostly dating from the 19th century when the city was at the height of its industrial might. The cemetery is entered through elaborate cast iron gates and over a bridge known popularly as the "Bridge of Sighs" under which a stream once flowed. It was here where St Mungo baptized his Christian converts. A path climbs to the summit of the hill from where there are excellent views over the city.

St Mungo Museum of Religious Life and Art (2 Castle Street, Glasgow G4 0RH, ☎ 141-553 2557, www.glasgowmuseums.com; open Mon-Thurs & Sat, 10am-5pm; Fri & Sun, 11am-5pm). The museum stands in the Cathedral Precinct on the site of the medieval Bishop's Castle and explores the importance of religion across the world down the ages. With such a large mission, the exhibits are necessarily selective. A highlight is the stunning painting *Christ of St John of the Cross* by Salvador Dalí. The painting looks down on the crucified Christ with a shoreline scene and fishing boats below. In addition to the Gallery of Religious Art, other galleries explore how religion is woven into people's daily lives, the ways religious beliefs have influenced Scottish society and the story of Glasgow Cathedral and the Bishop's Castle.

The museum also houses Britain's first permanent Japanese Zen Garden and has a café and shop.

Glasgow City Chambers (George Square, Glasgow G2 1DU, ☎ 141-287 4018, fax 141-287 5666; open Mon-Fri, 9am-4:30pm; free guided tours subject to availability and council business). The stunning headquarters of Glasgow City Council is over 100 years old and is the city's finest example of 19th-century architecture. Commanding the wide expanse of George Square, the chambers took six years to build, engaging skilled workers from as far afield as Italy and France, and finally opened in 1889. The extravagance of the Chambers wouldn't stand a chance of being approved in a public building nowadays: marble, gold, ornate plasterwork, alabaster, half-ton chandeliers, mahogany fittings and fine works of art. The marble staircase (the fullest marble staircase in Western Europe), magnificently tiled Councillors' corridor, library with 11-foot-high walnut bookcases, and sumptuous Banqueting Hall that could engulf a medium-sized office block are accessible to the public in daily organized tours (or alternatively glimpsed as backdrops to films ostensibly set in the Vatican or Kremlin!). Despite its splendor, the building remains very much a working office.

Provand's Lordship (3 Castle Street, Glasgow G4 0RB, ☎ 141-552 8819, fax 141-552 4744, www.glasgowmuseums.com; open Mon-Thurs & Sat, 10am-5pm; Fri & Sun, 11am-5pm). An outstanding example of 15th-century domestic architecture and the oldest house in Glasgow. It was built by Bishop Andrew Muirhead in 1471 as a manse for the cathedral's canons or priests. Several impressive displays featuring period furniture and artifacts vividly recreate home life in the Middle Ages.

Merchant Square (71-73 Albion Street, Glasgow G1 1RB, ☎ 141-552 5908, fax 141-553 1520). At the heart of Glasgow's historic Merchant City, the covered square offers shopping, dining and events in a 19th-century courtyard setting.

Hutchesons' Hall (NTS; 158 Ingram Street, Glasgow G1 1EJ, ☎ 141-552 8391, fax 141-552 7031, hutchesonshall@nts.org.uk; open 20 Jan-24 Dec, Mon-Sat, 10am-5pm; adult/concession £2/£1). Built in 1802-05 to a design by David Hamilton, this is one of the most elegant landmarks in central Glasgow. A major reconstruction in 1876 by John Baird heightened the hall and provided an impressive staircase. Portraits of Glasgow worthies hang from the interior walls. There is a multimedia exhibition, Glasgow Style, and works for sale by Glasgow designers.

The Tenement House (NTS; 145 Buccleuch Street, Garnethill, Glasgow G3 6QN, ☎ 141-333 0183, tenementhouse@nts.org.uk; open Mar-Oct, 1-5pm; adult/concession/family £3.50/£2.60/£9.50). Glasgow, more than any other Scottish city, is associated with tenement blocks used to house its armies of workers. The traditional Scottish tenement is a stone building of three stories or more with one or more homes on each floor. This first floor flat is typical of tenements in late Victorian times; it was the home of Miss Agnes Toward, a shorthand typist, for over 50 years from 1911-65. The flat comprises four

Glasgow

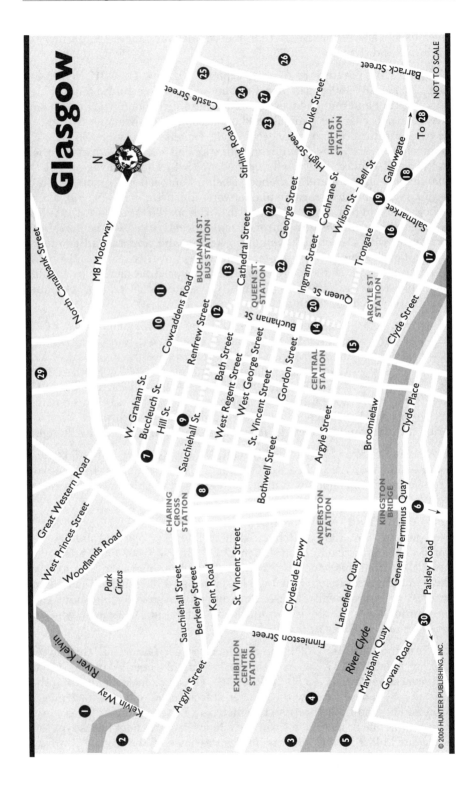

Glasgow

N

NOT TO SCALE

© 2005 HUNTER PUBLISHING, INC.

Glasgow Map Key

1. The Hunterian Museum & Art Gallery, Glasgow University
2. Museum of Transport, Kelvingrove Art Gallery & Museum
3. The Tall Ship SV *Glenlee*
4. Scottish Exhibition & Conference Centre,
   Clyde Auditorium (the Armadillo)
5. Prince's Dock, Glasgow Science Centre
6. The Burrell Collection, Pollok House, House for an Art Lover
7. Tenement House
8. King's Theatre
9. Glasgow School of Art, McLellan Galleries, Glasgow Film Theatre
10. Piping Centre, Theatre Royal, Pavillion Theatre
11. Glasgow Caledonian University
12. Glasgow Royal Concert Hall
13. Buchanan Galleries
14. The Lighthouse
15. St. Enoch Centre
16. Tron Theatre
17. Glasgow Green, People's Place
18. Barras Market
19. Tolbooth Steeple
20. Gallery of Modern Art & Royal Exchange Square, Princes Square
21. Hutchesons' Hall, City Chambers, George Square
22. Strathclyde University
23. Provand's Lordship
24. Glasgow Cathedral, St. Mungo Museum of Religious Life and Art
25. Royal Infirmary
26. Necropolis
27. St. Mungo Heritage Centre
28. Celtic Park
29. Start of Forth & Clyde Canal and Walkway
30. To Greenock & Glasgow Airport

Glasgow

atmospheric rooms that retain most of their original features, such as bed recesses, range stove, coalbunker and gently hissing gas lighting. The furniture, furnishings and, most strikingly, Miss Toward's personal possessions, including original jars of jam (one retaining contents dating back to 1929!), soaps and bottles of bathroom toiletries, recreate a fascinating picture of domestic life in the early 20th century. The flat is quite small but don't be surprised if you find yourself spending an inordinately long time just soaking up the atmosphere, particularly if you get chatting with the knowledgeable guides.

People's Palace (Glasgow Green, Glasgow G40 1AT, ☎ 141-554 0223, fax 141-550 0892, www.glasgowmuseums.com; open Mon-Thurs & Sat, 10am-5pm; Fri & Sun, 11am-5pm). This superb museum recounts the story of ordinary Glasgow people from 1750 to the present and is popular with visitors and locals alike. Informative displays, vivid recreations and fascinating narrations breathe life into the work, rest and play of Glaswegians as their city expanded into the second city of the British Empire, only to decline again a century later. Discover how a family lived in a typical one-room tenement flat. Be gripped by the award-winning film on Clyde shipbuilding. Learn the basics of Glasgow's unique accent and humor ("patter") through the wit and utterings of famous patter merchants Stanley Baxter, Billy Connolly and Rab C Nesbitt, not to mention its children's songs and street rhymes. Ye couldnae get bored here! The attached, airy palm-filled glasshouse of the Winter Gardens is the perfect place to relax over a coffee or light meal.

St Andrew's in the Square (1 St Andrew's Square, Glasgow G1 5PP, ☎ 141-559 5902, fax 141-559 5370, www.cafe-source.co.uk). A beautiful 18th-century church and one of the finest examples of neo-Baroque church architecture in Scotland. The gilded plasterwork interior was recently refurbished and the church reopened as a performance space for Scottish music, concerts and ceilidhs. The square is an elegant oasis of calm in the hustle and bustle of the city center; St Andrew's also boasts an excellent café (see Café Source in *Where To Eat*, page 169).

Museum of Transport (1 Bunhouse Road, Kelvin Hall, Glasgow G3 8DP, ☎ 141-287 2720, fax 141-287 2692, www.glasgowmuseums.com; open Mon-Thurs & Sat, 10am-5pm; Fri & Sun, 11am-5pm). This comprehensive collection of vehicles and models tells the story of transport by land and sea, from horse-drawn carriages to motorcycles, fire engines, railway engines, buses, boats and motorcars. Highlights include a recreation of Kelvin Street in 1938 and an impressive display of locomotives, train carriages and trams. Upstairs, a huge display of model ships evokes the glory days of Clyde shipbuilding, which produced great ocean liners such as *Queen Mary* (1936), *Queen Elizabeth* (1940) and *Queen Elizabeth 2* (1967), as well as the former Royal Yacht *Britannia* (now decommissioned and berthed in Leith – see the Edinburgh chapter).

Kelvingrove Art Gallery & Museum. Exhibiting everything from fine art to dinosaurs, the gallery has been Glasgow's star attraction (voted by Glaswegians as their favorite building) and the most popular free visitor attraction in Scotland. Unfortunately, the gallery closed in June 2003 for refurbishment that is expected to take at least three years. Call the gallery (☎ 141-287 2699) or the Tourist Board (☎ 141-204 4480), or check the link at www.glasgowmuseums.com, for updated information on its reopening.

During refurbishment, the best of Kelvingrove's art collection – including works by Botticelli, Turner, Rembrandt, Reubens and Mackintosh – is on display at **McLellan Galleries** (270 Sauchiehall Street, Glasgow G2 3EH, ☎ 141-565 4137, fax 141-565 4111, www.glasgowmuseums.com; open Mon-Thurs & Sat, 10am-5pm; Fri & Sun, 11am-5pm, regular guided tours available Mon-Fri).

Gallery of Modern Art (Queen Street, Glasgow G1 3AH, ☎ 141-229 1996, fax 141-204 5316; open Mon-Wed & Sat, 10am-5pm; Thurs, 10am-8pm; Fri & Sun, 11am-5pm) Set in the elegant Royal Exchange Building, four galleries display paintings, sculptures, photographs and other works by Scottish and international artists. Changing displays and a program of temporary exhibitions mean there is always something new to see. The basement houses a café and library.

■ The Mackintosh Legacy

Charles Rennie Mackintosh (1868-1928) was born one of 11 children in the Townhead area of Glasgow, near the cathedral. He met Margaret Macdonald, his future wife, at the Glasgow School of Art and much of his work involves their collaboration.

Mackintosh took much of his inspiration from Scottish traditions and nature and blended them with Art Nouveau, long vertical lines and the simplicity of Japanese forms. His distinctive style is striking in its handling of light and space (often "hurrying" people through darkened areas into bright, open spaces), the skillful use of color and the treatment of rooms as complete works of art, down to individual fittings and even doorplates. Many of his furniture pieces have themselves become design icons.

The **Charles Rennie Mackintosh Society** (Queen's Cross Church, 870 Garscube Road, Glasgow G20 7EL, ☎ 141-946 6600, fax 141-945 2321, info@crmsociety.com, www.crmsociety.com) can provide further information and also organizes tours. The society's headquarters at **Queen's Cross Church** (the only church designed by Mackintosh) also has a library and shop.

Glasgow School of Art (167 Renfrew Street, Glasgow G3 6RQ, ☎ 141-353 4526, fax 141-353 4746, shop@gsa.ac.uk, www.gsa.ac.uk, www.mackintoshshop.co.uk; entry is by guided tour only, Mon-Fri, 11am & 2pm; Sat, 10:30am & 11:30am; adult/concession £5/£4). Charles Rennie Mackintosh's architectural masterpiece occupies a whole central city block. Built at the turn of the last century it remains a working art school. Hour-long guided tours visit rooms containing many well-known pieces of furniture in this fascinating building, the highlight of which is the superb Mackintosh library. Along the way learn about Mackintosh's life and see his transformation of everyday objects, such as chairs, tables, doors and even number plaques, into works of art. In addition to items designed exclusively for the building, the school also has a collection of other pieces by Mackintosh, including architectural drawings, watercolors and furniture.

The Mackintosh House at Glasgow University's **Hunterian Art Gallery** (see below, ☎ 141-330 5431, fax 141-330 3618, hunter@museum.gla.ac.uk, www.hunterian.gla.ac.uk; open Mon-Sat, 9:30am-5pm; closed 12:30-1:30pm). The interiors of 6 Florentine Terrace (address was later changed to 78 Southpark Avenue), the Glasgow home of Charles and Margaret Mackintosh from 1906-1914, have been reassembled within the university's art gallery (the actual house was demolished in the 1960s). The reconstructed home is furnished with the Mackintoshes' own furniture – all to the architect's own design – and furnished as closely as possible to the original.

Hunterian Museum & Art Gallery (Museum, Gilbert Scott Building, University Avenue, Glasgow G12 8QQ, ☎ 141-330 4221, fax 141-330 3617; Art Gallery, 82 Hillhead Street, Glasgow G12 8QQ, ☎141-330 5431, fax 141-330 3618; hunter@museum.gla.ac.uk, www.hunterian.gla.ac.uk; open Mon-Sat, 9:30am-5pm). Housed in Glasgow University's magnificent Gilbert Scott building, the Hunterian is Scotland's oldest public museum. Exhibits include a meteorite that fell on Glasgow in 1804, the 325-million-year-old Bearsden shark, dinosaurs, gems, coins and Roman artifacts from the Antonine Wall. In addition to its renowned Mackintosh House, the Art Gallery also houses paintings by Rembrandt and Whistler, Scottish art and changing displays from one of the most important print collections in Scotland. Both the Museum and Art Gallery hold temporary exhibitions during the year – call for details or pick up a free copy of the *Glasgow Galleries Guide* (found in museums and galleries).

House for an Art Lover (Bellahouston Park, 10 Dumbreck Road, Glasgow G41 5BW, ☎ 141-353 4770, fax 141-353 4771, info@houseforanartlover.co.uk, www.houseforanartlover.co.uk; open April-Sept, Sun-Thurs, 10am-4pm and Sat, 10am-3pm; Oct-Mar, Sat-Sun, 10am-4pm; winter times may vary, call ahead; adult/concession/family £3.50/£2.50/£7). The Mackintosh Exhibition rooms were realized by contemporary artists and craftspeople from a 1901 portfolio created by Mackintosh for a competition to create a "House for an art lover: a grand house in a thoroughly modern style." Set in beautiful parkland adjacent to walled gardens, the house features a permanent exhibition of decorative rooms furnished in Mackintosh's colors and textiles, the Art Lovers' Shop and café.

The Lighthouse (11 Mitchell Lane, Glasgow G1 3LX, ☎ 141-221 6362, fax 141-221 6395, enquiries@thelighthouse.co.uk, www.thelighthouse.co.uk; open Mon & Wed-Sat, 10:30am-5pm; Tues, 11am-5pm; Sun, noon-5pm; adult/concession/child £3/£1.50/£0.80). The former Glasgow Herald Building is now home to Scotland's award-winning Centre for Architecture, Design and the City. The Mackintosh Interpretation Centre exhibits original objects, interactive displays and architectural models representing the best of local, national and international architecture and creative design. The Mackintosh Tower with its spiral staircase provides excellent views over Glasgow's rooftops. There are regular events, talks and workshops in addition to a café-bar and shop.

Martyrs' School (Parson Street, Glasgow G4 0PX, ☎/fax 141-552 2356, www.glasgowmuseums.com; open Mon-Sat, 10am-5pm; Sun, 11am-4pm). Built on the street where Mackintosh was born, the school is one of Mackintosh's earliest buildings and was opened in 1897 as a public primary school for children of the surrounding Townhead area. The red sandstone construction is topped by three ventilators with decorative finials. The interior has fine tile work and impressive roof trusses.

Scotland Street School Museum (225 Scotland Street, Glasgow G5 8QB, ☎ 141-287 0500, fax 141-287 0515, www.glasgowmuseums.com; open Mon-Thurs & Sat, 10am-5pm; Fri & Sun, 11am-5pm). Mackintosh designed this impressive building, his last major Glasgow commission, in 1903-06 for the School Board of Glasgow. The restored building now houses a museum telling the story of education in Scotland from 1872 to the late 20th century, and includes leaded glass towers, a magnificent tiled entrance hall, period classrooms, exhibitions and activity programs.

■ Pollok Country Park

 After a short journey from central Glasgow, the peaceful 361-acre Pollok Country Park provides solitude, delightful country walks and two of the city's major attractions: **The Burrell Collection** and **Pollok House**. Frequent buses run from Union Street in central Glasgow to the Pollokshaws Road entrance of the park, and a regular train service runs from Glasgow Central to Pollokshaws West. It is then an enjoyable 15-minute walk to the attractions, or take the courtesy bus. Don't be alarmed by the sound of dogs barking – the park is also home to the Strathclyde police-dog center.

The Burrell Collection (Pollok Country Park, 2060 Pollokshaws Road, Glasgow G43 1AT, ☎ 141-287 2550, fax 141-287 2597, www.glasgowmuseums.com; open Mon-Thurs & Sat, 10am-5pm; Fri & Sun, 11am-5pm). A collection of some 9,000 works of art gifted by Glasgow shipping magnate Sir William Burrell (1861-1958) and his wife Constance. For most of his life Burrell was an avid collector of art, most notably medieval European Art, Oriental ceramics and bronzes and European paintings. Later in life Burrell also started to collect ancient art.

Colorful tapestries and stained glass show the details of medieval life, along with furniture, paintings, sculpture, armour and weapons. The collection also boasts medieval altars, tombs and stone windows and doorways. Rugs, ceramics and metalwork represent Islamic art and there is also a large collection of Chinese and other Oriental ceramics. Paintings on display include works by Bellini, Rembrandt and the French Impressionists.

Burrell specified that the collection should be housed away from the pollution of the city center. In 1967, Anne Maxwell MacDonald's gift of her estate to the city provided the perfect setting for the building later designed to house the collection. There are daily guided tours, a restaurant and museum shop.

Pollok House (NTS; Pollok Country Park, 2060 Pollokshaws Road, Glasgow G43 1AT, ☎ 141-616 6410, fax 141-616 6521, pollokhouse@nts.org.uk; open year-round, 10am-5pm; admission April-Oct, adult/concession/family £5/£3.75/£13.50; admission free Nov-March). Experience life in one of Scotland's most impressive Edwardian country houses at the turn of the last century. The Maxwells of Pollok lived on this site for 700 years until the 1950s and in 1966 donated their estate, including the Palladian mansion in its walled gardens, to the city. The house is furnished with antique furniture, ceramics, glass and silver and also houses the largest collection of Spanish paintings in the UK and works by William Blake. The suite of servants' quarters in the basement corridor is particularly evocative. Look for the photo of the 1905 staff dance, which shows just how big an army of servants was needed to maintain the house. The Servants' Hall café is decorated in such

Glasgow

period style it's difficult to tell it isn't another display room. In the grounds are peaceful walks through the gardens and an old stable courtyard.

■ In & Around Glasgow

Glasgow Science Centre (50 Pacific Quay, Glasgow G51 1EA, ☎ 141-420 5000, fax 141-420 5011, admin@glasgowsciencecentre.org, www.glasgowsciencecentre.org; 10am-6pm; adult/concession/family £6.95/£4.95/£18.95; including IMAX Theatre £9.95/£7.45/£32.95). The futuristic riverside complex resembles a rocket launch pad. It comprises a science mall, IMAX Theatre and the Glasgow Tower (see below). The spectacular design perfectly complements the striking auditorium ("armadillo") in the SECC complex across the river.

It's no small achievement that the Science Centre's interior displays match its dazzling exterior. The ultra-modern science mall presents over 300 hands-on displays and experiments that will enthral visitors for hours. Discover how we explore and experience the world around us, examine scientific solutions to real-world problems and find out how science impacts our everyday lives. Engaging and informative exhibits cover forces and motion, space science, communication, materials, structures and physiology. Mini laboratories allow real-life experiments and the thrilling planetarium shows make learning about science and technology as much fun as it will ever be. The egg-shaped IMAX Theatre boasts Scotland's largest film screen (80 x 60 feet) and takes you to exotic destinations such as the ocean depths or the summit of Everest.

At the time of writing, the 417-foot (127-m) **Glasgow Tower** was suffering teething problems and remained closed. The tower, Scotland's tallest free-standing structure, houses galleries on the city's past and future and provides a great view over the city. Its innovative design will allow it to rotate fully once the technical problems are corrected (hopefully by the time of your visit).

The Tall Ship at Glasgow Harbour (100 Stobcross Road, Glasgow G3 0QQ, ☎/fax 141-222 2513, info@thetallship.com, www.thetallship.com; open Mar-Oct, 10am-5pm; Nov-Feb, 11am-4pm; adult/concession £4.50/£3.25, children free with paying adult). Voyage back in time to the days of sail aboard the three-masted barque SV *Glenlee*. Taking to the water in 1896 as a bulk-cargo carrier, the *Glenlee* circumnavigated the globe four times and survived the fearsome waters of Cape Horn 15 times. Beautifully restored, she is now one of only five Glasgow-built sailing ships still afloat. Displays chart Glasgow's development into the world's foremost shipbuilder and provide a glimpse of the crew's cramped and often treacherous life at sea. There are also regular events, a riverside restaurant, café and nautical souvenir shop.

Glasgow Botanic Gardens (730 Great Western Road, Glasgow G12 0UE near the Hillhead underground station, ☎ 141-334 2422, fax 141-339 6964; gardens open dawn-dusk; glasshouses open 10am-4:45pm). The gardens provide education, conservation and research as well as displaying a famous range of glasshouses. The main glasshouse range contains a collection of tropical plants, including orchids, begonias and ferns.

Fossil Grove (Victoria Park, Glasgow G14 1BN, ☎ 141-287 2000, www.glasgowmuseums.com; open April-Sept, noon-5pm). Glasgow's most ancient attraction represents a corner of an ancient forest preserved in stone. The 11 curious tree stumps, discovered in 1887, are the fossilized remains of a giant clubmoss – a plant that grew here 330 million years ago. This area was once a vast, swampy, tropical forest; debris from these forests formed the coal seams that helped Glasgow develop into a major industrial city.

Museum of Piping (The National Piping Centre, 30-34 McPhater Street, Cowcaddens, Glasgow G4 0HW, ☎ 141-353 0220, fax 141-353 1570, reception@thepipingcentre.co.uk, www.thepipingcentre.co.uk; open May-Sept, 10am-4:30pm; Oct-Apr, closed Sunday; adult/concession £3/£2). Set within the National Piping Centre, the museum records the history and music of Scotland's national instrument. There is an audio tour, video presentation, shop and bi-monthly magazine, *Piping Today.*

Scottish Football Museum (Hampden Park, Glasgow G42 9BA, ☎ 141-616 6139, fax 141-616 6101, info@scottishfootballmuseum.org.uk; open Mon-Sat, 10am-5pm & Sun, 11am-5pm, subject to events; museum & stadium tour adult/concession £7.50/£3.75; museum only £5/£2.50). Refurbished at a cost of £63 million, Hampden – Scotland's national stadium – hosted the 2002 final of the European Champions League (won by Real Madrid). The stadium also houses the Scottish Football Museum, containing trophies, medals, jerseys and boots worn by football heroes down the years, together with part of the old home dressing room and a section of the old press box. Also available are tours to the changing rooms and warm up area, players' tunnel, cup presentation area and royal box. You probably need to be a football (soccer) fan to fully appreciate the museum, although most sports enthusiasts should find the stadium tour fascinating.

If you have an Old Firm affiliation, you'll probably want to head straight to the hallowed ground of the respective Glasgow giant:

Celtic Football Club (Celtic Park, Glasgow G40 3RE, ☎ 141-551 4308, fax 141-551 8106, visitorexperience@celticfc.co.uk, www.celticfc.net; 11am-2:30pm; adult/concession £8.50/£5.50; no tours on match days). Take a stadium tour to experience the history and passion of Celtic, the green half of Glasgow's "Old Firm," viewing trophies, jerseys and other memorabilia.

Rangers Football Club (Ibrox Stadium, 150 Edmiston Drive, Glasgow G51 2XD, ☎ 870-600 1972, fax 870-600 1978, www.rangers.co.uk; tours Thurs-Fri, 10:30am-12:30pm and 2:30pm; Sun, 10:30am-4:30pm; adult/concession £7/£5). The blue half of Glasgow's "Old Firm" also provides stadium tours.

Glasgow

THE "OLD FIRM" GAME

Legendary Liverpool football manager Bill Shankly once made the famous quote that football (soccer) is much more serious than a matter of life and death. There is no better illustration of this than the fierce rivalry between Glasgow's "Old Firm" – Celtic and Rangers – whose clashes ignite the city with their passion, furious intensity and inevitable controversy.

The sectarian divide between the rival supporters dates back to a time when Catholics would support Celtic and Protestants would support Rangers, but the vast majority of today's rivalry is only loosely based on religion. Such has been the monotonous domination the Glasgow giants hold over Scottish football that there have been moves for them to play in the English league. However, irrespective of whether they meet in the Scottish league, English league or European competition, every time Celtic and Rangers take to the same pitch is likely to be a fiery occasion.

■ City Tours

Open-Top Bus Tours

City Sightseeing Glasgow (153 Queen Street, Glasgow, G1 3BJ, ☎ 141-204 0444, fax 141-248 6582, info@scotguide.com, www.scotguide.com; regular daily departures from George Square; adult/concession/child/family £8/£6/£3/£19.50). Guided sightseeing tours by open-top bus to many of Glasgow's top visitor attractions. Hop-on, hop-off capability makes this an ideal way to get around the city, and tour tickets provide a second day's travel on the tour bus at no additional cost, with discounted entry to several attractions.

Walking Tours

 Mercat Glasgow (25 Forth Road, Bearsden G61 1JT, ☎/fax 141-586 5378, info@mercat-glasgow.co.uk, www.mercat-glasgow.co.uk; adult £6-£7, discounts available). Horror- and history-themed Glasgow tours, which can include a light buffet, drinks and quiz. Bookings are sometimes required – phone to check.

Journeyman Tours (☎ 800-093 9984, bookings@journeymantours.co.uk, www.journeymantours.co.uk). Excellent Glasgow tours departing from the War Memorial, George Square. The "Secrets of the Merchant City" tour describes the characters, architecture and important events that influenced the old city (Sun-Thurs, 7:30pm; adult/concession/child £5/£4/£2.50). "The Glasgow Fling" is a superb evening of bizarre stories, laughs, drinks and dance in Glasgow's oldest pubs and ceilidh clubs (Fri-Sat, 7pm-12 midnight; £15 including tour, drink and ceilidh admission).

■ Entertainment

Glasgow offers a huge range of entertainment for concert-goers, opera aficionados, theater lovers and dance fans. Spectacular productions by **Scottish Opera**, avant garde performances at the **Citizens Theatre**, the **RSNO Summer Proms** (see below), innovative dances from **Scottish Ballet**; and annual festivals such as the **West End Festival**, **International Jazz Festival** and **Celtic Connections**, reinforce Glasgow's reputation as one of Europe's most vibrant cultural capitals.

TIP: *The best guide to entertainment in Glasgow (and Edinburgh) is* The List *(www.list.co.uk), a twice-monthly magazine listing and reviewing film, music, theater, dance, art, clubs, sport and other events, available from newsagents (£2.20).*

■ Theater & Concerts

The Arches (253 Argyle Street, Glasgow G2 8DL, ☎ 141-565 1023, fax 141-565 1001, info@thearches.co.uk, www.thearches.co.uk). A varied artistic program of theater, music, nightclubs, exhibitions, fashion and cultural festivals in an unusual venue – a series of Victorian railway arches.

Citizens Theatre (119 Gorbals Street, Glasgow G5 9DS, ☎ 141-429 0022, fax 141-429 7374, info@citz.co.uk, www.citz.co.uk). Housed in a Victorian auditorium with two modern studio theaters, this producing company has a strong reputation for presenting British and European classics.

Glasgow Royal Concert Hall (2 Sauchiehall Street, Glasgow G2 3NY, ☎ 141-353 8000, fax 141-353 8001, www.grch.com). The city's most prestigious venue offers a variety of performances by world-famous artists and events throughout the year.

Scottish Exhibition & Conference Centre (Glasgow G3 8YW, ☎ 141-248 3000, fax 141-226 3423, info@secc.co.uk, www.secc.co.uk). Located on the north bank of the River Clyde, the **SECC** is an ultra-modern hall that looks like a cross between an armadillo and a croissant, and hosts a variety of rock, pop and classical concerts, conferences, events and exhibitions.

Royal Scottish National Orchestra (73 Claremont Street, Glasgow G3 8EP, ☎ 141-225 3500, fax 141-225 3505, info@rsno.org.uk, www.rsno.org.uk). Scotland's national symphony orchestra is based in Glasgow and performs regularly at the Glasgow Royal Concert Hall. Events include the **Summer Proms** in June, classical concerts October to April, and contemporary and popular music throughout the year.

Scottish Ballet (261 West Princes Street, Glasgow G4 9EE, ☎ 141-331 2931, fax 141-331 2629, promo@scottishballet.co.uk, www.scottishballet.co.uk) Scotland's national dance company performs regularly at the **Theatre Royal** (282 Hope Street, Glasgow G2 3QA, ☎ 141-332 3321) and at other venues throughout Scotland.

Scottish Opera (39 Elmbank Crescent, Glasgow G2 4PT, ☎ 141-332 9000, fax 141-221 8812, info@scottishopera.org.uk, www.scottishopera.org.uk). Scotland's national opera company is based at the **Theatre Royal** (282 Hope Street, Glasgow G2 3QA, ☎ 141-332 3321) and regularly tours Edinburgh, Aberdeen and Inverness.

■ Cinema

 Glasgow Film Theatre (12 Rose Street, Glasgow G3 6RB, ☎ 141-332 8128, fax 141-332 7945, info@gft.org.uk, www.gft.org.uk). One of Britain's original and most successful independent art house cinemas. Housed within a wonderful post-Art Deco building, the theater shows the best of world-wide films, new British and Scottish releases, classic genres and special events.

■ Comedy

The Stand Comedy Club (333 Woodlands Road, Glasgow G3 6NG, ☎ 870-600 6055, fax 141-337 3976, www.thestand.co.uk). Offers live contemporary comedy from Wednesday-Sunday. Weekend shows feature good-quality stand-up.

■ Shopping

Glasgow is the largest retail center in the UK outside London and offers everything from ultra-modern shopping complexes such as **Buchanan Galleries**, the **St Enoch Centre** (Europe's largest glass structure) and designer boutiques to open air markets, the specialty shops of the Merchant City and the antique and rare book shops hidden in the lanes of the West End. Away from the city, the area's market towns and villages boast antique shops, craft workshops and garden centers.

Antiques & Art

Tim Wright Antiques (147 Bath Street, Glasgow G2 4SQ, ☎/fax 141-221 0364, www.timwright-antiques.com). Glasgow's largest antique shop has been established for over 30 years and has six showrooms.

Cyril Gerber Fine Art (148 West Regent Street, Glasgow G2 2RQ, ☎ 141-221 3095/204 0276, fax 141-248 1322). Specialists in British paintings from the 19th and 20th centuries, including regular stocks of "Scottish colorists" and the "Glasgow Boys," a group of young painters whose work challenged 19th-century artistic traditions (see the **Burrell Collection**, page 159).

F.W. Holroyd Gallery (9-11 George Street, Glasgow G1 1PY, ☎ 141-552 2024, fax 141-552 2025, www.holroydgallery.co.uk). Framing gallery that also sells original watercolors, prints and oil paintings, with a tax-free facility for non-EU visitors.

Clothing & Highland Dress

Geoffrey (Tailor) Kiltmakers (309 Sauchiehall Street, Glasgow G2 3HW, ☎ 141-331 2388, fax 141-332 0506, enquiries@geoffreykilts.co.uk, www.geoffreykilts.co.uk). One of Scotland's top kiltmakers and Highland outfitters, which recently launched its own range of 21st-century kilts and has its own weaving mill next to Edinburgh Castle.

Hector Russell – R.G. Lawrie (110 Buchanan Street, Glasgow G1 2JN, ☎ 141-221 0217, fax 141-204 3971, www.hector-russell.com). Highland dress specialist offering woolens, tartans, cashmere knitwear, souvenirs and jewelry.

Scottish Goods & Specialty Gifts

Gift Merchant (5 Merchant Square, 71-73 Albion Street, Glasgow G1 1NY, ☎/fax 141-552 8269). A large selection of quality gifts situated in the historic Old Fruitmarket within the Merchant City.

Stockwell Bazaar (67 Glassford Street, Glasgow G1 1UB, ☎ 141-552 5781, fax 141-553 1925, www.stockwellbazaar.co.uk). Specialist retailer of porcelain, china, crystal, gifts, cookware and collectibles, with world-wide export and tax-free services available.

Jewelers

Henderson The Jeweller (217 Sauchiehall Street, Glasgow G2 3EX, ☎ 141-331 2569, fax 141-331 1665, www.hendersonjewellers.co.uk). Situated in a historic building designed by Charles Rennie Mackintosh, Henderson stocks extensive ranges of diamonds, jewelry and gifts, many based on Mackintosh's designs.

Orro (12 Wilson Street, Merchant City, Glasgow G1 1SS, ☎ 141-552 7888, fax 141-552 8987). Minimalist shop with innovative, contemporary jewelry collections from leading international designers.

Markets

The Barras (between Gallowgate and London Road, near Glasgow Green, ☎ 141-552 4601, fax 141-552 4997, manager@glasgow-barras.com, www.glasgow-barrowland.com; open Sat-Sun, 9am-5pm). Glasgow's famous weekend market has 1,000 traders and 150 shopkeepers selling all manner of goods from labyrinthine indoor malls and outdoor stalls. Search for bargains, including bric-a-brac, clothing, food, music and even fireplace surrounds and other home furnishings. Cries of "Bacca!" and "Tobacco!" from stall-less vendors of cigarettes and packet tobacco parody the once mighty tobacco lords who once made Glasgow great.

Paddy's Market (The Bridgegate, alternatively the "Briggait," Glasgow). This well-known street market gained its name from the impecunious Irish immigrants who frequented it. Its rough-and-ready appearance, miscellaneous goods on offer (everything from a second-hand cardigan to a Charles Rennie Mackintosh fireplace) and haphazard stall arrangement have made its name synonymous with any untidy place.

Glasgow

■ Where To Stay

City Center

Hotels

Langs Hotel (2 Port Dundas Place, Glasgow G2 3LD, ☎ 141-333 1500, fax 141-333 5700, www.langshotel.co.uk; B&B ££££). Located in the heart of Glasgow's buzzy theater district, Langs is a stylish, contemporary hotel providing spacious, well-designed accommodation in bright, loft-style rooms. Bedrooms have all the latest in entertainment technology and the **Oshi Spa** is very popular. The fresh fruit at breakfast is excellent.

Thistle (Cambridge Street, Glasgow G2 3HN, ☎ 141-332 3311, fax 141-332 4050, glasgow@thistle.co.uk, www.thistlehotels.com/glasgow; B&B £££). A modern, high-quality hotel well located for central shopping and entertainment. There is a health club and free parking.

Arthouse Hotel (129 Bath Street, Glasgow G2 2SY, ☎ 141-221 6789, fax 141-221 6777, info@arthousehotel.com, www.arthousehotel.com; B&B ££££). The 1911 building was restored in 1999 to provide spacious and beautifully chic, almost extravagant, accommodation. The busy **Arthouse Grill** serves everything from simple grills and salads to fine dining.

Bewleys Hotel (110 Bath Street Glasgow G2 2EN, ☎ 141-353 0800, fax 141-353 0900, gla@bewleyshotels.com, www.bewleyshotels.com; B&B ££££). Modern hotel in the heart of the city with spacious and well-equipped bedrooms.

Malmaison (278 West George Street, Glasgow G2 4LL, ☎ 141-572 1000, fax 141-572 1002, glasgow@malmaison.com, www.malmaison.com; B&B ££££). A striking, converted Greek church in the heart of the business district. The rooms and suites are individually designed, some with mezzanines, others with French windows. All have CD players, personal bars and city art. The atmospheric **Brasserie Bar** in the vaulted basement serves classic French food and excellent wines.

Milton Hotel & Leisure Club (27 Washington Street, Glasgow G3 8AZ, ☎ 141-222 2929, fax 141-270 2301, sales@miltonhotels.com, www.miltonhotels.com; B&B £££-££££). New, city center hotel with a choice of feng shui-designed bedrooms or luxury apartments. The hotel has superb leisure facilities, including pool, sauna, steam room, Jacuzzi and gym.

Pipers' Tryst Hotel (30-34 McPhater Street, Cowcaddens, Glasgow G4 0HW, ☎ 141-353 5551, fax 141-353 1570, hotel@thepipingcentre.co.uk, www.thepipingcentre.co.uk; B&B ££). The

HOTEL PRICE CHART	
Per person, per night, based on double occupancy in high season. B&B rate includes breakfast; DB&B includes dinner and breakfast.	
£	Under £20
££	£21-£35
£££	£36-£50
££££	£51-£80
£££££	Over £80

cozy hotel is next to the National Piping Centre and offers quality accommodation and the **Pipers' Tryst Café Bar**, which serves an all-day menu of light lunches, snacks and evening meals (with live Celtic music on Saturday nights).

Quality Hotel (99 Gordon Street, Glasgow G1 3SF, ☎ 141-221 9680, fax 141-226 3948, enquiries@quality-hotels-glasgow.com, www.quality-hotels-glasgow.com; B&B ££). Large, traditional hotel next to Central Station. Historic claims to fame include: John Logie Baird transmitted the first television pictures from here in 1927, Winston Churchill once reserved a whole floor and Roy Rogers booked a room for his horse Trigger while staying here. Horses aren't so welcome nowadays but it's a fine hotel nevertheless.

Radisson SAS (301 Argyle Street, Glasgow G2 8DL, ☎ 141-204 3333, fax 141-204 3344, reservations.glasgow@radissonsas.com, www.radissonsas.com; B&B £££-££££). Large and imposing hotel in the heart of Glasgow. The interior boasts a contemporary, designer style with chic finishes and there is a large leisure club and choice of restaurants and bars.

Tulip Inn (80 Ballater Street, Glasgow G5 0TW, ☎ 141-429 4233, fax 141-429 4244, info@tulipinnglasgow.co.uk, www.tulipinnglasgow.co.uk; B&B ££). A modern functional hotel on the south bank of the river a short walk from the city center. **Bibo** bistro provides good value, though limited choice dining.

Guest Houses & B&Bs

 The Flower House B&B (33 St Vincent Crescent, Glasgow G3 8NG, ☎ 141-204 2846, fax 141-226 5130, sweaterheads@bigfoot.com, www.scotland2000.com/flowerhouse; B&B ££). This restored 1846 Victorian listed building retains many original architectural features and is furnished with fine antiques and period furniture. The attractive bedrooms are individually styled, some with brass beds and chandeliers. Breakfast is served in your room.

McLays Guest House (264-276 Renfrew Street, Charing Cross, Glasgow G3 6TT, ☎ 141-332 4796, fax 141-353 0422, info@mclays.com, www.mclays.com; B&B ££). The hotel is in the heart of Glasgow and comprises three interlinked townhouses. There are 62 rooms, of which 39 have private bathrooms.

Merchant Lodge (52 Virginia Street, Glasgow G1 1TY, ☎ 141-552 2424, fax 141-552 4747, themerchant@ukonline.co.uk, www.the-merchant-lodge.sagenet.co.uk; B&B ££). In the heart of the Merchant City, one of Glasgow's oldest buildings – the former home of a tobacco lord – boasts a private cobbled courtyard and one of the last stone turnpike stairs still in use. It provides reasonable accommodation with a good breakfast menu.

The Old School House (194 Renfrew Street, Glasgow G3 6TX ☎ 141-332 7600, fax 141-332 8684, jamesjoyes@oldschoolhouse.freeserve.co.uk; B&B ££). An attractive, listed Georgian villa set in its own gardens provides cozy, reasonably priced accommodation.

Victorian House Hotel (212 Renfrew Street, Glasgow G3 6TX, ☎ 141-332 0129, fax 141-353 3155, info@thevictorian.co.uk, www.thevictorian.co.uk;

Glasgow

B&B ££). Set in a terrace of traditional townhouses, the hotel offers individually-styled bedrooms, some with polished pine floors, and a spacious, pine-beamed breakfast room, which serves a great menu, including kippers, smoked haddock, haggis and potato scones.

West End

Hotels

One Devonshire Gardens (1 Devonshire Gardens, Glasgow G12 0UX, ☎ 141-339 2001, fax 141-337 1663, www.onedevonshiregardens.com; B&B £££££). An intimate, top-quality hotel offering timeless elegance, sophisticated luxury and Michelin-starred cuisine – probably the best hotel in Glasgow. There are only 39 bedrooms but they're huge, and combine traditional splendor with modern chic. Celebrity chef Gordon Ramsay is in charge at the hotel's **Amaryllis** restaurant.

Guest Houses & B&Bs

Kirklee Hotel (11 Kensington Gate, Glasgow G12 9LG, ☎ 141-334 5555, fax 141-339 3828, kirklee@clara.net, www.scotland2000.com /kirklee; B&B ££). The imposing Edwardian house boasts many period features, including an ornate doorway, paneled hallway, original art and antique furniture. The bedrooms aren't quite as ornate but are very comfortable.

Number Thirty Six (36 St Vincent Crescent, Glasgow G3 8NG, ☎ 141-248 2086, fax 141-221 1477, no36@no36.co.uk, www.no36.co.uk; B&B ££). The artistically designed bedrooms are furnished in natural woods and fabrics and include double walk-in showers. A continental breakfast is served in your room.

Sandyford Hotel (904 Sauchiehall Street, Glasgow G3 7TF, ☎ 141-334 0000, fax 141-337 1812, info@sandyfordhotelglasgow.com, www.sandyfordhotelglasgow.com; B&B ££). This long-established hotel offers simple but comfortable bedrooms with polished pine floors. There is unrestricted parking to the side and rear.

The Town House (4 Hughenden Terrace, Glasgow G12 9XR, ☎ 141-357 0862, fax 141-339 9605, hospitality@thetownhouseglasgow.com, www.thetownhouseglasgow.com; B&B ££-£££). An attractive hotel set in a high-ceilinged townhouse. The interior is elegant and comfortable, with a real fire in the lounge, spacious bedrooms and seafood choices at breakfast. There is limited room service of home-made soup and sandwiches, and ample free parking.

■ Where To Eat

You can easily eat your way around the world in Glasgow, as the city's culinary renaissance continues unabated. The greatest concentration of eateries is around **Byres Road** in the West End, where the student population ensures cheap, stylish places to eat. The **Merchant City**

contains most of the expensive designer brasseries, although many of the central bars serve good food at reasonable prices.

City Center

L'Ariosto Restaurant (92-94 Mitchell Street, Glasgow G1 3NQ, ☎ 141-221 0971/221 8543, fax 141-226 5718, info@lariosto.com, www.lariosto.com; lunch ££, dinner £££). Traditional Italian restaurant serving some of the finest and freshest food in Glasgow in a friendly, relaxed atmosphere. There is live music Tuesday-Saturday evenings.

Art House Grill (129 Bath Street, Glasgow G2 2SY, ☎ 141-221 6789, fax 141-221-6777, info@arthousehotel.com, www.arthousehotel.com; ££). A stylish fusion of international cuisine in a fresh, contemporary setting and lively atmosphere.

Babbity Bowster (16-18 Blackfriars Street, Glasgow G1 1PE, ☎ 141-552 5055, fax 141-552 7774; lunch £, dinner ££-£££). A wonderful late-18th-century Robert Adam building housing an ever-popular café-bar, which serves a traditional Scottish and French menu with flair. Upstairs the **Schottische** restaurant serves fine Scottish food, including diet-busting puddings, at reasonable prices.

La Bonne Auberge (161 West Nile Street, Glasgow G1 2RL, ☎ 141-352 8310, fax 141-332 7447, www.labonneauberge.co.uk; ££). High-quality, good-value food served in a charming brasserie.

Café Source (1 St Andrew's Square, Glasgow G1 5PP, ☎ 141-548 6020, fax 141-548 6029, www.cafesource.co.uk; £-££). A stylish and cozy bar-bistro set below an elegant converted church in a quiet city center square. An interesting menu includes mussels, oysters, toasted sandwiches, reasonably priced main courses and a wide selection of wines, beers and malts.

Canton Express (407 Sauchiehall Street, Glasgow, ☎ 141-332 0145; £). No-frills, reasonable quality, cheap and filling Chinese fast food served until the early hours.

City Merchant (97-99 Candleriggs, Glasgow G1 1NP, ☎ 141-553 1577, fax 141-553 1588, www.citymerchant.co.uk; ££). Top-quality Scottish meat and game, superb fish and seafood, served in a good atmosphere with excellent value two and three-course set menus.

Glasgow Noodle Bar (482 Sauchiehall Street, Glasgow, ☎ 141-333 1883; £). Cheap and cheerful Oriental fast food eaten from disposable containers with plastic chopsticks or forks – perfect after a heavy night on the town.

Café Mao (84 Brunswick Street, Glasgow G1 1ZZ, ☎ 141-564 5161, fax 141-564 5163,

DINING PRICE CHART	
Indicates the price per person for a full meal, excluding drinks. Generally three courses, though fixed menus of five or more courses may be available.	
£	Under £10
££	£11-£20
£££	£21-£30
££££	£31-£40

Glasgow

info@cafemao.com, www.cafemao.com; ££-£££). A good range of fish, meat and vegetarian dishes cooked in an exotic Asian fusion style.

Rococo (202 West George Street, Glasgow G2 2NR, ☎ 141-221 5004, fax 141-221 5006, res@rococoglasgow.com, www.restaurantrococo.com; lunch ££, dinner £££-££££). Intimate surroundings, stylish décor and classic dishes skilfully cooked with contemporary flavors combine to create one of Glasgow's finest restaurants.

West End

Air Organic (36 Kelvingrove Street, Glasgow, ☎ 141-564 5200; ££-£££). Set above a pub, the ultra-cool bistro serves great organic food, including great Thai and Japanese dishes and excellent sushi.

Amaryllis (1 Devonshire Gardens, Glasgow G12 0UX, ☎ 141-337 3434, fax 141-339 0047, amaryllis@gordonramsay.com; open Wed-Sun, bookings recommended; ££££). Not much more needs to be said about Amaryllis other than it's run by Gordon Ramsay, probably Britain's best chef, and that it's located in One Devonshire Gardens, probably Glasgow's finest hotel.

Mr Singh's India (149 Elderslie Street, Glasgow G3 7JR, ☎ 141-221 1452, fax 141-248 6504; lunch £, dinner ££). Kilted waiting staff serve innovative and exotic Indian cuisine. Reserve on weekends.

Mother India (28 Westminster Terrace, Glasgow G3 7RU, ☎ 141-221 1663, fax 141-221 2217; lunch £, dinner ££). Excellent Indian cooking, including a strong vegetarian selection, at affordable prices, served in a friendly and informal atmosphere. There are cheap set lunch and early evening menus, but you need to bring your own alcohol as they have no drinks license.

Stravaigin (28 Gibson Street, Kelvinbridge, Glasgow G12 8NX, ☎ 141-334 2665, fax 141-334 4099, mailbox@stravaigin.com, www.stravaigin.com; ££-£££). Exotic Asian flavors meet prime Scottish ingredients to produce top-quality food. Upstairs is a café-bar where you can sample some of that fabulous food at more affordable prices.

There is an extension to the successful theme at **Stravaigin 2** (8 Ruthven Lane, Glasgow G12 9BG, ☎ 141-334 7165, fax 141-357 4785, mailbox@stravaigin2.com, www.stravaigin.com; ££-£££).

Ubiquitous Chip (12 Ashton Lane, Glasgow G12 8SJ, ☎ 141-334 5007, fax 141-337 1302, enquiries@ubiquitouschip.co.uk, www.ubiquitouschip.co.uk; lunch £££, dinner ££££). A multi award-winning restaurant that remains a city favorite for top notch Scottish food, especially venison and seafood, served in a plant-filled, covered courtyard patio. There is also a phenomenal wine list and 150 malt whiskies. The upstairs bistro, **Upstairs at the Chip**, isn't quite as magical but is slightly easier on the budget (lunch ££, dinner £££).

Pubs & Bars

Glasgow has one of the liveliest pub and bar scenes in Britain, with everything from traditional Glaswegian pubs to the plushest contemporary bars. Shrinking violets and others not prepared to party should steer well clear of

Sauchiehall Street (pronounced "sockie-hall") on Friday or Saturday evenings.

Traditional Bars

 Babbity Bowster (16-18 Blackfriars Street, Glasgow G1 1PE, ☎ 141-552 5055, fax 141-552 7774). Atmospheric café-bar with a beer garden, buzzy atmosphere, wide selection of real ales and great food. There is also regular traditional Scottish music.

Blackfriars (36 Bell Street, Glasgow, ☎ 141-552 5924). A Merchant City favorite that serves a vast range of beers, lagers and excellent pub grub *(£)*. There is also live music and comedy on weekends and that inimitable Glasgow atmosphere.

The Horse Shoe Bar (17 Drury Street, Glasgow, ☎ 141-229 5711). The classic Victorian gin palace's bar is the longest in the UK, so it shouldn't take long to get served with a fine real ale. There is an incredibly good-value lunch (three courses £3.20) served until 2:30pm.

Molly Malones (224 Hope Street, Glasgow G2 2UG, ☎/fax 141-332 2757). Traditional bar-restaurant serving hearty food and good craic (banter). There is nightly live entertainment ranging from traditional Scottish/Irish folk to Celtic rock.

Scotia (112 Stockwell Street, Glasgow G1 4LW, ☎ 141-552 8681). Low ceilings and wooden beams support the Scotia's status as Glasgow's oldest pub (1792). It has great folk music on weekends, and is popular with writers, poets and drinking thinkers (or thinking drinkers).

Uisge Beatha (232-246 Woodlands Road, Glasgow, ☎ 141-564 1596). This old-style bar is full of stuffed animals and quirky décor but more importantly offers a selection of 120 whiskies ("uisge beatha" is Gaelic for "water of life," better known as whisky!).

Modern Bars

Bargo (80 Albion Street, Glasgow, ☎ 141-553 4771). Stylish designer bar serving excellent value bar snacks and good-quality meals (£-££).

Corinthian (191 Ingram Street, Glasgow G1 1PA, ☎ 141-552 1101, fax 141-559 6826, info@corinthian.uk.com, www.corinthian.uk.com). A stunning Victorian interior housed within a magnificent domed building provides a cocktail bar, piano bar and casual restaurant-café (dining ££-£££).

Malmaison Brasserie Champagne Bar (278 West George Street, Glasgow G2 4LL, ☎ 141-572 1003, fax 141-572 1002, glasgow@malmaison.com, www.malmaison.com). A super-stylish (you enter by descending a grand spiral staircase) but relaxed bar.

Nice 'N' Sleazy Bar Café (421 Sauchiehall Street, Glasgow G2 3LG, ☎/fax 141-333 0900). Glasgow's alternative music scene hangout, with live bands most nights.

Outside Glasgow

Outside Glasgow

■ Attractions & Sights

Paisley Abbey (Abbey Close, Paisley PA1 1JG, ☎ 141-889 7654, fax 141-887 3929, www.paisleyabbey.org.uk; open Mon-Sat, 10am-3:30pm, Sun for services only). The magnificent abbey was founded in 1163 when Walter Fitzalan, High Steward to David I, signed a charter to found a Cluniac priory. The priory achieved abbey status in 1245 although much of the original building was burned in 1307 by Edward I of England during the Wars of Independence. The abbey was restored during the 14th century but disaster struck again when the tower collapsed in 1553, destroying the roof. The roof remained open for the next 300 years until 1858 when repair work began. The abbey contains a memorial to **Marjorie Bruce**, daughter of Robert the Bruce and wife of Walter Stewart. Her son **Robert II** became the first Stewart king. Marjorie, along with Robert II's wives and Robert III, is buried at the abbey. In addition to the royal tombs the abbey also has beautiful stained glass windows, the **Barochan Cross** and fine choir stalls.

At the time of the Reformation, in 1560, the monastery was disbanded and the walled-off nave became Paisley's parish church. The transepts and choir remained in ruins until the late 19th and early 20th centuries when they were restored to create one of the finest churches in Scotland.

Coats Observatory (49 Oakshaw Street West, Paisley PA1 2DE, ☎ 141-889 2013, fax 141-889 9240, www.renfrewshire.gov.uk; public viewing Oct-Mar, Thurs, 7:30pm-9:30pm, weather permitting). This stunning working Victorian observatory was built by the Coats family in 1883. There are displays on astronomy, astronautics, seismology and meteorology.

Clydebuilt (The Scottish Maritime Museum at Braehead, King's Inch Road, Glasgow G51 4BN; ☎ 141-886 1013, fax 141-886 1015, www.scottishmaritimemuseum.org; open Mon-Thurs & Sat, 10am-6pm; Sun, 11am-5pm; adult/concession/family £3.50/£1.75/£0.80). A fascinating museum describing the development of Glasgow and the River Clyde from the early days of the tobacco, sugar and rum trades, through iron and heavy industry to one of the most important eras in the city's history: shipbuilding. A realistic demonstration shows men riveting and painting the side of a ship. Scale models show several of the famous vessels built on the Clyde. Interactive displays allow visitors to try their hand at piloting a ship into port (not as easy as it sounds!), loading cargo without capsizing the vessel, handling a welding gun and riveting. A highlight is the newsreel footage reflecting on the demise of Clyde shipbuilding – a film that has brought tears to the eyes of former Clyde shipbuilders. This is an excellent museum but it can be infuriatingly difficult to find, lost as it is among huge shopping warehouses with inadequate signposting. It's off the M8 (Junction 26 eastbound or Junction 25a westbound); head for the Braehead Shoping Centre and Green parking area.

■ Adventures

On Foot

Only 30 minutes by car from central Glasgow, **Clyde Muirshiel Regional Park** (Calder Glen Road, By Lochwinnoch, Renfrewshire, ☎ 1505-842 882, fax 1505-613 605, info@clydemuirshiel.co.uk, www.clydemuirshiel.co.uk) provides a wide variety of walks and trails in over 100 scenic square miles. Tracks and trails provide easy access to woods, hills and moors with fine views over the Firth of Clyde. The Barytes Mine track walk extends 2½-five miles. There is an information point, gift shop, ranger service and events. See the web site for map and directions.

The 40-mile (65-km) **Clyde Walkway** links Glasgow city center to New Lanark in South Lanarkshire. The walkway begins near the Science Centre and extends through the scenic Clyde Valley, passing the spectacular Falls of Clyde.

The **Forth & Clyde Canal** stretches 35 miles to link Scotland's east and west coasts via Grangemouth on the River Forth and Bowling on the River Clyde. A circular, six-mile route between Craigmarloch and Twechar (Quarry Inn) lets walkers combine an 18th-century towpath with the 2nd-century Antonine Wall.

The **North Calder Heritage Trail** is a new 10-mile trail across North Lanarkshire. It starts at Summerlee Heritage Park (Heritage Way, Coatbridge ML5 1QD, ☎ 1236-431 261, www.northlan.gov.uk), a 25-acre site displaying industrial and social life from the 19th/20th centuries. From there the route follows the Monkland Canal and North Calder Water to Hillend Reservoir, east of Airdrie.

On Wheels

The **Glasgow to Loch Lomond Cycleway** is a popular 21-mile (34-km) route for both cyclists and walkers. The route starts at **Bell's Bridge** opposite the Scottish Exhibition and Conference Centre (SECC), half a mile west of central Glasgow. The route runs west parallel to the **River Clyde**, following a disused railway line from Partick through Whiteinch, Scotstoun and Yoker to Clydebank. From there it follows the towpath of the Forth & Clyde Canal through Dalmuir and Old Kilpatrick to Bowling. The stretch from Bowling is an off-road path leading to Dumbarton, capital of the ancient kingdom of Strathclyde. **Dumbarton castle** (HS; ☎ 1389-732 167) was an important medieval stronghold and entry point to western Scotland. From Dumbarton the route follows the banks of the River Leven to its source in Loch Lomond at Balloch.

The cycleway passes close to many stations on the Glasgow-Balloch railway line so if cycling becomes too strenuous you can travel the rest of the way by train. These run every half-hour, daily, and cycles are carried free of charge.

On Water

Clyde Marine Cruises (Victoria Harbour, Greenock PA15 1HW, ☎ 1475-721 281, fax 1475-888 023, enquiries@clyde-marine.co.uk, www.clyde-marine.co.uk). View the Cumbrae Isles and Arran's peaks from the sea, or cruise through the Kiles of Bute, along the way looking out for seals, porpoises and seabirds.

 The **Waverley** (Anderston Quay, Glasgow G3 8HA, ☎ 845-130 4647, fax 141-248 2150, info@waverleyexcursions.co.uk, www.waverleyexcursions.co.uk; July-Aug, departures from Glasgow Fri-Mon). *Waverley*, the world's last seagoing paddle steamer, was built on the Clyde in 1947. Today it offers gentle day, afternoon and evening cruises to the peaceful lochs and islands from the Firth of Clyde.

Pride o' The Clyde (Broomielaw/Braehead, Glasgow G1 4NR, ☎ 7711-250 969, fax 141-778 6635, alex@clydewaterbusservices.co.uk, www.clydewaterbusservices.co.uk; adult/concession £3/£2 one way, £5/£3.50 return). The Clyde water bus departs from the city center (bottom of Jamaica Street, under Central Station Bridge) and takes 30 minutes to reach Braehead Shopping Centre.

Seaforce (The Tall Ship, Glasgow Harbour, 100 Stobcross Road, Glasgow G3 8QQ, ☎/fax 141-221 1070, info@seaforce.co.uk, www.seaforce.co.uk). A powerboat tour is an unusual way to see Glasgow, the estuary and sea lochs. Tours last 30 minutes to four hours.

SHIPBUILDING ON THE CLYDE

Between the 1860s and 1960s the reputation of Clyde shipbuilding was unsurpassed and the region became one of the world's greatest shipbuilding areas. Yards lined the banks of the river and produced thousands of ships, including some of the most famous liners and warships ever built: *Lusitania*, *Aquitania*, *Queen Mary*, *Queen Elizabeth*, *Queen Elizabeth 2*, the former Royal Yacht *Britannia*, HMS *Ramillies* and HMS *Hood*. The Clyde's reputation for quality and innovation made it particularly popular with the Admiralty, and almost a quarter of all Royal Navy ships built between 1868 and 1914 were built on the Clyde.

The depression of the 1930s hit the shipyards badly and even the fanfare launch of the *Queen Mary* in 1934 only served to raise false hopes of a new dawn. Wartime demand for ships, weapons and munitions kept the yards busy but shipbuilding was already in terminal decline. Success made the yards complacent and reluctant to modernize; unions resisted changes to working practices. The yards became uncompetitive and shipbuilding orders went elsewhere. Yards amalgamated and many closed. Of the more than 30 yards that once prospered along the Clyde and employed thousands, only two survive – ghosts of the glory days of Clyde shipbuilding.

On Horseback

 Ardgowan Riding Centre (Bankfoot Farm, Inverkip, Greenock PA16 0DT, on the A78 between Greenock and Inverkip, ☎ 1475-521 390, fax 1475-529 288, info@ardgowan-riding.co.uk, www.riding-ardgowan.co.uk). A variety of riding activities, including show-jumping, cross-country, hacks through a private country estate and lessons for all levels.

■ Golf

 The Glasgow area is not an obvious golf destination but has over 80 parkland, moorland and heathland courses ranging from championship venues to testing nine-hole courses. **Haggs Castle** on Glasgow's south side was the venue for the Glasgow Classic, later to become the Bell's Scottish Open.

Greenock Golf Course (18-hole inland, 5,888 yards; Forsyth Street, Greenock PA16 8RE, one mile southwest of Greenock on the A8, ☎ 1475-720 793, fax 1475-791 912; green fees £20-£25). Testing moorland course with trees defining many of the tight fairways and small undulating greens, and the odd stream and bunker to catch the unwary.

Haggs Castle Golf Course (18-hole inland, 6,426 yards; 70 Dumbreck Road, Dumbreck, Glasgow G41 4SN, three miles southwest of Glasgow on the M77, ☎/fax 141-427 1157; green fees £35). A challenging, wooded parkland course used as a venue for both the Scottish National Championships and Scottish Open.

Pollok Golf Course (18-hole inland, 6,358 yards; 90 Barrhead Road, Glasgow G43 1BG, four miles southwest of Glasgow on the A762, ☎ 141-632 4351, fax 141-649 1398; green fees £32-£40). Mature wooded, parkland course founded in 1892 and set in the **Pollok Estate**, which includes the **Burrell Gallery** and **Pollok House**.

■ Wildlife Watching

Lochwinnoch RSPB Nature Reserve (18 miles west of Glasgow, between Paisley and Largs, ☎ 1505-842 663; reserve open at all times, Visitor Centre open 10am-5pm; adult/concession/child/family £2/£1/£0.50/£4). Lying within the Clyde Muirshiel Regional Park (see page 173), Lochwinnoch is one of the few wetland sites remaining in west Scotland. There is a viewing tower with telescopes giving good views over the marshland, home to wildfowl and goosanders in the winter and great-crested grebes and lapwings in the spring.

■ Shopping

Edinburgh Woollen Mill (New Lanark World Heritage Site, South Lanarkshire ML11 9DB, ☎ 1555-662 322). One of the largest Edinburgh Woollen Mill outlets in Scotland offers a wide selection of traditional & contemporary knitwear, country classics, gifts and souvenirs.

Outside Glasgow

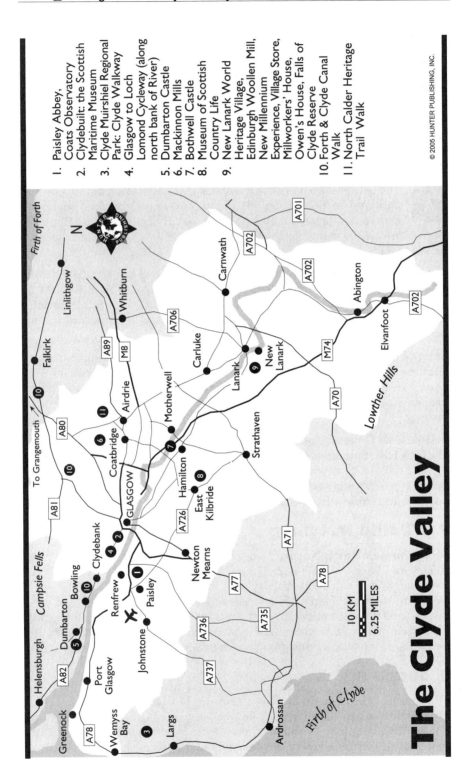

1. Paisley Abbey,
   Coats Observatory
2. Clydebuilt: the Scottish
   Maritime Museum
3. Clyde Muirshiel Regional
   Park: Clyde Walkway
4. Glasgow to Loch
   Lomond Cycleway (along
   north bank of River)
5. Dumbarton Castle
6. Mackinnon Mills
7. Bothwell Castle
8. Museum of Scottish
   Country Life
9. New Lanark World
   Heritage Village,
   Edinburgh Woollen Mill,
   New Millennium
   Experience, Village Store,
   Millworkers' House,
   Owen's House, Falls of
   Clyde Reserve
10. Forth & Clyde Canal
    Walk
11. North Calder Heritage
    Trail Walk

© 2005 HUNTER PUBLISHING, INC.

The Clyde Valley

Mackinnon Mills (Kirkshaws Road, Coatbridge ML5 4SL, ☎ 1236-440 702, fax 1236-426 193). A wide selection of clothing, gifts, linen, footwear and a large golf shop together with a designer zone selling labels such as DKNY, YSL and Helly Hansen. There is free parking, a restaurant and coffee shop.

Clyde River Valley

 The River Clyde played a vital role in the development of Glasgow but it also left its influence on the upstream towns and communities (southeast of Glasgow). Nowhere was this influence felt more strongly than at **New Lanark**, where the power of the river was harnessed to sustain an enterprising mill village – now a World Heritage Site – with a nearby gorge and spectacular waterfall (see page 179).

 INFORMATION SOURCES: There are tourism offices at **Hamilton** (Road Chef Services, M74 northbound, Hamilton, ☎ 1698-285 590, fax 1698-891 494, hamilton@seeglasgow-.com), **Lanark** (Horsemarket, Ladyacre Road, ☎ 1555-661 661, fax 1555-661 143, lanark@seeglasgow.com), **Biggar** (155 High Street, Biggar, ☎/fax 1899-221 066; open Easter-Oct) and **Abington** (Welcome Break Motorway Service Area, M74 Junction 13, Abington, ☎ 1864-502 436, fax 1864-502 571, abington@seeglasgow.com).

■ Attractions & Sights

 Bothwell Castle (HS; Uddingston, off the B7071, ☎ 1698-816 894; open April-Sept, 9:30am-6:30pm; Oct-Mar, 9:30am-4:30pm; closing days vary in winter, call ahead; adult/concession/child £2.50/£1.60/£0.75). The ruins of Scotland's mightiest and finest 13th-century stone castle occupy a beautiful and peaceful setting overlooking the River Clyde. Built of local red sandstone, its walls glow in sunlight. The oldest part of the castle is the great donjon, a four-story keep built for Walter of Moray who became **Lord of Bothwell** in 1242. The castle was besieged, captured and recaptured several times and badly damaged during the wars with England in the early 14th century. In its last siege in 1337, the Scots recaptured the castle and partly destroyed it, although some of the original keep survives.

Most of the castle dates from the 14th-15th centuries, built by the Earls of Douglas who acquired the Lordship of Bothwell in around 1362. They patched up the original keep but built the remainder of their lodgings on the opposite side of a new courtyard. The ruins of their chapel retain their high arched windows. Fireplaces and even latrine towers in the great hall and other chambers help you imagine life in a medieval castle. The castle had become abandoned ruins by the 17th century and now houses a noisy population of pigeons.

Museum of Scottish Country Life (Wester Kittochside, Philipshill Road, East Kilbride G76 9HR, ☎ 1355-224 181/131-247 4377, fax 1355-571 290, kittochside@nms.ac.uk, www.nms.ac.uk/countrylife; open 10am-5pm; adult/concession £3/£1.50, children free). An impressive museum, based around a traditional, working farm, showing how people lived and worked in Scotland's countryside. The museum is set in 170 acres of unspoiled farmland and takes visitors back to the 1950s – when traditional farming with horses was just being replaced by tractors and combine harvesters. The museum comprises an exhibition building and separate farm.

The exhibition houses displays on the land (people have farmed Scottish land for at least 6,000 years), farming tools (including the oldest known grain threshing machine in the world and the largest collection of combine harvesters in Europe) and the everyday lives of Scotland's farmers.

A short walk away (or drive on a tractor-drawn cart) is the farm worked for over 400 years by 10 generations of the Reid family. The Georgian farmhouse was built for the 6th Laird in around 1783 and expanded in the early 20th century. It is still furnished with the original Reid family possessions and gives a good impression of their surprisingly comfortable existence. Lambs and cattle are still farmed here, albeit not on a large scale, and visitors can watch cows being milked and lambs being fed. There are daily demonstrations of 1950s farming techniques together with a full program of events and displays such as vintage tractors, Clydesdale horses, ploughing, seed time, haymaking and harvest. Many activities are seasonal – call for information.

New Lanark World Heritage Village (New Lanark Mills, Lanark ML11 9DB, ☎ 1555-661 345, fax 1555-665 738, visit@newlanark.org, www.newlanark.org; open 11am-5pm; adult/concession/family £5.95/£3.95/£16.95). An award-winning 200-year-old cotton mill village set in a dramatic gorge. New Lanark was founded in 1785 by David Dale as an industrial settlement of cotton-spinning mills (powered by water from the nearby Falls of Clyde) and tenement-style housing for its workforce. By 1820, New Lanark had become Britain's largest cotton manufacturer and supported a population of 2,500. After the mill closed in 1968 the buildings fell into disrepair, to be later rescued and beautifully restored as a visitor attraction and World Heritage Site. The village now has about 180 inhabitants.

Under the enlightened management of **Robert Owen** (son-in-law of founder David Dale) from 1800-1825, New Lanark became famous as a model society. Owen sought to realize his utopian dream of a community founded on "universal harmony." Seeking to improve the quality of life of his employees in addition to making profits, he reduced working hours, banned child labor and set up a store where villagers could buy goods cheaply, using the shop's profits to finance a new school and the intriguingly named "Institute for the Formation of Character" where workers could attend evening classes and social events.

Historic exhibits and innovative displays present the New Lanark story in several ways and vividly recreate the mill village of the 1820s. The **New Millennium Experience**, an audiovisual ride, is guided by a girl named Harmony who has traveled back from the year 2200. Housed in the same mill building is a massive working 19th-century spinning mule whose output is still sold commercially and has been used to make woolens used in the *Harry Potter* films.

The **Village Store** sold coal, clothing, household goods, food and drink. The **Millworkers' House** recreates the spartan tenements and crowded living conditions from the 1820s to the 1930s. In contrast the refurbished rooms of **Owen's House**, including his study, sitting room, nursery and basement kitchen, give an insight into the mill owner's more lavish lifestyle. A display beside the kitchen tells the story of Owen's failed attempt to create a utopian community in the USA (**Historic New Harmony**, 344 W. Church Street, New Harmony, Indiana 47631, USA, ☎ 812-682 4488, www.usi.edu).

Robert Owen's **School** recreates a classroom from the 1820s and a separate exhibition hall tells the story of the village's restoration. Also housed in the school building is possibly the most touching of the site's displays, **Annie McLeod's Story**, in which the "ghost" of Annie describes the life of the 10-year-old mill girl in the 1820s. The innocent cheerfulness with which she describes her long working hours, strict working regime and cramped living conditions (which would outrage many today but at the time represented radical social reform and a good life) could easily bring a tear to your eye! It also makes you wonder what life must have been like in the "dark satanic mills" of the time.

There is a large coffee shop, huge Edinburgh Woollen Mill store, and a gift shop that sells the Aran wool spun at the mill; there are also several smaller craft outlets around the village. Allow at least half a day to fully explore the site and leave time to walk to the Falls of Clyde (see below).

The Falls of Clyde. These three picturesque waterfalls, which powered New Lanark's success as a mill town and inspired many famous writers and painters, can be reached from New Lanark via a riverside path. The first set of falls – **Dundaff Lin** – lies just above the village. Twenty minutes up the path, uphill from the hydroelectric station, lies **Corra Linn**. Though no Niagara Falls, this is Britain's largest waterfall at 88 feet (27 m). Its sight inspired painters such as JMW Turner and Jacob More and inspired Wordsworth to describe it as "the Clyde's most majestic daughter." An additional 20-minutes-walk up the path lies **Bonnington Linn**, the final set of falls. These falls are now, sadly, often diminished in flow through usage for energy generation but still flow freely on a small number of "Waterfall Days."

■ Golf

Lanark Golf Course (18-hole moorland, 6,306 yards; The Moor, Whiteless Road, Lanark ML11 7RX, off the A73 on the east side of the town, ☎/fax 1555-663 219; green fees £26-£40). Dating from 1851, this is a demanding moorland course open to the prevailing wind.

Clyde River Valley

■ Wildlife Watching

 The Falls of Clyde Reserve (New Lanark ML11 9DB, ☎ 1555-665 262, fallsofclyde@swt.org.uk, www.swt.org.uk; admission free) Don't miss the peregrine falcons – The Reserve maintains a peregrine viewpoint between the second and third falls. Telescopes at the manned lookout provide good views of the rare birds. The best time to view peregrines is mid-May to mid-June when the new chicks are being fed in the nest. The birds are harder to observe in winter when they are more often hunting away from the nest. The reserve comprises a mosaic of ancient woodland and meadow, dissected by the Clyde and its majestic waterfalls. You can view over 100 species of birds and there is a comprehensive ranger service and summer events program.

■ Where To Stay & Eat

See *Accommodation* and *Dining* price charts on pages 166 and 169.

 New Lanark Mill Hotel (New Lanark Mills, Lanark ML11 9DB, ☎ 1555-667 200, fax 1555-667 222, hotel@newlanark.org, www.newlanark.org; B&B £££, dinner ££). Comfortable accommodation in a converted 18th-century cotton mill, which retains many original features such as Georgian windows, barrel-vaulted ceilings and even heavy lifting machinery in corridors! Although surrounded by native woodland and close to the Falls of Clyde, the overwhelming selling point is being able to wake up in a World Heritage Site and enjoy its atmosphere in peace and quiet away from the crush of the day crowds. For those who prefer to prepare some or all of their own meals, "Waterhouses" with kitchens are also available.

Argyll, Stirling & The Trossachs

The Stirling region extends from the **Firth of Forth** in the east to **Loch Lomond** in the west, and is mainly hilly, although it reaches 3,192 feet in Ben Lomond. The city of **Stirling** commands a strategic position in Scotland's narrow central belt where most of the country's natural highways converge, and has as a result been the scene of many battles. It was here that **William "Braveheart" Wallace** and **Robert the Bruce** won independence for Scotland.

West of Stirling lies **Argyll**, a beautiful mountainous region that marks the boundary between the Highlands and Lowlands. Sea lochs break up its deeply indented Atlantic coastline; inland are numerous freshwater lochs, the largest of which is **Loch Awe**. Off the coast lie the myriad islands of the **Inner Hebrides**. The climate is wet but temperate; the average temperature is similar to that of the Isle of Wight off southern England.

The Scottish nation was born in Argyll. The *Scotti* invaders arrived here from Ireland in the 6th century and established their Gaelic-speaking Dalriada kingdom at Dunadd, so laying the foundations for modern-day Scotland. More recently, Clan Campbell was for a long time the all-powerful force in the region, and the Dukes of Argyll still live in the elegant, turreted castle in Inveraray.

DON'T MISS

Visit **Stirling Castle**, Scotland's grandest and most historic fortress.

Take a boat trip or kayak away from **Loch Lomond's** bonnie, bonnie (but crowded) banks to its beautiful islands.

Relax in the whitewashed, lochside town of **Inveraray**.

Tour the unspoiled tranquility of the **Kintyre Peninsula**.

Walk or cycle along the banks of beautiful **Loch Katrine**.

Walk in the **Trossachs**, starting with the short hike up to Creag an Tuirc and its glorious view over Balquhidder Glen.

Take a boat trip on **Loch Etive** to see seals and possibly golden eagles.

Best Freebie: Cluster of ancient monuments in **Kilmartin Glen**.

Argyll, Stirling & The Trossachs

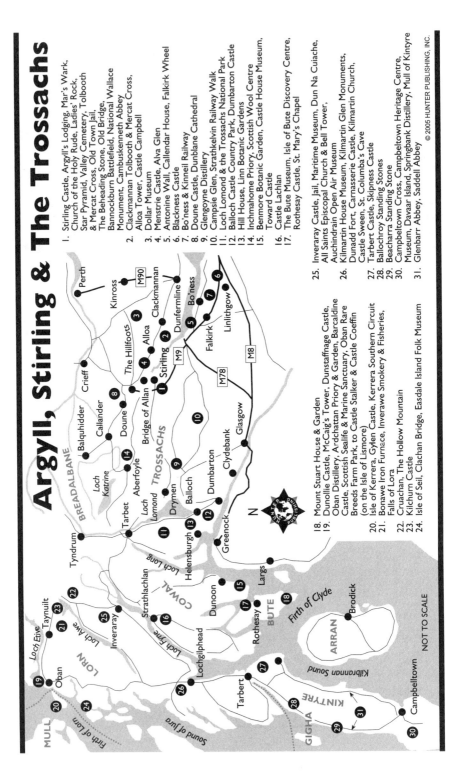

1. Stirling Castle, Argyll's Lodging, Mar's Wark,
   Church of the Holy Rude, Ladies' Rock,
   Star Pyramid, Valley Cemetery, Tolbooth
   & Mercat Cross, Old Town Jail,
   The Beheading Stone, Old Bridge,
   Bannockburn Battlefield, National Wallace
   Monument, Cambuskenneth Abbey
2. Clackmannan Tolbooth & Mercat Cross,
   Alloa Tower, Castle Campbell
3. Dollar Museum
4. Menstrie Castle, Alva Glen
5. Antonine Wall, Callendar House, Falkirk Wheel
6. Blackness Castle
7. Bo'ness & Kinneil Railway
8. Doune Castle, Dunblane Cathedral
9. Glengoyne Distillery
10. Campsie Glen, Strathkelvin Railway Walk
11. Loch Lomond & the Trossachs National Park
12. Balloch Castle Country Park, Dumbarton Castle
13. Hill House, Linn Botanic Gardens
14. Inchmahome Priory, Scottish Wool Centre
15. Benmore Botanic Garden, Castle House Museum,
    Toward Castle
16. Castle Lachlan
17. The Bute Museum, Isle of Bute Discovery Centre,
    Rothesay Castle, St. Mary's Chapel

18. Mount Stuart House & Garden
19. Dunollie Castle, McCaig's Tower, Dunstaffnage Castle,
    Oban Distillery, Ardchattan Priory & Garden, Barcaldine
    Castle, Scottish Sealife & Marine Sanctuary, Oban Rare
    Breeds Farm Park, to Castle Stalker & Castle Coeffin
    (on the Isle of Lismore)
20. Isle of Kerrera, Gylen Castle, Kerrera Southern Circuit
21. Bonawe Iron Furnace, Inveraray Smokery & Fisheries,
    Falls of Lora
22. Cruachan, The Hollow Mountain
23. Kilchurn Castle
24. Isle of Seil, Clachan Bridge, Easdale Island Folk Museum
25. Inveraray Castle, Jail, Maritime Museum, Dun Na Cuiache,
    All Saints Episcopal Church & Bell Tower,
    Auchindrain Open Air Museum
26. Kilmartin House Museum, Kilmartin Glen Monuments,
    Dunadd Fort, Carnasserie Castle, Kilmartin Church,
    Castle Sween, St. Columba's Cave
27. Tarbert Castle, Skipness Castle
28. Ballochroy Standing Stones
29. Beacharra Standing Stone
30. Campbeltown Cross, Campbeltown Heritage Centre,
    Museum, Davaar Island, Springbank Distillery, Mull of Kintyre
31. Glenbarr Abbey, Saddell Abbey

Stirling & Environs

Nestled among green, rolling hills and farmland on Scotland's narrow central waistband lies the former town of Stirling, which became Scotland's newest city in 2002, as part of the Queen's Golden Jubilee celebrations.

From medieval days, Stirling (whose name means "place of strife") was strategically the most important town in Scotland: to control the nation you had first to control Stirling. To the west lay treacherous marshes; to the east the broadening estuary of the **River Forth** offered no easy crossing below Stirling Bridge. All key north-south routes passed through Stirling, commanded by its magnificent cliff-top castle, and the town became known as the brooch or clasp of Scotland – the Key to the Kingdom.

The great battles of the Wars of Independence – when Scotland struggled to free itself from English domination – took place around Stirling: at **Stirling Bridge** in 1297 and **Bannockburn** in 1314. The ramparts of Stirling Castle overlook seven battlegrounds.

Clustered beneath the castle, **Stirling's Old Town** (based around Broad Street, St John Street and St Mary's Wynd) retains much of the character and feel of a medieval town with its cobbled streets lined with medieval and Renaissance homes and buildings. Stirling's town wall is the finest surviving town wall in Scotland and was built in defense against Henry VIII of England who was seeking to force a marriage between the infant Mary, Queen of Scots and his son Edward.

Nearby rises the prominent **National Wallace Monument** that commemorates Scotland's greatest patriot, Sir William Wallace, who was popularized in the film *Braveheart*.

 INFORMATION SOURCES: Argyll, the Isles, Loch Lomond, Stirling & Trossachs Tourist Board is at **Old Town Jail**, St John Street, Stirling FK8 1EA, ☎ 1786-445 222, fax 1786-461 994, info@scottish.heartlands.org, www.visitscottishheartlands.org.

There are three additional tourism offices in and around Stirling. **Royal Burgh of Stirling Visitor Centre**, Castle Esplanade, Stirling FK8 1EH, ☎ 870-720 0622, fax 1786-451 881, info@rbsvc.visitscotland.com; open year-round; **41 Dumbarton Road**, Stirling FK8 2QQ, ☎ 870-720 0620, fax 1786-450 039, info@stirling.visitscotland.com; open year-round; **Motorway Service Area** at the M9/M80 Junction 9, ☎ 870-720 0621, info@pirnhall.visitscotland.com; open April-Oct.

■ Special Events

Stirling Highland Games (July; ☎ 1786-474 933, fax 1786-466 716). Traditional Highland Games with fun fair, stalls and other events.

■ Attractions & Sights

Stirling Castle (HS; top of Castle Wynd, Stirling, ☎ 1786-450 000; open April-Sept, 9:30am-6pm; Oct-Mar, 9:30am-5pm, last admission 45 minutes before closing; adult/concession/child £8/£6/£2). One of the grandest of all Scottish castles for its situation on a commanding rocky outcrop, its splendid architecture (some of the finest Renaissance architecture in Europe), decorative stonework and many complete buildings. Stirling Castle has often featured in film and TV productions, including *Tunes of Glory, Colditz* and *Deacon Brodie.*

The first reference to the castle alludes to Alexander I's endowment of a chapel within the castle between 1107 and 1115. The castle changed hands many times during the Wars of Independence, most famously in 1297 when patriots William Wallace and Andrew Murray won it back from the English king, Edward I, after the Battle of Stirling Bridge, and in 1314 when Robert the Bruce took Stirling at the Battle of Bannockburn.

The **Great Hall** was built by James IV around 1500 and is the finest and largest surviving medieval hall in Scotland – so vast it has five fireplaces. It has recently been restored to its original medieval appearance. Mary, Queen of Scots was crowned in the **Chapel Royal** in 1543 when she was only nine months old. There has been a chapel on this site since soon after 1100; the present building dates from 1594.

The early Renaissance splendor of the Palace is believed to be the work of French masons brought to Scotland by James V. The palace apartments surround the **Lion's Den**. Both James III and James IV kept lions and other exotic wild beasts for entertainment and the enclosed square is believed to have been used for exercising the animals.

The **Stirling Heads**, carved wooden roundels originally placed on the ceiling of the King's Outer Chamber, are the finest surviving examples of Renaissance wood sculpture in Scotland. The carvings depict mythical figures and portraits of court characters such as the jester.

The medieval kitchens were excavated in the 1920s and the torch-lit kitchen tableaux recreate the fashion for serving pre-baked pies filled with live birds (immortalized in the nursery rhyme *Sing a Song of Sixpence*).

Stirling is reputedly one of Scotland's most haunted castles; its many ghouls include a Green Lady, a Pink Lady, a kilted ghost and a chilling presence in the Elphinstone Tower, which allegedly once housed a torture chamber. There are interesting displays on the castle's history and an attractive café.

Argyll's Lodging (HS; top of Castle Wynd, Stirling, ☎ 1786-431 319; open April-Sept, 9:30am-6pm & Oct-Mar, 9:30am-5pm, last admission 30 minutes before closing; adult/concession/child £3.30/£2.50/£1.20, free with paid admission to Stirling Castle). Superb mansion built in about 1630 around an earlier core structure and extended by the Earl of Argyll in the 1670s. It is probably the finest townhouse of its period in Scotland; restoration of its principal rooms approximates their late-17th-century appearance.

New Lanark Mills, Clyde River Valley

Above: Glasgow's Armadillo auditorium

Below: Temple Wood Stone Circle, Kilmartin Glen

Above: Castle Stalker, Loch Laich, Appin

Below: Inveraray Castle, home of the Dukes of Argyll

Grave Slabs, Kilmartin Church

Mar's Wark (Castle Wynd, Stirling). A remarkable Renaissance mansion built for James VI in 1570 and subsequently used as the town workhouse. The mansion was never completed and now only the impressive façade can be seen.

Church of the Holy Rude (St John Street, Stirling Old Town; open May-Sept, 10am-5pm). Stirling's principal church for more than 500 years and site of James VI's coronation in 1567. Parts of the nave and tower date from 1456-70; the church features magnificent stained glass windows and one of Scotland's few surviving medieval open-timber roofs.

Ladies' Rock, Star Pyramid & Valley Cemetery (access from Castle Wynd or Castle Esplanade). Ladies' Rock, now in the Castle Cemetery, was once a favorite vantage point for watching royal tournaments in the valley below. The nearby Star Pyramid remembers all those martyred while seeking religious freedom.

Tolbooth & Mercat Cross (Broad Street, Stirling Old Town). The tolbooth, the administrative heart of the Old Town, was built in 1703-5 and has a rare example of a Dutch pavilion roof. Outside in Broad Street stands the Mercat Cross, once the focus of the town's trading activities.

Old Town Jail (St John Street, Stirling FK8 1EA, ☎ 1786-450 050, fax 1786-471 301; open April-Sept, 9:30am-5pm; earlier closing times Oct-Mar, call for schedule; adult/concession/family £5/£3.25/£13.25 for living-history tours). The corridors and cells of the 19th-century prison introduce you to jail life, the town's hangman and many jailers and inmates. The top of the jail has great views over Stirling Old Town. Handset audio commentaries are available in five languages.

The Beheading Stone (Gowan Hill, Stirling, access from Upper Castlehill or Back Walk). Gruesome reminder of capital punishment in times past and thought to have witnessed the execution of various important figures, including in 1425, Murdoch, Duke of Albany and former Regent of Scotland.

Old Bridge An impressive late-15th- to early-16th-century bridge, the southern arch of which was blown up during the 1745 Rising to prevent the Jacobite army from entering the town, and rebuilt in 1749.

Royal Burgh of Stirling Visitor Centre (Castle Esplanade, Stirling, ☎ 1786-479 901/462 517; open April-Oct, 9:30am-6pm & Nov-Mar, 9:30am-5pm). Exhibits and a multi-lingual audiovisual presentation tell the story of Stirling from the earliest times to the present day, including the Wars of Independence and everyday life in the medieval town.

Bannockburn (NTS; Glasgow Road, Stirling FK7 0LJ, ☎ 1786-812 664, fax 1786-810 892; site open at all times, Heritage Centre open April-Oct, 10am-5:30pm; earlier closing times Nov-Mar; adult/concession/family £3.50/£2.60/£9.50). This historic battlefield is where, on 23rd-24th June 1314, King Robert the Bruce routed the superior forces of Edward II to win the Scots' freedom from English domination. Near the Heritage Centre is the famous Borestone site, marked by an impressive equestrian statue of the

Bruce, which was the Scottish King's command post before the battle. The Centre contains a period exhibition and audiovisual presentation.

National Wallace Monument (Abbey Craig, Causeway-head, two miles north of Stirling, ☎ 1786-472 140, fax 1786-461 322, nationalwallacemonument@aillst.ossian.net; open year-round, hours vary seasonally; adult/concession £5.50/£3.50). Towering memorial to Scotland's national hero William Wallace (1267-1305) and his epic struggle for a free Scotland, which formed the plot for the film *Braveheart*. Displays explain Wallace's tactics and provide an insight into the battles. Exhibits include Wallace's two-handed sword and a recreation of his eventual trial. Climb the 246 steps to the top of the 220-foot tower (already perched on top of a hill) for a superb view.

SCOTLAND'S "BRAVEHEART"

In the late 13th century, Edward I of England ruled Scotland with a mixture of tyranny, terror and political trickery. **William Wallace**, an impassioned patriot, waged a guerrilla-style campaign to free the Scots and finally confronted the English at Stirling Bridge in 1297. Despite his army being vastly outnumbered, Wallace's tactics won the Scots a resounding victory and the English fled in disarray. Wallace was eventually betrayed to the English in 1305 and brutally executed in London.

Cambuskenneth Abbey (one mile east of Stirling off the A907; view exterior only). The only substantial survivor of this once-great Augustinian house is the fine detached tower; it is notable as the scene of Robert the Bruce's parliament in 1326 and as the burial place of James III and his Queen.

■ Adventures

CNDo Scotland (32 Stirling Enterprise Park, Springbank Road, Stirling FK7 7RP, ☎/fax 1786-445 703, info@cndoscotland.com, www.cndoscotland.com). Established outdoor operator offering walking, scrambling and climbing by the day, weekends and longer.

■ Golf

Stirling Golf Course (18-hole inland, 6,123 yards; Queens Road, Stirling FK8 3AA, ☎ 1786-464 098, fax 1786-450 748; green fees £28). Testing rolling parkland course with magnificent views of Stirling Castle, Ben Lomond and the Fintry Hills.

■ Where To Stay

Hotels

Barn Lodge (Croftside Farm, Pirnhall, Stirling FK7 8EX, ☎ 1786-813 591, fax 1786-816 138, sales@thebarnlodgestirling.co.uk, www.thebarnlodgestirling.co.uk; B&B ££-£££). Quiet and spacious accommodation (room only**YOU LIST B&B, WHY ROOM ONLY?**) in two recently converted barns on a working farm three miles from Stirling.

Park Lodge Hotel (32 Park Terrace, Stirling FK8 2JS, ☎ 1786-474 862, fax 1786-449 748, info@parklodge.net, www.parklodge.net; B&B £££). Victorian-Georgian mansion overlooking the park and castle. The bedrooms have antique furniture and paintings.

The Portcullis (Castle Wynd, Stirling FK8 1EG, ☎ 1786-472 290, fax 1786-446 103, theportcullis@aol.com, www.theportcullishotel.com; B&B £££, dinner £££).
Refurbished hotel, dating from 1787, set in a former school next to Stirling Castle. There is a beer garden in summer and log fire in winter.

HOTEL PRICE CHART	
Per person, per night, based on double occupancy in high season. B&B rate includes breakfast; DB&B includes dinner and breakfast.	
£	Under £20
££	£21-£35
£££	£36-£50
££££	£51-£80
£££££	Over £80

Guest Houses & B&Bs

Ashgrove House (2 Park Avenue, Stirling FK8 2LX, ☎/fax 1786-472 640, ashgrovehouse@strayduck.com, www.ashgrove-house.com; open Mar-Oct; B&B ££). Elegantly restored Victorian townhouse two minutes' walk from the town center.

Southfield (2 Melville Terrace, Stirling FK8 2ND, ☎ 1786-464 872, ebrodiesouthfield@tinyworld.co.uk; B&B ££). Comfortable bedrooms in a fine Georgian townhouse within walking distance of the Old Town.

Burns View (1 Albert Place, Stirling FK8 2QL, ☎/fax 1786-451 002, m.watt@totalise.co.uk; B&B ££). Spacious Victorian detached house in central Stirling.

Firgrove (13 Clifford Road, Stirling FK8 2AQ, ☎ 1786-475 805, fax 1786-450 733, firgrove@stirling.co.uk, www.firgrove.stirling.co.uk; B&B ££). Elegant Victorian villa five minutes' walk to Stirling town center with spacious and relaxing bedrooms and an attractive breakfast room.

Forth Guest House (23 Forth Place, Riverside, Stirling FK8 1UD, ☎ 1786-471 020, fax 1786-447 220, www.forthguesthouse.freeserve.co.uk; B&B ££). Georgian townhouse near the bus and rail stations.

Number 10 (Gladstone Place, Stirling FK8 2NN, ☎/fax 1786-472 681, cameron-10@tinyonline.co.uk, www.cameron-10.co.uk; B&B ££). Modernized Victorian house with well-decorated bedrooms and an attractive breakfast room.

■ Where To Eat

DINING PRICE CHART	
Indicates the price, per person, of a full meal, excluding drinks. Generally three courses, though fixed menus of five or more courses may be available.	
£	Under £10
££	£11-£20
£££	£21-£30
££££	£31-£40

Barnton Bar & Bistro (3½ Barnton Street, Stirling FK8 1HF, ☎ 1786-461 698; £). Café-bar that's popular with students and serves freshly cooked snacks and meals, including good all-day breakfasts.

The Birds and The Bees (Easter Cornton Road, Causewayhead, Stirling FK9 5PB, ☎ 1786-473 663; ££). Award-winning bar and bistro on the edge of Stirling with real ales, log fire and French boules.

La Ciociara (41 Friars Street, Stirling FK8 1HA, ☎ 1786-451 552; lunch £, dinner ££). Informal Italian bar-bistro serving meals, coffee and great ice cream.

Darnley Coffee House (18 Bow Street, Stirling FK8 1BS, ☎ 1786-474 468; £). Great specialty teas, coffees and home baking.

Olivia's (5 Baker Street, Stirling FK8 1BJ, ☎/fax 1786-446 277; lunch £, dinner ££). A pleasant, informal restaurant close to the historic heart of Stirling. The modern Scottish menu features good local produce well cooked with imagination.

Victoria's Coffee Shop (15 King Street, Stirling FK8 1DN, ☎ 1786-479 867; £). Friendly, traditional coffee shop with light meals and home baking to eat in or take away.

Clackmannanshire & the Ochil Hills

Clackmannanshire is one of Scotland's smallest districts. **Clackmannan**, the former county town, has a famous tower and marketplace with a tolbooth and 16th-century Mercat Cross (it's a nice walk from the tower through the main street to the church). **Alloa** is a large modern town with the impressive and recently renovated Alloa Tower (see page 189). Alloa also celebrates its heritage as a major brewing center with regular real ale festivals.

The streams spilling down the steep slopes of the Ochil Hills once powered a host of mills in the **Hillfoots**, the string of flower-decked villages (Menstrie, Alva, Tillicoultry, Dollar and Muckhart) that line the southern edge of the Ochils. This region was at the forefront of the thriving 19th-century textile industry and once employed the majority of the local population.

Menstrie is an attractive village with the remains of a 16th-century castle. **Alva** is a small former weaving town sheltering at the foot of the Ochils. **Tillicoultry** is a traditional village beneath Mill Glen, which once boasted 12 textile mills. **Dollar** is a picturesque small town nestling at the foot of Dollar Glen, overlooked by Castle Campbell. **Muckhart** is a tiny but attractive village renowned for its floral displays.

The **Ochils** loom large overhead and are a paradise for hillwalkers, with winding paths leading through steep-sided glens to cascading waterfalls. The more adventurous can attempt the "round of the nine" (peaks over 2,000 feet).

 INFORMATION SOURCES: There is a tourism office in Alva at **Mill Trail Visitor Centre**, West Stirling Street, Alva FK12 5EN, ☎ 870-720 0605, fax 1259-763 100, info@alva.visitscotland.com; open year-round.

■ Attractions & Sights

 **Alloa Tower** (NTS; Alloa Park, Alloa FK10 1PP, ☎ 1259-211 701, fax 1259-218 744; open April-Oct, 1-5pm; adult/concession/family £3.50/£2.60/£9.50). The 14th-century tower is the largest surviving keep in Scotland. This was home to generations of the Earls of Mar, hosts and guardians of many Scots monarchs. The tower retains original medieval features, including the dungeon, first-floor well and magnificent oak roof timbers, and has also seen major alterations, including the early-18th-century sweeping Italianate staircase and dome.

Castle Campbell (HS; at the head of Dollar Glen, 10 miles east of Stirling on the A91, ☎ 1259-742 408; open April-Sept, 9:30am-6:30pm; days/times vary the rest of the year, call ahead; adult/concession/child £3/£2.30/£1). This late-15th-century fortress was formerly known as the "Castle of Gloom." It is beautifully sited between two ravines at the head of Dollar Glen. John Knox is said to have preached here in the 16th century and there is a well-preserved 15th-century tower (which survived Cromwell's sacking of the castle in 1654). The approach to the castle is via a 20-minute walk up Dollar Glen, a deep tree-filled gorge with waterfalls and mossy rocks.

Clackmannan Tower (Clackmannan, off the A907; external viewing only). This 14th-century keep, later enlarged, was a residence of the Bruce family from 1365 to 1772. In 1787, the widow of the last laird knighted the poet Robert Burns in the castle with Robert the Bruce's sword. The main surviving part is the tower house, and there remain extensive traces of courtyards, buildings and gardens around it. Although not open to the public, the tower is worth visiting for its historic significance.

Tolbooth A local Sheriff built Clackmannan's tolbooth in the 16th century when he tired of having to put up prisoners in his own home. Only the belfry tower now remains.

Dollar Museum (Castle Campbell Hall, 1 High Street, Dollar FK14 7AY, ☎ 1259-742 895; open April-Dec, Sat, 11am-1pm & 2-4:30pm; Sun, 2-4:30pm). Permanent displays on the history of Dollar village and Devon Valley Railway, together with a program of temporary exhibitions.

Menstrie Castle (Castle Street, Menstrie, call Alloa Tower, ☎ 1259-211 701; open Easter Sunday & May-Sept, Wed & Sun, 2-5pm). The castle is a small three-story L-plan tower house dating from the late 16th century. Sir William

Alexander, founder of the colony of Nova Scotia in Canada, was born here in 1567.

■ Adventures

 Alva Glen is a short but strenuous walk up a narrow meandering glen typical of the southern edge of the Ochil Hills. Start from Alva at the parking area at the north end of Brook Street and follow the signs for Alva Glen – north of the main road (A91) between Stirling and Tillicoultry. From the top of Brook Street, follow the path through the woods. Cross the stream and turn left. Climb the steps to follow the line of an old water pipe under the glen path. The path is mostly well-surfaced and criss-crosses the stream. At the third bridge the path swings up the hill in a series of switchbacks, finally reaching a viewpoint high above the glen. Go through the kissing gate (a gate that swings freely between two stationary posts, it is designed for easy use by walkers, but won't allow livestock through), take the high-level path back around the hill, and down a steep path to the edge of the golf course (take care in wet conditions). Cross an old wall via a stile to return to the start (1½ hours; easy/moderate).

■ Where To Stay & Eat

See *Accommodation* and *Dining* price charts on pages 187 and 188.

 East Mill Bank (25 Ochil Road, Alva FK12 5JT, ☎/fax 1259-760 281; B&B £-££). High-standard B&B with period features, antiques and views of Alva Glen, the Ochils and the Wallace Monument.

Wyvis (70 Stirling Street, Tillicoultry FK13 6EA, ☎ 1259-751 513, wyvis@btopenworld.com; B&B ££, dinner ££). Comfortable accommodation in a converted Victorian mill-worker's cottage close to the Ochil Hills, offering a warm welcome and excellent breakfasts.

Leys Farm (Muckhart FK14 7JL, ☎ 1259-781 313; B&B £). Modern, quietly situated farmhouse B&B with lovely views all around.

Falkirk

Falkirk is a sizeable modern town with good shopping in two covered malls and pedestrianized mews. Its history stretches back to the 2nd century when the Romans built the Antonine Wall to try to contain the unruly Picts. More recently, the Forth & Clyde and Union Canals played key roles during the industrial revolution, carrying raw materials and finished products. These canals are now connected by the incredible Falkirk Wheel – the world's first rotating boat lift.

 INFORMATION SOURCES: The **Falkirk tourism office** is at 2/4 Glebe Street, Falkirk FK1 1HX, ☎ 870-720 0614, fax 1324-638 440, info@falkirk.visitscotland.com; open year-round. There is also a tourism office at **Bo'ness** at the Car Park, Seaview Place, Bo'ness EH51 0AJ, ☎/fax 870-720 0608, info@boness.visitscotland.com; open April-Sept.

■ Attractions & Sights

Antonine Wall. In AD 141, after marching north again into Scotland, the Romans built a new wall to replace their more southerly Hadrian's Wall. The Antonine Wall represented the northernmost frontier of their empire and ran across the Forth-Clyde Valley from Bo'ness in the east to Old Kilpatrick in the west. The wall was made of turf-covered stone and was some 10 feet high and 13 feet thick. A deep ditch protected the wall's northern side and there were at least 17 forts and 40 smaller fortifications running along its southern side.

Remains of the wall can be seen in various places. The best-preserved is **Rough Castle** (signposted from the B816 between Bonnybridge and High Bonnybridge), containing a length of rampart and ditch together with the earthworks of a fort and short length of military way. The Romans only held the wall for 20 years before they gave up trying to subdue the indomitable Picts and retreated farther south.

Blackness Castle (HS; four miles northeast of Linlithgow, off the A904, ☎ 1506-834 807; open April-Sept, 9:30am-6:30pm; days/hours vary the rest of the year; adult/concession/child £2.50/£1.90/£0.75). Dating from the 1440s, Blackness was massively strengthened in the 16th century into a formidable artillery fortification, whose south-facing walls are 18 feet thick. The castle surrendered to Cromwell after suffering extensive damage; after repair, it became an ammunition depot in the 1920s. The roof of the central tower provides good views over the River Forth and the moody fortress provided the setting for the 1991 film version of *Hamlet*, starring Mel Gibson.

Callendar House (Callendar Park, Falkirk FK1 1YR, ☎ 1324-503 770, fax 1324-503 771, callendar.house@falkirk.gov.uk, www.falkirkmuseums.demon.co.uk; open Mon-Sat, 10am-5pm; April-Sept also open Sun, 2-5pm, last admission 4pm; adult/concession/child £3/£1.50/£1). Imposing mansion with a 600-year-old history set in magnificent grounds. There are costumed interpreters, exhibitions and a Georgian garden, and the restored Georgian kitchen serves good food.

Falkirk Wheel (Lime Road, Tamfourhill, Falkirk FK1 4RS, ☎ 1324-619 888, ☎ booking 870-050 0208, fax 1324-671 224, info@thefalkirkwheel.co.uk, www.thefalkirkwheel.co.uk; year-round, times vary seasonally; adult/concession/child/family £8/£6/£4/£21). The world's first and only rotating boat lift is a beautiful piece of modern engineering and sculpture. It takes about 15 minutes to lift and lower boats 115 feet (35 m) between the Union Canal (upper) and the Forth & Clyde Canal (lower). The 45-minute "Falkirk Wheel Experience Boat Trip" lets you take the incredible journey on board one of a fleet of specially designed boats. Sail into the bottom caisson of the Wheel, ascend to join the Union Canal and then cruise through the Roughcastle tunnel beneath the Antonine Wall before returning to the Wheel and descending back down to the Visitor Centre. The trips are very popular; you're advised to book a day ahead.

Bo'ness & Kinneil Railway (Bo'ness Station, Union Street, Bo'ness EH51 9AQ, ☎ 1506-822 298, enquiries@railway.srps.org.uk, www.srps.org.uk; open July-Aug (closed Mon) and most weekends in spring/autumn; adult/concession/child/family £7.50/£6/£4/£19). A 3½-mile steam train journey to the caverns of Birkhill Mine with conducted tours of the caverns and its 300-million-year-old fossils.

■ Where To Stay

See *Accommodation* and *Dining* price charts on pages 187 and 188.

 Arbuthnot House (Dorrator Road, Camelon, Falkirk FK1 4BN, ☎ 1324634 785, stay@arbuthnotnothouse.com, www.arbuthnothouse-.com; B&B ££). High-quality B&B offering comfortable accommodation and a quiet garden.

Darroch House (Camelon Road, Falkirk FK1 5SQ, ☎ 1324-623 041, fax 1324-626 288; B&B ££). Spacious, peaceful accommodation in a large house standing in nine acres of grounds, 10 minutes' walk from the town center.

■ Where To Eat

 Comma Bar Café (14 Lint Riggs, Falkirk FK1 1DG, ☎ 1324-611 669, fax 1324-613 258; lunch £, dinner £-££). Popular and stylish eatery serving coffees, lunches, snacks and evening meals.

Pierre's Restaurant (140 Grahams Road, Falkirk FK2 7BZ, ☎ 1324-635 843; closed Sun-Mon; ££-£££). Classic French cuisine in a friendly, informal atmosphere.

The Campsies & Strathallan

The landscape around Stirling is lush and fertile, with the peaceful slopes of the Campsies and rolling farmlands of Strathallan. Scattered towns and villages create a rich tapestry of rural Scotland. The town of **Doune** boasts an imposing 14th-century castle, once a favorite royal hunting retreat. **Bridge of Allan** is a former spa town with broad, tree-lined streets on the banks of the Allan Water, its parklands now occupied by Stirling University. The Campsie Fells reach nearly 2,000 feet and provide a scenic backdrop to the numerous colorful villages in the area. **Killearn** has attractive 18th- and 19th-century cottages and a 103-foot-high obelisk. Tucked away at the foot of the Campsies is the pretty village of **Fintry**. Some two miles east of Fintry village on the B818 Denny Road, the Endrick cascades 94 feet over rocky ledges in an impressive waterfall – the Loup of Fintry. The delightful village of **Kippen** was once home to a laird who declared himself "King of Kippen."

 INFORMATION SOURCES: There is a tourism office in Dunblane at Stirling Road, Dunblane FK15 9EP, ☎/fax 870-720 0613, info@dunblane.visitscotland.com; open May-Sept.

■ Attractions & Sights

Doune Castle (HS; Doune, 10 miles northwest of Stirling, ☎ 1786-841 742; open April-Sept, 9:30am-6:30pm; Oct-Mar, Sat-Wed, 9:30am-4:30pm; adult/concession/child £3/£2.30/£1). A magnificent medieval castle, and probably the best preserved in Scotland. Dating from the late 14th century, this courtyard castle was built for the Regent Albany at a strategic crossroads on the Edinburgh-Inverlochy and Glasgow-Inverness routes. A massive curtain wall encloses a large courtyard dominated by a square gatehouse tower. The restored Lord's Hall with its minstrels' gallery, cavernous Great Hall and huge kitchen create a sense of what life in the castle must have been like. The castle was for many years a royal residence but is now more famous as the set for much of the 1975 cult film *Monty Python and the Holy Grail*.

Dunblane Cathedral (HS; Dunblane FK15 0AQ, ☎ 1786-823 388; open Sun, from 1:30pm; admission free). One of Scotland's noblest medieval churches, with fine sandstone detailing in Gothic style. The cathedral dates from the 13th century, although the lower part of the tower is Romanesque. The cathedral was restored in 1889-93.

Dunblane boasts an impressive cathedral but will, sadly, long be remembered for the horrific primary-school massacre that took place there in 1996.

Glengoyne Distillery (Dumgoyne, near Killearn G63 9LB, on the A81 between Glasgow and Stirling, ☎ 1360-550 254, fax 1360-550 094, www.glengoyne.com; open Mon-Sat, 10am-4pm; Sun, noon-4pm; regular tour/VIP tour £3.95/£5, children free). A beautiful distillery that offers you a dram in a superb reception room before you tour the distillery. The whisky is clear and smooth, unusually made from air-dried (rather than peat-smoke-dried) barley.

■ Adventures

On Foot

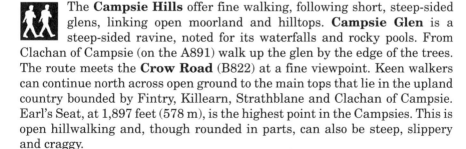

The **Campsie Hills** offer fine walking, following short, steep-sided glens, linking open moorland and hilltops. **Campsie Glen** is a steep-sided ravine, noted for its waterfalls and rocky pools. From Clachan of Campsie (on the A891) walk up the glen by the edge of the trees. The route meets the **Crow Road** (B822) at a fine viewpoint. Keen walkers can continue north across open ground to the main tops that lie in the upland country bounded by Fintry, Killearn, Strathblane and Clachan of Campsie. Earl's Seat, at 1,897 feet (578 m), is the highest point in the Campsies. This is open hillwalking and, though rounded in parts, can also be steep, slippery and craggy.

The **Queen's View** provides a splendid panorama north to Loch Lomond and its surrounding mountains and is reached by a moderately sloping path leading from a parking area on the A809, opposite Strathblane. Walking a farther mile west leads to the **Whangie**, a strange geological structure comprising a 30-foot-deep gully and a rocky ridge said to be a miniature reflection of the famous Black Cuillins on the Isle of Skye.

Strathkelvin Railway Walk stretches from Strathblane and skirts the Campsie Fells, Lennox Forest, Glazert Water and Kilsyth Hills on well-made paths along a disused railway track-bed. The route provides up to 13 miles of pleasant walking for all abilities and is also suitable for bikes and wheelchairs. Walk as much or as little as you wish.

On Horseback

 Drumbrae Riding School (Drumbrae, Bridge of Allan FK9 4LT, ☎ 1786-832 247). Riding instruction for all levels and trekking through beautiful countryside.

On Water

The Campsies offer good coarse and game fishing, including the River Endrick (☎ 141-221 0068), the Carron Valley Reservoir (☎ 1786-442 000), Swanswater Fishing (☎ 1786-814 805) and North Third Trout Fishery (☎ 1786-471 967).

■ Golf

 Campsie Golf Course (18-hole inland, 5,517 yards; Crow Road, Lennoxtown G66 7HX, on B822, three-quarters of a mile out of Lennoxtown, ☎ 1360-310 244; green fees £15). A beautiful and challenging parkland course sitting at the foot of the Campsie Fells and enjoying stunning views.

■ Where To Stay & Eat

See *Accommodation* and *Dining* price charts on pages 187 and 188.

 Glenardoch House (Castle Road, Doune FK16 6EA, ☎ 1786-841 489, stay@glenardochhouse.com, www.glenardochhouse.com; open May-Sept; B&B ££). Comfortable, spacious bedrooms in an 18th-century country house with riverside gardens close to Doune Castle.

Sunnylaw House (1 Upper Glen Road, Bridge of Allan FK9 4PX, ☎ 1786-833 429, sunnylawhouse@sol.co.uk, www.sunnylawhouse.co.uk; B&B ££, dinner ££). Interesting 19th-century villa with its own small tower. The rooms are pretty and there is the option of evening meals.

Cross Keys Hotel (Main Street, Kippen FK8 3DN, ☎ 1786-870 293, crosskeys@kippen70.fsnet.co.uk; B&B ££, dinner £-££). Traditional country inn with open fires, real ales and home-cooked local produce.

Sealladh Ard (Station Brae, Kippen FK8 3DY, ☎ 1786-870 291, ann@bandb-stirling.com, www.bandbstirling.com; B&B ££). Charming B&B in Kippen serving homemade breads and preserves at breakfast.

Culcreuch Castle Hotel (Fintry G63 0LW, ☎ 1360-860 228/860 555, fax 1360-860 556, info@culcreuch.com, www.culcreuch.com; B&B £££, dinner

£££). Elegant accommodation and traditional Scottish cuisine in a 700-year-old castle set in 1,600 acres of parkland near the beautiful village of Fintry.

Fintry Inn (Main Street, Fintry, ☎ 1360-860 224; B&B ££, dinner £-££). The mid-18th-century inn serves excellent bar meals and has live music most weekends. It also has rooms and can arrange fishing on its own stretch of the River Endrick.

Black Bull Hotel (2 The Square, Killearn G63 9NG, info@the-blackbull-killearn.co.uk; B&B ££, dinner ££). Small country hotel with a public bar, bistro and grill.

Loch Lomond

Loch Lomond is one of Scotland's most famous lochs, its "bonnie, bonnie banks" often celebrated in song and verse from Scott's *The Lady of the Lake* to the traditional *Wild Mountain Thyme*. It's the largest area of freshwater in Britain (although Loch Ness contains more water) and is home to Scotland's first National Park. Just 20 miles from Glasgow, Loch Lomond is a very popular destination.

From its craggy, fjord-like northern depths to the broad, shallow reaches of the south, studded with tiny wooded islands, Loch Lomond perfectly epitomises the contrast between the rugged Highlands and more mellow Lowland hillsides. The loch's easily defended islands first attracted human habitation. Medieval Christian evangelists such as St Kentigerna and St Kessog established monasteries on several of the islands.

The **Loch Lomond & the Trossachs National Park**, Scotland's first National Park, stretches from Balloch in the south to Tyndrum in the north, encompassing both the Queen Elizabeth and Argyll Forest Parks and much of the Cowal Peninsula.

Drymen is a beautiful and tranquil village huddled around a traditional village green. Although best known as a staging post on the West Highland Way, Drymen is well worth visiting in its own right. Once favored by Rob Roy (who is said to have frequented the village's ancient Clachan Inn), Drymen is now a popular stop for coach parties, which can temporarily rouse the village from its sleepiness, as can the pipe band that plays on the green on Thursday evenings in July and August.

On the western shore is the picture-postcard village of **Luss**, which in summer is ablaze with floral color. This delightfully preserved conservation village has a fine beach and is the home of Scottish Television's *High Road* soap. The loch's eastern shore is dominated by the brooding mass of Ben Lomond, the most southerly Munro and Scotland's most climbed mountain. At the south of the loch, the farming community of **Gartocharn** is known for the great view afforded by the short climb up Duncryne Hill (known locally as "the Dumpling").

At the unspoiled northern end of the loch, Arrochar stands by the head of Loch Long, encircled by rugged mountain peaks, the best known of which is

Ben Arthur (known locally as "The Cobbler"), which is a Mecca for hillwalkers.

 INFORMATION SOURCES: There are tourism offices in **Balloch** (Balloch Road, Balloch G83 8LQ, ☎ 870-720 0607, fax 1389-751 704, info@balloch.visitscotland.com; open April-Oct), **National Park Gateway Centre** (Loch Lomond Shores, Balloch G83 8LQ, ☎ 870-720 0631, fax 1389-722 177, info@lochlomond.visitscotland.com; open year-round), **Drymen** (Drymen Library, The Square, Drymen G63 0BD, ☎ 870-720 0611, fax 1360-660 751, info@drymen.visitscotland.com; open May-Sept) and **Tarbet** (Main Street, Tarbet G83 7DE, ☎ 870-720 0623, info@tarbet.visitscotland.com; open April-Oct).

■ Special Events

 Balloch (Loch Lomond) **Highland Games** (Jul; ☎ 1389-754 995) Traditional Highland Games in Balloch Castle Country Park.

Lomond Folk Festival (Jul/Aug; ☎ 1389-757 561, www.lomondfolkfestival.com). Weekend of traditional music on the banks of Loch Lomond.

■ Attractions & Sights

Balloch Castle Country Park (Balloch G83 8LX, ☎ 1389-722 600; open Easter-Oct; admission free). Rather touristy country park offering parkland, lochside walks, a walled garden and Loch Lomond interpretation.

Loch Lomond Shores (Old Luss Road, Balloch G83 8QW, ☎ 1389-721 500/722 406, fax 1389-720 603, info@lochlomondshores.com, www.lochlomondshores.com; open April-Sept, 10am-5pm, 6pm weekends; & Oct-Mar, 10am-4pm, 5pm weekends; adult/concession/family £5.95/£3.75/£16.50). Situated on the southern shore of the loch, this new visitor attraction offers a gateway and National Park information center; a shopping arcade, including the only Jenners outlet outside Edinburgh; and Drumkinnon Tower, fashioned as a modern-day castle and housing two shows (both included in admission; see below), several drinking and dining options and stunning loch viewing areas; follow signs to Balloch and then signs for Loch Lomond Shores.

The **Small Theatre** displays an animatronic show following the history, myths and legends of the loch through the eyes of an otter, and will appeal to families. Even better is *Legend of Loch Lomond*, a 40-minute giantscreen drama following the story behind the famous song *Loch Lomond*. Set at the time of the 1745 Jacobite Rising, the drama weaves the story of a brave Highland soldier and his love for a Lowland lady, set against the breathtaking backdrop of the loch. A moving story, awe-inspiring scenery and instantly recognizable tune combine to produce a superb multimedia experience.

Loch Lomond Shores has a full program of events, such as craft fairs, pipe bands and charity events, and hosts a farmers' market on the third Sunday of each month with offerings such as fresh organic vegetables, delicious seafood, artisan cheeses and beer brewed using Loch Lomond water.

■ Adventures

 The lack of competing nearby peaks exaggerates the sense of height from the summit of **Ben Lomond** and allows unencumbered panoramas you might expect to have to work harder for. As Scotland's most southerly Munro, Ben Lomond makes an ideal day-trip from Edinburgh or Glasgow.

The path climbs steadily from behind the Rowardennan Visitor Centre. Once above the conifer forest, the views over Loch Lomond and later the Trossachs become increasingly more striking. Approaching the summit ridge, the path steepens and soon it's sky rather than mountain that surrounds you. If you walk above the path to the edge of the ridge (which you don't have to do to reach the summit), the vertical drop-offs further enhance the sense of the high mountains. Return by the same route or, more interestingly, continue on the path beyond the summit down a steeper route that passes closer to Loch Lomond (4-5 hours; easy/moderate).

Cruach Tairbeirt is an undulating walk through woodland offering excellent views down Loch Long, Loch Lomond and across to Ben Lomond and the Arrochar Alps. Start in Arrochar where you should park in the main parking area at the south of the village. Leave the village near the telephone box and follow a path that climbs steeply. The gradient soon relents and the path undulates for about a mile. Continue straight ahead at two path junctions. After the second junction, the path climbs steeply once again. The path turns right and traverses along the hillside, passing a viewpoint to reach a footbridge across a stream. Turn right and follow the path steeply downhill to re-cross the stream after 400 yards. Continue along the path to rejoin the outward route near the station, from where you can return to Arrochar (3 hours; easy).

Loch Lomond Seaplanes (☎ 1436-675 030/870-242 1457, info@lochlomondseaplanes.com, www.lochlomondseaplanes.com). Scotland's first commercial seaplane operator has a variety of tours over Loch Lomond and the Trossachs, and, with the ability to land on both land and water, will provide transport to some of Scotland's most remote areas.

Cruise Loch Lomond (The Boatyard, Tarbet, Loch Lomond G83 7DG, ☎ 1301-702 356, fax 1301-702 636, enquiries@cruiselochlomond.com, www.cruiselochlomondltd.com). Cruises from Tarbet to the quiet northern end of Loch Lomond aboard twin-decked cruisers with bar facilities and a full commentary.

Macfarlane & Son (The Boatyard, Balmaha G63 0JQ, ☎ 1360-870 214, ☎ mobile 7818-022 242, boatyard@macfarlaneandson.co.uk, www.balmahaboatyard.co.uk). Cruises on Loch Lomond with the local postman in his mail boat. Boats and fishing rods are also available for rent.

Sweeney Cruises (Balloch G83 8SS, ☎ 1389-752 376, fax 1389-721 082, john_sweeney@talk21.com, www.sweeney.uk.com). One-hour boat trips on Loch Lomond leave hourly during the summer. 2½-hour cruises to Luss are also available, including an hour ashore at the village, and evening cruises during July and August.

Loch Lomond Water Ski Club (Balloch, Loch Lomond, ☎ 1389-753 000; open April-Sept). Skiing and lessons for members and non-members of all levels. A slalom course is available.

Can You Experience (11 Haldane Terrace, Balloch G83 8ER, ☎ 1389-602 576, info@canyouexperience.com, www.canyouexperience.com). Outdoor activities company based at Loch Lomond Shores offering guided canoe, cycling and walking trips around the Loch Lomond area, including canoe trips to the loch's diverse, beautiful and historic islands. Short-term canoe and bike rental are also available and, for the more adventurous, longer guided canoe trips, including three-day trips paddling the entire length of Loch Lomond or even paddling three lochs to travel from Balloch to Stirling. Walking, cycling and canoeing around Loch Lomond's superb scenery has to be one of the most pleasant ways to get an all-body workout!

Lomond Activities (64 Main Street, Drymen, By Loch Lomond G63 0BG, ☎ 1360-660 066, info@lomondactivities.co.uk, www.lomondactivities.co.uk). Bikes and fishing tackle for rent.

■ Where To Stay & Eat

See *Accommodation* and *Dining* price charts on pages 187 and 188.

Drymen

Winnock Hotel (The Square, Drymen G63 0BL, ☎ 1360-660 245, fax 1360-660 267, info@winnockhotel.com, www.winnockhotel.com; B&B £££, dinner ££). Wonderfully atmospheric 18th-century coaching inn on Drymen's village green; run on environmentally friendly principles. There are ceilidhs every Sunday from June to mid-September, regular Scottish nights, and murder mystery evenings. The cozy bar serves a wide range of malt whiskies and real ales.

Croftburn (Croftamie, Drymen G63 0HA, ☎ 1360-660 796, fax 1360-661 005, enquiries@croftburn.co.uk, www.croftburn.co.uk; B&B £-££, dinner ££). Spacious B&B accommodation in an attractive 200-year-old former gamekeeper's cottage. Evening meals are available.

Easter Drumquhassle Farm (Gartness Road, Drymen G63 0DN, ☎ 1360-660 893; B&B ££, dinner ££). B&B in a quiet rural setting with excellent views. Evening meals are available.

Buchanan Arms Hotel (Drymen G63 0BQ, ☎ 1360-660 588, fax 1360-660 943, www.buchananarms.co.uk; B&B £££, lunch ££, dinner £££). Former coaching inn with a quiet location and comfortable rooms.

Clachan Inn (The Square, Drymen G63 0BG, ☎ 1360-660 824; £-££). Established in 1734 (Rob Roy MacGregor's sister was the first licensee), the cozy Clachan claims to be Scotland's oldest inn. It serves good food and real ales.

Drymen Pottery (The Square, Drymen, ☎ 1360-660 458, fax 1360-660 211; lunch £, dinner ££). Delightful restaurant and coffee shop serving all-day food, including snacks, home baking, filled rolls and pizzas. A carry-out service is available, and there is a pub, plus a pottery studio and shop.

Balloch

Gowanlea Guest House (Drymen Road, Balloch G83 8HS, ☎ 1389-752 456, fax 1389-710 543, gowanlea@aol.com; B&B £-££). Reasonably priced, high-quality accommodation in a family-run guest house.

Sheildaig Farm (Upper Stoney Mollen Road, Balloch G83 8QY, ☎ 1389-752 459, fax 1389-753 695, lesley@sheildaigfarm.co.uk, www.sheildaigfarm.co.uk; B&B ££, dinner ££). Comfortable courtyard bedrooms in a delightful country house set in nearly 30 acres of scenic farmland. There is a bar and excellent dinners are available (non-residents should book ahead).

Station Cottages (Balloch Road, Balloch G83 8SS, ☎ 1389-750 759, fax 1389-710 501, scottages@bigfoot.com; B&B ££, dinner ££). Delightful B&B accommodation in Victorian former station cottages, with evening meals available.

Loch Lomond Shores (Old Luss Road, Balloch G83 8QW, ☎ 1389-721 500, fax 1389-720 603, info@lochlomondshores.com, www.lochlomondshores.com; £-££). Three dining outlets allow plenty of choice; the 6th floor **Viewing Gallery Café** is hard to beat, with its superb elevated view over the loch.

Maid of the Loch (The Pier, Pier Road, Balloch G83 8QX, ☎ 1389-711 865, fax 1389-711 958, www.maidoftheloch.co.uk; open Easter-Oct, Nov-Easter, Sat-Sun; lunch £-££). Café, restaurant and bar aboard Loch Lomond's historic (though permanently berthed) paddle steamer.

Stables Restaurant (Roundabout Inn, Carrochan Road, Balloch G83 8BW, ☎ 1389-752 148, fax 1389-755 032, info@stablesrestaurant.com, www.stablesrestaurant.com; ££). A choice of light, informal brasserie meals or elegant fine dining in the restaurant.

Luss

Doune of Glen Douglas Farm (Luss G83 8PD, ☎/fax 1301-702 312, dounefarm@aol.com; B&B ££). B&B in an 18th-century house on a 6,000-acre sheep farm surrounded by great views.

Hill of Camstraddan Farm (Luss G83 8NX, ☎ 1436-860 262; B&B £-££). Farmhouse B&B on a friendly family-run hill farm within easy walking distance of Luss village.

Inverbeg Inn (Inverbeg, Luss G83 8PD, ☎ 1436-860 678, fax 1436-860 686, info@inverbeginn.co.uk, www.inverbeginn.co.uk; B&B £££, dinner ££-£££). The hotel is surrounded by beautiful scenery and offers a choice of bedrooms ranging from cozy, inn-style to sumptuous. The traditional dining room serves fresh local produce or you can eat more lightly in the bar with its real ales and good choice of whiskies.

Coach House Coffee Shop (Luss G83 8NN, ☎ 1436-860 341, fax 1436-860 336; £). A lovely coffee shop in the heart of Luss with a comfortable sofa, log fire, coffees, home baking and light meals.

Waters Edge Cottage (Duck Bay, Arden, near Luss G83 8QZ, ☎ 1389-850 629, fax 1389-850 549, www.watersedgecottage.co.uk; B&B ££). Charming Victorian lochside cottage furnished with antiques and curios. The individually styled bedrooms all have views of Loch Lomond and there is a good breakfast choice.

Ardlui

Ardlui Hotel (Ardlui G83 7EB, ☎ 1301-704 243, fax 1301-704 268, reception@ardlui.co.uk; B&B £££, dinner ££). Country-house hotel set at the magnificent head of Loch Lomond offering traditionally decorated rooms, bar meals and restaurant dining.

The Stagger Inn (Inverarnan, Ardlui G83 7ZZ, ☎ 1301-704 274; open April-Sept, plus weekends year-round; £-££). The inn combines a good menu, including excellent steaks and traditional cooking, and great views.

Arrochar

Dalkusha House (Arrochar, Loch Long G83 7AA, ☎ 1301-702 234, fax 1301-702 990, dalkusha@aol.com; B&B ££). B&B in a beautiful house set in large gardens. The sitting room has good loch views.

Ferry Cottage (Ardmay, Arrochar, Loch Long G83 7AH, ☎ 1301-702 428, fax 1301-702 729, ferrycottagebb@aol.com; B&B ££, dinner ££). Renovated 200-year-old cottage overlooking Loch Long and the Arrochar Alps, with pleasant rooms and evening meals available.

Village Inn (Arrochar, Loch Long G83 7AX, ☎ 1301-702 279, fax 1301-702 458, villageinn@maclay.co.uk, www.maclay.com; B&B ££). Refurbished inn with open log fires and individually styled bedrooms furnished with traditional furniture. The restaurant serves excellent local seafood, Angus beef and venison and the bar serves real ales and a wide whisky selection.

Dumbarton

The southern shores of Loch Lomond open into a broad, fertile valley. The fast-flowing **River Leven**, a noted salmon and sea trout river, flows from Loch Lomond through this valley, joining the **River Clyde** at the ancient town of Dumbarton. Dominating the town's skyline is the majestic ruin of **Dumbarton Castle** sitting atop a volcanic plug overlooking the estuary.

 INFORMATION SOURCES: The tourism office is at **Milton** on the A82 northbound, ☎/fax 870-720 0612, info@milton.visitscotland.com; open year-round.

■ Attractions & Sights

Dumbarton Castle (HS; Dumbarton, on the A82, ☎ 1389-732 167; open April-Sept, 9:30am-6:30pm; in winter, days/times vary; adult/concession/child £2.50/£1.90/£0.75). The castle is spectacularly situated on a 240-foot-high volcanic plug and witnessed several phases of development. Only the portcullis arch above the guard house (14th century) and the guardhouse itself (circa 1580) remain of the original stone structure. The castle was a medieval royal residence but was surrendered without a fight when Oliver Cromwell arrived in 1652. The Governor's House and King George's Battery, which dominate the Clyde side of the rock, date from 1735.

■ Shopping

Antartex Village (Lomond Industrial Estate, Heather Avenue, Alexandria G83 0TP, ☎ 1389-752 393, fax 1389-750 656). Watch Antartex sheepskins being made in the workshop and browse clothing, whisky, Scottish foods and gifts.

■ Where To Stay & Eat

See *Accommodation* and *Dining* price charts on pages 187 and 188.

Dumbuck House Hotel (Glasgow Road, Dumbarton G82 1EG, ☎ 1389-734 336, fax 1389-742 270, reservations@dumbuckhousehotel.com, www.dumbuckhousehotel.com; B&B £££, dinner ££). A 19th-century mansion set in landscaped gardens with stylishly refurbished bedrooms. There is a good restaurant serving natural local produce.

Helensburgh

Helensburgh is a holiday town named after the wife of Sir Robert Colquhoun, who founded the town at the end of the 18th century. The town has wide, tree-lined streets, a long promenade, parks and gardens. Wealthy Glaswegian merchants commissioned **Hill House**, Charles Rennie Mackintosh's domestic masterpiece, in upper Helensburgh.

INFORMATION SOURCES: The tourism office is at Clock Tower, The Pier, Helensburgh G84 7NY, ☎ 870-720 0615, info@helensburgh.visitscotland.com; open April-Oct.

■ Getting Here

By Car

Helensburg is on the A814 between Dumbarton and Ardgartan.

By Ferry

Strathclyde Passenger Transport (☎ 870-608 2608) operates a passenger-only ferry between Gourock and Kilcreggan, near Helensburgh (crossing time 40 minutes).

■ Attractions & Sights

Linn Botanic Gardens (Cove, By Helensburgh G84 0NR, ☎ 1436-842 242; open Mar-Oct, gardens, dawn to dusk; nursery, 11am-5pm; adult/concession/child £3/£2.50/£2). Formal ponds, extensive water garden, herbaceous borders, glen with waterfalls, cliff garden, rockery and terrace with views down the Firth of Clyde.

Hill House (NTS; Upper Colquhoun Street, Helensburgh G84 9AJ, ☎ 1436-673 900, fax 1436-674 685; open April-Oct, 1:30pm-5:30pm, weekday morning visits for pre-booked groups; adult/concession/family £7/£5.25/£19). Sitting high above the Clyde, this is Charles Rennie Mackintosh's finest domestic creation. Mackintosh designed not only the house and garden but also much of the furniture and all the interior fittings and decorative schemes.

■ Where To Stay

See *Accommodation* and *Dining* price charts on pages 187 and 188.

 Ava Lodge (44 Glasgow Street, Helensburgh G84 8YH, ☎ 1436-677 751, fax 1436-677 830, norma@cantello.prestel.co.uk; B&B ££). B&B in a comfortable Victorian villa well placed for the town, stations and seafront.

Longleat (39 East Argyle Street, Helensburgh G84 7EN, ☎ 1436-671 041, longleathouse@aol.com; B&B £). Traditional Victorian Scottish villa enclosed within pretty walled gardens with good views over the River Clyde.

Strone House (Glen Fruin, near Helensburgh G84 8YT, ☎/fax 1436-810 719, mac.ayres@lineone.net; B&B ££, dinner ££). Attractive beamed cottage with streamside gardens. Evening meals are available. The cottage with kitchen is occasionally let, when B&B is not available.

■ Where To Eat

 Famous Coffee House (102 West Princes Street, Helensburgh G84 8XD, ☎ 1436-672 005; £). Award-winning teas and coffees and an all-day menu, including homemade soups, light meals and ice cream.

Mira Mare (82 West Clyde Street, Helensburgh G84 8BB, ☎ 1436-673 766; closed Sun evening & Mon; ££). Extensive Italian menu, lunchtime specials and traditional Sunday lunches.

Upper Crust Restaurant (88a West Clyde Street, Helensburgh G84 8BB, ☎ 1436-678 035; dinner Tues-Sat; ££). Restaurant specializes in Scottish seafood and game, although vegetarian choices are also available.

The Trossachs

The Trossachs is a beautiful and unspoiled area of craggy peaks, shimmering lochs and deep-cut, forested glens – the Highlands in miniature. Its name derives from the Gaelic, meaning "crossing place" – where boats were hauled between **Loch Achray** and **Loch Katrine**.

The popular holiday town of **Callander** is set beneath high, wooded crags and is the eastern gateway to the Loch Lomond & the **Trossachs National Park**. Its main street is lined with tourist shops selling woolens, tartan, whisky and gifts. At the northern end of Loch Lubnaig is the small village of **Strathyre** (whose name means "sheltered valley"), surrounded by forested hillsides and overlooked by **Ben Sheann**.

The sleepy hamlet of **Balquhidder** lies at the head of Loch Voil, surrounded by glorious mountain scenery. The short climb up to the famous **Creag an Tuirc** viewpoint with its sweeping view down beautiful Balquhidder Glen is well worth the moderate effort. This is the heart of Rob Roy Country and his grave lies in the churchyard at Balquhidder, marked with the defiant motto, *MacGregor Despite Them*.

Aberfoyle is a traditional community on the banks of the River Forth and provides the southern gateway to the National Park. The drive north from Aberfoyle, over the winding Duke's Pass (named after Rob Roy's arch rival the Duke of Montrose), offers great views of tranquil lochs, forest and heather. Loch Katrine – which now provides Glasgow's water supply – inspired Sir Walter Scott to write *The Lady of the Lake*.

ROB ROY

Rob Roy MacGregor (1671-1734) is to some a folk hero, to others a notorious outlaw. Cattle trader, cattle thief and blackmailer, he led one of Scotland's wildest clans – **Clan MacGregor**. After falling out with their Campbell feudal lords, the MacGregors were evicted, outlawed and their name banned. Rob Roy and his clansmen resorted to raiding and plundering Campbell property, using their intimate knowledge of the wild Trossachs hills to outwit the Redcoat soldiers sent after them. The MacGregors' sudden raids were so skilful they became known as the "Children of the Mist."

 INFORMATION SOURCES: There are tourism offices in **Aberfoyle** (Trossachs Discovery Centre, Main Street, Aberfoyle, ☎ 870-720 0604, info@aberfoyle.visitscotland.com; open April-Oct & weekends only Nov-Mar) and **Callander** (Rob Roy & Trossachs Visitor Centre, Ancaster Square, Callander FK17 8ED, ☎ 870-720 0628, fax 1877-330 784, info@callander.visitscotland.com; open Mar-Dec & weekends only Jan-Feb).

■ Special Events

Callander Highland Games (July; ☎ 1877-330 184, fax 1877-330 228). Traditional Highland Games incorporating the World Heavyweight Championships.

■ Attractions & Sights

Rob Roy & Trossachs Visitor Centre (Ancaster Square, Callander, ☎ 1877-330 342, fax 1877-330 784, robroy&t@aillst.ossian.net; open year-round, hours vary seasonally; adult/concession/family £3.25/£2.25/£8.75). Discover the dramatic story of Rob Roy MacGregor – part freedom fighter, part blackmailer, part politician and part Robin Hood. There is an interesting audiovisual presentation and a reconstructed 18th-century farmhouse.

Balquhidder Kirk & Rob Roy's Grave (Balquhidder, off the A84). The ruins of Balquhidder Kirk date from 1631. It was built on the site of a pre-Reformation chapel once visited by King James IV. The new parish church dates from 1853 and its graveyard is the final resting place of Rob Roy MacGregor (1671-1734).

 **Inchmahome Priory** (HS; on an island in the Lake of Menteith, reached by ferry from Port of Menteith, four miles east of Aberfoyle, off the A81, ☎ 1877-385 294; open April-Sept from 9:30am, last outward sailing at 5:15pm; adult/concession/child £3.50/£2.50/£1.20, including ferry) is the beautifully situated ruin of an Augustinian monastery founded in 1238 by Walter Comyn, the Earl of Menteith. The young Mary, Queen of Scots was brought here briefly to hide after the Battle of Pinkie in 1547. The Reformation saw the land and buildings pass into secular hands and the priory gradually declined.

Moirlanich Longhouse (near Killin, ☎/fax 1567-820 988; open Easter Sun & May-Sept, Wed & Sun, 2pm-5pm; adult/concession £2/£1). An outstanding example of a traditional 19th-century cruck-frame cottage (built using naturally-curved timbers to create an A-frame) and byre (small barn or shed). The building has had little alteration since the last of three generations of the Robertson family left in 1968 and retains many original features such as box beds. A small adjacent building houses an exhibition and collection of original clothing.

Scottish Wool Centre (off Main Street, Aberfoyle FK8 3UQ, ☎ 1877-382 850, fax 1877-382 854; open year-round, hours vary seasonally; adult/concession/family £4/£3/£9). Learn the story of Scottish wool and browse through wide selections of woolens and knitwear. Try your hand at spinning or watch sheepdog demonstrations (daily in summer); in spring, children can handle and feed lambs and baby goats.

■ Adventures

On Foot

Creag an Tuirc (pronounced "creg-an-turk") is reached by a short, moderately steep walk from Balquhidder Kirk leading to a rocky outcrop; this was once a rallying place of Clan Maclaren. The path is well signposted from the church and passes through an area of forest before opening up. A cairn marks the viewpoint, from where there are sensational views beyond the pretty village of Balquhidder to Loch Voil and the Braes of

Balquhidder. The climb takes around 20 minutes and the view from the top for the little effort required is a real bargain (1 hour; easy).

A short but steep climb to the summit of **Ben A'an**, a well-loved and prominent Trossachs landmark. Despite its relative lack of height (1,300 feet), the summit offers spectacular views down Loch Katrine to the Cobbler and Ben Lomond, and back to Loch Achray and Loch Venachar. On a clear day you can even see the Campsie Hills and Dumgoyne.

From Callander, head west on the A821 toward Loch Katrine, continuing past Brig o'Turk to a church, beyond which is a parking area on the left with signs for Ben A'an. Cross the road and head up the rocky path climbing steadily through pine woodland. The path climbs steeply, crosses a wooden bridge then levels off, meandering through the trees. Cross a couple of streams, start to climb again and finally leave the trees, whereupon the shapely, conical peak of Ben A'an comes into view. This is the start of an extremely steep path leading to the summit. Rocky steps make the first part of the ascent relatively easy, but the path deteriorates to rough earth and loose stones. Just before the summit a path splits off to the left (a steeper path used by rock climbers), but stay on the main path to the top (2 hours; moderate).

Towering over the Trossachs, rugged **Ben Venue** (2,385 feet/727 m) offers marvelous views of Loch Katrine, Loch Achray and Loch Venachar. To the north, you can see Ben More, the Crianlarich Hills and Ben Lawers.

A path leads up Ben Venue from behind the Loch Achray Hotel just past the Loch Katrine road. Turn left at the first fork and continue straight ahead at the crossroads. The wide track now becomes a path. Rejoin a forestry road for a short distance and look for a waymarked path to the right. Walk uphill on a path through forest and cross a stile to reach open moorland. Continue toward the lowest point on the skyline, with the stream on your left. Past a cairn the path turns right toward Ben Venue's twin summits (3-4 hours; moderate).

An excellent road hugs the **Loch Katrine** shore from Trossachs Pier in the south over the northeastern shore to Stronachlachar on the western shore. It's a private water-board road and great for walking or cycling. The best way to tackle the walk is to take the *Walter Scott* steamer (see below, *On Water*) to Stronachlachar and then walk back, along the way passing tumbling streams and beautiful woodlands (5-6 hours; moderate).

Aberfoyle Golf Course (18-hole inland, 5,218 yards; Braeval, Aberfoyle FK8 3UY, ☎ 1877-382 493; green fees £15-£25). Heathland course with beautiful views and superb greens.

On Wheels

 Trossachs Cycle Hire (Trossachs Holiday Park, By Aberfoyle FK8 3SA, ☎ 1877-382 614, fax 1877-382 732, info@trossachsholidays-.co.uk, www.trossachsholidays.co.uk). Bikes for rent with helmets provided free. Mountain bike leader also available for group tours.

Wheels Cycle Hire & Sales (Invertrossachs Road, Callander FK17 8HW, ☎ 1877-331 100, fax 1877-331 200, scotcycle@aol.com, www.scottish-cycling.co.uk). Bikes for rent and on-site hostel accommodation.

On Water

Forest Hills Watersports (Forest Hills Resort, Kinlochard, Aberfoyle FK8 3TL, ☎ 1877-387 775, www.goforth.co.uk). Sailing, canoeing and mountain biking, with boat rental and fishing also available. Courses and instruction are available.

Standing Waves Leisure (Forestry Cabin, Main Street, Strathyre FK18 8NA, ☎ 1877-384 361; open April-Nov). Kayaks and canoes for rent; lessons and courses are available.

Lake of Menteith Fishery (Port of Menteith FK8 3RA, ☎ 1877-385 664; open April-Oct). The Lake of Menteith is one of Scotland's top trout fisheries (fly-casting for browns and rainbows) and is set in beautiful and historic surroundings.

Steamship *Sir Walter Scott* (Trossachs Pier, Loch Katrine, By Callander, FK17 8HZ, ☎ 1877-376 316, lochkatrine@scottishwater.co.uk, www.lochkatrine.co.uk; Easter-Oct, sailings Thurs-Tues, 11am, stopping at Stronachlachar; and 1:45pm & 3:15pm daily, no stops; adult/concession/family, round trip £6.80/£4.80/£14.76). Cruise beautiful Loch Katrine aboard a historic steamship that has sailed these waters for over a century. Bicycle rental is available for half- or full-day, £8/£12, from **Katrinewheelz**, ☎ 1877-376 284; you may take your own bike aboard the steamer for £0.50 if you want to cycle the pretty lochside path in one direction (from/to Stronachlachar).

■ Where To Stay & Eat

See *Accommodation* and *Dining* price charts on pages 187 and 188.

Aberfoyle

 Crannaig House (Trossachs Road, Aberfoyle FK8 3SR, ☎/fax 1877-382 276, info@crannaighouse.com, www.crannaighouse.com; B&B ££, dinner ££). B&B in a secluded Victorian house in Aberfoyle village. Evening meals are available.

Forth Inn (Main Street, Aberfoyle FK8 3UQ, ☎ 1877-382 372, fax 1877-382 488, phil@forthinn.com, www.forthinn.com; B&B £££). Atmospheric inn with comfortable bedrooms and excellent cuisine served in the cozy, traditional dining room.

Town House Hotel (16 Main Street, Aberfoyle FK8 3UG, ☎ 1877-382 216, townhousehotel@talk21.com; B&B ££, dinner ££). Family-run restaurant with rooms set in beautiful surroundings, offering reasonably priced evening meals emphasizing fresh Scottish produce.

Inchrie Castle/Covenanters Inn (Aberfoyle, ☎ 1877-382 347, fax 1877-382 785, enquiries@inchriecastle.co.uk, www.innscotland.com; DB&B ££££). Comfortable bedrooms; teas, bar meals, restaurant and ceilidh nights in the cozy, oak-beamed inn where a group of Scots signed the Second Covenant to "secure a Parliament for Scotland."

Callander

Brook Linn Country House (Leny Feus, Callander FK17 8AU, ☎/fax 1877-330 103, derek@blinn.freeserve.co.uk, www.brooklinn-scotland.co.uk; open Easter-Oct; B&B ££). Quality B&B accommodation in an attractive Victorian house set in pretty gardens with great views.

Conservatory Seafood Restaurant with Rooms (Ballachallan, Cambusmore, Callander FK17 8LJ, ☎/fax 1877-339 190, enquiries@ballachallan.co.uk, www.ballachallan.co.uk; open mid-Feb through Dec, restaurant open Wed-Sun; B&B ££, dinner ££). A traditional stone farmhouse set peacefully in its own grounds near Callander. The spacious bedrooms are full of character and include the room where Sir Walter Scott supposedly wrote *The Lady of the Lake*. The light and airy conservatory overlooks tranquil countryside and serves a wide selection of fresh fish, shellfish and Scottish meats.

Leny House (Leny Estate, Callander FK17 8HA, ☎ 1877-331 078, fax 1877-331 335, res@lenyestate.com, www.lenyestate.com; open April-Oct; B&B £££-££££). Opulent B&B accommodation in a grand historic estate house enjoying great views over mountains and glens. Guest accommodation includes spacious four-poster bedrooms, fine antiques, tapestries and open fires. Accommodation with kitchen is also available.

Lubnaig House (Leny Feus, Callander FK17 8AS, ☎/fax 1877-330 376, info@lubnaighouse.co.uk, www.lubnaighouse.co.uk; open May-Oct; B&B ££). Fine Victorian house with lovely bedrooms, three guest lounges, including the delightful Garden Room, and tranquil views.

Waverley Hotel (88-94 Main Street, Callander FK17 8BD, ☎ 1877-330 245, fax 1877-331 120, enquiries@thewaverleycallander.com, www.thewaverleycallander.com; B&B ££, dinner ££). Family-run hotel renowned for fine food and cask ales. The hotel hosts an annual beer festival and has regular live entertainment.

Lade Inn (Kilmahog, By Callander FK17 8HD, ☎ 1877-330 152, fax 1877-331 878, www.theladeinn.com; £-££). Friendly traditional pub serving a wide choice of whiskies, cask-conditioned real ales and home-cooked food. There is live music (ceilidh or live bands) on Saturday evenings.

Strathyre/Balquhidder

Creagan House (Strathyre FK18 8ND, ☎ 1877-384 638, fax 1877-384 319, eatandstay@creaganhouse.co.uk, www.creaganhouse.co.uk; open Mar-Jan; B&B £££, dinner £££). A converted farmhouse dating to 1638 that oozes charm and character. The lounge is inviting and atmospheric, with exposed stone walls and cozy nook behind a wooden dresser. The five guestrooms are decorated with nice touches such as antique furniture, books and CDs. Gordon and Cherry Gunn don't show guests the dining room until dinner, when newcomers invariably gasp on entering the magnificent baronial room with its massive fireplace. Gordon's culinary skills match the splendor of the room and can be accompanied by wines from a surprisingly extensive list.

Ardoch Lodge (Strathyre FK18 8NF, ☎/fax 1877-384 666, ardoch@btinternet.com; open Easter-Oct; B&B ££-£££, dinner £££). Attractive spacious bedrooms with good mountain views, quietly set in 12 acres. High-quality evening meals are available.

Monachyle Mhor (Balquhidder, Lochearnhead FK19 8PQ, ☎ 1877-384 622, fax 1877-384 305, info@monachylemhor.com, www.monachylemhor.com; open Feb-Dec; B&B £££, lunch ££, dinner ££££). Rose-washed country home set amid farmland with open fires and wonderful views. The French-influenced modern Scottish restaurant serves local fish, meat and game.

Breadalbane

The ancient Celtic earldom of Breadalbane straddles the northern border of the Loch Lomond & the Trossachs National Park. Its name derives from the Gaelic meaning "high country of Scotland" and it is home to the grandest and wildest mountain scenery in the park. Its great sweeping mountains and tumbling waterfalls are the realm of deer and eagles. This is where the Highlands begin.

The pretty village of **Killin** lies beneath impressive mountains at the head of Loch Tay. The celebrated **Falls of Dochart** spill through the heart of the village. Breadalbane abounds with folk history and tales of mythical Celtic heroes and medieval saints, all of which can be explored at Killin's **Breadalbane Folklore Centre**.

Lochearnhead has a lovely lochside setting and is a leading watersports center. **Crianlarich** is a tiny, strung-out village along the West Highland Way, overlooked by **Ben More**.

 INFORMATION SOURCES: There are tourism offices in **Killin** (Breadalbane Folklore Centre, Falls of Dochart, Killin FK21 8XE, ☎ 870 720 0627, fax 1567-820 764, info@killin.visitscotland.com; open Mar-Oct) and **Tyndrum** (Main Street, Tyndrum FK20 8RY, ☎ 870 720 0626, info@tyndrum.visitscotland.com; open April-Oct).

■ Special Events

Killin Highland Games (Jul; ☎ 1567-820 224, fax 1567-820 819). Traditional Highland Games with side shows, amusements and stalls.

■ Attractions & Sights

Breadalbane Folklore Centre (St Fillan's Mill, Killin FK21 8XE, ☎ 1567-820 254, fax 1567-820 764, killin@aillst.ossian.net; open Mar-May & Oct, 10am-5pm; July-Aug, 9:30am-6:30pm; Jun & Sep, 10am-6pm; adult/concession/child/family £2/£1.25/£5.25). Housed in a restored watermill overlooking the Falls of Dochart, the Centre gives a fascinating insight into the rich folklore and fables of ancient Breadalbane – the high country of Scotland. A touch-screen book of local folklore tells a number of tales, including *The Piper's Pool*, the *Black Laird of Glenorchy*, the *Lairig Eirie Ghost* and the *Witch of Strath Fillan*. Separate displays record the lives of local clans: the MacGregors (of Rob Roy fame), MacLarens, MacNabs and Campbells. An atmospheric exhibition describes the life of St Fillan, an early Celtic evangelist whose relic is reputed to have inspired Robert the Bruce on the eve of Bannockburn.

Falls of Dochart. Tumbling through the heart of the pretty village of Killin, the celebrated and much-photographed (though far from thundering) falls cascade beneath the bridge and flow around the island of **Inchbuie** (or *Innes Buie*), the traditional burial place of clan MacNab.

■ Adventures

The ascent of **Ben Lui** (3,710 feet/1,130 m) is one of the best walks in the area. The walk starts from Tyndrum Lower Station, from where you follow the track in Glen Cononish. Follow the riverbank as far as Coire Laoigh (between Ben Lui and Ben Oss), from where the ascent to the summit via the southeastern ridge is fairly straightforward (7 hours; moderate).

Quad Ventures (Auchtertyre, Tyndrum, Crianlarich FK20 8RU, ☎ 1838-400 229, www.quadventures.co.uk; £25 for an hour). Quad bike tours on remote tracks leading high into the hills.

Drummond Estates Boat Hire (Ardveich Bay, Lochearnhead FK19 8PZ, ☎ 1567-830 400, fax 1567-830 265, open mid-Mar through early Oct). Rentals of 15-foot boats equipped with outboards, oars and lifejackets. £15 for four hours, £29 for eight hours.

Lochearnhead Watersports Centre (Lochearnhead FK19 8PR, ☎ 1567-830 330, fax 1567-830 434; open Easter-Oct). Waterskiing, dinghy sailing, Canadian canoes and kayaks for rent.

■ Golf

Killin Golf Course (9-hole parkland, 5,066 yards; Killin FK21 8TX, ☎/fax 1567-820 312, info@killingolfclub.co.uk, www.killingolf-club.co.uk; green fees £15). A gem of a parkland course hidden in the breathtaking Breadalbane Hills.

■ Where To Stay & Eat

See *Accommodation* and *Dining* price charts on pages 187 and 188.

Ewich House (Strathfillan, Crianlarich FK20 8RU, ☎/fax 1838-300 300, enquiries@ewich.co.uk, www.ewich.co.uk; B&B ££, dinner ££). Expanded around an early 19th-century farmhouse, Ewich (pronounced "you-wick") provides tranquil, comfortable accommodation within yards of the West Highland Way. There are lovely views, particularly from the rear toward Ben Challum. The friendly proprietors, Liz and Brian, produce tasty home cooking using locally sourced produce. Liz's homemade muesli is excellent and breakfasts are enlivened by Jim, the colorful local Post Bus driver, who drops by for tea during his morning round.

Station Tea Room (Crianlarich FK20 8QN, ☎ 1838-300 204, fax 1838-300 242; open Mar-Oct; £). An ideal place for a snack or light meal amid beautiful mountain scenery.

Dall Lodge Country House Hotel (Killin FK21 8TN, ☎ 1567-820 217, fax 1567-820 726, connor@dalllodgehotel.co.uk, www.dalllodgehotel.co.uk; open Mar-Oct; B&B ££). Late-Victorian country mansion set on the banks of River Lochay at the head of Loch Tay. Four-poster rooms are available and the elegant dining room has stunning views to Ben Lawers and River Lochay.

Killin Hotel (Killin FK21 8TP, ☎ 1567-820 296, fax 1567-820 647, info@killinhotel.eu.com, www.killinhotel.eu.com; B&B ££, dinner ££). Comfortable riverside hotel with an excellent restaurant, informal bistro and roaring fires in the lounge and public bars.

Breadalbane House (Main Street, Killin FK21 8UT, ☎ 1567-820 134, fax 1567-820 798, info@breadalbanehouse.com; B&B ££). Comfortable accommodation in an attractive house with good breakfasts and dinner available by arrangement.

Fairview House (Main Street, Killin FK21 8UT, ☎ 1567-820 667, info @fairview-killin.co.uk, www.fairview-killin.co.uk; B&B ££, dinner ££). Elegant Victorian villa providing comfortable bedrooms and a relaxing lounge. A four-course evening meal is available, except Wednesday and Sunday, (pre-booking required).

Cowal Peninsula

The Cowal Peninsula lies between **Loch Fyne** in the west and **Loch Long** in the east. This little visited area of hills, forests, deep glacial lochs and narrow winding roads is home to attractive villages like Tighnabruaich, and Lochgoilhead. Built around two sheltered bays, Dunoon is Cowal's principal town. It grew in the late 19th century to cater to visitors and boasts a range of hotels, shops and eateries. There isn't much reason to stay in Dunoon, unless you are here for the annual Cowal Gathering, the town's famous Highland Games.

■ Getting Here

Caledonian MacBrayne (☎ 1475-650 100, www.calmac.co.uk) and **Western Ferries** (☎ 1369-704 452, www.western-ferries.co.uk) both sail car ferries from Gourock near the end of the M8 motorway across the Firth of Clyde to Dunoon. Both take 20 minutes; the CalMac ferry runs from Gourock to Dunoon and drops you closest to the town; the Western Ferries boat sails from Gourock (McInroy's Point) to Dunoon Hunter's Quay.

There's also a CalMac ferry from Rhubodach on the Isle of Bute to Colintraive in Cowal (crossing time five minutes).

INFORMATION SOURCES: There are tourism offices in **Dunoon** (7 Alexandra Parade, Dunoon PA23 8AB, ☎ 870-720 0629, fax 1369-706 085, info@dunoon.visitscotland.com; open year-round) and **Ardgartan** (Glen Croe, By Arrochar G83 7AR, ☎/fax 870-720 0606, info@ardgartan.visitscotland.com; open April-Oct).

■ Special Events

 Cowal Highland Gathering (last Fri-Sat in Aug; 54 Hillfoot Street, Dunoon PA23 7DT, ☎ 1369-703 206, info@cowalgathering.com, www.cowalgathering.com). The largest and one of the most spectacular Highland Games featuring the World Highland Dancing Championships, over 150 massed bands, solo piping, track and heavy athletics and shinty tournaments (see page 64).

■ Attractions & Sights

Benmore Botanic Garden (by Dunoon PA23 8QU, ☎ 1369-706 261, fax 1369-706 369, benmore@rbge.org.uk, www.rbge.org.uk; open Mar-Oct, 10am-5pm; April-Sept til 6pm); adult/concession/child/family £3.50/£3/£1/£8). The gardens include an avenue of giant redwoods, over 250 rhododendron species, a stunning view over the Holy Loch, and mountainside trails. There is also a shop and café.

Castle House Museum (Castle Gardens, Dunoon PA23 7HH, ☎ 1369-701 422, info@castlehousemuseum.org.uk, www.castlehousemuseum.org.uk; open Easter-Oct, Mon-Sat, 10:30am-4:30pm & Sun, 2pm-4:30pm; adult/concession £1.50/£1, children free with paid adult). In a historic building, in rooms furnished in the Victorian style, are collections of models and photographs exploring the history of Cowal and Dunoon, from ancient times to the heyday of the Clyde steamers. Nothing now remains of the ancient castle except the hill on which it stood (now Castle Gardens).

Castle Lachlan (Strathlachlan, on the eastern shore of Loch Fyne between Otter Ferry and Strachur). This ruined 15th-century castle, set on a promontory on the eastern shore of Loch Fyne, was the ancestral home of Clan Lachlan. The clan chief was killed at Culloden in 1746, after which the castle was ravaged by the Campbells and ordered to be destroyed. Many of the rooms and doorways have been closed up but it's picturesque from the outside.

> **NOTE:** The "New" Castle Lachlan is an 18th-century house on the Lachlan estate, updated in the Scottish Baronial style in the late 19th century, which offers rooms on a weekly or long-weekend basis (www.scottscastles.com/lachlan).

Toward Castle (two miles south of Innellan on the A815). This ruined 15th-century castle stands near the southern tip of the peninsula and was the scene of the massacre of 200 Lamont clansmen by the Campbells in 1646.

■ Adventures

Quadmania (Stronchullin Farm, Blairmore, By Dunoon PA23 8TP, ☎/fax 1369-810 246, info@quadmaniascotland.co.uk, www.quadmaniascotland.co.uk). Quad bike treks across 2,600 acres of farmland and woodland. £35 for 1½-hour trek (minimum age 16).

Tighnabruaich Sailing School (Tighnabruaich PA21 2AH, ☎/fax 1700-811 717, enquiries@tssargyll.co.uk, www.tssargyll.co.uk; May-Sept). Daily, weekend and weekly courses in dinghy sailing and windsurfing for all levels on the sheltered waters of the Kyles of Bute.

Yellow Water Taxi (Lochgoilhead PA24 8AH, ☎ 1301-703 382; May-Sept; adult/child £9/£6). Depart from Ardentinny (20 minutes from Dunoon) and travel at speed to Lochgoilhead, where you have time for lunch before returning. You may see seals on the way. Booking essential.

Ardroy Outdoor Education Centre (Lochgoilhead PA24 8AE, ☎ 1301-703 391/703 353, fax 1301-703 479, ardroy.oec@btinternet.com, www.outdooreducation.co.uk). Weekend trips include canoeing, kayaking, hillwalking, climbing, abseiling, orienteering, archery and gorge walking. From £75.

■ Golf

Cowal Golf Course (18-hole inland, 6,063 yards; Ardenslate Road, Dunoon PA23 8IB, ☎/fax 1369-705 673, info@cowalgolfclub.co.uk, www.cowalgolfclub.co.uk; green fees £24-£34). Founded in 1891, this heathland course overlooks the Firth of Clyde and Dunoon and provides an enjoyable golfing test with great views of the Isle of Arran and Ailsa Craig.

■ Where To Stay

See *Accommodation* price chart on page 187.

Enmore Hotel (Marine Parade, Kirn, Dunoon PA23 8HH, ☎ 1369-702 230, fax 1369-702 148, info@enmorehotel.co.uk, www.enmorehotel.co.uk; open mid-Feb to mid-Dec; B&B ££££, dinner ££-£££). Built in 1875 as a retreat for a wealthy Glasgow businessman, this small hotel has luxurious bedrooms, some with four-poster beds, others with whirlpool baths, a renowned restaurant and three lounges.

Dhailling Lodge (155 Alexandra Parade, Dunoon PA23 8AW, ☎ 1369-701 253, fax 1369-701 340, fraser@dhaillinglodge.com, www.dhaillinglodge.com; B&B ££, lunch £, dinner ££). Victorian villa overlooking the Firth of Clyde. There is a patio, garden and intimate dining room serving a limited but excellent dinner menu.

Lyall Cliff Hotel (141 Alexandra Parade, East Bay, Dunoon PA23 8AW, ☎/fax 1369-702 041, info@lyallcliff.co.uk, www.lyallcliff.co.uk; open Jan-Oct; B&B ££, dinner ££). Small hotel with an excellent seafront location and pretty garden. Most bedrooms have sea views. The hotel has music weekends in the spring and autumn.

Royal Hotel (Tighnabruaich PA21 2BE, ☎ 1700-811 239, fax 1700-811 300, info@royalhotel.org.uk, www.royalhotel.org.uk; B&B £££, dinner ££). Situated on the edge of the Kyles of Bute, the Royal has beautifully furnished bedrooms and public areas and high-quality dining in its brasserie and restaurant with fish and game the specialty.

■ Where To Eat

See *Dining* price chart on page 188.

 Chatters Restaurant (58 John Street, Dunoon PA23 8BJ, ☎ 1369-706 402; open Mar-Dec, Wed-Sat; lunch £-££, dinner ££-£££). French-influenced Scottish cooking capably presented in a pleasant, informal atmosphere.

Di Marco's Café Bar & La Cantina Restaurant (200 Argyll Street, Dunoon PA23 7HA, ☎ 1369-703 595/705 550, info@lacantinadimarcos.co.uk, www.lacantina-dimarcos.co.uk; closed Mon; £-££). Italian restaurant serving home-baked pizza, authentic pasta, and a good selection of wines and beers.

The Lorne Bar (249 Argyll Street, Dunoon PA23 7QT, ☎ 1369-705 064; £). Family-run traditional pub serving good bar meals, fine ales and a good selection of whiskies. There is weekend entertainment.

The Yachtsman (Victoria Parade, West Bay, Dunoon PA23 7HN, ☎ 1369-704 428; open Mar-Nov; £). Licensed seafront coffee shop and restaurant serving good food at reasonable prices.

Anselmo's Fish & Chips (36 Hillfoot Street, Dunoon PA23 7DT, ☎ 1369-703 849; £). Fish and chips shop with lunchtime specials and a few tables.

Isle of Bute

Bute is one of the most accessible west coast islands and has a long history stretching back to its first settlers in 2000 BC. Early people left standing stones at **Ettrick Bay**, the ancient chapel of **St Blane** and the Iron Age fort at **Dunagoil**. **Rothesay**, the island's only town, has the impressive Gothic castle of **Mount Stuart**, as well as many fine Victorian buildings dating from Bute's heyday as a holiday resort, including the refurbished **Winter Garden** and ornate public toilets. Rothesay gave its name to Scotland's premier dukedom in 1398, a title held today by Prince Charles.

 INFORMATION SOURCES: The tourism office is at Isle of Bute Discovery Centre, Winter Gardens, Victoria Street, Rothesay, Isle of Bute PA20 0AT, ☎ 870-720 0619, fax 1700-505 156, info@rothesay.visitscotland.com; open year-round.

■ Special Events

Isle of Bute Jazz Festival (Apr/May; Bute Discovery Centre, Rothesay, Isle of Bute, ☎ 1700-502 151, fax 1700-505 156). A top event attracting great performers, this is one of Scotland's most popular jazz weekends.

Bute Highland Games (next-to-last Saturday in August; ☎ 1700-831 610, evenings). Traditional Highland Games with a full program of pipe bands, Highland dancing and athletic events.

■ Getting Here

 Caledonian MacBrayne (☎ 1475-650 100, www.calmac.co.uk) operates car-ferry services from Colintraive in Cowal to Rhubodach (crossing time five minutes) and from Wemyss Bay in Ayrshire to Rothesay (crossing time 35 minutes).

■ Attractions & Sights

The Bute Museum (Stuart Street, Rothesay, Isle of Bute, ☎ 1700-505 067, open April-Sept, Mon-Sat, 10:30am-4:30pm; Sun, 2:30pm-4:30pm; Oct-Mar, Tues-Sat, 2:30pm-4:30pm; adult/concession/child £1.50/£1/£0.50). The museum houses displays on Clyde steamers, geology, archaeology and other aspects of local history.

Isle of Bute Discovery Centre (The Winter Garden, Rothesay, Isle of Bute PA20 0AH, ☎ 870-720 0619, fax 1700-505 156, info@rothesay.visit-scotland.com). Housed in the restored 1924 Winter Garden, the exhibition provides a good introduction to Bute in addition to tourist information.

 **Mount Stuart** (Mount Stuart, Isle of Bute PA20 9LR, ☎ 1700-503 877, fax 1700-505 313, contactus@mountstuart.com, www.mountstuart.com; open Easter & May-Aug, house 11am-5pm; gardens, 10am-6pm; closed Tues & Thurs; adult/concession/child/family £7/£5.50/£3/£16). A spectacular Victorian Gothic mansion surrounded by 300 acres of grounds and gardens. Mount Stuart is the home of the Marquess of Bute, whose family descends from Robert the Bruce. The mansion occupies the site of a previous mansion that was destroyed by fire in 1877. The ornate interior includes a lavish use of marble (including a magnificent marble hall and white marble chapel), fine works of art and other treasures. There is an audiovisual presentation, exhibition gallery, guided and waymarked walks, shop and restaurant.

Rothesay Castle (HS; Rothesay, Isle of Bute, ☎ 1700-502 691; open April-Sept, 9:30am-6:30pm; Oct-Mar, 9:30am-4:30pm, closed some days in winter, call ahead; adult/concession/child £2.50/£1.90/£0.75). This 13th-century castle commands the town of Rothesay on Bute and is surrounded by a circular curtain wall within its water-filled moat. The castle was a favorite residence of the Stewart kings until the Duke of Argyll's men burned it in a revolt in 1685. It remained abandoned until 1816 when the Marquis of Bute began restoration work.

St Blane's Chapel (above Dunagoil at the southern end of the island). The charming and tranquil ruin of a 12th-century Romanesque chapel set within an early Christian monastery founded by St Blane. There is evidence of much earlier settlements on this site; tombs record the names of two 7th-century bishops and three 8th-century abbots.

St Mary's Chapel (HS; Rothesay High Kirk, High Street, Rothesay; open 8am-5pm; closed Fridays Oct-Mar; admission free). The late-medieval remains of the chancel of the Parish Church of St Mary, which was recently re-roofed to protect its fine tombs.

Scalpsie Bay in the southwest is home to a seal colony. Bute's central **lochs** attract huge numbers of wintering greylag geese, as well as large numbers of teal and goldeneye ducks.

■ Adventures

Bute Sailing School (The Crows Nest, 3 Castle Street, Port Bannatyne, Isle of Bute PA20 0ND, ☎ 1700-504 881; open Mar-Nov). Sailing courses, day-sails and adventure cruises (to the Inner Hebrides, Irish coast and St Kilda) aboard a luxury offshore yacht.

■ Where To Stay & Eat

See *Accommodation* and *Dining* price charts on pages 187 and 188.

The Ardyne – St Ebba Hotel & Restaurant (37/38 Mount Stuart Road, Rothesay, Isle of Bute PA20 9EB, ☎ 1700-502 052, fax 1700-505 129, ardyne.hotel@virgin.net, www.rothesay-scotland.com; B&B ££, dinner ££). Imposing Victorian hotel with superb seafront views. The hotel has comfortable accommodation and a good restaurant.

Bayview Hotel (21/22 Mount Stuart Road, Rothesay, Bute PA20 9EB, ☎ 1700-505 411, fax 1700-505 416, bayview.hotel@tinyworld.co.uk; open Feb-Nov; B&B ££, dinner £). Friendly Victorian hotel with good views over Rothesay Bay, offering reasonably priced full board (no single supplements).

Port Royal Hotel (37 Marine Road, Port Bannatyne, Isle of Bute PA20 0LW, ☎ 1700-505 073, stay@butehotel.com, www.butehotel.com; B&B ££, dinner ££). Waterfront Russian-style tavern with refurbished rooms, award-winning real ales, Tsarist-influenced menu and performances by visiting Russian musicians. A genuine taste of Russia on a Scottish island.

Balmory Hall (Ascog, Isle of Bute PA20 9LL, ☎/fax 1700-500 669, enquiries@balmoryhall.com, www.balmoryhall.com; B&B ££££). A grand and secluded Victorian mansion built in Italian villa style, with spacious and elegant accommodation.

St Blanes Hotel (Kilchattan Bay, Isle of Bute PA20 9NW, ☎/fax 1700-831 224; B&B ££, dinner £). Unusual 19th-century building by the water's edge at the south of the island. Facilities include a four-poster room, restaurant and beer garden.

The Black Bull (3 West Princes Street, Rothesay, Isle of Bute PA20 9AF, ☎ 1700-502 366, fax 1700-504 466; £). Bute's oldest pub is situated opposite Rothesay harbor and serves good food and beer.

Craigmore Pier Licensed Tearoom & Restaurant (Mount Stuart Road, Rothesay, Isle of Bute PA20 9LD, ☎/fax 1700-502 867; lunch £, dinner ££-£££). Fresh, homemade fare served with unrestricted sea views.

The Kettledrum Bistro/Café (32 East Princes Street, Rothesay, Isle of Bute PA20 9DN, ☎ 1700-505 324; £-££). Pleasant café overlooking Rothesay harbor that serves coffees, snacks and three-course meals.

Oban & Lorn

Oban

Oban (from the Gaelic for "little bay") is an attractive, bustling fishing port set in a peaceful bay protected by the **Isle of Kerrera**, beyond which lie the green island of **Lismore**, the **Isle of Mull** and mountains of the **Morvern Peninsula**. **Dunollie Castle**, which has stood sentinel over the northern entrance to the bay for six centuries, is now a picturesque ruin. Also north of the town is a sandy beach at **Ganavan**.

As the main ferry port for the Hebrides, Oban is known as the "Gateway to the Isles." The town can get quite busy with visitors, but retains the feel of a genuine town rather than a tourist trap. Despite there not being many attractions in the town itself, Oban is a pleasant town to spend time in, and has several good eateries to try.

 INFORMATION SOURCES: The tourism office is at Argyll Square, Oban PA34 4AN, ☎ 870-720 0630, fax 1631-564 273, info@oban.visitscotland.com; open year-round.

■ Special Events

Highlands & Islands Music & Dance Festival (May; 2 Etive Park, Connel, By Oban, ☎ 1631-710 787). A major competitive arts festival featuring Highland dancing, singing and instruments.

Argyllshire Gathering (Oban Games – fourth Wed & Thurs in Aug; ☎/fax 1631-562 671, www.obangames.com). One of the oldest Highland Games, including visitors' races and shinty (see page 64).

■ Attractions & Sights

Dunollie Castle (Corran Esplanade, Oban). Originally dating from the 7th century, the present ruins of the seat of Clan MacDougall date from the 15th century.

McCaig's Tower (signposted up Craigard Road from George Street in central Oban). Founded in 1900 by John Stuart McCaig, arts critic, philosophical essayist, banker and Oban resident, the tower resembles the thin outer wall of a coliseum. Although a complete circle, funds ran out to complete the roof and the structure resembles a crown overlooking Oban. The wonderful view across Oban is worth the fairly steep walk up to the tower.

Oban Distillery (Stafford Street, Oban PA34 5NH, ☎ 1631-572 004, fax 1631-572 011; open year-round, days and hours vary seasonally; last tour one hour before closing; admission £4). Oban Distillery is unusual in being sited in the center of a bustling town, and as a result is one of the easiest to tour. The single malt has a character in between the light mainland style and the peaty, complex island style.

■ Adventures

 Puffin Dive Centre (Port Gallanach, Oban PA34 4QH, ☎ 1631-566 088, fax 1631-564 142, info@puffin.org.uk, www.puffin.org.uk). Award-winning dive training center offering courses for all levels of diver and trial dives for novices.

Gordon Grant Tours (Waterfront, Railway Pier, Oban PA34 4AL, ☎ 1631-562 842, fingal@staffatours.com, www.staffatours.com). Excursions to the "Three Isles" of Mull, Iona and Staffa, and tours to the Treshnish Isles.

Achnalarig Riding Stables (Achnalarig Farm & Stables, Glencruitten, Oban PA34 4QA, ☎ 1631-562 745, ☎ 7748-708 141 mobile). Riding, trekking and lessons for all ages and abilities.

■ Entertainment

 McTavish's Kitchen (34 George Street, Oban, ☎ 1631-563 064, oban@mctavishs.com, www.mctavishs.com; open May-Sept, nightly, 8pm-10pm; adult/child £2/£1 if dining, show only £4/£2) has shows of traditional Scottish music and dance, with à la carte or fixed-price menus, and great views across the bay.

O'Donnell's Irish Bar (Breadalbane Street, Oban PA34 5NZ, ☎ 1631-566 159, odonnellsoban@aol.com) has live Irish music most nights in summer.

■ Shopping

The Iona Shop (2 Queens Park Place, Oban PA34 5RS, ☎ 1631-562 071, fax 1631-562 600, info@ionashop.com, www.ionashop.co.uk). Third-generation family business specializing in quality Scottish jewelry and gifts, including a fine Celtic wedding ring collection and products from some of the smallest local workshops.

The Kitchen Garden (14 George Street, Oban PA34 5SB, ☎ 1631-566 332). Delicatessen offering a fine range of gourmet Scottish foods and a restaurant and coffee shop upstairs.

■ Where To Stay

Hotels

 The Manor House (Gallanach Road, Oban PA34 4LS, ☎ 1631-562 087, fax 1631-563 053, manorhouseoban@aol.com, www.manorhouse-oban.com; B&B ££££, dinner £££). Built in 1780 as the principal residence of the Duke of Argyll's Oban estate, The Manor House is one of Oban's best hotels, and occupies a quiet position with magnificent views over the bay. The late-Georgian exterior, with an attractive glasshouse to one side, and elegant interior finished in rich colors and fine wood paneling, create a stylish country-house ambience. The rooms are very high-quality and the excellent restaurant rightly wins awards.

Kings Knoll Hotel (Dunollie Road, Oban PA34 5JH, ☎ 1631-562 536, fax 1631-566 101, kingsknoll@aol.com, www.kingsknollhotel.co.uk; open Feb-Dec; B&B ££, dinner £-££). Small, family-run hotel overlooking the bay. The bedrooms and public lounges are pleasantly styled and there is a choice of restaurant and bar dining.

Queens Hotel (Esplanade, Oban PA34 5AG, ☎ 1631-562 505, fax 1631-566 217, queens@british-trust-hotels.com, www.british-trust-hotels.com; B&B £££, dinner ££). A friendly hotel with nicely decorated bedrooms and lounges and excellent sea and hill views. There is a good restaurant.

Soroba House Hotel (Oban PA34 4SB, ☎ 1631-562 628, fax 1631-566 900, enquiry@sorobahouse.co.uk, www.sorobahouse.co.uk; B&B £££). This attractive 18th-century, white-painted hotel was once the home of John Stuart McCaig, builder of McCaig's Tower. The hotel stands in 10 acres of land and has luxurious guest suites. The Queen and Prince Philip have dined in the restaurant.

Guest Houses & B&Bs

HOTEL PRICE CHART	
Per person, per night, based on double occupancy in high season. B&B rate includes breakfast; DB&B includes dinner and breakfast.	
£	Under £20
££	£21-£35
£££	£36-£50
££££	£51-£80
£££££	Over £80

La Cala (Ganavan Road, Oban PA34 5TU, ☎/fax 1631-562 741, lacala@zoom.co.uk; open Mar-Oct; B&B ££). Beautiful, white-washed Georgian-style house set in attractive gardens by the sea with views to the islands.

Glenara Guest House (Rockfield Road, Oban PA34 5DQ, ☎ 1631-563 172, fax 1631-571 125, info@glenara-oban.com, www.glenara-oban.com; B&B ££). B&B in an individually furnished house featuring antique pine king-size beds and a large collection of the owner's objets d'arts.

Greencourt Guest House (Benvoulin Lane, Oban PA34 5EF, ☎ 1631-563 987, fax 1631-571 276, relax@greencourt-oban.fsnet.co.uk, www.greencourt-oban.fsnet.co.uk; B&B ££). Pleasant accommodation in a quiet residential area close to the center of Oban. The bright dining room has good views toward Oban Bay.

Hawthornbank Guest House (Dalriach Road, Oban PA34 5JE, ☎ 1631-562 041, hawthornbank@aol.com; B&B ££). Attractive Victorian villa offering high levels of comfort, including an attractive four-poster room.

Kathmore Guest House (Soroda Road, Oban PA34 4JF, ☎ 1631-562 104, fax 1631-570 067, wkathmore@aol.com, www.kathmore.co.uk; B&B £-££). Comfortable B&B accommodation in an attractive whitewashed cottage a short walk from the town center. The guest lounge leads to an outside decking area and light snacks are served in the evening.

Invercairn (Musdale Road, Kilmore, By Oban PA34 4XX, ☎/fax 1631-770 301, invercairn.kilmore@virgin.net, www.invercairn.com; open April-Sept; B&B ££). Modern bungalow in a picturesque setting next to an ancient Pictish cairn, from which the house takes its name. A delicious tea with home baking awaits you on arrival.

■ Where To Eat

The Gathering Restaurant (Breadalbane Street, Oban PA34 5NZ, ☎ 1631-565 421/564 849, gatheringoban@aol.com; open Easter-Christmas; lunch £, dinner ££). A banqueting hall built in 1882 for Scottish nobility and visiting royalty, that serves good food using local seafood, beef and game. The attached **O'Donnell's Irish Bar** (☎ 1631-566 159, odonnellsoban@aol.com; £) serves lunches and bar meals with live music most nights.

The China Restaurant (39 Stafford Street, Oban, ☎ 1631-563 575; ££). Good-quality Chinese restaurant opposite Oban Distillery.

Ee'usk Fish Café (102 George Street, Oban PA34 5NT, ☎ 1631-565 666, fax 1631-570 282; lunch £-££, dinner ££-£££). Excellent seafood bistro with a buzzy atmosphere.

The Kitchen Garden (14 George Street, Oban PA34 5SB, ☎ 1631-566 332; £-££). Delicatessen selling fine gourmet foods with an upstairs restaurant serving all-day snacks and meals.

Light of India Tandoori Restaurant (43 Stevenson Street, Oban PA34 5NA, ☎ 1631-563 728; £-££). Established Indian restaurant that offers a takeaway service.

The Manor House (Gallanach Road, Oban PA34 4LS, ☎ 1631-562 087, manorhouseoban@aol.com, www.manorhouse-oban.com; lunch ££, dinner £££).

DINING PRICE CHART	
Indicates the price per person for a full meal, excluding drinks. Generally three courses, though fixed menus of five or more courses may be available.	
£	Under £10
££	£11-£20
£££	£21-£30
££££	£31-£40

High-quality traditional Scottish cuisine in an elegant dining room overlooking Oban Bay.

Mondo's (60 George Street, Oban, ☎ 1631-565 078, fax 1631-564 492; ££). Lively, modern restaurant serving hand-made pasta, fresh local seafood and daily baked bread, with a good wine list.

Oban Fish & Chip Shop (116 George Street, Oban PA34 4NT, ☎ 1631-562 426; £). Traditional chippie that also serves pizzas, pasta and coffees.

Shellfish Bar (Railway Pier, Oban; £). Oban's famous seafood stall sells fish, shellfish and sandwiches.

Studio Restaurant (Craigard Road, Oban PA34 5NP, ☎ 1631-562 030, fax 1631-566 227; open April-Oct; ££). Cozy restaurant up a hill from the main street, with good-quality à la carte and set menus covering traditional, continental and Oriental dishes, and specializing in local seafood and prime Aberdeen Angus steaks.

Waterfront Restaurant (1 The Waterfront, Railway Pier, Oban, ☎/fax 1631-563 110, www.waterfront-restaurant.co.uk; open mid-Mar to Christmas; ££). Stylish modern Scottish cooking with a Mediterranean influence, serving local seafood, Scottish beef and venison.

Isle of Kerrera

Kerrera is a tranquil little island whose northern end faces Oban, across the bay. The only cars on the island are those owned by the 30 or so islanders so it's pretty quiet. Kerrera has some great scenic walking, particularly on the south end of the island.

■ Getting Here

A daily **passenger ferry** (☎ 1631-563 665) operates to Kerrera from Gallanach, two miles south of Oban.

■ Attractions & Sights

Gylen Castle (approached by a track at the south of the island – turn left at the junction where the path straight ahead leads to the Tea Garden & Bunkhouse). The path passes a rocky beach before climbing steeply up to the L-plan tower house, dating from 1587, clinging to a headland that falls away steeply on all sides. The castle was besieged and burned by Major-General Leslie's Covenanter Army during the Wars of the Covenant in 1647. All the resident MacDougalls were killed during the attack or after surrendering.

■ Adventures

The best way to experience the island is to walk the **Kerrera Southern Circuit**, a six-mile circular route. Traveling clockwise you soon reach Horseshoe Bay, where Alexander II died in 1249 while trying to retake western Scotland from the Norwegians. Continuing past the left turn (leading to the castle) and beyond the Tea Garden, you reach Kerrera's rocky southern coast, before cutting across a shoulder of land to walk along a high footpath with superb views west to Mull and north along the island's length. As you near completion of the circuit, there is the option of extending the walk to take in the north end of the island. This takes you past the boatyard at Ardantrive, looking across to Oban. Standing on high ground at the northern tip of Kerrera is an obelisk memorial to David Hutcheson, one of the founders of what is now the ferry company Caledonian MacBrayne (3 hours; easy).

Kerrera Sea Adventures (Ardchore Farm, Isle of Kerrera PA34 4SX, ☎/fax 1631-563 664, roderickmaceachen@kerrerasea.fsnet.co.uk) has hour-long RIB trips around the island.

■ Where To Stay & Eat

See *Accommodation* and *Dining* price charts on pages 218 and 219.

 Kerrera Tea Garden & Bunkhouse (Lower Gylen, Isle of Kerrera PA34 4SX, ☎ 1631-570 223, info@kerrerabunkhouse.com, www.kerrerabunkhouse.com; bunkhouse £; lunch £; dinner ££, pre-booked groups only). Excellent light meals cooked using organic vegetables are available April-Sept. Basic accommodation is available throughout the year. Reservations recommended, particularly in winter.

Loch Etive & North Lorn

 Loch Etive is a famously attractive sea loch that stretches 20 miles from the mountains of **Glen Coe** to the **Falls of Lora** at Connel Bridge. A beautiful, though in places challenging, walk follows the loch's northern shore all the way to Glen Coe. The **River Awe**, which flows into the loch at Taynuilt, provides good salmon fishing while its sloping banks offer good walking and picnic opportunities.

Taynuilt (in Gaelic "Tigh an Uillt" meaning "house by the stream") is a lovely, peaceful village nestling on the southern shore of Loch Etive at the foot of Ben Cruachan. Taynuilt has for centuries been a staging post and resting place for drovers and travelers.

Connel is a small community at the mouth of Loch Etive, overlooking the Falls of Lora. Across Connel Bridge lies the peaceful hamlet of North Connel, home to the 13th-century **Ardchattan Priory**. Appin is a small community just north of Loch Creran with the picturesque **Castle Stalker** on an offshore islet. Nearby, tiny **Port Appin** is a delightful coastal village with great views of **Loch Linnhe** and the **Morvern Hills** and some lovely local walks. A ferry runs from Port Appin to the Isle of Lismore.

■ Attractions & Sights

Ardchattan Priory & Garden (Oban PA37 1RQ, on Loch Etive, six miles northeast of Oban off the A828, ☎ 1796-481 355; open April-Oct, 9am-6pm; priory admission free, garden £2, children free). A ruined Valliscaulian priory founded in 1231 by Sir Duncan MacDougall, who also built nearby Dunstaffnage Castle. The priory underwent a religious revival in the early 16th century after rebuilding but fell into disuse after the Reformation of 1560. The cloisters and refectory were subsequently incorporated into a private house lived in by descendants of Alexander Campbell, the last prior. The ruins of the chapel and graveyard lie beyond the front garden through a gate in the northeastern corner. A lean-to shelter houses some early carved stones, including 15th- and 16th-century grave slabs. Colin Campbell of Glenure (the "Red Fox" and victim of the famous Appin Murder) is buried in the transept. The extensive gardens mostly date from this century and are known for their rhododendrons, azaleas and Scots pines.

THE APPIN MURDER

In 1752, the British government was still reeling from the Jacobite rebellions and sought to repress those clans whose loyalties were suspect. Prominent among those in the West Highlands were the Stewarts of Appin, ardent supporters of Bonnie Prince Charlie. The divided loyalties of Appin clans were further exacerbated by the traditional deep animosity between the Stewarts and the Campbells, the latter staunch Hanoverian monarchists.

In May 1752, Colin Campbell of Glenure (the "Red Fox") was traveling through the Wood of Lettermore on official government business when he was shot from behind and killed. Allan Breck Stewart, a well-known troublemaker and chief suspect, could not be found. Despite there being no evidence against him, James Stewart – "James of the Glen" – was arrested, convicted of the murder and hanged in November 1752, his rotting body and eventually skeleton hung for three years to deter others.

Some firmly believe that certain members of Clan Stewart know the true killer's identity to this day. In 1911, the Stewart Society erected a monument to James of the Glen on a knoll beside the present Ballachulish Bridge – the site of the execution.

Dunstaffnage Castle (HS; by Dunbeg village, three miles north of Oban off the A85, ☎ 1631-562 465; open April-Sept, 9:30am-6:30pm; Oct-Mar, Sat-Wed, 9:30am-4:30pm; adult/concession/child £2.50/£1.90 /£0.75). Commanding a rocky outcrop against the imposing backdrop of Ben Cruachan, Dunstaffnage castle is an impressive curtain-walled fortification that once guarded the important west coast sea lanes. Its strategic site has been defended for nearly 1,500 years and the castle is believed to have held the Stone of Destiny during the Viking invasions. A MacDougall lord built the castle in the 13th century, although Robert the Bruce captured it in 1309. In 1470, the Lordship of Lorn together with custody of Dunstaffnage passed to the Campbells of Argyll, in whose family ownership it remains.

Dunstaffnage was burned in 1685 during a failed uprising by the 9th Earl of Argyll against James VII. Following the Jacobite Rising of 1745,

Dunstaffnage was garrisoned by government forces and became the temporary prison of Flora MacDonald in 1746 after she helped Bonnie Prince Charlie flee in the aftermath of Culloden. Despite being a ruin (apart from the gatehouse, which isn't open to the public!), this is a worthwhile castle visit. A short walk from the castle into the woods is the ruined chapel that shows fine architectural detailing.

Bonawe Iron Furnace (HS; between Taynuilt and Loch Etive, off the A85, ☎ 1866-822 432; open April-Sept, 9:30am-6:30pm; adult/concession/child £3/£2.30/£1). Founded in 1753 by ironmasters from the English Lakeland, Bonawe is the most complete charcoal-fueled ironworks in Britain and occupies a beautiful setting beside Loch Etive. The most successful of the blast furnaces set up in the Highlands in the 17th and 18th centuries, Bonawe remained in almost continuous operation for over a century before ceasing production in 1876. Iron ore was imported from the south for smelting with charcoal fuel, which was plentifully available from the surrounding woods. The pig iron was shipped back to forges in the south for manufacture into finished products. A waymarked trail takes visitors around the various stages of production and detailed information panels explain the process.

Inverawe Smokery & Fisheries (Inverawe, near Taynuilt PA35 1HU, ☎ 1866-822 446, fax 1866-822 274, info@inverawe.co.uk, www.inverawe.co.uk). Traditional smokery, fisheries and country park with a shop, tearoom, exhibition and nature trails.

Scottish Sealife & Marine Sanctuary (Barcaldine, Connel, By Oban PA37 1SE, ☎ 1631-720 386, oban@sealsanctuary.co.uk, www.sealsanctuary.co.uk; open Feb-Easter, 10am-5pm, Easter-Oct, 10am-6pm, Nov-Jan, Sat-Sun, 10am-5pm, last admission one hour before closing, closed three weeks in Dec; adult/concession/child/family £6.95/5.95/4.95/23.5). Close encounters with hundreds of sea creatures, including resident otters and seals. There are regular talks and demonstrations of otter, seal and shark feeding, a shop and reasonably priced restaurant.

Castle Stalker (Loch Laich, Appin, ☎ 1631-730 234; visits by appointment only). A small but picturesque tower house sited on an islet, the Rock of the Cormorants, at the mouth of Loch Laich. It was built in the mid-15th century by Sir John Stewart, Lord of Lorn and, being only reachable by boat, was highly defendable. It is best viewed on the approach to Appin on the A828 Oban-Fort William road and from the quieter Appin-Port Appin road.

Cruachan The Hollow Mountain (Cruachan Power Station, Dalmally PA33 1AN, six miles east of Taynuilt on the A85, ☎ 1866-822 618, fax 1866-822 509, visit.cruachan@scottishpower.plc.uk; open Easter-Nov, 9:30am-5pm; to 6pm in August; adult/concession/child £3/£2.75/£1.50). A unique guided tour inside the power station explains the workings of the hydro-electric station, which generates electricity from a dammed reservoir half-way up Ben Cruachan. Travel deep underground – by electric bus – to view the turbines in their vast cavern.

Falls of Lora (Connel Bridge, Loch Etive). An underwater ledge at the point where Loch Etive meets the sea causes a tidal cascade (the only one in Britain) under certain tidal conditions.

■ Adventures

On Wheels

Port Appin Bikes (9 Shuna View, Port Appin PA38 4DG, ☎ 1631-730 391) has bikes for rent for £10 per day and £45 per week.

On Foot

Clach Thoull to Port Appin is a delightful little walk, perfect as a pre-dinner stroll. The path starts from the gateway opposite the side entrance to the Airds Hotel parking area. The path soon opens out to provide views down the Firth of Lorn and across to the Isle of Lismore. The track passes several interesting sections of cliffs, caves and the sea arch from which the walk takes its name ("rock with a hole"). Seals, and less often otters, can be seen on the rocks here. Continue on the path to Port Appin pier and beyond to return to the starting point (30 minutes; easy).

On Horseback

 Lettershuna Riding Centre (Appin PA38 4BN, ☎ 1631-730 227, fax 1631-730 551, lettershunarc@aol.com; £15 for an hourly ride). Rides and treks in the Appin area that can include, subject to tides, riding out beside Castle Stalker.

On Water

Loch Etive Cruises (Taynuilt Pier, ☎ 1866-822 430, fax 1866-822 555, lochetive@aol.com; Easter-Oct, days, rates and length of cruises vary seasonally; adult/child/family from £5/£3/£13 to £9/£5/£23). Cruises aboard *Anne of Etive* from Taynuilt Pier to the head of Loch Etive, on the way soaking up dramatic mountain scenery and viewing a great variety of wildlife, including a close-up view of a seal colony and possibly golden eagles.

Sea Otter **Cruises** (Dunstaffnage Marina, Dunbeg, By Oban PA37 1PX, ☎ 191-489 7127, ☎ 7801-130 044 mobile, fax 191 489227, info@seaotter.co.uk, www.sea-otter.co.uk). Boat charter, diving and wildlife cruises around the Hebrides and cruises along the Caledonian Canal. Daycharters or live-aboard.

■ Where To Stay & Eat

See *Accommodation* and *Dining* price charts on pages 218 and 219.

 Airds Hotel (Port Appin, Appin PA38 4DF, ☎ 1631-730 236, fax 1631-730 535, airds@airds-hotel.com, www.airds-hotel.com; DB&B £££££+). Originally a 1720s ferry inn, the delightful Airds Hotel justifiably wins regular acclaim for the relaxing elegance of its rooms and its superb restaurant – one of the finest tables in Scotland. Two elegant lounges warmed by log fires and furnished with comfy sofas induce peace and relaxation, as does the cozy conservatory, particularly in evening candlelight. The views across Loch Linnhe are glorious and early morning tea is a nice touch. The hotel runs specialist painting and cookery weeks.

Isle of Eriska (Ledaig, By Oban PA37 1SD, ☎ 1631-720 371, fax 1631-720 531, office@eriska-hotel.co.uk, www.eriska-hotel.co.uk; closed Jan; B&B £££££, dinner ££££). A 300-acre private island approached by a causeway over the Atlantic. Log fires, wood-paneled rooms, deep sofas and large, comfortable guest rooms induce calm and relaxation. Morning coffee and afternoon tea are civilized touches evoking more a country-house party than a hotel. For the active there is a modern sports complex in an outlying building that offers swimming pool, gym, spa, sauna and steam room. Tennis, clay pigeon shooting and a 9-hole golf course are also available on the island. One of Eriska's unforgettable attractions takes place nightly after dinner when badgers come to be fed on the steps of the bar.

Blarcreen House (Ardchattan, By Oban PA37 1RG, ☎/fax 1631-750 272, enquiries@blarcreenfarm.com, www.blarcreenfarm.com; open Mar-Dec; B&B £££, dinner £££). Approached by a picturesque six-mile drive along the northern shore of Loch Etive, Blarcreen occupies a peaceful, lochside spot surrounded by sheep pastures. Beautiful spacious rooms are elegantly furnished in classic traditional style and provide uninterrupted views over the loch and/or Beinn Duirinnis. The innovative dinner menu uses seasonal local produce and the excellent, mountainous breakfasts guarantee you will never leave hungry!

Ards House (Connel, By Oban PA37 1PT, ☎ 1631-710 255, info@ardshouse.com, www.ardshouse.com; B&B ££). A traditional Victorian villa attractively set by the loch. The bedrooms are beautifully furnished and the spacious drawing room has a grand piano. There is a good breakfast menu.

Lochside Cottage (Fasnacloich, Appin PA38 4BJ, ☎/fax 1631-730 216, us@lochsidecottage.fsnet.co.uk, www.lochsidecottage.fsnet.co.uk; B&B ££, dinner ££-£££). Comfortable accommodation set picturesquely on the shore of a lochan (small lake), with panoramic views across the hills of Glen Etive. The dinner menu highlights local produce and there is a log fire for after-dinner relaxing.

Polfearn Hotel (Taynuilt PA35 1JQ, ☎ 1866-822 251, polfearn@aol.com, www.polfearnhotel.com; B&B ££, dinner ££-£££). Situated at the foot of Ben Cruachan, the hotel enjoys superb views with the River Awe running to one side and Loch Etive lapping on the shingle beach to the front. There are comfortable rooms with views and delicious home cooking (don't miss the *moules marinières* using Loch Etive mussels).

Robin's Nest (Main Street, Taynuilt PA35 1JE, ☎ 1866-822 429; £). Delightful village tearoom serving home baking and light lunches, including great soups and sandwiches.

Hawthorn Restaurant (Benderloch, By Oban, PA37 1QS north of Connel near Tralee Beach, ☎ 1631-720 777; closed Mon; ££). Comfortable 100-year-old crofthouse serving good Scottish cuisine and fresh local seafood.

Isle of Lismore

Lismore is a long, narrow island 10 miles long by a mile wide, lying in Loch Linnhe. Its Gaelic name, *lios mor*, means "the great garden." The island is rich in historical sites bearing testament to the people who settled here thousands of years ago. Several small communities are scattered on the island and there is one "main" road, off which run tracks leading to several sheltered bays with great views.

■ Getting Here

 Caledonian MacBrayne (☎1631-566 688/1475-650 100) operates a car ferry from Oban to Achnacroish at the southern end of Lismore (daily except Sun, crossing time 45 minutes; ferry schedules allow day-visitors around six hours on the island).

Argyll & Bute Council (☎ 1631-562 125/1546-602 127, www.argyll-bute.gov.uk) operates a passenger ferry from Port Appin to Point in the north of Lismore; it operates year-round but a day's notice is required Nov-Mar; crossing time 10 minutes; ferry schedules (see web site for details) allow you to stay about 12 hours on the island; bicycles are carried free.

■ Attractions & Sights

There are three ruined castles on Lismore: **Tirfuir Castle**, a Pictish broch, or tower, stands on a high point overlooking the Lynn of Lorn, and is visible from the Oban ferry as it nears Achnacroish pier. On the west side of the island stands **Castle Coeffin**, known for its Viking connections. Farther south is 13th-century **Achinduin Castle**, which faces the Sound of Mull.

■ Adventures

Castle Coeffin. Take the ferry to Point in the north of Lismore. Follow the (only) road south, ignoring the right turn to Port Ramsey reached after half an hour. The road leads up onto open fields and St Moluag's stone (where the saint sat every day). Farther along the road is the 14th-century parish church that was once part of a much larger cathedral. There is beautiful stained glass and a wealth of local family history in the graveyard. Shortly after the church, take the farm track leading across the island to a cliff. Follow the track at the southern end of the scarp, which brings Coeffin Castle into view. The path descends to a muddy valley and then to the castle. The grass inside the castle walls is a perfect spot for a picnic (2½ hours; easy).

Bike rental is available in Lismore with advance booking (☎ 1631-760 213), or from **Port Appin Bikes** (☎ 1631-730 391).

■ Where To Stay & Eat

See *Accommodation* and *Dining* price charts on pages 218 and 219.

The Schoolhouse (Baligarve, Isle of Lismore PA34 5UL, two miles from the Port Appin ferry, ☎ 1631-760 262; B&B £, DB&B ££). Accommodation and home cooking, including evening meals. Vegetarian options and packed lunches are also available.

Loch Awe & South Lorn

Loch Awe is the longest inland loch in Scotland, fed by the River Orchy, which is itself born in the landscape around Loch Tulla and Inveroran. Dotted along the shores of Loch Awe are small villages, handsome estates and mansions. The loch is studded with small islands and crannogs rich with history, and is renowned for trout and pike fishing. At its head stands the picturesque ruin of Kilchurn Castle.

Craobh Haven (pronounced "croof-harven") is a small village clustered around a man-made marina with views to the Isles of Shuna, Luing and Scarba. **Ardfern** is a busy marina set amid superb scenery on Loch Craignish.

■ Attractions & Sights

Kilchurn Castle (HS; at the northeastern head of Loch Awe, best accessed by boat; open year-round). A substantial ruined fortress magnificently situated at the head of Loch Awe, whose reflected image framed against a backdrop of mountains and low clouds is one of Scotland's most famous and inspiring views. The castle was built in 1550 as a square tower and much enlarged in 1693 to incorporate the first specially built barracks in Scotland. Access by land is difficult and the best way to reach the castle is by the steamer ferry that sails regularly from Loch Awe Pier (☎ 1838-200 440).

Oban Rare Breeds Farm Park (Glencruitten, Oban PA34 4QB, ☎ 1631-770 608, fax 1631-770 604, info@obanrarebreeds.com, www.obanrarebreeds.com; open mid-Mar through Oct, 10am-6pm; Nov-Dec, Sat-Sun, 11am-4pm; adult/concession/family £6/£4/£18). "Rare" is a relative term. If you come here hoping to see white rhinos and giant pandas you'll be badly disappointed. However, if you're an aficionado of the rarer breeds of sheep, such as Castlemilk and Soay, this is the place to visit. Also on display are pigs, poultry, deer and – almost as token exotica – a llama and alpaca. Children will love the barn, where they can see lambs in spring and handle rabbits and guinea pigs.

AUTHOR'S TIP: *If it's a choice between the Rare Breeds Farm and nearby Scottish Sealife & Marine Sanctuary (see* Loch Etive & North Lorn*), opt for the latter.*

■ Adventures

On Horseback

 Appaloosa Holidays (Craobh Haven, By Lochgilphead PA31 8QR, ☎ 1852-500 632/500 270, appaloosaholidays@talk21.com). Horseback trekking, picnics, pub rides (an easygoing ride with a pub meal as your reward), and lessons on an unspoiled coastal estate.

On the Water

 Loch Awe Boating & Fishing Centre (Ardbrecknish, By Dalmally PA33 1BH, ☎/fax 1866-833 256). Rental facilities for motor (from £6 per hour) and row boat fishing (from £3 per hour).

Lochaweside Marine (11 Dalavich, By Taynuilt PA35 1HN, ☎ 1866-844 209) Motor- and rowboat rental for fishing and pleasure trips on Loch Awe.

Loch Awe Steam Packet Co (Ardanaiseig, Kilchrenan, By Taynuilt PA35 1HE, ☎ 1838-200 440/1866-833 333, fax 1866-833 222, ardanaiseig@clara.net; open April-Nov, 10am-5pm). Cruises on the hour from Loch Awe Pier to Kilchurn Castle aboard the steamboat Lady Rowena and cruiseboat Flower of Scotland.

Craignish Cruises (Ardfern Yacht Centre, Musgan, Craobh Haven, By Lochgilphead PA31 8UA, ☎ 1852-500 540; closed Jan). Wildlife and fishing trips, water taxi services and private charters aboard Sea Leopard to view Corryvreckan whirlpool, Scarba, Jura and the Garvellachs. Adult/child £6/£4 per hour.

Farsain Cruises (Craobh Haven, By Lochgilphead PA31 8UA, ☎ 1852-500 664). Daily wildlife trips to the Gulf of Corryvreckan and Inner Hebridean islands, and ferry, diving and fishing services.

■ Where To Stay & Eat

See *Accommodation* and *Dining* price charts on pages 218 and 219.

 Galley of Lorne Inn (Ardfern, By Lochgilphead PA31 8QN, between Oban and Lochgilphead, ☎ 1852-500 284, galleyoflorne@aol.com, www.galleyoflorne.co.uk; B&B £££, dinner ££). Situated on the tranquil shores of Loch Craignish, this 18th-century droving inn retains much character and a cozy, relaxed ambience. The bedrooms are simple but comfortable and most have loch views. The atmospheric, log fire-warmed **Galley Bar** is a lively meeting place for locals, visitors and yachtsmen. The restaurant serves fresh, local seafood and own-grown vegetables and the bar food is high on quality and value.

Lunga (Craobh Haven, By Lochgilphead PA31 8QR, between Oban and Lochgilphead, ☎ 1852-500 237, fax 1852-500 639, colin@lunga.demon.co.uk, www.lunga.com; B&B ££). Colin Lindsay MacDougall, the Laird of Lunga, offers both serviced and cook-for-youself accommodation in the imposing 15th-century house his family has occupied for over 300 years. Lunga is set on a 3,000-acre estate; the rooms are spacious and atmospheric, and include the splendid long-time apartment of the late Dowager Duchess of Argyll. The Laird, whose family boasts royal connections, is a fascinating host and provides a wealth of information on local attractions, many off the standard tourist trails.

Loch Melfort Hotel (Arduaine, By Oban PA34 4XG, ☎ 1852-200 233, fax 1852-200 214, reception@lochmelfort.co.uk, www.lochmelfort.co.uk; B&B £££, dinner ££). A reasonable hotel with sea views and decent bedrooms. The restaurant serves fresh local produce, particularly fish and shellfish, meats and cheeses, and has large panoramic windows looking over Asknish Bay.

Crafty Kitchen Café & Craft Shop (Ardfern, By Lochgilphead PA31 8QN (between Oban and Lochgilphead), ☎ 1852-500 303, fax 1852-500 689; £). Delightful village café serving all-day homemade food, and particularly renowned for gooey cakes and puddings – especially those containing chocolate! The shop sells Scottish and ethnic crafts.

Isle of Seil

Seil is an attractive small island with pretty seascapes, a leisurely pace of life and an interesting history. The island was settled as early as 5000 BC and numerous prehistoric remains include two forts – **Dun Mucaig** and **Dun Earn** – on the west coast. St Brendan "The Navigator" founded his first church on Seil 20 years before St Columba arrived on Iona. The island has been featured in several films, including *A Ring of Bright Water* and *Kidnapped*.

■ Getting Here

Located 12 miles south of Oban, Seil is reached by road via Clachan Seil (off the A816 at Kilninver) over Thomas Telford's famous **Clachan Bridge** – the "Bridge over the Atlantic." The bridge dates from 1792, its elegant high arch designed to allow sailing ships to pass beneath. The island has four main communities: **Clachan**, **Balvicar**, **Cuan** and **Ellenabeich**.

WHO'S WHO? *Thomas Telford, born in 1757, began his career at the age of 14 as a stonemason's apprentice. After a time in Edinburgh, he moved to London where he worked as a general builder and surveyor, and developed a reputation as an engineer. His best-known works include bridges, canals and roads.*

NOTE: Ellenabeich, the island's main community, at its western tip, is often called Easdale, which is – confusingly – also the name of a small island reached by boat from Ellenabeich.

■ Attractions & Sights

Scottish Slate Islands Heritage Trust Heritage Centre (Ellenabeich, By Oban PA34 4RQ, ☎ 1852-300 449, fax 1852-300 473; open April-Jun & Sep, Mon-Sat, 10:30am-5:30pm; Sun, 10:30am-5pm; longer hours in July-Aug; adult/concession/child £1.50/£1.25/£0.25). Exhibition of photos, models and pictures showing life in the islands in the 19th/20th centuries.

SLATE QUARRYING ON SEIL AND EASDALE

The economies of Seil and Easdale revolved around slate quarrying for roof tiles. Easdale slates were shipped all over the world and Iona Abbey is roofed with them. The lines of whitewashed cottages on the islands today (squat, built end-on to the wind) once housed the hundreds of people the industry employed at its height. The community of Ellenabeich itself was a separate island until the narrow strip of sea separating it from Seil was filled in with quarry waste. Much of the island of Easdale has been quarried away. The industry was effectively ended by a winter storm on 22nd November 1881, which broke through and flooded the 250-foot-deep quarries.

Easdale Island Folk Museum (Isle of Easdale, By Oban PA34 4TB, ☎/fax 1852-300 370; open April-Oct, 10:30am-5:30pm; adult/concession/child £2/1.5/0.5). Museum tells the story of the slate industry and the island's people in the 18th/19th centuries. Argyll & Bute Council (☎ 1546-602 127) runs a daily passenger-only ferry service operates between Ellenabeich and Easdale Island. Sailing times are displayed at the pier.

■ Adventures

Porpoise Charters (Dunaverty, Easdale, By Oban PA34 4RF, ☎ 1631-567 007 days, 1852-300 203 evenings). Flexible trips, cruises, diving parties and underwater photography expeditions.

Sea.fari Adventures (Easdale Harbour, Isle of Seil, By Oban, ☎/fax 1852-300 003, www.seafari.co.uk). Exciting RIB (Rigid Inflatable Boat) cruises to explore the local waters, including the Gulf of Corryvreckan and remote islands, and to view wildlife.

■ Shopping

Highland Arts Studios (Isle of Seil, By Oban PA34 4RF, ☎ 1852-300 273, fax 1852-300 271). Aladdin's cave of a crafts shop and exhibition of works by the late C. John Taylor. You'll need to dodge the bus tours, though. Get your timing wrong and you could get stuck in the shop for a very long time.

■ Where To Stay & Eat

See *Accommodation* and *Dining* price charts on pages 218 and 219.

 Willowburn Hotel (Clachan, Isle of Seil, By Oban PA34 4TJ, ☎ 1852-300 276, fax 1852-300 597, willowburn.hotel@virgin.net, www.willowburn.co.uk; open mid-Mar through Nov; DB&B ££££). Situated just 300 meters from the Atlantic Bridge, the Willowburn offers peace and quiet in comfortable rooms and good food with views in its restaurant.

Seafood & Oyster Bar (Ellenabeich Harbour, Isle of Seil, By Oban PA34 4RQ, ☎ 1852-300 121, oysterbar@easdale.fsbusiness.co.uk; £-££). An excellent and atmospheric restaurant serving superb oysters and mussels (weather-dependent) and award-winning fish and chips. There is a great sea view from the conservatory at the back. No credit cards.

Tigh an Truish Inn (Isle of Seil, By Oban, ☎ 1852-300 242; lunch £, Dinner, Easter-Oct only, ££). A traditional 18th-century inn just over the Clachan Bridge from the mainland that serves real ales and good bar meals. Its name means the "House of Trousers," as islanders traveling to the mainland reputedly changed here out of their kilts, which had been banned after Culloden.

Inveraray & Mid-Argyll

The history of the Scottish nation has its roots in the tranquil, unspoiled glens and wooded hills of Mid-Argyll. The tribe of Scots from Ireland established its kingdom of Dalriada at **Dunadd**, near Lochgilphead, in the ancient land of the native Picts. The two peoples merged over time but it was the settlers' name that would, some 300 years later, be adopted by what is now known as Scotland. Long before these events, prehistoric settlers left magnificent sculptures and monuments in Kilmartin Glen, from Bronze Age cup and ring engravings to cairns and standing stone circles.

Inveraray

Inveraray is a beautiful little town, its whitewashed stone cottages stunningly set on the northern shore of Loch Fyne. Inveraray was the most important town in Argyll for 300 years and is overlooked by a suitably graceful castle, for generations the seat of Clan Campbell. The original town of Inveraray occupied the site between the present castle and the sea and had a church, tolbooth and no fewer than 43 taverns! In 1744, the Duke of Argyll decided to replace his ruined old castle with a splendid new mansion. He demolished the old town to make room for landscaped gardens and laid out the present town a half-mile to the south – Britain's first planned town. There's lots to see and do in and around the town, although Inveraray is also a great place to just relax and do nothing.

INFORMATION SOURCES: The tourism office is at Front Street, Inveraray PA32 8UY, ☎ 870-720 0616, fax 1499-302 269, info@inveraray.visitscotland.com; open year-round.

■ Attractions & Sights

Inveraray Castle (Inveraray PA32 8XE, ☎ 1499-302 203, fax 1499-302 421, enquiries@inveraray-castle.com, www.inveraray-castle.com; open June-Sept, Mon-Sat, 10am-5:45pm; Sun, 1pm-5:45pm; last admission 5pm; limited hours in April, May & Oct, call ahead; adult/concession/child/family £5.50/£4.50/£3.50/£14). This fairytale castle is the home of the Duke of Argyll, whose family represents the senior branch of Clan Campbell. A castle has stood on these grounds since the early 15th century when the family moved from Loch Awe to Inveraray. The present castle dates from 1745-85 and replaced an earlier fortified keep. Its less fortified design (by Roger Morris and Robert Mylne) with fine turreted spires at the corners, reflects the start of more settled times in Scotland. Displays include a famous armory collection, French tapestries, ornate Scottish and European furniture, other works of art and a genealogical display in the Clan Room.

High on a hill behind the castle is **Dun Na Cuiache**, the "Watch Tower," a folly built by the Duke of Argyll in 1748. A circular track leads up to the tower from near the castle and makes a great walk on a clear day.

Inveraray Jail (Church Square, Inveraray PA32 8TX, ☎ 1499-302 381, fax 1499-302 195, info@inverarayjail.co.uk, www.inverarayjail.co.uk; open April-Oct, 9:30am-6pm; Nov-Mar, 10am-5pm; last admission one hour before closing; adult/concession/child/family £5.75/£3.75/£2.80/£15.70). Informative panels, gripping exhibits and life-like recreations tell the story of crime and punishment in Scotland from the 16th century. Discover the gruesome punishments meted out before prison sentences became commonplace. A re-creation of an early 19th-century courtroom is realistic and absorbing. The recreations in the cells of the Old and New Prisons are so realistic they're almost spooky. Fortunately, the costumed wardens are friendly and informative.

Inveraray Maritime Museum on the *Arctic Penguin* (The Pier, Inveraray PA32 8UY, ☎ 1499-302 213; open April-Sept, 10am-6pm; Oct-Mar, 10am-5pm; adult/concession/child/family £3.60/£2.60/£2/£10). One of the world's last iron sailing ships, this three-masted schooner now houses a maritime museum. Naval memorabilia, archive footage and hands-on activities evoke life on the high seas. Contrast the luxury of steam-yacht quarters with the horrors on board emigrant and slave ships. Graphic displays in the lower hold depict the hardships suffered aboard during the Highland Clearances.

The Bell Tower, All Saints Episcopal Church (Inveraray, ☎ 1499-302 259; open May-Sept, 10am-1pm & 2pm-5pm; adult/concession/family £2/£0.75/£4). Ascend the 126-foot tower by an easy staircase to see and hear Scotland's finest bells (a Mecca for visiting ringers from the world over) and to gain an excellent view.

Auchindrain Museum of Country Life (Auchindrain Township, By Inveraray PA32 8XN, ☎ 1499-500 235; open April-Sept, 10am-5pm; adult/concession/child/family £3.80/£3/£1.80/£9.50). A restored original Highland

Above: Kilchurn Castle, Loch Awe

Below: Slate workers' cottages, Ellenbeich, Isle of Seil

Queen's View, Loch Tummel, Pitochry

Above: Glamis Castle

Below: Strathisla Distillery, Keith

Above: Crow-stepped gables, Crail, East Neuk

Below: Arbroath Signal Tower Museum

township that escaped the infamous Clearances and was farmed until 1962, Auchindrain is typical of the traditional Highland communities that are now long gone. Several of Auchindrain's cottages (especially MacCallum's House), barns, stables, workshops and other buildings have been furnished and equipped to original standards and provide a fascinating glimpse of the stark life and rugged work of the Victorian Highlander. There is also a museum of farming and farming implements through the ages.

■ Adventures

Argyll Riding (Dalchenna Farm, Inveraray PA32 8XT, ☎ 1499-302 611, fax 1499-302 233, info@horserides.co.uk, www.horserides.co.uk). Trekking, hacking, clinics and lessons, half-day and full-day rides and riding holidays.

■ Shopping

Inveraray Woolen Mill (The Anvil, Inveraray PA32 8UY, ☎ 1499-302 166). Quality knitwear, country clothing, whisky and gifts in a late 18th-century former blacksmith's house.

■ Where To Stay & Eat

See *Accommodation* and *Dining* price charts on pages 218 and 219.

 Loch Fyne Hotel & Leisure Club (Inveraray PA32 8XT, ☎ 1499-302 148, fax 1499-302 348, lochfyne@crerarhotels.com, www.british-trust-hotels.com; B&B ££££, dinner ££). Comfortable, historic hotel superbly situated beside the tranquil shores of Loch Fyne, a short distance from the heart of Inveraray. The hotel served as headquarters for Combined Operations Training during World War II and hosted the only War Cabinet meeting outside Downing Street (London). Eminent visitors included King George VI, Winston Churchill, General Eisenhower, General de Gaulle and Viscount Mountbatten. The spacious rooms in the old (front) wing are named after local distilleries and offer stunning views over the loch. The leisure club includes a swimming pool, spa bath, sauna and steam room.

George Hotel (Main St East, Inveraray PA32 8TT, ☎ 1499-302 111, fax 1499-302 098, www.thegeorgehotel.co.uk; B&B ££, dinner ££). Long-established family-run hotel whose history is reflected in the décor of its rooms. Original solid flagstone floors and four roaring log and peat fires create a perfect setting for good food (especially West Highland beef, lamb and local seafood), real ales and a choice of 100 malt whiskies.

Creag Dhubh (Inveraray PA32 8XT, ☎ 1499-302 430, www.creagdhubh.com; open Feb-Nov; B&B £-££). Family-run B&B in an attractive house with superb views across its garden to Loch Fyne.

Minard Castle (Minard, By Inveraray PA32 8YB, ☎/fax 1546-886 272, reinoldgayre@minardcastle.com, www.minardcastle.com; open April-Oct; B&B ££££). Stylish B&B in a 19th-century castle beside Loch Fyne, with spacious and beautifully furnished bedrooms and public rooms. The 144-acre estate offers fishing and attractive walks.

Loch Fyne Oyster Bar (Clachan, Cairndow PA26 8BL, ☎ 1499-600 236, fax 1499-600 234, oysterb@lochfyne.com, www.loch-fyne.com; ££-£££). Award-winning seafood restaurant, shop and smokehouse. There is home baking, an all-day kipper breakfast and an excellent wine list.

A WORD TO
THE WISE

TIP: *A great option on a sunny day is to take a cup of homemade soup and a pie (together about £2) from the **Pier Shop** (opposite Inveraray Pier) down to the Loch Fyne waterfront.*

Lochgilphead & Kilmartin

Lochgilphead sweeps attractively around a bay on Loch Fyne. There isn't much to see here, but it makes a good stopping point on any journey to or from Kintyre. The **Crinan Canal**, built by Thomas Telford in the early 19th century, provides yachts with a popular shortcut between Loch Fyne and the waters of the Hebrides.

Magical Kilmartin Glen, an unassuming area north of Lochgilphead, has an extraordinary and diverse concentration of archaeological treasures. Over 150 prehistoric sites and around 200 other ancient monuments cluster within a six-mile radius of the quiet Kilmartin village. These include impressive burial cairns, enigmatic rock carvings, mysterious stone circles, three castles and the remains of the fortress of the first Scottish kings at Dunadd.

INFORMATION SOURCES: The tourism office is at Lochnell Street, Lochgilphead PA30 8JN, ☎ 870-720 0618; fax 1546-606 254, info@lochgilphead.visitscotland.com; open April-Oct.

■ Attractions & Sights

Kilmartin House Museum (Kilmartin PA31 8RQ, ☎ 1546-510 278, fax 1546-510 330, museum@kilmartin.org, www.kilmartin.org; open 10am-5:30pm; adult/child/family £4.50/£1.50/£10). The award-winning museum, housed in what was the church manse, traces thousands of years of human activity across the Kilmartin valley and is an excellent starting point for your exploration of the glen's archaeology. Find out about the lives of the early hunters, farmers and warriors who left such rich remains in the area. View local artifacts, hear prehistoric music, taste wild food or relax in the green oak conservatory. The vibrant visitor center includes a powerful audio-visual presentation, *The Valley of Ghosts*.

Kilmartin Glen Monuments – The earliest traces of human habitation of Kilmartin Glen date back to 3000 BC. Many of the most impressive are at **Temple Wood**, within a short walk of the first parking area south of Kilmartin village (on the right side of the road heading south). The South Cairn at **Nether Largie**, a Megalithic chambered tomb entered between two vertical stones, is believed to be the earliest cairn in the valley. Ancient pottery and burned bones were excavated from this site in 1864. Additional chambered cairns were built along the valley floor over the next 1,500 years and created the **Linear Cemetery**, which runs for over a mile from Kilmartin to Ri Cruin. Across a field are the **Nether Largie Standing Stones** and a short distance away stands the lower but fairly complete **Temple Wood Stone Circle**.

At **Ballymeanoch**, a short distance south of Temple Wood, is another complex that includes standing stones, cairns and a carved rock. Kilmartin boasts many prehistoric rock carvings, principally cup and ring marks – small indentations (cup marks) encircled by one or more rings – again dating from 3000 BC. Although of fundamentally simple appearance, these enigmatic designs can be quite complex and very individual. The site at Achnabreck has the largest cluster of such carvings anywhere in Britain.

By 500 AD, Kilmartin lay at the heart of the early Scottish Kingdom of Dalriada. Built high on a rocky outcrop approachable by a rough track (from the main road, heading south of Kilmartin village), **Dunadd Fort** maintains a brooding presence over the surrounding countryside. Reputed to be the capital of the kingdom, this is the probable site where early Scottish Kings were inaugurated. A rock near the summit bears a footprint and hollowed out basin, believed to have been used in the inauguration of the Kings of Dalriada, and a Pictish boar carving.

Carnasserie Castle (HS; two miles north of Kilmartin off the A816; open at all times; admission free). The late-16th-century home of John Carswell (Rector of Kilmartin and subsequently Bishop of Argyll and the Isles) who translated John Knox's liturgy into Gaelic in 1567. Built in 1565, the castle is an important building of its time, combining a medieval tower and great hall in one layout. Though ruined, it is still possible to see much of the detailed stonework and carvings.

Kilmartin Church houses a number of great crosses dating from the 8th century and late Middle Ages. The graveyard contains an impressive collection of grave slabs dating mainly from the 14th-18th centuries, mostly the work of Loch Awe sculptors.

Castle Sween (HS; Knapdale off the B8025, on the eastern shore of Loch Sween; admission free). The ruin of one of the earliest stone castles in Scotland, dating from the late 11th to early 12th century and extended in the 15th century. The castle is superbly sited, looking past nearby islands and down the Sound of Jura toward Ireland, but is blighted by an eyesore of a caravan park that sprawls around it.

St Columba's Cave (Knapdale, south of Lochgilphead, on the upper reaches of Loch Caolisport). This cave is traditionally thought to have been used by the famous saint during his 6th-century crusade from Ireland. An altar on a rock shelf, carved crosses and a large font-shaped basin all suggest the saintly presence.

■ Adventures

Argyll Trail Riding (Brenfield Farm, Ardrishaig, near Lochgilphead PA30 8ER, ☎ 1546-603 274, fax 1546-603 225, info@brenfield.co.uk, www.brenfield.co.uk; open April-early Oct). Explore the remote splendor of the West Highlands on horseback through a superb range of weeklong trail rides.

■ Where To Stay & Eat

See *Accommodation* and *Dining* price charts on pages 218 and 219.

Lochgilphead

Argyll Hotel (Lochnell Street, Lochgilphead PA31 8JN, ☎ 1546-602 221, fax 1546-603 576; B&B ££). A small village inn with comfortable budget rooms, refurbished steak house and bar.

Stag Hotel & Restaurant (Argyll Street, Lochgilphead PA31 8NE, ☎ 1546-602 496, fax 1546-603 549, www.staghotel.com; B&B £££, dinner ££). Good basic hotel with clean rooms, bar and restaurant serving local produce.

Bellanoch House (Crinan Canal, By Lochgilphead PA31 8SN, ☎ 1546-830 149, stay@bellanochhouse.co.uk, www.bellanochhouse.co.uk; B&B ££, dinner ££). Historic Gothic listed mansion with stunning Atlantic views over Loch Crinan. A former church, the mansion served as a schoolhouse for 150 years from the 1820s. The refurbished interior is exquisite and full of period features and antiques. Delicious evening meals are available.

Corbiere (Achnabreac, near Lochgilphead PA31 8SG, ☎ 1546-602 764; B&B £-££). Spacious and peaceful B&B rooms with great views to the Crinan Canal.

The Stables (Argyll Street, Lochgilphead, ☎ 1546-602 674; £-££). Restaurant with a takeaway service.

Tayvallich Inn (by Lochgilphead PA31 8PR, ☎ 1546-870 282, fax 1546-870 333; lunch ££, dinner £££). Friendly bar-restaurant on the shores of Loch Sween serving lunches and dinners, including fresh scallops, mussels, oysters and prawns.

Kilmartin

Kilmartin Hotel (Kilmartin, By Lochgilphead PA31 8RQ, ☎ 1546-510 250, info@kilmartin-hotel.com; www.kilmartin-hotel.com; B&B ££, dinner £-££). Attractive 19th-century hotel in Kilmartin village with six comfortable bedrooms. There is a good choice from the bar and restaurant menus, featuring traditional Scottish and seafood dishes. The bar also offers real ales and over 40 whiskies.

Dunchraigaig House (Kilmartin, By Lochgilphead PA31 8RG, ☎ 1546-605 209, dunchraig@aol.com; B&B ££). A comfortable and attractive house set in two acres of garden and grounds in Kilmartin Glen, close to Dunchraigaig Cairn and opposite the Ballymeanoch standing stones.

Kintyre Peninsula

Despite the massive chart success of ex-Beatle Paul McCartney's song *Mull of Kintyre*, the main tourist routes continue to bypass the Kintyre peninsula, whose tranquil beauty remains unspoiled and unexplored (although rumor has it that tourism on the Isle of Mull flourished thanks to Sir Paul!). Swept by the warm Gulf Stream, the Kintyre Peninsula is almost an island, and juts out into the Irish Sea almost due south. The west coast is rugged, with glorious beaches, crashing surf and stunning views to the Inner Hebrides. The more gently scenic east coast offers superb views to Arran.

Kintyre joins the rest of Argyll at the pleasant fishing village of Tarbert, which sits on a narrow land strip between West Loch Tarbert and East Loch Tarbert. The Viking Magnus Barefoot (King of Norway) could claim any land he "sailed" around, and made his men drag his longship across the isthmus to claim Kintyre in 1098. Centuries later, Robert the Bruce repeated the feat to celebrate victory over the English.

■ Getting Here

By Air

Machrihanish Airport (Campbeltown; ☎ 1586-553 797) hosted military operations until 1997, and its 10,000-foot runway is the longest in Europe. **Loganair** (☎1586-552 571, www.loganair.co.uk) now operates a scheduled service from here to Glasgow.

By Ferry

Caledonian MacBrayne (☎ 1475-650 100, www.calmac.co.uk) operates a car-ferry service from Port Ellen/Port Askaig on Islay to Kennacraig (crossing takes about 2 hours).

Scenic Drive

The drive down Kintyre's east coast from **Whitehouse** to **Campbeltown** (signposted from Whitehouse) twists and turns its way over heather-clad hills, through lush glens and forests, by sandy shores and over rocky headlands. It isn't the easiest of drives, being almost all single-lane with several steep ascents and descents, sharp bends and blind summits. However, it is very scenic, and you have the constant companion of the **Kilbrannan Sound** and superb profile views of **Arran's** mountain landscape.

The A83 south from **Inveraray** runs all the way to **Campbeltown**, about 60 miles.

Tarbert & North Kintyre

Tarbert is overlooked by a ruined castle and has a couple of interesting galleries and good places to eat. Farther south, a single-lane road twists and meanders its way down the east coast, over heather-clad hills and through lush glens and forests. The west coast is rugged and has some glorious empty beaches, crashing Atlantic surf and the backdrop of the Paps of Jura. The tiny village of Skipness sits at the northern end of Kilbrannan Sound and has a 13th-century castle and historic chapel. A ferry leaves from nearby Claonaig to Arran (Lochranza).

 INFORMATION SOURCES: The tourism office is on Harbour Street, Tarbert PA29 6UD, ☎ 870-720 0624, 1880-820 082, info@tarbert.visitscotland.com; open April-Oct.

■ Attractions & Sights

Tarbert Castle (signposted from Harbour Street up a short but steep path just left of Loch Fyne Gallery). Tarbert's first royal castle was probably built in the 13th century, but only the ruin of a fortified tower now remains, comprising a cellar and four levels. James IV visited the castle in 1494 and the tower house was constructed around this time. By the 16th century the castle was under the guardianship of the Earls of Argyll and later became a stronghold of Clan Campbell. The castle was derelict by the mid-18th century. Be careful as the ruins are in a dangerous condition. The view over Tarbert is arguably more impressive than the castle itself.

Skipness Castle (from Tarbert follow the signs south to Claonaig and then Skipness). Standing on the eastern side of Kintyre and enjoying views to the Isle of Arran, the castle is believed to date from the early 13th century, with later fortifications during the 13th, 14th and 16th centuries. Little is known about the castle's early history, although it occupies a strategic site. In 1261, it was held by Dugald McSween on behalf of the Lords of the Isles, and remained under the MacDonalds until forfeited in 1493 when it reverted to the crown and became another Campbell stronghold. The castle buildings incorporate a curtain wall, hall house, chapel and tower house. The castle was abandoned in the 17th century and is now a ruin. In the late 13th and early 14th century, Kilbrannan Chapel (St Brendan's Chapel) was constructed on the nearby shoreline and there are a number of ancient burial slabs in the surrounding graveyard.

Ballochroy Standing Stones – On a raised beach just north of Ballochroy, near Clachan, these three stones mark a straight line running northeast to southwest. The stones and are believed to represent one of the most important sites in the West of Scotland. From the stones, the midsummer sun sets behind Ben Cora on the Isle of Jura and the midwinter sun sets behind the Isle of Cara to the south of Gigha.

Beacharra Standing Stone – This 16-foot (5-m) stone is the tallest standing stone in Kintyre and is situated near Beacharr Farmhouse, south of Tayinloan.

■ Adventures

An Tairbeart Trekking (on A83, just south of Tarbert, ☎ 1880-820 333, fax 1880-820 042; open Easter-Oct). Riding tours through woodlands and across open hills on native Eriskay and Highland ponies, from an hour to a day. Minimum age 12; maximum weight 14 stone (a stone is equal to 14 pounds, so 14 stone is just under 200 lbs).

Barrglen Equitation Centre (Arnicle Farm, Glenbarr, By Tarbert PA29 6UZ, ☎ 1583-421 397). Small riding stable set on a 5,000-acre sheep farm offering beach and moorland rides, lessons and farmhouse accommodation.

■ Wildlife Watching

 Ronachan Point (signposted on the A83 between Kennacraig and Tayinloan). The name means "point of the seals" and it's certainly that. Common seals can easily be seen, almost from your car, on the smooth rocks just offshore.

■ Shopping

 Loch Fyne Gallery (Harbour Street, Tarbert PA29 6UD, ☎/fax 1880-820 390, gallery@tarbertlochfyne.com). The gallery sells an above-average range of paintings and prints, books, maps, jewelry, music, crafts and gifts.

■ Where To Stay & Eat

See *Accommodation* and *Dining* price charts on pages 218 and 219.

 Balinakill Country House Hotel (Clachan, near Tarbert PA29 6XL, ☎ 1880-740 206, fax 1880-740 298, info@balinakill.com, www.balinakill.com; closed mid-Nov to mid-Dec; B&B £££, dinner £££). A classy Victorian mansion with elegant wood paneling, ornate plasterwork, antiques, high ceilings and huge windows, set amid six acres of tranquil parkland. Bedrooms are individually and stylishly furnished and many boast real log fires. Guests face a difficult choice between relaxing in their rooms, in one of the two elegant lounges or the cozy bar. Also expect to spend considerable time mulling over Angus's delicious dining options, cooked with flair using fresh local seafood and game. It's no surprise that visitors voted Balinakill the Stirling/Argyll Hotel of the Year 2003.

Dunultach (Clachan, near Tarbert PA29 6XW, ☎ 1880-740 650, fax 1880-740 296, contact@dunultach.co.uk, www.dunultach.co.uk; open Mar-Oct; B&B ££, dinner ££-£££). B&B in an attractive 1900 manse beautifully situated with views over the Sound of Jura. The breakfasts are good and evening meals are available by arrangement.

Stonefield Castle Hotel (Tarbert PA29 6YJ, ☎ 1880-820 836, fax 1880-820 929, enquiries@stonefieldcastle.co.uk, www.stonefieldcastle.co.uk; DB&B £££££). The baronial-style hotel dates from 1837 and sits majestically in 60 acres of woodland overlooking Loch Fyne. The period interior oozes elegance and gracious living. The excellent restaurant serves succulent fresh seafood, Argyll lamb, Buccleuch beef and homegrown vegetables, although you'll probably remember the sensational view from the dining room even more.

Victoria Hotel (Barmore Road, Tarbert PA29 6TW, ☎/fax 1880-820 236, info@victarbert.com, www.victarbert.com; B&B ££, dinner ££). Distinctive, yellow-painted hotel on the Tarbert harborside. The bedrooms have recently been refurbished, there's a good candlelit conservatory restaurant and the lively bar is popular with locals and visiting yachtsmen.

West Loch Hotel (By Tarbert PA29 6YF, ☎ 1880-820 283, fax 1880-820 930, westlochhotel@btinternet.com; B&B ££, dinner ££). An attractive 18th-century former coaching inn, with comfortable rooms, open fires and a renowned cozy restaurant offering high-quality Tarbert seafood, Scottish beef and local game.

Columba Hotel (East Pier Road, Tarbert PA29 6UF, ☎/fax 1880-820 808, www.columbahotel.com; B&B £££, lunch ££, dinner £££). The hotel has a peaceful lochside setting, well-furnished cozy bedrooms and log fires. Locally caught langoustines and scallops feature in the restaurant and bar menus.

Ca' Dora Café (Harbour Street, Tarbert; £). This excellent harbor-front café serves inexpensive meals, snacks and delicious ice cream.

Anchorage Restaurant (Harbour Street, Tarbert PA29 6UD, ☎ 1880-820 881, mail@anchoragetarbert.co.uk; open Feb-Dec; £££). Small, intimate restaurant produces fresh, colorful food with an accent on seafood, beef and lamb cooked in a simple, classic style. The blackboard menu changes daily according to the local catch.

Kilberry Inn (Kilberry, By Tarbert PA29 6YD, ☎ 1880-770 223, relax@kilberryinn.com, www.kilberryinn.com; open April-Oct, closed Mon; B&B £££, dinner ££). Cozy, traditional stone cottage providing comfortable accommodation and wonderful food (booking recommended), including daily specials.

Skipness Castle Seafood Cabin (Skipness Castle, Skipness, By Tarbert PA29 6XU, ☎ 1880-760 207, fax 1880-760 208; open late May through Sept; £-££). Seafood specials, home baking and takeaways in magnificent surroundings.

Isle of Gigha

Gigha (pronounced "gee-a" with a hard "g") is a small, low-lying, fertile island between Kintyre and Islay. It is famous for ancient standing stones and burial sites and the celebrated **Achamore Gardens** (☎ 1583-505 254; open year-round, dawn-dusk; admission by donation). The gardens boast 50 acres of natural woodland and large walled gardens, and were founded by Colonel Horlick (of the famous drinks family). The banks of rhododendrons, azaleas, camellias and rarer exotic shrubs, particularly between March and June, are a delight for garden lovers.

From end to end, there are traces of ancient dwellings and burial sites. Most are difficult to find and you'll almost certainly need local help to find them let alone interpret them. The carved stones in and around Kilchattan are only a short walk from the ferry, and there is a fine view from the old church. The island store rents cycles, although you can walk to most places, nowhere being more than three miles from the ferry.

■ Getting Here

By Ferry

Caledonian MacBrayne (☎ 1475-650 100) operates a regular car ferry from Tayinloan to Gigha (20 minutes).

■ Golf

 Gigha Golf Course (9-hole inland, 5,042 yards-18 holes; Isle of Gigha PA41 7AA, ☎ 1583-505 254, fax 1583-505 244; green fees £10). Pay and play or join as a country member to enjoy magnificent views on a fine 9-hole course.

■ Where To Stay & Eat

See *Accommodation* and *Dining* price charts on pages 218 and 219.

The Gigha Hotel (☎ 1583-505 254, fax 1583-505 244, hotel@isle-of-gigha.co.uk, www.isle-of-gigha.co.uk; B&B £££, dinner ££). A short walk from the ferry, the only hotel on the island is renowned for its good Scottish food and lively all-day bar.

Post Office Guest House (Isle of Gigha PA41 7AA, ☎ 1583-505 251, postoffice@gigha.net, www.gigha.net; B&B £, dinner £-££). The island's post office/store offers guest house accommodation above the shop, with a cozy residents' lounge warmed by an open fire and traditional dining room. You can also rent bikes for £3 per hour/£10 per day.

Campbeltown & Mull of Kintyre

On the east coast of Kintyre is the popular holiday village and fishing harbor of Carradale, nestled at the heart of a network of forest and coastal walks. Kintyre's main town is Campbeltown in the south. This is where the 7th Earl of Argyll built a castle overlooking the natural harbor in the early 17th century and developed the economy by encouraging migration from the Scottish Lowlands. Campbeltown was at one time the Scotch whisky capital and boasted a remarkable 34 distilleries, although today only two remain and only one is operational. Farther south lies the famous Mull (tip) of Kintyre itself, from which the hills of Antrim in Northern Ireland are clearly visible, just 12 miles away. According to legend, St Columba landed here during his great pilgrimage and left his footprints in a rock near Southend.

 INFORMATION SOURCES: The tourism office is at MacKinnon House, The Pier, Campbeltown PA28 6EF, ☎ 870-720 0609, fax 1586-553 291, info@campbeltown.visitscotland.com; open year-round.

Kintyre Peninsula

■ Special Events

 Mull of Kintyre Music Festival (Aug; ☎ 1586-551 053, fax 1586-554 972; www.mokmf.com). Popular festival of traditional Scottish and Irish music, concerts, free pub sessions, street entertainment and ceilidhs.

■ Attractions & Sights

 **Glenbarr Abbey** (Glenbarr, By Tarbert PA29 6UT, ☎ 1583-421 247, fax 1583-421 255; open Easter to mid-Oct, 10am-5:30pm, closed Tues; adult/concession £2.50/£2). This 18th-century house is the home of the Lairds of Glenbarr and is set in attractive grounds with riverside and woodland walks. Exhibits include 19th-century fashions, antique toys, an original Spode dinner service, china collections, family jewelry, patchworks and a thimble collection. The Laird Angus MacAlister and his wife Jeanne MacAlister, Lady Glenbarr, conduct house tours personally.

Saddell Abbey (Saddell, five miles south of Carradale on the B842). The tranquil ruins of a 12th-century Cistercian abbey founded by Somerled, Lord of the Isles, and worshipped in for some 300 years. The abbey was cruciform in shape but all that remains today is part of the north transept, the presbytery and a small section of the refectory. A shelter next to the entrance displays some fine sculptured stonework dating from the 15th century, including a cross, six tombstones and five effigies.

Campbeltown Cross (bottom of Main Street, facing the harbor, Campbeltown). This 14th-century cross is the finest example of medieval carving in Kintyre. It is believed to have been carved at Saddell Abbey or on Iona and stood in the graveyard at Kilkivan (near Machrihanish) before being moved to Campbeltown around 1680. It remained there as a market cross, in front of the town hall, until it was removed for safety during World War II, before being re-erected on its present site.

Campbeltown Heritage Centre (Lorne Street Church, Big Kiln, Campbeltown PA28 6JU, ☎ 1586-551 400; open April-Oct, Mon-Sat, noon-5pm & Sun, 2-5pm; adult/concession/child £2/£1.50/£1). A treasure-trove of information on the cultural and economic history and development of southern Kintyre. Located in a former church (the Tartan Kirk), exhibits include a working model of the former Campbeltown to Machrihanish light railway and displays on the whisky industry (there were once 34 distilleries in Campbeltown), herring fishing and the 6th-century St Kieran, "Apostle of Kintyre."

Campbeltown Museum (Hall Street, Campbeltown, ☎ 1586-552 366 or 367; open Tues-Sat, 10am-1pm & 2-5pm; til 7:30 pm Tues & Thurs). The museum contains specimens with geological, archaeological and cultural connections to Kintyre.

Springbank Distillery (Campbeltown PA28 6EJ, ☎ 1586-552 085, fax 1586-553 215; open April-Sept, Mon-Thurs, tours 2pm by arrangement only; adult/child £3/free). The only fully operational survivor of the 34 distilleries that once made Campbeltown the capital of Scotch whisky. Dating from 1828 and still in the ownership of the founding Mitchell family, Springbank maintains an idiosyncratically traditional production process that uniquely covers all stages from peating its barley to bottling the whisky. Connoisseurs revere the output as a hugely impressive and distinctive malt.

Davaar Island (at the mouth of Campbeltown Loch). At the north of the island is a Stevenson-built lighthouse, while to the south is Crucifixion Cave with its famous dream-inspired painting of the death of Christ. Local artist Archibald MacKinnon created the painting in 1887 as an act of piety after a shipwreck. You reach the island on foot at low tide via a shingle causeway called the Dorlin, the crossing taking around 45 minutes. On reaching the island, go to the caves on the right – the painting is in the fifth of seven caves. Because of the rocks, it takes a good 30 minutes to reach the caves. Check the tide times at the tourism office and allow for this in planning your return journey. Bring a torch to illuminate the cave. Don't try to reach the lighthouse from the caves – the route is very rocky and dangerous. Apart from the lighthouse cottage and a small herd of wild goats, Davaar is uninhabited.

Mull of Kintyre (reached by an appropriately long and winding single-track road south from Campbeltown). A remote headland rising a massive 300 feet from the sea and immortalized by Paul McCartney in his song *Mull of Kintyre*. The ex-Beatle still owns four farms nearby. A lighthouse has stood here since 1788; you are now only 12 miles from the coast of Ireland, which is visible on a clear day.

■ Adventures

Mull of Kintyre Equestrian Centre (Homeston, Campbeltown, ☎ 1586-552 437, lorna@ridescotland.com, www.ridescotland.com). Hacking and trail riding (covering 100 miles in a week) over quiet beaches, forest and moorland, with accommodation and dining available. Fishing and clay shooting are also available.

■ Golf

Machrihanish Golf Course (18-hole links, 6,225 yards; Machrihanish, Campbeltown PA28 6PT, ☎ 1586-810 213/810 277, fax 1586-810 221, secretary@machgolf.com, www.machgolf.com; green fees £30-£40). The remote Machrihanish course has yet to be widely discovered but is one of Scotland's finest links. Its first hole has been described as the "world's greatest opening hole" by no less a legend than Jack Nicklaus.

■ Wildlife Watching

Uisead Point at Machrihanish (follow the road through Machrihanish to where it ends close to the Marine Research Station; parking is restricted). This is the best place in Kintyre for watching seabirds and migrants. Almost 200 species have been recorded here. Seals and otters are regularly seen, and porpoises and whales occasionally. Walk south along the coast for half a mile to reach a dramatic bay backed by an amphitheatre of cliffs – the Gauldrons. The stupendous four miles of beach at Machrihanish is open to the pounding Atlantic surf and is backed by spectacular sand dunes and machair (a seaside flower meadow). Waders and seabirds feed along the coast here.

The area between Campbeltown and Machrihanish is known as The Laggan and is one of the largest lowland areas in Argyll. Huge numbers of geese winter here and can easily be seen from the main roads.

Campbeltown Loch is often visited by dolphins and seals and the Dorlin Laggan, overlooked by Davaar Island is an accessible site from which to view teal, wigeon, seabirds and waders.

The rugged cliffs around the Mull of Kintyre hide a wealth of birdlife, including gannets, puffins, storm petrels and peregrine falcons.

Cruises

Kintyre Marine & Fishing Charters (Dunaskomel, High Askomil, Campbeltown PA28 6EN, ☎ 1586-553 511, meg.gannon@btinternet.com; open April-Oct; adult/child from £10/7). Boat trips from Campbeltown to Sanda Island (including a visit to the restaurant-tavern) and fishing charters.

■ Shopping

Torrisdale Castle Tannery (Carradale, Campbeltown PA28 6QT, ☎/fax 1583-431 233, machall@torrisdalecastle.com, www.torrisdalecastle.com). Unique in its use of traditional organic tanning techniques largely abandoned elsewhere, Torrisdale's sheepskin and deerskin rugs are distinctively natural and free from chemicals or smells. Hand methods are used throughout and the skins are produced in a wide range of natural colors.

■ Where To Stay & Eat

See *Accommodation* and *Dining* price charts on pages 218 and 219.

Carradale

 Carradale Hotel (Carradale PA28 6RY, ☎/fax 1583-431 223, carradaleh@aol.com, www.carradalehotel.com; B&B ££, dinner ££). Peaceful small hotel with good sea views. There is a sauna, fishing, riding, a good restaurant and a wide selection of fine wines and whiskies.

Dunvalanree Guest House (Port Right Bay, Carradale PA28 6SE, ☎ 1583-431 226, fax 1583-431 339, house@milstead.demon.co.uk, www.dunvalanree.com; B&B ££-£££, dinner ££). Standing in gardens on the edge of Port Righ Bay, Dunvalanree enjoys good views over Kilbrannan Sound to the Isle of Arran and around Carradale Bay and Forest. There is a comfortable guest lounge, log fires and a spacious dining room serving fresh local Kintyre produce. The hotel can collect you from Machrihanish airport.

Kiloran Guest House (Carradale PA28 6QG, ☎ 1583-431 795; B&B £-££, dinner £). B&B in a pretty Victorian house overlooking fields toward Carradale Bay, with good home cooking and reasonably priced evening meals available.

Mains Farm (Carradale PA28 6QG, ☎ 1583-431 216; open April-Oct; B&B £). Comfortable B&B accommodation in a traditional farmhouse with open fires and good views.

Campbeltown

Argyll Hotel (Bellochantuy, By Campbeltown PA28 6QE, ☎/fax 1583-421 212, info@argyllhotel.co.uk, www.argyllhotel.co.uk; B&B ££, dinner ££). Built in 1785 as a coaching inn, the charming Argyll Hotel was once owned by the Duke of Argyll and was visited by the Duke of Windsor (Edward VIII) in the 1930s. The hotel provides comfortable, relaxing accommodation and excellent dining beside a long stretch of empty beach. The airy conservatory restaurant enjoys westerly views over the nearby islands of Islay, Jura and Gigha, and the jaw-dropping sunsets alone bring many visitors to the hotel. Caravan and camping facilities are also available.

The Ardshiel Hotel (Kilkerran Road, Campbeltown PA28 6JL, ☎ 1586-552 133, fax 1586-551 422, reservations@ardshiel.co.uk, www.ardshiel.co.uk; B&B ££, dinner ££). Originally built in 1877 as the home of a local whisky baron, the bedrooms are pleasantly furnished and the restaurant serves good home cooking emphasizing local seafood and game.

Ballygreggan Farm (Drumlemble, Campbeltown PA28 6PW, ☎ 1586810 211; B&B ££). B&B in a family-run farm on the road between Campbeltown and Machrihanish.

Westbank Guest House (Dell Road, Campbeltown PA28 6JG, ☎/fax 1586-553 660; B&B £-££). Quietly situated Victorian villa within walking distance of the town center.

Low Cattadale (Southend, By Campbeltown PA28 6RN, ☎ 1586-830 205; open Mar-Nov; B&B £). Well-furnished B&B rooms in a farmhouse set in beautiful surroundings close to the Mull of Kintyre.

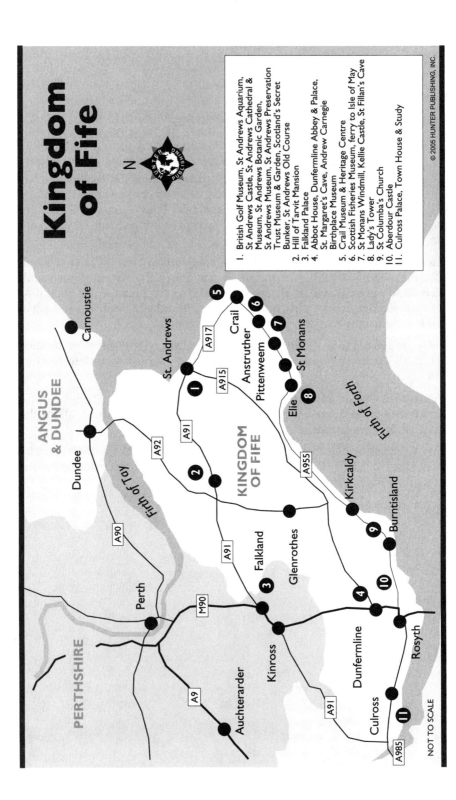

Kingdom
of Fife

N

1. British Golf Museum, St Andrews Aquarium, St Andrews Castle, St Andrews Cathedral & Museum, St Andrews Botanic Garden, St Andrews Museum, St Andrews Preservation Trust Museum & Garden, Scotland's Secret Bunker, St Andrews Old Course
2. Hill of Tarvit Mansion
3. Falkland Palace
4. Abbot House, Dunfermline Abbey & Palace, St. Margaret's Cave, Andrew Carnegie Birthplace Museum
5. Crail Museum & Heritage Centre
6. Scottish Fisheries Museum, ferry to Isle of May
7. St Monans Windmill, Kellie Castle, St Fillan's Cave
8. Lady's Tower
9. St Columba's Church
10. Aberdour Castle
11. Culross Palace, Town House & Study

© 2005 HUNTER PUBLISHING, INC.

Carnoustie

ANGUS & DUNDEE

Dundee

PERTHSHIRE

Perth

Firth of Tay

A90

A9

Auchterarder

M90

Kinross

A91

Falkland

Glenrothes

A92

A91

A917

St. Andrews

A915

Crail

Anstruther

Pittenweem

St Monans

Elie

KINGDOM
OF FIFE

Firth of Forth

A955

Kirkcaldy

Burntisland

Dunfermline

Culross

Rosyth

A91

A985

NOT TO SCALE

Eastern Scotland

Eastern Scotland spans **Fife, Perth-shire, Angus** and **Aberdeenshire**. The region is blessed with richly contrasting scenery: a varied coastline, rolling countryside, tranquil lochs and forested mountains. Threaded along the coast are some of Scotland's most attractive towns and villages. The pretty fish-

ing villages of the north Moray coast are little visited compared with the better known red-roofed East Neuk villages on the south Fife coast. Inland, the scenery of the Angus and Perthshire glens is reminiscent of the Highlands that begin for real not far beyond their borders.

DON'T MISS

Play golf at **St Andrews Old Course** or just walk the famous links.

Tour the delightful East Neuk fishing villages, particularly **Crail**, and don't miss the **Scottish Fisheries Museum** in Anstruther.

Glimpse the 16th- and 17th-century time capsule that is **Culross**, one of Scotland's loveliest old towns.

Visit **Dunfermline Abbey**, burial site of Robert the Bruce, and the nearby Abbot House.

Soak up the history at **Falkland Palace**, former home of Stewart monarchs.

Best Freebie: **St Margaret's Cave**, Dunfermline.

Kingdom of Fife

Fife is best known for the town of St Andrews, but it also boasts delightful fishing villages strung out along its East Neuk coastline.

The region's gently rolling countryside makes it ideal for cycling, further aided by 300 miles of cycle routes along quiet country lanes, disused railway lines and forest tracks (www.fife-cycleways.co.uk).

St Andrews

Picturesque St Andrews was once the ecclesiastical capital of Scotland, although only glorious ruins now remain of its once-mighty cathedral and palace. The town is nowadays better known as the "Home of Golf" and attracts golfing fanatics from the world over. It is the seat of the game's governing body – the **Royal and Ancient Golf Club** – and home of the world's most famous course – the **Old Course**.

According to legend, St Andrews grew as a religious site after St Rule, a Greek monk, brought relics of St Andrew here. Celtic monks built the church of St Mary on the Rock, whose remains still stand near the harbor. Many pilgrims visited the shrine of St Andrew, who became Scotland's patron saint and whose saltire cross (diagonal white cross on a blue background) was adopted as the national flag. For centuries afterwards, St Andrews remained at the religious heart of the nation, and its castle witnessed many of the bloodiest episodes of the Reformation.

St Andrews is also home to Scotland's first university, by royal appointment since Prince William, elder son of Prince Charles and the late Diana, Princess of Wales, began studying here in 2001.

 INFORMATION SOURCES: Kingdom of Fife Tourist Board is at 70 Market Street, St Andrews KY16 9NU, ☎ 1334-472 021, fax 1334-478 422, standrewstic@kftb.ossian.net, www.standrews.com/fife.

■ Special Events

St Andrews Golf Week (Apr; ☎ 1334-478 639, www.linksgolfstandrews.com). Celebrate golf at the game's home, with rounds on several courses, including the Old Course, coaching and gala dinner.

St Andrews Highland Games (last Sun in Jul; ☎ 1334-476 305). Traditional Highland Games.

St Andrew's Week (Nov; ☎ 1334-472 021). Four days of festivities, including food, drink, music and art, culminating in St Andrew's Day (30 Nov).

■ Getting Here

By Air

Eastern Scotland is served by international airports in Edinburgh, Glasgow and Aberdeen (see page 30), and by a regional airport in Dundee (www.scotairways.com).

By Rail

The nearest station to St Andrews is **Leuchars**, from where there are regular buses to St Andrews. **ScotRail** (☎ 845-755 0033, www.scotrail.co.uk); **National Rail Enquiries** (☎ 845-748 4950).

By Car

 The A90 follows the coast from Edinburgh to Aberdeen, and the A96 continues northwest to Inverness. St Andrews is off the A91, coming south from Dundee, or the M90/A91 from Perth or Edinburgh.

Parking in St Andrews

Much of the parking in central St Andrews is controlled by a Voucher parking system. You can buy parking vouchers (scratch cards) from many local shops, which you validate by scratching off the relevant panel and displaying it in your vehicle.

■ Attractions & Sights

British Golf Museum (Bruce Embankment, St Andrews KY16 9AB, ☎ 1334-460 046, fax 1334-460 064, www.britishgolfmuseum.co.uk; open Easter to mid-Oct, 9:30am-5:30pm, mid-Oct to Easter, Thurs-Mon, 11am-3pm; adult/concession/child/family £4/£3/£2/£9.50). Learn the history of golf at the home of golf. The museum traces the game's development from the Middle Ages to the present day, looking at the tournaments, players and equipment that have helped make golf the game it is today. Exhibits cover the development of the Royal and Ancient Golf Club, the history of the Open Championship and clubs and balls down the ages. Watch videos of classic Open Championships and get close to players in the Modern Gallery, which displays equipment used in important championships and personal memorabilia. The museum should interest golfers and non-golfers alike.

St Andrews Aquarium (The Scores, St Andrews KY16 9AS, ☎ 1334-474 786, fax 1334-475 985, info@standrewsaquarium.co.uk, www.standrewsaquarium.co.uk; open Easter-Oct, 10am-6pm, phone for winter opening hours; adult/concession/child £5.50/£4.50/£3.75). Medium-sized aquarium providing an introduction to life beneath the waves, from seahorses to sharks, octopus to eels and rays to seals. Over 30 exhibition tanks display hundreds of species, including deadly piranhas.

St Andrews Castle (HS; The Scores, St Andrews KY16 9AR, ☎ 1334-477 196; open April-Sept, 9:30am-6:30pm; Oct-Mar, 9:30am-4:30pm; adult/concession/child £4/£3/£1.25 includes admission to Cathedral, below). The castle dates from the 13th century and replaced the original castle, destroyed during the Wars of Independence. Most of the present ruin dates from 1400-1560. The castle served as a palace, fortress and prison. Just the thought of being imprisoned in its underground "bottle-dungeon," hollowed from solid rock, is terrifying.

The castle stood at the forefront of the Reformation and witnessed some grizzly events. Protestant reformer George Wishart was burned at the stake at the instigation of Cardinal Beaton, who was himself later killed and his body hung from the battlements. Following Beaton's death, the castle was besieged in 1546-47. The attackers built a mine (tunnel) to enter the castle and the pro-Reformation defenders dug a counter-mine to keep them out. These tunnels are the finest examples of medieval siege techniques in Europe and it's fascinating to compare the large, deliberate tunnel dug by the attackers with the twisting, cramped tunnel dug desperately by the defenders. Reformer John Knox preached in the castle during the siege but was captured and exiled when the castle was finally taken. A trip into the mine and coun-

Kingdom of Fife

ter-mine is fascinating, but be warned – you have to crouch fairly low to get through the tunnels.

 St Andrews Cathedral (HS; The Pends, St Andrews KY16 9QL, ☎ 1334-472 563; open April-Sept, 9:30am-6:30pm; Oct-Mar, 9:30am-4:30pm; adult/concession/child £4/£3/£1.25, includes castle admission). St Andrews was once the largest cathedral in Scotland and its majestic ruins still provide a vivid impression of the huge scale of the complex. The precinct walls are particularly well preserved and sections of the domestic ranges also survive. It's possible to climb a narrow spiral staircase to the top of **St Rule's Tower**, part of the first church built on the site in the early 12th century, for an excellent view over the town (obtain a token from the visitor center).

The **Cathedral Museum** houses an excellent collection of early and later medieval sculpture, grave slabs, cross slabs, ornate shafts of high crosses and other relics found on the site. Most notable is the **St Andrews Sarcophagus**, a royal burial shrine dating from the late 8th century (the time of the Picts) and one of the finest examples of early medieval European sculpture.

St Andrews Botanic Garden (Canongate, St Andrews KY16 8RT, ☎ 1334-476 452, www.st-andrews-botanic.org; open May-Sept, 10am-7pm; Oct-Apr, 10am-4pm; glasshouses close 4pm year-round; adult/child £2/£1). 18 acres of rare and beautiful plants displayed under glass and in the open.

St Andrews Museum (Kinburn Park, Doubledykes Road, St Andrews KY16 9DP, ☎ 1334-412 690, fax 1334-413 214, museums.east@fife.gov.uk; open April-Sept, 10am-5pm; Oct-Mar, 10:30am-4pm). Museum telling the story of the town from medieval to modern times, through temporary exhibitions and a program of events, workshops and activities.

St Andrews Preservation Trust Museum & Garden (12 North Street, St Andrews KY16 9PW, ☎ 1334-477 629, curator.saptmuseum@virgin.net; open Easter weekend, then end of May through Sept & St Andrew's Week, 2-5pm). Charming 16th-century house containing displays and reconstructions on the history of St Andrews, and a sheltered garden.

Scotland's Secret Bunker (Troywood, Crown Buildings, By St Andrews KY16 8QH, ☎ 1333-310 301, fax 1333-312 040, mod@secretbunker.co.uk, www.secretbunker.co.uk; open April-Oct, 10am-6pm, last admission 5pm; adult/concession/child/family £6.95/£5.65/£3.95/£19.50). Discover the twilight world of the government during the Cold War through a fascinating underground labyrinth. This bunker is encased in 15 feet of reinforced concrete 100 feet beneath an ordinary-looking farmhouse. It's from here that government and military officials would have run the country had the UK been attacked by a nuclear strike.

■ Adventures

Fifeoffroad (Kinkell House, St Andrews KY16 8PN, ☎ 1334-472 003, fax 1334-475 248, info@fyfeoffroad.com, www.fyfeoffroad.com). Quad biking and off-road driving.

Kinshaldy Riding Stables (Kinshaldy Farm, Leuchars, near St Andrews KY16 0DR, ☎ 1334-838 527). Exciting beach gallops, forest rides and instruction for all ages.

■ Golf

 Fife has been at the heart of golf for 500 years; the St Andrews New Course dates from 1895 and the revered Old Course is much older. Fife has 45 courses, from the Open and championship qualifying links to several reasonably priced municipal courses.

St Andrews Old Course (18-hole links, 6,609 yards; St Andrews Links Trust, Pilmour House, St Andrews KY16 9SF, ☎ 1334-466 666, fax 1334-477 036, reservations@standrews.org.uk, www.standrews.org.uk; green fees £75-£110). This is the world-famous course, where the game began around 1400. The Old Course has hosted 26 Open Championships and the event will return here in 2005.

PLAYING THE OLD COURSE

Unlike many other prestigious golf venues, the Old Course is public and not the property of an exclusive club. As the world's most famous course, it is immensely popular; close to 42,000 rounds are played on it each year. The course is closed on Sundays when there is the surreal spectacle of the general public walking dogs across its hallowed greens and fairways and even building sand castles in bunkers.

Getting to play a round can be hit or miss (although your golf game certainly can't be – you need a handicap certificate: maximum 24 for men, 36 for ladies) and a little planning will greatly increase your chances. Ideally, book in writing or by fax up to two years ahead to the Reservations Office at the above address; applications are allocated in November the year before play.

Around half of all starting times enter into a ballot drawn daily for the following day (the Saturday draw is for Monday). Telephone or apply in person before 2pm on the day before you want to play (for a minimum of two). The ballot is typically five- to seven-times oversubscribed so it's not ridiculously unlikely you'll get to play if you're in the area for a few days. The results appear by 4pm on the Internet, at the clubhouse, the starters' boxes, caddie pavilion, local golf clubs and Tourist Information Centre.

Local hotels are allocated tee-off times, and you might be able to secure one as a guest. The best way for a single golfer to play is to arrive at the course as early as possible in the morning. The starter will try to join the single with the first available two- or three-ball group.

Kings Barns Golf Links (18-hole links, 7,126 yards; Kingsbarns, By St Andrews KY16 8QD, ☎ 1334-460 860, fax 1334-460 877, info@kings-barns.com, www.kingsbarns.com; green fees £125-£135). One of Fife's newest courses (opened 2000) with spacious fairways, rolling and twisting through dune ridges and hollows, and large greens.

Scotscraig Golf Course (18-hole links, 6,550 yards; Golf Road, Tayport, By St Andrews DD6 9DZ, ☎ 1382-552 515, fax 1382-553 130, scotscraig@scottishgolf.com, www.scotscraig-golfclub.co.uk; green fees £38-£44). Regularly used for Open qualification, Scotscraig is a gem of a course and you can play 36 holes for the price of 18.

National Golf Academy (Drumoig, Leuchars, near St Andrews KY16 0DW, ☎ 1382-541 144, fax 1382-541 133, sngc@scottishgolf.com, www.scottishgolf.com). Golf and leisure facility incorporating coaching, indoor and outdoor practice areas, driving range and large shop.

A WORD TO
THE WISE

WARNING: *The many bags of expensive golf clubs in St Andrews unfortunately attract professional thieves. Always take your clubs into your hotel and never leave them in your car (even locked in the trunk).*

■ Entertainment

Byre Theatre (Abbey Street, St Andrews KY16 9LA, ☎ 1334-475 000, fax 1334-475 370, enquiries@byretheatre.com, www.byretheatre.com). Varied program of contemporary and classic drama, music, dance, opera and comedy. There's also a nice café and restaurant (☎ 1334-468 720).

■ Shopping

St Andrews Pottery Shop (4 Church Square, St Andrews KY16 9NN, ☎/fax 1334-477 744, youngs@pottery52.freeserve.co.uk). Wide selection of pottery and other gifts, including tiles, jewelry, wall plaques and Cretan terracotta pots.

■ Where To Stay

Hotels

MacDonald Rusacks Hotel (Pilmour Links, St Andrews KY16 9JQ, ☎ 870-400 8128, fax 1334-477 896, rusacks@macdonald-hotels.co.uk, www.macdonaldhotels.co.uk; B&B £££££). Stylish hotel overlooking the 1st tee and 18th green of the Old Course. Originally opened in 1887, the hotel reflects the golfing traditions of its unique location.

New Hall (University of St Andrews, 79 North Street, St Andrews KY16 9AD, ☎ 1334-462 000, fax 1334-465 555, holiday@st-andrews.ac.uk, www.escapetotranquillity.com; B&B ££). Good-quality en-suite accommodation in a student hall with all-day coffee shop, dining room and bar.

Old Course Hotel (St Andrews KY16 9SP, ☎ 1334-474 371, fax 1334-477 668, reservations@oldcoursehotel.co.uk, www.oldcoursehotel.co.uk; B&B £££££+). Large, elegant hotel and spa overlooking the Old Course and St Andrews coast. Facilities include lavish accommodation and relaxation facilities and the chance to play the hotel's Duke's Course. Wear smart dress and a tie in the excellent restaurant.

Rufflets Country House Hotel (Strathkinness Low Road, St Andrews KY16 9TX, ☎ 1334-472 594, fax 1334-478 703, reservations@rufflets.co.uk, www.rufflets.co.uk; B&B £££££). Delightful, turreted country-house hotel set in 10 acres of landscaped grounds a mile out of St Andrews. Privately owned and run by the same family since 1952, there are individually decorated bedrooms, spacious public rooms and fine dining and grill menus.

Inn at Lathones (Largoward, By St Andrews KY9 1JE, ☎ 1334-840 494, fax 1334-840 694, lathones@theinn.co.uk, www.theinn.co.uk; B&B ££££). Cozy, refurbished 400-year-old coaching inn provides modern, comfortable rooms and serves great food.

Guest Houses & B&BS

The Old Station (Stravithie Bridge, St Andrews KY16 8LR, ☎/fax 1334-880 505, info@theoldstation.co.uk, www.theoldstation.co.uk; B&B £££-££££). The delightful Sheila and Paul Briggs provide very comfortable accommodation in their attractive converted Victorian station, including superbly cooked, candlelit breakfasts in the conservatory set on what used to be the station platform. For the ultimate stay, a restored railway carriage provides two luxurious and wonderfully romantic suites. Get onboard, but book early if you want a carriage suite on a weekend – they're very popular!

Aslar Guest House (120 North Street, St Andrews KY16 9AF, ☎ 1334-473 460, fax 1334-477 540, enquiries@aslar.com, www.aslar.com; B&B £££). Characterful house with beautiful bedrooms, including the Master, Four Poster and Turret Suite. There is free Internet access and DVD players in all bedrooms.

Cambo House (Kingsbarns, By St Andrews KY16 8QD, ☎ 1333-450 054, fax 1333-450 987, cambo@camboestate.com, www.camboestate.com; B&B £££). Grand style B&B on an extensive estate close to St Andrews, with magnificent furniture and a four-poster bedroom.

Hamilton Hall (University of St Andrews, 79 North Street, St Andrews KY16 9AD, ☎ 1334-462 000, fax 1334-465 555,

HOTEL PRICE CHART	
Per person, per night, based on double occupancy in high season. B&B rate includes breakfast; DB&B includes dinner and breakfast.	
£	Under £20
££	£21-£35
£££	£36-£50
££££	£51-£80
£££££	Over £80

holidays@st-andrews.ac.uk, www.escapetotranquillity.com; B&B ££). Basic student accommodation with shared bathrooms and superb views over the golf courses and sea. Breakfast and a bar are available but no evening meals.

Little Carron Cottage (Little Carron Gardens, St Andrews KY16 8QN, ☎ 1334-474 039, fax 1334-472 398, info@littlecarroncottage-standrews.com, www.littlecarroncottage-standrews.com; B&B £££). Quietly situated, delightful former farmhouse with three suites, each with private sitting rooms. There are candlelit organic breakfasts and real log fires. No credit cards.

■ Where To Eat

See *Dining* price chart, next page.

 Balaka Restaurant (Alexandra Place, St Andrews KY16 9XD, ☎ 1334-474 825, fax 1334-476 548, info@balaka.co.uk; ££). Excellent, award-winning Bangladeshi restaurant that uses own-grown spices.

Doll's House (3 Church Square, St Andrews KY16 9NN, ☎ 1334-477 422, fax 1334-474 487, mail@dolls-house.co.uk, www.dolls-house.co.uk; ££). Relaxed, buzzy, candlelit restaurant in the heart of old St Andrews. There is a changing menu of Scottish and French-influenced dishes.

Grange Inn (Grange Road, St Andrews KY16 8LJ, ☎ 1334-472 670, fax 1334-472 604; £-££). Charming pub-restaurant overlooking St Andrews Bay, with rooms dating from the 17th and 18th centuries, and decent Scottish food cooked to order.

Russell Hotel (26 The Scores, St Andrews KY16 9AS, ☎ 1334-473 447, fax 1334-478 279, enquiries@russellhotelstandrews.co.uk, www.russellhotelstandrews.co.uk; lunch ££, dinner £££). The hotel's small candlelit dining room offers imaginative, well-prepared Scottish and international dishes.

The Seafood Restaurant (below The Scores, St Andrews KY16 9AS, ☎ 1334-479 475, fax 1334-479 476, www.theseafoodrestaurant.com; lunch ££, dinner £££). The newly opened sister establishment of the celebrated St Monans restaurant enjoys a spectacular waterside location overlooking the West Sands.

St Andrews Links Clubhouse (West Sands Road, St Andrews KY16 9XL, ☎ 1334-466 666, fax 1334-466 664, linkstrust@standrews.org.uk, www.standrews.org.uk; ££). The recently refurbished restaurant on the world-famous links offers a wide range of dishes, including fresh seafood and chargrilled steaks.

The Vine Leaf (131 South Street, St Andrews KY16 9UN, ☎/fax 1334-477 497, vineleaf@tesco.net, www.vineleafstandrews.co.uk; closed Sun-Mon; £££). Popular, bustling non-smoking restaurant overlooking a secluded herb garden in the heart of St Andrews. Specialties include seafood, Scottish beef, game and gourmet vegetarian dishes. Reservations strongly advised.

Cupar

Cupar has a long history; the town was Fife's market center and seat of justice from medieval times. It is now a bustling town with good shopping and leisure facilities.

■ Attractions & Sights

Hill of Tarvit Mansion House (NTS; Cupar KY15 5PB, ☎/fax 1334-653 127, hilloftarvit@nts.org.uk; house open April-Sept, 1-5pm; Oct, Sat-Sun, 1pm-5pm; gardens open year-round, 9:30am-sunset; house & gardens adult/concession/family £5/£3.75/£13.50). Fine Edwardian mansion containing impressive French, Scottish and Chippendale furniture, Dutch paintings and Flemish tapestries. There is a restored Edwardian laundry, delightful formal gardens, tearoom and gift shop.

■ Adventures

Barbarafield Riding School (Barbarafield Farm, Craigrothie, By Cupar KY15 5PU, ☎/fax 1334-828 223, www.barbarafield.co.uk) offers instruction and hacking across beautiful farmland, including pub rides.

■ Where To Stay & Eat

Peat Inn (Cupar KY15 5LH, ☎ 1334-840 206, fax 1334-840 530, stay@thepeatinn.co.uk, www.thepeatinn.co.uk; restaurant closed Sun-Mon; B&B ££££, lunch ££, dinner ££££). Cozy and enduringly popular restaurant with rooms, providing beautifully styled suites, exceptional Scottish cooking and an excellent wine list. Not cheap but it's probably the best restaurant in Fife.

Todhall House (Dairsie, near Cupar KY15 4RQ, ☎ 1334-656 344, fax 1334-650 791, info@todhallhouse.com, www.todhallhouse.com; open Mar-Oct; B&B ££, dinner ££). Handsome country house standing in extensive lawns with a walled garden, providing quality accommodation and traditional Scottish cuisine.

Westfield Mansion House (Westfield Road, Cupar KY15 5AR, ☎ 1334-655 699, fax 1334-650 075, westfieldhouse@standrews4.freeserve.co.uk, www.standrews4.freeserve.co.uk; B&B £££). Top-quality B&B in a handsome Georgian mansion set in beautiful grounds and retaining many period features such as antique cornices and marble fireplaces.

Chapel House (Kettlebridge, near Cupar KY15 7TU, ☎/fax 1337-831 790,

DINING PRICE CHART	
Indicates the price, per person, of a full meal, excluding drinks. Generally three courses, though fixed menus of five or more courses may be available.	
£	Under £10
££	£11-£20
£££	£21-£30
££££	£31-£40

www.chapelhouse.com; B&B ££££). A beautiful Georgian house set in 10 acres of grounds, including a tennis court and trout pool. The bedrooms are huge and guests have the run of four reception rooms, drawing room and oak-paneled billiard room. Evening meals are available.

Ostlers Close (25 Bonnygate, Cupar KY15 4BU, ☎ 1334-655 574, www.ostlersclose.co.uk; lunch £££, dinner ££££). Established restaurant serving imaginative menus of Scottish cuisine using local shellfish, game, free range ducks and organic vegetables and herbs.

Falkland

The history of Falkland dates back to medieval times when it was the home of the Earls of Fife, their ancient castle having stood in the gardens of the present Royal Palace. The town was a favorite of the Stewart kings from James I onwards, who enjoyed hunting deer in the great forest that once covered the area. **Falkland Palace** dominates the town. Built as the principal royal hunting lodge in 1501-41 by James IV and James V, it boasts the world's oldest tennis court.

With a royal household to supply, the weaving industry flourished in Falkland, later developing into handloom weaving. The cottages of these weavers can still be seen, many with small, irregularly spaced windows. As you walk around the town keep a lookout for telltale marriage lintels over doorways, which indicate the joining of two families, usually inscribed with a marriage date.

■ Attractions & Sights

Falkland Palace (NTS; Falkland, By Cupar KY15 7BU, ☎ 1337-857 397, fax 1337-857 980; open Mar-Oct, Mon-Sat, 10am-6pm & Sun, 1pm-5pm; adult/concession/child/family £7/£5.25/£5.25/£19). Falkland Palace was the Balmoral of its day. As the country residence and hunting lodge of eight Stewart monarchs, including Mary, Queen of Scots, it retains a palpable sense of history. Built in 1501-41, the palace is an excellent example of Renaissance architecture and royalty last lived here in 1651. The keepership subsequently descended to the Crichton Stuart family that still occupies the palace today.

The ornate **Chapel Royal** remains a place of worship and beside the chapel is a stunning Tapestry Gallery (containing 17th-century Flemish tapestries) forming the processional route from the king's apartments to the chapel. A small but cozy library houses family portraits together with photos of the Queen and Prince Charles, both of whom have visited. The King's Room and Queen's Room are recreations to show what royal apartments might have looked like.

The palace gardens include the site of the original 12th-century castle and well. The intriguing **Royal Tennis Court** is 450 years old – the world's oldest. Modern players continue a real tennis tradition that has included royalty from James V to Charles II, the last royal to live here. A video attempts to explain the game's complicated rules, although the clatter of the ball bouncing on the ceiling often drowns out the sound.

■ Golf

 Ladybank Golf Course (18-hole heathland, 6,754 yards; Annsmuir, Ladybank, Cupar KY15 7RA, between Falkland and Cupar, ☎ 1337-830 814, fax 1337-831 505, ladybankgc@aol.com, www.ladybankgolf.co.uk; green fees £40). The heathland-style course is regularly used for Open qualifying. Advance booking recommended, and no jeans allowed.

■ Where To Stay & Eat

See the *Accommodation* and *Dining* price charts on pages 253 and 255.

 Covenanter Hotel (High Street, Falkland KY15 7BU, ☎ 1337-857 224, fax 1337-857 163, www.covenanterhotel.com; B&B ££, dinner ££). Small 18th-century coaching inn close to the palace. The restaurant and bistro serve good food.

Honeysuckle Cottage (1 Victoria Place, Falkland KY15 7AU, ☎/fax 1337-858 600, jesspattersongrant@amserve.com; B&B £-££). Charming and quiet cottage B&B with pleasant bedrooms and bright guest lounge.

Wester Cash Farmhouse (Strathmiglo, Auchtermuchty by Falkland KY14 7RG, ☎/fax 1337-860 215, info@westercash.co.uk, www.westercash.co.uk; open April-Oct; B&B ££). Comfortable B&B in a 200-year-old farmhouse set on a 400-acre farm.

Greenhouse Restaurant (High Street, Falkland KY15 7BU, ☎/fax 1337-858 400, greenhouse.restaurant@ukgateway.net, www.greenhouserestaurant.com; closed Mon-Tues; lunch £, dinner ££). Organic restaurant with modern décor that makes all its dishes freshly on the premises.

Kind Kyttock's Kitchen (Cross Wynd, Falkland KY15 7BE, ☎ 1337-857 477, fax 1337-857 379; lunch ££). Delightful tearoom in a charming 17th-century cottage serving homemade soups, excellent home baking and pancakes.

Dunfermline

Dunfermline (which means "fortress by the crooked stream") was Scotland's ancient capital for more than 500 years. It was already a fortified settlement when in 1060 Malcolm III (Malcolm Canmore) chose the town for his new royal residence. His second wife, Queen Margaret (later canonized), established a religious community here and built a new church, on the site of the nave of the present abbey.

Dunfermline's 11th-century abbey is the final resting place of King Robert the Bruce and was the post-Iona burial site of the Scottish monarchy. After James VI/I moved his court to London in 1603, Dunfermline declined throughout the

17th century until the rise of the 18th-century weaving industry. The great industrialist and philanthropist **Andrew Carnegie** was born in Dunfermline in 1835 and his birthplace cottage is now a museum celebrating his life.

 INFORMATION SOURCES: The tourism office is at 1 High Street, Dunfermline KY12 7DL, ☎ 1383-720 999, fax 1383-625 807, kftb@dunfermlinetic.fsnet.co.uk; open year-round.

■ Attractions & Sights

Abbot House (Maygate, Dunfermline KY12 7NE, ☎ 1383-733 266, fax 1383-624 908, dht@abbothouse.fsnet.co.uk, www.abbothouse.co.uk; open year-round, 10am-5pm; adult/concession/child £3/£2/£1.25, including tea/coffee and cake). This is the oldest house in Dunfermline. The main room (Presence Chamber) includes fragments of an original wall mural dating from the 1570s, together with a traceried window that dates the house to 1450-60. The *Spirit in the Stones* audiovisual presentation tells the story of the house's friendly ghost. The shrine of Saint Margaret, the jewel-encrusted reliquary of Scotland's saintly queen, evokes the vitality of the Benedictine abbey she founded. More modern exhibits include the "Poison Chalice," the replica of the glass goblet that the United Kingdom's first monarch believed could magically warn of the presence of poison, and the "Lochgelly Tawse," the teacher's leather strap that once ruled the schoolrooms of Scotland. Well-meaning but amateur volunteer guides take visitors around the display rooms. Spend time on your own to make the most of your visit.

 **Dunfermline Abbey & Palace** (HS; St Margaret Street, Dunfermline KY12 7PE, ☎ 1383-739 026; open April-Sept, 9:30am-6:30pm; hours limited Oct-Mar, call ahead; closes 12:30-1:30pm daily; Abbey Church closed Oct-Apr; adult/concession/child £2.50/£1.90/£0.75). The remains of a great Benedictine abbey founded by Saint Margaret in the 11th century. The remains of her church lie beneath the present superb nave, built in Romanesque style in the 12th century. Eight Scottish kings lie in the abbey. Most notably, Robert the Bruce's tomb and memorial plaque lie beneath the pulpit of the present parish church, which has the king's name carved around its tower. Substantial ruins of the abbey buildings remain, including the vast refectory.

Next to the abbey stands the ruin of the royal palace built from the monastery guesthouse and altered in the 16th century for James VI. As at the abbey at Holyrood in Edinburgh, the royal palace eventually became more important than the abbey itself. This was the birthplace of Charles I, the last monarch born in Scotland (born 1600, reigned 1625-1649?); in 1603, when James VI succeeded to the English crown, the Scottish royal family moved to England. The palace fell into ruin, with most of what can be seen today dating from the 16th century.

St Margaret's Cave (Chalmers Street Car Park, Dunfermline, ☎ 1383-313 838/314 228; open Easter-Sept, 11am-4pm; admission free). The cave in which St Margaret, Queen of Scotland, used to pray. Originally on the banks of the Tower Burn, the cave was built over and is now 86 steps below ground. Information panels, some with audio handsets, line the tunnel leading down to the cave; church music evocatively plays in the background.

MARGARET, SCOTLAND'S SAINTLY QUEEN

Margaret was a Saxon princess (granddaughter of Edward the Confessor of England) born in Hungary who married King Malcolm III of Scotland. Three of her eight children – Edgar, Alexander and David – became Scottish kings. Margaret founded a small priory in Dunfermline, and in 1128 her son David I began to build a great abbey (Dunfermline Abbey) over the site of his mother's church. In 1916, fragments of Margaret's church were found below the nave of the abbey.

Margaret died in 1093 and was canonized by Pope Innocent IV in 1250, largely because of miracles attributed to her name. Her relics and name have been the subject of worship ever since. After Margaret's canonization, a shrine was built to house her remains, turning Dunfermline into a pilgrimage center, second in Scotland only to St Andrews. The pilgrimage to St Margaret's Cave became an annual event that at its height attracted up to 18,000 Roman Catholics. Organized pilgrimages stopped in 1974, although individuals still make personal pilgrimages to the cave.

Andrew Carnegie Birthplace Museum (Moodie Street, Dunfermline KY12 7PL, ☎ 1383-724 302, fax 1383-721 862; open April-Oct, Mon-Sat, 11am-5pm & Sun, 2-5pm; adult/concession £2/£1, children free). The Birthplace Cottage and adjoining Memorial Hall tell the inspiring story of how a weaver's son became the king of the steel industry and greatest benefactor of his time.

■ Adventures

 Waterskiscotland (Townhill Country Park, Townhill, By Dunfermline KY12 0HT, ☎ 1383-620 123, fax 1383-620 122, info@waterskiscotland.co.uk, www.waterskiscotland.co.uk). Training and practice site for the national waterskiing team where one-to-one instruction is available for all abilities.

■ Where To Stay & Eat

See the *Accommodation* and *Dining* price charts on pages 253 and 255.

 Davaar House Hotel & Restaurant (126 Grieve Street, Dunfermline KY12 8DW, ☎ 1383-721 886, fax 1383-623 633, enquiries@davaarhouse-hotel.com, www.davaar-house-hotel.com; restaurant closed Sun; B&B £££, dinner £££). Traditionally furnished small hotel that serves a menu of Scottish cuisine that changes daily.

Garvock House Hotel (St John's Drive, Transy, Dunfermline KY12 7TU, ☎ 1383-621 067, fax 1383-621 168, sales@garvock.co.uk, www.garvock.co.uk; B&B £££, lunch ££, dinner £££). Elegant country house tucked away in woodland with stylish bedrooms and a reputation for fine food.

Town House Restaurant (48 East Port, Dunfermline KY12 7JB, ☎ 1383-432 382, 1383-432 381, info@townhouserestaurant.co.uk, www.townhouserestaurant.co.uk; ££). Bright designer furnishings and original stonework provide the setting for an eclectic European menu.

East Neuk

"A fringe of gold on a beggar's mantle," was how James II of Scotland described the picturesque East Neuk. "Neuk" is the old Scots for "corner" and East Neuk refers to the coastal strip skirting Fife's southeastern peninsula, with its little towns and villages built around sheltered bays and surrounded by rich farmland. This string of quaint fishing villages has colorful cottages with whitewashed walls, red-pantile roofs and stepped gable ends. Their cobbled, winding streets lead to secluded harbors where small boats unload their catches as they have done for centuries. Trading salted fish and agricultural produce with Europe made these communities among the richest in Scotland. In addition to pretty villages, the East Neuk also boasts some of the finest beaches, watersports and sea angling in Fife.

■ Crail

Crail is the oldest of the East Neuk towns. It received Royal Burgh status in the 12th century and developed around its picturesque harbor, where fishing boats still land mostly shellfish, and its 12th-century castle (where Crail House now stands). The town's **Marketgate** became one of the largest marketplaces in medieval Europe, and the Mercat Cross still stands there with a 17th-century shaft. Streets of 17th and 18th-century houses retain many traditional features of East Neuk dwellings, including outside stairs and distinctive crow-stepped gables. Many houses have marriage lintels built above their doors or into walls, showing the initials of the first owners and the date of the building or their marriage.

INFORMATION SOURCES: The tourism office is at Crail Museum & Heritage Centre, 62-64 Marketgate, Crail KY10 3TL, ☎/fax 1333-450 869, crailtic@uk2.net; open April-Sept.

Special Events

Crail Festival (Jul; ☎ 1333-450 316). Varied program of music, dance, art and competitions.

Attractions & Sights

Crail Museum & Heritage Centre (62/64 Marketgate, Crail KY10 3TL, ☎ 1333-450 869; open April-Sept, Sat-Sun & public holidays, 2-5pm; in summer also open Sat 10am-1pm). Museum telling the story of the town, its seafaring tradition, 200-year-old golf course and airfield history. There are also weekly guided walks around Crail from the last Sunday in June through August, departing at 2:30.

Golf

Crail Balcomie (18-hole links, 5,922 yards; Balcomie Clubhouse, Crail KY10 3XN, ☎ 1333-450 686, fax 1333-450 416, info@crailgolfingsociety.co.uk, www.crailgolfingsociety.co.uk; green fees £32-£40). Delightful and spectacularly located course designed by the legendary Old Tom Morris of St Andrews.

Shopping

Crail Pottery (75 Nethergate, Crail KY10 3TX, ☎ 1333-451 212, www.crail-pottery.com). Family-run pottery producing a wide range of stoneware and brightly colored earthenware, including mugs, cooking pots, salad sets and planters. All pieces are hand-thrown, decorated, glazed and fired on-site.

Where To Stay & Eat

See the *Accommodation* and *Dining* price charts on pages 253 and 255.

Barnsmuir Farmhouse B&B (Crail KY10 3XB, 1333-450 342, fax 1333-451 729; B&B £-££). Jacobean farmhouse set on a family-run working farm (bathrooms are shared).

Denburn House (1 Marketgate North, Crail KY10 3TQ, ☎ 1333-450 253, denburn@fsbdial.co.uk; B&B £-££). B&B and cook-for-yourself accommodation in an attractive 18th-century house with a peaceful walled garden, comfortable guest lounge and great sea views.

Honeypot Guest House & Tearoom (6 High Street South, Crail KY10 3TD, ☎/fax 1333-450 935, info@honeypotcrail.net; open Mar-Oct, closed Tues; £). Small guest house with a tearoom serving home baking, teas, coffees, soups and snacks.

The Marine (54 Nethergate South, Crail KY10 3TZ, ☎ 1333-450 207, fax 1333-450 272, standrews.marine@which.net; B&B ££). Guest house with nice rooms and great views of the sea and Isle of May.

Reilly Crab & Lobsters (☎ 1333-450 476/450 523; open April-Oct, closed Mon; £-££). The small wooden stall on Crail harbor serves delicious dressed crab (from £3) and fresh lobster.

■ Anstruther

Anstruther (pronounced "enster") is East Neuk's largest town and is a popular holiday destination. The town developed from monastic beginnings, although life here has always revolved around the sea. Herring fishing was one of the mainstays of town trade and Anstruther grew into one of Scotland's busiest ports. Fishing boats still work in the harbor they now share with an increasing number of pleasure craft.

As with the rest of the East Neuk, much of Anstruther's trade was with Europe, although not all of it was legal! Wine, tobacco, cloth and sugar were smuggled up the Dreel Burn under the 16th-century Smuggler's Inn, and linen and coal were smuggled out. Jacobite conspirators met at the inn in 1715.

 INFORMATION SOURCES: The tourism office is at Scottish Fisheries Museum, Harbourhead, Anstruther KY10 3AB, ☎/fax 1333-311 073, anstruthertic@uk2.net; open April-Oct.

Attractions & Sights

Scottish Fisheries Museum (St Ayles, Harbourhead, Anstruther KY10 3AB, ☎/fax 1333-310 628, info@scottish-fisheries-museum.org, www.scottish-fisheries-museum.org; open April-Sept, Mon-Sat, 10am-5:30pm & Sun, 11am-5pm; Oct-Mar, Mon-Sat, 10am-4:30pm & Sun, noon-4:30pm, last admission one hour before closing; adult/concession £3.50/£2.80, children free with paid adult). Fascinating museum telling the story of Scottish fishing and its people from the earliest days to the present. Follow the industry that has played such a major role in Scotland's development from primitive fishing in dugout boats through sail and herring fishing, to whaling and steam-powered boats. Particularly attention-grabbing are the many actual fishing vessels and the original wheelhouse on display, real-life models of boats and a working steam engine, recreations of cabins, a historic boatyard and fisherman's cottage. Two excellent videos take you to sea through the eyes of North Sea fishermen and many fine paintings and photographs bring to life Scotland's rich fishing heritage. The museum also houses the memorial to Scottish fishermen lost at sea and has an extensive library and archive open by appointment. Don't be surprised if you end up spending several hours in this absorbing museum.

Wildlife Watching

 Isle of May (☎ 1333-310 103, info@isleofmayferry.com, www.isleofmayferry.com; May-Oct; adult/concession/child £14/£12/£6). The Isle of May was the base of early Christian missionaries. You can see remains of a 7th-century chapel and the Beacon, the oldest lighthouse in Scotland (1636). The island is today an important wildlife sanctuary, home to thousands of puffins, shags, guillemots, razorbills, terns and other seabirds, and a large grey seal colony. May to early July are the best months to see breeding seabirds. You can see grey seals year-round, but the best month is October when they pup. Six miles off the coast, reached by the *May Princess* from Anstruther (see page 261), approximately one hour each way with two to three hours on the island.

Where To Stay & Eat

See the *Accommodation* and *Dining* price charts on pages 253 and 255.

Spindrift Hotel (Pittenweem Road, Anstruther KY10 3DT, ☎/fax 1333-310 573, info@thespindrift.co.uk, www.thespindrift.co.uk; B&B ££, dinner ££). Restored Victorian sea captain's stone house. The much-requested top floor "Captain's Room" was the private room of the house's original owner, who designed the room as a replica of a shipmaster's cabin. Quality, home-cooked evening meals are available.

Smugglers Inn (High Street East, Anstruther KY10 3DQ, ☎ 1333-310 506, fax 1333-312 706, smuggs106@aol.com; ££). Historic, 300-year-old family-run inn serving home-cooked dishes, fresh seafood and traditional Scottish dishes, either in the cozy, harbor-view bar or dining room.

Anstruther Fish Bar & Restaurant (42/44 Shore Street, Anstruther KY10 3AQ, ☎ 1333-310 518, fax 1333-311 919, www.anstrutherfishbar.co.uk; £-££). Award-winning fish and chip shop (haddock and chips is the specialty), which generates lengthy queues throughout the day. It can often be quicker to eat in than wait in the takeaway line.

The Cellar (24 East Green, Anstruther KY10 3AA, ☎ 1333-310 378, fax 1333-312 544; £££-££££). Established restaurant renowned for its fresh seafood, Scottish beef and excellent wines. Booking recommended.

Dreel Tavern (16 High Street West, Anstruther KY10 3DL, ☎ 1333-310 727, fax 1333-310 577, dreeltavern@aol.com; £-££). 16th-century inn serving real ales, bar lunches and evening meals, including fish, homemade pies, steaks and filled baguettes.

■ Pittenweem

Pittenweem's history dates back to the 7th century and St Fillan may have lived here while converting local Picts to Christianity. Ecclesiastical connections continued in medieval times when monks from St Ethernan's Priory on the Isle of May moved to Pittenweem Priory in the 13th century to escape marauding pirates. Pittenweem harbor is at the heart of the East Neuk fishing industry; it is busiest early in the morning when catches are sold at the new fish market built in 1994.

Attractions & Sights

Kellie Castle (NTS; Pittenweem KY10 2RF, ☎ 1333-720 271, fax 1333-720 326; castle open Easter & June-Sept, 1-5pm; garden open year-round, 9:30am-sunset; adult/concession/family £5/£3.75/£13.50). A superb example of Lowland domestic architecture, believed to date from 1360, although most of the present buildings date from the late 16th and early 17th centuries. The castle features a Victorian nursery, old kitchen, ornate plaster ceilings, painted paneling and a lovely 17th-century organic walled garden.

St Fillan's Cave (Cove Wynd, Pittenweem, ☎ 1333-311 495; open year-round, key from Gingerbread Horse Coffee Shop, 9 High Street). Legend tells that St Fillan lived and worshipped in this dark chamber beneath the rocks in Pittenweem, his writing guided by a mysterious light emanating from his left arm. The cave was dedicated to his name, although some historians dispute whether he was ever there.

Where To Stay & Eat

See the *Accommodation* and *Dining* price charts on pages 253 and 255.

 Harbour Guest House (14 Mid Shore, Pittenweem KY10 2NL, ☎ 1333-311 273, guesthouse@pittenweem.com, www.pittenweem-.com; B&B ££). Simple but pleasant accommodation overlooking the harbor.

Anchor Inn (42 Charles Street, Pittenweem, ☎ 1333-311 326; ££). Intimate, candlelit dining room with natural stone walls that serves fresh local meat, game, seafood and vegetarian options.

Larachmhor Tavern (6 Mid Shore, Pittenweem, ☎ 1333-311 200; £). The tavern serves light meals, including prawns in butter, toasties, filled rolls and soup.

■ St Monans

St Monans is a typical East Neuk fishing village, its traditional cottages built with outside stairs, crow-stepped gables and red-pantiled roofs hugging the sea wall on the edge of the shoreline. The village took its name from a shrine said to contain the relics of St Monan (the Irish missionary companion of St Adain), which achieved fame for its healing powers.

Boats have fished from the village since its foundation and still land lobster and crab. The village's other traditional industry was boat building, which has recently been revived on a small scale.

 St Monans Windmill (St Monans, ☎ 1334-412 933, fax 1334-413 214, museums.east@fife.gov.uk; open July and August, noon-4pm). An unusual reminder of Fife's short-lived salt industry, which was abandoned by 1823. The windmill evaporated seawater in iron pans and the extracted salt was sold from Pittenweem harbor. If you miss the regular opening time, a key is available at the Post Office, West Shore, ☎ 1333-730 240, and at the Spar Shop, West Street, ☎ 1333-730 315.

The Seafood Restaurant (16 West End, St Monans KY10 2BX, ☎ 1333-730 327, fax 1333-730 508, info@theseafoodrestaurant.com, www.theseafoodres-taurant.com; closed Mon; lunch ££, dinner £££). Harbor-side restaurant serving fantastic seafood with views to match.

■ Elie & Earlsferry to Lower Largo

Earlsferry dates from the 11th century, and golfers have played its links since the 16th century. Elie grew up around a bay offering safe anchorage, protected by an island and causeway. Lower Largo was the birthplace of **Alexander Selkirk,** the real-life castaway whose adventures formed the subject of Daniel Defoe's *Robinson Crusoe.*

Attractions & Adventures

Lady's Tower (Ruby Bay, Elie). Lady Janet Anstruther, wife of the laird of Ardross and Elie, built Lady's Tower as her summerhouse in the late 18th century. She enjoyed naked bathing in the sea and sent a bell-ringer around the town to warn townspeople to keep away.

Chain Walk is a highly enjoyable coastal walk at **Kincraig Point** involving some (occasionally steep) scrambling up and down rocks aided by stainless-steel chains fixed to the cliffs. Tackle the chain walk on a falling tide – around one hour after high tide is a good time to start the walk (check in Earlsferry for tide times).

To start the walk, drive from Elie to Earlsferry. Continue past the right turn that leads to the golf course to the end of the road, marked by a series of wooden stakes to your right indicating parking bays. Follow the track that continues across the golf course to the beach where you turn right toward the cliffs. Sections of the ascending/descending ground can be as much as 25-30 feet above ground level and the chains can be slippery in wet conditions. There is no safe escape route if caught by an incoming tide – stay put until conditions change. The hardest section of the chain walk is the first part – if you don't like the look of the traverse into the inlet, turn back here. Along the walk, you pass pebble beaches, open views of the sea and basalt columns and can peer into two caves. Return on the path over the cliffs or, if you really enjoyed clambering up and down the chains (and if tidal conditions are still favorable), retrace your steps (1-2 hrs; moderate).

Elie Watersports (The Harbour, Elie, ☎ 1333-330 962, info@eliewatersports.com, www.eliewatersports.com; end of May to early Sept). Equipment rental and instruction in a wide range of watersports – windsurfing, sailing, canoeing, pedaloes, waterskiing and banana or rubber ring rides – in the sheltered water of Elie Bay.

 Lundin Golf Course (18-hole links, 6,394 yards; Golf Road, Lundin Links KY8 6BA, ☎ 1333-320 202, fax 1333-329 743, secretary@lundingolfclub.co.uk, www.lundingolfclub.co.uk; green fees £37-£47). Alhough not easy, Lundin can be enjoyed by golfers of all abilities and offers beautiful views. The course has been a venue for Open qualification.

Where To Stay & Eat

See the *Accommodation* and *Dining* price charts on pages 253 and 255.

 Elms Guest House (14 Park Place, Elie KY9 1DH, ☎/fax 1333-330 404, info@elms-elie.co.uk, www.elms-elie.co.uk; open April-Oct; B&B ££). Attractive Victorian house with pleasant bedrooms and a conservatory lounge. There is also a cottage in the garden, with a kitchen for those who want to cook for themselves.

Ship Inn (The Toft, Elie KY9 1DT, ☎ 1333-330 246, fax 1333-330 864, info@ship-elie.com, www.ship-elie.com; B&B ££). Cozy, informal bar set in a converted boathouse overlooking the bay. The inn serves decent, no-nonsense food and is renowned for its steaks and seafood platter. There is also basic guest house accommodation.

Bouquet Garni (51 High Street, Elie KY9 1BZ, ☎ 1333-330 374, fax 1333-330 364; lunch £, dinner £££). Excellent Scottish cooking prepared with flair and French influences.

Crusoe Hotel (2 Main Street, Lower Largo KY8 6BT, ☎ 1333-320 759, fax 1333-320 865, relax@crusoehotel.co.uk, www.crusoehotel.co.uk; B&B £££, dinner ££). Based in the coastal village of Lower Largo, birthplace of Alexander Selkirk, the castaway whose real-life adventures were immortalized in Daniel Defoe's *Robinson Crusoe*, this is a comfortable and historic hotel set right on the sandy beach. Beamed ceilings and nautical fittings maintain an olde worlde ambience. The restaurant and bar serve good food and many rooms enjoy magnificent views over the beach.

Old Manor Country House Hotel (Lundin Links, near Lower Largo KY8 6AJ, ☎ 1333-320 368, fax 1333-320 911, enquiries@oldmanorhotel.co.uk, www.oldmanorhotel.co.uk; B&B ££££, lunch ££, dinner ££££). Picturesquely set overlooking a championship golf course and Largo Bay, the hotel has pretty bedrooms, comfortable lounges, fine dining and an informal bistro. The menu specialties are fresh fish, seafood and Aberdeen Angus steaks.

Kirkcaldy & Around

Kirkcaldy (pronounced "kir-coddy"), the "Lang Toun," dates from the 11th century and is one of Scotland's oldest towns. Economist **Adam Smith** was born here in 1723 as was architect **Robert Adam** five years later. The town lacks major visitor attractions but is Fife's main shopping town. Every April Kirkcaldy holds the **Links Market**, reputedly Europe's longest street fair.

Burntisland is a mix of busy harbor, popular seaside resort and historic buildings that reflect the town's long and eventful history. Prehistoric people were the first to make use of its natural harbor before the Picts built a fort on Dunearn Hill. Oliver Cromwell's troops besieged the town and garrisoned here from 1651.

In **St Columba's Church**, which dates from 1594, the town boasts the earliest post-Reformation church still in regular use. Its unusual square design and elaborate lofts and pews make the church unique. It was here in 1601 that King James VI authorized the first translation of the Bible into English.

The Victorians called **Aberdour** the "Fife Riviera" and flocked here to holiday on its Silver Sands, a sheltered and secluded sandy beach. The town has a 14th-century castle, near which stands a small church begun in the 12th century and dedicated to St Fillan, the Irish Saint who was Abbot of Pittenweem.

 INFORMATION SOURCES: The tourism office is at 19 Whytescauseway, Kirkcaldy KY1 1XF, ☎ 1592-267 775, fax 1592-203 154, kirkcaldyoffice@kftb.fsbusiness.co.uk; open year-round.

■ Special Events

Kirkcaldy Links Market (April only; ☎ 1592-414 221). Europe's longest street fair provides a mile of fairground attractions and rides.

■ Attractions & Sights

Aberdour Castle (HS; Aberdour KY3 0SL, ☎ 1383-860 519; open April-Sept, 9:30am-6:30pm; Oct-Mar, 9:30am-4:30pm, opening times limited in winter, call ahead; adult/concession/child £2.50/£1.90/£0.75). Aberdour is the ruined 13th-century seat of the Douglas Earls of Morton, extended in the 15th to 17th centuries. The castle probably started life as a hall house, one large room above a basement. The addition of another story and garret, probably in the 15th century, gave the appearance of a tower house. A massive piece of masonry has collapsed from a top corner of the tower and lies at a crazy angle on the ground. The kitchen retains its enormous fireplace and oversize stone mortar for crushing and grinding food. The grounds contain a well kept though plain walled garden and a fine circular doocot (dovecote) shaped like a beehive whose stone nesting boxes are still well preserved. The castle holds weddings, as does the nearby small church of St Fillans, and it's not uncommon to hear contests between wedding pipers.

■ Where To Stay & Eat

See the *Accommodation* and *Dining* price charts on pages 253 and 255.

Balbirnie House Hotel (Balbirnie Park, Markinch village, By Glenrothes KY7 6NE, ☎ 1592-610 066, fax 1592-610 529, info@balbirnie.co.uk, www.balbirnie.co.uk; B&B £££££, dinner ££££). Grand Georgian mansion (built 1777) set in 416 acres of estate, offering spacious and luxurious accommodation, fine dining and an impressive wine list.

Gruinard Guest House (148 Kinghorn Road, Burntisland KY3 9JU, ☎ 1592-873 877, gruinard@dircon.co.uk, www.gruinardguesthouse.co.uk; open Mar-Nov; B&B ££). Attractive, stone cottage retaining many original features such as log fires and natural wood paneling. Tea and home baking are served on arrival. B&B22-27

Kingswood Hotel (Kinghorn Road, near Burntisland KY3 9LL, ☎ 1592-872 329, fax 1592-873 123, rankin@kingswoodhotel.co.uk, www.kingswoodhotel.co.uk; B&B £££, dinner ££). Attractive Victorian hotel with individually styled bedrooms, including one with a four-poster bed.

Delicate Essence & The Ramblers Rest Tearoom (253 High Street, Burntisland KY3 9AQ, ☎/fax 1592-873 103; £-££). Delicatessen and tearoom serving snacks, traditional meals and Orkney ice cream.

Aberdour Hotel (38 High Street, Aberdour KY3 0SW, ☎ 1383-860 325, fax 1383-860 808, reception@aberdourhotel.co.uk, www.aberdourhotel.co.uk; B&B ££, dinner ££). Historic 17th-century hotel and coaching inn with well-decorated bedrooms and the cozy, reasonably priced **Mortimer's Deep** restaurant.

Cedar Inn (20 Shore Road, Aberdour KY3 0SW, ☎ 1383-860 310, fax 1383-860 004, enquiry@cedarinn.co.uk, www.cedarinn.co.uk; B&B £££). Comfortable accommodation and good-quality dining in a bar popular with locals.

Culross & North Queensferry

Culross (pronounced "koo-ross") is one of Fife's loveliest old towns and provides a wonderful insight into Scottish domestic life in the 16th and 17th centuries. Its cobbled streets are lined with little houses – some painted white, others rich yellow – that converge on the Mercat Cross in the heart of the town. St Mungo, patron saint of Glasgow, was born in Culross, according to legend after his mother – the King of Lothian's exiled daughter Thenew – was washed ashore here.

The area has a long association with coal mining. The Cistercian monks of the now-ruined Culross Abbey were the first to mine coal here and the nearby **Longannet Colliery** is Scotland's last deep mine. From Culross harbor, called the **Sandhaven**, ships took salt and coal to the Low Countries and Baltic throughout the 16th century, bringing back as ballast the red pantiles that attractively roof many of the town's houses.

Culross Palace, Town House & Study (NTS; Culross KY12 8JH, ☎ 1383-880 359, fax 1383-882 675; open Good Friday-Sept, noon-5pm; adult/concession/family £5/£3.75/£13.50). Culross Palace was built from 1597 to 1611 and is a fine restoration of a merchant's townhouse. It features original interiors, painted woodwork, 17th- and 18th-century furniture and furnishings, and a fine pottery collection. A splendid 17th-century kitchen garden behind the palace cultivates plants known to grow at that time. The Town House dates from 1626 and for many years housed the town's local government. The ground floor was a debtors' prison while "witches" were imprisoned in the attic. The Study was built in 1610 and is believed to have been used by Bishop Leighton of Dunblane on visits to Culross in the 17th century. The **Outlook Tower** – his study room – gives excellent views over the Forth. Next to the Study stands the **Mercat Cross**, where trade was conducted and proclamations read. It dates from 1588, although the shaft was replaced in 1902.

Deep Sea World (Battery Quarry, North Queensferry, Fife KY11 1JR, ☎ 1383-411 880, fax 1383-410 514, info@deepseaworld.co.uk, www.deepseaworld.com; open year-round, April-Oct, 10am-6pm; winter weekdays, 10 am-5 pm; last entry one hour before closing; adult/concession/child/family £8.25/£6.50/£6/£27). Activities and demonstrations include divers hand-feeding sharks, frenzied piranha feeds, touch-pool, reptiles and the opportunity to control an underwater camera carried by a model boat on the lagoon.

Perthshire

Perthshire lies at the heart of Scotland, which makes it easy to get to and a good base from which to explore. Despite its compact size, it offers an enormous range of beautiful and varied landscapes, from heather moors and rocky Munro summits to vast lochs, rushing rivers and densely forested hillsides. What is particularly striking about the landscape, and indeed also the region's towns and villages, is just how pristine and unspoiled everything appears – the unblemished vistas of mountain peaks, conifer forest and sparkling water wouldn't look out of place in British Columbia.

 INFORMATION SOURCES: Perthshire Tourist Board is at Lower City Mills, West Mill Street, Perth PH1 5QP, ☎ 1738-450 600, fax 1738-444 863, info@perthshire.co.uk, www.perthshire.co.uk.

DON'T MISS

Discover ancient lifestyles and try Iron Age crafts at the **Crannog Centre** on Loch Tay.

Admire the **Queen's View**, Loch Tummel – often photographed but even better in real life.

Walk the **Pass of Killiecrankie**, a beautiful wooded gorge and historic battle site.

Tour **Blair Castle**, home of the Atholl Highlanders, Europe's last private army.

Best Freebie: Tour enchanting **Edradour Distillery**.

Adventures

It is perhaps the region's accessibility and enormous variety of terrain that makes it one of the most popular destinations in Scotland for outdoor activities, as evidenced by the many activity operators based here. Contact the **Perthshire Activity Line** (☎ 1577-861 186, www.perthshire.co.uk/adventure) if you need help narrowing down the choice.

■ Big Tree Country

 Perthshire is renowned for its remarkable **forests** and **woodland**. In some areas it's still possible to see how Scotland must have looked thousands of years ago when a huge forest of pine, birch and juniper cloaked the Highlands. Remnants of this ancient Caledonian forest still survive, for example at the **Black Wood of Rannoch** (to the west of Schiehallion), where you can see majestic pines up to 350 years old.

Perthshire

Perthshire's high and mighty trees boast a cast of reputed record breakers, including:

World's tallest hedge – Meikleour beech hedge (height 100 feet/30 m), 10 miles east of Dunkeld on the A93;

Europe's oldest living thing – Fortingall yew (estimated over 3,000 years old), also the largest yew tree in Europe (girth 56.5 feet/17 m), 10 miles west of Aberfeldy;

Britain's tallest tree – Douglas fir near the Hermitage (height 212 feet/65 m), one mile west of Dunkeld on the A9;

Britain's widest conifer – Wellingtonia at Cluny House Gardens (girth 36 feet/11 m), three miles east of Aberfeldy, between Weem and Strathtay.

Lush summer greenery gives way to the blazing reds and golds of autumn, one of the best times to visit Perthshire. An **"Autumn colors"** telephone line (☎ 1796-472 215, pitlochrytic@perthshire.co.uk) provides up-to-the-minute information on where to find the best autumn colors and operates Oct to mid-Nov.

Perth developed printing, dyeing, linen, glass and drinks industries, and is now a busy market town. It is the focus of the region's agriculture and is the location of a number of cattle auctions, including the internationally famous February bull sales.

Perth

Perth is a cosmopolitan city beautifully set on the banks of the **River Tay**. With a history stretching back over 8,000 years, Perth has always been one of Scotland's most important political, judicial and commercial centers. It served as the nation's capital from the 12th century until the murder of James I here in 1437. Forty-two Scottish kings were crowned at Scone on the city's outskirts.

■ Special Events

Perth Festival of the Arts (May; ☎ 1738-472 706, www.perthfestival.co.uk). Ten-day festival of opera, classical music, jazz, dance, comedy and drama, featuring some famous performers.

Perth Show (Aug; ☎ 1738-623 780, www.perthshow.co.uk). Agricultural show, including trade stands, crafts and food, competitions, exhibitions and rare breeds.

Perth Highland Games (Aug; ☎ 1738-627 782, www.highland-games.org.uk). Traditional Highland Games.

■ Attractions & Sights

Scone Palace (Perth PH2 6BD, ☎ 1738-552 300, fax 1738-552 588, visits@scone-palace.co.uk, www.scone-palace.co.uk; open April-Oct, 9:30am-5:30pm, last admission 4:45 pm, evening and winter tours by

Perthshire

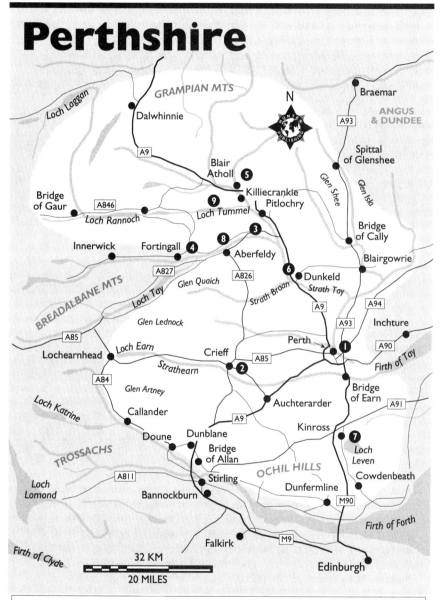

1. Scone Palace, St John's Kirk, Elcho Castle, Huntingtower Castle
2. Famous Grouse Experience, Discover the Highland Drovers
3. Blair Athol Distillery, Eradour Distillery
4. Fortingall Yew
5. The Soldier's Leap, Blair Castle
6. Dunkeld Cathedral
7. Lochleven Castle
8. Dewar's World of Whisky, Castle Menzies, Scottish Crannog Centre
9. Queen's View

arrangement; adult/concession/child/family £6.75/£5.70/£3.80/£18). Poised above the River Tay, Scone Palace (pronounced "scoon") was the ancient crowning site of Scots kings. Standing on the site of a former 12th-century abbey (destroyed in the Reformation), the palace dates largely from the early 19th century and echoes the original monastic building in its Gothic styling. In its grounds stood the **Stone of Destiny** (the original is in Edinburgh – a replica now stands at Scone), on which kings were crowned from 838 until Edward I unceremoniously removed the Stone to England in 1296.

The palace is today the home of the Earl of Mansfield. The splendid interior includes beautiful state dining and drawing rooms, a **Long Gallery** dating from 1580, and wonderful treasures, including bedhangings stitched by Mary, Queen of Scots (possibly while imprisoned at Lochleven Castle), fine porcelain, clocks, ivories and a fabulous collection of papier-mâché objets d'art. The expansive grounds include the **Murray Star Maze**.

THE STONE OF DESTINY

 The Stone of Destiny stood at Scone for nearly 500 years, on **Moot Hill** ("hill of belief"), an ancient mound in front of the palace (kings were not enthroned at Scone Palace – no house existed here before 1580). From the time of Kenneth MacAlpin, who created the Kingdom of Scone in the 9th century, until the 13th century, all the Kings of Scots were crowned on Moot Hill, seated upon the Stone, fulfilling an ancient prophecy:

Except old seers do feign, and wizard wits be blind,
the Scots in place must reign, where they this stone shall find.

Robert the Bruce declared himself King of Scots here on 25th March 1306. The last coronation held at Scone was that of **King Charles II** as King of Scots on 1st January 1651, some nine years before he returned to the English throne.

According to legend, the Stone was either Jacob's pillow or came to Scotland with the daughter of an Egyptian pharaoh. It was most likely a royal stone brought from Antrim to Scone by Kenneth MacAlpin, 36th King of Dalriada. King Edward I seized the Stone in 1296 and carted it off to Westminster Abbey in London, although some say that Stone was a fake and monks had hidden the true Stone. Scottish Nationalists removed the Stone from Westminster in 1950 and returned it to Scotland, where it turned up in the grounds of Arbroath Abbey. The Stone was restored to Scotland in 1996 and moved to Edinburgh Castle.

St John's Kirk (St John's Street, central Perth, www.st-johns-kirk.co.uk; open May-Sept, Mon-Sat, 10am-4pm; June-Sept, also open Sun, noon-2pm; £1 donation requested). This fine church stands in the heart of Perth and, though founded in 1126, largely dates from the 15th century. It was here in

May 1559 that Protestant reformer John Knox preached his famous sermon against idolatry that sparked the Reformation.

■ Around Perth

Elcho Castle (HS; near Perth, five miles north of Bridge of Earn off the A912, ☎ 1738-639 998; open April-Sept, 9:30am-6:30pm; adult/concession/child £2.20/£1.60/£0.75). A handsome and complete 16th-century fortified mansion with three projecting towers. The original wrought-iron grilles protecting the windows are still in place.

Huntingtower Castle (HS; Huntingtower, Perth PH1 3JR, two miles west of Perth off the A85, ☎ 1738-627 231; open April-Sept, 9:30am-6:30pm; Oct-Mar, call ahead for days/times; adult/concession/child £2.50/£1.90/£0.75). Two complete towers, dating from the 15th and 16th centuries, joined by a three-story 17th-century range of buildings. The hall of the eastern tower has a fine painted ceiling.

■ Adventures

Scottish Aero Club (Perth Airport, Scone, ☎ 1738-550 044, fax 1738-553 097) uses modern microlight technology and offers trial flights and courses.

■ Where To Stay

Hotels

Ramada Jarvis Hotel (West Mill Street, Perth PH1 5QP, ☎ 1738-628 281, fax 1738-643 423; B&B ££). Pleasant mid-range hotel converted from a 15th-century water mill situated in a quiet corner of central Perth.

Salutation Hotel (34 South Street, Perth PH2 8PH, ☎ 1738-630 066, fax 1738-633 598, salessalutation@strathmorehotels.com, www.strathmore-hotels.com; B&B ££). One of Scotland's oldest hotels (dating from 1699) and reputedly Bonnie Prince Charlie's headquarters during the 1745 Rising. The hotel offers quality accommodation in refurbished rooms and fine dining in the magnificent Adam Restaurant.

Guest Houses & B&Bs

Abercrombie Guest House (85 Glasgow Road, Perth PH2 0PQ, ☎/fax 1738-444 728; B&B ££). Attractive, well-furnished Victorian townhouse with award-winning B&B facilities.

Beechgrove Guest House (Dundee Road, Perth PH2 7AQ, ☎/fax 1738-636 147, beechgroveg.h@sol.co.uk, www.smoothhound.co.uk/hotels/beechgr; B&B ££).

HOTEL PRICE CHART	
Per person, per night, based on double occupancy in high season. B&B rate includes breakfast; DB&B includes dinner and breakfast.	
£	Under £20
££	£21-£35
£££	£36-£50
££££	£51-£80
£££££	Over £80

Perthshire

Peaceful former manse with pleasant guest rooms, set in scenic gardens.

Dunallan Guest House (10 Pitcullen Crescent, Perth PH2 7HT, ☎/fax 1738-622 551, enquiries@dunallan.co.uk, www.dunallan.co.uk; B&B ££). Charming rooms; evening meals available.

Blackcraigs Farmhouse B&B (Scone, By Perth PH2 7PJ, ☎/fax 1821-640 254, millar@blackcraigs.fsworld.co.uk, www.blackcraigs.com; B&B £-££). Quiet 18th-century farmhouse set in well-maintained gardens with views to surrounding hills. There is an open fire in the residents' lounge and salmon and trout fishing are available nearby.

The Linn B&B (3 Duchess Street, Stanley, By Perth PH1 4NG, ☎/fax 1738-828 293; B&B £). Picturesque house set beside the village green with well-furnished rooms and a comfortable lounge.

Otterstones B&B (Burnmouth Ferry, Stanley, By Perth PH1 4QF, ☎/fax 1738-827 837, info@otterstones.co.uk, www.otterstones.co.uk; B&B ££). Pretty house set on the banks of the Tay, next to Stanley village, six miles from Perth. All rooms have river views.

■ Where To Eat

See the *Dining* price chart, next page.

 63 Tay Street (63 Tay Street, Perth PH2 8NN, ☎ 1738-441 451, fax 1738-441 461, www.63taystreet.co.uk; lunch ££, dinner ££££). New-ish restaurant with a fast-growing reputation for fresh, nouvelle cuisine served in a calm and minimalist setting.

Perth Theatre Restaurant (Perth Theatre, 185 High Street Perth PH1 5UW, ☎ 1738-472 709, fax 1738-624 576; lunch £, dinner ££). Innovative and traditional Scottish cooking served in the period feel of the Victorian Theatre.

Let's Eat (77-79 Kinnoull Street, Perth PH1 5EZ, ☎ 1738-643 377, fax 1738-621 464, enquiries@letseatperth.co.uk, www.letseatperth.co.uk; closed Sun-Mon; lunch ££, dinner £££). This bistro-style restaurant is probably Perth's top eatery and offers high-quality, modern Scottish cuisine with classic influences.

Macmillan Coffee Shop (Quarrymill, Woodland Park, Perth PH2 7HQ, ☎ 1738-633 890; open May-Sept, Mon-Sat; £). Reasonably priced soups, sandwiches, home baking and snacks in a traditional tearoom run by volunteers in aid of cancer relief.

Willows Coffee Shop (12 St Johns Place, Perth PH1 5SZ, ☎ 1738-441 175, fax 1738-637 200; £). Reasonably priced all-day menu with daily specials in a central café setting.

Crieff & Strathearn

Strathearn, the valley of the **River Earn**, lies right on the geological fault line that separates the Scottish Lowlands from the Highlands. The bustling town of Crieff has always provided an important link between the Lowlands and Highlands and its history dates back to Roman times when it was the main north-south crossing point on the River Earn. Throughout the Middle Ages, it was an important political and judicial center and developed into a lively cattle trading town for Highlanders bringing their cattle to Lowland trysts. In the 19th century, Crieff became a fashionable holiday resort and the town retains a relaxed affluence with many services catering mainly to visitors.

■ Special Events

Crieff Highland Games (Aug; ☎ 1738-627 782, www.crieff-highland-games.co.uk). Traditional Highland Games.

 INFORMATION SOURCES: The tourism office is at **High Street**, Crieff PH7 3HU, ☎ 1764-652 578, fax 1764-655 422, criefftic@perthshire.co.uk; open year-round.

■ Attractions & Sights

 Famous Grouse Experience (Glenturret Distillery, The Hosh, Crieff PH4 7HA, ☎ 1764-656 565/845-045 1800, fax 1764-654 366, www.famousgrouse.com; open year-round, 9am-6pm; til 6:30 in July-Aug; adult/concession/child £6/£5/£3). Fairly touristy whisky experience taking in a distillery tour, tasting, shop and bar.

Discover the Highland Drovers (Crieff Visitor Centre, Muthill Road, Crieff PH7 4HQ, ☎ 1764-654 014, www.crieff.co.uk; year-round, 10am-4:30pm; adult/concession/family £2.50/£1.50/£6). Exhibition following the 300-year-old history and long journeys of the Highland drovers, who drove black cattle through the Highlands and made Crieff the crossroads of Scotland at the turn of the 18th century. There is also a garden center, shop and restaurant.

■ Where To Stay & Eat

Crieff Hotel (45-49 East High Street, Crieff PH7 3HY, ☎ 1764-652 632, fax 1764-655 019, customerservices-@crieff-hotel.com, www.crieffhotel.com; B&B ££, dinner £). Pleasant hotel in central Crieff with bar lunches and suppers available in the **Haggis & Sporran** restaurant. Beauty and aromatherapy treatments are available.

Crieff Hydro Hotel (Crieff PH7 3LQ, ☎ 1764-655 555, fax 1764-653 087, enquiries@crieffhydro.com, www.crieffhydro.com; B&B ££££, dinner £££). Quality

DINING PRICE CHART	
Indicates the price per person for a full meal, excluding drinks. Generally three courses, though fixed menus of five or more courses may be available.	
£	Under £10
££	£11-£20
£££	£21-£30
££££	£31-£40

Perthshire

hotel set in 900 acres of estate, with a wide choice of room types, and spa, leisure and beauty facilities.

Four Seasons Hotel (St Fillans, Loch Earn PH6 2NF, ☎ 1764-685 333, fax 1764-685 444, info@thefourseasonshotel.co.uk, www.thefourseasonshotel.co.uk; open Mar-Jan; B&B £££, dinner £££). High-quality 19th-century hotel delightfully set on the banks of Loch Earn. There are great views down the loch and imaginative menus; six log cabins with bunkrooms are also available.

Galvelmore House B&B (5 Galvelmore St, Crieff PH7 4BY, ☎/fax 1764-655 721, katy@galvelmore.co.uk, www.galvelmore.co.uk; B&B £-££). Comfortable Georgian house with well-furnished guest rooms and a wood-paneled lounge warmed by a log fire.

Merlindale B&B (Perth Road, Crieff PH7 3EQ, ☎/fax 1764-655 205, merlin.dale@virgin.net; open Feb-Dec; B&B ££, dinner £££). Elegant Georgian house offering sunken baths, garden Jacuzzi and a Scottish library.

The Bank Restaurant (32 High Street, Crieff PH7 3BS, ☎/fax 1764-656 575, info@thebankrestaurant.co.uk; lunch £, dinner ££). Modern Scottish cooking in a former bank building run by husband and wife team Bill and Lilias McGuigan.

Pitlochry, Aberfeldy, Loch Tay & Loch Tummel

Pitlochry is an attractive town surrounded by densely wooded mountains. It owes its existence to Victorian tourism and modern-day visitors continue the tradition of flocking to the town. Despite its popularity and the many hotels, restaurants and shops that cater mainly to visitors, Pitlochry retains a pleasant atmosphere and is an excellent base from which to explore Perthshire and beyond. To the north of the town is the impressive, white **Blair Castle**. To the west above **Loch Tay**, Perthshire's largest loch, rises **Ben Lawers**, its highest mountain.

The 18th-century town of Aberfeldy grew up around its **Wade's Bridge** and has become a popular holiday destination. The area around the town is rich in natural heritage and includes the yew tree in **Fortingall** churchyard, which at over 3,000 years old is believed to be Europe's oldest living thing. Fortingall itself is a very pretty, sleepy village at the mouth of Glen Lyon.

■ Special Events

Atholl Highlanders Parade, Atholl Gathering & Highland Games (May; ☎ 1796-481 207, www.blair-castle.co.uk). Annual parade and inspection of the Atholl Highlanders and their pipe band by the Duke of Atholl, and traditional Highland Games.

INFORMATION SOURCES: There are tourism offices at Pitlochry (22 Atholl Road, Pitlochry PH16 5BX, ☎ 1796-472 215/472 751, fax 1796-474 046, pitlochrytic@perth-shire.co.uk) and Aberfeldy (The Square, Aberfeldy PH15 2DD, ☎ 1887-820 276, fax 1887-829 495, aberfeldytic@perthshire.co.uk); both open year-round.

■ Attractions & Sights

Blair Athol Distillery (Pitlochry PH16 5LY, ☎ 1796-482 003, fax 1796-482 001; open Easter-Sept, Mon-Sat, 9:30am-5pm; plus Sun noon-5pm, June-Sept; shorter hours in fall and winter; admission £4). An attractive old distillery producing whisky for the Bells blend. Tours explain the production of malt whisky and the blender's art; admission includes a discount voucher for the shop.

 **Blair Castle** (Blair Atholl, Pitlochry PH18 5TL, ☎ 1796-481 207, fax 1796-481 487, office@blair-castle.co.uk, www.blair-castle.co.uk; open April-Oct, 9:30am-5pm; call for schedule in winter; adult/concession/child/family £6.50/£5.50/£4/£16.75). Dating from 1269, beautiful, bright white Blair Castle has been the home of the Dukes and Earls of Atholl for over 700 years. The castle is steeped in history; its 30 display rooms, ranging from the cozy Tullibardine bedroom dedicated to the Jacobite members of the family, to the superb wood-paneled ballroom, exhibit huge collections of fine objects, arms, hunting trophies, china, lace, furniture and pictures. The 8th, 9th and 10th Dukes all died without heirs and the title has moved considerably sideways. However, Blair Castle remains home to the last private army in Europe – the **Atholl Highlanders**, whose annual parade takes place in late May.

The castle's **Hercules Garden** is a nine-acre walled enclosure developed by the second Duke in the mid-18th century and contains landscaped ponds, fruit trees, vegetable beds and herbaceous borders, overlooked by a statue of Hercules. **Pony trekking** (☎ 1796-481 568), **ranger-guided walks** (☎ 1796-481 355, www.athollestatesrangerservice.co.uk) and **fishing, shooting and stalking** (☎ 1796-481 355, www.athollestates.co.uk) are available on the estate.

Dewar's World of Whisky (Aberfeldy Distillery, Aberfeldy PH15 2EB, ☎ 1887-822 010, fax 1887-822 012, worldofwhisky@dewars.com, www.dewarswow.com; open Easter-Oct, Mon-Sat, 10am-6pm & Sun, noon-4pm; Nov-Easter, Mon-Sat, 10am-4pm; adult/concession/child/family £5/£3/£2.50/£12). A complete whisky experience taking in a tour of Aberfeldy Distillery, an interactive journey through the Dewar's story from the 1890s, a peek into the first master blender's room, whisky trivia, nosing and tasting. There is also a shop and coffee shop.

Edradour Distillery (Pitlochry PH16 5JP, ☎ 1796-472 095, fax 1796-472 002, www.edradour.co.uk; open Mar-Oct, Mon-Sat, 9:30am-5pm & Sun, noon-5pm; Nov-Dec, Mon-Sat, 10am-4pm, call to check opening times in

Perthshire

Jan-Feb). Scotland's smallest (legal!) distillery produces only 12-15 barrels per week (the next smallest produces around 45). With its neat 150-year-old white-painted buildings clustered in a pocket glen, Edradour is one of the most picturesque distilleries. It offers free tours and its 12-year-old single malt is very drinkable! The distillery is 2½ miles from Pitlochry; follow signs from the A924 Pitlochry-Moulin road.

Fortingall Yew (Fortingall, 10 miles west of Aberfeldy). In the heart of Scotland stands the oldest living thing in Europe. Experts guess the Fortingall Yew to be anywhere between 3,000 and 9,000 years old. Visible today are the relics and offspring of the original tree that was recorded in 1769 as having a girth of 56.5 feet (17 m).

 Killiecrankie & the Soldier's Leap (NTS; Killiecrankie, By Pitlochry PH16 5LG, ☎/fax 1796-473 233; site open at all times, visitor centre open April-Oct, 10am-5:30pm; July-Aug, 9:30am-6pm; £2 parking). On 27th July 1689, the Killiecrankie Pass echoed with the sound of battle cries and gunfire as a Jacobite army led by John Graham of Claverhouse ("Bonnie Dundee") defeated government forces under veteran soldier General Hugh Mackay. Dundee had raised the Highlanders and set up headquarters at nearby Blair Castle (see above). When Dundee heard Mackay was leading some 4,000 men through the narrow pass, he led his own much smaller army onto higher ground from where they defeated the government troops in only 40 minutes. Sadly, Dundee was killed in the battle; without his leadership the Highlanders were defeated at Dunkeld shortly afterwards and the rising collapsed.

According to legend, in the flight of government troops from Killiecrankie, one soldier, Donald MacBean, made a spectacular escape. Pursued by a group of Highlanders, MacBean abandoned his horse, climbed onto rocks and leapt 18 feet (5.5 m) across the fast-flowing River Garry. On her visit in 1844 Queen Victoria declared the leap "impossible." Decide for yourself. The visitor center provides information on Killiecrankie's natural history and on the 1689 battle. The site is three miles north of Pitlochry on the B8079.

Castle Menzies (Weem, Aberfeldy PH15 2JD, ☎ 1887-820 982; open Easter to mid-Oct, Mon-Sat, 10:30am-5pm; Sun, 2-5pm; last admission 4:30pm; adult/concession/child £3.50/£3/£2). Fine example of a 16th-century Z-plan fortified tower house. The stronghold and home of the Chiefs of Clan Menzies for over 400 years, the castle witnessed many turbulent events. Bonnie Prince Charlie stayed here on his journey to Culloden in 1746. The castle is 1½ miles from Aberfeldy on the B846 to Loch Tummel.

Queen's View (seven miles west of Pitlochry on the B8019, ☎ 1796-473 123; £1 fee includes parking and audiovisual presentation). The spectacular view down **Loch Tummel**, with its islets and gently sloping, densely-wooded banks, toward the peak of **Schiehallion**, is one of the most famous and most photographed in Scotland, but don't let that deter you – the reality is even better than the images. Queen Victoria took tea here in 1866, but the viewpoint actually commemorates Queen Isabella, wife of Robert the Bruce. The nearby visitor center (open end-Mar to Oct, 10am-6pm) tells the story of the people and forests in Highland Perthshire through an exhibition and audiovisual show, and provides information on the surrounding **Tay Forest Park**.

Scottish Crannog Centre (Kenmore, South Loch Tay, Aberfeldy PH15 2HY, ☎ 1887-830 583, fax 1887-830 876, info@crannog.co.uk, www.crannog.co.uk; open mid-Mar to Oct, 10am-5:30pm; until 4pm in Nov; adult/concession/child/family £4.25/£3.85/£3/£13). Crannogs are ancient loch dwellings dating from around 5,000 years ago, found throughout Scotland and Ireland. They were built by Iron Age farmers out in water for defense and land use; people lived in crannogs until the 17th century. Today they appear as tree-covered islands or hide as submerged stony mounds. Researchers have built a life-size crannog in a style typical of the 18 so far discovered in Loch Tay: timber roundhouses supported on piles driven into the lochbed. Surprisingly spacious, the heather- and skin-lined walls and central hearth create a warm, cozy interior. An exhibition displays ancient house timbers and other original objects and explains the construction process. Outside, watch and then try out Iron Age crafts, including wool spinning, woodturning with primitive tools and fire lighting without matches. This is a fascinating insight into ancient lifestyles and visitors of all ages will love the hands-on ancient crafts. There is also a full program of themed events, and weekly summer evening concerts of traditional music played by a log fire (book early).

■ Scenic Drives

Little-visited **Glen Lyon** is the longest enclosed glen in Scotland (34 miles long) and hides some of Perthshire's finest views. The long single-lane road leading to its heart deters many, but provides a wonderful experience for the intrepid. The drive provides superb scenery and the chance to see the picturesque village of **Fortingall** with its 19th-century thatched cottages, ancient church and *very* ancient yew tree.

■ Adventures

On Foot

 The **Pass of Killiecrankie** is a splendid walk through a narrow, densely wooded gorge bustling with wildlife. Start from the visitor center (£2 parking fee) three miles north of Pitlochry on the B8079, which provides information on Killiecrankie's natural history as well as the famous battle of 1689. Follow the path beside the River Garry past the old viaduct to the footbridge with an excellent view down the pass. If you want a longer walk, it's possible to follow the path all the way to Pitlochry (1 hour; easy).

The elegantly shaped **Schiehallion** mountain (3,554 feet/1,083 m) formed the basis of early experiments to measure the mass of the earth and gave birth to geographical contour lines. Not content with such fame, Schiehallion also provides the attractive backdrop to the classic Queen's View vista.

From the A9 take the B8019 west to Tummel Bridge (past the Queen's View). Turn south at Tummel Bridge and after several miles take the right turn signposted "Schiehallion Road." Follow this road to the Braes of Foss parking area (not to be confused with the smaller, earlier Forest Enterprise layby, which is also signposted Braes of Foss) where the walk begins.

From the parking area, follow the obvious path up the hillside. After 45 minutes to an hour, the path divides into two: a messy, wide stone path continues upwards while an easier looking dirt path forks to the right. Stay on the stone path as the dirt path requires a later scramble up a stone wall. The terrain becomes progressively rocky as you reach Schiehallion's broad and boulder-strewn ridge. Take care picking your way through the rocks to the craggy summit as the path here becomes distinctly less obvious – although the rocks are fairly solid and there are some cairns to help keep you on the right track (4-5 hours; moderate).

On Wheels

You can rent mountain bikes locally from **Atholl Mountain Bike Hire** (Old School Park, Blair Atholl, By Pitlochry, ☎ 1796-473 553, ambh@james-stewart.co.uk).

On Water

Loch Tay Boating Centre (Pier Road, Kenmore, Loch Tay PH15 2HG, ☎ 1887-830 291, fax 1887-830 414, boats@loch-tay.co.uk, www.loch-tay.co.uk). Fishing, canoeing and powerboat or cruiser rental on Loch Tay. Mountain bikes are also available for rent.

Multi-Activity Operators

 Active8s Canyoning (The Coachyard, Aberfeldy PH15 2AS, ☎ 1887-829 292, info@activ8s.com, www.activ8s.com). Outdoor activities, particularly rafting and canyoning – descending gorges and natural water flumes – and rope lowers over a waterfall.

Beyond Adventure (Eilean Riabhach, Alma Avenue, Aberfeldy PH15 2BL, ☎ 1887-829 202, email@beyondadventure.co.uk, www.beyondadventure.co.uk). Tailor-made trips in the Scottish wilderness, specializing in open canoeing (from weeklong adventures on Rannoch Moor to half-day trips on the River Tay) and ski touring.

Croft-Na-Caber (Loch Tay, By Aberfeldy PH15 2HW, ☎ 1887-830 588, fax 1887-830 649, info@croftnacaber.com, www.croftnacaber.com). A wide variety of water sports and other activities on the banks of Loch Tay, including power boating, boat cruises, windsurfing, sailing, canoeing, jetbiking, waterskiing, kayaking, river rafting, quad bike treks, archery and mountain biking.

Dunolly Adventure Outdoors (Taybridge Drive, Aberfeldy PH15 2BP, ☎ 1887-820 298, fax 1887-829 842, info@dunollyadventures.co.uk, www.dunollyadventures.co.uk). Activity operator offering accommodation and a choice of archery, gorge walking, river rafting, hillwalking, orienteering, mountain biking and nature walks.

■ Golf

Pitlochry Golf Course (18-hole heathland, 5,811 yards; Golf Course Road, Pitlochry PH16 5QY, ☎ 1796-472 792, fax 1796-473 599; green fees £18-£21).

A varied and interesting heathland course with winding fairways climbing up the hillside across gorges and valleys.

Taymouth Castle Golf Course (18-hole parkland, 6,066 yards; Kenmore, Aberfeldy PH15 2NT, ☎/fax 1887-830 228; green fees £22-£26). The course is laid out through mature parkland with gentle slopes providing an interesting challenge.

■ Entertainment

Pitlochry Festival Theatre (Pitlochry PH16 5DR, ☎ 1796-484 626, boxoffice@pitlochry.org.uk, www.pitlochry.org.uk). Acclaimed and extensive programs of drama and comedy that attract audiences from all over the country. The summer season runs from May to mid-October; visiting shows and other events from October through April.

■ Where To Stay

See the *Accommodation* price chart on page 273.

Pitlochry

Killiecrankie Hotel (Killiecrankie, By Pitlochry PH16 5LG, ☎ 1796-473 220, fax 1796-472 451, enquiries@killiecrankiehotel.co-.uk, www.killiecrankiehotel.co.uk; B&B ££££, lunch £, dinner £££). Originally built as the dower house for the Atholl Estate and subsequently used as a manse (private residence for the local minister), Killiecrankie is an elegant hotel offering high-class, tranquil accommodation and haute cuisine in beautiful surroundings. The charming owners Tim and Maillie Waters are prominent and ensure an informal, friendly ambience. This is one of the best hotels in a region burgeoning with good hotels. Not surprisingly, many guests are repeat visitors.

Moulin Hotel & Brewery (Moulin, By Pitlochry PH16 5EW, ☎ 1796-472 196, fax 1796-474 098, enquiries@moulinhotel.co.uk, www.pitlochryhotels.co.uk/moulinhotel; B&B ££, dinner ££). Dating from the late 17th century, this atmospheric hotel just outside Pitlochry has spacious rooms, log fires, a restaurant overlooking floodlit gardens and a stream, as well as its own brewery, which you can tour.

Atholl Palace (Pitlochry PH16 5LY, ☎ 1796-472 400, fax 1796-473 036, info@athollpalace.com, www.athollpalace.co.uk; B&B £££££, dinner ££-£££). Grand Victorian hotel set in 48 acres of wooded parkland with refurbished bedrooms, turret suites, spacious lounges and log fires.

Green Park Hotel (Clunie Bridge Road, Pitlochry PH16 5JY, ☎ 1796-473 248, fax 1796-473 520, bookings@thegreenpark.co.uk, www.thegreenpark.co.uk; B&B £££, lunch ££, dinner £££). The hotel is set beside Loch Faskally at the western edge of Pitlochry, with quality guest rooms and great views.

East Haugh House (East Haugh, By Pitlochry PH16 5JS, ☎ 1796-473 121, fax 1796-472 473, easthaugh@aol.com, www.easthaugh.co.uk; B&B £££, din-

Perthshire

ner £££). Attractive 17th-century turreted stone house set in lawned gardens, owned by chef/patron Neill McGowan for 14 years. There are nice rooms and the menu includes Western Isles seafood and local game (often shot by Neill himself!).

Dunfallandy House (Logierait Road, Pitlochry PH16 5NA, ☎ 1796-472 648, fax 1796-472 017, dunfalhse@aol.com, www.dunfallandy-house.com; B&B £££). Secluded and elegant Georgian mansion offering great views from its lovely guest rooms. The breakfast specialty is porridge topped with brown sugar, whisky and cream; evening meals are available by arrangement.

Easter Dunfallandy Country House B&B (Pitlochry PH16 5NA, ☎ 1796-474 128, fax 1796-474 446, sue@dunfallandy.co.uk, www.dunfallandy.co.uk; B&B ££, dinner ££). Top-quality B&B accommodation in a beautiful, peaceful country house with spacious, charming rooms and hearty breakfasts, including home-made preserves and freshly baked bread. Home baking awaits you on arrival.

Ferryman's Cottage B&B (Port-na-Craig, Pitlochry PH16 5ND, ☎/fax 1796-473 681, kath@ferrymanscottage.fsnet.co.uk; B&B ££). 250-year-old former home of the ferry boatman, in a beautiful setting with cozy rooms.

Ptarmigan House (Blair Atholl, By Pitlochry PH18 5SZ, ☎/fax 1796-481 269, gordon@ptarmiganhouse.co.uk, www.ptarmiganhouse.co.uk; B&B ££). Stylish, modern guest rooms in a Victorian shooting lodge.

Aberfeldy

Balnearn House (Crieff Road, Aberfeldy PH15 2BJ, ☎ 1887-820 431, fax 1887-829 064, enquiries@balnearnhouse.com, www.balnearnhouse.com; B&B ££). Beautiful guest house set in sheltered gardens, with nice rooms, panoramic lounge and evening meals by arrangement.

Tigh'n Eilean Guest House (Taybridge Drive, Aberfeldy PH15 2BP, ☎/fax 1887-820 109, info@tighneilean.com, www.tighneilean.com; B&B ££, dinner ££). Elegant Victorian house overlooking the River Tay with cozy guest rooms (one with a Jacuzzi), lounge with open fire and evening meals by arrangement.

Loch Tay

Ardeonaig Hotel (South Loch Tay Side, By Killin FK21 8SU, ☎ 1567-820 400, fax 1567-820 282, info@ardeonaighotel.co.uk, www.ardeonaighotel.co.uk; B&B £££-££££, dinner £££). The hotel has a beautiful, secluded setting on the south shore of Loch Tay with views across to the summit of Ben Lawers. On offer are calming rooms, great food, a bar where you can meet the locals and private salmon fishing on the loch as well as access to beats on the Dochart and Tay rivers.

Kenmore Hotel (The Square, Kenmore, Loch Tay PH15 2NU, ☎ 1887-830 205, fax 1887-830 262, reception@kenmorehotel.co.uk, www.kenmorehotel.co.uk; B&B ££-£££, dinner £££). The hotel claims to be Scotland's oldest inn, established in 1572, around which the "model" village of Kenmore was built from 1760. The hotel has a delightful lochside setting, cozy atmosphere, log fires and conservatory restaurant overlooking the river.

Loch Tummel

Bunrannoch House (Kinloch Rannoch, By Pitlochry PH16 5QB, ☎ 1882-632 407, bun.house@tesco.net, www.bunrannoch.co.uk; B&B ££). Attractive Victorian shooting lodge offering comfortable accommodation, complimentary afternoon tea and evening meals by arrangement (preceded by complimentary drinks).

Dunalastair Hotel (The Square, Kinloch Rannoch, By Pitlochry PH16 5PW, ☎ 1882-632 218, fax 1882-632 371, info@dunalastair.co.uk, www.dunalastair.co.uk; B&B ££, dinner ££). Traditional hotel with comfortable guest rooms and relaxing lounges with log fires.

Loch Tummel Inn (Strathtummel, By Pitlochry PH16 5RP, ☎/fax 1882-634 272; B&B £££). Old coaching inn set amid beautiful scenery three miles west of the Queen's View.

■ Where To Eat

See the *Dining* price chart on page 275.

 The Loft Restaurant & Bistro Wine Bar (Golf Course Road, Blair Atholl, By Pitlochry PH18 5TE, ☎ 1796-481 377, fax 1796-481 511; lunch £, dinner ££). Elegant Scottish cuisine in an atmospheric setting of wood beams, stone walls and oak flooring, with a conservatory bar and a roof terrace. Reservations essential.

The Old Armoury (Armoury Road, Pitlochry PH16 5AP, ☎ 1796-474 281, fax 1796-473 157; lunch £, dinner £££). Delightful family-run restaurant serving accomplished and innovative Scottish cooking with a New Zealand influence (particularly noticeable in the wine list!).

Pitlochry Festival Theatre (Pitlochry PH16 5DR, ☎ 1796-484 600, fax 1796-484 616; lunch £, dinner £££). Lunchtime buffets and evening table d'hôte menus of modern Scottish cuisine, enjoyed with elevated views over the River Tummel.

Portnacraig Inn (Portnacraig, Pitlochry, ☎ 1796-472 777, fax 1797-472 931, portnacraig@talk21.com; £-££). Charming 17th-century riverside inn and restaurant overlooking the River Tummel, below the Festival Theatre.

Victoria's Restaurant & Coffee Shop (45 Atholl Road, Pitlochry PH16 5BX, ☎ 1796-472 670, fax 1796-472 373; ££). Charming, family-owned coffee shop and restaurant offering a cosmopolitan daily menu.

Blairgowrie, Dunkeld & Glenshee

Blairgowrie is the second largest town in Perthshire. It sits on the **River Ericht**, which once powered a dozen spinning mills. The fertile farmlands of Blairgowrie and East Perthshire stretch from the River Tay to the high

Perthshire

Grampian Mountains. The region is famous for its berries and soft fruits and their harvest attracts visitors from far and wide.

Dunkeld is a small town set amid hills and forests on the banks of the **River Tay**. Its history dates back to the 6th century when a monastery was founded beside the Tay. Kenneth MacAlpin, the first King of Scots, moved the bones of St Columba from Iona to a church at Dunkeld around 850, establishing the town as the first ecclesiastical capital of medieval Scotland. The entire medieval town was burned to the ground in 1689 during the Battle of Dunkeld, between the Jacobite forces of Bonnie Dundee and the local garrison. From the ashes were built the picturesque "Little Houses of Dunkeld" in the early 18th century. From the lawn of **Dunkeld Cathedral**, there is a wonderful view down to the Tay, taking in the Telford Bridge and whitewashed little houses. Near Dunkeld is **Birnam Wood**, made famous in Shakespeare's Macbeth, although the town itself only dates from Victorian times.

North of Blairgowrie, the road leads to the mountains of Glenshee, which provide the terrain for Scotland's largest ski lift system and a range of year-round sports such as abseiling, hang gliding and mountain biking.

 INFORMATION SOURCES: There are tourism offices at Blairgowrie (26 Wellmeadow, Blairgowrie PH10 6AS, ☎ 1250-872 960, fax 1250-873 701, blairgowrietic@perth-shire.co.uk) and Dunkeld (The Cross, Dunkeld PH8 0AN, ☎ 1350-727 688, fax 1350-728 875, dunkeldtic@perthshire-.co.uk); both open year-round.

■ Special Events

Blairgowrie Highland Games (September; ☎ 1250-872 960, www.blair-highlandgames.co.uk). Highland Games that include the world's longest tug o' war rope.

■ Attractions & Sights

Dunkeld Cathedral (HS; Dunkeld village; free). The cathedral is beautifully situated on the banks of the Tay. Construction was begun in the 12th century, and additions were made up to the 16th century. The choir is now the parish church, although the 15th-century nave and tower are ruined.

 **Beatrix Potter Exhibition** (Birnam Institute, Station Road, Birnam, By Dunkeld PH8 0DS, ☎ 1350-727 674, fax 1350-727 748, admin@birnaminstitute.com, www.birnamin-stitute.com; open year-round, 10am-5pm; admission free). Beatrix Potter spent many childhood holidays in Birnam; this exhibition celebrates her life and work through displays and interactive activities.

■ Adventures

On Snow

 Glenshee (Cairnwell, Braemar AB35 5XU, ☎ 13397-41320, fax 1339741665, info@ski-glenshee.co.uk, www.ski-glenshee.co.uk). Glenshee (meaning "valley of the fairies") flanks the UK's highest mountain pass, formerly one of the main historic drove routes from the Highlands to the Lowlands. Skiing began here in the late thirties; the first lifts consisted of simple rope tows driven by the rear wheels of motorcycles or tractors. Things have moved on considerably since those days and Glenshee now boasts Scotland's largest lift system, extending across four mountains and three valleys.

The size of the area translates into the widest range of skiable terrain of any of the Scottish resorts, from gentle cruises to steep plunges and from wide bowls to narrow gullies. Several lifts access different ski areas directly from road level, which helps disperse skiers and minimize queuing.

Much of the beginners' skiing is accessed directly from road level, after which there is a large selection of greens and easy blues. The Bunny Run provides an easy but lengthy cruise from a high mountain start down to the principal beginners' area.

With 26 blue and red runs scattered throughout the region, Glenshee is best suited to intermediates. Strong skiers invariably gravitate toward **Glas Maol** with its steep and remote slopes that have been used for the British Speed Skiing Championships. In good conditions, the **Tiger** can provide challenging mogul skiing, and the **Slalom** is an interesting descent.

SKIING GLENSHEE

- Base elevation: 2,132 feet (650 m)

- Skiing range: 2,132 feet (650 m) to 3,504 feet (1,068 m)

- Pisted runs: 25 miles (40 km)

- Longest run: 1¼ miles (2 km)

- Maximum vertical descent: 1,500 feet (457 m)

- Lifts: 23

- Runs: 38 (easy: 26%, intermediate: 34%, difficult: 34%, very difficult: 6%)

- Mountain restaurants/cafés: 3

- Snow reports: ☎ 13397-41628, BBC Ceefax page 421, www.ski-glenshee.co.uk.

On Horseback

Kirkmichael Riding (Kirkmichael, Blairgowrie PH10 7NX, ☎ 1250-881 309, rebecca@kirkmichaelriding.co.uk, www.kirkmichaelriding.co.uk). Riding

Perthshire

over heather-clad hills and through pine forests, with faster rides for experienced riders; lessons available.

Multi-Activity Operators

 For a variety of activities, contact **Nae Limits** (The Chalet, Tay Terrace, Dunkeld PH8 0AQ, ☎ 1350-727 242, enquiry@naelimits.co.uk, www.naelimits.co.uk). Choices include cliff jumping, whitewater rafting, kayaking, canyoning/gorge walking, climbing, abseiling, quad biking, gorge crossing and "spheremania" – bouncing and screaming your way down a hillside strapped inside a large inflated ball.

■ Golf

 Glenisla Golf Course (18-hole parkland, 6,402 yards; Pitcrocknie, Alyth, near Blairgowrie PH11 8JJ, ☎ 1828-632 445, fax 1828-633 749, info@golf-glenisla.co.uk, www.golf-glenisla.co.uk; green fees £22-£26). The beautiful, undulating course is set in 180 acres of parkland in the Strathmore valley and is particularly testing on the back nine.

■ Where To Stay

See the *Accommodation* price chart on page 273.

Hotels

 Dalmunzie House (Spittal of Glenshee, Blairgowrie PH10 7QG, ☎ 1250-885 224/6, fax 1250-885 225, reservations@dalmunzie.com, www.dalmunzie.com; B&B £££, lunch £, dinner £££). A stylish baronial country house set in a 6,500-acre estate, Dalmunzie (pronounced "dal-mung-ee" with a soft "g") combines old fashioned comfort with a wide range of on-site activities, including golf (the house has its own course), tennis, walking, mountain biking, stalking, fishing and clay pigeon shooting. The beautiful guest rooms are individually styled and include four-poster beds, huge baths and rooms set delightfully in turrets. The restaurant serves gourmet dining with a menu that changes daily.

Glenshieling House Hotel (Hatton Road, Rattray, Blairgowrie PH10 7HZ, ☎ 1250-874 605, glenshielinghouse@btopenworld.com, www.glenshielinghouse.co.uk; B&B ££, dinner ££). A large Victorian country house set in gardens and woodland, with cozy rooms and an intimate conservatory bar.

Lands of Loyal Hotel (Loyal Road, Alyth, near Blairgowrie PH11 8JQ, ☎ 1828-633 151, fax 1828-633 313, reservations@landsofloyal.com, www.landsofloyal.com; B&B £££, dinner £££). Impressive Victorian mansion with a magnificent hall modeled on the interior of the RMS *Mauretania*. The hotel offers stylish accommodation, fine dining, log fires and a liberal use of oak panelling.

Kinloch House Hotel (Kinloch, By Blairgowrie PH10 6SG, ☎ 1250-884 237, fax 1250-884 333, reception@kinlochhouse.com, www.kinlochhouse.com; B&B ££££, lunch ££, dinner ££££). Luxurious Victorian house standing in 25 acres of woodland with stylish accommodation and high-quality dining.

Hilton Dunkeld House (Dunkeld PH8 0HX, ☎ 1350-727 771, fax 1350-728 924, reservations_dunkeld@hilton.com, www.hilton.com; DB&B ££££). The former home of the Duke of Atholl stands in 280 acres of woodland and has luxurious bedrooms, a pool and leisure complex. The extensive outdoor facilities at the Dunkeld Park Activity Centre include fishing, shooting and off-road driving. The hotel hosts a dinner dance on Saturdays and a ceilidh on Sunday evenings.

Guest Houses & B&Bs

 Duncraggan (Perth Road, Blairgowrie PH10 6EJ, ☎ 1250-872 082, fax 1250-872 098; open Mar-Oct; B&B £, dinner ££). Picturesque guest house offering reasonably priced dinner, bed and breakfast.

Birnam Wood House (Perth Road, Birnam, By Dunkeld PH8 0BH, ☎ 1350-727 782, fax 1350-727 196, bob@birnamwoodhouse.co.uk, www.birnamwoodhouse.co.uk; B&B ££, dinner £££). Attractive house combining period furniture with contemporary features. There is an excellent breakfast menu and evening meals are available by arrangement.

Letter Farm (Loch of the Lowes, Dunkeld PH8 0HH, ☎ 1350-724 254, fax 1350-724 341, letterlowe@aol.com, www.letterfarm.co.uk; closed Apr; B&B ££). Family-run stock farm providing peaceful B&B accommodation with large beds, log fire and delicious home baking.

Old Stables (2 Losset Road, Alyth, near Blairgowrie PH11 8BT, ☎ 1828-632 547, eileen@oldstables.com, www.oldstables.com; B&B ££). A converted 19th-century farmstead with stone wall, timber-lined ceiling and wood-burning fire provides comfortable B&B accommodation. Guest e-mail facilities are available.

The Pend (5 Brae Street, Dunkeld PH8 0BA, ☎ 1350-727 586, fax 1350-727 173, molly@thepend.sol.co.uk, www.thepend.com; B&B ££, dinner £££). Award-winning B&B set within an elegant and Georgian house full of character. There are beautiful guest rooms (though bathrooms are not en-suite) and fine dining.

■ Where To Eat

See the *Dining* price chart on page 275.

 Cargills Restaurant & Bistro (Lower Mill Street, Blairgowrie PH10 6AQ, ☎/fax 1250-876 735, lunch £-££, dinner ££). Lively, informal bistro serving modern Scottish cuisine, a selection of daily specials and an extensive wine list.

Cornerstone Restaurant & Coffee Shop (23 High Street, Blairgowrie PH10 6DA, ☎ 1250-872 038; closed Sun; lunch £). Traditional family-run restaurant serving teas, coffees, snacks and early suppers, and with preserves for sale.

The Dome Restaurant (20 Leslie Street, Blairgowrie PH10 6AH, ☎ 1250-874 888; £-££). Family-run restaurant in charming surroundings serving morning coffee, snacks and meals.

Perthshire

The Oven Bistro (Drumnacree House Hotel, St Ninian's Road, Blairgowrie PH11 8AP, ☎/fax 1828-632 194, www.drumnacreehouse.co.uk; ££). Bistro-restaurant decorated in warm Mediterranean colors, and featuring a wood-burning oven that lets you watch your meal being cooked.

Katie's Tearoom (Perth Road Birnam, By Dunkeld PH8 0AA, ☎ 1350-727 223, fax 1350-727 154; £). Coffees, teas, soups, filled croissants and home baking. Internet stations and patio seating are available.

Palmerston's Coffee House & Bistro (20 Atholl Street, Dunkeld PH8 0AR, ☎ 1350-727 231; £). Homemade food and baking, specializing in local produce with specialty teas, coffees and good wines.

Loch Leven & South Perthshire

Loch Leven, the largest loch in the Scottish Lowlands is the main feature of south Perthshire. The loch is renowned for its fishing and is also an important nature reserve, attracting around 15,000 migrating geese every autumn.

 INFORMATION SOURCES: There are tourism offices at **Kinross** (Heart of Scotland Visitor Centre, Service Area, Junction 6, M90, Kinross KY13 7NQ, ☎ 1577-863 680, fax 1577-863 370, kinrosstic@perthshire.co.uk) and **Auchterarder** (90 High Street, Auchterarder PH3 1BJ, ☎ 1764-663 450, fax 1764-664 235, auchterardertic@perthshire.co.uk); both open year-round.

■ Attractions & Sights

 **Lochleven Castle** (HS; on an island in Loch Leven, accessible by boat from Kirkgate Park in Kinross, ☎ 7778-040 483; open April-Sept, from 9:30am; last outward sailing at 5:15pm; adult/concession/child £3.5/2.5/1.2, including ferry). A short ferry ride takes you to the island castle where Mary, Queen of Scots was imprisoned in 1567 for almost a year before charming her young jailer into setting her free. The tower is late-14th- to early-15th-century, on one side of an irregular courtyard.

■ Wildlife Watching

 The Vane Farm, Loch Leven RSPB Centre (☎ 1577-862 355; reserve open at all times, visitor center open daily, 10am-5pm; adult/concession/child/family £3/£2/£0.50/£6). Loch Leven is home to more breeding ducks than anywhere else in inland Europe. From later summer until spring, tens of thousands of other wildfowl, including pink-footed and greylag geese and whooper swans, use it as a stopover.

■ Adventures

 Loch Leven is possibly Scotland's most famous angling water, famous for its brown trout and additionally stocked with high-quality rainbows. Contact **Loch Leven Fisheries** (The Pier, Kinross KY13 8AS, ☎ 1577-863 407, fishing@green-hotel.com) for information on permits and boat rental.

Scottish Gliding Centre (Portmoak Airfield, Scotlandwell, By Kinross KY13 9JJ, ☎ 1592-840 543) offers daily flying, weather permitting, and lessons.

■ Golf

 Gleneagles PGA Centenary (18-hole heathland, 6,558 yards; Auchterarder PH3 1NF, ☎ 1764-662 231, fax 1764-662 134, resort.sales@gleneagles.com, www.gleneagles.com; green fees £60-£95). The famous PGA Centenary Course is a classic designed by Jack Nicklaus and combines the best of the neighboring King's (heathland, 6,471 yards) and Queen's (woodland, 5,965 yards) courses. A feature of the PGA Centenary Course – apart from its challenge – is the feast of views of the straths (river valleys) and rugged mountains in which the course is set.

■ Entertainment

 Bein Inn (Glenfarg, near Kinross PH29PY, ☎ 1577-830 216, fax 1577-830 211, david@beininn.com, www.beininnmusic.com). Artists perform live classic rock, folk and blues throughout the year.

■ Where To Stay & Eat

See the *Accommodation* and *Dining* price charts on pages 273 and 275.

 Cairn Lodge Hotel (Orchil Road, Auchterarder PH3 1LX, ☎ 1764-662 634, fax 1764-664 866, info@cairnlodge.co.uk, www.cairnlodge.co.uk; B&B ££££, dinner £££). Attractive whitewashed hotel with spacious bedrooms, elegant public areas and formal and informal dining.

Gleneagles Hotel (Auchterarder PH3 1NF, ☎ 1764-662 231, fax 1764-662 134, resort.sales@gleneagles.com, www.gleneagles.com; B&B £££££+, dinner ££££). One of Scotland's finest hotels, world-famous for its luxurious facilities and golf courses. There is every luxury you could want and a wide range of leisure facilities, including pools, gym, riding, shooting, fishing, falconry, off-road driving and, of course, golf. The Andrew Fairlie restaurant serves the finest French cuisine in dreamy 1920s surroundings. Gleneagles is a large hotel (270 rooms) but the staff try hard to minimize the large hotel feeling.

Grouse & Claret (Heatheryford, Kinross KY13 0NQ, ☎ 1577-864 212, fax 1577-864 920, grouseandclaret@lineone.net; B&B £££, lunch ££, dinner £££). Popular country restaurant mixing modern Scottish cooking with subtle oriental flavors. Detached accommodation is available, with some bedrooms overlooking the trout lochans.

Muirs Inn Kinross (49 Muirs, Kinross KY13 8AU, ☎/fax 1577-862 270; B&B ££, dinner ££). Traditional inn with comfortable accommodation and home-cooked Scottish and international cuisine.

Carlin Maggies Restaurant (191 High Street, Kinross KY13 8DB, ☎/fax 1577-863 652; closed Sun pm & Mon; lunch ££, dinner ££-£££). Good food with an international accent at lunchtime and more traditional Scottish evening menu.

Angus & Dundee

The Angus landscape is mainly mountainous, with areas of peaceful rolling hills, a low-lying coastal belt and fertile agricultural plain stretching across it. The area is dotted with attractive towns (notably **Kirriemuir** and **Arbroath**) and picturesque villages (notably **Glamis** and **Edzell**) and contains several old castles, such as Glamis, Brechin and Edzell. In the north are the five **Angus Glens**. Although not of Highland proportions, they're not far short and offer beautiful scenery and tranquility with few visitors.

DON'T MISS

Visit **Arbroath Abbey**, birthplace of Scotland's eloquent Declaration of Independence, then taste delicious Arbroath Smokies in the *Fit o' the Toon*.

Relax in **Glamis**, with its royal castle and lovely folk museum.

Explore **Pictavia**, Scotland's finest museum on the mysterious Picts, or "painted people."

Unwind in peaceful **Edzell** village, with its castle and pretty riverside walks.

Tour the scenic **Angus Glens**.

Best Freebie: **Arbroath Museum**, housed in the historic signal tower.

 INFORMATION SOURCES: Angus & Dundee Tourist Board is at 21 Castle Street, Dundee DD1 3AA, ☎ 1382-527 527, fax 1382-527 551, enquiries@angusanddundee.co.uk, www.angusanddundee.co.uk.

Dundee

Dundee is Scotland's fourth-largest city and has a superb setting on the banks of the **River Tay**. Its jute industry once employed 50,000 people and shaped the life of the city more than a century ago. Its main square is dominated by **Caird Hall**, a 2,400-seat concert and conference hall, and features fountains and a café terrace. **The Law**, the remains of an ancient volcanic plug and site

Angus & Dundee

1. Broughty Castle, Broughty Ferry, RRS Discovery, HM Frigate Unicorn, Dundee University Botanic Garden, Mills Observatory, Sensation, Verdant Works, Camperdown Wildlife Centre
2. Arbroath Abbey, Arbroath Museum
3. Brechin Cathedral & Round Tower, Caledonian Railway, Pictavia
4. House of Dun, Montrose Air Station Museum, Montrose Basin Wildlife Centre
5. Glamis Castle, Angus Folk Museum, Meigle Sculptured Stones
6. Restenneth Priory, Aberlemno Sculptured Stones
7. Edzell Castle
8. J.M. Barrie's Birthplace, Camera Obscura, Kirriemuir Gateway to the Glens Museum
9. Glenesk Folk Museum
10. Reekie Linn Falls
11. Kilbo Pass

Angus & Dundee

of a hill fort, is the highest point in Dundee at 571 feet. It's well worth climbing to gain an excellent view over the city.

Four miles east of Dundee is **Broughty Ferry**, a pretty seaside suburb sitting imposingly at the mouth of the Tay. Sometimes described as "upmarket Dundee," the town was where wealthy jute merchants chose to build their mansions. Before the arrival of the jute barons, the town was just another cluster of fishermen's cottages in the harbor under the shadow of Broughty Castle, now an interesting local history museum.

■ Getting Here

By Air

Dundee Airport (☎ 1382-662 200) has scheduled service from London City. The city center is a £3 taxi ride from the airport.

By Road

Dundee is reached via the A90 from Perth or Aberdeen, the A92 from Edinburgh, or the coastal routes through Perthshire or the Kingdom of Fife.

■ Attractions & Sights

RRS *Discovery* (Discovery Point, Discovery Quay, Dundee DD1 4XA, ☎ 1382-201 245, fax 1382-225 891, www.rrsdiscovery.com; open April-Oct, Mon-Sat, 10am-6pm & Sun, 11am-6pm; Nov-Mar, Mon-Sat, 10am-5pm & Sun, 11am-5pm; adult/concession/child/family £6.25/£4.70/£3.85/£17). The RRS (Royal Research Ship) *Discovery* was one of the last wooden three-masted ships built in Britain, and the first constructed specifically for scientific research. Step aboard Captain Scott's exploration vessel and join Scott, Shackleton and other heroic explorers on their epic voyages. Interactive and multimedia galleries and original polar exploration equipment bring to life their adventures. The restored Captain's Bridge provides a good view of the ship's decks and River Tay; discounted combined ticket with Verdant Works available (see below).

Dundee University Botanic Garden (Riverside Drive, Dundee DD2 1QH, ☎ 1382-647 190, fax 1382-640 574, www.dundeebotanicgardens.co.uk; open Mar-Oct, 10am-4:30pm; til 3:30, Nov-Feb; adult/concession/family £2/£1/£5). The 28-acre gardens present a wide range of plants, fine collections of conifers and broad-leaved trees and shrubs, tropical and temperate glasshouses, water and herb gardens featuring indigenous plants and collections from around the world. There is an interpretation center, guided tours by prior arrangement, plants for sale, coffee shop and gift shop.

Mills Observatory (Glamis Road, Balgay Park, Dundee DD2 2UB, ☎ 1382-435 967, fax 1382-435 962, mills.observatory@dundeecity.gov.uk, www.dundeecity.gov.uk/mills; open April-Sept, Tues-Fri, 11am-5pm & Sat-Sun, 12:30-4pm; Oct-Mar, Mon-Fri, 4-10pm & Sat-Sun, 12:30-4pm; admission to planetarium adult/concession/child £1/£0.50/£0.50, observatory and displays free). The UK's only full-time public observatory houses a Victorian 250-mm Cooke refracting telescope, small planetarium and display areas.

Observe the night sky, view the planetarium show and learn more through the displays, audiovisual presentations and interactive computer.

HM Frigate *Unicorn* (Victoria Dock, Dundee DD1 3JA, ☎ 1382-200 900, fax 1382-200 923, mail@frigateunicorn.org, www.frigateunicorn.org; open April-Oct, 10am-5pm; Nov-Mar, Wed-Fri, noon-4pm & Sat-Sun, 10am-4pm; adult/concession/family £3.50/£2.50/£9.50). The *Unicorn* is the oldest British-built warship still afloat and the world's last intact warship from the days of sail. Launched in 1824, the *Unicorn* carried 46 guns and was only decommissioned in 1968. Changing displays and exhibitions help you imagine life on board and the hardships at sea.

Sensation (Greenmarket, Dundee DD1 4QB, ☎ 1382-228 800, staff@sensation.org.uk, www.sensation.org.uk; open daily from 10am, last entry 4pm; adult/concession/family £6.50/£4.50/£20). Interactive, hands-on exhibits devoted to an exploration of the five senses, including a gyro to experience weightlessness, experiments to test your hearing and taste buds and a bird's-eye view of the world.

Verdant Works (West Henderson's Wynd, Dundee DD1 5BT, ☎ 1382-225 282, fax 1382-221 612, www.verdantworks.com; open April-Oct, Mon-Sat, 10am-6pm & Sun, 11am-6pm; Nov-Mar, Wed-Sat, 10:30am-4:30pm & Sun, 11am-4:30pm; adult/concession/child/family £5.95/£4.45/£3.85/£17; inquire about combined ticket with RRS *Discovery*, above). Experience Dundee, its people and the jute industry in one of Europe's top industrial museums. Set in a working jute mill, original working machinery, computer displays and interactive activities tell the story of the trade from its Indian-sub-continent beginnings to the end product in all its various forms.

Broughty Castle (Castle Approach, Broughty Ferry, Dundee DD5 2TF, ☎ 1382-436 916, fax 1382-436 951, broughty@dundeecity.gov.uk, www.dundeecity.gov.uk/broughtycastle; open year-round, 10am-4pm; 12:30-4pm Sun; closed Mon, Oct-Mar). The castle was built in 1496 on a rocky promontory but fell into ruin in the 18th century, only to be rebuilt in the 1860s as part of the coastal defense system. The castle houses a local history museum that charts the landscape, geology and natural history of the area and the history of the local people.

■ Wildlife Watching

Camperdown Wildlife Centre (Coupar Angus Road, Dundee DD2 4TF, ☎ 1382-432 661/431 811, fax 1382-431 810, camperdownpark@dundeecity.gov.uk; open Mar-Sept, 10am-4:30pm; Oct-Feb, 10am-3:30pm; adult/child/family £2.40/£1.90/£6.70). Home to more than 75 species of Scottish and European wildlife, including brown bears, lynx, arctic foxes and the rare pine marten. Special events, such as animal handling and animal feeding days, are ever-popular with children.

■ Where To Stay

Hotels

HOTEL PRICE CHART	
Indicates the standard price of accommodation per person, per night, based on double occupancy in high season. B&B rate includes breakfast; DB&B includes dinner and breakfast.	
£	Under £20
££	£21-£35
£££	£36-£50
££££	£51-£80
£££££	Over £80

Apex City Quay Hotel & Spa (1 West Victoria Dock Road, Dundee DD1 3JP, ☎ 1382-202 404, fax 1382-201 401, dundee@apexhotels.co.uk, www.apexhotels.co.uk; B&B £££). Recently opened, city center hotel offering stylish contemporary rooms, great dining and a range of leisure and treatment facilities.

Hilton Dundee (Earl Grey Place, Dundee DD1 4DE, ☎ 1382-229 271, fax 1382-200 072, www.hilton.com; B&B £££). High-quality hotel on the banks of the River Tay, with an excellent restaurant, pool, leisure club and river views.

Queen's Hotel (160 Nethergate, Dundee DD1 4DU, ☎ 1382-322 515, fax 1382-202 668, enquiries@queenshotel-dundee.com, www.queenshoteldundee.com; B&B ££££). One of Dundee's original central hotels, the stylish Queen's has recently been totally refurbished and remains a firm favorite at the upper end of the market.

Fisherman's Tavern Hotel (10-16 Fort Street, Broughty Ferry, By Dundee DD5 2AD, ☎ 1382-775 941, fax 01382-477 466, bookings@fishermans-tavern-hotel.co.uk, www.fishermans-tavern-hotel.co.uk; B&B ££). Attractive 17th-century fisherman's cottage, with a picturesque seaside setting and cozy nooks and fireplaces, converted to a pub in 1827. The hotel serves excellent bar food and real ales.

Guest Houses & B&Bs

Aberlaw Guest House (230 Broughty Ferry Road, Dundee DD4 7JP, ☎/fax 1382-456 929, aberlawguesthouse@btinternet.com, www.aberlawguesthouse.btinternet.co.uk; B&B ££). An imposing Victorian villa set in gardens on the outskirts of Dundee and incorporating a magnificent leaded stained glass window. The attractively furnished interior includes very comfortable guestrooms.

Brook House (86 Brook Street, Broughty Ferry, By Dundee DD5 1DQ, ☎ 1382-779 166, reception@brookhouseguesthouse.co.uk, www.brookhouseguesthouse.co.uk; B&B ££). B&B in a detached stone villa with pleasant guest rooms, including one with a four-poster.

■ Where To Eat

Byzantium Restaurant (13 Hawkhill, Dundee DD1 5DL, ☎ 1382-228 866, ssouliman@aol.com; closed Mon; ££-£££). Award-winning fresh seafood and authentic Mediterranean dishes.

Howies Restaurant (25 South Tay Street, Dundee DD1 3NR, ☎ 1382-200 399, www.howies.uk.com; £-££). Stylish restaurant set on two floors serving modern Scottish dishes. Four guestrooms are also available.

The Kittiwake (8 Dalhousie Road, Broughty Ferry, By Dundee DD5 2SQ, ☎ 1382-735 901; lunch £, dinner ££). Excellent traditional cuisine, real ales and an extensive choice of wines, quietly set among mature gardens.

DINING PRICE CHART	
Indicates the price per person for a full meal, excluding drinks. Generally three courses, though fixed menus of five or more courses may be available.	
£	Under £10
££	£11-£20
£££	£21-£30
££££	£31-£40

Murrays Fish & Chip Shop (23 Gray Street, Broughty Ferry, By Dundee DD5 2BH, ☎ 1382-738 117; £). Seaside fish and chips you shouldn't miss.

Royal Arch (285 Brook Street, Broughty Ferry, By Dundee DD5 2DS, ☎ 1382-779 741, thebar@royal-arch.co.uk, www.royalarch.co.uk; £-££). Hearty, reasonably priced food and real ales in a traditional town pub.

The Pear Tree (Burnhead Farm, Auchterhouse, By Dundee, ☎/fax 1382-320 266; closed Mon; £-££). Homemade pizza and pasta, chargrilled steaks and fajitas.

Rancho Pancho (2 Mattocks Road, Wellbank, By Dundee DD5 3PJ, ☎ 1382-350 328, www.ranchopancho.com; ££). Authentic Mexican dishes, including tacos, burritos and fajitas with, of course, margaritas, tequila and sangria.

Carnoustie

Carnoustie is famous for its great golf course, which has periodically hosted the Open Championship since 1931. Local boy Paul Lawrie memorably won the 1999 Open at Carnoustie after shooting a superb final round and play-off.

 INFORMATION SOURCES: The tourism office is at 1b High Street, Carnoustie DD9 6RL, ☎ 1241-852 258; open April-Sept.

■ Golf

 Carnoustie Championship Golf Course (18-hole links, 6,941 yards; Links Parade, Carnoustie DD7 7JE, ☎ 1241-853 789, fax 1241-852 720, golf@carnoustiegolflinks.co.uk, www.carnoustiegolf-links.co.uk; green fees £70-£95). Magnificent and challenging Open Championship venue renowned for having the toughest finish in golf. Jean Van de Velde, who lost the 1999 Open on the closing holes of his final round will testify to this.

■ Where To Stay & Eat

See the *Accommodation* and *Dining* price charts on page 294 and 295.

Carnoustie Golf Course Hotel & Resort (The Links, Carnoustie DD7 7JE, ☎ 1241-411 999, fax 1241-411 998, enquiries@carnoustie-hotel.com, www.carnoustie-hotel.com; B&B £££££, dinner ££££). Luxurious golf resort adjoining the 1st tee and 18th green of the Championship Course, with spacious, high-quality rooms and excellent wining and dining. There is a state-of-the-art spa and leisure facilities. Guests enjoy guaranteed tee-off times on the Championship Course.

Lochlorian House (13 Philip Street, Carnoustie DD7 6ED, ☎ 1241-852 182, fax 1241-855 440, hotellochlorian@aol.com; B&B ££). Centrally located family-run hotel with a large garden and good restaurant.

Station Hotel (Station Road, Carnoustie DD7 6AR, ☎ 1241-852 447, fax 1241-855 605, enquiry@stationhotel.uk.com, www.stationhotel.uk.com; B&B ££). Established family-run hotel offering comfortable accommodation and good food. The bars are popular with both locals and visitors.

Carlogie Farmhouse (Carnoustie DD7 6LD, ☎ 1241-853 128, fax 1241-857 308; B&B ££). Spacious farmhouse B&B in idyllic country surroundings, with private trout fishing for guests.

Old Manor (Panbride, Carnoustie DD7 6JP, ☎/fax 1241-854 804, enquiries@oldmanorcarnoustie.com, www.oldmanorcarnoustie.com; B&B ££). B&B in a restored country manor house set in large gardens. There are good sea views and well-furnished rooms named after local castles.

11 Park Avenue (Carnoustie DD7 7JA, ☎/fax 1241-853 336, parkavenue@oz.co.uk, www.11parkavenue.co.uk; closed Sun-Mon; lunch ££, dinner £££). Small, informal restaurant serving high-quality food skilfully cooked from homemade and locally sourced ingredients.

Arbroath

Taking its name from the **Brothock Burn** that once powered its flax mills, Arbroath is the largest town in Angus. It is a popular holiday resort and active fishing port. The town has a pretty harbor, sandy beach, cliff-top walks and the beautiful ruins of its **abbey**, where in 1320 Scotland's nobles swore their independence from England in the famous "Declaration of Arbroath." The town has long earned its living from the sea and there has been a harbor here since the 14th century. Most of the fishing activity is focused around the *Fit o' the Toon*, the picturesque harbor area (bounded by Commerce Street/Hill Road and Market Gate). The area's tiny smokehouses continue to produce Arbroath's famous delicacy, the **Arbroath Smokie** (haddock smoked slowly over burning wood chips), which is delicious hot or cold.

INFORMATION SOURCES: The tourism office is at Market Place, Arbroath DD11 1HR, ☎ 1241-872 609, fax 1241-878 550; open year-round.

■ Special Events

Arbroath Sea Fest (Aug; ☎ 1241-870 563/872 632 from TB). Vibrant mixture of seafood, sea creatures and street theater.

■ Attractions & Sights

 **Arbroath Abbey** (HS; central Arbroath, just off the A92, ☎ 1241-878 756; open April-Sept, 9:30am-6:30pm; Oct-Mar, 9:30am-4:30pm; adult/concession/child £3.30/£2.50/£1). The impressive ruins of a Tironensian monastery founded by William I (the Lion) in 1178. William died before the abbey was completed and is buried beneath the high altar with a memorial to him at the crossing.

The church is laid out in the usual cross shape facing east. Parts of the church and domestic buildings are well preserved, notably the sacristy, abbot's house and gatehouse range. The sacristy is the most complete part of the church to survive, and contains a small chamber that might have served as a strongroom. Another doorway above the entrance to the small ground floor chamber leads to a room that may have been a secure treasury. The abbot house is one of the best preserved in Scotland and survived the Reformation because it could easily be used for other purposes. The interior contains oak panels and tracery frieze once part of a fine paneled room embellished with wall paintings, fragments of which survive.

DECLARATION OF INDEPENDENCE

Edward I of England's harsh lordship over Scotland led to the Wars of Independence. Despite Robert the Bruce's victory at Bannockburn in 1314, the war continued for many years. When Pope John XXII attempted to proclaim a truce in 1317, Robert's position became severely weakened when he was excommunicated for refusing to accept the proposed truce and ignoring papal letters not addressing him as king. A letter to the pope from the nobles of Scotland was the diplomatic solution and in 1320 Abbot Bernard drafted the letter that subsequently became known as the *Declaration of Arbroath*:

. . . for, as long as but a hundred of us remain alive, never will we on any conditions be brought under English rule. It is in truth not for glory, nor riches, nor honours that we fight, but for freedom – for that alone, which no honest man gives up but with life itself . . .

This famous quote has inspired future generations and was used as the basis for the American Declaration of Independence.

Angus & Dundee

After the Reformation in 1560, the abbey became a quarry when much of its stone was used to build the town's tolbooth and many houses. But Arbroath remained an important site – when Scottish nationalists stole the Stone of Destiny from London in 1950, they left it in Arbroath Abbey.

There is an excellent visitor center to help you understand what was a hugely impressive complex. Audiovisual screens tell the story of the abbey; other information panels recount important episodes from Scottish history and describe the monastic way of life. After the introduction, climb to the bright viewing gallery for an overview of the splendid ruins before exploring the site. The abbey is famously associated with the stirring 1320 Declaration of Arbroath, which asserted Scotland's independence from England, and whose story is told in **The Pen is Mightier than the Sword** exhibition in the gatehouse range.

Arbroath Museum (Ladyloan, Arbroath DD11 1PU, ☎ 1241-875 598; open year-round, Mon-Sat, 10am-5pm; plus Sun, 2-5pm in July-Aug). Housed in the elegant signal tower for offshore **Bellrock Lighthouse**, this great little museum brings to life Arbroath's maritime and social history with models and recreations. Exhibits describe seafaring, fishing and the development of the famous Arbroath Smokie. Another display tells the fascinating story behind the Bell Rock Lighthouse, located on a treacherous reef 11 miles southeast of Arbroath (just visible to the naked eye on a clear day). Estimates suggest the reef claimed 100 vessels in 10 years before Robert Stevenson built the lighthouse in 1807. Bell Rock is the oldest surviving offshore lighthouse and its construction was a tremendous feat of engineering, as its reef is only exposed above the sea for a few hours each day and work could only be carried out during the relative calm of summer.

Lunan Bay (six miles north of Arbroath, off A92) has one of Scotland's best beaches, overlooked by the ruined stone tower of 15th-century **Red Castle**. The castle replaced an even earlier fortress built in the 12th century for William I (the Lion), who used it for hunting. The castle remained in royal ownership until given to the Earl of Ross by Robert the Bruce. Watch out for the loose masonry.

■ Cruise Operators

Inchcape Marine Services (7 Old Shorehead, Arbroath DD11 1BB, ☎ 1241-874 510, ☎ 7752-470 621 mobile, April-Oct), and *Mari Dawn* (6 Osborne Terrace, Arbroath DD11 1QP, ☎ 1241-873 957, ☎ 7796-497 232 mobile, year-round), offer sea fishing and pleasure cruises, including trips to Bell Rock; rod rental available.

■ Where To Stay

See the *Accommodation* chart on page 294.

 Ethie Castle (Inverkeilor, By Arbroath DD11 5SP, ☎ 1241-830 434, fax 1241-830 432, kmydemorgan@aol.cm, www.ethiecastle.com; B&B £££, dinner £££). Truly atmospheric accommodation in a 14th-century sandstone castle built by the Abbot and monks of Arbroath

Abbey. The castle was immortalized by Sir Walter Scott as **Knockwinnoch** in his novel *The Antiquary*. Climb the tower for a splendid view of the area. The public rooms and guest suites, almost wings, are appropriately spacious and finely decorated. The main dining room is impressive but eating in the smaller dining room, with its high ceiling and blazing log fire, is much cosier. The castle is, of course, haunted.

Five Gables B&B (Elliot, Arbroath DD11 2PE, ☎ 1241-871 632, fax 1241-873 615, www.fivegableshouse.co.uk; B&B £-££). Former clubhouse overlooking Arbroath Golf Course, with nice rooms, landscaped gardens and superb sea views from the airy breakfast room.

Scurdy Guest House (33 Marketgate, Arbroath DD11 1AU, ☎ 1241-872 417, fax 1241-874 603; B&B £-££). Spacious, central guest house with a restaurant renowned for delicious home baking, local seafood and great steaks.

■ Where To Eat

See the *Dining* price chart on page 295.

The Old Brewhouse (1-3 High Street, Arbroath DD11 1BE, ☎/fax 1241-879 945, www.oldbrewhouse.com; £-££). Harbor-side pub set in a 17th-century fisherman's cottage that serves good food, including Angus beef, local seafood and interesting veggie options. There are outside tables for sunny days and cozy log fires for cold ones.

Sugar & Spice (9-13 High Street, Arbroath DD11 1BE, ☎ 1241-437 500, mail@sugarandspiceshop.co.uk; £-££). Elegant tearoom and sun terrace serving snacks and light meals. Housed within a delightful Victorian sweet shop, the waitresses are dressed as parlour maids. The shop sells gifts and period children's toys as well as sweets.

The But 'n' Ben (Auchmithie, By Arbroath DD11 5SQ, ☎ 1241-877 223; closed Tues; ££). Award-winning cottage restaurant serving traditional Scottish cooking using fresh local produce, especially fish and shellfish.

Gordon's Restaurant (Main Street, Inverkeilor by Arbroath DD11 5RN, ☎ 1241-830 364, gordonsrest@aol.com, www.gordonsrestaurant.co.uk; lunch ££, dinner ££££). The beautiful, intimate restaurant provides the perfect setting for top-quality food expertly cooked, using fresh local fish, meat and vegetables. A small number of comfortable guestrooms are available; restaurant open to guests only on Mondays.

Brechin & Montrose

Brechin stands on the **South Esk** and was once an ancient market town. Its cathedral is famous for its distinctive 11th-century round tower, one of only two such towers on the Scottish mainland. The Picts – Scotland's "Painted People" – occupied this area centuries earlier, and nearby Pictavia (see next page) is Scotland's foremost exhibition describing these mysterious people.

Montrose is the northernmost coastal town in Angus, and for centuries life here has been focused around its natural harbor. The town is at the mouth of a tidal lagoon and boasts Scotland's widest high street. Montrose Air Station (see next page) was the first operational air station in Britain and the museum commemorates the RAF pilots of both world wars.

 INFORMATION SOURCES: There are tourism offices at Brechin (Brechin Castle Centre, Haughmuir, Brechin DD9 6RL, ☎ 1356-623 050) and Montrose (Bridge Street, Montrose DD10 8AB, ☎ 1674-672 000); both are open April to September.

■ Attractions & Sights

Brechin Cathedral & Round Tower (signposted in central Brechin; open year-round, 9am-5pm). Brechin has its roots in the medieval cathedral and earlier Celtic monastery, first recorded in the late 10th century. In the mid-12th century King David I made the church one of Scotland's cathedrals and Norman-style alterations were made to reflect its new status. Rebuilt and altered at various times it achieved its present form in 1900-01. The cathedral is best known for its Irish-style round bell tower, one of only two in mainland Scotland (the other is at Abernethy). Built in the 11th century as a refined, freestanding tower, it stands 106 feet tall. The finest feature is the upward-tapering doorway edged with mouldings, which stands well above ground level to protect the monastery's precious relics and manuscripts. When the new cathedral was built in the 13th century, the tower was absorbed into its southwest corner.

Caledonian Railway (The Station, Park Road, Brechin, Angus DD9 7AF, ☎ 1356-622 992, www.caledonianrailway.co.uk; Sundays from last in May to second in September, and special holiday trips; adult/concession/child/family £5/£4/£3/£16). Heritage steam train running four miles through the rolling Angus countryside from the Victorian Brechin Station to Bridge of Dun.

Pictavia (Brechin, just off the A90, ☎ 1356-626 241, www.pictavia.org.uk; open April-Sept, Mon-Sat, 9:30am-5:30pm & Sun, 10:30am-5:30pm: Oct-Mar, Sat, 9am-5pm & Sun, 10am-5pm; adult/concession/family £3.5/£2.25/£10). A superb and well-thought-out museum that skilfully deals with the fascinating but mysterious Pictish tribes, the ancient warrior people who inhabited Scotland nearly two thousand years ago. The Picts left few clues about themselves apart from a legacy of magnificent standing stones carved with pictures and strange symbols. This absorbing exhibition goes a long way toward unravelling some of the mysteries of these people who the Romans called the "painted people" because they painted and tattooed their bodies. Examine replicas of beautifully carved Pictish stones and listen to interpretations of their possible meanings. Listen to music played on Pictish instruments and marvel at finely wrought Pictish jewelry studded with gems. Have a go at solving the riddles of Pictish symbolism using the excellent interactive touch-screen cyber symbols game. Learn the history of the Battle of Dunnichen, which laid the foundations of modern-day Scotland.

House of Dun (NTS; Montrose DD10 9LQ, ☎ 1674-810 264, fax 1674-810 722, houseofdun@nts.org.uk; tours noon-5 pm, daily in July and August;

Fri-Tues only, April-June & Sept; adult/concession/family £7/£5.25/£19). Built in 1730 by William Adam for David Erskine, Lord Dun, the house is particularly noted for its superb plasterwork, a particular feature of the Saloon. His wife, Lady Augusta Kennedy-Erskine, was the daughter of King William IV, and many royal mementos from that period are scattered throughout the house. There is a Victorian walled garden, woodland walk, restaurant and shop. There are also good views over the **Montrose Basin Nature Reserve**.

Montrose Air Station Museum (Waldron Road, Broomfield, Montrose DD10 9BB, ☎ 1674-673 107, fax 1674-674 210, info@RAFmontrose.org.uk, www.RAFmontrose.org.uk; open Sun, noon-5pm, other days by arrangement; adult/concession £2/£1.50). Montrose became operational – the first of the government's 12 air stations – in 1913. Many famous pilots trained or served at Montrose during the two world wars, including "The Few" who fought in the Battle of Britain. The museum displays historical photographs, uniforms, memorabilia and RAF archive material.

■ Adventures

Brechin Castle Equestrian (East Lodge, Maulesden, Brechin DD9 6RL, ☎/fax 1356-623 262, info@bcequestrian.com, www.bcequestrian.com) offers lessons and hacking for all ages and abilities.

■ Golf

Montrose Medal Course (18-hole links, 6,496 yards; Traill Drive, Montrose DD10 8SW, ☎ 1674-672 932, fax 1674-671 800, secretary@montroselinks.co.uk, www.montroselinks.co.uk; green fees £18-£20). A majestic, traditional links course that has hosted numerous important tournaments in its long history.

■ Wildlife Watching

Montrose Basin Nature Reserve (Montrose Basin Wildlife Centre, Rossie Braes, Montrose DD10 9TJ, ☎ 1674-676 336, fax 1674-678 773). The unpolluted 2,100-acre enclosed estuary of the South Esk river has been virtually untouched by industrial development and provides a rich feeding ground for thousands of resident and migratory birds, including **eider ducks**, and **pink-footed** and **greylag geese**. **Otters** are also sighted here.

■ Where To Stay & Eat

See the *Accommodation* and *Dining* price charts on pages 294 and 295.

Brathinch Farm (By Brechin DD9 7QX, ☎ 1356-648 292, fax 1356-648 003; B&B £). B&B in an attractive 18th-century farmhouse with a large garden set on a working arable farm between Brechin and Edzell.

36 The Mall (36 The Mall, Montrose DD10 8SS, ☎ 1674-673 646, enquiries@36themall.co.uk, www.36themall.co.uk; B&B ££). B&B in an elegant

Victorian townhouse with spacious, airy rooms furnished with natural pine. There is an excellent breakfast menu.

Woodston Fishing Station (St Cyrus, Montrose DD10 0DG, ☎/fax 1674-850 226, info@woodstonfishingstation.co.uk, www.woodstonfishingstation.co.uk; B&B ££). Beautifully furnished B&B rooms decorated with Victorian antiques, superbly set atop a grassy cliff overlooking the sea. The breakfasts are impressive and evening meals are also available.

Roo's Leap (2 Traill Drive, Montrose DD10 8SW, ☎ 1674-672 157; ££-£££). Aussie restaurant set on Montrose Golf Course, offering a vast menu, including burgers and prime steaks.

Glamis

Glamis (pronounced "glarms") is a sleepy, picturesque village mentioned in Shakespeare's *Macbeth*. It boasts a striking royal castle (the childhood home of Queen Elizabeth, the late Queen Mother) and the excellent **Angus Folk Museum** housed in a row of charming 18th-century cottages.

■ Special Events

Forfar Highland Games (Jun; ☎ 1307-465 605, www.glamis-castle.co.uk). Traditional Highland Games taking place at Glamis Castle.

Glamis Vintage Vehicle Extravaganza (Jul; ☎ 1307-840 393, www.glamis-castle.co.uk). Annual car show in beautiful Glamis, with lots of stands and events.

■ Attractions & Sights

Glamis Castle (Glamis, Angus DD8 1RJ, ☎ 1307-840 393, www.glamiscastle.co.uk; open 10:30 am to 5:30 pm, late March-Oct; from 10 am in July and August; last entry 4:45pm; adult/concession/child/family £6.70/£5/£3.50/£18). Glamis Castle is the family home of the Earls of Strathmore and has been a royal residence since 1372. The present castle was built in the late 17th century around the remnants of a 14th-century keep; its fairytale turrets reflects the French château style. Evidence suggests that Malcolm II, the grandfather of Duncan, was murdered at Glamis in 1034 in an incident immortalized by Shakespeare in *Macbeth*. Glamis is one of the most haunted castles in Scotland, having played host to at least a dozen spirits, of which the most famous is the Grey Lady, who still regularly appears in the chapel.

Glamis was the childhood home of the late **Queen Mother** and birthplace of the late **Princess Margaret**. Though open to visitors, the castle remains a family home. Historic paintings, furniture, porcelain and tapestries are on display with weapons and coats of arms, and the castle has a sealed-up secret room. In addition to the main castle tour are the **Old Coach House** and **Elizabeth of Glamis** (devoted to the late Queen Mother) exhibitions. The grounds were landscaped toward the end of the 18th century and contain a beautiful **Italian garden** and **nature trail**. Guided tours run every 10-15 minutes and take around an hour.

Angus Folk Museum (NTS; Kirkwynd, Glamis DD8 1RT, ☎ 1307-840 288; open noon to 5 pm, daily in July-Aug, Fri-Tues only, April-June & Sept; adult/concession/family £5/£3.75/£13.50). A beautiful row of low-roofed 18th-century cottages containing fine collections of domestic and agricultural exhibits showing how local people once lived. Old Madge's room recreates a combined kitchen, living room and bedroom with box beds, and there are recreations of a rural kitchen, classroom and manse parlour from the late 19th century. Other exhibits include hunting rifles, costumes, musical instruments, butter and cheese making, domestic appliances and utensils, and an exhibition of handloomed linen (once a major cottage industry in Angus). A separate courtyard of barns presents a display called "Life on the Land," containing agricultural implements, a recreated farmworkers' bothy, stable and smiddy, a restored 19th-century hearse from Kirkton of Glen Isla and a model of a traction engine – the "Lawton Lad."

Meigle Sculptured Stones (HS; Meigle village, six miles southeast of Glamis off the A94, ☎ 1828-640 612; open April-Sept, 9:30am-6:30pm, closed 12:30pm-1:30pm; adult/concession/child £2.20/£1.60/£0.75). A magnificent collection of 30 sculptured stones, dating from the 8th-11th centuries, discovered in or by the parish church.

■ Where To Stay & Eat

See the *Accommodation* and *Dining* price charts on pages 294 and 295.

 Castleton House Hotel (By Glamis DD8 1SJ, ☎ 1307-840 340, hotel@castletonglamis.co.uk, www.castletonglamis.co.uk; B&B ££££, dinner £££). Luxurious, cozy country-house hotel set in 10 acres of gardens. There are six spacious and well furnished guest rooms, including a four-poster room. Homegrown vegetables, fruit and free range eggs feature strongly on the excellent menu.

Hatton of Ogilvy Farm (Hatton of Ogilvy, Glamis DD8 1UH, ☎/fax 1307-840 229, hattonogilvy@talk21.com; open April-Oct; B&B £-££). B&B on a peaceful family farm five minutes from the castle.

Forfar

Forfar might be the county town of Angus but it boasts few visitor attractions apart from the ruins of **Restenneth Priory**. The town's greatest claim to fame is probably the "Forfar Bridie," a meat-filled pastry traditionally eaten by farm workers.

 INFORMATION SOURCES: The tourism office is at East High Street, Forfar DD9 6RL, ☎ 1307-467 876; open April-Sept.

■ Attractions & Sights

Restenneth Priory (HS; one mile northeast of Forfar off the B9134 Brechin road; open at all times; admission free). Restenneth lies at the heart of the old Pictish kingdom. It's thought to date from around 1100, although little is known of its early history. The priory housed a small community of Augustinian canons, priests who lived a monastic life. The priory was never strong and its community had virtually disappeared before the Reformation in 1560. As early as 1501 there were attempts to divert its income to the newly founded Chapel Royal in Stirling Castle.

Aberlemno Sculptured Stones (Aberlemno village, six miles northeast of Forfar on the B9134 Brechin road; open April-Oct, covered in winter; admission free). A magnificent range of Pictish sculptured stones, three of which stand alongside the road. The fourth, a cross-slab, stands in the churchyard and is one of the finest Dark Age sculptures in Europe, with interlaced decoration, Pictish symbols and battle scene.

■ Where To Stay & Eat

See the *Accommodation* and *Dining* price charts on pages 294 and 295.

 Royal Hotel (Castle St, Forfar DD8 3AE, ☎/fax 1307-462 691, reception@royalhotelforfar.co.uk, www.royalhotelforfar.co.uk; B&B £££). Refurbished former coaching inn in central Forfar. Ask to see your room first as some are nicer than others.

West Mains of Turin Farmhouse (Rescobie, By Forfar DD8 2TE, ☎/fax 1307-830 229, cjolly3@aol.com; open Mar-Oct; B&B £-££). B&B on an attractive 400-acre stock farm with views over **Rescobie Loch**, grazing cows and pedigree sheep. There are Highland ponies to go trekking on and evening meals by arrangement. The farmhouse is four miles east of Forfar on the B9113 Montrose road.

Edzell

Edzell is a lovely, peaceful village entered through the 19th-century **Dalhousie Arch**. Tenants and friends erected the arch in 1887 in memory of the 13th Earl of Dalhousie and his Countess, who died within a few hours of each other. At the nearby approach to **Glen Lethnot** stands the picturesque ruin of **Edzell Castle** with its attractive walled Renaissance garden – the **Pleasance**.

■ Attractions & Sights

Edzell Castle (HS; near Edzell village, six miles north of Brechin on the B966, ☎ 1356-648 631; open April-Sept, 9:30am-6:30pm; Oct-Mar, 9:30am-4:30pm, call ahead for winter hours; adult/concession/child £3/£2.30/£1). A beautiful castle complex surrounded by attractive gardens. Sir David Lindsay's walled garden dates from 1604; the late-medieval tower occupies the site of an earlier castle, possibly with domestic buildings around it, and a defensible courtyard. Owners progressively enlarged the castle into the fortified mansion whose ruins remain today. The last Lindsay Laird of Edzell sold the estate to the Earl of Panmure in 1715, but the earl soon lost it after supporting the Jacobite rebellion of that year. In 1764, the castle was gutted for its building materials and fell into ruin. It has a summerhouse, bathing pavilion, wall recesses for heraldic groupings and attractive carved panels that are unique in Britain.

■ Adventures

Gannochy Bridge is a stone bridge one mile north of Edzell on the B966. The walk to the **Rocks of Solitude** begins through a blue wooden door in the wall of the Burn House, just by the bridge (not through the famous Dalhousie Arch). The shaded, overhung path runs through pretty woodland beside the **River Esk**. Red squirrels, frogs and otters can occasionally be seen. Cross a number of wooden bridges and pass several salmon pools and many potential picnic spots on the way to the small gorge (1.5 hours; easy).

The **Burn House** in Glen Esk, two miles north of Edzell, was built in 1791 by Lord Adam Gordon on the left bank of the River North Esk.

■ Where To Stay & Eat

See the *Accommodation* and *Dining* price charts on pages 294 and 295.

Glenesk Hotel (High Street, Edzell DD9 7TF, ☎ 1356-648 319, fax 1356-647 333, gleneskhotel@btconnect.com, www.gleneskhotel.co.uk; B&B £££, dinner £-££). High-quality family-run hotel with tastefully decorated public areas and extensive leisure facilities, including pool, sauna and spa.

Panmure Arms Hotel (52 High Street, Edzell DD9 7TA, ☎/fax 1356-648 950, david@panmurearmshotel.co.uk, www.panmurearmshotel.co.uk; B&B ££). Refurbished family-run hotel with pleasant rooms.

Doune House B&B (24 High Street, Edzell DD9 7TA, ☎ 1356-648 201, johna@cameron21.freeserve.co.uk; B&B £). Victorian house with spacious guest rooms and delicious home baking on arrival.

Inchcape B&B (High Street, Edzell DD9 7TF, ☎ 1356-647 266, alison.mcm@btinternet.com; B&B £-££). Comfortable guest rooms in a late Victorian house.

The Coffee Shop Edzell (Edzell Tweed Warehouse, 1 Dunlappie Road, Edzell DD9 7UB, ☎ 1356-648 348; £). Attractive coffee shop serving home baking, snacks, excellent sandwiches and light lunches, set within a large shop selling tweeds, tartans, knitwear and gifts.

Kirriemuir

Kirriemuir, the "Gateway to the Glens," is a pretty, red sandstone town perched on a hill. Its narrow winding cobbles lead you to a statue of Peter Pan

– in memory of the town's most famous son, **JM Barrie**. The restored Camera Obscura that Barrie gifted to the town provides a unique panorama over the town and surrounding hills.

 INFORMATION SOURCES: The tourism office is at Cumberland Close, Kirriemuir DD8 4EF, ☎ 1575-574 097; open April-Sept.

■ Attractions & Sights

JM Barrie's Birthplace (NTS; 9 Brechin Road, Kirriemuir DD8 4BX, ☎ 1575-572 646; open noon-5 pm, daily in July-August; Fri-Tues only, April-June & Sept; adult/concession/family £5/£3.75/£13.50). This two-story house was the birthplace of JM Barrie (1860-1937), author of *Peter Pan*. The upper floors are furnished as they may have appeared when Barrie lived there. Next door is an exhibition, "The Genius of JM Barrie," about the author's literary and theatrical works. The outdoor washhouse is said to have been his first theater.

 NOTE: *Your admission fee for the Barrie Birthplace includes entry to the Camera Obscura, and vice versa. If the Barrie Birthplace is closed on the day of your visit, admission to the Camera Obscura is reduced.*

Camera Obscura (NTS; Kirrie Hill, Kirriemuir, follow signs from town center; ☎ 1575-572 646; open noon to 5 pm, April-Sept; last viewing 4:40pm; adult/concession/family £5/£3.75/£13.50). The Kirriemuir Camera Obscura is one of only three in Scotland. It was gifted to the town by author JM Barrie in 1929 and is housed in a turret room in the Kirriemuir Hill cricket pavilion. It consists of a dark room (*camera obscura* is Latin for "darkened chamber"), through which light gathered from a roof-mounted mirror reflects onto a saucer-shaped viewing table. The views on a clear day can be staggering and include the Ochil Hills, Ben Ledi, Ben Lui, Ben Lawers, the Grampian foothills and the Angus Glens. Admission is weather-dependent – call to check before visiting.

Kirriemuir Gateway to the Glens Museum (The Townhouse, 32 High Street, Kirriemuir DD8 4BX, ☎ 1575-575 479, kirriegateway@angus.gov.uk; open July-Aug, Mon-Wed & Fri-Sat, 10am-5pm; Sun 2-5pm; Sep-Jun, Mon-Wed & Fri-Sat, 10am-5pm; Thurs, 1-5pm). Displays highlight the wildlife, geology, places, legends, history and life in the town of Kirriemuir and its surroundings, especially the western Angus glens: Glen Isla, Glen Prosen and Glen Clova. Interactive touch-screen displays visit the glens and explore Kirriemuir.

■ Adventures

 Pathead Stables & Nursery (Pathead Farm, 2 Forfar Road, Kirriemuir DD8 5BY, ☎ 1575-572 173). Riding stable and tack shop with a nursery selling plants.

■ Where To Stay & Eat

See the *Accommodation* and *Dining* price charts on pages 294 and 295.

 Airlie Arms Hotel (St Malcolm's Wynd, Kirriemuir DD8 4HB, ☎ 1575-572 847, fax 1575-573 055, info@airliearms-hotel.co.uk, www.airliearms-hotel.co.uk; B&B ££). Traditional 17th-century coaching inn with pleasant rooms and a bright, airy restaurant serving good Scottish cuisine.

Muirhouses Farm B&B (Cortachy, By Kirriemuir DD8 4QG, ☎ 1575-573 128, www.muirhousesfarm.co.uk; B&B ££). A mid-19th-century farmhouse on a working livestock and arable farm, with spacious and traditionally decorated guest rooms.

Woodlands (2 Lisden Gardens, Brechin Road, Kirriemuir DD8 4DW, ☎ 1575-572 582; B&B ££). B&B in a large modern bungalow with views over the Strathmore Valley.

The Angus Glens

Although lacking the towering drama of their more illustrious Highland counterparts, the five Angus Glens that spill through the north of the region are beautiful, atmospheric and unspoiled – some of Scotland's best-kept scenic secrets. The glens include 10 Munro summits and miles of narrow, twisting roads. It's worth taking time to explore them all, though Glen Clova is probably the most beautiful, followed by Glen Esk. If you want to escape from it all, visit Glen Lethnot.

■ Special Events

Angus Glens Walking Festival (Jun; ☎ 1382-527 527). A popular new event involving guided walks through the glens.

■ The Glens

Glen Esk (off the B966 north of Edzell). Glen Esk is the longest and one of the most scenic of the Angus Glens and has a deep track carved through it by the **River North Esk**. A road threads its way through the glen as far as **Loch Lee** in the eastern Grampians, with **Mount Keen** rising in the northern background to over 3,000 feet.

At the head of the glen, the delightful **Glenesk Folk Museum** (The Retreat, Glenesk DD9 7YT, ☎ 1356-670 254; open noon-6pm, Easter-Oct; Sat-Sun only, Easter-June; adult/child £2/£1) has a fascinating collection of local exhibits, handicrafts and artifacts, and a welcome tearoom.

Glen Lethnot (off the B966 south of Edzell). This little-visited glen is hidden behind a maze of country lanes northwest of Brechin. It has a General Wade bridge and a whisky trail used by smugglers who once secreted their illicit stills in the corries.

WHO'S WHO? *General Wade created a network of roads and a number of bridges across the Highlands for the benefit of the British army. The first roads were along the Great Glen, and connected Inverness and Fort William with Dunkeld and Crieff.*

Glen Clova/Glen Doll (B955 from Kirriemuir). This most beautiful of glens is accessed from Kirriemuir via Dykehead. The road loops round the upper section of the glens so you can drive up one side of the river and return on the other. At the head of Glen Clova is Glen Doll, from where ancient narrow roads and footpaths lead into the heart of the **Cairngorm Mountains**.

Glen Prosen (B955 from Kirriemuir, turn left at Dykehead). Thickly wooded slopes cloak Glen Prosen in green. A narrow, twisty road runs up the western side of the glen, along the side of which stands a cairn dedicated to Antarctic explorers Edward Wilson (who lived in the glen) and Robert Falcon Scott.

Glen Isla (B951 from Kirriemuir). Glen Isla is the most westerly of the Angus Glens and the only one with a through road. In gorged woodland at the foot of the glen are the **Reekie Linn Falls**. Nearby is the delightful **Peel Farm Coffee & Crafts** (Lintrathen, By Kirriemuir DD8 5JJ, ☎ 1575-560 205, enquiries@peelfarm.com, www.peelfarm.com; open May-Oct), which offers delicious homemade baked goods and unusual crafts and gifts.

The glen road passes **Loch of Lintrathen**, summer home of ospreys and winter home of varied wildfowl, then takes you across the **Blackwater Reservoir** dam before leading toward **Glenshee**.

■ Adventures

A superb walk crosses the **Kilbo Pass** between Glen Clova and Glen Prosen, two of the most scenic Angus glens. It's a full-day, linear walk so you need to arrange transportation for your return trip. The walk starts from the Glen Doll Forest Enterprise parking area, accessed from the B955 from Kirriemuir.

Set off northwest past Acharn Farm, through a gate and onto the forest track. Turn west (left) just beyond the Mountain Rescue post, cross the bridge over White Water and continue west on the track for a mile. Turn southwest onto the old path and begin to ascend through the forest. Shortly after reaching the Burn of Kilbo you cross the deer fence and climb up the path on the northwest side of Corrie Kilbo, above the Shank of Drumfollow. Beyond the pass the path turns south down the Shank of Drumwhallo. Continue beyond Cairn Dye and enter the forest at King's Seat. The path crosses Prosen Water leading down to Kilbo (marked by a ruined cottage) and into Glen Prosen, before returning to the north bank and continuing through a gate. Continue for two miles to

Glenprosen Lodge where the paved road starts. Glenprosen village is another 2½ miles along this road (5-7 hours; moderate).

A steep five-mile (eight-km) climb through **Glen Clova to and above Loch Brandy** (shorter if you only go as far as the loch itself). Loch Brandy is one of a pair of corrie lochs on the north side of Glen Clova above the Glen Clova Hotel. This is where the two legs of the B955 (on either side of the river) meet and cross the River South Esk. Two well-defined paths lead to the loch and then complete a circle high above it, giving excellent views of Glen Clova and the Eastern Grampians to Lochnagar and Mount Keen (5 hours; moderate).

■ Where to Stay & Eat

See the *Accommodation* and *Dining* price charts on pages 294 and 295.

 Idyllically located at the head of the glen is the **Glen Clova Hotel** (Glen Clova, By Kirriemuir DD8 4QS, ☎ 1575-550 350, fax 1575-550 292, hotel@clova.com, www.clova.com; B&B ££), a charming old drover's inn offering character, relaxation and beautiful scenery. The rooms are cozy, and include a bridal suite, and field sports such as hands-on hawking are available. There is a simple all-day menu with more elaborate evening choices.

Brandy Burn House/Stables Café/Bar (Glen Clova, By Kirriemuir DD8 4QS, ☎ 1575-550 203, info@glenclova.co.uk, www.glenclova.co.uk; B&B £) is a beautiful former manse secluded in the heart of Glen Clova that provides home baking, snacks, malt whiskies and B&B accommodation.

Lochside Lodge (Bridgend of Lintrathen, By Kirriemuir DD8 5JJ, ☎ 1575-560 340, fax 1575-560 202, enquiries@lochsidelodge.com, www.lochsidelodge.com; closed Mon; B&B ££, lunch ££, dinner £££). A converted farmstead by Lintrathen Loch provides spacious, comfortable accommodation in the converted hayloft and serves delicious food in the **Roundhouse Restaurant** and **Steading Bar**.

Glenmarkie Guest House, Health Spa & Riding Centre (Glen Isla PH11 8QB, ☎ 1575-582 295, holidays@glenmarkie.freeserve.co.uk, www.glenmarkie.co.uk; B&B ££). A beautiful house set in wonderful scenery in upper Glen Isla with relaxing rooms, home cooking, horseback riding, and health and beauty therapies.

Purgavie Farm (Lintrathen, By Kirriemuir DD8 5HZ, ☎/fax 1575-560 213, purgavie@aol.com; B&B ££, dinner ££). Homely B&B accommodation on a working farm peacefully set near Lintrathen Loch (on which fishing is available). Traditional home-cooking is available.

Aberdeenshire & Moray

Scotland's northeast regions stretch from the high **Cairngorm Mountains**, through pristine rolling countryside carpeted with thick forest, passing castles and whisky distilleries, down to a rugged coastline dotted with tiny fishing communities.

The region's fertile lowland farming country has earned Aberdeenshire the title "Scotland's larder." Aberdeen Angus beef is famous the world over. The pure mountain water flowing through the area is a major reason for Aberdeenshire and Moray being home to more than half of Scotland's whisky distilleries, including **Glenfiddich**, **Macallan** and **Cardhu**.

Aberdeen is the region's largest city, and the third-largest in Scotland. While Edinburgh and Glasgow are world-class tourism magnets in their own right, the city of Aberdeen lacks a comparable concentration of visitor attractions (despite the undoubted charms of Old Aberdeen), and has to content itself with being a gateway for Aberdeenshire as a whole. No visit to Aberdeen would be complete without exploring its countryside, which is hugely rich in scenery and heritage.

 INFORMATION SOURCES: Aberdeen & Grampian Tourist Board, Exchange House, 26-28 Exchange Street, Aberdeen AB11 6PH, information ☎ 1224-288 828; accommodation ☎ 1224-288 825; fax 1224-288 838, info@agtb.org or info@aberdeen-grampian.com, www.aberdeen-grampian.com.

DON'T MISS

Explore **Aberdeen**, the "Granite City," particularly Old Aberdeen with its 17th-century Provost Skene's House and grand university buildings.

Visit **Dunnottar Castle**, perched magnificently on a huge rock over the sea.

Tour Speyside's whisky distilleries, starting with **Strathisla**, possibly Scotland's prettiest distillery.

Tour the region's many striking **castles**, particularly Crathes, Drum, Fraser and Craigievar.

Experience the splendor of **Royal Deeside** and **Balmoral Castle**.

Visit Moray's **coastal villages**, particularly Portsoy, Pennan and Crovie.

Best Freebie: Tour **Pluscarden Abbey** or, at the opposite end of the spiritual spectrum, **Glenfiddich Distillery**.

Getting Here

■ By Air

Aberdeen Airport (☎ 1224-722 331, www.baa.co.uk/aberdeen) is seven miles northwest of the city. Flights arrive from throughout the UK, including daily flights from London, as well as international destinations such as Amsterdam, Dublin and Paris. A taxi from the airport to the city costs £10-£12.

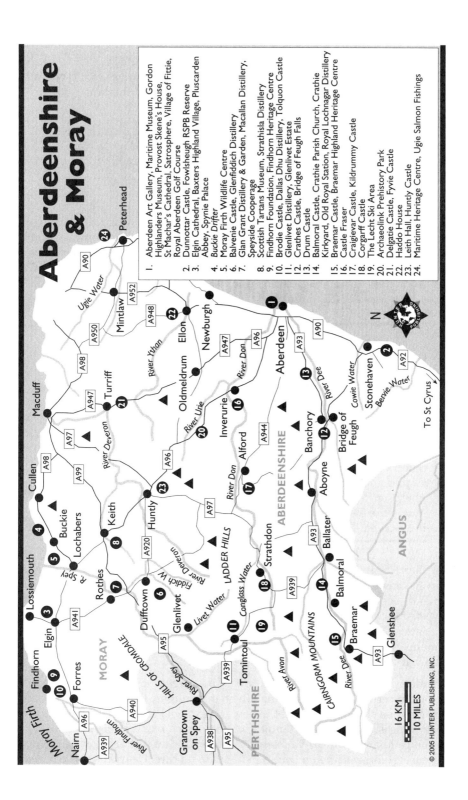

Aberdeenshire & Moray

1. Aberdeen Art Gallery, Maritime Museum, Gordon Highlanders Museum, Provost Skene's House, St Machar's Cathedral, Satrosphere, Village of Fittie, Royal Aberdeen Golf Course
2. Dunnottar Castle, Fowlsheugh RSPB Reserve
3. Elgin Cathedral, Baxters Highland Village, Pluscarden Abbey, Spynie Palace
4. Buckie Drifter
5. Moray Firth Wildlife Centre
6. Balvenie Castle, Glenfiddich Distillery
7. Glan Grant Distillery & Garden, Macallan Distillery, Speyside Cooperage
8. Scottish Tartans Museum, Strathisla Distillery
9. Findhorn Foundation, Findhorn Heritage Centre
10. Brodie Castle, Dallas Dhu Distillery, Tolquon Castle
11. Glenlivet Distillery, Glenlivet Estate
12. Crathes Castle, Bridge of Feugh Falls
13. Drum Castle
14. Balmoral Castle, Crathie Parish Church, Crathie Kirkyard, Old Royal Station, Royal Lochnagar Distillery
15. Braemar Castle, Braemar Highland Heritage Centre
16. Castle Fraser
17. Craigievar Castle, Kildrummy Castle
18. Corgarff Castle
19. The Lecht Ski Area
20. Archaeolink Prehistory Park
21. Delgatie Castle, Fyvie Castle
22. Haddo House
23. Leith Hall, Huntly Castle
24. Maritime Heritage Centre, Ugie Salmon Fishings

© 2005 HUNTER PUBLISHING, INC.

16 KM

10 MILES

■ By Ferry

NorthLink Ferries (☎ 845-600 0449, www.northlinkferries.co.uk) operates luxury car-ferry services to Aberdeen from Orkney and Shetland.

■ By Road

Aberdeen, on the coast, can be reached via the A90 or A92 north from Dundee, or the A96, which cuts inland after following the Moray Firth out of Inverness.

Aberdeen

Aberdeen, Scotland's third-largest city, is known for many things, notably granite, oil and fish. It is no ordinary city, not least because, being hemmed in physically by mountains to the south and west, it has traditionally looked to the sea for its commerce and fortune. Also unusually for a city, Aberdeen enjoys two miles of exquisite sandy beach.

OLD ABERDEEN

Old Aberdeen provides an oasis of tranquility and historic architecture, in contrast to Aberdeen's busy center, with its preserved ancient houses, town plan and fine, cobbled **High Street**. Once a separate burgh, Old Aberdeen is now one of the most charming parts of the city.

Don't miss **King's College** – the heart of Aberdeen University – an imposing building erected around the famous **Quadrangle**. King's College Chapel, used for daily worship for five centuries, houses a collection of 15th-century ornamentation. The King's College Visitor Centre tells the story of the 500-year-old university. Other Old Aberdeen highlights include the **Art Gallery**, **Marischal College**, **Maritime Museum**, **Provost Skene's House**, the **harbor** and **Union Street** – all within easy walking distance.

The North Sea oil and gas bonanza arrived in the 1970s. Although oil activity may have peaked, Aberdeen remains Europe's energy capital and should continue to benefit from its "black gold" for many years to come. The city has invested its windfall wisely: Aberdeen enjoys high employment and a surprising lack of urban squalor. In addition to getting rich from oil, Aberdeen remains one of the country's main fishing ports, and working boats fill its busy harbor.

Aberdeen isn't called the Granite City for no reason. Its grey stonework is instantly recognizable, sparkling silver in sunlight, particularly after rain. The city has skilfully blended the new with the old and has retained its core Scottishness, resisting any temptation to develop into a mini-Houston. With the oil companies' offices deliberately located in the western part of the city, Aberdeen has preserved a traditional feel to its core. Central Aberdeen comprises mostly low-rise, granite buildings set around the long, broad backbone of Union Street, with tight lanes around the harbor – understated Scandinavia rather than high-rise Texas.

INFORMATION SOURCES: The tourism office is at 23 Union Street, Aberdeen AB11 5BP, ☎ 1224-288 828, fax 1224-288 838, aberdeen@agtb.org; open year-round.

■ Attractions & Sights

Aberdeen Art Gallery (Schoolhill, Aberdeen AB10 1FQ, ☎ 1224-523 700, fax 1224-632 133, info@aagm.co.uk; Mon-Sat, 10am-5pm & Sun, 2-5pm). The splendid gallery opened in 1885 and its elegant marble-lined interior displays collections of modern art, works by the Impressionists and Scottish colorists, contemporary crafts, Aberdeen silver and decorative art. There is a program of special exhibitions, events and activities, an excellent gallery shop and café.

Aberdeen Maritime Museum (Shiprow, Aberdeen AB11 5BY, ☎ 1224-337 700, fax 1224-213 066, info@aagm.co.uk; Mon-Sat, 10am-5pm & Sun, noon-3pm). The museum tells the story of Aberdeen's long relationship with the sea, including collections on shipbuilding, fast sailing ships, fishing, port history and the North Sea oil industry.

Fittie is a well preserved fishing village at the mouth of the **River Dee**. The village is a microcosm of fishing life in times past: navigation lamps light doorways; ships in bottles decorate windows; and colorful sheds line the centers of both village squares. Next to the beach are poles, from which nets were hung out to dry.

Gordon Highlanders Museum (St Luke's, Viewfield Road, Aberdeen AB15 7XH, ☎ 1224-311 200, museum@gordonhighlanders.com, www.gordonhighlanders.com; open April-Oct, Tues-Sat, 10:30am-4:30pm & Sun, 1:30-4:30pm; adult/concession/child £2.50/£1.50/£1). Paintings, uniforms, weapons, colors, trophies and 12 Victoria Crosses tell the story of the region's regiment and its kilted soldiers. There is also an audiovisual presentation, shop and tearoom.

St Machar's Cathedral (The Chanonry, Old Aberdeen, Aberdeen AB24 1RQ, ☎ 1224-485 988, administration@stmachar.com, www.stmachar.com; open 9am-5pm; Church of Scotland services 11am & 6pm every Sunday). A fine example of a fortified cathedral, the best view being obtained from inside the West Gate. The distinctive twin towers reflect the fashion of 14th-century tower houses with walls thick enough to enclose spiral staircases and battlements at the tower heads. A church has stood here since around 580. According to legend, Machar, a companion of St Columba of Iona, founded a church here at the request of God, who asked him in a dream to establish his church where a river curves into the shape of a bishop's crosier (which the River Don does just below where the cathedral now stands). The heraldic ceiling of the nave dates from 1520 and provides a vision of the political situation of Scotland and Christendom in the early 16th century.

Provost Skene's House (Guestrow, Aberdeen AB10 1AS, between Broad Street and Flourmill Lane; ☎ 1224-641 086, fax 1224-632 133, info@aagm.co.uk; Mon-Sat,10am-5pm & Sun, 1pm-4pm). One of Aberdeen's few surviving examples of early burgh architecture. Dating from 1545, the house displays an attractive series of period room settings, furnishings and painted ceilings, from the 17th-century great hall, Regency parlour and Edwardian nursery to the Georgian dining room. There are displays on local history, coins and archaeology and The Cellar serves snacks and refreshments.

Satrosphere (179 Constitution Street, Aberdeen AB24 5TU, ☎ 1224-640 340, fax 1224-622 211, info@satrosphere.net, www.satrosphere.net; Mon-Sat, 10am-5pm & Sun, 11:30am-5pm; adult/concession £5.25/£3.75). Hands-on exhibition of science and technology for all ages, with a café and science shop.

■ Adventures

Hayfield Riding Centre (Aberdeen AB15 8BB, ☎ 1224-315 703, fax 1224-313 834, info@hayfield.com, www.hayfield.com). One of Scotland's top riding establishments offers recreational riding and instruction for beginners to professionals, and residential riding holidays.

■ Golf

Royal Aberdeen Golf Course (18-hole links, 6,850 yards; Balgownie Links, Links Road, Bridge of Don, By Aberdeen AB23 8AT, ☎ 1224-702 571, fax 1224-826 591, admin@royalaberdeengolf.com, www.royalaberdeengolf.com; green fees £75-£85). Set among hill, sand and sea, the Balgownie is a perfect example of a demanding links course and not for the faint-hearted.

■ Where To Stay

See the *Accommodation* price chart on page 294.

Hotels

Palm Court Hotel (81 Seafield Road, Aberdeen AB15 7YX, ☎ 1224-310 351, fax 1224-312 707, info@palmcourt.co.uk; B&B ££-£££). Restored mid-range West End hotel with a traditional atmosphere.

The Queen's Hotel (51-53 Queen's Road, Aberdeen AB15 4YP, ☎ 1224-209 999, fax 1224-209 009, enquiries@the-queens-hotel.com, www.the-queens-hotel.com; B&B £££). Friendly, family-run hotel in Aberdeen's West End, five minutes from the city center.

Atholl Hotel (54 King's Gate, Aberdeen AB15 4YN, ☎ 1224-323 505, fax 1224-321 555, info@atholl-aberdeen.co.uk, www.atholl-aberdeen.com; B&B £££, dinner ££). High-quality privately-owned hotel targeting both the business (ADSL lines in all rooms) and leisure traveler. There is an excellent restaurant and good bar meals.

Marcliffe at Pitfodels (North Deeside Road, Pitfodels, Aberdeen AB15 9YA, ☎ 1224-861 000, fax 1224-868 860, info@marcliffe.com, www.marcliffe.com; B&B £££££, dinner ££££). Contemporary styling combines with antiques and baronial detailing to produce a luxurious hotel standing in eight acres of wooded grounds. There is exquisite dining accompanied by extensive selections of wines and spirits.

Maryculter House Hotel (South Deeside Road, Maryculter, By Aberdeen AB12 5GB, about eight miles west of Aberdeen; ☎ 1224-732 124, fax 1224-733 510, info@maryculterhousehotel.com, www.maryculterhousehotel.com; B&B £££, dinner ££). Home to the Knights Templar, Maryculter House dates from 1227 and retains many original features. The staff are very friendly, the food's great and the bedrooms very comfortable, but the highlight is the magnificent Cocktail Bar dating from 1225, with its spectacular high beamed ceiling and open hearth fire – the perfect place to relax with a coffee or dram.

Norwood Hall Hotel (Garthdee Road, Cults, Aberdeen AB15 9FX, ☎ 1224-868 951, fax 1224-869 868, info@norwood-hall.co.uk, www.norwood-hall.co.uk; B&B £££). Occupying the site of the 15th-century Pitfodels Castle, this Victorian mansion is set in seven acres of wooded grounds three miles from Aberdeen. The rooms are grand and there is fine dining in the Tapestry Dining Room.

Old Mill Inn (South Deeside Road, Maryculter, By Aberdeen AB12 5FX, about eight miles west of Aberdeen; ☎ 1224-733 212, fax 1224-732 884, info@oldmillinn.co.uk, www.oldmillinn.co.uk; B&B ££, lunch £, dinner ££). Historic 200-year-old family-run country inn, extensively refurbished, on the edge of the River Dee. The inn is next to Old Mill Antiques showrooms and Storybook Glen.

Guest Houses & B&Bs

 Arkaig Guest House (43 Powis Terrace, Aberdeen AB25 3PP, ☎ 1224-638 872, fax 1224-622 189, pat@arkaig.co.uk, www.arkaig.co.uk; B&B ££). Friendly guest house with comfortable, well-decorated rooms and a pretty garden courtyard. Dinner is available by prior arrangement.

Jays Guest House (422 King Street, Aberdeen AB24 3BR, ☎/fax 1224-638 295, alice@jaysguesthouse.co.uk, www.jaysguesthouse.co.uk; B&B ££-£££). High-quality guest house renowned for its friendly atmosphere and personal attention of the owners.

Royal Crown Guest House (111 Crown Street, Aberdeen AB11 6HN, ☎ 1224-586 461, fax 1224-575 485, b&b@royalcrown.co.uk, www.royal-crown.co.uk; B&B £-££). Comfortable and pleasantly furnished city center guest house.

West Lodge Guest House (Norwood Hall, Garthdee Road, Cults, By Aberdeen AB15 9FX, ☎ 1224-861 936; B&B £-££). Charming accommodation set quietly in a converted coach house.

■ Where To Eat

See the *Dining* price chart on page 295.

 Ashvale Fish Restaurant (42-48 Great Western Road, Aberdeen, ☎ 1224-596 981; £). You can't come to Aberdeen without trying a traditional fish-and-chip restaurant, and this is one of the best.

La Bonne Baguette (Correction Wynd, Aberdeen, ☎ 1224-644 445; £-££). French style café-brasserie close to the major shopping area.

Les Amis (58-60 Justice Mill Lane, Aberdeen, ☎ 1224-584 599, fax 1224-584 599; closed Sun; ££). Small, family-run French restaurant specializing in seafood.

Lj's (46-52 Schoolhill, Aberdeen AB10 1JQ, ☎ 1224-635 666, fax 1224-635 777; ££). Relaxed informality over two floors of retro styling with a jazzy influence, and an extensive, varied menu.

Nargile Restaurant (77-79 Skene Street, Aberdeen, ☎ 1224-636 093; ££-£££). Well-regarded, family-run restaurant serving some of the best Eastern Mediterranean/Turkish-style food in Scotland.

Old Blackfriars (52 Castlegate, Aberdeen, ☎ 1224-581 922; £-££). Award-winning real ale pub that serves good bar meals.

Shiso Brasserie (8 Golden Square, Aberdeen, ☎ 1224-624 324, fax 1224-624 109, indulge@shiso.co.uk, www.shiso.co.uk; ££). All-day food, great daytime deli and evening fine dining.

Silver Darling (Pocra Quay, North Pier, Aberdeen AB11 5DQ, ☎ 1224-576 229; £££-££££). A superb restaurant overlooking the harbor entrance, specializing in French-flavored seafood.

Slains Castle Pub & Restaurant (14-18 Belmont Street, Aberdeen, ☎ 1224-631 877; £-££). Traditional, heart-of-the-city pub with an unusual, eerie gothic influence.

Via Milano ("The Galleria," Bon Accord Street, Aberdeen, AB11 6FB, ☎ 1224-593 222, fax 1224-594 666, mail@viamilano.co.uk, www.viamilano.co.uk; ££-£££). Authentic Italian cooking.

Yangtze River Chinese Restaurant (8 Bridge Street, Aberdeen, ☎ 1224-583 377; ££). Aberdeen's original Chinese restaurant.

Stonehaven

Stonehaven is an attractive seaside resort with a picturesque, sheltered harbor busy with sailboats. The **Tolbooth Museum** is a notable quayside building and the ruined cliff-top fortress of **Dunnottar Castle** is a "must see." Nearby, the **Fowlsheugh Seabird Colony** is the largest on the British mainland.

INFORMATION SOURCES: The tourism office is at 66 Allardice Street, Stonehaven AB39 2AA, ☎ 1569-762 806, stonehaven@agtb.org; open Easter-Oct.

■ Special Events

Stonehaven Fireball Festival (31 Dec; 63 Barclay Street, Stonehaven AB39 2AR, ☎ 1569 764 647/762 300, www.stonehavenfireballs.co.uk). Stonehaven's unique way of welcoming the New Year, with 45 marchers swinging fireballs above their heads.

■ Attractions & Sights

 Dunnottar Castle (Dunnottar, two miles south of Stonehaven on the A92, ☎ 1569-762 173; open Easter-Oct, Mon-Sat, 9am-6pm & Sun, 2-5pm; Nov-Mar, Fri-Mon, 9am-sunset; adult/child £3.50/£1). An ancient fortress perched dramatically on a cliff-top, Dunnottar is one of the most significant historical buildings in Scotland. From the earliest times, this imposing rock was a stronghold; in 1297 William Wallace burned the fortress, complete with its English garrison. Sir William de Keith, the Grand Marischal of Scotland, built the present tower in the late 14th century. For 300 years, the castle was home to the Keiths, royal counsellors and one of the richest and most powerful families in Scotland. Mary, Queen of Scots and her son King James VI both visited several times. The castle's finest hour came in 1650 when its garrison safeguarded the Scottish crown jewels, the "Honours of Scotland," during a siege by Cromwell's Roundheads. Infamously, 167 Covenanters were imprisoned here in terrible conditions in 1685 – the vault where they were kept can be seen today as it was then.

■ Wildlife Watching

 Fowlsheugh RSPB Reserve (three miles south of Stonehaven, signposted off the A92, ☎ 1224-624 824; open at all times; admission free). The Fowlsheugh cliffs are packed with breeding seabirds in the spring and summer, particularly **guillemots**, **razorbills** and **kittiwakes**, with smaller numbers of **fulmars**, **gulls** and **puffins**. From May to July, evening boat trips visit the cliffs from Stonehaven.

■ Where To Stay & Eat

See the *Accommodation* and *Dining* price charts on pages 294 and 295.

 The Creel Inn (Catterline, Stonehaven AB39 2UL, ☎ 1569-750 254, info@thedreelinn.co.uk, www.thecreelinn.co.uk; B&B ££). Perched on cliffs in the fishing village of Catterline and overlooking the bay and harbor, the inn offers comfortable rooms and great seafood in an original fisherman's cottage with open fires and beamed ceiling.

Heugh Hotel (Westfield Road, Stonehaven AB39 2EE, ☎ 1569-762 379, fax 1569-766 637, kevin@heughhotel.com, www.heughhotel.com; B&B £££). A beautiful granite baronial mansion owned and run by the Hermanns family since 1984. The oak paneling and fireplace set the tone for luxury and quiet elegance, and there is fine dining with a good wine selection.

Ship Inn Hotel (5 Shorehead, Stonehaven AB39 2JY, ☎ 1569-762 617; B&B ££). Privately-owned inn overlooking Stonehaven harbor with a good restaurant specializing in local fish.

Arduthie House (Ann Street, Stonehaven AB39 2DA, ☎ 1569-762 381, fax 1569-766 366, arduthie@talk21.com; B&B ££). Elegant, centrally located guest house offering a guest lounge, sun lounge and four-poster bed.

Lairhillock Inn & Restaurant (Netherley, By Stonehaven AB39 3QS, ☎ 1569-730 001/730 220, fax 1569-731 175, www.lairhillock.co.uk; lunch £, dinner ££-£££). Hearty bar lunches and a top-quality evening menu, served in an atmospheric 200-year-old inn with authentic rustic décor and a log fire.

Sandy's Fish & Chips (28 Market Square, Stonehaven, ☎ 1569-763 234; £). High-quality chippie established 20 years, with a weekend delivery service.

Elgin

Lying at the heart of Moray, Elgin was an ancient provincial capital, although its importance is now much reduced. Its highlight is the ruin of a magnificent medieval cathedral, the "Lantern of the North." Nearby you can witness monastic life in practice at **Pluscarden Abbey**. Prince Charles and his father, the Duke of Edinburgh, both studied at nearby **Gordonstoun School**.

 INFORMATION SOURCES: The tourism office is at 17 High Street, Elgin IV30 1EG, ☎ 1343-542 666, fax 1343-552 982, elgin@agtb.org; open year-round.

■ Attractions & Sights

Elgin Cathedral (HS; in Elgin on the A96, ☎ 1343-547 171; open April-Sept, 9:30am-6:30pm; Oct-Mar, 9:30am-4:30pm; call ahead for winter schedule; adult/concession/child £3/£2.30/£1, discounted joint ticket available with Spynie Palace, below). This is the superb ruin of one of Scotland's most beautiful and impressive cathedrals, named the Lantern of the North. It was founded in 1224. Much of the work at Elgin is in the rich late-13th-century style, though much modified after being burned by the Wolf of Badenoch in 1390. The best-surviving sections are the south transept, two western towers and re-roofed octagonal chapter house (meeting room for the canons). After the Reformation of 1560, the cathedral was neglected in favor of the much simpler parish church of St Giles. In 1561, the cathedral's interior was "cleansed" of many items associated with the old religious ways. In 1567, lead was stripped from the roof, allowing the inevitable process of decay to begin.

Baxters Highland Village (Fochabers IV32 7LD, ☎ 1343-820 393, fax 1343-820 286, info@baxters.co.uk, www.baxters.com; open April-Dec, 9am-5:30pm; Jan-Mar, 10am-5pm). Since its establishment in 1868, Baxters has become an internationally renowned producer of fine foods, mostly jams and soups, that are popular with the British Royal Family. The product talks and tastings are an excellent way to discover the ever-developing range. George Baxter's original village shop has been recreated with products from the time. Several modern shops sell food and drink, kitchen utensils, clothing, home furnishings and Scottish gifts and, from October, there is a Christmas shop. The restaurants, of course, serve many Baxters products.

Pluscarden Abbey (Pluscarden, Elgin IV30 3UA, ☎ 1343-890 257, fax 1343-890 258, monks@pluscardenabbey.org, www.pluscardenabbey.org; 9am-5pm). The impressive Abbey of Our Lady, Saint John the Baptist and Saint Andrew in Pluscarden was founded by Alexander II in 1230 for Valliscaulian monks, and is Britain's only medieval abbey still inhabited by monks. The strict rule (no mattresses, sparse diet, silence, etc) of the Valliscaulian order combined the solitude of the Carthusians with the common life of the Cistercians and the rule of Saint Benedict dictating life.

In 1390, Alexander Stewart (the "Wolf of Badenoch") sacked the priory and over the next three centuries the priory fell into disuse, in 1682 suffering the indignity of being used as a stone quarry for the construction of St Giles Church in Elgin. In 1948, the priory was re-founded by the Benedictine monks of Prinknash Abbey in Gloucestershire, England, who took up residence. The central tower, chapter house and domestic buildings were repaired and in 1974 the priory was elevated to the status of abbey. White-habited monks continue to live, work and pray at the abbey, which remains a place of total peace and tranquility. Retreats are available for visitors.

Spynie Palace (HS; two miles north of Elgin off the A941, ☎ 1343-546 358; open April-Sept, 9:30am-6:30pm; Oct-Mar, 9:30am-4:30pm; call ahead for winter schedule; adult/concession/child £2.20/£1.60/£0.75 or combine with Elgin Cathedral, above). The now-ruined palace was the domain of the bishops of Moray from the 14th century to 1686. Dominated by the massive tower built by Bishop David Stewart (1461-77), there are spectacular views over Spynie Loch.

Buckie Drifter (Maritime Heritage Centre, Freuchny Road, Buckie AB56 1TT, ☎ 1542-834 646, fax 1542-835 995, www.moray.org/bdrifter; open April-Oct; 10 am-5 pm, Mon-Sat; noon-5 pm, Sun; from 10 am Sundays in July-Aug; adult/concession/family £2.75/£1.75/£8). A journey back in time to the days when the herring was king and Buckie was the premier herring fishing port in Scotland. Walk along a 1920s quayside and climb aboard a replica Buckie Drifter, watch rare 1930s archive film of the drifters fishing and try several hands-on activities.

■ Wildlife Watching

 The **Moray Firth Wildlife Centre** (Spey Bay, Fochabers IV32 7PJ, ☎ 1343-820 339, fax 1343-829 109, enquiries@mfwc.co.uk, www.mfwc.co.uk; open April-Oct, 10:30 am-5 pm; weekends only, Feb-March). Spey Bay is renowned for its variety of wildlife, which includes otters, ospreys, dolphins, porpoises, minke whales and seals. Housed in a former salmon-fishing station, the Wildlife Centre provides an exhibition of local wildlife, shop and café.

Sailingwild (East Harbour Basin, Lossiemouth Harbour, Lossiemouth, ☎/fax 1343 829-244, info@sailingwild.com, www.sailigwild.com, April-Oct, £25 for a two-hour cruise) offers trips aboard the sailing yacht *Dolphinicity*, with the chance to see whales, dolphins, seals and marine birds.

■ Shopping

Johnstons Cashmere Visitor Centre (Newmill, Elgin IV30 4AF, ☎ 1343-554 099, fax 1343-554 080, enquiries@johnstonscashmere.com, www.johnstonscashmere.com). Exhibition, audiovisual presentation and factory tours tell the story of cashmere from its roots in the wilds of Asia. There is also a mill shop and coffee shop.

■ Where To Stay & Eat

See the *Accommodation* and *Dining* price charts on pages 294 and 295.

Hotels

 Laichmoray Hotel (Maisondieu Road, Elgin IV30 1QR, ☎ 1343-540 045, fax 1343-540 055, enquiries@laichmorayhotel.co.uk, www.laichmorayhotel.co.uk; B&B £££, dinner ££-£££). Central family-run hotel with a good restaurant and bar meals served in the whisky theme lounge and conservatory.

Mansefield House Hotel (Mayne Road, Elgin, 1343-540 883, fax 1343-552 491, reception@themansefield.com, www.themansefield.com; B&B £££, dinner £££). A former manse built in 1837-39, offering individual, contemporary styling and some four-poster rooms. The à la carte menu emphasizes classic Scottish dishes and uses local produce, including Moray seafood.

Mansion House Hotel (The Haugh, Elgin IV30 1AW, ☎ 1343-548 811, fax 1343-547 916, reception@mhelgin.co.uk, www.mansionhousehotel.co.uk; B&B ££££, dinner £££). Modern accommodation combined with old world charm in a peaceful riverside setting.

Guest Houses & B&Bs

The Lodge Guest House (20 Duff Avenue, Elgin IV30 1QS, ☎ 1343-549 981, fax 1343-540 527, thelodgeguesthouse@talk21.com, www.beeandbee.com; B&B £-££). Imposing and distinctive town house set in a large mature garden. There are great breakfasts and the guest lounge has a turreted window, books and magazines and a selection of malt whiskies.

"Parrandier" – The Old Church of Urquhart (Meft Road, Urquhart, By Elgin IV30 8NH, ☎/fax 1343-843 063, www.oldkirk.co.uk; B&B ££, dinner ££). A beautifully and imaginatively converted church dating from 1843, set quietly in two acres of gardens atop a small hill. The building retains many original church features (as well as a civil-wedding license) and enjoys uninterrupted views of the surrounding countryside. The first-floor guest lounge/dining room is a magnificent space in what was the church gallery. B&B (dinner by prior arrangement) accommodation and an apartment with kitchen are available.

The Pines Guest House (East Road, Elgin IV30 1XG, ☎ 1343-552 495, fax 1343-556 424, enquiries@thepinesguesthouse.com, www.thepinesguesthouse.com; B&B ££). Elegant and refurbished Victorian town house with tastefully furnished bedrooms, including a popular four-poster room. A la carte breakfasts are served in the magnificent dining room.

Dufftown, Rothes & Keith

Dufftown, Rothes and Keith lie in the heart of Speyside's malt whisky country. **Glenfiddich**, which produces around a quarter of Scotland's malt whisky output, is close to Dufftown. **Strathisla** in Keith is one of the most picturesque of all distilleries. Keith, an important agricultural center, also houses the **Scottish Tartans Museum**. Rothes was originally a crofting township and boasts **Glen Grant Distillery** with its beautiful gardens.

SPEYSIDE MALT WHISKY TRAIL

Speyside is home to more than half of Scotland's whisky distilleries and its Malt Whisky Trail – marked by white on brown signs – links seven distilleries and a cooperage. A leaflet is available from local tourism offices (www.maltwhiskytrail.com).

■ Special Events

Spirit of Speyside Whisky Festival (Apr/May; ☎ 1343-542 666, enquiries@spiritofspeyside.com, www.spiritofspeyside.com). Celebration of whisky, including tastings, distillery visits, food, music and other themed entertainment.

Dufftown Highland Games (Jul; ☎ 1340-820 342/820 265, www.dufftownhighlandgames.org). Traditional Highland games, including hill race, Highland dancing and massed pipe bands, concluding with massed pipe bands in the town square.

Autumn Speyside Whisky Festival (Sep; ☎ 1304-821 097, whiskyfestival@dufftown.co.uk, www.dufftown.co.uk). In case you missed out in May!

Spirit of Speyside Walking Festival (Oct; ☎ 1343-820 339, fax 1343-829 109, enquiries@mfwc.co.uk, www.walkingfestival.net). Themed walks (history, whisky, etc) throughout Speyside and Moray for all levels.

 INFORMATION SOURCES: The tourism office is at The Clock Tower, The Square, Dufftown AB55 5AD, ☎ 1340-820 501, dufftown@agtb.org; open Easter-Oct.

■ Attractions & Sights

Dufftown

Balvenie Castle (HS; in Dufftown on the A941, ☎ 1340-820 121; open April-Sept, 9:30am-6:30pm; adult/concession/child £2.20/£1.60/£0.75). A ruined courtyard castle whose enclosure was first owned by the Comyns. A curtain wall was added in the 13th century and further enhancements made in the 15th and 16th centuries.

Glenfiddich Distillery (Dufftown AB55 4DH, ☎ 1340-820 373, fax 1340-822 083, www.glenfiddich.com; open Mon-Fri, 9:30am-4:30pm; plus Sat, 9:30am-4:30pm & Sun, noon-4:30pm, from Easter to mid-Oct). Five generations after the first spirit flowed in 1887, Glenfiddich remains one of the few Scotch whisky producers still in the hands of its founding family. Glenfiddich's distinctive triangular bottle is the best-selling single malt (accounting for around a quarter of the single malt market). The audiovisual presentation/distillery tour is particularly worthwhile as Glenfiddich is one of only three distilleries that still bottles on-site (the others being Springbank in Kintyre and Bruichladdich on Islay).

Rothes

Glen Grant Distillery & Garden (Elgin Road, Rothes AB38 7BS, ☎ 1340-832 118; open April-Oct, Mon-Sat, 10am-4pm & Sun, 12:30-4pm; admission £3, including a shop voucher). Founded in 1840 by John and James Grant and inspired by James's son "The Major," the distillery produces a light, floral malt with a clear color. The restored Victorian garden is more noteworthy than the distillery; don't miss the gorge walk, where you can enjoy a dram from the "Major's safe" in the heather-thatched pavilion.

The Macallan Distillery (Easter Elchies, Craigellachie, near Rothes AB38 9RX, ☎ 1340-872 280 www.themacallan.com; open Easter-Oct, Mon-Sat, 9am-6pm; Nov-Easter, Mon-Fri, 9am-5pm). High on a hill overlooking the River Spey with views across to Ben Rinnes, the distillery nestles within the Easter Elchies Estate and produces one of the most highly regarded Scotch malt whiskies.

Speyside Cooperage (Dufftown Road, Craigellachie, near Rothes AB38 9RS, ☎ 1340-871 108, fax 1340-881 437, enquiries@speysidecooperage.co.uk, www.speysidecooperage.co.uk; open year-round, Mon-Fri, 9:30am-4pm; adult/concession/child/family £3.10/£2.50/£1.80/£8.50). Family-run business that has been making oak casks for Speyside's whisky distilleries for three generations. Watch the cooperage in operation and even try building a "demonstration" cask. There is an audiovisual presentation, exhibition, shop and tastings.

Keith

Scottish Tartans Museum (Institute Hall, 138 Mid Street, Keith, ☎ 1542-888 419; open April-Nov, Mon-Sat, 11am-3pm, until 4 pm in July and August; adult/concession/child/family £2.50/£2/£1.50/£7). Trace the history and development of tartan and kilts, with over 700 tartans and 1,000 artifacts on display.

Strathisla Distillery (Seafield Avenue, Keith AB55 5BS, ☎ 1542-783 044, fax 1542-783 039; open April-Oct, Mon-Sat, 10am-4pm & Sun, 12:30-4pm; admission £5, including a shop voucher). Founded in 1786, Strathisla is Scotland's oldest working distillery. It's also one of the most picturesque, with its tranquil setting, old-fashioned visitor rooms and quaint waterwheel beneath its pagoda towers. Start with a coffee and shortbread, then take the self-guided distillery tour before finishing with a tutored nosing and dram of the smooth, flavorful Strathisla single malt or Chivas Regal blend. If you're planning to tour only one distillery in Speyside, tour this one.

■ Where To Stay

See the *Accommodation* and *Dining* price charts on pages 294 and 295.

 Tannochbrae Guest House (22 Fife Street, Dufftown AB55 4AL, ☎ 1340-820 541, info@tannochbrae.co.uk, www.tannochbrae.co.uk; B&B £-££). Converted Victorian villa with walled gardens, fountains, ponds and waterfalls. The restaurant serves good, reasonably priced food using the best local ingredients, with vegetables and herbs from the garden.

Archiestown Hotel (Archiestown, By Aberlour AB38 7QL, between Rothes and Dufftown; ☎ 1340-810 218, fax 1340-810 239, rml@archiestownhotel.co.uk, www.archiestownhotel.co.uk; open Feb-Dec; B&B £££, ££). Attractive, traditionally furnished village hotel with an informal bistro overlooking a pretty walled garden. Lunch, supper, morning coffee and afternoon tea are available and non-residents are welcome. There is a log fire in the sitting room and an extensive selection of reading.

Ben Aigen Hotel (51 New Street, Rothes AB38 7BJ, ☎ 1340-831 240, fax 1340-831 921; B&B ££). Chef-owned, family-run hotel offering traditional charm and comfortable bedrooms. The wholesome home cooking includes fresh Moray seafood and local venison, accompanied by real ales and malts.

Craighurst B&B (Seafield Avenue, Keith AB55 5BS, ☎/fax 1542-888 389; B&B ££). Two en-suite bedrooms in a fine Victorian house set in a peaceful garden.

■ Where To Eat

See the *Dining* price chart on page 295.

 A Taste Of Speyside (10 Balvenie Street, Dufftown AB55 4AB, ☎/fax 1340-820 860; open Mar-Oct, closed Sun; lunch ££, dinner £££). Cozy family-run restaurant, specializing in wholesome local food and offering around 70 local malt whiskies.

Boogie Woogie Gifts & Coffee Shop (2 Regent Square, Keith AB55 5DX, ☎ 1542-888 077, fax 1542-888 037, info@boogiewoogieshop.com, www.boogiewoogieshop.com; £). Simple, freshly prepared food, including homemade soups, sandwiches, hot bacon rolls, cakes and salads.

Findhorn

Findhorn is a picturesque coastal village that has long attracted watersports lovers. It now also attracts visitors with more spiritual interests to its unique **Findhorn Foundation**, dedicated to personal growth, sustainability and communal living.

 INFORMATION SOURCES: The nearest tourism office is at 116 High Street, Forres IV36 0NP, ☎ 1309-672 938, forres@agtb.org; open Easter-Oct.

■ Attractions & Sights

Findhorn

Findhorn Foundation (The Park, Findhorn, Forres IV36 3TZ, ☎ 1309-690 311, fax 1309-691 301, reception@findhorn.org, www.findhorn.org; daily tours throughout the summer starting at 2pm). From its inception in 1962, the Findhorn Foundation has become the hub of a major international community, providing courses on personal and spiritual growth, ecology, sustainability and community living. Around 14,000 visitors attend courses, workshops and conferences each year. The community is developing an eco-village incorporating "breathing wall" construction, turf roofs and whisky barrel houses. The community grows organic vegetables, uses innovative biological sewage treatment (the first plant of its kind in Europe) and generates power from its wind generator.

Findhorn Heritage Centre (Findhorn village, next to Culbin Sands Hotel, ☎ 1309-690 349/690 659; open May-Sept, 2-5pm; Sat-Sun only in May & Sept, daily June-Aug; donations requested). A private venture by local residents, based in two former salmon-fishery huts. The first is laid out as a salmon-fisher's bothy of days gone by, and the second contains exhibits and displays tracing Findhorn's development from prehistoric times to the present. A restored icehouse is being added to the exhibits at this writing, and may be open by the time you visit.

Forres

Brodie Castle (NTS; Brodie, Forres IV36 2TE, ☎ 1309-641 371, fax 1309-641 600, brodiecastle@nts.org.uk; castle open April-Sept, noon-4pm; daily in July-Aug; Sun-Thurs only in May, June & Sept; grounds open year-round, 9:30am-sunset; adult/concession/family £5/£3.75/£13.50, £1 parking). Set in peaceful parkland, the Z-plan tower house dates from the 16th century and houses a magnificent collection of art, furniture, porcelain and a 6,000-volume library. The grounds are famous for their impressive spring daffodils, and there are several woodland walks, one of which runs alongside a large pond overlooked by wildlife observation hides (to view swans and cygnets).

Dallas Dhu Historic Distillery (HS; one mile south of Forres off the A940, ☎ 1309-676 548; open April-Sept, 9:30am-6:30pm; call ahead for winter schedule; adult/concession/child £3.50/£2.60/£1). Built in 1898 to supply malt whisky for Wright and Greig's "Roderick Dhu" blend, the distillery is now a perfectly preserved time capsule of the distiller's art. See and hear how whisky was made through an audiovisual presentation and free audio guide, then sample a dram.

Tolquon Castle (HS; Pitmedden, By Ellon, 15 miles north of Aberdeen on the A920, ☎ 1651-851 286; open April-Sept, 9:30am-6:30pm; call ahead for winter schedule; adult/concession/child £2.20/£1.60/£0.75). The original early-15th-century tower built for the Forbes family was enlarged in 1584-89 with a large mansion around a courtyard. The castle is noted for its ornamented gatehouse.

■ Where To Stay & Eat

See the *Accommodation* and *Dining* price charts on pages 294 and 295.

 Knockomie Hotel (Grantown Road, Forres IV36 2SG, ☎ 1309-673 146, fax 1309-673 290, stay@knockomie.co.uk, www.knocko-mie.co.uk; B&B ££££, lunch ££, dinner £££). High-quality country-house hotel with 15 bedrooms individually decorated with soft furnishings and period furniture, some with four-poster beds, others with patios. The first-rate restaurant and informal bistro both serve traditional Scottish cuisine.

Kimberley Inn (Findhorn, ☎ 1309-690 492; £-££). The inn serves daily bar meals, including fresh local seafood and vegetarian options.

Ramnee Hotel (Victoria Road, Forres IV36 3BN, ☎ 1309-672 410, fax 1309-673 392, ramneehotel@btconnect.com, www.ramneehotel.net; B&B ££££, lunch £, dinner £££). Traditional town hotel set in two acres with spacious rooms, including four-poster beds. There is a choice of fine or informal dining.

Sherston House B&B (Hillhead, Forres IV36 2QT, ☎ 1309-671 087, fax 1343-850 535; B&B ££). Traditional house set in secluded gardens and grounds, with views across Findhorn Bay.

Tormhor B&B (11 High Street, Forres IV36 1BU, ☎/fax 1309-673 837, www.tormhor.com; open Mar-Oct; B&B £). Edwardian villa overlooking the fountains of Grant Park. The bedrooms are comfortable and cozy and there is a varied breakfast menu.

Tomintoul

Tomintoul (pronounced "tomin-towel") stands on the road between Deeside and Speyside, close to the **Cairngorm Mountains** and **Cromdale Hills**. It was established in 1776 by Alexander, 4th Duke of Gordon, and is attractively laid out with a long main street and central square. The **Glenlivet Estate**, **Glenlivet Distillery** and **Lecht** ski area are all nearby.

 INFORMATION SOURCES: The tourism office is at The Square, Tomintoul AB37 9ET, ☎/fax 1807-580 285, tomintoul@agtb.org; open Easter-Oct.

■ Special Events

Tomintoul Highland Games (July; ☎ 1807-580 246). Traditional Highland Games.

■ Attractions & Sights

Glenlivet Distillery (Glenlivet, Ballindalloch, near Tomintoul AB37 9DB, ☎ 1340-821 720, www.theglenlivet.com; open April-Oct, Mon-Sat, 10am-4pm; Sun, 12:30-4pm; admission £3). Whisky has been produced in the Livet valley since 1824. The distillery has an exhibition, guided tour, gift shop and café.

■ Adventures

Glenlivet Estate (Estate Office, Main Street, Tomintoul AB37 9EX, ☎ 1807-580 283, fax 1807-580 319, www.crownestate.co.uk/1601_glenlivet). The 58,000-acre Glenlivet Estate lies between the Ladder and Cromdale hills on the edge of the Cairngorms and is part of the Crown Estate. Its rolling hills provide a wonderful terrain for the outdoor enthusiast.

ADVENTURES ON GLENLIVET

Walking & Cycling: The estate provides over 100 miles of waymarked paths and cycle tracks, described in a free leaflet obtainable from the Estate Office.

Deerstalking & Grouse-shooting: Certain paths may be affected by roe deerstalking activities in the evening and early morning during April-June, and by grouse shooting at any time (except Sundays) from 12th August- September. If you are planning to walk or cycle, take care not to disturb shooting activities – check with the Ranger to find out whether your intended route will be affected.

Horseback riding: Lessons and trekking are available at St Bridget's Farm (Tomintoul, ☎ 1807-580 210).

Fishing: The rivers Avon (pronounced "arn") and Livet are major tributaries of the renowned Spey and provide quality salmon (12th February-30th September) and trout (15th March-30th October). Fishing is not permitted on Sundays by tradition. The fishing rights on Glenlivet are leased to local hotels and fishing associations, which can provide permits. For more information contact the Estate Ranger at ☎ 1807-580 283.

■ Where To Stay & Eat

See the *Accommodation* and *Dining* price charts on pages 294 and 295.

 Glen Avon Hotel (The Square, Tomintoul AB37 9ET, ☎ 1807-580 218, fax 1807-580 733, enquiries@glenavon-hotel.co.uk, www.glenavonhotel.co.uk; B&B ££). Small, family-run inn offering basic but pleasant accommodation. There is restaurant and bar food, and beer brewed locally at the Tomintoul brewery.

Gordon Hotel (The Square, Tomintoul AB37 9ET, ☎ 1807-580 206, fax 1807-580 488, reservations@whiskytrail.com, www.whiskytrail.com; open April-Oct; B&B £££, dinner ££). The hotel has spacious, comfortable rooms. The restaurant emphasizes Scottish favorites cooked with local produce; the separate bar menu concentrates on hearty homemade dishes.

Findron Farm B&B (Tomintoul, Ballindalloch AB37 9ER, ☎/fax 1807-580 382, enquiries@findronfarmhouse.co.uk, www.findronfarmhouse.co.uk; B&B £). A delightful, high standard B&B based on a 200-acre beef-cattle farm a short distance from Tomintoul. A cozy guest lounge and bright conservatory/breakfast room complement the well-furnished bedrooms. Afternoon tea with homemade cakes is a real treat.

Mace Foodstore (34 Main Street, Tomintoul AB37 9EX, ☎ 1807-580 205; £). Sells hot takeaways (the steak pies are excellent) and sandwiches throughout the day.

Croft Inn (Glenlivet, Ballindalloch, near Tomintoul AB37 9DP, ☎ 1807-590 361; ££). An 18th-century inn looking out over Ben Rinnes with a large garden and restaurant sunroom. The varied menu features local meats, game and fish, and the bar offers over 50 malt whiskies to enjoy by the cozy peat fire.

Royal Deeside & Donside

It was so calm and so solitary, it did me good as one gazed around; and the pure mountain air was most refreshing. All seemed to breathe freedom and peace, and to make one forget the world and its sad turmoils.

From Queen Victoria's *Highland Journals*, 8th September 1848.

The **River Dee** rises at 4,000 feet (1,219 m) on the vast plateau of Braeriach in the heart of the Cairngorm Mountains and flows 85 miles (136 km) through mountains and moorland, forests and farmland to the North Sea at Aberdeen. The Dee's clear waters provide famous salmon fishing and important income for the local economy. To the north of the Dee, the **River Don** follows a shorter, almost parallel course.

■ Victorian Heritage Trail

The Dee Valley became known as **Royal Deeside** after its long association with the Royal Family, which began during the reign of Queen Victoria. The Victorian Heritage Trail – marked by white-on-brown signs with a Queen Victoria profile – takes you to castles, distilleries and viewpoints, By Royal appointment! A leaflet is available from local tourism offices.

Royal Deeside Walking Week (May; ☎ 13397-55467, info@royal-deeside.org.uk, www.royal-deeside.org.uk) helps you enjoy a stroll or something more strenuous through the spectacular scenery of Royal Deeside with other walkers and guides.

■ Banchory

Banchory is a Deeside holiday town with a museum and good range of shops and facilities. Salmon can be seen leaping up the falls at the **Bridge of Feugh**. Nearby are the impressive castles of **Crathes** and **Drum**.

INFORMATION SOURCES: The tourism office is at Bridge Street, Banchory AB31 5SX, ☎ 1330-822 000, banchory@agtb.org; open Easter-Oct.

Attractions & Sights

Crathes Castle (NTS; Banchory AB31 5QJ, ☎ 1330-844 525, fax 1330-844 797, crathes@nts.org.uk; castle open April-Sept, 10am-5:30pm; Oct, 10am-4:30pm; grounds open year-round, 9am-sunset; adult/concession/family £9/£6.50/£23, plus £2 parking). Crathes is the seat of the ancient Burnett family, granted the lands of Leys by Robert the Bruce in 1323. The castle, a fine example of a 16th-century tower house, was built in two stages: the first two floors in 1552-54 and the top two floors in 1594-96. The castle contains many fine period rooms; the top-floor gallery, with its wood paneling and garden views, is particularly impressive. The walled gardens, with their magnificent yew hedges, and woodland gardens make for interesting strolls around the grounds. The castle has a licensed restaurant.

Drum Castle (NTS; Drumoak, By Banchory AB31 5EY, ☎ 1330-811 204, fax 1330-811 962, drum@nts.org.uk, www.drum-castle.org.uk; open April-Sept, 12:30-5:30pm; June-Aug opens at 10am; adult/concession/family £7/£5.25/£19, plus £2 parking). The castle's tower dates from 1286 and is one of the oldest and best-preserved tower houses surviving in Scotland. A small extension was built in the 15th century, and the main Jacobean mansion was built in the 17th century. A gallery and courtyard were added in Victorian times. Alexander, the 17th laird, hid for three years in a tiny secret room after escaping from the Battle of Culloden. The tower's sturdy walls (up to 13 feet/4m thick) reflect turbulent times during the Wars of Independence. The tower's low hall was incorporated into the Jacobean mansion house and later the Victorian library; the rest of the tower (which originally housed the laird's chambers, and is accessible by a narrow stair) was abandoned and remains in its medieval state. The Irvine family lived here until 1975. The grounds contain a pretty walk through ancient oak woodland and an old walled garden with a collection of historic roses. There is also a tearoom.

Where To Stay & Eat

See the *Accommodation* and *Dining* price charts on pages 294 and 295.

Douglas Arms Hotel (22 High Street, Banchory AB31 5SR, ☎ 1330-822 547, fax 1330-825 989, gogsmac@aol.com, www.douglasarms.co.uk; B&B ££). Victorian coaching inn dating from 1840-50 with eight comfortable bedrooms, two bars and a restaurant. The inn is one of the oldest buildings in Banchory.

Raemoir House Hotel (Raemoir, Banchory AB31 4ED, ☎ 1330-824 884, fax 1330-822 171, www.raemoir.com; B&B £££, lunch ££, dinner £££). Stylish and

Dunfermline Abbey

Above: Toward Isle of Skye from Dun Caan, Raasay

Below: Village of Crovie on the Moray coast

Above: Evocative Glenfinnan Monument

Below: Coire Mhic Fhearchair, Torridon

Above: View from Glen Coe toward Ben Nevis

Below: Sandy cove in northwest Sutherland

romantic baronial mansion dating from around 1750 and set in 3,500 acres of forest and parkland. The individually styled rooms are sumptuous and luxurious. The beautiful, candlelit **Oval Ballroom** (dining room) serves top-quality food. Light lunches, tea and after dinner coffee are served in the magnificent **Morning Room** with its high ceiling and Victorian paneling.

Village Guest House (83 High Street, Banchory AB31 5PJ, ☎ 1330-823 307, www.guest-house83.freeserve.co.uk; B&B ££). Comfortable accommodation in a tartan-furnished Victorian house.

The Milton Restaurant (Crathes, Banchory AB31 5QH, ☎ 1330-844 566, fax 1330-844 666, reservations@themilton.co.uk, www.themilton.co.uk; lunch £, dinner ££-£££). All-day fine dining, including innovative evening menus using local seasonal ingredients. Reservations advisable on weekends.

St Tropez Restaurant (22D Bridge Street, Banchory, ☎ 1330-822 216; closed Sun; dinner £££). Classic French seafood restaurant that also serves excellent duck and Scottish beef.

Migvie House (By Logie Coldstone, Aboyne, between Banchory and Ballater, AB34 4XL, ☎ 13398-81313, fax 13398-81635; open Mar-Oct; B&B ££). Attractive house nestling in quiet grounds with antiques, country furnishings, wood fires and fine mountain views. Breakfast includes homemade bread and preserves, and eggs from the owners' hens.

Struan Hall (Ballater Road, Aboyne AB34 5HY, ☎/fax 13398-87241, struanhall@zetnet.co.uk, www.struanhall.co.uk; open Jan-Oct; B&B ££). High-quality accommodation set quietly in two acres of woodland garden, close to the village of Aboyne.

■ Ballater

Ballater is a picturesque village framed by the River Dee and an impressive backdrop of forested mountains. Ever since Queen Victoria and Prince Albert first came to **Balmoral**, the village has enjoyed a long Royal association. Members of the Royal Family can often be seen in local shops during the summer, and many Royal Warrants are displayed in the village. Even the local fish and chip shop boasts royal connections! The **Old Royal Station** is a finely restored exhibition describing the history of royal rail travel to the village. Near Ballater is the hamlet of **Crathie**, famous for the church (Crathie Kirk) the Royal Family attends when in residence, and Royal Lochnagar Distillery.

INFORMATION SOURCES: There are tourism offices at Ballater (The Old Royal Station, Station Square, Ballater AB35 5RB, ☎ 13397-55306, fax 13397-54088, ballater@agtb.org; open year-round) and **Crathie** (The Car Park, Crathie, Ballater, ☎ 13397-42414, crathie@agtb.org; open Easter-Oct).

Special Events

Ballater Victoria Week & Highland Games (Aug; ☎ 13397-55467, ☎ 13397-55771, info@royal-deeside.org.uk, www.royal-deeside.org.uk). Celebrate Ballater's history and royal connections, with a program of music, theater and the Ballater Highland Games.

Attractions & Sights

Balmoral Castle (Balmoral, Ballater AB35 5TB, ☎ 13397-42534, fax 13397-42034, info@balmoralcastle.com, www.balmoralcastle.com; open April-Jul, 10am-5pm; adult/concession/child £5/£4/£1, parking £0.50). Queen Victoria and her consort Prince Albert fell in love with the castle, which was originally a 16th-century tower house, and bought it in 1852. Victoria treasured the freedom and peace she found at Balmoral, her "dear paradise." She and Albert completed the present castle in 1855 and it remains the Scottish holiday home of the Royal Family, who visit each summer and early autumn. The driveway to the castle is lined with towering conifers. The grounds, garden, carriage room and ballroom exhibition are open to the public and there are also shops, walks and café.

AUTHOR'S NOTE: *Be clear that there is no castle tour at Balmoral. Photographs and memorabilia in the ballroom exhibition are as far as you will get within the Royal residence.*

QUEEN VICTORIA AND BALMORAL

Queen Victoria and her beloved consort Prince Albert paid their first visit to the Scottish Highlands in 1842 and so began a royal holiday tradition that continues to this day. In September 1848, on her very first night at Balmoral, the queen wrote delightedly in her journal: "It was so calm and so solitary... All seemed to breathe freedom and peace, and to make one forget the world and its sad turmoils." Over the next seven years, the present Balmoral castle was built to accommodate the growing Royal Family. Those halcyon days were shattered in 1861 when Prince Albert fell sick of typhoid and died three weeks later. The Queen was desolate and subsided into a deep mourning that lasted decades. As the years progressed, she spent more and more time at Balmoral – a month in May and as much as three months in autumn – because it was so full of her happiest memories and provided the solitude she craved.

Crathie Parish Church – "Crathie Kirk" (Crathie; open April-Oct, Mon-Sat, 9:30am-5pm & Sun, 12:45pm-5pm, Sunday service 11:30am, all welcome; admission free). Crathie Kirk is one of the best known parish churches in Scotland because of its long association with the Royal Family. Queen Victoria worshipped in the previous church for 45 years and participated enthusiastically in plans for the new church. Built of local granite, the new church was dedicated in the presence of Queen Victoria in June 1895.

The church is cruciform in plan, with a semi-circular apse to the east. The interior is Gothic, and has round granite pillars supporting four pointed arches at the crossing of the nave and transepts. The Queen and Royal Family regularly worship here when residing at Balmoral; they traditionally use the south transept and south porch. The church contains many gifts and memorials presented by the Royal Family.

Crathie Kirkyard The kirkyard contains the ruins of the pre-Reformation church. Among the graves of local farmers and shepherds are tombstones erected by Queen Victoria in memory of her faithful retainers. An interpretive board in the kirkyard gives more detailed information.

The Old Royal Station (Station Square, Ballater, ☎ 13397-55306; open year-round; July-Aug, 9:30am-7pm; hours are shorter in other months, call ahead). Restored Victorian railway station containing fascinating displays on its 100 years as the scene of frequent arrivals and departures by the Royal Family and their guests, including the unique **Royal Waiting Room**. Queen Victoria first visited Ballater in October 1866, and over the years almost every member of European royalty visited Victoria at Balmoral. Five subsequent generations of British royalty used Ballater station until 15th October 1965; Queen Elizabeth II made the last royal train journey from the station before it closed the following year.

Royal Lochnagar Distillery (Crathie, Ballater AB35 5TB; ☎ 13397-42700, fax 13397-42702; open May-Sept, Mon-Sat, 10am-5pm; Sun, noon-4pm; Oct-Apr, Mon-Fri, 11am-4pm; admission £4, including a shop voucher). John Begg founded the beautifully situated distillery in 1845. Three years later Queen Victoria, Prince Albert and their two young sons visited and were given a distillery tour.

To get to the distillery, cross Balmoral Bridge and continue uphill past the castle. After your visit, you might find people peering into your car as you drive back across Balmoral Bridge assuming you've just had tea with the Queen.

Adventures

On Foot

 The **Deeside Railway** line to Ballater closed in 1966 and its railbed is now a walkway and cycle path. Starting from Station Square, gain the platform and track and follow it out of town. The track soon becomes a delightful fenced path. Cross the A93 road and pass the ruined 15th-century church and graveyard of Kirkton of Tullich on your left. The Dee appears on your right and stays in view to Cambus o'May with its elegant suspension bridge. Past the colorful Cambus Cottage, there is a fine view of the wide sweep of the river. The path becomes a straight, broad sandy track, fringed by birch and pine trees, and rejoins the road at Dinnet. Return by the same route or catch the bus back to Ballater (perhaps after visiting the inn in Dinnet) (2-3 hours one-way; easy).

The **Pannanich Woods Circular Walk** is a steep climb through woodland to a surprisingly impressive view of Ballater and the Dee Valley. From Ballater village, cross the bridge over the Dee to the road junction. Cross the road and take the path opposite, which rises left (northeast) up the hill, turning right when you reach the forestry track. The path turns left and climbs uphill through woods to the radio mast and viewpoint. Retrace your steps from the viewpoint to the track and follow it left, steadily downhill. You emerge at a small parking area on the South Deeside Road, from where you can complete the loop by following a forest track back to the road and Ballater Bridge (2 hours; moderate).

You can arrange deerstalking and game shooting through **Scotsport Travel**, Turner Hall Shooting Lodge, Cambus o'May, near Ballater AB35 5SD, ☎ 13397-55032, fax 13397-55908, scotsportuk@compuserve.com.

On Water

The salmon fishing on the **River Dee** is world-famous; to the north of the Dee, the **River Don** follows a shorter, almost parallel course. Inquire at the tourism center or at your hotel.

On Wheels

You can rent mountain bikes from **Wheels & Reels** (2 Braemar Road, Ballater AB35 5RL, ☎ 13397-55864).

In the Air

Deeside Gliding Club (Aboyne Airfield, Dinnet AB34 5LB, ☎/fax 13398-85339, office@deesideglidingclub.co.uk, www.deeside.gliding-club.co.uk) offers high altitude and cross-country flights over the beautiful Deeside area. Trial lessons (£50) and glider rental are available.

On Horseback

 Balmoral Castle (☎ 13397-42534, fax 13397-42034, trek-king@balmoralcastle.com, www.balmoralcastle.com; April-Jul, daily except Thurs, 10am & 2pm, £30 for two hours; full-day treks departing at 10am and returning at 4pm, for experienced riders, £70). Pony trekking over the Queen's Scottish estate on Balmoral's stalking ponies. Minimum age 12, no experience needed for the two-hour treks. Advance booking recommended.

Balmenach Pony Trekking (Balmenach, Pass of Ballater, Ballater, ☎ 13397-55660, info@balmenachtrekking.co.uk, www.balmenachtrek-king.co.uk). Traffic-free treks from a half-hour to four hours or more for riders of all abilities aged 12 and over.

Glen Tanar Equestrian Centre (Glen Tanar, Aboyne AB34 5EU, ☎ 13398-86448). Lessons and one- to two-hour rides along riverside, woodland and mountain trails in Royal Deeside.

Where To Stay & Eat

See the *Accommodation* and *Dining* price charts on pages 294 and 295.

Darroch Learg Hotel (Braemar Road, Ballater AB35 5UX, ☎ 13397-55443, fax 13397-55252, info@darrochlearg.co.uk; open Feb-Dec; B&B £££-££££, lunch £££, dinner ££££). Attractive hotel enjoying great views from its position high up on a rocky hillside. The hotel offers quality accommodation and excellent modern Scottish cooking.

Glen Lui Hotel (Invercauld Road, Ballater AB35 5RP, ☎ 13397-55402, fax 13397-55545, infos@glen-lui-hotel.co.uk, www.glen-lui-hotel.co.uk; B&B ££, dinner ££). Mid-range country-house hotel offering good views and inexpensive dining.

The Green Inn (9 Victoria Road, Ballater AB35 5QQ, ☎ 13397-55701, fax 13397-56357, info@green-inn.com, www.green-inn.com; B&B ££, dinner £££). Seriously good regional Scottish cooking with international influences. Comfortable guestrooms are also available.

Hilton Craigendarroch (Braemar Road, Ballater AB35 5XA, ☎ 13397-55858, fax 13397-55447, www.hilton.com; B&B ££££, dinner ££-£££). Set in 29 acres of woodland, the hotel offers stylish accommodation, a choice of restaurants and country club facilities, including pools, sauna, gym and beauty salon.

Monaltrie Lodge (Bridge Square, Ballater AB35 5QJ, ☎/fax 13397-55296, bhepburn@talk21.com, www.castlesandgolfcottages.co.uk; B&B ££). Traditional Victorian villa originally the lodge for nearby Monaltrie House. The rooms are well-equipped and comfortable and the generous decanter of sherry is a nice touch. Dinner, by prior arrangement, is skilfully prepared using fresh local produce.

Belvedere Guest House (Station Square, Ballater AB35 5QB, ☎ 13397-55996, fax 13397-55110, flora-ingram@freeuk.com; B&B ££). Reasonably priced guest house with a delightfully furnished traditional interior.

Rowan Tree Restaurant (Netherley Place, Ballater AB35 5QE, ☎ 13397-55191, hayarchie@aol.com, www.rowantree-restaurant-ballater.co.uk; ££). Freshly baked cakes and scones every day and a daily specials board.

Silver Teapot (8 Bridge Street, Ballater AB35 5QP, ☎ 13397-55694; £). Homemade soups, home baking, baked potatoes, toasties and bacon rolls.

Station Restaurant (Station Square, Ballater, ☎ 13397-55050; £-££). Popular coffee shop and restaurant in the Old Royal Station serving home baking and fresh food all day.

■ Braemar

Braemar is the eastern gateway to the Cairngorms and most famous for its world-renowned Highland Games – the **Braemar Gathering** – which is attended by the Royal Family. **Braemar Castle** and **Highland Heritage Centre** are also worth a visit.

INFORMATION SOURCES: The tourism office is at The Mews, Mar Road, Braemar AB35 5YP, ☎ 13397-41600, fax 13397-41643, braemar@agtb.org; open year-round.

Special Events

Braemar Telemark Festival (Mar; 13 Huntly Cottages, Aboyne AB34 5HD, ☎ 13398-86520/13397-41242, info@telemarkfestival.co.uk, www.tele-markfestival.co.uk). International "free heel" ski event with competitions, demonstrations and instruction on the slopes of Braemar and Glenshee.

Braemar Gathering (first Sat in Sep; Braemar Royal Highland Society, Coilacriech, Ballater AB35 5UH, ☎/fax 13397-55377, info@braemarga-thering.org, www.braemargathering.org). The most famous of Highland Games attracts huge crowds and marks the grand finale of the Highland Games calendar. Advance booking is essential if you want a seat.

Attractions & Sights

Braemar Castle (half a mile northeast of Braemar on the A93, ☎ 13397-41219, fax 13397-41252, invercauld@freenet.co.uk, www.brae-marcastle.co.uk; open April-Oct, 10am-6pm; closed Fridays except in July-Aug; adult/concession/child £3.50/£3/£1.50). An impressive castle built in 1628, Braemar was used by Hanoverian troops after the 1745 Rising and later transformed into a private residence by the Farquharsons of Invercauld. The L-plan castle is protected by a star-shaped curtain wall, and its central round-tower has barrel-vaulted ceilings and an underground prison. The interior contains fine furniture, paintings and curios such as a section of a plaid worn by Bonnie Prince Charlie.

Braemar Highland Heritage Centre (Mar Road, Braemar AB35 5YL, ☎ 13397-41944; admission free). An audiovisual presentation and informa-tion panels explain the famous Braemar Gathering and its royal patronage. There is also a specialist clan and tartan shop.

Where To Stay & Eat

See the *Accommodation* and *Dining* price charts on pages 294 and 295.

 Braemar Lodge Hotel (Glenshee Road, Braemar AB35 5YQ, ☎/fax 13397-41627, info@braemarlodge.co.uk, www.braemarlodge.co.uk; B&B ££). Former Victorian shooting lodge offering homely accommo-dation, good local cuisine and the cozy **Malt Lounge**, offering a choice of 80 whiskies. Log cabins and a bunkhouse are also available.

Callater Lodge Hotel (9 Glenshee Road, Braemar AB35 5YQ, ☎ 13397-41275, fax 13397-41345, bookings@hotel-braemar.co.uk, www.hotel-braemar.co.uk; B&B ££). Pretty Victorian villa standing in spa-cious grounds offering good home cooking and evening meals by arrange-ment.

Gordon's Tearoom & Restaurant (20 Mar Road, Braemar, ☎ 13397-41247; £). Family-run tearoom and restaurant serving traditional Scottish break-fasts, snacks and main meals, with daily specials available.

■ Donside

North of Royal Deeside is Donside, an area that is also beautiful but much more peaceful and less visited. Donside is rich in scenery and heritage, particularly boasting **Corgarff**, **Craigievar**, **Fraser** and **Kildrummy** castles, and hosts the famous **Lonach Gathering**.

Special Events

Lonach Gathering (fourth Saturday in August; Lonach Highland and Friendly Society, Railway Cottage, Bellabeg, Strathdon AB36 8UL, ☎ 19756-51297/51302, enquiries@lonach.info, www.lonach.org). Lonach is one of the oldest Highland Games and incorporates the march of The Men of Lonach in full Highland dress, armed with pikes and battleaxes. Comedian Billy Connolly owns a house nearby, and in recent years has invited showbiz friends to the event, including Steve Martin, Judi Dench and Robin Williams.

 INFORMATION SOURCES: There are tourism offices at Alford (Old Station Yard, Main Street, Alford AB33 8FD, ☎ 19755-62052, alford@agtb.org; open Easter-Sept) and **Inverurie** (18 High Street, Inverurie AB51 3XQ, ☎ 1467-625 800, inverurie@agtb.org; open year-round).

Attractions & Sights

 **Castle Fraser** (NTS; Sauchen, Inverurie AB51 7LD, ☎ 1330-833 463, fax 1330-833 819, castlefraser@nts.org.uk; open April-Sept, Fri-Tues, noon-5:30pm; from 11am in July-Aug; adult/concession/family £7/£5.25/£9, £2 parking). Built in 1575-1636 by the 6th laird, Michael Fraser, the castle is the most elaborate Z-plan fortress in Scotland. The interior houses many historic furnishings, family portraits and embroidery. The strikingly simple **Great Hall** is often used for concerts and events. The walled garden features shrubs, flowers, wall-trained fruit and vegetables. There are waymarked estate walks through mixed woodland and open farmland, and a tearoom.

Corgarff Castle (HS; Corgarff, eight miles west of Strathdon on the A939, ☎ 1975-651 460; open year-round; April-Sept, 9:30am-6:30pm; off-season schedule varies, call ahead; adult/concession/child £3/£2.30/£1). A lonely 16th-century towerhouse isolated on a bleak moor, whose allure and historical importance far outweigh its stark appearance. Above a storage basement was the main room – the hall – over which was a large private chamber and garret. Other buildings, including a stable, bakehouse and brewhouse, are clustered around the tower, sheltering within a stone perimeter wall. Corgarff's eventful history saw 24 residents burned to death in 1571 when the castle was set ablaze by supporters of the deposed Mary, Queen of Scots. Jacobite supporters of the exiled James VII burned the castle again in 1689 to prevent its use by the forces of William of Orange. The castle played a prominent role in the Jacobite Risings of 1715 and 1745 and, after Culloden, became a military barracks. Low pavilions were added, together with a star-shaped defensive wall with musket slits. Inside the castle is a re-creation of a soldiers' barrack room from 1750. The castle's final role was to control illicit whisky smuggling (ironically, a previous tenant operated a distillery here) between 1827 and 1831, when the last garrison pulled out.

Craigievar Castle (NTS; Alford AB33 8JF, ☎ 13398-83635, fax 13398-83280; castle open April-Sept, Fri-Tues, noon-5:30pm; grounds open year-round, 9:30am-sunset; adult/concession/family £9/£6.50/£23, £1 parking). Craigievar is a fairytale castle exemplifying the best of Scottish baronial architecture; its simple lower towers contrast wonderfully with the turrets, cupolas and corbelling that embellish the roofline. Built in 1626, the castle houses a great collection of family portraits and 17th- and 18th-century furniture. The castle remains largely as it was when last occupied as a family home by the Forbes-Sempills in 1963.

Kildrummy Castle (HS; Kildrummy, 10 miles southwest of Alford on the A97, ☎ 1975-571 331; open April-Sept, 9:30am-6:30pm; adult/conces-sion/child £2.20/£1.60/£0.75). The ruin of a fine 13th-century courtyard castle with a curtain wall, four round towers, hall and chapel. The ancient seat of the Earls of Mar, Kildrummy was where the 1715 Jacobite Rising was orga-nized, and it was dismantled after the rising failed.

Adventures

 The Lecht (Strathdon AB36 8YP, ☎ 1975-651 440, fax 1975-651 426, info@lecht.co.uk, www.lecht.co.uk). The Lecht straddles the Cockbridge-Tomintoul road in the Eastern Cairngorms. With a top station at only 2,551 feet (778 m) it is Scotland's lowest ski area but compen-sates for this with the largest snowmaking facilities. Its low elevation some-times provides protection from the winds that blight Scottish skiing and allows The Lecht to open when higher, more exposed resorts can't. Being cov-ered in heather rather than rocks, The Lecht also requires less snow coverage to be skiable and is often the first of the Scottish resorts to open (occasionally in October!). The best skiing is usually found in January-February.

SKIING THE LECHT

- Base elevation: 2,090 feet (637 m)

- Skiing range: 2,090 feet (637 m) to 2,551 feet (778 m)

- Pisted runs: 12 miles (20 km)

- Longest run: ½ mile (0.9 km)

- Maximum vertical descent: 700 feet (213 m)

- Lifts: 15

- Runs: 21 (easy 33%, intermediate 33%, difficult 30%, very difficult 4%)

- Mountain restaurants/cafés: 1

- Snow reports: ☎ 19756-51440, BBC Ceefax page 421, NECR Radio 102.6 FM, www.lecht.co.uk.

The majority of the skiing is on the north-facing valley face. Unusually, most lifts operate from road level. Runs (really just one run replicated several times) are short and not that challenging, but are perfect for beginners and early intermediates who can cruise on wide slopes accessed by four easy tows.

The **Falcon** and **Harrier** lifts, and the **Buzzard** lift on the southfacing side of the valley, access more interesting runs for better skier. With a low risk of avalanches and getting lost (all descents finish at the road), skiers can investigate areas away from the marked trails on both sides of the valley. For wannabe racers, The Lecht offers race training each weekend.

Shopping

Goodbrand Knitwear (Corgarff, Strathdon AB36 8YL, ☎ 19756-51433, fax 19756-51442, mail@highlandtradingpost.co.uk, www.highlandtradingpost.co.uk). Knitwear, textiles, jewelry, books, Scottish music and gifts, as well as equipment rental and instruction in skiing the Lecht. An excellent café serves fresh sandwiches and home baking.

Where To Stay & Eat

See the *Accommodation* and *Dining* price charts on pages 294 and 295.

 Colquhonnie Hotel (Strathdon AB36 8UN, ☎ 19756-51210, fax 19756-51347, colquhonnie@aol.com, www.colquhonnie-hotel.co.uk; B&B ££, dinner ££). Friendly, family-run hotel sitting on a natural terrace with excellent views over the Don valley. Close to the whisky and castle trails, the hotel enjoys nine miles of fine trout and some salmon fishing. Log fires warm the lounge (which incorporates a small antiques shop) and bar, and the romantic dining room serves excellent home-cooked meals. The 200-year-old hotel began life as a coaching inn and is believed to be haunted by the bagpipe-playing ghost of one of three consecutive lairds killed supervising the construction of neighboring Colquhonnie Castle.

Kildrummy Castle Hotel (Kildrummy, By Alford AB33 8RA, ☎ 19755-71288, fax 19755-71345, bookings@kildrummycastlehotel.co.uk, www.kildrummycastlehotel.co.uk; open Feb-Dec; B&B ££££, dinner £££). Top-quality accommodation in a converted mansion set in acres of gardens and woodland. Oak-paneled walls and ceilings, wall tapestries, hand-carved staircase and roaring log fires complete the scene and the restaurant serves excellent local cuisine.

Porter's Organic Restaurant (Burnett Arms Hotel, Kemnay, near Inverurie, ☎ 1467-642 208; ££-£££). Excellent organic restaurant.

Northeast Aberdeenshire

Aberdeen's northeast corner is varied and little visited. Many of its communities have grown up beside the sea, leaving the coastline with a legacy of castles, fishing communities and tiny harbors, their buildings often brightly painted as traditional protection against salty winds. These picturesque villages (such as **Portsoy**, **Crovie** and **Pennan**) and larger fishing ports (such as **Peterhead** and **Fraserburgh**) are interspersed between deserted beaches and high cliffs teeming with birdlife.

Castle Trail. Aberdeenshire has more castles per acre than any other region of Britain, mostly of the turreted fairytale variety rather than colossal medieval fortresses. The Castle Trail – marked by white-on-brown signs with a blue castle logo – links together a collection of the finest, including **Craigievar, Castle Fraser, Fyvie** and **Corgarff**. You don't have to stick rigidly to the official trail, though. Several of the region's finest castles – including **Crathes, Drum** and the Royal castle of **Balmoral** – aren't on the Castle Trail.

AUTHOR'S TIP: *If you plan to visit Aberdeenshire's castles, you'll save money by buying passes from the **National Trust for Scotland** (☎ 131-243 9300, www.nts.org.uk) and / or Historic Scotland (☎ 131-668 8600, www.historic-scotland.net), which manage many of the heritage properties in the area. A brochure is available from tourism offices.*

Coastal Trail. Aberdeenshire's northeast coast is unspoiled, varied and dotted with small fishing communities huddled around tiny, often ancient, harbors. The Coastal Trail – marked by white-on-brown signs with a blue anchor logo – takes you on a coastal journey from **Findhorn** to **St Cyrus** (a total distance of 166 miles, although you can drive shorter sections of the trail). Pick up a brochure at local tourism offices.

INFORMATION SOURCES: The tourism office is at 9a The Square, Huntly AB54 8BR, ☎ 1466-792 255, huntly@agtb.org; open Easter-Oct.

■ Attractions & Sights

Archaeolink Prehistory Park (Oyne, Insch AB52 6QP, 10 miles northwest of Inverurie, ☎ 1464-851 500, fax 1464-851 544, info@archaeolink.co.uk, www.archaeolink.co.uk; open April-Oct, 11am-5pm; adult/concession/child/family £4.25/£3.50/£3/£13). Explore ancient history, from Stone Age settlements to a Roman marching camp, with interactive displays, reconstructions, craft demos, *Myths and Legends* exhibition and audiovisual presentation. There is a gift hall and coffee shop.

Delgatie Castle (Delgatie, Turriff AB53 5TD, 37 miles northwest of Aberdeen, ☎/fax 1888-563 479, www.delgatiecastle.com; open April-Oct, 10am-5pm; adult/concession £3/£2). Eleventh-century castle with fine original 16th-century painted ceilings and unusually wide turnpike stair built within the thickness of the wall. The castle has been owned by the Hay family for most of the last 650 years, since it was taken from the Earl of Buchan in 1314 after the Battle of Bannockburn.

Fyvie Castle (NTS; Fyvie, Turriff AB53 8JS, 25 miles northwest of Aberdeen, ☎ 1651-891 266, fax 1651-891 107; castle open April-Sept, Fri-Tues, noon-5pm; from 11am in July-Aug; grounds open year-round,

9:30am-sunset; adult/concession/family £7/£5.25/£19, £2 parking). Fyvie was once a royal stronghold, one of a chain of fortresses throughout medieval Scotland, and is associated with many ghosts and legends. The oldest part of the castle dates from the 13th century and within its walls is a great wheel stair. 17th-century paneling and plaster ceilings survive in the **Morning Room** as do the opulent Edwardian interiors created by the first Lord Leith of Fyvie. There are collections of portraits, arms and armour and 17th-century tapestries. The grounds and loch were landscaped in the early 19th century. The 18th-century walled garden has been redeveloped to show the variety of fruits and vegetables that can be grown in the Scottish climate; the castle also has a tearoom.

Haddo House (NTS; Ellon AB41 7EQ, 19 miles north of Aberdeen; ☎ 1651-851 440, fax 1651-851 888, haddo@nts.org.uk; house open Jun-Aug, 11am-4:30pm, days vary, call ahead; garden open year-round, 9:30am-6pm; adult/concession/family £7/£5.25/£19). This grand house is unusual for Aberdeenshire in that it was not built as a castle. Dating from 1732 and refurbished in the 1880s, Haddo blends neat Georgian lines with sumptuous Victorian interiors. The house is noted for its fine furniture, paintings and objets d'art. Personal portraits, monuments and memorabilia relating to the Gordon family (who have lived at Haddo for over 400 years) are scattered throughout the house and grounds. There is also a tearoom.

Leith Hall (NTS; Huntly AB54 4NQ, 34 miles northwest of Aberdeen, ☎ 1464-831 216, fax 1464-831 594, leithhall@nts.org.uk; house open Easter weekend and May-Sept, Fri-Tues, noon-5pm; garden open year-round, 9:30am-sunset; adult/concession/family £7/£5.25/£19). Charming family home built in the style of a small castle; collections include furniture, artwork, tapestry, military memorabilia and personal items relating the history of the Leith-Hay family over the last four centuries. At the top of the garden is a **Chinese moon gate** that provides superb views of the surrounding hills. Nearby is a small collection of Pictish stones. On the grounds are waymarked woodland walks, 18th-century stables, an icehouse and a tearoom.

Huntly Castle (HS; in Huntly on the A96, ☎ 1466-793 191; open April-Sept, 9:30am-6:30pm; hours vary in other months, call ahead; adult/concession/child £3.30/£2.50/£1). Impressive ruin of a castle in a beautiful setting by the **River Deveron**. The castle was the stronghold of the Gordon family and its architectural details, including fine heraldic sculpture and inscribed stone friezes, are particularly fine.

■ Peterhead

Peterhead is Europe's busiest fishing port with over 400 boats and a bustling daily fish market. The **Maritime Heritage Centre** (The Lido, South Road, Peterhead, ☎ 1779-473 000; open June-Aug, Mon-Sat, 10:30am-5pm; Sun, 11:30am-5pm; adult/concession/family £3/£2/£7) tells the story of the town and its people's connections with fishing and whaling.

Ugie Salmon Fishings (Golf Road, Peterhead AB42 6NF, ☎ 1779-476 209, fax 1779-471 475, sales@ugie-salmon.co.uk, www.ugie-salmon.co.uk), Scotland's oldest salmon fish-house, sells directly to the public from its web site or its 400-year-old building on the banks of the River Ugie.

Adventures

Slains Castle & the Bullers of Buchan is an excellent coastal walk offering cliff paths, plentiful birdlife and the dramatic ruins of "Dracula's Castle." From Cruden Bay, walk along the track toward Port Erroll to join the coastal footpath, signposted to the Bullers of Buchan and beyond. Slains Castle soon comes into view. Its striking cliff-top position holds extra menace, as it was supposedly Bram Stoker's inspiration for Dracula's lair. The castle is a vast mansion built by the Earls of Errol in 1836 on the site of a smaller 16th-century fortress. Continue northwards to reach the cliffs and natural arches known as the Bullers of Buchan. The path follows the edge of a 200-foot (60-m) cliff that provides nesting for thousands of seabirds, including kittiwakes, fulmars, gannets and occasionally puffins. The noise from the birds and the crashing waves can be tremendous (3-4 hours; easy).

Golf

Cruden Bay Golf Course (18-hole links, 6,396 yards; Aulton Road, Cruden Bay, By Peterhead AB42 0NN, ☎ 1779-812 285, fax 1779-812 945, cbaygc@aol.com, www.crudenbaygolfclub.co.uk; green fees £55-£65). A historic course offering old-fashioned links golf of the highest quality.

Where To Stay & Eat

See the *Accommodation* and *Dining* price charts on pages 294 and 295.

Palace Hotel (Prince Street, Peterhead AB42 1PL, ☎ 1779-474 821, fax 1779-476 119, info@palacehotel.co.uk, www.palacehotel.co.uk; B&B ££, dinner ££). Not in fact a palace but a reasonably priced mid-range hotel with an attractive brasserie and lively bar-diner.

Invernettie Guest House (South Road, Peterhead AB42 0YX, ☎/fax 1779-473 530, kathleen@invernettie.co.uk, www.invernettie.co.uk; B&B ££). Comfortable guesthouse accommodation with all facilities wheelchair-accessible.

■ Fraserburgh

Fraserburgh is a major fishing port with great sandy beaches. The first Scottish lighthouse was built here in 1787 and, now decommissioned, forms part of the **Museum of Scottish Lighthouses**.

INFORMATION SOURCES: The tourism office is at 3 Saltoun Square, Fraserburgh AB43 9DA, ☎ 1346-518 315, fraserburgh@agtb.org; open Easter-Oct.

Attractions & Sights

Kinnaird Head Castle Lighthouse & **Museum of Scottish Lighthouses** (Kinnaird Head, Stevenson Road, Fraserburgh AB43 9DU, ☎ 1346-511 022, fax 1346-511 033, enquiries@lighthousemuseum.demon.co.uk, www.lighthousemuseum.co.uk; open year-round; hours vary seasonally; adult/concession/child/family £4.75/£4/£2/£12). Kinnaird Head was the Northern Lighthouse Board's first lighthouse (1787), and the only one ever to be built on top of a castle. It was reconstructed and developed in the early 19th century by the Stevenson family. Decommissioned in 1991, the original lighthouse and engine room are now preserved as they were when last in use. The museum houses a large collection of lighthouse lenses and equipment and tells the story of the Stevenson lighthouse-engineering dynasty. Guided climbs to the top of the lighthouse let you see impressive views of the Buchan Coast and port of Fraserburgh.

Where To Stay & Eat

See the *Accommodation* and *Dining* price charts on pages 294 and 295.

 Tufted Duck Hotel (St Combs, By Fraserburgh AB43 8ZS, ☎ 1346-582 481, fax 1346-582 475; B&B ££). Quiet hotel in the coastal village of St Combs, with views over the sea and freshly prepared meals.

White Horse Hotel & Restaurant (65 High Street, Strichen, By Fraserburgh AB43 6SQ, ☎ 1771-637 218, fax 1771-637 940, info@whhr.co.uk, www.whhr.co.uk; B&B ££, dinner ££-£££). The hotel has small but reasonably priced rooms. The à la carte and bar menus offer Scottish cooking with a modern influence and there is informal folk music on Tuesday evenings.

Galleon Bar Diner & Crows Nest Restaurant (145-147 Shore Street, Fraserburgh, ☎ 1346-517 308/515 354; ££). Bar-diner and restaurant offering an extensive menu from snacks to à la carte dining, with excellent views of the harbor and surrounding area. There is weekend entertainment.

Heath-Hill Restaurant & Bar (Muir Road, Memsie, By Fraserburgh, ☎ 1346-541 492; ££). Restaurant set in a barn that specializes in local meat and fish.

■ Pennan & Crovie

Pennan is a delightful old smugglers' village set at the foot of high cliffs. Its cluster of whitewashed buildings was the location for the 1983 film *Local Hero*, and its famous phone box is a listed historic monument. Nearby **Aberdour Bay** has sandy beaches, extensive sea caves and a 10th-century church associated with St Columba.

Crovie (pronounced "crivie") is a tiny village of simple stone, slate and pantiled houses occupying a narrow coastal strip at the base of high cliffs. This austere settlement was established by families cleared from the Highlands after the Jacobite Risings of 1715 and 1745. The coastal strip is so tightly squeezed between the cliffs and sea that villagers can only reachs their houses from a footpath along the sea wall. The original buildings sit gable-end to the sea to present the least resistance to the winter gales that sweep the coast. A severe storm in January 1953 washed away much of the sea wall and destroyed or badly damaged several houses. Residents moved away and

Crovie ceased to be an active fishing village, becoming instead a holiday village.

Adventures

The **Crovie & Troup Head** walk explores a fascinating coastal area dotted with tiny villages squeezed between the sea edge and high cliffs. Start at the small parking area at the Crovie viewpoint. Walk down the steep hill and steps into Crovie. Explore the village, then return to the foot of the steps, this time turning left, over a footbridge, past the house and up the track. Turn left at the junction, past Drumohr, and left again at the next junction on a stony track to Crovie Farm. Continue to the next junction and turn left up to North-field Farm. Past the farm, a track leads to a gateway into a field. Follow the right-hand edge of the field to the trig pillar on Troup Head. These 360-foot (110-m) cliffs are home to as many as 100,000 breeding seabirds, including guillemots, kittiwakes, razorbills and fulmars.

Return to the farm and back onto the road. Pass the junction (on the right) where you came down and continue to Protston, where you turn right to Stonewells. Keep left past the farm buildings and continue on a grassy track between fences, marked by a green arrow. The track drops downhill and bends sharply through a gully. Go through a gate, past Mink Howe, to a track where you turn left until you regain the Crovie road. Turn left and return uphill to the parking area (3-4 hours; easy/moderate).

■ Macduff, Banff & Portsoy

Macduff is a fishing port at the mouth of the **River Deveron** that is noted for impressive cliff scenery and a marine aquarium with a unique open-air central tank. Banff is a historic coastal town with many restored 18th-century buildings. Nearby is the splendid **Duff House**, now an outpost of the National Galleries of Scotland. Portsoy is an atmospheric conservation village build around an attractive 17th-century harbor. The village hosts a popular traditional boat festival each July.

Special Events

Scottish Traditional Boat Festival (Jul; The Old Mill Office, Burnside Street, Portsoy AB45 2QN, ☎ 1261-842 951, contact@scottishtraditionalboatfestival.co.uk, www.scottishtraditionalboatfestival.co.uk). Revel in the maritime and cultural heritage of the region through a program of sailing and maritime demonstrations, music, food, dance, crafts, ceilidh and concert.

INFORMATION SOURCES: The tourism office is at Collie Lodge, Banff AB45 1AU, ☎ 1261-812 419, banff@agtb.org; open Easter-Oct.

Attractions & Sights

Duff House (HS; Banff AB45 3SX, ☎ 1261-818 181, duff.house@aberdeenshire.gov.uk, www.duffhouse.com; April-Oct, 11am-5pm; Nov-Mar, Thurs-Sun, 11am-4pm; adult/concession £4.50/£3.50). A magnificent early-Georgian mansion designed by William Adam and acknowledged as his masterpiece. The house has been refurbished as a **Country House Gallery** – a collection of artwork displayed as it would be in a private home – in the care of the National Galleries of Scotland. In addition to works of art and an impressive library, Duff House has a shop, café and woodland walks.

Macduff Marine Aquarium (11 High Shore, Macduff AB44 1SL, ☎ 1261-833 369, fax 1261-831 052, macduffaquarium.ed@aberdeenshire-.gov.uk, www.marine-aquarium.com; open year-round, 10am-5pm; adult/concession/child/family £4.20/£2.35/£1.80/£10.70). An aquarium complex built around its principal attraction – a large central tank open to the sky and filled with fish, invertebrates and seaweeds. Watch talks, audiovisual presentations and divers feeding the fish. Other displays include a splash tank, rock pools, octopus display, ray pool and touch-pools where you can come to grips with some of the smaller inhabitants of the Moray Firth's waters.

Adventures

Faraway Riding & Recreation Centre (Forgue, near Huntly AB54 6DH (15 miles south of Banff), ☎ 1466-730 358, admin@farawayrrc.com, www.farawayrrc.com) offers riding instruction and hacking over rolling countryside and forestry tracks.

For the serious rider, **Highland Horseback** (Easter Bodylair, Glass, Huntly AB54 4XR, ☎/fax 1466-700 304, sales@highlandhorseback.co.uk, www.highlandhorseback.co.uk; £1,470/£785 per person, all-inclusive) offers two options for long trail rides: the "Long Ride" – 200 miles in eight days from Huntly to Kintail on the west coast; and the "Short Ride" – 100 miles in four days comprising either half of the "Long Ride."

Where To Stay & Eat

See the *Accommodation* and *Dining* price charts on pages 294 and 295.

 County Hotel (32 High Street, Banff AB45 1AE, ☎ 1261-815 353, fax 1261-818 335, enquiries@thecountyhotel.com, www.thecounty-hotel.com; B&B ££, dinner ££-£££). Elegant Georgian house overlooking the bay. Authentic French cuisine is served in the stylish **L'Auberge** restaurant and bistro.

St Helens Guest House (Bellevue Road, Banff AB45 1BJ, ☎/fax 1261-818 241, watt@sthelensbanff.demon.co.uk, www.sthelensbanff.demon.co.uk; B&B ££). Spacious accommodation in a large Victorian house with secluded gardens. Dinner is available by arrangement.

Boyne Hotel (2 North High Street, Portsoy AB45 2PA, ☎/fax 1261-842 242, enquiries@boynehotel.co.uk, www.boynehotel.co.uk; B&B ££). Cozy family-run hotel 100 yards from Portsoy's 17th-century harbor. There are two dining rooms, lounge, public bar and cocktail bar complete with small dance floor. Lunches, high teas and dinners are served daily using fine local produce.

Academy House B&B (School Road, Fordyce, near Portsoy AB45 2SJ, ☎ 1261 842 743, www.fordyceaccommodation.com; B&B ££, dinner ££). Stylish and cozy Victorian country house converted from a former schoolhouse. Dinner is available, although you need to supply your own wine.

Harbour Café (Macduff Harbour, ☎ 1261-833 393; £). Breakfast, lunch, sandwiches and baked goods.

Milo's Restaurant (2 Crook-o-ness Street, Macduff AB44 1TR, ☎ 1261-831 222, ££). A small but good-quality restaurant overlooking the harbor, serving lunches, bar suppers, high teas (weekends) and fine à la carte menus of Scottish cuisine with French influences. Reservations advised.

Moray View Tearoom (2 Duff Street, Macduff, ☎ 1261-833 425; £-££). First-floor tearoom overlooking the harbor that serves snacks, baked treats and three-course lunches.

The Shore Inn (48 Church Street, Portsoy AB45 2QR, ☎ 1261-842 831, fax 1261-842 833; £-££). Lovely atmospheric inn right on the historic harbor, where locals eat and drink. Bar meals are available all day in summer and on weekends in winter. The huge breakfasts are especially popular. Reservations are required for dinner.

The Highlands & Skye

The Highlands encapsulate everything that is glorious about Scotland's wide, empty spaces. This is where the superlatives of history, legend, romance, culture and magnificent scenery collide in a peerless landscape of spectacular mountains, rushing rivers, heather moors, glassy lochs, ancient clans and proud castles. Woven through this magical tapestry are spellbinding tales of human endeavour stretching back into the mists of time. This is exhilarating wilderness at its most heartwrenchingly beautiful.

As chief supporters of the Jacobite claim to the British throne, Highlanders suffered cruel persecution when their cause was violently snubbed out on the battlefield of Culloden. Clans were stripped of their power; tartans and even bagpipes were prohibited. Property was seized and those who weren't forced off their land then were evicted in the Highland Clearances of the 19th century, when tenant farmers (crofters) were driven out to make way for sheep. Happily, Highland culture continues to flourish through the Gaelic language, piping, ceilidhs and a full schedule of Highland games.

CROFTING

Crofting is a unique system of smallholding and living off the land (defined by over a century of legislation beginning with the Crofters' Act of 1886) that recognizes the distinctive nature of traditional land tenure in the Highlands and Islands. Despite traditionally providing only a limited income in return for a great deal of hard work, crofting has proved a sustainable system of land use and has demonstrated an ability to bind communities together. Without crofting, it is likely that much of the Highlands and Islands would be almost empty of people.

A croft comprises a small plot of land and a share in common grazings. Crofts are organized into townships, which are managed communally. Crofters enjoy security of tenure and the right to a fair rent. Because of the usually low level of income, many crofters supplement their land-based income with a variety of other activities, for example fishing, fish farming or local services.

What most people associate with "Scottishness" – tartan kilts, whisky, bagpipes and tossing the caber – are Gaelic traditions descended from the Highlands. That such traditions should survive at all, let alone be so etched in the psyche, is testimony to the irrepressible resolve and determination of Highlanders – qualities that still fire the Scots' pride in their roots and their fierce patriotism.

 INFORMATION SOURCES: Highlands of Scotland Tourist Board is at Peffery House, Strathpeffer IV14 9HA, ☎ 845-225 5121, fax 1997-421 168, info@host.co.uk, www.visithighlands.com.

Getting Here

■ By Air

 Inverness Airport (☎ 1667-464 000) is the main aerial gateway to the Highlands and is just over 1¾-hours' flight from London. The airport is eight miles from the city of Inverness. There is a regular bus service, and taxis cost around £10.

British Airways (☎ 870-850 9850, www.ba.com; from London-Gatwick) and **easyJet** (www.easyjet.com; from London Gatwick and London-Luton) fly daily to Inverness. British Airways also flies to Inverness from Glasgow, Edinburgh and several regional Scottish airports.

Highland Airways (☎ 1667-462 664, www.highlandairways.co.uk) flies to Inverness from Glasgow, Benbecula, Stornoway and Sumburgh.

Eastern Airways (☎ 1652-680 600, www.easternairways.com) flies to Inverness from Birmingham and Manchester.

The Highlands has a second airport at **Wick** (☎ 1955-602 215). **Eastern Airways** (see above) flies to Wick from Aberdeen, and **Loganair** (☎ 845-773 3377, www.loganair.co.uk) flies to Wick from Edinburgh and Kirkwall. Wick Airport is around a mile from the town. Taxis cost around £3.

■ By Rail

 Rail service (**ScotRail**, ☎ 845-755 0033, www.scotrail.co.uk) from Inverness to Kyle of Lochalsh, Inverness to Wick and Thurso, Glasgow to Fort William and Fort William to Mallaig (where steam rains run in the summer) provides excellent transport links through some of Scotland's most spectacular scenery. The **Strathspey Steam Railway** (☎ 1479-810 725) operates from Aviemore to Boat of Garten.

The **Highland Council** (☎ 1463-702 458, fax 1463-702 606, public.transport@highland.gov.uk) publishes a free map showing all travel in the Highlands (also the Western Isles and Orkney).

■ By Ferry

Caledonian MacBrayne (☎ 1475-650 100, www.calmac.co.uk) operates car-ferry services to Ullapool and Skye from the Outer Hebrides, and

NorthLink Ferries (☎ 845-600 0449, www.northlinkferries.co.uk) operates car-ferry services to Scrabster from Orkney.

■ By Car

 From Edinburgh, the motorway (M90) runs to Perth, where you can pick up the A90 toward Dundee and Aberdeen. From Glasgow, the A80 and M80 will take you to Stirling.

■ By Bus

The **Postbus** service (☎ 845-774 0740, www.royalmail.com/postbus) carries passengers on its mail-delivery routes in rural areas where little or no other public transport is available. Given the isolation of many areas of the Highlands, Postbuses can be an important and enjoyable mode of travel if you don't have a car.

Inverness

Inverness, the vibrant capital of the Highlands, straddles the banks of the **River Ness** where it meets the **Moray Firth**, and was elevated to city status as part of the Millennium celebrations. Eleventh-century King Duncan of Shakespeare's *Macbeth* fame had his castle in Inverness, but nothing remains of that today. The *Macbeth* link is more commonly (but erroneously) made to nearby Cawdor Castle (see *Nairn*, page 357).

Inverness became a sizeable town in late Georgian and early Victorian times when the Highland cattle trade flourished and canal and rail links were established through the Great Glen. The prosperity from this era left a legacy of grand, riverside houses, many of which are now hotels and guest houses.

You struggle to name many attractions to keep visitors busy in Inverness for more than a day. However, with its wide range of good restaurants, shopping and entertainment, the city maintains a soft spot in many visitors' hearts. Inverness also makes a great base from which to explore nearby attractions such as **Cawdor Castle**, **Culloden** and **Fort George** – not to mention **Loch Ness** – and farther afield into the Highlands.

Inverness

DON'T MISS

Walk to Inverness's delightful **Ness Islands**.

Explore the beautiful native pine forests of **Glen Affric**.

Feel your spine tingle at **Culloden Battlefield**.

Watch dolphins from the ramparts of **Fort George**.

Take a tour of fairytale **Cawdor Castle**.

Best Freebie: **Inverness Museum**.

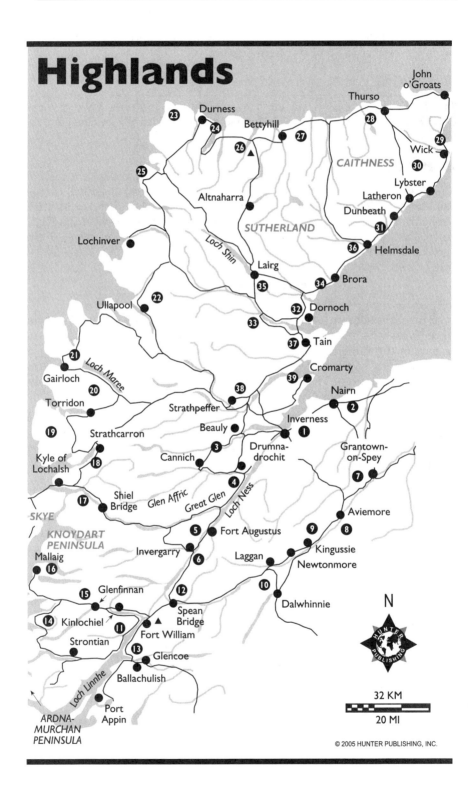

Highlands

John o'Groats

Thurso

Durness 23
24
Bettyhill 26 27
25

CAITHNESS 28

Wick 29
30

Lybster
Altnaharra Latheron
Dunbeath

SUTHERLAND 31

Lochinver
Loch Shin
Lairg 36 Helmsdale
22
Ullapool 35
34 Brora
33 32 Dornoch
37 Tain
21 Loch Maree
Gairloch 39 Cromarty
20
Torridon 38 Nairn
19 Strathpeffer 2
Strathcarron Beauly Inverness
Kyle of 3 Drumna- 1 Grantown-
Lochalsh 18 Cannich drochit on-Spey
17 4 7
Shiel
Bridge Glen Affric Great Glen Loch Ness
SKYE Aviemore
KNOYDART 5 Fort Augustus 9 8
PENINSULA
Mallaig Invergarry 6 Laggan Kingussie
16 Newtonmore
15 Glenfinnan 12 10 Dalwhinnie
14 Kinlochiel 11 Spean
Strontian Bridge
13 Fort William
Glencoe
Ballachulish
Loch Linnhe
Port
Appin
ARDNA-
MURCHAN
PENINSULA

N

32 KM

20 MI

© 2005 HUNTER PUBLISHING, INC.

Highlands Map Key

1. Inverness Museum & Art Gallery, Inverness Cathedral, Inverness Castle, Hootananny Highland World Exhibition, Inverness Floral Hall, Culloden Battlefield
2. Cawdor Castle & Gardens, Cawdor Big Wood, Fort George, Nairn Museum
3. Aigas Dam Fish Lift, Beauly Priory, Beauly Centre, Glen Affric Forest
4. Urquhart Castle, Corrimony Chambered Cairn & Stone Circle, Loch Ness 2000 Exhibition Centre, Original Loch Ness Monster Visitor Centre
5. Clansman Centre, Caledonian Canal Heritage Centre, Fort Augustus Rare Breeds Croft
6. Glengarry Visitor Centre, Invergarry Castle, Well of the Seven Heads, Clan Cameron Museum
7. Grantown Museum & Heritage Trust
8. Cairngorm Brewery, Cairngorm Mountain, Cairngorm Reindeer Centre, Strathspey Steam Railway, Rothiemurchus Estate
9. Highland Wildlife Park (Kincraig), Highland Folk Museum (Kingussie & Newtonmore), Ruthven Barracks, Working Sheepdogs, Waltzing Waters Aqua Theatre
10. Dalwhinnie Distillery
11. West Highland Museum, Ben Nevis Distillery, Inverlochy Castle
12. Commando Memorial, Achnacarry House
13. Glencoe & North Lorn Folk Museum, Glencoe Visitor Centre
14. Castle Tioram
15. Glenfinnan Monument, Glenfinnan Station Museum, Treasures of the Earth
16. Land, Sea & Islands Centre, Mallaig Heritage Centre, Mallaig Marine World
17. Eilean Donan Castle, Kyle Station Visitor Centre
18. Attadale Gardens & Nursery, Smithy Heritage Centre
19. Bealach na Ba Pass
20. Beinn Eighe National Nature Reserve, Coire Mhic Fhearchair Walk
21. Gairloch Heritage Museum, Inverewe Garden
22. Ullapool Museum & Visitor Centre, The Hydroponicum
23. Cape Wrath
24. Smoo Cave, Allt Smoo Waterfall
25. Handa Island Nature Reserve
26. Ben Loyal, Loch Loyal
27. Strathnaver Museum
28. Dounreay Visitor Centre
29. Caithness Glass
30. Grey Cairns of Camster, Waterlines Visitor Centre
31. Dunbeath Heritage Centre
32. Historylinks Museum
33. Croick Church
34. Dunrobin Castle & Gardens, Brora Heritage Centre, Clynelish Distillery
35. Falls of Shin
36. Timespan Heritage Centre
37. Glenmorangie Distillery, Tain Through Time, Tarbat Discovery Centre
38. Highland Museum of Childhood
39. The Black Isle, Cromarty Courthouse Museum, Hugh Miller's Cottage, Black Isle Brewery (Munlochy), Groam House Museum (Rosemarkie)

Inverness

Special Events

Highland Festival (June; ☎ 1463-719 000, info@highlandfestival.org.uk, www.highland-festival.co.uk). Music, dance and theater celebrating Highland culture at various venues in and around Inverness.

Inverness Highland Games & Tattoo (July; ☎ 1463-724 262, fax 1463-712 850). Highland Games on the banks of the River Ness, featuring all the traditional heavy events, Highland dancing, piping and traditional music.

Highland Food & Drink Festival (Oct; info@highlandfeast.co.uk, www.highlandfeast.co.uk). A four-day feast of traditional fine food, drink and culture.

 INFORMATION SOURCES: The tourism office is at Castle Wynd, Inverness IV2 3BJ; open year-round.

Attractions & Sights

■ Museums & Historic Sites

Inverness Museum & Art Gallery (Castle Wynd, Inverness IV2 3EB, ☎ 1463-237 114, fax 1463-225 293, enquiries@invernessmuseum.com, www.invernessmuseum.com; open Mon-Sat, 9am-5pm). A small museum displaying the heritage of Inverness and the Highlands, with exhibits showing the landscape, wildlife and archaeology of the region. The interactive "Hands on the Highlands" gallery, which includes a rooftop camera, quern for corn grinding and hundreds of artifacts to handle, will particularly appeal to children. Changing exhibitions of art and culture are displayed in the gallery.

Inverness Cathedral (Ness Walk, Inverness, ☎/fax 1463-225 553, www.invernesscathedral.co.uk). This was the first new cathedral to be built in Britain after the Reformation, consecrated in 1874. There are regular services throughout the year and summer recitals.

 Inverness Castle (between Castle Street and Castle Wynd, Inverness). This elevated position high above Inverness was the site of a royal castle from the 12th century. The original timber castle was replaced by a high stone tower in the 16th century. The castle was the northern stronghold of early Scottish royal authority during clan wars and civil strife until 1726, when General Wade enlarged it into a Hanoverian fort. Prince Charles Edward Stuart's Jacobite army blew up the castle in 1746 and its only remains are a deep well and sections of a bastion wall. The present structure was built in 1834, with the north block added in 1847, and serves as the Sheriff Courthouse and County Hall.

The castle is the setting for the popular **Castle Garrison Encounter** (☎ 1463-243 363, fax 1463-710 755; Mar-Oct, Mon-Sat, 10am-5pm; Sun, 2:30-4:30pm; adult/child £4.50/£3), which introduces you to costumed soldiers from the Hanoverian army of 1746 and offers you a chance to sign up!

Hootananny Extravaganza (67 Church Street, Inverness IV1 1ES, ☎ 1463-233 651, fax 1463-233 678, music@hootananny.com, www.hootananny.com; shows Mon-Sat, 12:30, 2, 3:30 and 7pm, adult/concession/child £4.75/£4.25/£3). Guided tour of the inner world of the Highlands lets you discover the secrets of the Gaeltoch – the Gaelic world – and how its people invented so much of what we associate with Scotland: kilts, whisky, tartan, ceilidhs, shinty, bagpipes, Highland games, etc. Start with a tasting of Highland spirits, wines and liqueurs. Try on kilts and sporrans. The recreated Highland home depicts life in 1960. Hear a welcome from a Gaelic-speaking robot. Watch a video of a ceilidh featuring bagpipes, fiddles and Gaelic song. Learn the six principles of the Scottish Highland Reel. There is also an atmospheric café-bar and shop.

Inverness Floral Hall (Bught Lane, Inverness IV3 5SS, ☎ 1463-713 553, fax 1463-222 599, enquiries@invernessfloralhall.com, www.invernessfloralhall.com; open April-Oct, 10am-5pm & Nov-Mar, 10am-4pm; closed two weeks in Dec; adult/concession £1.50/£1). A subtropical oasis of winding paths, watercourses, fountains and ponds of koi (Japanese carp) swimming below a cascading waterfall, all in a climate-controlled environment. The landscaping includes an array of exotic plants and cacti and there is an attractive outdoor display garden. A coffee shop serves home baking.

Culloden Battlefield (NTS; Culloden Moor, By Inverness IV2 5EU, on the B9006, five miles east of Inverness; ☎ 1463-790 607, fax 1463-794 294, culloden@nts.org.uk; site open at all times; visitor center open year-round; spring through fall, 9am-5pm, longer in summer; winter, 11am-4pm; adult/concession/family £5/£3.75/£13.50). This is the evocative scene of the Battle of Culloden – the last major battle fought on the British mainland. It was here, on the sleet-filled morning of 16th April 1746, that the Jacobite army of Prince Charles Edward Stuart ("Bonnie Prince Charlie") was crushed in less than an hour by the larger, better-drilled and better-equipped Government forces commanded by the Duke of Cumberland, so ending the last and most spectacular of the Jacobite Risings.

An excellent presentation recounts the story behind the battle, and an exhibition displays many period arms and other items, including several used at Culloden. The bleak moor has been restored to its state at the time of the 1746 battle and is without doubt one of the most poignant locations in Scotland. Towering standards mark the lines of the opposing forces across the heather-clad, boggy ground that so crucially hindered the Jacobites' "Highland charge." Plaques indicate the positions of individual regiments and clans. The turf and stone dykes that also played a crucial part in the battle (by constricting the Jacobites and, when breached, allowing Government forces to attack from the side) have been reconstructed on their original site. **Leanach Cottage**, which survived the battle fought around it, holds living history presentations during the summer. Most haunting are the scattered gravestones engraved with the names of Highland clans that lost men here (1,200 of the 5,000-strong Jacobite army perished at Culloden and another 3,000 people died in the ensuing carnage) and the Field of the English, a memorial to the 400 Government troops who fell. Even those with no interest in history can't fail to be moved by the atmosphere of the field.

Clava Cairns (HS; six miles east of Inverness, 300 yards east of Culloden Battlefield, ☎ 1667-460 232). Believed to date from 2000 BC or earlier, Clava Cairns form a well-preserved Bronze Age cemetery complex of passage cairns, ring cairns, kerb cairn and standing stones in a beautiful setting. There are also the remains of a chapel of unknown date.

■ Open-Top Bus Tours

City Sightseeing Inverness (☎ 1463-224 000, www.city-sightseeing.com; late May-late Sept; Inverness tour, adult/child £5/£2.50; Culloden/Cawdor/Fort George tour, adult/child £8.50/£3.50; tickets valid for travel over 24 hours). Hop-on, hop-off city and history tours departing from the tourism office on Bridge Street.

Adventures

■ On Foot

 Ness Islands provides a delightful riverside walk that's perfect for an early morning or evening stroll. Start at **Ness Bank** on the eastern bank of the River Ness in Inverness and continue away from the city center along **Ladies Walk**. Cross the bridges onto the Ness Islands at the signposts. Cross to the western bank and return to the city center. You can occasionally see seals during the walk and watch anglers fishing for salmon – not bad for a short stroll from a busy city center (30-45 minutes; easy).

■ On Wheels

You can rent cycles at **Highland Cycles**, 16A Telford Street, Inverness IV3 5JZ, ☎/fax 1463-234 789, tbikesueaguy@aol.com.

■ On Water

Inverness Dolphin Cruises (Shore Street Quay, Shore Street, Inverness IV1 1NF, ☎ 1463-717 900; Mar-Oct, 10:30am-4:30pm, later in summer; adult/concession/child/family £10/£8/£7.50/£40). Cruise from Inverness to view the Moray Firth **dolphins**, and possibly also **ospreys**, **red kites** and **seals**. This is a good way to try to see the dolphins if you're short of time; otherwise, take a pair of binoculars to Chanonry Point on the Black Isle or Fort George for cheaper, often equally good views.

Jacobite Cruises (Tomnahurich Bridge, Glenurquhart Road, Inverness IV3 5TD, ☎ 1463-233 999, fax 1463-710 188, info@jacobite.co.uk, www.jacobite.co.uk; cruises April-Dec). Cruise Loch Ness with traditional music and evocative storytelling to enhance the atmosphere. Mini-coaches take you to the loch from Inverness (make reservations at the Tourist Information Centre, Castle Wynd); there is on-board catering and a bar. Evening party cruises are available.

Caley Cruisers (Canal Road, Inverness IV3 8NF, ☎ 1463-236 328, fax 1463-714 879, info@caleycruisers.com, www.caleycruisers.com). Pilot your own motor-cruiser on the Caledonian Canal on weekly or short-break charters. No experience is necessary as full instruction is given.

Golf

Inverness Golf Course (18-hole inland, 6,256 yards; Culcabock Road, Inverness IV2 3XQ, ☎ 1463-239 882, clubmanager@inverness-golfclub.co.uk, www.invernessgolfclub.co.uk; green fees £33). A well-maintained course, established in 1883, with a modern clubhouse and facilities.

Loch Ness Golf Course (18-hole inland, 6,772 yards; Castle Heather, Inverness IV2 6AA, ☎ 1463-713 335, fax 1463-712 695, info@golflochness.com, www.golflochness.com; green fees £15-£30). Interesting course on the outskirts of Inverness that provides a good test for all abilities.

Entertainment

■ Performances & Theater

Eden Court Theatre (Bishop's Road, Inverness IV3 5SA, ☎ 1463-234 234, fax 1463-732 689, boxoffice@eden-court.co.uk, www.eden-court.co.uk). Year-round program of theater, cinema and art, with restaurant and bars.

Scottish Showtime (Spectrum Centre Theatre, 1 Margaret Street, Inverness, ☎ 1349-830 930, fax 1349-830 999, showtime@nessie.org.uk, www.scottishshowtime.com; June-early Sep, 8:30pm-10:30pm). Scotland's longest-running show has been performed for over 30 years: a fast-moving and colorful evening of traditional song, dance, music and humor.

■ Music & Clubs

Blackfriars Pub (93-95 Academy Street, Inverness IV1 1LX, ☎ 1463-233 881, www.blackfriars-pub.co.uk). One of the better traditional pubs for live music, with Mon/Wed ceilidh dances and music on most other nights. Cask ales and reasonably priced bar meals are available.

Hootananny (67 Church Street, Inverness IV1 1ES, ☎ 1463-233 651, fax 1463-233 678, music@hootananny.com, www.hootananny.com; admission £2 for non-diners). Traditional live music and entertainment in an atmospheric club in the heart of Inverness. Live Scottish music every night spring-autumn, Wed-Sun in winter, and dining at candlelit tables.

Johnny Foxes (26 Bank Street, Inverness IV1 1QU, ☎ 1463-236 577, www.johnnyfoxes.co.uk). Based on the legend of the renowned Irish poacher, this large pub-restaurant is always busy and loud, with live music most nights of the week.

Market Bar (Off Church Street entrance to the Victorian Market). Downstairs is a smoky locals' bar and upstairs is live-music.

Falcon Square is a venue for piping and other open-air concerts.

Shopping

Celtic Spirit (14 Church Street, Inverness IV1 1EA, ☎ 1463-714 796, www.celtic-spirit.co.uk). Products for the mind and body, including books and tapes, aromatherapy, crystals, flower essences and Orkney-inspired jewelry, plus evening talks and workshops (reservations recommended).

Chisholms (47-51 Castle Street, Inverness IV2 3DU, ☎ 1463-234 599, fax 1463-223 009, info@kilts.co.uk, www.kilts.co.uk). Established, highly regarded traditional kiltmaker.

James Pringle Weavers (Holm Mills, Dores Road, Inverness IV2 4RB, ☎ 1463-223 311, fax 1463-231 042). Established in 1798, Pringle is one of the oldest working mills in Scotland. Watch cloth being made and weave your own tartan (over age 16 only) on the "have a go" handloom. The shop sells tartan, shoes, knitwear, Scottish foods, souvenirs, golf equipment and whisky (with free tastings).

Leakey's Café & Bookshop (Church Street, Inverness, ☎ 1463-239 947). This superb second-hand bookshop is one of Scotland's largest, with an inventory of over 100,000 books, maps and prints. Situated in an 18th-century Gaelic Church, the shop is heated by a massive central wood stove. Coffee, lunch and afternoon tea are served in its delightful upstairs café.

■ Markets

Farmers', craft and continental markets regularly take place in Inverness High Street. Contact the tourism office for dates.

Victorian Market (Queensgate/Academy Street/Union Street, Inverness). Rebuilt in 1890 after being destroyed by fire, the ornate Victorian arcades house an eclectic collection of shops and a café.

Where To Stay

HOTEL PRICE CHART	
Per person, per night, based on double occupancy in high season. B&B rate includes breakfast; DB&B includes dinner and breakfast.	
£	Under £20
££	£21-£35
£££	£36-£50
££££	£51-£80
£££££	Over £80

■ Inverness

Glenmoriston Town House (20 Ness Bank, Inverness IV2 4SF, ☎ 1463-223 777, fax 1463-712 378, glenmoriston@cali.co.uk, www.glenmoriston.com; B&B ££££). Stylish riverbank hotel with individually styled bedrooms, an airy conservatory for coffee or lunch, and high-quality restaurant.

Palace Milton Hotel & Leisure Club (Ness Walk, Inverness IV3 5NE, ☎ 1463-223 243, fax 1463-236 865, sales@miltonhotels.com, www.miltonhotels.com; B&B £££). The river-view rooms of this recently refurbished traditional hotel are very popular – check availability when booking. Leisure facilities include a pool, gym, spa and sauna.

Moyness House (6 Bruce Gardens, Inverness IV3 5EN, ☎/fax 1463-233 836, stay@moyness.co.uk, www.moyness.co.uk; B&B £££). Friendly, five star guest house in a peaceful location a short distance from the heart of Inverness. Proprietor Richard Jones is a great source of information on local attractions and eateries.

Talisker Guest House (25 Ness Bank, Inverness IV2 4SF, ☎ 1463-236 221, fax 1463-234 173, taliskerguesthouse@btinternet.com; B&B ££). Morag and Norman Brown provide comfortable B&B accommodation on the banks the river, with interesting, light breakfast options as well as the traditional fry-up.

Ivybank Guest House (28 Old Edinburgh Road, Crown, Inverness IV2 3HJ, ☎/fax 1463-232 796, ivybank@talk21.com, www.ivybankguesthouse.com; B&B ££). Charming Georgian house close to the center of Inverness with original open fireplaces, paneled, beamed hall, mahogany staircase, four-poster beds and a bathroom in the turret.

Ness Bank House (7 Ness Bank, Inverness IV2 4SF, ☎/fax 1463-232 939, nessbankgh@btinternet.com, www.nessbankguesthouse.co.uk; B&B ££). B&B in a Georgian house beside the River Ness.

Millwood House (36 Old Mill Road, Inverness IV2 3HR, ☎ 1463-237 254, fax 1463-719 400, www.scotlandaccommodation.com; open Jan-Nov; B&B £££). Cozy traditional cottage with log fires, antiques and fresh flowers about 15 minutes' walk from central Inverness.

Ho Ho Hostel (23a High Street, Inverness IV1 1HY, ☎ 1463-221 225, www.hohohostel.force9.co.uk; £ excluding breakfast). Budget accommodation set in a splendid central building that once housed the aristocratic Highland Club. Internet access is available.

■ Outside Inverness

Bunchrew House Hotel (Inverness IV3 8TA, ☎ 1463-234 917, fax 1463-710 620, enquiries@bunchrew-inverness.co.uk, www.bunchrew-inverness.co.uk; B&B ££££, lunch £££, dinner ££££). Surrounded by 20 acres of woodland by the seashore, you'd never know you were only three miles from Inverness. The turreted 17th-century mansion offers elegant rooms with four-poster beds, log fires, a cozy bar and excellent food served in a magnificent dining room overlooking the water.

Culloden House (Culloden, Inverness IV2 7BZ, ☎ 1463-790 461, fax 1463-792 181, info@cullodenhouse.co.uk, www.cullodenhouse.co.uk; B&B £££££+, dinner ££££). Culloden House was requisitioned by Bonnie Prince Charlie as his lodging and headquarters prior to the fateful battle in 1746. Today, the imposing Palladian country house stands in 40 acres of tranquil lawns and parkland, with stylish bedrooms and two excellent restaurants.

Where To Eat

DINING PRICE CHART

Indicates the price per person for a full meal, excluding drinks. Generally three courses, though fixed menus of five or more courses may be available.

£	Under £10
££	£11-£20
£££	£21-£30
££££	£31-£40

Café 1 (75 Castle Street, Inverness IV2 3EA, ☎ 1463-226 200, fax 1463-716 363, info@cafe1.net, www.cafe1.net; lunch £, dinner ££). Popular bistro whose open-plan kitchen produces high-quality Scottish cooking from local produce.

Castle Restaurant (41-43 Castle Street, Inverness IV2 3DU, ☎/fax 1463-230 925; £-££). Neither cheap nor very cheerful, but popular with locals for all-day dining.

Chez Christophe (16 Ardross Street, Inverness IV3 5NS, ☎ 1463-717 126; £££). Serves the best food in Inverness, with impeccable ingredients, cooking and presentation, although it can feel rather formal.

Delices de Bretagne (Stephens Brae, Inverness-Eastgate, ☎ 1463-712 422; closed in winter; lunch £, dinner ££). Authentic French restaurant serving light daytime snacks (including great crêpes) and an evening à la carte menu.

Harlequin Bar & Restaurant (1-2 View Place, Inverness IV2 4SA, top of Castle Street, ☎ 1463-718 178; ££). Great food in a cozy, intimate atmosphere overlooking the castle and river, with entertainment and live music in the downstairs bar.

Johnny Foxes (26 Bank Street, Inverness IV1 1QU, ☎ 1463-236 577, www.johnnyfoxes.co.uk; ££). Large, busy modern pub-restaurant. The prices are higher than the average pub, but the food is better too.

Mustard Seed (16 Fraser Street, Inverness IV1 1DW, ☎ 1463-220 220, fax 1463-220 323, info@themustardseedrestaurant.co.uk, www.themustardseedrestaurant.co.uk; lunch £, dinner ££). Very popular restaurant, attractively set in a converted church hall with a stove, chimney and balcony overlooking the river. The food never disappoints.

Nico's Bistro & Wine Bar (Glen Mhor Hotel, 9-12 Ness Bank, Inverness IV2 4SG, ☎ 1463-234 308; ££). Cozy, informal dining in a Victorian Oak Room.

Riva Ristorante Italiano (4-6 Ness Walk, Inverness, ☎ 1463-237 377; ££). Tuscan-style bistro with high-quality traditional and modern Italian dishes across the river from Inverness Castle. Upstairs is **Pazzo's**, a lively pizzeria serving hand-thrown pizzas.

River Café & Restaurant (10 Bank Street, Inverness IV1 1QY, ☎ 1463-714 884, www.rivercafeandrestaurant.co.uk; ££). Home-cooked meals and home baking served in a cozy, friendly setting beside the river.

Riverhouse (1 Greig Street, Inverness IV3 5PT, ☎/fax 1463-222 033; closed Mon; £££). First-class contemporary Scottish cooking in an intimate setting. Specialties include local seafood and prime Highland beef.

Rocpool (1 Ness Walk, Inverness IV3 5NE, ☎ 1463-717 274, www.rocpool.com; ££). Reasonably priced contemporary and tapas menus served by friendly staff in an airy, modern setting. The tapas plates are great for grazing.

La Tortilla Asesina (99 Castle Street, Inverness IV2 3EA, ☎ 1463-709 809; £-££). Authentic and atmospheric Spanish tapas bar, café and restaurant serving a variety of Spanish food and drink.

Clachnaharry Inn (17-19 High Street, Clachnaharry, about a mile north-west of Inverness on the A862 toward Beauly; ☎ 1463-239 806; £) Delightfully atmospheric old coaching inn that serves real ales and good food.

Nairn

The Victorian seaside resort of Nairn sits on the south shore of the **Moray Firth** with views over the **Black Isle**. The town was once an active fishing port but its harbor now primarily berths leisure craft. The harbor doesn't exactly buzz with bars and cafés, which is disappointing given the glorious expanses of beach stretching away on either side. The sands extend east to the **RSPB Bird Reserve** and beyond to **Culbin Forest**.

The conservation village of **Cawdor** lies five miles south of Nairn. The castle is understandably the chief draw, but the village, lying mainly to the west of the castle, is also well worth a stroll. The church was built in 1619 by the Thane of Cawdor in gratitude for his deliverance from a shipwreck. The tavern serves excellent ales and good food.

 INFORMATION SOURCES: The tourism office is at The Library, 68 King Street, Nairn IV12 4AU; open year-round.

Attractions & Sights

 Cawdor Castle (between Inverness and Nairn on the B9090 off the A96, ☎ 1667-404 615, fax 1667-404 674, info@cawdorcastle.com, www.cawdorcastle.com; open May-early Oct, 10am-5:30pm, last admission 5pm; adult/concession/child/family £6.50/£5.50/£3.70/£19.20) is a fairytale castle, romantically (though incorrectly) linked by Shakespeare with *Macbeth*. The **Thanes of Cawdor** built the castle in the late 14th century as a private fortress, and it remains the Cawdor family home. The medieval tower was built around a legendary holly tree. Although the castle has evolved over 600 years, later additions, mainly dating from the 17th century, maintained the Scottish style, with slate roofs, walls of mellow local stone, and crow-stepped gables . Fine furniture, portraits and pictures, interesting objects and outstanding tapestries give the interior an intimate feel. Outside are three gardens, the **Cawdor Big Wood** and a nine-hole golf course. There is a restaurant, gift shop, bookshop and wool shop.

AUTHOR'S TIP: *A family feud delayed the start of the 2003 season by a month. Call in advance to check that the castle is open before traveling any distance.*

SHAKESPEARE'S MACBETH AND CAWDOR CASTLE

Shakespeare wrote *The Tragedie of Macbeth* in the spring of 1606. The murder of King Duncan (which is central to the play) took place on 14th August 1040, and is believed by some to have happened at Cawdor Castle (Duncan had his castle at Inverness). However, as the castle was not built until the late 14th century, it is impossible for King Duncan to have lost any blood here.

Fort George (HS; six miles west of Nairn, near Ardersier village on the B9006, off the A96; ☎ 1667-460 232; open year-round, 9:30am-6:30pm, Oct-Mar closes at 4:30pm; last admission 45 minutes before closing; adult/concession/child £6/£4.50/£1.50). A well-thought-out military attraction made all the more interesting by its slightly surreal setting in an active barracks (your bags may be searched on entry). Fort George was built for George II of England following the Battle of Culloden to suppress further Jacobite risings (although that threat never reappeared). The 42-acre fort is one of the most outstanding artillery fortifications in Europe. Completed in 1769 after 20 years' construction, Fort George has served as an active military garrison ever since. Reconstructed barrack rooms show the squalid conditions in which rank-and-file soldiers lived in 1780, their improved conditions in 1868 (single beds!) and an altogether more comfortable officer's lodging from 1813. The **Seafield Collection** is an outstanding display of muskets, pikes and swords. The light, airy chapel was an afterthought but is noteworthy, not least for the bagpipe-playing angel on one of its stained glass windows. Living-history presentations provide an eye-opening insight into the life of a soldier, and the sizeable **Regimental Museum** provides a superb display of military memorabilia, including arms, uniforms and no fewer than 16 Victoria Crosses. The self-guided audio tour is first-rate and free, and a regular trolley bus ("train") takes you around the fort if you don't want to walk.

If you tire of the military displays, the fort's ramparts are one of the best vantage points from which to watch the playful **Moray Firth dolphins**. Binoculars provide the best view, but dolphins often swim just offshore and can be seen clearly without them.

Nairn Museum (Viewfield House, Viewfield Drive, Nairn IV12 4EE, ☎ 1667-456 791, fax 1667-455 399, www.nairnmuseum.co.uk; open end-Mar through Oct, Mon-Sat, 10am-4:30pm; adult/child/family £2/£0.50/£4). In a Georgian house set amid parkland, the museum tells the story of Nairnshire and its people, with displays on local and natural history, archaeology, geology and temporary exhibits. The **Fishertown collection** highlights Nairn's fishing heritage.

Adventures

■ On Foot

Riverside Walk to Cawdor & Castle Trails is an attractive walk along the River Nairn, from Nairn harbor to Cawdor village about five miles away. If you wish to walk farther, from Cawdor you have a choice of waymarked nature trails within the woods surrounding the castle. These vary in length from ¾ mile to five miles; most start from the Flower Garden (1½-3 hours; easy).

After the tenant farmers were driven out of **Culbin Forest** by an immense sandstorm in 1694, Scots and Corsican pines were planted to try to stabilize the sand dunes. The pines flourished and soon became a haven for many plant, animal and bird species normally only found in more ancient forests. The Forestry Commission has established a network of waymarked paths and tracks through the forest, with access points at East Beach, Cloddymoss and Wellhill parking areas.

A 12-mile circular walking or cycling route starts from the **East Beach** parking area in Nairn or can be joined at **Cloddymoss**. Several walks radiating from the **Wellhill** parking area, a mile beyond Kintessack, include an **All Abilities** trail and the **Flowers of the Forest** trail that guides walkers to the shore through Culbin's plant life.

■ On Water

Phoenix (5 Newton Gate, Nairn IV12 4TS, ☎ 1667-456 078, ☎ 7050-214 127 mobile; cruises April-Sept). Boat trips depart from Nairn harbor to view seals at Ardersier and dolphins in the Moray Firth.

Golf

Nairn Golf Course (18-hole links, 6,721 yards; Seabank Road, Nairn IV12 4HB, ☎ 1667-453 208, fax 1667-456 328, bookings@nairngolfclub.co.uk, www.nairngolfclub.co.uk; green fees £50-£70). Founded in 1887 and extended by Archie Simpson, Old Tom Morris and James Braid, Nairn is one of the top courses in the UK and hosted the Walker Cup in 1999.

Wildlife Watching

The ramparts at Fort George are one of the best vantage points from which to view the playful **Moray Firth dolphins** that regularly pass by. They're often just off the fort and can easily be seen with the naked eye. If they're on the opposite shore by Fortrose you'll need binoculars to see them clearly. If you can't see them, ask any of the soldiers or workers at the fort as there are certain times of day when tides are more favorable for the dolphins.

Nairn's varied landscapes provide a good range of habitat for diverse wildlife, particularly birds. **Buzzards** can be seen in rural areas, hovering on the air or perched on fence posts. **Lapwings** give impressive tumbling displays. **Oystercatchers** probe the fields for worms during the spring and summer. **Graylag** or **pink-footed geese** migrating from Iceland's Arctic tundra fly past from October to April, and stop to feed on leftover grain in stubble fields.

Culbin Sands Nature Reserve (on the south shore of the Moray Firth, one mile east of Nairn; ☎ 1463-811 186, tourism information, www.rspb.org-.uk/reserves) forms one of the largest shingle-and-sand-dune bars in Britain, behind which lies extensive salt marsh. Much of the area is remote and unspoiled, and large numbers of sea ducks can be seen offshore in winter. **Bar-tailed godwits, oystercatchers** and **knots** flock at high tide.

Entertainment

 Head up the road to Inverness if you're looking for entertainment. The closest thing to nightlife to be found in Nairn is **Jacko's** (44 Harbour Street, Nairn IV12 4NU, ☎ 1667-452 743), a friendly pub that serves good food and presents regular live music with a hint of Irish.

Where To Stay & Eat

See the *Accommodation* and *Dining* price charts on pages 354 and 356.

 Aurora Hotel (2 Academy Street, Nairn IV12 4RJ, ☎ 1667-453 551, fax 1667-456 577, aurorahotelnairn@aol.com; B&B ££-£££, dinner ££). A small, good-value family-run hotel offering comfortable rooms and a selection of authentic pasta, fish and meat dishes in the dining room or conservatory.

Boath House Hotel & Spa (Auldearn, By Nairn IV12 5TE, ☎ 1667-454 896, fax 1667-455 469, wendy@boath-house.demon.co.uk, www.boath-house.com; B&B ££££). A restored Regency house set in 20 acres, with six elegantly designed guestrooms and a full range of beauty treatments in the spa. The grounds include a beautiful lake and tranquil walled kitchen garden.

The Braighe (Albert Street, Nairn IV12 4HQ, ☎ 1667-453 285, info@the-braighe.com, www.thebraighe.co.uk; B&B ££). Cozy and intimate house with lovely, well-equipped bedrooms and a breakfast menu, including haggis on toast (with or without whisky), local sausages and scrambled eggs with smoked salmon.

Ceol Mara (Links Place, Nairn IV12 4NH, ☎ 1667-452 495, fax 1667-451 531, ceolmara15@aol.com, www.ceolmara.co.uk; B&B £-££). Friendly B&B enjoying great views over the award-winning beach and links course to the Moray Firth beyond.

Sunny Brae Hotel (Marine Road, Nairn IV12 4EA, ☎ 1667-452 309, fax 1667-454 860, enquiries@sunnybraehotel.com, www.sunnybraehotel.com; open Mar-Nov; B&B £££, lunch ££, dinner £££). Excellent family-run hotel beautifully situated in private gardens close to the beach with uninterrupted views over the Moray Firth from many rooms. There is a very good restaurant.

Cawdor Tavern (The Lane, Cawdor, Nairn IV12 5XP, ☎ 1667-404 777; lunch £, dinner ££). Acclaimed country pub-restaurant serving modern Scottish cuisine in elegant surroundings.

Classroom Bistro (1 Cawdor Street, Nairn IV12 4QD, ☎/fax 1667-455 999; lunch £, dinner ££). Coffees, teas and baking served all day as well as lunches and dinners.

Harbour Café (Harbour Street, Nairn, ☎ 1667-461 051; £). Serves the best ice cream in town, in addition to freshly cooked meals and home baking to eat in or take away.

Taste of Moray (Gollanfield, Inverness IV2 7QT (on the A96 road to Inverness), ☎ 1667-462 340, fax 1667-461 087, www.tasteofmoray.co.uk; lunch £, dinner ££). Seafood/steak restaurant that also serves breakfasts, morning coffee and afternoon tea and has a food hall and gift/cook shop.

Beauly & Glen Affric

The picturesque village of Beauly (pronounced "byoo-lee") lies some 10 miles west of Inverness at the head of the **Beauly Firth**, and is surrounded by high mountains, rivers and some of the most scenic glens in Scotland. The area has been inhabited for at least 4,000 years, as evidenced by the remains of crannogs – man-made islands – in the Firth, and duns and vitrified forts in the surrounding hills. Remnants of the ancient **Caledonian forest**, dominated by grand Scots pines and birch trees, cover many of the glens' lower slopes, particularly in Glen Affric and Glen Strathfarrar.

Beauly probably takes its name from the 13th-century priory around which it grew. An alternative theory suggests that Mary, Queen of Scots visited in 1564 and described it as a "beau lieu," meaning beautiful place. The priory monks founded the original harbor on the **River Beauly,** which continued in use until the First World War and contributed to the town's prosperity.

Glen Affric, from the Gaelic meaning "dappled ford," is a magnificent forest of native Caledonian pines, many 200-300 years old, set among spectacular mountains, lochs and waterfalls – unquestionably one of the most beautiful glens in Scotland. These ancient woodlands are direct descendants of trees that first colonized the area after the last Ice Age some 8,000-10,000 years ago. Centuries of destruction by felling, fire and grazing have reduced the ancient Caledonian forest to less than 1% of its original area.

North of Glen Affric lie two more scenic glens: **Glen Cannich** and **Glen Strathfarrar**. These also thread deep into the mountains from Strathglass, through which the **River Glass** flows to join with the **River Farrar** and become the River Beauly. To visit this area, take the A862 from Inverness for Beauly.

Access to Glen Affric and Glen Cannich is unrestricted, but the Glen Strathfarrar road is private and you must obtain permission from the gatekeeper (☎ 1463-761 260) to drive along it (walkers and cyclists have free access).

Attractions & Sights

Aigas Dam Fish Lift (three miles west of the A862 on the A831; Mon-Thurs, 10-11am & 3-4pm; Fri, 10-11am & 2:30-3:30pm). Watch the intriguing spectacle of fish, mainly salmon, being lifted up to pass over a massive dam. A passage holding the fish trying to swim upstream is flooded with water. When the water in the passage reaches the height of the dam, the fish continue upstream. A plaque at the dam provides a full explanation.

Beauly Centre (High Street, Beauly IV4 7JQ, ☎ 1463-783 444, beaulycentre@btinternet.com; open March-Oct, 10am-6pm & Nov-Feb, Wed-Sun, 10am-4pm; adult/child £2/£1). An old village store with exhibitions and demonstrations on spinning, dyeing and loom weaving, plus local history and clan research.

Beauly Priory (HS; Beauly, ☎ 1667-460 232; open mid-June through Sept, 9:30am-6:30pm; admission free). The priory was founded by the Valliscaulian order in 1230. The priory became a Cistercian home around 1510. A plaque recounts the visit of Mary, Queen of Scots in 1564 during her travels through the Highlands. The Priory was abandoned after the Reformation; the lead roof was removed, and it's believed Cromwell used a quantity of the Priory's stones for buildings, including a fort, in Inverness in 1652.

Adventures

■ On Foot

The Forestry Commission has produced several excellent waymarked trails through the Glen Affric forest.

Dog Falls, **Coire Loch** and **Viewpoint Walks** follow well-maintained and signposted paths, with numerous information panels along the way. Each is a self-contained walk (the Dog Falls and Coire Loch routes are circular, the Viewpoint route is linear) that can be done on its own, although you can combine any two together or do all three if you want a longer trail.

All three walks start from the first of the parking areas in Glen Affric. From the A831 at Cannich take the single-lane road into Glen Affric; follow this for two miles past the Fasnakyle Power Station and leave your car at the parking area on your left (with toilets and picnic tables).

The Dog Falls walk climbs steeply into the heart of pine forest that has recently been regenerated after years of overgrazing. The Coire Loch walk passes a beautiful woodland lochan; this is an important breeding site for many dragonfly species, and crested tits are also common here. Walking to the viewpoint rewards you with the classic Affric view (1-3 hrs; easy).

At **Plodda Falls**, water tumbles down a sheer drop of over 100 feet (30 m) in a gorge surrounded by established broadleaf and pine forest. Viewing platforms above and below the falls let you get up close. From the A831 at Cannich follow the signs for and through Tomich village to the parking area about four miles beyond. The circular walk passes through some magnificent Douglas fir and European larch trees planted in the late 19th century. The Douglas firs are some of the tallest in Scotland, many measuring over 210 feet (65 m), and are occasionally felled for ship masts (30 minutes; easy).

Fit trekkers will enjoy the **Glen Affric Traverse**; it takes you along ancient drove roads and trails running between the east and west coasts of Scotland. The Youth Hostel at Allt Beithe (Glen Affric, By Beauly IV47 7ND, ☎ 870-155 3255) makes a convenient halfway stop; it can be popular, so make a reservation in advance.

If you don't want to do the entire traverse, a four- to six-hour alternative, also on forest paths, will take you on a scenic circuit of Loch Affric. If taking photos, do the circuit in the direction that will give you the best light conditions while you're on the southern shore, as this is where you'll get the best shots (2 days; moderate/difficult).

■ On Horseback

Braeside Trekking Centre (Ardendrain, Kiltarlity, Beauly IV4 7HS, ☎ 1463-741 525). Small, informal stable catering to all riding levels, including rides through forest and over moorland.

Highland Trekking & Trail Riding (Cougie, Tomich, Cannich, Beauly IV4 7LY, ☎ 1456-415 323). Trekking and trail riding through the stunning forests, mountains and rivers of the Glen Affric Nature Reserve.

■ On Water

The area is most famous for its salmon, particularly in the **River Beauly** and its tributaries, the **Farrar** and **Glass**. Several hill lochs also offer good brown trout fishing. You can buy permits in Beauly, Cannich, Tomich, Strathfarrar and Inverness.

Farrar Fishing (Culligran Estate, Glen Strathfarrar, Struy IV4 7JX, ☎/fax 1463-761 285; open April to mid-Oct, Mon-Sat) offers fly fishing for salmon and trout on the Farrar and Glass rivers.

Golf

Aigas Golf Course (9-hole inland, 4,878 yards-18 holes; Mains of Aigas, By Beauly IV4 7AD, ☎ 1463-782 942, fax 1463-782 423, info@aigas-holidays.co.uk, www.aigas-holidays.co.uk; green fees £13-£15). Situated at the foot of Strathglass and opened in 1993, Aigas has been designed as a family course, with large, high-quality greens subtly blending into the beautiful landscape.

Wildlife Watching

Glen Affric is a haven for wildlife. The Scots pine and birch woodlands are home to **red squirrels**, **stoats**, **weasels**, **badgers** and **foxes**. **Pine martens** have increased their numbers over the last decade, but their nocturnal habits make good sightings difficult.

 Trout and **salmon** can be seen jumping below the dam at Kilmorack or using the fish lift that bypasses Aigas dam. **Otters** can occasionally be seen and the Beauly Firth is well known for wintering birds such as **whooper swans**.

Red deer are a common sight on the open slopes above the tree line, as are birds of prey, including **buzzards**, **red kites**, **sparrowhawks**, **peregrines** and occasional **golden eagles**. The bird population also includes **crested tits**, **Scottish crossbills**, **black grouse** and the increasingly rare **capercaillie**. Easier to spot are the water birds such as **dippers** and **black throated divers**.

The mountain tops are home to **blue hares**, **ptarmigans** and **dotterels**. Glen Affric is home to some of the rarest **dragonflies** in Europe, including the Northern emerald.

Shopping

Made in Scotland (Station Road, Beauly IV4 7EH, ☎ 1463-782 578, fax 1463-782 409, mis@enterprise.net, www.madeinscotland.uk.com). Scottish crafts and gifts, gallery and a good restaurant (££).

Moniack Castle (Inverness IV5 7PQ, seven miles west of Inverness on the A862 Beauly Road; ☎ 1463-831 283, fax 1463-831 419, mail@moniack-castle.co.uk, www.moniackcastle.co.uk). The castle has been the ancestral home of the Frasers since 1580. The present generation maintains centuries-old traditions of making country wines from wildflowers, fruits and tree sap, as well as creating marmalades, sauces and preserves. Guided tours are available to the kitchen, fermenting and bottling rooms, and cellars, with tastings and an audiovisual presentation on harvesting and wine making. A mail-order service is available.

Where To Stay & Eat

See the *Accommodation* and *Dining* price charts on pages 354 and 356.

 Lovat Arms Hotel (Beauly IV4 7BS, ☎ 1463-782 313, fax 1463-782 862, lovat.arms@cali.co.uk, www.lovatarms.com; B&B £££, lunch ££, dinner £££). Family-run hotel whose two restaurants serve traditional local produce, including beef, lamb and venison from its own farm.

Priory Hotel (The Square, Beauly IV4 7BX, ☎ 1463-782 309, fax 1463-782 531, reservations@priory-hotel.com, www.priory-hotel.com; B&B £££, dinner ££). Comfortable hotel in Beauly's picturesque village square. Dine from the à la carte dinner menu or informally in The Comm, the hotel's in-house pub.

Tomich Hotel (Tomich, near Cannich, By Beauly IV4 7LY, ☎ 1456-415 399, fax 1456-415 469, tomich@tomich.freewire.co.uk, www.tomichhotel.co.uk; B&B £££, dinner ££). Traditional Victorian stone hunting lodge in a conservation village at the edge of the Glen Affric Forest Reserve. On offer are comfortable rooms, good food, blazing log fires, a wide selection of malt whiskies and free use of the nearby indoor swimming pool.

Ardgowan Lodge (Wester Phoineas, By Beauly IV4 7BA, ☎/fax 1463-741 745, info@ardgowanlodge.co.uk, www.ardgowanlodge.co.uk; open Mar-Oct; B&B ££). Part of a former Victorian coach house and stables, the attractive lodge sits in two acres of secluded gardens and has been pleasantly furnished inside and out. Breakfast includes interesting fish options.

Comar Lodge (Cannich, By Beauly IV4 7NB, ☎/fax 1456-415 251, ianmure@aol.com, www.comarlodge.co.uk; B&B ££, dinner ££). Built in 1740 for Clan Chisholm, this listed building stands at the mouth of Glen Affric and has large rooms with lovely views.

Loch Ness & The Great Glen

The **Great Glen** is a system of lochs and rivers stretching 62 miles (100 km) from Inverness in the northeast to Fort William in the southwest. It was formed 380 million years ago from massive fracture movements of the earth's crust, which continue to produce minor earth tremors today. Huge glaciers and meltwater carved out the deep trough of the glen from weakened rock some 20,000 years ago. As they retreated, the glaciers deposited rocks and debris that formed the present-day system of rivers and lochs.

DON'T MISS

Explore the peaceful southern shore of **Loch Ness** and visit the falls at **Foyers**.

Unwind in peaceful **Fort Augustus**.

Take a **barge cruise** on Loch Ness and the Caledonian Canal.

Best Freebie: Walk or cycle sections of the **Great Glen Way**, particularly walking through the woods on the south shore of Loch Oich and cycling the Dark Mile to Loch Arkaig.

The **Caledonian Canal** was engineered to provide ships with a sheltered alternative to voyaging around the stormy north Scottish coast. With the natural rivers too shallow for traffic, cuttings were dug to link the chain of four lochs, which are, from east to west, **Loch Dochfour**, **Loch Ness**, **Loch Oich** and **Loch Lochy**.

Designed by Thomas Telford (among whose many works are the churches now housing the Ullapool Museum and the Iona Heritage Centre), the Caledonian Canal was completed in 1822 after 19 years of work. Cargo ships long ago outgrew its capacity and it is now the preserve of recreational traffic and occasional fishing vessels. Flanked by imposing mountains, misty woods and romantic castles, the canal is one of Scotland's most beautiful waterways.

Barges make great bases from which to explore the Caledonian Canal and surrounding Highlands. Either of the two main barges operating on the canal will provide you with a superbly enjoyable cruise taking in the sensational scenery between Inverness and Fort William. Go with *Fingal of Caledonia* if you want to combine cruising with activities, art or music. *Scottish Highlander* focuses more on luxury and pampering, with leisurely day-trips by support vehicle. For full details, see page 49 in the *Introduction*.

Although Loch Ness is less than two miles wide, its north and south shores are quite different. Over millions of years, the landmasses to the north and south of the Great Glen fault have slid many miles sideways. High peat levels turn the loch's mysterious waters black just feet below the surface. These darkened depths provide Nessie, the mythical Loch Ness Monster, with plenty of room in which to avoid detection. Steep, densely forested valley sides plunge into the loch's murky waters. Heather and rhododendrons carpet areas of open country dotted with isolated houses, while sheep graze quietly in clearings.

THE LOCH NESS MONSTER

Although Nessie sightings date back to the 6th century, it is the modern-day sightings that capture the public imagination. The road built around the loch in the 1930s opened the floodgates for new sightings, in the water and on land, spreading the Nessie legend far beyond the local community. Numerous research projects have tried to solve the mystery (several are ongoing) but have each time been defeated by the scale, and in particular the depth, of the loch's dark waters, and the numerous underwater caves that many believe provide sanctuary from sonar detection. Although several underwater photographs have been taken that seem to show unmistakable dinosaur-like bodies and fins, the myth of Nessie was severely dented when the famous "surgeon's picture" was admitted to be a fake on the surgeon's deathbed.

Monster or not, the local economy is thriving on the back of the myth with Drumnadrochit alone supporting two monster exhibitions. Review the evidence and make up your own mind!

Drumnadrochit

A pleasant though unremarkable lochside village that can justifiably be accused of cashing in on Loch Ness mythology, with not one but two Monster exhibitions.

INFORMATION SOURCES: The tourism office is at The Car Park, Drumnadrochit IV63 6TX; open year-round.

■ Attractions & Sights

Urquhart Castle (HS; two miles south of Drumnadrochit on the A82, ☎ 1456-450 551; open year-round, 9:30am-6:30pm, April-Sept; shorter hours in winter; last admission 45 minutes before closing; adult/concession/child £6/£4.50/£1.20). The splendid ruin of Urquhart Castle stands proudly on an isolated promontory near Drumnadrochit. Boats drop anchor in its bay in 30 feet of water but just a little farther out, the bottom plummets dramatically to 750 feet (230 m), the maximum recorded depth in the loch. A castle has stood on this site since the 12th century, and this is thought to have been the stronghold of Bude, king of the Picts whom Saint Columba visited in the 6th century. The story of Saint Columba's visit records the first mention of the Loch Ness Monster (Aquatalis Bestia) from whose jaws one of his monks had a narrow escape.

The castle was built in the 1230s and was one of the largest in Scotland. It once commanded the whole upper part of the Great Glen and was the mighty stronghold of kings and clan chiefs for 500 years. Edward I of England seized the castle in 1296 during the Wars of Independence, and the MacDonald Lords of the Isles sacked it in 1545. Government redcoats blew up the castle and left it to fall into decay after the failed Jacobite Rising of 1689. Most of the existing buildings date from the 14th century, although the Grant Tower, the best-preserved part of the complex, is 16th century. There is an excellent new visitor complex with audiovisual presentation, interpretation, shop and café.

Corrimony Chambered Cairn & Stone Circle (HS; Glen Urquhart, signposted off the A831 from Drumnadrochit, ☎ 1667-460 232). The excavated chambered cairn was built around 2000 BC as a passage grave encircled by 11 standing stones, and is a good example of a prehistoric burial tomb. There is an explanation panel at the site.

AUTHOR'S TIP: *Drumnadrochit has two Loch Ness Monster exhibitions, the "2000" and the "Original". For those who don't want to visit both, the "2000" is stronger on scientific background and the "Original" is stronger on myths and legends.*

Loch Ness 2000 Exhibition Centre (Drumnadrochit IV63 6TU, ☎ 1456-450 573, fax 1456-450 770, info@loch-ness-scotland.com, www.loch-ness-scotland.com; open year-round, 9am-6pm; closes 8pm summer, 3:30pm winter; adult/concession/child/family £5.95/£4.50/£3.50/£14.95). A high-tech multimedia presentation leads you through 500 million years of natural history, myth and legend relating to Loch Ness and the "Nessie" legend. The presentation uses special effects, archive footage and original expedition equipment, and was written by Loch Ness expert and leader of the **Loch Ness Project** Adrian Shine (who has researched Loch Ness for 30 years). There is also genealogy, a kilt maker, whisky shop and restaurants.

Original Loch Ness Monster Visitor Centre (Loch Ness Lodge Hotel, Drumnadrochit IV63 6TU, ☎ 1456-450 342, fax 1456-450 429, donald@lochness-centre.com, www.lochness-centre.com; open year-round, 9am-5pm; til 8pm summer, 4pm winter; adult/concession/child/family £4.75/£4/£3.25/£12). Review the facts and documented evidence from photographs, descriptions and film footage and make up your own mind about the existence or otherwise of the monster. The exhibition cinema brings you facts and explanations about "Nessie" in eight languages, immersing you in the depths of the mystery. Also examine the historical and cultural background of the area. There is a gift shop, coffee shop and restaurant.

> **DID YOU KNOW?** *At 23 miles (39 km) long and more than 750 feet (229 m) deep, Loch Ness is the largest body of fresh water in Britain – it contains more water than all the lakes and reservoirs in England and Wales combined.*

■ Adventures

On Foot

Follow the **Abriachan Shielings** route taken by summer herders driving their cattle to hilltop grazing grounds and enjoy great views across Loch Ness and out to sea. Start from the village hall at Abriachan, above the northwest coast of Loch Ness. Take the road toward Balchraggan and climb steadily for 30 minutes through birch and pine woodland. Follow the right path at the fork and you will soon see the turf-roofed *shieling* (herdsman's hut) ahead.

Continue along the hill path past large circles of turf mounds – possibly the remains of ancient shielings. Turn sharply left to return along the edge of woodland. Descend one of the steep roads that meet the road to Corryfoyness to reach a superb viewpoint over the Great Glen. Alternatively, continue along the edge of the woodland to return by the path you came up (2 hours; moderate).

The **Divach Falls** have a drop of over 100 feet (30 m) and have inspired artists such as John Phillips, whose painting of the falls now hangs in Buckingham Palace. Start at the tourism office in Drumnadrochit, turn right along the main road and take the first right along Pitkerrald Road. Continue along the path at the foot of the hill toward the site of Balmacaan House. At the end of this path, turn right onto the road with River Coiltie on your left. Follow the road across a bridge and uphill to the falls. Return by the same route but instead of returning to Balmacaan, stay on the path and pass through the historic village of Lewiston, built by Sir James Seafield to improve housing for the people on his estate (3 hours; easy).

On Wheels

You can rent mountain bikes at **Wilderness Cycles** (Fiddler's Café Bar, The Green, Drumnadrochit, ☎ 1456-450 223), together with safety equipment and maps. Reserve using the "Dial-a-bike" service and they'll deliver the bike to your door at no additional cost.

On Horseback

Highland Riding Centre (Borlum Farm, Drumnadrochit IV63 6XN, ☎ 1456-450 220, fax 1456-450 358). One to three-hour hacks overlooking Loch Ness, plus instruction and show jumping in the indoor riding school or outdoor all-weather arena.

On Water

Loch Ness Fishing (The Glen B&B, Drumnadrochit IV63 6TX, ☎ 1456-450 279, ☎ 7831-372 229 mobile, bwynne@madasafish.com). Bruce Wynne runs trips on Loch Ness to fish for brown trout, sea trout and salmon from his traditional 27-foot cobble boat, with all tackle provided. Clay pigeon shooting is also available.

Jacobite Cruises (Tomnahurich Bridge, Glenurquhart Road, Inverness IV3 5TD, ☎ 1463-233 999, fax 1463-710 188, info@jacobite.co.uk, www.jacobite.co.uk; April-Dec). Cruises depart Clansman Harbour on the northeastern shore of the loch; catering and a bar onboard. Coach and cruise tours also depart from Inverness (make reservations at the TIC, Caste Wynd), and there are evening party cruises.

Loch Ness Cruises (The Original Loch Ness Visitor Centre, Drumnadrochit IV3 6UR, ☎ 1456-450 395, fax 1456-450 785, cruises@lochnesscruises.com, www.lochness-cruises.com; cruises April-early Jan). Hourly cruises aboard *Nessie Hunter*, fully equipped with radar, sonar, GPS, underwater cameras and video.

■ Shopping

Loch Ness Clay Works (Goshem Studio, Bunloit, near Drumnadrochit: follow the single-lane road from Lewiston Bridge between Drumnadrochit and Castle Urquhart; ☎ 1456-450 402). Nestled in a peaceful crofting community high above Loch Ness is a tiny clay-works that produces beautiful pottery pieces, including bowls, plates and charming oil lamps. Browse the cozy gallery and watch the artists at work, and come prepared with cash (no credit cards) – you'll almost certainly want to buy something.

■ Where To Stay & Eat

See the *Accommodation* and *Dining* price charts on pages 354 and 356.

Drumnadrochit Hotel (Drumnadrochit IV63 6TU, ☎ 1456-450 202, fax 1456-450 793, fraser@nessie.sol.co.uk; B&B ££, dinner ££). Sixteen en-suite bedrooms, budget accommodation in four-person rooms and good food.

Fiddler's Café Bar (Main Street, Drumnadrochit IV63 6TX, ☎ 1456-450 678, fax 1456-450 258; closed Jan; £-££). Lively, family-run restaurant serving Scottish dishes such as whisky salmon, venison casserole and rabbit stew, washed down with a fine selection of local beers.

Fort Augustus

The attractive village of Fort Augustus at the western extreme of Loch Ness marks the midway point of the Caledonian Canal. The village developed around the fort, which was built in 1720 by General Wade to subdue the Highlanders and was named after the king's son, William Augustus, the Duke of Cumberland (who became known as "The Butcher" after his ruthless pursuit of vanquished Highlanders after Culloden). Benedictine monks founded a monastery at Fort Augustus and later ran a boarding school there until 1993. The monks left abruptly in November 1998 and the abbey closed. It has reverted to the Lovat Estate and its future is not yet clear. A five-flight set of locks dominates the village, beside which run some excellent bars, restaurants, shops and heritage exhibitions.

 INFORMATION SOURCES: The tourism office is at The Car Park, Fort Augustus PH32 4DD; open Easter-Oct.

■ Attractions

Clansman Centre (Fort Augustus PH32 4BD, ☎/fax 1320-366 444, clansman.centre@talk21.com, www.scottish-swords.com; open April-Oct, 10am-6pm; adult/concession £3/£2.50). Fascinating live presentations on ancient Highland life, with clothing and weapons demonstrations. Swords, axes, targes (shields) and clothing are available for sale (and can be made to order), as well as Celtic jewelry, CDs and books. Presentations are usually on the hour but may be more frequent in high season.

Caledonian Canal Heritage Centre (Ardchattan House, Canalside, Fort Augustus PH32 4BA, ☎ 1320-366 493, fax 1320-366 505; open year-round, 10am-5pm; daily in summer, Sun-Thurs only from Oct-May). A small exhibition displaying the history and development of the Caledonian Canal from its conception to present-day refurbishment.

Fort Augustus Rare Breeds Croft (Rowan Lea, Auchterawe Road, Fort Augustus PH32 4BW, By the River Oich near the tourism office; ☎ 1320-366 433; open Mar-Oct, 10am-6pm; adult/concession/family £2/£1.50/£5). A display of Highland cattle, Shetland sheep, Soay sheep, red deer, pheasants, Highland ponies, as well as some not-so-rare breeds. Be warned that the park is a bit of a walk from the roadside entrance.

■ Adventures

 Cruise Loch Ness (Knockburnie, Inchnacardoch, Fort Augustus, ☎ 1320-366 277, fax 1320-366 221, mackenzie@cruise.demon.co.uk, www.cruiselochness.com; cruises April-Oct, 10am-7pm). Cruise in comfort aboard the *Royal Scot*, a custom-built ship equipped with sonar equipment projecting a fascinating view of life under the loch's mysterious depths onto two large television screens. Drinks and light snacks are served in the bar.

■ Golf

Fort Augustus Golf Course (9-hole inland, 5,454 yards; 18 holes of play; Markethill, Fort Augustus PH32 4DS, ☎ 1320-366 660, secretary@fagc.co.uk, www.fagc.co.uk; green fees £12). A beautifully located course along the banks of the Caledonian Canal, curiously grazed by a flock of sheep – hitting one qualifies for a free ball!

■ Shopping

Imray Shop (Fort William Road, Fort Augustus PH32 4BD, ☎/fax 1320 366 724, imray@imray.demon.co.uk, www.imray.demon.co.uk). Collections of Scottish needlecraft, chess sets, books, clan-related items and Scottish gifts, including pewter gifts with Celtic and Charles Rennie Mackintosh designs.

Clog & Craft Shop (Invermoriston, By Fort Augustus IV63 6YA, ☎/fax 1320-351 318). An eclectic assembly of clogs, deer horns, hides, native taxidermy and Celtic leather goods.

■ Where To Stay & Eat

See the *Accommodation* and *Dining* price charts on pages 354 and 356.

Lovat Arms Hotel (Fort William Road, Fort Augustus PH32 4DU, ☎ 1320-366 366, fax 1320-366 677, lovatarms@ipw.com, www.ipw.com/lovatarms; B&B £££). Historic hotel standing on the site of Kilwhimen Barracks, with spacious bedrooms featuring antique furnishings, and a comfortable guest lounge.

Caledonian House (Station Road, Fort Augustus PH32 4BQ, ☎1320-366 236, cal@ipw.com, www.ipw.com/cal; B&B £). Delightful B&B in the heart of Fort Augustus on the banks of the Caledonian Canal.

Bothy Restaurant & Bar (Canalside, Fort Augustus PH32 4BA, ☎ 1320-366 710, bothybar@aol.com, www.lochnessrestaurant.co.uk; lunch £, dinner ££). Set in a traditional 18th-century stone building along the banks of the Caledonian Canal, the Bothy serves freshly cooked food, including homemade steak pies, scallops, mussels and oysters. The lively bar sometimes has live music – call to check the schedule.

Lock Inn & Gilliegorm Restaurant (Canalside, Fort Augustus PH32 4AU, ☎ 1320-366 302; lunch £, dinner ££). Atmospheric, traditional inn beside the locks at Fort Augustus that is so cozy (once you're in you won't want to move) it's often difficult to find anywhere to sit down. A fine menu includes excellent mussels.

Glenmoriston Arms Hotel (Invermoriston, near Fort Augustus IV63 7YA, ☎ 1320-351 206, fax 1320-351 308, reception@glenmoristonarms.co.uk, www.lochnessglen-moriston.co.uk; B&B ££). Comfortable bedrooms, including a four-poster room with Jacuzzi bath, and dining by candlelight.

Loch Ness & The Great Glen

South Shore

Most visitors to Loch Ness charge up and down the busy A82 along the loch's north shore. A much better alternative is the single-lane road on the south shore, which takes you away from the crowds and closer to the loch. The road is rugged in places but takes you up high for panoramic views over the Great Glen, and passes close to the sleepy village of **Foyers**.

■ Adventures

 The sleepy village of Foyers lies on the peaceful south shore of Loch Ness. A short, well-maintained path down a steep gorge leads to two viewpoints across from **Foyers Falls** with their 80-foot drop. The walk starts opposite the post office/village store.

For a longer (30-minute) walk, retrace your steps from the viewpoints toward Foyers village. Instead of climbing back to the village, continue on the path, which leads to the Lower Falls via another spectacular view over the gorge. The path is well kept and fences protect against drop-offs. Follow this path through woodland, past a former aluminum factory and a fish farm to reach the loch shores. You can retrace your steps or follow another 20-minute woodland walk around **Foyers Bay** and back along **Foyers River** (20 minutes, graded easy).

■ Where To Stay & Eat

See the *Accommodation* and *Dining* price charts on pages 354 and 356.

 Foyers Bay House (Lower Foyers IV2 6YB, ☎ 1456-486 624, fax 1456-486 337, carol@foyersbay.co.uk, www.foyersbay.co.uk; B&B ££, dinner £). Impressive Victorian villa secluded in wooded grounds of pine and rhododendrons next to the Falls of Foyers. There are comfortable bedrooms and a delightful conservatory dining room.

Loch Oich & Loch Lochy

West of Fort Augustus are the pristine locks at **Kytra** and **Cullochy**, two of the most attractive on the canal. Ancient tracks and footpaths weave between the remains of a railway track. Past Aberchalder Bridge is Loch Oich, the smallest, highest and shallowest loch in the Caledonian Canal. With its peaceful seclusion and intimate, wooded shores, it's also the most picturesque. West of Laggan Locks lies Loch Lochy, which – though wider and less visually interesting than Loch Oich – offers some excellent walking and fishing.

Attractions & Sights

Glengarry Visitor Centre (Invergarry, on the A87 Loch Oich-Skye road, ☎ 1809-501 424, www.glengarry.net/visitor; open Easter-Sept, 10:30am-4:30pm; admission £1, children free). Housed in a log cabin, exhibits tell the story of the glen in three themes: the MacDonells of Glengarry, the emigrations to Glengarry County in Canada and the legacy of the Ellice Family as landlords after the MacDonells left.

Invergarry Castle (midway along the north shore of Loch Oich). Seventeenth-century stronghold of the Chief of the Glen Garry MacDonnells (MacDonalds), said to have been built by workers passing stones hand-to-hand, down from the shoulder of Ben Tee, the highest mountain in the area. The castle is of L-plan design and has five stories, peeking out over dense woods. Invergarry sheltered Bonnie Prince Charlie before and after Culloden, and has been in a ruined state since shortly after the fateful battle. There is no admittance to the castle as the structure is in a dangerous state, but it's a nice walk along the shore of the loch to get there.

Well of the Seven Heads (just north of Laggan Locks beside the A82, near the southern tip of Loch Oich). This well with a memorial above it tells a gruesome story. After an uncle and his six sons murdered two young relations of the Chief of MacDonnell, revenge was ordered on the seven perpetrators. Sixty men arrived at the murderers' house and carried out the execution. Their seven heads were removed and washed in this spring before being presented before the Chief in Invergarry Castle.

WHO'S WHO? *The MacDonnell execution was carried out at Inverlair, which later became famous as one of the prisons where Rudolf Hess, the deputy Nazi leader, was held after escaping to Scotland in May 1941.*

Clan Cameron Museum (Achnacarry, By Spean Bridge PH34 4EJ, ☎ 1397-712 090, clancam1@aol.com, www.clan-cameron.org; open April to mid-Oct, 1:30-5pm, July-Aug opens 11am; adult/concession £3/£1.50, children free). The museum celebrates the history of the clan and its role in the 1745 Jacobite Rising – after which Cameron of Lochiel, the Clan Chief, went into exile in France with Prince Charles Edward Stuart. There are also displays on the Second World War commandos who trained at nearby Achnacarry, and the Queen's Own Cameron Highlanders.

Adventures

■ On Foot

Sections of the **Great Glen Way** (see page 365) provide excellent shorter routes for those who don't want to walk its entire length. The section from Cullochy Lock to Laggan Locks follows General Wade's 18th-century military road through the forest reserve, a beautiful six-mile walk along the wooded south shore of Loch Oich. This section is particularly quiet as no cyclists are allowed on this side of Loch Oich. The route passes a disused railway line and you can see two massive trees growing through what was once a station platform. Midway around the loch you can peer through dense trees to the remains of Invergarry Castle, poking above the woods on the opposite side of the loch.

■ On Wheels

If you don't wish to cycle the entire 80 miles of the **Great Glen Cycle Route**, you can pick and choose sections to suit the length and grade of ride you're looking for. Most are off-road and the route is well sign-posted.

One of the prettiest sections to cycle is from Laggan to Gairlochy, a distance of about 12 miles. The forest track of gravel and shale hugs the north side of Loch Lochy and mostly undulates gently, with a couple of steeper climbs and descents. The hillsides throughout the forest are home to red deer and birds of prey.

Another beautiful route is the **Dark Mile and Loch Arkaig** route. From Gairlochy, take the B8005, following the sign to Achnacarry. The road skirts the head of Loch Lochy before veering left to Clunes and the Dark Mile – where the branches of beech trees growing across the narrow road keep out the daylight. At the end of this is the Witches' Pool at Cia-Aig falls. A stone staircase leads to the top of the falls, which were used as a location in the film *Rob Roy*. A short distance to the west is Achnacarry House, which billeted commandos on basic training during World War II and is the home of Cameron of Lochiel (the 27th Chief of Clan Cameron). The road continues for an additional 14 scenic miles beside the long and deep Loch Arkaig.

The **Tomdoun-Kinlochhourn road** twists for a wonderful 22 miles through deserted Glen Garry and is the longest, and probably the most beautiful, cul-de-sac in Britain. The one-lane road weaves westward beside the shores of Loch Garry and Loch Quoich before descending dramatically between glacier-worn rocks to the head of fjord-like Loch Hourn. The changing scenery includes sweeping forests, mountains and lochs, and you'll almost certainly see deer around Loch Quoich. Kinlochhourn was once a thriving fishing village but is today a haven for walkers (tackling the superb 18-mile route to Inverie; see page 410), kayakers, deer stalkers and fishermen.

■ On Horseback

Highland Icelandic Horse Trekking (Loch Arkaig, By Spean Bridge PH34 4EL, ☎ 1397-712 783, kirsty@icelandichorses.fs-net.co.uk, www.highland-icelandic.com; rides from £18 for an hour). Try riding an Icelandic horse, which, in addition to walk, trot and canter, has a four-beat gait called the tolt, similar to a walk but with speeds matching a canter. Experienced riders can enjoy fast rides over mountain paths. There is a weight limit of 15 stone (210 pounds) and you need to book a day ahead.

■ Multi-Activity Operator

Monster Activities (Great Glen Water Park, South Laggan, By Spean Bridge PH34 4AE, at the northeastern end of Loch Lochy; ☎ 1809-501 340, info@monsteractivities.com, www.monsteractivities.com) offers whitewater rafting, kayaking/canoeing, sailing, motor boating, wake boarding, water skiing and jet biking, and land-based activities such as walking, abseiling, shooting and archery.

Where To Stay & Eat

See the *Accommodation* and *Dining* price charts on pages 354 and 356.

 Glengarry Castle Hotel (Invergarry, Loch Oich PH35 4HW, ☎ 1809-501 254, fax 1809-501 207, castle@glengarry.net, www.glengarry.net; open Mar-Nov; B&B £££, dinner £££). A classy Victorian country house that enjoys a dreamy, romantic setting in spectacular grounds beside Loch Oich, one of the prettiest lochs in the Highlands. Log fires, wood paneling and stylish bedrooms add to the reverie. Afternoon cream tea overlooking the loch is an unforgettable experience. To either side of a small stone jetty are enchanting woodland walks along the shore, totally overhung by the branches of mosscovered trees. In one direction are sheep pastures and towering Scots Pines, and in the other, the ruins of Invergarry Castle. The hotel offers fishing, rowing and tennis and is an idyllic spot to pause on any journey through the Great Glen.

Corriegour Lodge Hotel (Loch Lochy, By Spean Bridge PH34 4EB, ☎ 1397-712 685, fax 1397-712 696, info@corriegour-lodge-hotel.com, www.corriegour-lodge-hotel.com; open Feb-Nov & New Year; B&B ££££, dinner ££££). Former hunting lodge transformed into an exquisite and acclaimed small hotel and restaurant that is very much family-owned and run. Proprietor Christian Drew extends the warmest of welcomes of the instant-friend variety while her son, Ian, works culinary wonders as head chef. The nine bedrooms are comfortable and well-styled, but the main attraction is the **Loch View Restaurant**. This magical candlelit dining room provides mesmerizing panoramas down Loch Lochy beneath the lofty peaks of the opposite shore, and is the perfect setting in which to savor Ian's innovative five-course evening menus.

Eagle Bar & Restaurant (beside Laggan Locks, ☎ 7789-858 567 mobile, or 7970-550 076; dinner ££). Dine aboard a beautifully decorated barge moored beside Laggan Locks, just east of Loch Lochy. Paintings, model ships and ornate woodwork create a wonderfully cozy atmosphere in which to eat (the specialty is seafood), have a drink or chat with Gordon, the affable owner. Booking is essential for dinner.

Strathspey & The Cairngorms

The strath (valley) of the **River Spey** runs through the area known as **Badenoch & Strathspey**. To the west lie the **Monadhliath Mountains**. To the east rise the rugged peaks of the **Cairngorms**, a mass of granite spreading over 160 square miles – the largest mountain range in Britain.

The area is dotted with pretty Highland villages that each have their own charm and character: **Dalwhinnie**, **Laggan**, **Kincraig**, **Newtonmore**, **Kingussie**, **Aviemore**, **Carrbridge**, **Boat of Garten**, **Nethy Bridge** and **Grantown-on-Spey**.

The **Cairngorms National Park** opened in September 2003. It is Scotland's second national park and the UK's largest at 1,400 square miles (3,800 square km). It stretches from Grantown-on-Spey to the heads of the Angus Glens and from Ballater to Dalwhinnie and Drumochter, including much of the Laggan area in the southwest and a large area of the Glenlivet estate and Strathdon/Glen Buchat. The national park is home to a quarter of Scotland's native woodland and is a refuge for a host of rare plants and creatures, including 25% of the UK's threatened species.

DON'T MISS

Walk the wooded shore of **Loch an Eilein** with its ruined island castle and ospreys (which you can also see at nearby Loch Garten).

Ride the funicular (or walk) up **Cairngorm Mountain**.

Get active walking or cycling in the **Cairngorm National Park**.

Best Freebie: Tour **Cairngorm Brewery**.

Grantown-on-Spey

Grantown-on-Spey is the capital of Strathspey and one of Scotland's earliest planned towns, with broad streets built around a granite Georgian square later lined with trees.

Dulnain Bridge is a small Highland village in the heart of Strathspey, centered on an 18th-century bridge. The village comprises two communities: Dulnain Bridge itself to the north of the bridge and the crofting community of Skye-of-Curr, which stretches for about a mile to the south.

Nethy Bridge has been a holiday village since Victorian times. Set beside ancient Caledonian pine forest and with the backdrop of the Cairngorms and hundreds of acres of Abernethy Forest, Nethy Bridge spans the lower reaches of the River Nethy a mile before it reaches the River Spey. The bridge itself, a classic Telford design, stands in the heart of the village.

Above: Cawdor Castle near Inverness

Below: Dunrobin Castle, Golspie

Above: Callanish Standing Stones, Isle of Lewis

Below: Whisky barrels, Glenmorangie Distillery, Tain

Round Church, Bowmore, Isle of Islay

Above: Finlaggan, Isle of Islay, seat of the Lords of the Isles

Below: Ferry at dawn, Craignure, Isle of Mull

INFORMATION SOURCES: The tourism office is at 54 High Street, Grantown-on-Spey PH26 3EH; open Easter-Oct.

Strathspey & The Cairngorms

■ Attractions & Sights

Grantown Museum & Heritage Trust (Grantown-on-Spey PH26 3HH, ☎/fax 1479-872 478; open Mar-Dec, Mon-Fri, 10am-4pm; plus Saturday in May-Oct; adult/concession/family £2/£1/£5). A museum telling the story of Grantown-on-Spey from 1765. There is a gift shop, Internet access and research facilities.

■ Adventures

 Woolly Mammoth Activities (40 Kylintra Crescent, Grantown-on-Spey PH26 3ES, ☎ 1479-873 716, enquiries@woolly-mammoth.co.uk, www.woolly-mammoth.co.uk) offers river canoe trips, climbing, hill-walking, gorge-walking, mountain biking and overnight expeditions.

Three waymarked paths start from the same point in **Anagach Wood**, easily accessible from the town. The popular Red Route winds its way through open pine woods and is ideal for a good morning or afternoon walk.

From the town square in Grantown, go down Forest Road. The walk starts at the small parking area at the end of the road. The route first follows one of General Wade's military roads and later undulates across fluvio-glacial deposits – clay with boulders deposited by the retreating ice and later re-sorted by water from the melting ice-front. Along the way notice the filled-in remnants of glacial lakes, recognizable by the long grass growing in them; they attract the roe deer living in the wood (2½ hours; easy).

■ Shopping

Speyside Heather (Skye of Curr, Dulnain Bridge PH26 3PA, ☎ 1479-851 359, fax 1479-851 396, enquiries@heathercentre.com, www.heathercentre.com). Heather and plant sales, antique shop, knitwear, craft and gift shop and **Clootie Dumpling Restaurant**.

■ Where To Stay & Eat

See the *Accommodation* and *Dining* price charts on pages 354 and 356.

 Dunallan House (Woodside Avenue, Grantown-on-Spey PH26 3PA, ☎/fax 1479-872 140, dunallan@cwcom.net; B&B ££). Situated on a quiet street close to the town center, Dunallan is a fine Victorian villa retaining many period features such as original fireplaces and stained glass windows. There is a Victorian bedroom and a Honeymoon Suite.

Muckrach Lodge Hotel (Dulnain Bridge, Grantown-on-Spey PH26 3LY, ☎ 1479-851 257, fax 1479-851 325, stay@muckrach.co.uk, www.muckrach.co.uk; B&B ££££, dinner £££). A beautifully located hotel with lovely rooms and a renowned conservatory restaurant with an excellent wine list.

Aviemore, Boat of Garten & Carrbridge

Aviemore should probably be renamed "Avie-less." The town was a small railway village until the 1960s when it became the new base for skiing in the Cairngorms. Unfortunately, the developers turned Aviemore into an ugly concrete sprawl that still tries vainly to pretend it's a trendy ski resort. There's very little reason to linger in Aviemore – the satellite villages of Carrbridge and Boat of Garten are only slightly farther away from Cairngorm and Rothiemurchus, and make infinitely more attractive bases.

Boat of Garten is a small quiet village named after the ferry that once carried passengers over the river. It is the home of the **RSPB Osprey Hide** and one terminus of the **Strathspey Steam Railway**.

Dating from 1717, the picturesque **Bridge of Carr** has long provided visitors with a memorable image of **Carrbridge** village, a pretty, age-old settlement with attractive woodland walks and the **Landmark Forest Heritage Park**.

 INFORMATION SOURCES: The tourism office is at Grampian Road, Aviemore PH22 1PP; open year-round.

■ Attractions & Sights

Cairngorm Brewery (Unit 12, Dalfaber Industrial Estate, Aviemore PH22 1PY, ☎ 1479-812 222, fax 1479-811 465, info@cairngormbrewery.com, www.cairngormbrewery.com; open year-round, Mon-Fri, 9am-5pm; tours Tues & Fri, 11am & 2pm). A brewery tour might make a refreshing change if you've overdone the whisky distillery tours. Taste the range of quality real ales and lightly carbonated filtered beer. Booking is advisable.

Cairngorm Mountain (Aviemore PH22 1RB, ☎ 1479-861 261, fax 1479-861 207, www.cairngormmountain.com). The spanking new funicular railway whisks you high onto a plateau on mighty Cairngorm Mountain. At the top is a mountain exhibition, alpine garden, viewing balcony and the highest restaurant in the UK. A couple of signposted walks take you out into the mountain habitat.

Cairngorm Reindeer Centre (Glenmore, Aviemore PH22 1QU, ☎ 1479-861 228, info@reindeer-company.demon.co.uk, www.reindeercompany.demon.co.uk; open Feb-Dec, with visits to the herd at 11am year-round, and at 2:30pm from May to Sept; adult/concession/family £6/£3/£18). Visit Britain's only reindeer herd, roaming freely in its natural environment. Follow the herder onto the hillside and reindeer grazings, and handle and feed the friendly animals. Separate reindeer fact from fiction, and visit **Santa's Bothy**, the reindeer paddocks and shop.

 Strathspey Steam Railway (Aviemore Station, Dalfaber Road, Aviemore PH22 1PY, ☎ 1479-810 725, fax 1479-812 220, information@strathspeyrailway.co.uk, www.strathspeyrailway.co.uk; open end-Mar through Oct). Take a journey back in time aboard a steam train between **Aviemore**, **Boat of Garten** and **Broomhill** (better known as "Glenbogle" station in the popular TV series *Monarch of the Glen*). The journeys aren't long but the unspoiled Highlands backdrop is spectacular. There is a buffet car on most trains (except Sat) and traditional Sunday lunch, dinner and festive holiday "Santa Train" departures are also available.

■ Adventures

On Foot

 Loch an Eilein Circuit (pronounced "loch-an-eelan," meaning "loch of the island") is a beautiful walk around a peaceful loch surrounded by an ancient Scots pine forest. The island has a dramatic ruined castle, linked with the unpopular 14th-century Alexander Stewart, son of King Robert II, known as the "Wolf of Badenoch." Turn off the Aviemore-Coylumbridge road and follow the signs to the parking area (with a charge). The path is clear and generally stays close to the loch. The castle was once a nesting site for ospreys and you might still see the birds fishing in the loch (1½-2 hours; easy).

A steep hill-climb provides superb views over the **Cairngorm** ski slopes. There is a funicular for skiers, but if you want to climb to the summit you'll have to make the hike from the base of the mountain – funicular passengers are numerous, and therefore aren't allowed to venture far from the top-station to minimize damage to the delicate environment (and funicular-assisted Munro-bagging is frowned upon!). Take warm clothing, as it can be cold on the top.

Take the road from Aviemore to Coylumbridge and follow the ski road up to Coire Cas. There is no clear path up the mountain. Walk along the floor of the corrie (hollow) beyond the ski base station. Pick your way across the slope up to the fences above Coire na Ciste (see below under *On Snow*) and onto the ridge up to the Ptarmigan Restaurant and funicular top-station. The going is steep but not difficult. Beyond the restaurant is a stepped path to the summit from where on a clear day there are superb views of the surrounding broad, rocky ridges and deep corries (3-4 hours; moderate).

 WARNING! *At the summit, don't venture onto any snow patches, particularly near the corrie edges. The snow is unstable and often forms cornices over the steep cliffs.*

On Wheels

 Rothiemurchus Mountain Bike Trails The network of estate roads and paths is excellent for cycling and mountain biking. You can rent cycles from **Inverdruie Mountain Bikes**, Rothiemurchus Visitor Centre, By Aviemore PH22 1QH, ☎ 1479-810 787, www.inverdruiemountainbikes.co.uk.

Highland Venture (Alvie & Dalraddy Estate, ☎ 1479-810 330; Rothiemurchus Estate, ☎ 1479-812 345, highlandventure@aol.com). Choose from two off-road quad bike treks, taking in tracks through Caledonian pine woodland and heather moor. The guided treks last an hour and riders should be over 12. Bring suitable outdoor clothing and gloves.

On Water

Many watersports are available in the area, including canoeing, rowing, windsurfing and sailing. The easiest way to get involved is to visit the well-established watersports center on Loch Morlich (www.lochmorlich.com), or contact one of the outdoor activity operators listed above.

The **River Spey** is the fastest flowing river in Europe and provides fine sea trout fishing, with well over 1,100 fish being taken each year. The **Abernethy Waters** comprise 15 pools over six miles of double bank fishing. Fly, spinning and bait are all allowed, although certain stretches are reserved for fly only when the river reaches a certain level. The **Aviemore Beat** offers two miles of single-bank fishing, and **Avielochan**, a peaceful 10-acre loch, provides excellent shore-, boat- and drift-fishing for brown and rainbow trout. Permits are required for most area fishing. For further information and tackle, contact **Allen's** (Deshar Road, Boat of Garten PH24 3BN, ☎ 1479-831 372).

Rothiemurchus Fishery (By Aviemore PH22 1QH, ☎ 1479-812 345, fax 1479-811 778, rothie@enterprise.net, www.rothiemurchus.net) offers salmon and sea trout fishing on the River Spey, stocked rainbow trout lochs with novice facilities, and boat fishing for brown trout and pike on tranquil lochs under the backdrop of the Cairngorms. Fly fishing, bait fishing and spinning are all permitted in specific areas; tackle for rent or sale and instruction are available if required.

On Snow

Cairngorm Mountain (Aviemore PH22 1RB, ☎ 1479-861 261, fax 1479-861 207, info@cairngormmountain.com, www.cairngormmountain.com). Rising above Loch Morlich and the ancient Caledonian pine forest of Glen More, Cairngorm Mountain rises to 4,084 feet (1,245 m) and is the UK's fifth highest peak. The skiing area has recently undergone a major improvement program and was voted "Most Improved European Resort 2003" by *The Good Ski Guide*.

The gleaming Cairngorm **funicular railway** whisks you up the mountain in comfort and is particularly useful for beginners who can now enjoy the nursery slopes on the top of the mountain without having to ski back down on steeper runs.

The skiing takes place in two adjoining valleys: **Coire Cas** and **Coire na Ciste** (pronounced "corrie-na-keest"). Coire Cas offers a range of runs for beginners and intermediates, including the enjoyable long and cruisy "M2." This valley also offers stiffer tests, including "White Lady," Cairngorm's signature run.

The **Ptarmigan Bowl** at the top of Coire na Ciste is an excellent gentle bowl for beginners. Farther down the valley the terrain becomes more challenging through the steep Ciste gully. **Coire Laogh Mor** is often used for off-piste skiing. Be careful if you choose to ski here – the area is not patrolled and is a special environment with protected landscape and wildlife. Experienced skiers and boarders can take advantage of the "Ambassador Service," which provides free daily tours of the area.

The refurbishment program created modern restaurants and mountain shops. The **Mountain Exhibition** at the top of the funicular is also worth a visit. Exhibits and a video explore how the mountains evolved, how wildlife adapted to survive such extreme conditions, climate change, folklore and the human impact on the mountain environment.

Of all the Scottish ski areas, Cairngorm offers the greatest range of accommodation, in Aviemore and the more interesting neighboring villages of Kingussie, Kincraig, Carrbridge and Boat of Garten.

SKIING CAIRNGORM MOUNTAIN

- Base elevation: 2,150 feet (655 m)

- Skiing range: 1,650 feet (500 m) to 3,800 feet (1,155 m)

- Runs: 19, totaling 23 miles (37 km): 16% easy, 32% intermediate, 47% difficult, 5% very difficult

- Longest run: 1.36 miles (2.2 km)

- Maximum vertical descent: 2,000 feet (610 m)

- Lifts: 16

- Mountain restaurants/cafés: 3

- Snow reports: ☎ 1479-861 261, BBC Ceefax page 421, Ski FM (96.6 FM in the Cairngorm area), www.cairngormmountain.com.

For a unique experience, visit the **Cairngorm Sleddog Adventure Centre** (☎ 7767-270 526 mobile, stewartsledk9@aol.com, www.sleddogs.co.uk; trips Oct-Apr; adult/child £45/£30, group discounts available). Isolated on the **Rothiemurchus Estate** (see next page) with the impressive backdrop of the Cairngorms stretching into the distance, and run by Alan and Fiona Stewart, it's the only facility of its kind in Britain. The Stewarts live in a tiny but cozy cottage surrounded by heather, forests, lochs and, best of all, miles and miles of ideal sledding terrain. The Stewarts' 30 or so dogs, mostly Siberian or Alaskan huskies, pointers and specially bred crosses, charmingly reside in individual used Macallan whisky barrels, each inscribed with its inhabitant's name.

After an introductory video and peek at the small museum, it's off to meet the beautiful and friendly dogs. Alan then demonstrates one of his routines for exercising the dogs, racing off into the forest on a powerful quad bike as a graceful charge of race-fit huskies thunders after him.

After helping Alan and Fiona to harness the dogs, it's finally time for an unforgettable sled ride through the forest. When snow lies on the ground, the dogs pull traditional wooden sleds. At other times, they pull all-terrain vehicles on wheels. Night-time trips can include a stop for a wee dram at the "Nip Inn," a small forest clearing, and close encounters with herds of red deer, but dress up warmly as night-time temperatures in the Cairngorms suit huskies better than humans. Also beware – the dogs are easy to fall in love with, so be prepared to leave the Stewarts with plans for a husky of your own! For those eager to learn more, the Stewarts also offer a two-day sledding course, which culminates in students driving a small dog team themselves. The three-hour "Ultimate Sleddog Adventure" runs three times daily.

In the Air

Cairngorm Gliding Club (Feshie Airstrip, Feshiebridge, Kincraig PH21 1NG, ☎ 1540-651 317, gliding@feshiebridge.freeserve.co.uk). Trial flights in a modern, dual-control glider, enjoying fabulous aerial views of the Cairngorms.

Multi-Activity Operators

Adventure Scotland (Croft House, Croftside, Aviemore PH22 1QJ, ☎ 870-240 2676, info@adventure-scotland.com, www.adventure-scotland.com) offers guided canoeing, kayaking, telemark skiing, ski touring, walking and climbing, together with coaching and all equipment.

Mountain Innovations (Fraoch Lodge, Deshar Road, Boat of Garten PH24 3BN, ☎ 1479-831 331, info@scotmountain.co.uk, www.scotmountain.co.uk) offers all-inclusive walking vacations (including snow-holing), navigation and winter-skills training, together with tailor-made multi-activity vacations.

Rothiemurchus Estate (By Aviemore PH22 1QH, ☎ 1479-812 345, fax 1479-811 778, rothie@enterprise.net, www.rothiemurchus.net). Lying at the heart of the Cairngorms, the Grant family's Rothiemurchus Estate provides a superb one-stop-shop for the outdoor enthusiast. The estate maintains a 31-mile (50-km) footpath network and offers free ranger-guided walks. The estate's stag-stalking season lasts July to October with September and October being the most important months. During this time, check with the rangers or visitor center (☎ 1479-812 345) to see whether your intended route is affected.

Many of the tracks are suitable for mountain biking and there are several suggested cycling routes through the forest. Anglers can fish for salmon and sea trout on the **River Spey**, and rainbow trout, brown trout or pike in quiet lochs. Clay pigeon shooting is available, together with game and pheasant shooting.

■ Golf

Boat of Garten Golf Course (18-hole inland, 5,967 yards; Nethybridge Road, Boat of Garten PH24 3BQ, ☎ 1479-831 282, fax 1479-831 523, boatgolf@enterprise.net, www.boatgolf.com; green fees £29-£34). A beautiful and demanding James Braid course set in magnificent Highland surroundings.

■ Wildlife Watching

 Loch Garten Osprey Centre (10 miles east of Aviemore, between Boat of Garten and Nethybridge off the B970, ☎ 1479-821 409, fax 1479-821 069, www.rspb.org.uk; open April-Aug, 10am-6pm; adult/concession/child/family £2.50/£1.50/£0.50/£5). Binoculars and telescopes let you watch these spectacular fish-eating birds of prey at close quarters from an environmentally-friendly visitor center. A CCTV system also relays live pictures from the treetop nests. The ospreys arrive, settle and lay eggs in late April/early May. The eggs hatch in late May/early June when the adults can be seen feeding the young. The young grow rapidly and in mid-July to mid-August take to the air for the first time. From mid-August, the young start to spend time away from the nest and then start to migrate to West Africa.

The bird hide at the **Rothiemurchus Fishery** (By Aviemore PH22 1QH, ☎ 1479-812 345, fax 1479-811 778, rothie@enterprise.net, www.rothiemurchus.net; adult/concession £1/£0.5) is a great spot for watching ospreys as they dive for fish from the estate's lochs.

■ Shopping

Loch an Eilein Pottery (Rothiemurchus, By Aviemore PH22 1PQ, ☎/fax 1479-810 837, penspots@btinternet.com, www.penspots.co.uk). Craft pottery that makes hand-thrown domestic terracotta mugs, jugs and bowls, glazed in hues of blue, green and turquoise.

■ Where To Stay & Eat

See the *Accommodation* and *Dining* price charts on pages 354 and 356.

 The Boat (Boat of Garten PH24 3BH, ☎ 1479-831 258, fax 1479-831 414, info@boathotel.co.uk, www.boathotel.co.uk; B&B ££££, lunch ££, dinner ££-£££). Charmingly set beside the quaint Boat of Garten station, now used by the Strathspey Steam Railway, The Boat is a top-quality hotel offering friendly, efficient service and peaceful views across the unspoiled Spey Valley. Guestrooms are spacious and well furnished, and the strikingly decorated restaurant serves award-winning cuisine. Lighter meals are available in the comfortable guest bar (which also offers 60 malt whiskies), and you can enjoy a drink with locals in the in-house public bar.

Hilton Coylumbridge (By Aviemore PH22 1QN, ☎ 1479-810 661, fax 1479-811 309, www.hilton.com; B&B £££, dinner ££). A huge hotel set in 65 acres of Rothiemurchus woodland with a wide choice of leisure activities, including two pools, live entertainment and "Fun House." Lodges have kitchens for those who want to cook for themselves.

Chapelton Steading (Boat of Garten PH24 3BU, ☎ 1479-831 327, chapelton@btinternet.com, www.boatofgarten.com/chapelton; open Mar-Oct;

B&B ££). Rural B&B accommodation in a converted barn with log fire, books, paintings and organic kitchen garden. Afternoon tea is served with home baking. Every night you stay entitles you to a £5 voucher against green fees at the Boat of Garten Golf Course.

Kincraig

Kincraig is a true Highland village and home of the **Highland Wildlife Park**. A wide range of watersports is available at **Loch Insh**.

■ Attractions and Sightseeing

Highland Wildlife Park (Kincraig PH21 1NL, ☎ 1540-651 270, fax 1540-651 236, info@highlandwildlifepark.org, www.highlandwildlife-park.org; Mar-Jun & Sep-Oct, 10am-6pm; July-Aug until 7pm; Nov-April until 4pm; adult/concession/child/family £8/£7/£5.50/£27, including audio guide). One of the better wildlife parks in the Highlands. Weather permitting, you'll discover the variety of animals found in present-day Scotland and meet the animals that roamed the land hundreds – sometimes thousands – of years ago. Animals in the park include red deer, Soay sheep, Highland cattle, polecat, wildcat, pine marten, capercaillie, red grouse, golden eagle, arctic fox, snowy owl, otter, beaver and badger. Wild boar, wolves and reindeer evoke the Scottish landscape of the past. Note: last admission two hours before closing.

■ Adventures

 Loch Insh Watersports (Kincraig PH21 1NU, ☎ 1540-651 272, fax 1540-651 208, enquiries@lochinsh.com, www.lochinsh.com) offers sailing, windsurfing, canoeing, mountain biking, family river trips, archery, dry-ski slope, fishing for salmon or trout, and forest trails. There are beach and picnic areas, log chalets with kitchens, B&B accommodation, restaurant and a balcony bar.

Alvie Stables (Alvie Estate, signposted off the B9152 one mile north of Kincraig, ☎ 7831-495 397 mobile, ☎ 1540-651 409 evenings). Good riding through miles of open countryside for novice and experienced equestrians.

Kingussie & Newtonmore

Kingussie (meaning "head of the pinewood") is the capital of Badenoch and nestles attractively beside the **River Spey** in the foothills of the Cairngorm and Monadhliath ranges. It was founded in the late 18th century by the Duke of Gordon and at that time was a small hamlet surrounded by a vast pine forest. The village houses one of the two **Highland Folk Museums** and on the opposite side of the River Spey stands the historic ruin of **Ruthven Barracks**.

Nestling beneath **Creag Dhu**, Newtonmore (meaning "the new township on the moor") was once dismissed by Queen Victoria as a "very poor village." Things have improved since then, and Newtonmore now has arts and crafts shops, tearooms, bars and restaurants spread along its main street. It makes a good base for walking and is the location of the second **Highland Folk Museum**, on the village outskirts.

 INFORMATION SOURCES: The tourism office is at Newtonmore Gallery, Main Street, Newtonmore PH20 1DA; open year-round.

■ Attractions & Sights

Highland Folk Museum: Housed at two sites, one in Kingussie and the other in Newtonmore, the museum introduces you to the world of the Highlander. Exhibits, activities and living history displays depict 400 years of Highland life, including clans, crofting and Gaelic culture. The **Kingussie** site presents the social history of ordinary Highlanders, with collections of domestic objects and a reconstructed blackhouse (a traditional house with double-thick stone walls and a thatched roof), mill and smokehouse; Duke Street, PH21 1JG, £2.50/£1.50/£15, open year-round, hours vary seasonally. At **Newtonmore**, costumed staff demonstrate traditional skills and crafts; buses provide free on-site transport; Aultlarie, PH20 1AY, £5/£3/£15, open early April through Oct. At both sites, hours vary seasonally; for details, ☎ 1540-661 307, fax 1540-661 631, highland.folk@highland.gov.uk, www.highlandfolk.com.

Ruthven Barracks (HS; one mile from Kingussie, signposted from the A9/A86 in Kingussie, ☎ 1667-460 232). The ruins of an infantry barracks built after the 1715 Jacobite Rising, with stables added by General Wade in 1734. The Comyn Lords of Badenoch built a castle here before the 14th century, but that was demolished in 1718 to build the barracks, and part of the curtain wall is all that survives. Bonnie Prince Charlie's Jacobite army captured the barracks in early 1746. After their crushing defeat at Culloden, the remnants of that force gathered here briefly to regroup, but were devastated by a message from their already-fled leader: "Let everyone seek his own safety in the best way he can."

Waltzing Waters Aqua Theatre (Newtonmore PH20 1DR, ☎ 1540-673 752; adult/concession/child £4/£3.50/£2). Choreographed water shows, synchronised with light and music; open late-Jan to mid-Dec, with 40-minute shows on the hour, 10am-4pm, plus 5pm & 8:30pm in July-Aug.

■ Adventures

Corrieyairack Pass: A superb walk over the General Wade road linking Ruthven Barracks near Kingussie with Fort Augustus in the Great Glen. With its bridges and hairpin bends, the pass was a remarkable feat of 18th-century engineering, but fell out of use after the modern road was built through Glen Spean in the 19th century. It's possible to walk selected sections of the route, and the entire 20-mile traverse makes an excellent and challenging walk; the pass itself should only be attempted between May and September as the road rises to 2,500 feet (769 m), and is impassable in winter.

Turn north off the A86 road at Laggan; from here you can drive as far as Garvamore with its bridge and ruined barracks. The route follows the old road up the switchbacks to the summit of the pass, where the views match the history. It's an eight-mile walk if you turn around here, and should take about five hours.

Wildcat Trail: A lovely waymarked circuit around Newtonmore, along the banks of the Spey, Calder and Allt na Feithe Buidhe rivers, with a fine stretch of moorland between the latter two. The route provides great views over Strathspey and the surrounding mountains. The trail was set up by the local community, which also operates the Wildcat Centre in the village; stop in before your hike for maps and information (3 hours; easy).

Working Sheepdogs (Leault Farm, Kincraig, Kingussie PH21 1LZ, ☎ 1540-651 310, www.leaultfarm.co.uk; May-Oct, demonstrations at 12pm & 4pm; plus 2pm in July-Aug; Nov-April by appointment; adult/child £4/£2). Watch sheepdogs performing herding maneuvers, and view sheep-shearing demonstrations. Meet collie pups, bottle-fed lambs and border collies, and learn training tips.

■ Golf

Kingussie Golf Course (18-hole inland, 5,615 yards; Gynack Road, Kingussie PH21 1LR, ☎ 1540-661 374, fax 1540-662 066, sec@kingussie-golf.co.uk, www.kingussie-golf.co.uk; green fees £20-£22). The course provides an excellent test of shot-making for all ability levels.

Newtonmore Golf Course (18-hole inland, 6,041 yards; Golf Course Road, Newtonmore PH20 1AT, ☎ 1540-673 878, fax 1540-670 147, secretary@newtonmoregolf.com, www.newtonmoregolf.com; green fees £20-£24). The course mostly lies along the banks of the River Spey and is surrounded by beautiful Highland scenery.

■ Wildlife Watching

Insh Marshes Nature Reserve (1½ miles east of Kingussie on the B970, ☎ 1540-661 518, www.rspb.org.uk; guided walks Thurs at 2pm from April through August, £2). Insh Marshes is the most important floodplain wetland in Britain, attracting nearly 1,000 pairs of breeding waders. In spring, lapwings, redshanks and curlews nest here. In winter the marshes flood, providing roosting and feeding for flocks of **whooper swans** and **greylag geese**. The best time to visit is November-June.

Two hides overlook the marsh. In spring and early summer, look for breeding waders and wildfowl on the floodplain and goldeneye on the lochs and river. Roe deer are ever-present and you can sometimes see buzzards and hen harriers overhead. In the autumn, look for red squirrels feeding on hazelnuts.

■ Where To Stay & Eat

See the *Accommodation* and *Dining* price charts on pages 354 and 356.

Kingussie

Avondale House (Newtonmore Road, Kingussie PH21 1HF, ☎ 1540-661 731, fax 1540-662 362, avondalehouse@talk21.com, www.avondalehouse.com; B&B ££). Small family-run hotel providing an excellent base for outdoor activities in the Cairngorm area. Owners Pat and Ray Morris have skied here for 30 years, and they and their two children are all instructors at Cairngorm Mountain. With interests also covering walking, climbing and sailing, there isn't much this family can't tell you about what to see and do in the area. Avondale (pronounced "arndale") offers pleasant, comfortable guest rooms, drying room, equipment store and repair workshop.

Columba House Hotel & Garden Restaurant (Manse Road, Kingussie PH21 1JF, ☎ 1540-661 402, fax 1540-661 652, reservations@columba-househotel.com, www.columbahousehotel.com; B&B ££, dinner ££). The hotel is set in secluded walled gardens; romantic bedrooms have four-poster beds and double baths; and there is a cozy bar, candlelit restaurant and al fresco dining on the patio in summer.

The Cross (Tweed Mill Brae, Ardbroilach Road, Kingussie PH21 1LB, ☎ 1540-661 166, fax 1540-661 080, relax@thecross.co.uk, www.thecross.co.uk; open Mar-Nov, restaurant closed Tues; B&B ££££, dinner ££££). Individually styled bedrooms are bright and spacious. The restaurant serves the best food in Kingussie, but it's not cheap. The master chef experiments quite successfully with less-common produce and herbs from the garden.

Scot House Hotel (Newtonmore Road, Kingussie PH21 1HE, ☎ 1540-661 351, fax 1540-661 111, enquiries@scothouse.com, www.scothouse.com; B&B ££, dinner £-££). Originally a 19th-century manse, the small hotel has reasonable rooms and a good restaurant with a cozy, well-stocked bar.

Laird's Bothy Hostel (68 High Street, Kingussie PH21 1HZ, ☎ 1540-661 334, fax 1540-662 063; £ excluding breakfast). Budget accommodation in the heart of Kingussie. The **Tipsy Laird Restaurant** (£-££) serves reasonably priced meals and bar snacks, washed down with real ales on tap.

Newtonmore

Monadhliath Hotel (Laggan Bridge, near Newtonmore PH20 1BT, ☎/fax 1528-544 276, monadhliath@lagganbridge.com, www.lagganbridge.com; B&B ££, dinner ££). Converted church manse set in its own grounds, recently refurbished but keeping its character. Meals are available in both the bar and restaurant.

Dalwhinnie & Loch Laggan

Sitting at 1,188 feet (362 m) above sea level, Dalwhinnie is the highest-elevation village in the Highlands. It grew around an inn built in 1729 on the "new" Perth-Inverness military road, and was a traditional meeting place for drovers; you can still walk the drove road from here to **Kinloch Laggan**. The town is home to Dalwhinnie, Scotland's highest distillery.

Enclosed by dark mountains, the landscape between **Loch Laggan**, **Loch Ericht** and **Loch Insh** is characterized by birch-fringed crags and glimpses of the **River Spey**. In between lie a scattering of communities, towns and villages. Laggan is a picturesque village where you can visit **Dun da Lamh**, an Iron Age fort.

■ Attractions & Sights

Dalwhinnie Distillery (Dalwhinnie PH19 1AB, ☎ 1540-672 219, fax 1540-672 228; open year-round, opening times vary seasonally so call ahead; last tour one hour before closing; admission £4, including a shop voucher). The highest distillery in Scotland sits exposed to the elements on the wide open sweep of the Drumochter Hills, and is often cut off in the severest weather. The heather honey taste of Dalwhinnie reflects the appearance of the hills in summer.

Lochaber

Stretching north from Appin in north Argyll, Lochaber boasts some of Scotland's finest mountain scenery, dominated by towering, wild mountains, unpopulated glens and picturesque lochs, liberally sprinkled with the seeds of legend. The **Road to the Isles** (A830) cuts through the region on its romantic journey to Mallaig and the Small Isles. Close to Fort William itself are **Ben Nevis**, Britain's highest mountain, and the western end of the **Caledonian Canal**.

DON'T MISS

Walk in the sublime, history-tinged landscapes of **Glen Coe**, **Glen Nevis** and **Glen Etive**.

See hauntingly beautiful **Glenfinnan**, where Bonnie Prince Charlie raised his standard to launch the final Jacobite rebellion.

Explore unspoiled **Ardnamurchan**, with its lonely lighthouse and striking **Castle Tioram**.

Discover the region's fascinating past at Fort William's excellent **West Highland Museum**.

Walk or sail to the wilderness of **Knoydart**.

Best Freebie: **Walking** and **climbing**, just about anywhere in the area.

Fort William & Glen Nevis

Lying peacefully by the shore of **Loch Linnhe**, Fort William commands an important position within the Highlands and Scotland. It is easily accessible from Glasgow and the central belt, and provides good access to the north via the Great Glen, west to Ardnamurchan and to the Hebrides via Mallaig. Reflecting its strategic location, the town has often played a significant role in Highland history and featured in many military campaigns.

Fort William attracts many visitors but retains a pleasant compactness and "real town" feel. It's largely a one-street town but the main pedestrianized thoroughfare is attractive and lined with traditional bars and interesting shops. Best of all, stunning Highland scenery almost encroaches into the town. The shortest of drives from Fort William will deposit you in the middle of nowhere, with **Ben Nevis** – Britain's highest mountain – soaring high above you.

■ Special Events

Lochaber Highland Games (July; ☎ 1397-772 885, fax 1397-772 660). Fort William's traditional Highland Games.

Ben Race (first Saturday in Sept) Annual dash up Britain's highest mountain.

 INFORMATION SOURCES: The tourism office is at Cameron Centre, Cameron Square, Fort William PH33 6AJ; open year-round.

■ Attractions & Sights

West Highland Museum (Cameron Square, Fort William PH33 6AJ, ☎ 1397-702 169, fax 1397-701 927, info@westhighlandmuseum.org.uk, www.westhighlandmuseum.org.uk; open Mon-Sat, 10am-5pm; in summer open Sun, 2-5pm; Oct-May closes at 4pm; adult/concession £3/£2, children free). This absorbing and deceptively diverse museum showcases the dramatic social and natural history of the West Highlands and islands, and deserves to be visited even if it isn't raining! Collections include early archaeological finds, local wildlife, tartans and costume, domestic utensils, local industries and weapons of war. The museum provides fascinating insights on timeless Highland chronicles such as the Massacre of Glencoe, Appin Murder and, above all, Bonnie Prince Charlie and the 1745 Jacobite Rising. Foremost among the Jacobite exhibits are personal items relating to the Prince and Flora MacDonald (who helped him escape in a boat "over the sea to Skye") and moving relics recovered from the Culloden battlefield.

 Inverlochy Castle (HS; two miles northeast of Fort William, off the A82; open year-round). The ruin of one of Scotland's earliest stone castles stands in the shadow of Ben Nevis, on the south bank of the River Lochy. One of the few Highland castles to survive largely unaltered since before the Wars of Independence, it was built around 1280 by the powerful Comyn family, although only occupied by them until 1308, after which it appears to have been abandoned and only occupied sporadically. The castle is of simple form, with a great curtain wall (almost 30 feet high) drawn about a square courtyard with a round tower (climbed by stairs within the tower walls) at each corner. The River Lochy protected one side of the castle while a river-fed moat protected the other three. The tower at the northwest corner is Comyn's Tower. Larger than the others and built in the most easily defended part of the castle (by the river) it probably formed the main accommodation of Lord Comyn.

Ben Nevis Distillery (Lochy Bridge, Fort William PH33 6TJ, ☎ 1397-702 476, fax 1397-702 768, colin@bennevisdistillery.com, www.bennevisdistillery.com; open year-round, Mon-Fri, 9am-5pm; Saturdays from Easter through Sept; and Sundays in July and August; adult/child £2/£1, redeemable against shop purchases). Video presentation introduced by "Hector McDram," distillery tour and tasting of goldmedal-winning whiskies in a superb setting in the shadow of Ben Nevis.

THE BEST BEN NEVIS VIEWPOINTS

The summit of Ben Nevis isn't visible from Glen Nevis. The best views are from:

- Torlundy and the Caledonian Canal at Corpach and Banavie, from where the 2,000-foot north face cliffs can be clearly seen

- The Commando Memorial off the A82 north of Spean Bridge

- The road to Lundavra (turn left as you leave Fort William on the A82 toward Crianlarich).

■ Adventures

On Foot

 The superb **Glen Nevis-Steall Falls** walk takes you deep into some of the finest Highland scenery, yet is only a short drive from Fort William. From the mini-roundabout on the eastern outskirts of Fort William (by the old distillery) take the turnoff for Glen Nevis and drive up the glen. Follow the road through beautiful scenery that gets progressively wilder. Ahead rise the peaks of **Stob Ban** and **Sgurr a Mhaim**, both with white quartzite scree on their upper slopes making them look as though they are snow-covered. The road becomes single-lane for the final few miles and can be busy in the summer, ending at a parking area where the walk starts.

From the end of the road, you can see ahead that the **River Nevis** has carved an impressive gorge through the mountains. A gradual climb through attractive mixed woodland takes you to a rocky stream crossing. Take care, it can be slippery. You can hear the river down to your right and the torrent can be deafening after heavy rain. Be careful – some places there is a considerable steep drop on the right, although the path is fairly wide. After crossing a large area of boulders, the path descends to the river. Suddenly you're standing at the edge of an upland meadow and the glen opens out before you against the backdrop of the **Steall Falls**. It's possible to cross the river on a three-strand wire bridge and continue on a boggy path past a small bothy to the bottom of the falls. A better option is to continue up the valley to the old **Steall ruins** (1½ hours; easy).

The granite massif of **Ben Nevis** is the highest mountain in Britain – 4,406 feet (1,344 m) – and its ascent is understandably popular. The summit path is fairly easy to follow and, although long, is not so steep that it can't be climbed with hands in pockets all the way. From Fort William take the A82 toward Inverness until you reach the mini-roundabout on the eastern outskirts of the town (by the old distillery). Follow the Glen Nevis turnoff for a short distance to the **Glen Nevis Visitor Centre** on your left, where the path begins.

Follow the path for a short distance along the river and cross the bridge. Double back beside **Achintee Farm** before turning away from the river and climbing gradually across the flank of **Meall an t-Suidhe**. As you gain height, views up and across Glen Nevis open up. At the second of two metal bridges you are about a quarter of the way up. The going gets a little rougher and steeper until the path turns to the left (keep to the main path – the apparent shortcut is steep and loose) and an easier, flatter section. You soon reach **Lochan Meall an t-Suidhe** – the "Halfway Lochan."

WARNING – SAFETY ON THE BEN

Ben Nevis can be dangerous: on average, eight people die on the standard route every year (more than on Everest) and many more are injured, mostly due to a lack of suitable clothing and equipment. Summit conditions are **sub-Arctic**. Freezing conditions can occur at any time of year, covering the summit in snow and making navigation very challenging, even for the experienced. Even on hot sunny days, **mist** and **gales** can blow in without warning. If you are in any doubt, turn around and retrace your steps.

Don't attempt the ascent without being properly equipped with **walking boots**, **raingear**, **compass**, **map**, **warm clothing**, **food** and **fluids**. You should ideally have some hillwalking experience, failing which you can hire a professional guide. If that is not possible, undertake the ascent on a weekend when there will be many other walkers to follow.

Check the **weather forecast** (posted at the Visitor Centre) before setting off. Leave early to allow enough time to enjoy the walk. Inform someone that you are planning to climb the mountain and let them know your expected time of return. For further information, contact the Ranger Service at **Glen Nevis Visitor Centre** (Fort William PH33 6PF, ☎ 1397-705 922, fax 1397-706 278, glen.nevis@highland.gov.uk).

The path turns back to the right and heads toward the **Red Burn** (a small stream). Avoid the path to the left as it leads under the north face. Just before you reach the Red Burn are the remains of the "Halfway House," formerly connected with the summit observatory – now also in ruins. You are halfway to the summit.

The path ascends the upper half of the mountain by a series of long zigzags. Keep to the main path, as the apparent shortcuts are steep and loose, and have been the scene of many accidents. The views become more and more impressive, particularly along **Loch Linnhe** and, on clear days, north and west to the islands of **Rum** and **Skye**.

As the path nears the summit, it passes close to the edge of the north face cliffs. Two large gullies – **Tower Gully** and **Gardyloo Gully** – are gouged into the plateau and are often covered with snow. Keep to the path and *do not* venture near these gullies: the snow covering is often just an unstable cornice. A short distance past the two gullies lies the summit, with its **cairn** and ruined **observatory**. In bad visibility, don't venture out of sight of the cairn and ruins.

Return by the same route. There are no other ways down except for experienced climbers. Take particular care over the lower rocky sections as most Ben Nevis accidents happen on the bottom half of the descent (5-8 hours; moderate, but lengthy).

THE BEN RACE

The race up Ben Nevis started in 1895 when a local hairdresser ran from Fort William High Street to the summit and back in two hours 41 minutes. Several local heroes subsequently lowered the record but the race ceased in 1904 with the closure of the observatory. The race was revived in 1934 and has now grown into a national event, run on the first Saturday each September. The record times are 1 hour 25 minutes (men) and 1 hour 43 minutes (women), both run in 1984.

DID YOU KNOW? *A Model T Ford was driven to the summit of Ben Nevis in 1911, the first ascent made by a car!*

On Wheels

The Nevis Range (Torlundy, Fort William PH33 6SW, ☎ 1397-705 825, fax 1397-705 854, info@nevis-range.co.uk, www.nevis-range.co.uk) offers mountain-biking for all abilities, including a downhill track with gondola access.

You can rent cycles and equipment, including downhill bikes and safety gear, at **Off Beat Bikes** (117 High Street, Fort William PH33 6DG, ☎ 1397-704 008, info@offbeatbikes.co.uk, www.offbeatbikes.co.uk).

In & On the Water

 The Underwater Diving Centre (An Aird, Fort William PH33 6AN, ☎ 1397-703 786, fax 1397-704 969, scuba@theunderwater-centre.com, www.diving.gb.net) offers wreck diving, one-day trial dives and trips in a yellow submarine to watch other divers on the wrecks.

Morzh: **The Submarine** (An Aird, Fort William PH33 6AN, ☎ 1397-703 786, fax 1397-704 969, enquiries@theunderwatercenter.com, www.theunderwatercenter.com). Explore the depths of Loch Linnhe in this two-man submarine, and even learn to pilot the vessel.

Crannog Cruises (Town Pier, Fort William PH33 6DX, ☎ 1397-700 714, www.crannog.net; April-Oct) will take you to Seal Island to view the seal colony and working fish farm. Trips to Fort William Bay and evening cruises up Loch Eil with optional buffet, as well as RIB trips and winter cruises on the Caledonian Canal, are also available.

On Snow

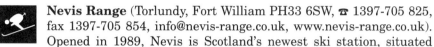 **Nevis Range** (Torlundy, Fort William PH33 6SW, ☎ 1397-705 825, fax 1397-705 854, info@nevis-range.co.uk, www.nevis-range.co.uk). Opened in 1989, Nevis is Scotland's newest ski station, situated seven miles north of Fort William on the northern slopes of **Aonach Mor** (pronounced "anak-mor," meaning "great ridge"). Rising to 4,006 feet, Aonach Mor is Britain's eighth-highest mountain and provides the highest skiing in Scotland. Ben Nevis, Britain's highest peak, is almost in-your-face from the higher stations on the mountain.

SKIING NEVIS

- Base elevation: 300 feet (91 m)

- Skiing range: 2,150 feet (650 m) to 4,006 feet (1,221 m)

- Pisted runs: 12 miles (20 km), total skiable: 22 miles (35 km)

- Longest run: 1¼ miles (2 km), 2½ miles (4 km) non-pisted

- Maximum vertical descent: 1,900 feet (580 m)

- Lifts: 12.

- Runs: 35 (easy: 20%, intermediate: 34%, difficult: 31%, very difficult: 15%)

- Mountain restaurants/cafés: 4

- Snow reports: ☎ 1397-705 825, BBC Ceefax page 421, Nevis Radio 96.6 FM, www.nevis-range.co.uk.

A modern gondola carries skiers up to the top station at 2,150 feet, from where another 11 lifts access a total of 35 runs. Most of the lifts service runs mainly for beginners and intermediates on the front (gondola) side of the mountain, mostly around the popular "Goose" area; one or two steeper challenges will test more advanced skiers and boarders. The horizontal Great Glen chairlift takes beginners (slowly) to an alternative easy piste served by a T-bar.

The opening up of the Back Corries with the installation of the Braveheart chairlift has increased the skiable area considerably and opened up an exciting and less used area of challenging skiing, on and off-piste, for intermediate and advanced skiers. The "Chancer" starts with a heart-stopping launch over a cornice, standing on top of which your ski tips reach out into thin air (like the celebrated "Tortin" run in Verbier, Switzerland), into a huge bowl-shaped snowfield. To really get away from it all, two unpatrolled routes, "Summit Gully" and "Spikes" take you down spectacular and lonely descents of the farthest extremes of the Back Corries.

On Horseback

Torlundy Farm Riding Centre (Torlundy, Fort William PH33 6SW, ☎ 1397-703 015, fax 1397-703 304, chris@gghc.demon.co.uk). Small-group riding (experienced riders preferred) around a farm breeding Highland cattle, ponies and sheep.

Multi-Activity Operators

Farr Cottage Activity Centre (Farr Cottage, Corpach, By Fort William PH33 7LR, ☎ 1397-772 315, fax 1397-772 247, mail@farrcottage.com, www.farrcottage.com) offers a range of outdoor activities – including rafting, canyoning, mountain biking, horse trekking, climbing, abseiling, walking, fishing and diving – and customized discovery tours (www.hiddenscotlandtours.com). The owner, Stuart, who guides the tours, is a knowledgeable and passionate Scot who has an infectious enthusiasm for Scottish history and culture, and has an expert knowledge of whisky. Farr Cottage offers a bar, meals and comfortable hostel accommodation.

Snowgoose Mountain Centre (The Old Smiddy, Station Road, Corpach, By Fort William PH33 7JH, ☎ 1397-772 467, fax 1397-772 411, info@highland-mountain-guides.co.uk, www.highland-mountain-guides.co.uk) offers courses and guiding in rock climbing, hill and ridge walking, scrambling, winter skills, mountain craft and watersports.

■ Golf

Fort William Golf Course (18-hole inland, 6,217 yards; Torlundy, Fort William PH33 6SN, ☎ 1397-704 464, www.fortwilliamgolf.co.uk; green fees £22). The surroundings will be a constant distraction on this course: the slightly elevated position provides excellent views to the north face of Ben Nevis, up the Great Glen and down Loch Linnhe.

■ Entertainment

McTavish's Kitchens (High Street, Fort William PH33 6AD, ☎ 1397-702 406, fax 1397-700 771, fortwilliam@mctavishs.com, www.mctavishs.com; nightly from May-Sept, 8-10pm; adult/child £4/£2, or £2/£1 with dinner; lunch £, dinner ££). Traditional music, featuring pipes and fiddles, Gaelic songs and dancing. Locals cringe but visitors love it. A full and reasonably priced menu is available.

The **Fort William High School Pipe Band** plays Tues & Thurs, June-Aug, from 7:30pm. Join the band outside McTavish's Kitchens and follow it along Fort William High Street.

■ Shopping

Ben Nevis Visitor Centre (Belford Road, Fort William PH33 6BZ, ☎ 1397-704 244). Outdoor clothing, knitwear and country casuals; Edinburgh crystal, Caithness glass, Scottish food and whisky. Trace your Scottish ancestry and take home some of your family tartan in anything from a scarf to a kilt. The coffee shop serves snacks and meals.

Hebridean Jewellery (95 High Street, Fort William PH33 6DG, ☎ 1397-702 033, www.hebridean-jewellery.co.uk). A wide range of Scottish-made Celtic and Pictish design jewelry, crafts, gifts and Celtic music.

Nevisport (Airds Crossing, High Street, Fort William PH33 6EJ, ☎ 1397-704 921, fax 1397-705 056, info@nevisport.com, www.nevisport.com). A large complex selling books, maps, gifts, clothing and equipment for the outdoor and mountain enthusiast. There is also a restaurant and bar.

Scottish Crafts & Whisky Centre (135-139 High Street, Fort William PH33 6EA, ☎ 1397-704 406, fax 1397-700 497). A better-than-average selection of Scottish gifts, food and clothing, with an excellent whisky selection and tempting discount offers.

■ Where To Stay

 Alexandra Hotel (The Parade, Fort William PH33 6AZ, ☎ 1397-702 241, fax 1397-705 554, salesalexandra@strathmorehotels.com, www.strathmorehotels.com; B&B £££). Mid-range hotel with an excellent location in central Fort William close to the station and shops. The hotel has comfortable rooms and friendly, helpful staff. Guests have use of the leisure facilities at nearby Ben Nevis Hotel (see below).

Ben Nevis Hotel & Leisure Club (North Road, Fort William PH33 6TG, ☎ 1397-702 331, fax 1397-700 132, salesbennevis@strathmorehotels.com, www.strathmorehotels.com; B&B £££). Large, mid-range hotel situated a short distance outside Fort William, with some rooms having great Ben Nevis views. The excellent leisure facilities include a 50-foot pool, Jacuzzi, gym, sauna and steam room.

West End Hotel (Achintore Road, Fort William PH33 6ED, ☎ 1397-702 614, fax 1397-706 279, welcome@westend-hotel.co.uk, www.westend-hotel.co.uk; B&B ££). Spacious hotel at the southwestern end of Fort William. The hotel has large, comfortable rooms, some with excellent views across Loch Linnhe, a large public bar and conservatory dining area.

Corrie Duff Guest House (Glen Nevis, Fort William PH33 6ST, ☎/fax 1397-701

HOTEL PRICE CHART	
Per person, per night, based on double occupancy in high season. B&B rate includes breakfast; DB&B includes dinner and breakfast.	
£	Under £20
££	£21-£35
£££	£36-£50
££££	£51-£80
£££££	Over £80

Lochaber

412; B&B £). Reasonably priced, friendly guest house just outside Fort William, close to the start of the Ben Nevis path.

Inverlochy Castle (Torlundy, Fort William PH33 6SN, ☎ 1397-702 177, or 1-888-424-0106 toll-free from US, fax 1397-702 953, info@inverlochycastle-hotel.com, www.inverlochycastlehotel.com; B&B £££££+, dinner ££££+). Secluded amid spectacular scenery in the foothills of Ben Nevis, and overlooking a private loch, Inverlochy Castle is one of the grandest and most luxurious hotels in the Highlands. It oozes timeless splendor from each of its individually styled rooms, the grand hall and renowned restaurant (jacket and tie required). Queen Victoria remarked, "I never saw a lovelier or more romantic spot." Few would disagree.

■ Where To Eat

DINING PRICE CHART	
Indicates the price per person for a full meal, excluding drinks. Generally three courses, though fixed menus of five or more courses may be available.	
£	Under £10
££	£11-£20
£££	£21-£30
££££	£31-£40

Crannog Seafood (Town Pier, Fort William PH33 6DX, ☎ 1397-705 589, fax 1397-700 134, www.crannog.net; £££). Lively seafood restaurant enjoying great loch views from its pier setting (a former bait house) and serving an extensive menu of fine seafood, meat and poultry.

Grog & Gruel (66 High Street, Fort William PH33 6AE, ☎ 1397-705 078, fax 1855-811 679, greatbeer@grogandgruel.co.uk, www.grogandgruel.co.uk; ££). Atmospheric pub restaurant serving reasonably priced Tex-Mex and traditional bar and restaurant menus.

Highland Star Chinese Restaurant (155 High Street, Fort William, ☎ 1397-703 905; lunch £, dinner £-££). Large selection of well-cooked Far Eastern dishes in a restaurant with excellent loch views; take-out available.

The Hot Roast Company (127 High Street, Fort William; £). Excellent café serving delicious hot roast (beef, pork, turkey and ham) rolls for £2.75.

Lochaber Siding (Travel Centre, An Aird, Fort William PH33 7NN, ☎ 1397-701 843; £). Coffee shop serving healthy, homemade food and home baking.

No 4 Restaurant (4 Cameron Square, Fort William, ☎ 1397-704 222, reservations@no4-fortwilliam.co.uk, www.no4-fortwilliam.co.uk; ££). Pleasantly decorated restaurant serving a well-crafted contemporary menu, including top-class game and seafood, and an impressive wine list.

The Stables Restaurant (Bank Street, Fort William PH33 6AX, ☎ 1397-700 730; lunch £-££, dinner ££-£££). Newer restaurant serving good Scottish cooking, including daily specials.

Glen Spean

The first major stop north of Fort William is **Spean Bridge**, a pleasant village boasting a good selection of local accommodation. A mile from the village stands the Commando Memorial (see below).

East of Spean Bridge the A86 heads through Glen Spean toward Loch Laggan and on to Strathspey and the Cairngorms, passing through the village of Roybridge. Just before Roybridge is **Glen Roy** – celebrated for an extraordinary landscape feature known as the "Parallel Roads." Once believed to be the work of fairies, the "roads" in fact mark the successive beaches of a glacial lake whose level dropped as the ice retreated.

■ Attractions & Adventures

The **Commando Memorial** (one mile north of Spean Bridge toward Inverness, just off the A82) keeps a lonely vigil high above Spean Bridge. This moving bronze monument, erected in 1952, is dedicated to the memory of the WWII commandos who trained at nearby Achnacarry House, home of Cameron of Lochiel. The memorial site is also one of the best vantage points from which to view Ben Nevis and other peaks in the Nevis and neighboring ranges.

THE COMMANDO TRAIL

The land around **Achnacarry House** was used for training during the Second World War. The Commando Trail, beginning at the **Clan Cameron Museum** near Spean Bridge, lets you see some of the facilities, including assault courses, firing ranges, marching grounds and field-craft areas.

Fishing Scotland (Roy Bridge PH31 4AG, ☎/fax 1397-712 812, gofishing@fishing-scotland.co.uk, www.fishing-scotland.co.uk). Guided "Learn to fly fish" vacations and excursions, including instruction and tackle. Spin and bait fishing are also available.

■ Shopping

Spean Bridge Mill (Spean Bridge PH34 4EP, ☎ 1397-712 260, info @speanbridgemill.com). Large selection of knitwear, textiles, food, gifts and souvenirs together with a superb whisky room. You can also discover the art of weaving (demonstrations Mon-Fri) and trace your clan history.

■ Where To Stay & Eat

See the *Accommodation* and *Dining* price charts on pages 395 and 396.

 Distant Hills Guest House (Spean Bridge PH34 4EU, ☎/fax 1397-712 452, enquiry@distanthills.com, www.distanthills.com; B&B ££, dinner ££). Popular, modern guest house set in spacious grounds on the outskirts of Spean Bridge. Margaret and Derek Pratt provide a warm, easy-going welcome, with helpful advice on how best to squeeze in plenty of the local attractions, and many guests make return visits. The comfortable bedrooms are all on ground level, allowing easy access for anyone with impaired mobility. Margaret creates tasty evening meals using local ingredients (don't miss the delicious homemade soups) and the breakfast bacon is particularly flavorsome.

Dreamweavers (Mucomir, By Spean Bridge PH34 4EQ, ☎ 1397-712 548, helen@dreamweavers.co.uk, www.dreamweavers.co.uk; B&B £, dinner £). The description "B&B" doesn't begin to describe the experience of staying at this tranquil house with wonderful views over mountains, fields and forests. The warm-hearted Helen Maclean provides services well beyond the call of duty, including holistic therapies, child-minding, story-telling and uplifting conversation into the small hours (the establishment was so named for a reason). Guests not only frequently return to Helen again and again, but many become personal friends.

Old Pines (Spean Bridge PH34 4EG, ☎ 1397-712 324, fax 1397-712 433, goodfood@oldpines.co.uk, www.oldpines.co.uk; restaurant closed Mon; DB&B £££££, lunch ££, dinner ££££). A celebrated, family-run establishment, blending an alpine chalet with a country cottage, set among mature Scots Pines with fine views over the Caledonian Canal. Bill and Sukie Barber combine a warm welcome with cozy rooms, deep sofas, an extensive library, fresh flowers and log fires. The excellent restaurant (bookings essential for dinner) uses organic produce, homegrown vegetables and herbs, homemade bread and pasta, home-smoked meats and fish, and locally gathered fungi to produce menus that leave guests and food critics drooling.

Glen Coe & Loch Leven

Magnificent Glen Coe is Scotland's most famous and atmospheric glen. It is not only a visual feast but also the stuff of legends – its romance, history and tragedy are almost tangible, particularly if you venture into its hills.

 INFORMATION SOURCES: Ballachulish Visitor Centre (Loan Fern, Ballachulish PH49 4JB, ☎ 1855-811 866, visitor-centre@ballachulish.fsnet.co.uk; open year-round). Excellent and friendly information source that also sells a good selection of jewelry, crafts, books, maps and music. There is a cash machine, Internet terminal and great coffee shop.

The drive to Glen Coe is itself out of the ordinary. Arriving from the south on the A82 you drive through moody Rannoch Moor, passing the beautifully formed sentinel of Buachaille Etive Mor ("Great Shepherd of Etive"), after which dark, foreboding mountains tower above you on all sides before closing in menacingly around you.

Sleepy **Glencoe village** sits in the shadow of the Pap of Glencoe, an attractive conical peak rising 2,430 feet. Heading east from the village, you reach the head of Loch Leven, where the famous West Highland Way winds through the peaceful village of **Kinlochleven**, famous in the past for its aluminum works.

THE GLENCOE MASSACRE

The end of the 17th century was an era of turmoil in Scotland. King William III and Queen Mary had replaced the Stewart King James VII, but many Scots – particularly in the Highlands – continued to support James and the Jacobite cause. Recognizing the resurgence of the Jacobites, William decided to test the loyalty of the clans by forcing them to swear an oath of allegiance by the end of 1691.

MacIain, chief of the MacDonalds of Glencoe, was delayed at Barcaldine by Government troops while on his way to Inverary to swear his oath and failed to sign until 6th January 1692. MacIain's oath was accepted in Inverary but rejected by Government officials who decided to punish him. Campbell of Glenlyon led a group of 128 soldiers who stayed with the MacDonalds for 12 days before turning on and murdering 38 of their hosts in the early hours of 13th February 1692. The massacre is particularly infamous because it involved the murder of hosts – "murder under trust."

A monument to the fallen MacDonalds was erected in Glencoe village. MacIain was buried on the island of Eilean Munde in Loch Leven. The massacre backfired on the Government and led to an increase in support for the Jacobites.

■ Attractions & Sights

Glencoe & North Lorn Folk Museum (Glencoe village PH49 4HS, ☎ 1855-811 664; open Easter & mid-May through Sept, Mon-Sat, 10am-5:30pm; adult/concession £2/£1.50, children free). Displays on local history, domestic and agricultural life set in a restored heather-thatched building in the heart of Glencoe village. Exhibits include Jacobite memorabilia, costumes, weapons, Victoriana, domestic bygones and agricultural implements.

Glencoe Visitor Centre (NTS; Glencoe PH49 4LA, ☎ 1855-811 307/811 729, fax 1855-812 010, glencoe@nts.org.uk; open April-Aug, 9:30am-5:30pm; Sep-Oct, 10am-5pm; Nov-March, 10am-4pm, Fri-Mon only in winter; adult/concession/family £3.50/£2.60/£9.50). An informative and enjoyable visitor experience tells the story of how the famous glen was formed and explores the landscape, wildlife and gripping history of clan massacres, royal visits and rebellions. The complex was constructed to be environmentally sustainable and has a shop, information point and a great café for lunches and snacks.

■ Adventures

Glen Coe boasts some of the finest walking in Scotland and includes easy, low-level walks as well as knife-edge ridges for the serious thrill seeker.

Behind and above sleepy Glencoe village the delightful **Glencoe-Lochan Trails** pass through lush woodland, and afford superb views. From the A82 take the minor road through Glencoe village. Cross the humpback bridge and take the road on your left, signposted for the hospital. Take the first turning on your right (away from the hospital) and continue along the track to the parking area, from where you have a choice of three walks.

Stay on the bottom path, through the gate and past the small lochan that often flowers with water lilies. Take the first turning right and then almost immediately left into the woods, following the markers to the lochan. Turn left to walk around the lochan clockwise. At the far end of the lochan the route meets a second path leading up a steep hill ("heart attack hill"), which gives splendid views from the top over **Loch Leven** and its surrounding hills and behind to the **Pap of Glencoe**. Descend steeply back to the path around the lochan and the parking area (1-1½ hours; easy).

The Lost Valley (Allt Coire Gabhail): This superb and fairly easy walk takes you into classic Glen Coe landscapes. From Glencoe village, head east on the A82 past **Loch Achtriochtan**. Once the road starts to ascend look for a large boulder on the right, which marks a gravel area where you can park. To the south rise the **Three Sisters of Glencoe**, from left to right Beinn Fhada, Gearr Aonach and Aonach Dubh. The **Lost Valley** rises between Beinn Fhada and Gearr Aonach.

Walk toward the Three Sisters, descending into the glen until you reach the old road. Turn left and continue until you reach a gravel path to your right. Take this route down to a wooden bridge that crosses the River Coe. Follow the path up and over the stile. From here there is a choice of two routes. The main track to the left is tougher, in places requiring some scrambling, but provides a picturesque riverside trail with views of waterfalls and pools. From where the two paths meet again, carefully traverse the river over stepping stones. Walk up the steepish bank to your right toward the green bank with some scree slopes up to the left. Carry on up toward the lip of the summit and into the Lost Valley, from where you have marvelous views of **Bidean nam Bian**, **Gearr Aonach** and **Beinn Fhada**. The MacDonalds reputedly hid their (often stolen!) cattle here and many of the clan fled here on the night of the infamous massacre in 1692. It's worth spending some time here to take in the hauntingly still surroundings, and you'll probably also see herds of red deer either in the valley or on the surrounding hills (2-3 hours; easy).

 Buachaille Etive Mor (pronounced "boockle-etiv-mor," meaning "great shepherd of Etive") is a beautiful name for a beautiful mountain. Rising majestically from flat moorland at the entrance to Glen Coe, "the Buachaille" is one of the most gorgeous peaks in Scotland. Although generally a climber's mountain, an easier route puts the summit within the reach of walkers who aren't afraid to scramble up occasional sections of steep scree. Climbing (and even more so descending) the scree can be challenging and uncomfortable, but the payback is considerable: the view across Rannoch Moor from the summit is breathtaking and even non-climbers have the chance to stand atop a truly magnificent mountain.

Start from Altnafeadh on the A82 road, marked by a white Scottish Mountaineering Club climbers' hut and across the road from the signposted path to Kinlochleven (part of the West Highland Way). Cross the bridge over the river and pass the climbers' hut. About 500 yards beyond the hut the path forks. Follow the right-hand fork, keeping to the right of the stream. The path rises steeply up the gully straight ahead of you. You can follow a path beside the stream, although this requires crossing the stream several times. A better option is to climb to the upper bank on the right. Take care on the steep scree slope as the gully narrows toward its head, topping out on a broad and not very steep ridge. The hardest part of the climb is now behind you. Head left (east then northeast) up the pink rocky scree. The ridge narrows and passes a couple of false summits before reaching the large summit cairn with views over Rannoch Moor and Glen Etive.

More challenging climbs exist up the imposing north face, including the noted Curved Ridge route, although these ascents are demanding and for experienced climbers only (4-5 hours; moderate/difficult).

Aonach Eagach (pronounced "anak-eager") is a spectacular serrated ridge whose three-mile traverse makes a superb day's ridge-scrambling for experienced hillwalkers. If you're up to it, you'll probably already know all about it (6-8 hours; difficult to very difficult).

WARNING! *The Aonach Eagach ridge is not for inexperienced walkers or anyone without a strong head for heights, as it is very narrow and testing in places and, sadly, regularly claims lives.*

On Snow

Glencoe Ski Centre (Kingshouse, Glencoe PH49 4HZ, ☎ 1855-851 226, fax 1855-851 233, info@ski-glencoe.co.uk, www.ski-glencoe.co.uk). Glencoe is Scotland's original ski area, opening its first lift on Meall A'Bhuiridh (meaning "hill of the roaring stag") in 1956. The ski area is isolated in some of Scotland's wildest and most spectacular Highland scenery, including the rocky peak of Buachaille Etive Mor, with a jaw-dropping view of Ben Nevis, Britain's highest peak, rising beyond the pristine wilderness of Rannoch Moor.

With seven lifts and 19 runs, Glencoe is one of Scotland's smaller ski areas, yet it boasts both Scotland's steepest piste (the Fly Paper) and longest descent (from Meall A'Bhuiridh back to the base station: 2,600 feet/792 m). The north-facing slopes and gullies holds snow well and a diversity of natural mountain terrain (from very mild and inviting to surprisingly steep and challenging, and also including two man-swallowing hollows called "haggis traps") will keep most skiers interested. Glencoe is also a named FIS (International Skiing Federation) World Speed Skiing venue.

The basic lift infrastructure and "no frills" approach fits perfectly with Glencoe's untamed surroundings. It could be this sense of raw wildness and being at one with nature that commands Glencoe's loyal, almost cult, following of ski aficionados.

SKIING GLENCOE

■ Base elevation: 1,000 feet (305 m)

■ Skiing range: 1,000 feet (305 m) to 3,636 feet (1,108 m)

■ Pisted runs: 12 miles (20 km)

■ Longest run: one mile (1.6 km)

■ Maximum vertical descent: 2,600 feet (792 m)

■ Lifts: 7

■ Runs: 19 (easy: 21%, intermediate: 32%, difficult: 37%, very difficult: 10%)

■ Mountain restaurants/cafés: 2

■ Snow reports: ☎ 1855-851 232, BBC Ceefax page 421, Nevis Radio 96.6 FM, www.ski-glencoe.co.uk.

On the Water

 Lochaber Watersports (West Harbour, West Laroch, Ballachulish, Glencoe PH33 6SA, ☎ 1855-821 391, fax 1855-821 052, tbuilder@aol.com, www.lochaberwatersports.co.uk). Large watersports complex offering a rental fleet of dinghies ("toppers" for one or two crew and "wanderers" for up to four), canoes and row boats, and you can also sail an ocean yacht on bareboat or skippered charter. Those without previous experience can take "taster" cruises, and there are also RIB (Rigid Inflatable Boat) cruises and sailing courses.

Vertical Descents (Inchree Falls, Onich, By Fort William PH33 6SD, eight miles south of Fort William on the A82; ☎ 1855-821 593, info@activities-scotland.com, www.activities-scotland.com; open May-Oct). Try your hand at canyoning (slithering down natural waterslides and jumping down waterfalls into foaming pools) and fun-yakking (running rapids in a two-person inflatable) under expert guidance.

Glencoe Cruises & Fishing Trips (Etive Cottage, Glencoe PH49 4HS, ☎/fax 1855-811 658). Admire Glencoe's stunning scenery from a cruise on Loch Leven, with private charters and fishing trips also available.

You can catch coalfish, dogfish, rock cod and codling from the shoreline of Loch Leven year-round. In the summer, you can expect to catch mackerel using spinners, feathers or bait. Good spots include the rocks near the Corran Ferry, below the gas station in North Ballachulish (a great spot for catching mackerel) and below Ballachulish Bridge from the old slipways.

There is salmon and sea trout fishing in local rivers, stocked rainbow trout in the Glencoe lochan and a number of hill lochs. Permits are available from local stores and newsagents. Fishing for salmon or sea trout is not allowed on Sundays and neither is fishing in or around river mouths on the sea lochs.

■ Wildlife Watching

Red and roe deer can frequently be seen on the hillside, high on the Three Sisters and in the Lost Valley. In autumn you can hear stags roaring in the hills. Red squirrels have not yet been displaced by the larger greys, and foxes, stoats, otters and weasels are also regularly seen. Pine martens, badgers and wildcats are still found in the area, although their nocturnal lifestyles make them difficult to spot.

Golden eagles are seen occasionally, particularly in remote areas such as Glen Etive. Buzzards are more common, and sparrowhawks, kestrels and peregrine falcons are also well established.

■ Scenic Drives

The drive through Glen Coe itself, particularly the gorge section between the Three Sisters and the Aonach Eagach ridge, is possibly the most spectacular drive in the area. However, the road can be busy and the high-speed traffic (when it isn't crawling) makes it difficult to savor the glen fully from a car. A better alternative is to drive south down **Glen Etive** (starting immediately east of Buachaille Etive Mor). The 12-mile-long single-lane takes you through one of Scotland's prettiest glens, toward the tranquil head of Loch Etive. The River Etive forms numerous pools and waterfalls along its way and you might also spot a golden eagle.

■ Shopping

Crafts & Things (Glencoe PA39 4HN, ☎ 1855-811 325, fax 1855-811 483, sales@glencoe.u-net.com, www.glencoe.u-net.com). Local crafts, woolens, unusual gifts for sale, and a pleasant café.

Great Glen Fine Foods (1-3 Old Ferry Road, North Ballachulish PH33 6RZ, ☎ 1855-821 277, fax 1855-821 577, info@greatglenfinefoods.co.uk, www.greatglenfinefoods.co.uk). Scottish specialty foods, including luxury jams and marmalades, preserves, fish and meats, whisky, wine, teas and coffees, chocolate and traditional confectionery, with free tasting of Islay tablet.

■ Where To Stay & Eat

See the *Accommodation* and *Dining* price charts on pages 395 and 396.

Gleann Leac Na Muidhe Farmhouse (Glencoe PH49 4LA, ☎/fax 1855-811 598, jeffanna@namuidhe.freeserve.co.uk, www.namuidhe.freeserve.co.uk; B&B ££). Anna and Jeff Amis provide a warm welcome to their beautifully modernized 200-year-old farmhouse (pronounced "glen-lak-na-moowie") located just down the glen from where the MacDonald chief MacIain met his end in the 1692 massacre. The name means "glen of the churning slabs," referring to the loud rumbling of rocks around submerged depressions heard after heavy rain. Elegant antiques add charm

404 ■ The Highlands & Skye

and atmosphere, and large windows look straight up to the serrated profile of the Aonach Eagach ridge. Two cottages with kitchens are also available. No credit cards.

The Isles of Glencoe Hotel & Leisure Centre (Ballachulish PH49 4HL, ☎ 1855-821 582, fax 1855-821 463, reservations@freedomglen.co.uk, www.freedomglen.co.uk; B&B ££££, dinner £££). Modern, efficient hotel nestling idyllically on a peninsula reaching into Loch Leven, close to its historic islands. The location commands a superb panorama over the loch toward the Pap of Glencoe. The spacious bedrooms enjoy loch and mountain views and the lochside conservatory restaurant serves fine dining with views to match. Leisure facilities include a pool, Jacuzzi, sauna, steam room, exercise room and solarium, and a ranger is available to organize activities.

Strathlachlan Guest House (Upper Carnoch, Glencoe PH49 4HT, ☎ 1855-811 244, fax 1855-811 873, info@theglencoeguesthouse.com, www.theglencoeguesthouse.com; B&B ££, dinner ££). Secluded a short distance from Glencoe village, Strathlachlan provides peaceful accommodation in unfussy double, twin and family rooms. The owners are great sources of information on local walking and climbing.

Macdonald Hotel (Fort William Road, Kinlochleven, near Glencoe PH50 4QL, ☎ 1855-831 539, fax 1855-831 416, availability@macdonaldhotel.co.uk, www.macdonaldhotel.co.uk; B&B ££, dinner ££). Comfortable, family-run hotel superbly situated at the head of Loch Leven and within a few strides of the West Highland Way. The restaurant serves hearty, reasonably priced meals but eat instead in the **Bothy Bar** (same menu) – the views down the loch, with mountains rising steeply on both sides, are stunning, and the westerly aspect ensures delicious sunsets. The bar also offers 50 malt whiskies. Look for the weird device resembling a Rastafarian vacuum cleaner – it's used to warm ski boots. Four-bunk lodges with kitchens are also available.

Clachaig Inn (Clachaig, Glencoe PH49 4HX, two miles southeast of Glencoe village; ☎ 1855-811 252, fax 1855-812 030, info@clachaig.com, www.clachaig.com; B&B £££, dinner £-££). Climbers' inn that resounds to live music and mountain bravado and has the curious notice at reception, "No Hawkers or Campbells."

King's House Hotel (Glencoe PH49 4HY, near the Glen Etive road; ☎ 1855-851 259; B&B ££-£££, dinner £-££). Isolated 17th-century hotel with magnificent mountain views. Though also popular with walkers and climbers, the King's House is generally quieter than the Clachaig.

Corrour Station Bunkhouse (Corrour, By Fort William PH30 4AA, ☎ 1397-732 236, fax 1397-732 275, stationhouse@corrour.co.uk, www.corrour.co.uk; £ excluding breakfast, dinner £-££). A quaint Victorian railway station/signal box on the West Highland Line that is best known for its remote location amid stunning scenery. There is no road access – you arrive by train or walk. Basic provisions are available in the shop (closed Wed).

Four Seasons Bistro & Bar (Inchree, Onich, near Fort William PH33 6SE, ☎ 1855-821 393, fax 1855-821 287, dine@fourseasonsbistro.co.uk, www.fourseasonsbistro.co.uk; dinner ££). Relaxed dining in peaceful, rural surroundings combining local game, seafood and vegetarian specials with Scottish ales and classic malt whiskies.

Laroch Bar & Bistro (East Laroch, Ballachulish PH49 4JB, ☎ 1855-811 900, fax 1855-811 834, www.bistro-bar.com; £-££). Reasonably priced food in an informal atmosphere with a wide selection of real ales and malt whisky.

Ardnamurchan Peninsula

The peaceful, unspoiled Ardnamurchan Peninsula lies west of Fort William and Loch Linnhe, stretching to the Atlantic in a blend of glen, mountain and sea loch. Along its southern coast run **Loch Sunart** and the **Sound of Mull**. To the north lie the **Small Isles** of Rum, Muck and Eigg. Ardnamurchan Point is the most westerly point on the British mainland and is noted for its storm-swept lighthouse and stunning seclusion.

South of **Glenuig** village, you can see the "Seven Men of Moidart" – a row of beech trees planted in memory of the men who accompanied Bonnie Prince Charlie on his journey to Scotland.

Continuing south, the road twists near the ruins of **Castle Tioram**, the magnificently sited ancient seat of the MacDonalds of Clan Ranald. Near Kilchoan stand the 13th-century ruins of **Mingary Castle**. From Kilchoan, the main town on the Ardnamurchan peninsula, a car ferry sails to Tobermory on Mull. Farther east, the village of Strontian is famous for its 18th-century lead mines, where the metallic element strontium was discovered in 1764.

 INFORMATION SOURCES: The tourism office is at Strontian, Acharacle PH36 4HZ; open from Easter through October.

■ Attractions & Sights

 Castle Tioram (Loch Moidart, signposted from the A861 north of Acharacle at Shiel Bridge). Perched on a rocky islet in Loch Moidart, this striking castle (pronounced "chee-rum") is reputedly where a girl known as James's Daughter, accused of stealing silver from the castle, was tied to rocks by her hair and left to drown. Repeatedly besieged and bombarded, the castle was burned in 1715 by its owner – the chief of Clanranald – to prevent it from falling into Hanoverian hands.

Cladh Chiarain (Bay of Camus Nan Geal, between Kilchoan and Glenborrodale on the B8007). A red-colored carved stone raised to commemorate St Ciaran, who died in Ireland in 548, and was possibly dedicated by St Columba himself.

Ardnamurchan Lighthouse (Ardnamurchan Point, Kilchoan, Acharacle PH36 4LN, ☎ 1972-510 210, fax 1972-510 396, davie@ardnamurchan.u-net.com, www.ardnamurchan.u-net.com; open April-Oct, 10am-5pm; adult/concession/family £2.50/£1.50/£7). Ardnamurchan continues to play a vital role ensuring the safety of ships navigating the Minch. The former head keeper's house is now an innovative learning center with interactive displays on lighthouses, weather and wildlife watching, and a virtual-reality trip to the top of the light tower, from which you can admire panoramic views via webcam over the nearby Inner Hebrides. The foghorn (on a platform on the rocks below the lighthouse) is a good place to try to spot whales and dolphins, and you'll really appreciate the cozy stone-walled café after the long journey here.

■ Adventures

 An attractive walk passes the atmospheric ruin of **Castle Tioram**, which stands in splendid isolation on an attractive islet in Loch Moidart. Access is either via the A830 Fort William-Mallaig road or via the Corran Ferry and A861 via Salen. North of Acharacle, at Shiel Bridge, look for a minor road signposted to Castle Tioram. The castle is reached via a tidal causeway, so visit it before or after the walk depending on the tides. From the castle, walk south (with the loch to your right) along the road until you reach the house, "Scuirduish;" cross a stile with the field to its right, and take an uphill track beside a metal water pipe. At the second tiny lochan, turn left and continue past Beinn Bhreac. Descend to the wooded shores of Loch Moidart, passing right of the ruined village of Briagh. The path joins the lochside path where you turn left to return to the castle (2 hours; easy/moderate).

The Ardnamurchan/Ardgour area is often ignored by walkers as it contains no Munros, but those who visit discover the region's excellent and quiet mountains. Arguably the best of these is **Garbh Bheinn**, which rises opposite the entrance to Loch Leven and provides great views toward the Glen Coe peaks and out over sea lochs. Travel south on the A861 for about six miles from the Corran Ferry, just beyond the junction with the B8043. Park at a short stretch of old road at the foot of Coire Iubhair, which provides the best ascent route, though not the shortest! Walk for 2½ miles along the glen on an easy path that gives good views toward the peak itself and its prominent classic ridge. From the head of the glen, follow the route to the left of the ridge up to the summit (6-7 hours; moderate).

■ Where To Stay & Eat

See the *Accommodation* and *Dining* price charts on pages 395 and 396.

 The Inn at Ardgour (Ardgour, near Fort William PH33 7AA, ☎ 1855-841 225, fax 1855-841 214, theinn@ardgour.biz, www.ardgour.biz; B&B £££, dinner ££). A charming and atmospheric inn (the name is pronounced "ard-gower") providing high-quality accommodation on the quiet northern shore of Loch Linnhe. Though just a five-minute crossing from the main A82 Fort William road to the ferry slipway just outside the front door, the inn enjoys a wonderful sense of peace and isolation, particularly after the last evening ferry. There are superb views down the loch toward Fort William in the distance.

Mallaig & The Road to the Isles

North of Fort William, the A830 heads west toward **Mallaig** along the famous **Road to the Isles**. This historic route winds through some of the most evocative Highland scenery and will forever be linked with Bonnie Prince Charlie and the doomed Jacobite Rising of 1745.

The village of **Glenfinnan** boasts not just a gorgeous setting at the head of **Loch Shiel** but also the viaduct – familiar to many from the *Harry Potter* films – carrying the West Highland railway line, and the heartrending **Glenfinnan Monument**, near the site where, in August 1745, clansmen first rallied to the standard of Bonnie Prince Charlie.

West of Glenfinnan, the road skirts **Loch Eilt** to reach **Loch nan Uamh**, where a stone cairn marks the bay where, in September 1746, the Prince left Scotland never to return. There are spectacular views out to **Skye** and the **Small Isles** as the road twists north past the sandy beaches of Arisaig. Mallaig, from where a ferry sails for Skye, is a traditional working fishing port marking the end of the Road to the Isles.

The nostalgic **Jacobite Steam Train** (West Highland Railway Company, ☎ 1463-239 026/1524-732 100, www.westcoastrailway.co.uk) operates between Fort William and Mallaig from mid-June to September. This is one of Britain's most scenic rail routes, made even more famous through its appearance in the *Harry Potter* films.

DID YOU KNOW?

DID YOU KNOW? *Plunging to a depth of 1,000 feet (over 300 m), remote Loch Morar, near Mallaig, is the deepest loch in Scotland. Like Loch Ness, it too allegedly has a monster hidden in its depths, dubbed "Morag."*

■ Special Events

Glenfinnan Games (Aug; ☎ 1397-722 234). Traditional Highland Gathering staged in the famous setting where the Jacobites raised their standard in 1745.

INFORMATION SOURCES: The tourism office is at Mallaig PH41 4SQ; open year-round.

■ The Jacobite Risings

The **Stuart** dynasty (spelled Stewart until the time of Mary, Queen of Scots) ruled Scotland from the late 14th century. On the death of Tudor Queen Elizabeth of England in 1603, James VI of Scotland was also crowned James I of England. In 1688, the birth of a son to the unpopular James VII (II of England) led to fears of a Catholic monarchy. James fled the country and the throne was offered to his daughter Mary and her Protestant husband, William of Orange.

But many Catholic Scots still supported the exiled Stuarts. The first Jacobite Rising (the term Jacobite derives from *Jacobus* – Latin for James) took place in 1689, but ended with the death of its leader, John Graham of Claverhouse ("Bonnie Dundee"). Jacobite unrest resurfaced with further failed risings in 1715 and 1719. The arrival in 1745 of the young and charismatic Prince Charles Edward Stuart – Bonnie Prince Charlie – led to renewed Jacobite hopes. Born in Rome in 1720, Charles was the elder son of the exiled King James VIII (III of England). He believed it was his destiny to restore the Stuarts to their rightful throne and in 1745 set sail for Scotland.

Initially, few Highland clan chiefs would support the Prince, who arrived at Glenfinnan in August 1745 with around 50 men. It was only when an additional 800 clansmen arrived behind Cameron of Lochiel that the Prince could raise his standard with genuine optimism. Two days later, the Jacobites headed south toward London. Confidence was high and the Highlanders won a decisive victory over the Government army at Prestonpans.

However, the expected support of the English Jacobites failed to materialize. By the time they reached Derby, morale was low and the Prince reluctantly agreed to retreat northwards. The Highlanders overcame General Hawley's forces at Falkirk in January 1746, but by then the Duke of Cumberland's Government forces were in hot pursuit. Both armies moved northwards for the inevitable final confrontation.

Despite his charisma, the Prince was an ineffective military commander. Bleak Culloden Moor was entirely the wrong terrain for the Jacobite troops since the boggy conditions hampered their traditional charge. Furthermore, as they faced the Duke's army, the Prince's men were hungry and exhausted after a night march to Nairn, a failed attempt to surprise the Government troops. The Government forces were stronger in number, better trained and better equipped. They turned the battle into a slaughter that lasted less than an hour.

After Culloden, the Prince became a fugitive with a considerable price on his head. He spent an additional five months in the Highlands and Hebrides, evading capture with the help of loyal supporters, the most famous of whom was **Flora MacDonald**, who dressed the Prince as her Irish maid Betty Burke to aid in his escape by boat to Skye.

The Prince finally left Scotland on 20th September 1746, never to return. He died in Rome in 1788, after a largely dissolute, drunken and lonely life that was the antithesis to the grand designs of his younger days. After Culloden, the Jacobites never rose again. The last recognized male of the Stuart line, Henry, Duke of York, died in Italy in 1807.

■ Attractions & Sights

Glenfinnan Monument (NTS; Glenfinnan PH37 4LT, on the A830, 18 miles west of Fort William; ☎/fax 1397-722 250, glenfinnan@nts.org.uk; site open year-round, visitor center open April-Jun & Sep-Oct, 10am-5pm; July-Aug, 9:30am-5:30pm; adult/concession £2/£1 plus £1 parking). Emotionally-charged monument to the Highlanders who supported Bonnie Prince

Charlie in his failed quest for the British throne, on the spot where the Prince raised his standard on 19th August 1745 to begin the last Jacobite Rising. Alexander MacDonald of Glenaladale, whose family had supported the Prince in his military campaign, built the monument in 1815. Even without its historical significance, the superb setting surrounded by glorious scenery at the head of Loch Shiel would impress. Add the fact that this is where the Prince was furtively rowed ashore to meet his supporters, and that he passed through Glenfinnan three more times as a fugitive after Culloden, and the site really stirs the soul. It's worth walking up the short path to the viewpoint on the hill beside the excellent visitor center. You can also climb the stairs to the top of the monument, but beware – the staircase is narrow and you need to climb through a small hatch to reach the only-slightly-larger viewing platform. Not for the large-framed!

 **Glenfinnan Station Museum** (Glenfinnan Railway Station, Glenfinnan PH37 4LT, ☎ 1397-722 295, fax 1397-701 292; open Easter & June-Sept, 9:30am-4:30pm, or by appointment; adult/child £0.50/£0.25). A fully operational station, close to the 21-arch viaduct of *Harry Potter* fame, has been restored as a museum for the unbelievably scenic West Highland Line.

Treasures of the Earth (Corpach, By Fort William PH33 7JL, four miles from Fort William on the A830/Mallaig road; ☎ 1397-772 283, fax 1397-772 133; open July-Sept, 9:30am-7pm; Oct-Jun, 10am-5pm; closed Jan; adult/concession/child £3.50/£3/£2). Gemstone, crystal and fossil collections displayed in simulated cave, cavern and mining scenes. The "Primeval World" exhibit includes a volcanic panorama and depicts the creation of crystals.

Land, Sea & Islands Centre (Arisaig, ☎ 1687-462 720, 7973-252 923 mobile, info@arisaigcentre.co.uk, www.arisaigcentre.co.uk; open April-Oct, Mon-Sat, 11am-3pm & Sun, noon-4pm; adult/child £2/£1). Exhibition on the culture, social and natural history of the area, including the warrior queen and secret wartime training, along with photographic displays and artifacts.

Mallaig Heritage Centre (Station Road, Mallaig PH41 4PY, ☎ 1687-462 085, info@mallaigheritage.org.uk, www.mallaigheritage.org.uk; open year-round; opening times vary seasonally, so call ahead; adult/concession £1.80/£1.20, children free). Museum telling the story of the "Rough Bounds" (as the rugged and historically inaccessible west Lochaber area has long been known) and the people who lived here, through an impressive collection of displays, models, photographs and film. Displays describe the building of the Mallaig railway, the Knoydart Clearance and the work of the Mallaig Lifeboat.

Mallaig Marine World (The Harbour, Mallaig PH41 4PX, ☎/fax 1687-462 292; open year-round except January, 9:30am-5:30pm; closed Sunday in winter, open later in summer; adult/concession/child/family £2.75/£2/£1.50/£7.50). Exhibition displaying some of the marine life found in Scottish waters, and providing an insight into the fishing industry that is so important to Mallaig.

A video, models, photos and equipment help bring the town's fishing tradition to life.

■ Adventures

Eda Frandsen (Doune, Knoydart, By Mallaig PH41 4PL, ☎ 1687-462 917, jamie@eda-frandsen.co.uk, www.eda-frandsen.co.uk). Unforgettable sailing trips to the Small Isles and remote Hebridean islands aboard a beautiful traditional wooden sailing boat. April-Sept; for full details, see *Introduction*, page 49.

Arisaig Marine (Arisaig Harbour PH39 4NH, ☎ 1687-450 224, fax 1687-450 678, info@arisaig.co.uk, www.arisaig.co.uk). Daily cruises from May to Sept, departing Arisaig 11am, visit the Small Isles to view wildlife and explore ashore.

Bruce Watt Cruises (East Bay, Mallaig PH41 4QG, ☎/fax 1687-462 320, brucewattcruises@aol.com, www.knoydart-ferry.co.uk). Ferry from Mallaig to Inverie and Tarbet (see below) is also available for other cruises and charters.

Loch Shiel Cruises (Marnoch, Roshven, Lochailort PH38 4NB, ☎/fax 1687-470 322, mobile 7801-537 617, sileas@highlandcruises.co.uk, www.highlandcruises.co.uk; cruises Easter to mid-Oct, private charters year-round). Wildlife and historical cruises from Glenfinnan aboard the MV *Sileas*, exploring the magnificent wilderness of Loch Shiel, with live commentary and regular wildlife sightings.

■ Where To Stay & Eat

See the *Accommodation* and *Dining* price charts on pages 395 and 396.

Glenfinnan Dining Car (Glenfinnan Railway Station, Glenfinnan PH37 4LT, ☎ 1397-722 300, fax 1397-722 363; open Easter-Oct, evenings from June onwards – call to check times; lunch £, dinner £-££). Breakfast, lunch, teas and classic evening meals served in a historic railway dining car that also provides interesting bunk-style accommodation (☎ 1397-722 295, £).

Knoydart

The lonely Knoydart Peninsula is one of the last areas of true wilderness remaining in Britain. It has an unhappy past and was "cleared" in 1853, its population shipped to Nova Scotia following the potato famine. A succession of 20th-century landowners exploited the area for short-term gain, although stability has hopefully returned since residents bought the land in the late 1990s. Knoydart remains little populated. Its main village of **Inverie** has significantly fewer than 100 inhabitants and can only be reached by boat or an 18-mile hike over a mountain pass. Knoydart's undisturbed scenery of mountains and coast is unsurpassed for walking and wildlife viewing – truly a miles-from-anywhere, get-away-from-it-all place.

■ Getting Here

Bruce Watt Cruises (East Bay, Mallaig PH41 4QG, ☎/fax 1687-462 320, brucewattcruises@aol.com, www.knoydart-ferry.co.uk) operates a ferry from Mallaig to Inverie on the Knoydart peninsula (year-round, Mon, Wed & Fri; plus Tues & Thurs from mid-May to mid-Sept).

■ Adventures

Knoydart has some of the most wild walking experiences in Scotland. **Kinlochhourn to Inverie**, a wonderfully scenic walk, is the only land-based route into the Knoydart wilderness. It's long (18 miles) and fairly tiring but is well worth the effort for its remarkable scenery. Start at Kinlochhourn and follow the scenic path beside the fjord-like **Loch Hourn**. The path is good, although occasionally muddy, and there are three short-but-steep hills to negotiate before the loch opens out into the extraordinary panorama of **Barrisdale Bay** (after about six miles), studded with small islands, and surrounded by towering mountains, with tranquil views to the peaks of Skye in the distance.

Beyond Barrisdale, the path crosses a vehicle bridge and climbs unrelentingly to the pass at **Mam Barrisdale**. From the summit, you look down over a lochan, beyond which you can make out Loch Nevis and the Isle of Rum in the distance. Follow this path all the way to Inverie (6-9 hours; difficult).

If you're not keen on walking 18 miles in a single day you have two options. You can stay at the small bothy in Barrisdale (£2.50 a night, bring food and a sleeping bag) and break the walk into two roughly equal days. Alternatively, just walk from Kinlochhourn to Barrisdale (the approach to Barrisdale is the most scenic section of the walk) and turn back before climbing the pass. The downside is that you would miss the chance to collapse in Britain's "most remote" pub with the most deserved pint you will ever drink.

A great additional walk is the ascent of the lonely, craggy summit of **Ladhar Bheinn** (pronounced "lar-ven"), one of Knoydart's most impressive hills, which you can reach from Barrisdale. At the vehicle bridge past the Barrisdale bothy, turn right and follow the rough track beside the shoreline towards the hillside.

Pick up an overgrown, but good-quality, stalkers' path that you follow into the beautiful **Coire Dhorrcail**. Continue along the path until you cross the **Allt Coire Dhorrcail** where you then make a trackless ascent to the ridge of Ladhar Bheinn. Continue along the ridge and over the subsidiary top to reach the summit (6 hours; moderate/difficult).

■ Wildlife Watching

Keep a lookout for **golden** and **white-tailed sea eagles** around Knoydart's mountains and passes. This unpopulated wilderness is perfect eagle territory.

■ Where To Stay & Eat

See the *Accommodation* and *Dining* price charts on pages 395 and 396.

 Pier House (Inverie, Knoydart, By Mallaig PH41 4PL, ☎ 1687-462 347, info@thepierhouseknoydart.co.uk, www.thepierhouseknoydart.co.uk; DB&B £££, dinner ££). There are four guestrooms, with the front rooms enjoying great views over Loch Nevis. The friendly, high-quality restaurant is renowned for its seafood (try the huge seafood platter), excellent local lamb, home baking and own-grown herbs and vegetables.

The Old Forge (Inverie, Knoydart, By Mallaig PH41 4PL, ☎ 1687-462 267, info@theoldforge.co.uk, www.theoldforge.co.uk; ££). The remotest pub on mainland Britain, according to the *Guinness Book of Records*, you reach the Old Forge either by boat (recommended) or by the 18-mile walk from Kinlochhourn described above (even more highly recommended, provided you're fit). The atmospheric bar serves real ales and great meals. There are live folk-music sessions and the resident fiddles, guitars, pennywhistles and other sundry instruments induce impromptu ceilidhs. It's well worth getting here, whichever way you can.

Lochalsh & The Isle of Skye

This region of superlatives is home to Scotland's most photographed castle (Eilean Donan) its most awe-inspiring island (Skye), which is itself crowned by the moodiest, most magical mountain range (Cuillin), and hides one of the most idolized whisky distilleries (Talisker). Woven around fjord-like sea lochs, inlets, bays and towering peaks are historic fortresses, picturesque villages and a population that retains strong Gaelic traditions.

DON'T MISS

Drive through scenic Glenelg to explore its **Iron Age brochs**.

Eat delicious **seafood**, especially mussels and langoustines (locally called "prawns," no matter how large).

Taste a dram of superlative Scotch whisky at **Talisker Distillery**.

Sail or walk to **Loch Coruisk** in Skye, nestling in a bowl beneath the brooding Black Cuillin.

Walk or climb **Skye's magnificent mountains**.

Visit the lovely island hideaway of **Raasay**.

Best Freebie: Watching **seals** and **otters** in Skye and Raasay.

Lochalsh

Bounded by **Loch Carron** to the north and **Loch Hourn** to the south, Lochalsh is an area of great beauty and picturesque Highland villages. The

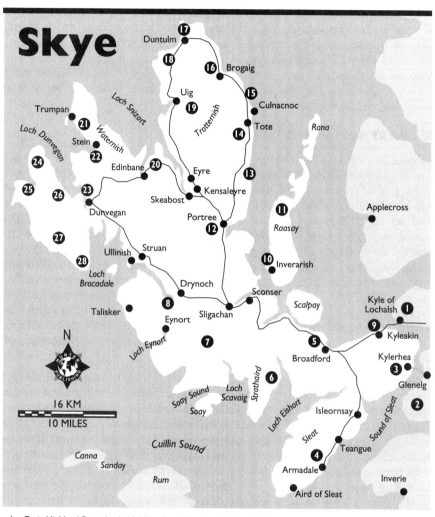

Skye

- Duntulm ⑰
- ⑱
- ⑯ Brogaig
- Uig ⑲
- ⑮
- Culnacnoc
- Trumpan
- ㉑
- Loch Snizort
- Waternish
- Trotternish
- Tote ⑭
- Rona
- Stein
- ㉒
- Edinbane ⑳
- Eyre
- ⑬
- Kensaleyre
- Skeabost
- ㉔
- ㉕ ㉖ ㉓
- Dunvegan
- Portree ⑫
- ⑪
- Applecross
- Raasay
- ㉗
- Ullinish Struan
- ⑩ Inverarish
- ㉘
- Loch Bracadale
- Drynoch
- Sconser
- Scalpay
- Kyle of Lochalsh ①
- Talisker
- ⑧
- Sligachan
- ⑨ Kyleakin
- Eynort
- Kylerhea
- N
- ⑦
- ⑤
- Broadford
- ③
- Loch Eynort
- Glenelg
- Strathaird
- ⑥
- Loch Scavaig
- 16 KM
- 10 MILES
- Soay Sound
- Loch Eishort
- Isleornsay
- ②
- Soay
- Sleat
- Sound of Sleat
- Canna
- Cuillin Sound
- Teangue
- Sanday
- ④
- Rum
- Armadale
- Inverie
- Aird of Sleat

1. Craig Highland Farm, Lochalsh Woodland Garden
2. Bernera Barracks, Glenelg Brochs (Towers)
3. Car Ferry, Otter Haven
4. Armadale Castle Gardens & Museum of the Isles, West Highland Heavy Horses Tours
5. Skye Environmental Centre, Serpentarium, World of Wood
6. Castle Keep
7. Cuillin Hills
8. Talisker Distillery
9. Skye Bridge, Brightwater Visitor Centre
10. Raasay House & Outdoor Centre, Iron Mine Ruin
11. Brochel Castle
12. An Tuireann, Aros Experience, Isle of Skye Soap Company
13. Storr Lochs, Old Man of Storr
14. Lealt Falls
15. Kilt Rock, Mealt Falls
16. Quiraing
17. Duntulm Castle
18. Museum of Island Life, Flora MacDonald Memorial
19. Fairy Glen
20. Edinbane Pottery
21. Trumpan Church Ruin
22. Skyeskyns
23. Dunvegan Castle, Giant MacAskill Museum
24. Borreraig Park
25. Toy Museum
26. Colbost Croft Museum
27. MacLeod's Tables
28. MacLeod's Maidens

approach from the east is through the spectacular **Glen Shiel**, beneath towering summits in all directions, including the imposing **Five Sisters of Kintail** – one of Scotland's most striking mountain ridges. Continuing on the Kyle of Lochalsh road, you pass through Dornie village, near which stands **Eilean Donan Castle** – Scotland's most photographed fortress and setting for many films. Picturesque **Plockton** was the setting of the BBC series *Hamish Macbeth* and boasts whitewashed houses and a palm-lined main street. The Kyle line, the scenic rail journey from Inverness to Kyle of Lochalsh, passes its finest scenery through this area.

■ Attractions & Sights

Eilean Donan Castle (Dornie, By Kyle of Lochalsh, IV40 8DX, ☎ 1599-555 202, fax 1599-555 262, info@eileandonancastle.com, www.eileandonancastle.com; open mid-March to mid-Nov, 10am-5:30pm, til 3:30 in March & Nov; adult/concession/child/family £4.50/£3.60/£1.50/£9.50). Stunningly located on an islet at the meeting point of lochs **Alsh**, **Duich** and **Long**, against the backdrop of the Isle of Skye, Eilean Donan, the ancestral seat of the MacKenzies of Kintail, is one of Scotland's most romantic castles despite being startlingly modern. Alexander II built the castle in the early 13th century to deter Viking invasions. Lieutenant Colonel John MacRae-Gilstrap largely rebuilt the present castle in 1912-32, after Government troops destroyed the previous castle in 1719, believing it was occupied by Jacobites. An understandably popular set for films, including *Highlander, Entrapment* and *The World is Not Enough*, Eilean Donan is one of the most photographed castles in Scotland.

Visitors can explore most parts of the castle with knowledgeable guides providing the story behind rooms and exhibits. An introductory exhibition displays the castle's early history, when it sat at the heart of the sea kingdom of the Lords of the Isles. The walls of the **Billeting Room** are up to 14 feet (4.26 m) thick. The massive walls and vast fireplace of the superb **Great Hall** (or Banqueting Hall) are a suitably grand setting for fine furniture, family portraits and Jacobite memorabilia including a lock of Bonnie Prince Charlie's hair. The recreated kitchen lets visitors experience the sights, sounds and smells during preparations for one of the first banquets to be held in the newly rebuilt castle in 1932. There is a visitor center, excellent café and gift shop.

Kyle Station Visitor Centre (Railway Station, Kyle of Lochalsh IV40 8AQ, ☎ 1599-534 824; open Easter-Dec, 10am-5:30pm, free). The famously scenic Kyle line runs from Inverness to Kyle of Lochalsh. This museum explains its history with railway memorabilia and short historical movie, together with many old photos of Kyle village. You can then take a trip along the line, perhaps stopping for lunch at a picturesque intermediate village. There is also a whisky shop.

Scenic Drives

Kintail marks the start of a great drive over the high pass of **Mam Ratagan** to **Glenelg**, from where a seasonal car ferry sails across the Sound of Sleat to

Kylerhea on Skye. Glenelg was the setting and inspiration for Gavin Maxwell's book (and film), *Ring of Bright Water*, and the area is still home to many otters. Glenelg is also renowned for the stark ruins of **Bernera Barracks**, built in the 1720s following the first Jacobite rebellion, and the ruins of three Iron Age brochs, including the well-preserved **Dun Telve**.

■ Adventures

 Loch Long Pony Trails (Allt-nan-Subh, Dornie, By Kyle of Lochalsh IV40 8DZ, ☎/fax 1599-588 230, macleod@u2.net). One- to five-hour small-group pony treks by the lochside or into the hills, with picnic rides also available.

■ Cruises

 Calum's Seal Trips (32 Harbour Street, Plockton IV52 8TN, ☎/fax 1599-544 306, plocktoncalum@aol.com; cruises Easter-Oct). Long-established boat operator guarantees you'll see seals or your money back! There are also regular sightings of otters, porpoises and, occasionally, dolphins.

Seaprobe *Atlantis* (The Pier, Kyle of Lochalsh IV40 8AF, ☎/fax 1471-822 716, 800-980 4846 freephone, www.seaprobeatlantis.com; regular cruises Mar-Oct). With its unique underwater observation deck, the UK's only semi-submersible passenger vessel provides fascinating underwater views of the Kyle of Lochalsh. See seals, otters, fish and kelp forests, and view the wreck of the 500-foot World War II minelayer HMS *Port Napier*. Above the waves, trips visit the protected seal and bird colonies on Seal Island.

■ Where To Stay & Eat

See the *Accommodation* and *Dining* price charts on pages 395 and 396.

 Kintail Lodge Hotel (Glenshiel, Kintail IV40 8HL, ☎ 1599-511 275, reception@kintaillodgehotel.co.uk, www.kintaillodgehotel.co.uk; B&B £££, dinner ££). As the only hotel (and public bar) for 10 miles, the Kintail Lodge has the market sewn up for walkers and climbers keen to bag the many local Munros. Converted from a former shooting lodge, the hotel stands at the foot of the Five Sisters of Kintail, on the shore of Loch Duich, and offers well-furnished bedrooms, home-cooked food and two cozy, well-stocked bars.

Plockton Hotel (Harbour Street, Plockton IV52 8TN, ☎ 1599-544 274, fax 1599-544 475, sales@plocktonhotel.co.uk, www.plocktonhotel.co.uk; B&B ££-£££, lunch £, dinner ££). Plockton's only waterfront hotel offers stylish modern rooms with magical views across the bay. The superb restaurant offers platters of the freshest prawns, fish and shellfish, and locally reared beef. The mussels in white wine sauce are superb.

Off the Rails (The Station, Plockton IV52 8YX, ☎ 1599-544 423, fax 1599-577 260, www.off-the-rails.co.uk; open Mar-Nov; ££). Small, cozy restaurant offering a variety of local and international dishes, and a respectable wine list.

Kyle Hotel (Main Street, Kyle of Lochalsh IV40 8AB, ☎ 1599-534 204, fax 1599-534 932, thekylehotel@btinternet.com, www.kylehotel.co.uk; B&B ££-£££, dinner ££). Comfortable hotel in Kyle village, with an à la carte restaurant and bar meals.

Lochalsh Hotel (Ferry Road, Kyle of Lochalsh IV40 8AF, ☎ 1599-534 202, fax 1599-534 881, mdmacrae@lochalshhotel.com, www.lochalshhotel.com; B&B £££). The hotel has reasonable rooms and even better views.

Dornie Hotel (Francis Street, Dornie, By Kyle of Lochalsh IV40 8DT, ☎ 1599-555 205, fax 1599-555 429, dornie@madasafish.com; B&B ££). Well located hotel close to Eilean Donan Castle.

 The Seafood Restaurant (Railway Station Buildings, Kyle of Lochalsh IV40 8AE, ☎ 1599-534 813, jann@the-seafood-restaurant.co.uk, www.the-seafood-restaurant.co.uk; open Mar-Oct; lunch £, dinner ££). Deliciously cooked fresh, local seafood served in a relaxed atmosphere. Booking essential.

Jac-o-bite Restaurant (Ault-na-Chruinne, Glenshiel, Kyle of Lochalsh IV40 8HN, ☎/fax 1599-511 347, jac.o.bite@btopenworld.com; open Easter-Nov; ££). Seafood, meat and game served at the foot of the Five Sisters of Kintail.

Waverley Restaurant (Main Street, Kyle of Lochalsh IV40 8AB, ☎ 1599-534 337; open Feb-Dec, evenings only; ££). Home-cooked local produce with à la carte and evening specials.

Isle of Skye

 Skye is one of the largest and most scenic of Scotland's islands, attracting visitors from the world over to its wild, rugged mountains, stunning seascapes and unspoiled, open spaces. The **Cuillin Mountains** at the heart of the island form a dramatic backdrop to many vistas. The Black Cuillins are made of gabbro (a tough volcanic rock) and form the most spectacular peaks and glacier-gouged corries – creating the ridges and sheer faces so loved by climbers. The neighboring Red Cuillins are made of pink granite that breaks down into harder-to-climb scree.

Skye has long been the Highland home of Clans MacLeod and MacDonald, and suffered Norse invasions and the sadness of the Highland Clearances. Most famously, Bonnie Prince Charlie and Flora MacDonald escaped here ("Speed bonnie boat like a bird on the wing . . . over the sea to Skye") following the Prince's defeat at Culloden.

The Gaelic culture retains a strong hold on Skye. The native language and traditional crofting way of life survive among the many tourist services and craft shops that have sprung up to cater to visitors. The opening of the **Skye Bridge** has taken away some of the magic and romance of the island (it's difficult to sing the *Skye Boat Song* as you're driving across a bridge), but only a little.

■ Special Events

Isle of Skye Pipe Band Festival (Jun; contact the tourism office). New but popular piping festival in Portree, attracting large crowds, especially for the massed bands in Somerled Square.

Edinbane Music Festival (Jul; ☎ 1470-532 436, info@edinbane-festival.com, www.edinbane-festival.com). A great weekend of music, fun and dance involving bands from near and far and a closing fire show.

Skye Festival (Jul; Ostaig House, Teangue, Isle of Skye IV44 8RQ, ☎ 1471-844 207, feis@cali.co.uk, www.skyefestival.com). Ten-day Gaelic and music festival, including ceilidhs, theater, workshops, dance and culture alongside the Sabhal Mòr Ostaig Gaelic college's own summer school.

Portree Highland Games (Aug; ☎ 1478-612 540, fax 1478-613 435). Traditional Highland Games with heavyweight competitions, dancing and piping competitions.

Skye & Lochalsh Food & Drink Festival (Sep; ☎ 1599-555 403/1478-612 137, shona@skyefood.co.uk, www.skyefood.co.uk). Food and drink festival highlighting the excellent local produce, with tastings, demonstrations and a ceilidh.

■ Getting Here

By Rail

Trains run from Inverness to **Kyle of Lochalsh**; you can walk across the road bridge (no charge) to Kyleakin or catch a bus across the bridge to Kyleakin, Portree or beyond.

By Car

Cars cross to the island by the **Skye Bridge** from Kyle of Lochalsh. This controversial bridge created an uproar by charging the highest toll-per-distance-traveled anywhere in the world. After continued protests, the toll was scrapped in late 2004.

By Ferry

Those looking for a more romantic passage to Skye than the bridge can still travel by traditional car-ferry.

The **Caledonian MacBrayne** (☎ 1475-650 100, www.calmac.co.uk) ferry from **Mallaig** to **Armadale** runs six to seven times a day in the summer (including high-season Sundays). The winter service is limited to two journeys a day (Mon-Fri only). Vehicle reservations are required; bikes are carried free of charge. CalMac also provides year-round sailings to Uig from North Uist and Harris (see their web site for sailing schedules).

The **Skye Ferry** *Glenachulish* (☎ 1599 511 302, www.skyeferry.co.uk) operates between Easter and October, including Sundays in high-season, with crossings from **Glenelg** to **Kylerhea** for passengers and up to six cars.

By Coach/Bus

Scottish Citylink (☎ 870-550 5050, www.citylink.co.uk) operates daily coach services to Kyleakin, Portree and Uig from Glasgow via Fort William, and to Portree from Inverness.

Car Rental

You can rent cars locally from **Ewen MacRae** (Dunvegan Road, Portree, Isle of Skye IV51 9HD, ☎ 1478-612 554, fax 1478-613 269, ewenmacraemotors@aol.com) or **Portree Coachworks** (Portree Industrial Estate, Portree, Isle of Skye, ☎ 1478-612 688, fax 1478-613 281, portreecoachworks@line-one.net, www.portreecoachworks.co.uk).

■ South Skye: Sleat & Broadford

The woods and green pastures of the Sleat Peninsula (it's pronounced "slate") contrast with the rugged mountains, bare rock and moors of so much of the rest of Skye. Close to Armadale are the ruins of **Armadale Castle** set among beautifully restored gardens. Traveling north, a short circular diversion brings you to the ruins of **Dunsgathaich Castle**, the oldest castle on Skye and former MacDonald stronghold.

Returning to the A851, the narrow road winds north past the sheltered harbor at Isle Ornsay and over moorland to Broadford. The **Bright Water Visitor Centre** at Kyleakin offers exclusive tours to the island nature reserve of Eilean Ban. The A887 runs southwest to **Elgol** (see *Scenic Drives*, next page), which enjoys outstanding views of the Cuillin Mountains.

Attractions & Sights

 Armadale Castle Gardens (Armadale, Sleat, Isle of Skye IV45 8RS, ☎ 1471-844 305, fax 1471-844 275, office@clandonald.com, www.clandonald.com; open April-Oct, 9:30am-5:30pm; adult/concession/family £4.50/£3/£14). Visit 40 acres of sheltered woodland garden dating back to the 17th century, set around the ruined Armadale Castle. The castle dates from the late 18th to early 19th century and was abandoned in 1925 when the family moved to a smaller residence nearby. Flora MacDonald married at Armadale in November 1750. Take a walk through expansive lawns, by herbaceous borders and landscaped ponds, follow woodland paths and nature trails through exotic trees, shrubs and flowers. The elegant stables now house a licensed restaurant and gift shop. The Celtic Cross-shaped **Museum of the Isles** charts the 1,300-year history of Clan MacDonald, from which the mighty Lords of the Isles descended, and the history of the Gaels. Genealogical archives let you delve into your own ancestry.

Bright Water Visitor Centre (The Pier, Kyleakin, Isle of Skye IV41 8PL, ☎/fax 1599-530 040, enquiries@eileanban.com; open April-Oct, Mon-Sat,

9:30am-5:30pm). Tour the wildlife haven on the island of Eilean Ban, beneath the Skye Bridge, with the **Stevenson lighthouse** and **Gavin Maxwell** (author of *Ring of Bright Water*) **museum**.

Scenic Drives

 The single-lane road from Broadford to Elgol is only 15 miles long, but can easily take upwards of an hour to drive as it winds its way through film-swallowing mountain and coastal scenery. It's worth stopping at the ruined pre-Reformation church of **Cill Chroisd** with its ancient graveyard. At Torrin, you pass the quarries producing the famous Skye Marble.

Adventures

On Foot

 Experience Skye Mountain Guides (Allt Slapin, Torrin, near Broadford, Isle of Skye IV49 9BA, ☎ 1471-822 018, www.experience-skye.co.uk). Guided walking on Skye and the Cuillins, mountain scrambles, classic climbs, ridge traverses, day-tours and courses.

Hebridean Pathways (PO Box 6340, Broadford, Isle of Skye IV49 9YA, ☎/fax 1471-820 179, 7712-577 121 mobile, darren@hebrideanpathways.co.uk, www.hebrideanpathways.co.uk). Walking, climbing and mountaineering guiding and instruction.

Skye Highs Mountain Guiding (3 Luib, Broadford, Isle of Skye IV49 9AN, ☎ 1471-822 116, mike.lates@skyeguides.co.uk, www.skyeguides.co.uk). Guiding walking, scrambling, rock climbing and abseiling for all levels.

Point of Sleat is a popular walk on good paths to the lighthouse at the southern point of Skye. Drive south from Armadale to the end of the road at Aird of Sleat, parking beside an old church. Go through the gate and follow the undulating moorland track that narrows as it descends toward the sea. The scenery changes from featureless moor to a splash of colors as the path follows a stream bordered by trees and flowers. The stream descends in two waterfalls, and the path crosses it several times.

The path narrows again as it passes through a gate and past some ruined crofts. Climb over a stile and continue past a tiny harbor and cottage. Turn left and follow the fence as it climbs up the hill, turns left and descends to some boggy ground. Turn right up the hill, along the direction of the peat cutting, to the high ground where the path becomes much clearer. You soon catch your first glimpse of the lighthouse. Follow the path across the cliffs with the sea on both sides. Steps lead up to the lighthouse from where there are excellent views of Rum and Eigg and the Cuillins in the distance (4 hours; easy).

On Wheels

You can rent cycles from **Fairwinds Bicycle Hire** (Elgol Road, Broadford, Isle of Skye IV49 9AB, ☎/fax 1471-822 270).

Lochalsh & The Isle of Skye

On Water

Skyak Adventures (13 Camus Cross, Isle Ornsay, Isle of Skye IV43 8QS, ☎ 1471-833 428, skyak@onetel.net.uk, www.skyakadventures.com). Sea kayak tours and skills training, with all equipment provided.

Fyne Leisure & Marine (Ornsay Edge, 15 Camus Cross, Isle Ornsay, Isle of Skye IV43 8QS, ☎ 1471-833 470, fleming.fyne@talk21.com). Classic yacht for skippered charter.

Sea.fari Adventures – Skye (Armadale Pier, Sleat, Isle of Skye IV45 8RS, ☎/fax 1471-833 316, info@whalespotting.co.uk, www.whalespotting.co.uk; cruises Mar-Oct, with year-round charters) RIB trips to spot whales and other wildlife, typically heading south down the Sound of Sleat, past the most southern tip of Skye and toward the Small Isles.

Seafood Cruises (☎ 1599-577 230, neillieach@yahoo.com). Enjoyable seafood and wildlife cruises from Kyleakin with Skye fisherman Neil MacRae. Pull mussels off Skye Bridge, buy langoustines from boats while they're fishing, catch scallops, crabs and all manner of fish, then enjoy your delicious bounty freshly cooked on board as you cruise Skye's magical waters. You'll see seals and occasional dolphins and whales.

Skye Jet Marine Adventures (☎ 800-783 2175 freephone, fax 1471-822 307, info@skyejet.co.uk, www.skyejet.co.uk). Wildlife adventure trips by RIB from Broadford Pier to see seals, seabirds and occasional dolphins and whales. Glass-bottom boat trips are also available.

On Horseback

West Highland Heavy Horses (7 Allt a'Tuath, Ardvasar, Sleat, Isle of Skye IV45 8RQ, ☎ 1471-844 759, 7769-588 565 mobile, annie@w-h-h-h.fsnet.co.uk). Tours in a covered horse-drawn cart, and trekking with heavy Clydesdale/shire horses.

Wildlife Watching

Kylerhea Otter Haven (Kylerhea – pronounced "kile-ray" – Isle of Skye, ☎ 1320-366 322; open 9am to one hour before dusk). A one-hour walk to an observation hide for unobtrusive wildlife viewing, which hopefully includes otters.

Shopping

Ragamuffin (The Pier, Armadale, Sleat, Isle of Skye IV45 8RS, ☎ 1471-844 217, fax 1471-844 225, www.ragamuffinonline.co.uk). High-quality knitwear, clothes and accessories ranging from elegant and traditional to outrageously modern; also jewelry, pottery and music.

■ East & North Skye: Portree & Trotternish

Portree, Skye's main town, is a pleasant, bustling port offering a good range of accommodation and services within its natural harbor. It was here that Bonnie Prince Charlie spent his last days in Scotland.

The Trotternish Peninsula stretches north of Portree and is some 20 miles long and eight miles wide. Trotternish is famous for its spectacular geological features such as the **Trotternish Ridge**, a 20-mile inland cliff (the longest landslip in Britain) winding down the heart of the peninsula. The ridge is studded with weird and wonderful rock formations, pinnacles and pillars, the most famous being the **Old Man of Storr**, **Kilt Rock** and the extraordinary pinnacles of the **Quiraing** (pronounced "kor-rang").

 INFORMATION SOURCES: The tourism office is at Bayfield House, Bayfield Road, Portree, Isle of Skye IV51 9EL; open year-round.

Attractions & Sights

Duntulm Castle (eight miles north of Uig; open at all times; admission free). The ruin of an ancient Pictish fort occupying an impressive coastal site. The castle changed hands between the MacLeods and MacDonalds and finally became the MacDonalds' principal dwelling in the 16th century. The ghost of Uisdean MacGillespie Chleirich is said to haunt the castle. Uisdean (Hugh) was a cousin of the Lord of the Isles, and plotted to take over the leadership of Clan MacDonald. He failed because of a careless blunder: he wrote a letter to a friend outlining his plot on the same day that he wrote a letter to his cousin declaring eternal friendship, but somehow mixed up the two letters. The Lord of the Isles received the letter outlining plans for his overthrow, captured Uisdean and left him to starve in Duntulm's highest tower.

Fairy Glen (two miles from Uig, along the road signposted to Sheader). This remarkable landscape of small conical hills divided by narrow, steep-sided valleys formed by a process of landslips and has a strange, magical atmosphere – you could easily imagine fairies live here. The steep crag overlooking Fairy Glen is called Castle Ewan and makes an enjoyable little scramble.

 Mealt Waterfall & Kilt Rock (17 miles north of Portree). The waterfall drops 300 feet toward the sea but often gets blown away on the wind before it reaches the ocean. This is also a popular viewpoint for Kilt Rock, where columns of dolerite, similar to the black basalt of Staffa, form what appear to be pleats in the cliff.

Skye Museum of Island Life (Kilmuir, Isle of Skye IV51 9UE, between Uig and Duntulm; ☎ 1470-552 206, www.skyemuseum.co.uk; open April-Oct, 9am-5:30pm May-Sept, other months call to check times; adult/child £1.75/£1). A cluster of seven thatched cottages portrays life on Skye about a century ago. The superb exhibits, particularly the evocative crofthouse kitchen and bedroom, relate mainly to the life of ordinary people, although there are also items connected with the 19th-century crofter rebellions, Bonnie Prince Charlie and Flora MacDonald, and weapons and Stone Age axe heads.

Lochalsh & The Isle of Skye

Adventures

On Foot

 Guiding on Skye & The Cuillin (4 Gedintailor, Braes, By Portree, Isle of Skye IV51 9NJ, ☎ 1478-650 380, info@guidingonskye.co.uk, www.guidingonskye.co.uk). Mountain guiding, Munros, classic scrambles, hill and coastal walks, including daily guiding and weekly courses.

Skyetrak Safari (Skeabost Farmhouse, By Portree, Isle of Skye IV51 9NP, ☎ 1470-532 436, fax 1470-532 436, skyetrak@lineone.net). Guiding, hill and coastal walking, as well as history, archaeology, wildlife and cultural tours.

Skye Walking Holidays (Duntulm Castle Hotel, Duntulm, Isle of Skye IV51 9UF, ☎ 1470-552 396, fax 1470-552 301, info@skyewalks.co.uk, www.skyewalks.co.uk; open Mar-Nov & New Year). Guided walking holidays exploring Skye's scenery and culture from a comfortable hotel base.

The full traverse of the **Trotternish Ridge** makes a superb 20-mile high-level walk that involves no climbing or scrambling, yet takes you into wild and primeval landscapes with panoramic views over the Cuillins, Outer Hebrides and the mountains of Wester Ross. Although you don't need climbing skills, only experienced walkers armed with a map and guidebook should undertake the full ridge walk. Allow two days for the full walk and check the weather report carefully before you leave – mist can often descend rapidly.

It's possible for less experienced walkers or those with less time to devote to enjoy the views from the ridge without walking its entire length. One option starts at Uig (by the newsagent) and takes you along the road through Glen Conon, a peaceful crofting valley set in a dramatic landscape. After two miles the road becomes a track and eventually disappears altogether, leaving you to plod through boggy ground (wear waterproof footwear) before you finally reach the ridge at one of its lowest points. From here there are great views in all directions, particularly north to the Quiraing.

Once on the ridge, turn right and continue along the cliff-top for a mile to the high point of Beinn Edra. From the top, descend south down beside the stream to the minor road at Balnaknock. The route then skirts down the south side of Glen Uig, emerging back onto the main road.

The Quiraing, the "round fold," is one of the most bizarre rock formations in Britain; it's hard to believe that geology alone could have created it. At its heart stands **The Table**, a high grassy plateau guarded by rock walls, which was used as a hiding place for cattle in the 15th and 16th centuries. Dwarfed on all sides by vertiginous spires and verdant walls, the plateau could be a playing field for the gods, but was used instead by locals to play shinty at New Year. You need a good head for heights, though, as some of the paths are narrow and it's a long way down!

From Portree take the A855 north to Brogaig where you follow a minor road to Uig. Continue past the cemetery and park at the highest point on the road. A path from the parking area leads northeast beside the escarpment to **The Prison** – a rocky peak on the right. Upwards to your left rises the impressive pinnacle of **The Needle**, guarding the narrow entrance to The Table. Climb up the steep scree slope and continue to the left of and behind The Needle to reach The Table – part of a gigantic landslip.

Return to the main path and turn north (left) to ascend to a ridge where you turn west (left). Carefully follow the path above the escarpment south (left) toward Meall na Suiramach, then southwestwards to return to the parking area (3 hours; moderate).

A good low-level walk to the **Duntulm Headland** starts at Duntulm (seven miles north of Uig), where you can explore the ruined castle then descend the steps to the shore and walk round the headland. You pass close to **Tulm Island**, just offshore, which teems with birdlife. The coast is initially gentle grassland, but turns to patterned cliffs as it veers eastward. You are now at the northernmost point on Skye, the best place on the island to spot whales and dolphins. Halfway along these cliffs is an old **coastguard station**. You can carry on until the shore meets the road again at Kilmaluag, cut across inland, or retrace your steps to Duntulm.

On Wheels

Island Cycles/Rod & Reel (The Green, Portree, Isle of Skye IV51 9BT, ☎ 1478-613 121) and **Skye Bicycle Hire** (Orasay, Uig, Isle of Skye IV51 9XU, ☎ 1470-542 316, barbara@orasay.freeserve.co.uk). There are no designated cycle routes on Skye, though many of the island's roads are quiet and not too steep, and well suited to cycling.

On Horseback

Portree Riding Stables (Garalapin, By Portree, Isle of Skye IV51 9LN, ☎ 1478-613 124, info@portreeriding.co.uk, www.portreeriding.co.uk). One-hour to all-day treks for all levels of rider, with qualified instructors and cross-country fences to try.

Skye Riding Centre (2 Suledale, Clachamish, By Portree, Isle of Skye IV51 9NY, ☎ 1470-582 419, horsetalk@skye-riding.co.uk, www.skye-riding.co.uk). Treks and rides through the heart of north Skye from half an hour to three hours.

In the Air

Isle of Skye Falconry (Kirklee, Kensaleyre, Snizort, By Portree, Isle of Skye IV51 9XE, ☎ 1470-532 489, www.isleofskye-falconry.co.uk). Handle and fly birds of prey to taste the ancient sport of kings, with hawk walks, hunting days and flying demonstrations available. Booking is essential.

On Water

Isle of Skye Adventure Cruises (12 Fraser Crescent, Portree, Isle of Skye IV51 9DR, ☎ 1478-613 161, jennifer-m@skye-boat-trips.com, www.skye-boat-trips.com; open Mar-Oct). Four- to eight-hour cruises from Portree aboard *Jennifer M*, a motor/sailing ketch.

Lochalsh & The Isle of Skye

Sky Waves (c/o "Diubaig," 9 Achachork, Portree, Isle of Skye IV51 9HT, ☎ 1478-612 461, www.skyewaves.com; open Mar-Oct). Anyone who enjoys a fast ride on the open water will enjoy taking a 9-meter RIB (rigid inflatable boat) on a high-speed voyage around Portree Bay, Raasay and Rona at speeds up to 50 knots. Waterproofs are provided.

Staffin Bay Cruises (Keepers Cottage, Staffin, Isle of Skye IV51 9JS, ☎/fax 1470-562 217, staffin.bay@virgin.net, www.trotternish.co.uk; open April-Oct). Hour-and-a-half cruises aboard a 30-foot motor cruiser exploring the Trotternish coastline, taking in views of the Trotternish Ridge, Outer Hebrides and mainland Torridon mountains. Also visit Kilt Rock and the seal colony at Flodigarry Island. Private charters and fishing trips are also available.

Golf

 Isle of Skye Sconser Course (9-hole links, 4,677 yards, 18 holes; Sconser, Isle of Skye IV48 8TD, ☎ 1478-650 414, isleofskye.golfclub @btinternet.com; green fees £15). Not a long course, but there are some challenging holes and good views over the Sound of Raasay.

Entertainment

Aros Heritage Centre (Viewfield Road, Portree, Isle of Skye IV51 9EU, ☎ 1478-613 649, www.aros.co.uk; open year-round, 9am-6pm; admission to exhibits, adult/concession/child/family £4/£3/£2/£10). Learn about Skye's history and culture and enjoy Gaelic evenings, music and films.

Skye Scene Highland Ceilidhs (Tigh Na Sgire, off Somerled Square, Portree, Isle of Skye, ☎ 1470-542 228, www.skyescene.co.uk; shows at 8 pm Mon & Wed, late May to early Sept; plus Tuesday in July and Aug; adult/concession/child £6/£5/£4). A great two-hour celebration of Gaelic music and culture performed by Skye artists at a traditional Highland ceilidh with bagpipes, fiddles, accordion and clarsach, Gaelic and Scottish songs, and an audiovisual presentation of the island's highlights.

Shopping

Isle of Skye Soap Co (Somerled Square, Portree, Isle of Skye IV51 9EH, ☎/fax 1478-611 350, sales@skye-soap.co.uk, www.skye-soap.co.uk). A delightful range of aromatherapy soaps handmade on-site using pure essential oils without added coloring.

Over the Rainbow (Quay Bay, Portree, Isle of Skye IV51 9DB, ☎/fax 1478-612 555, skyeknitwear@fsbdial.co.uk, www.skyeknitwear.com). Studio-manufactured luxury knitwear and clothing, with Scottish textiles, throws, rugs and tartans, soft furnishings, jewelry, art and prints.

Skye Batiks (The Green, Portree, Isle of Skye IV51 9BT, ☎ 1478-613 331, fax 1478-613 338, info@skyebatiks.com, www.skyebatiks.com). Funky Celtic and Viking-inspired batiks for home and body, with outrageously colorful hand-loomed cotton smocks, shirts, soft tweed garments, exclusive jewelry and hand-carved wood. Enjoy a free coffee or tea while you browse.

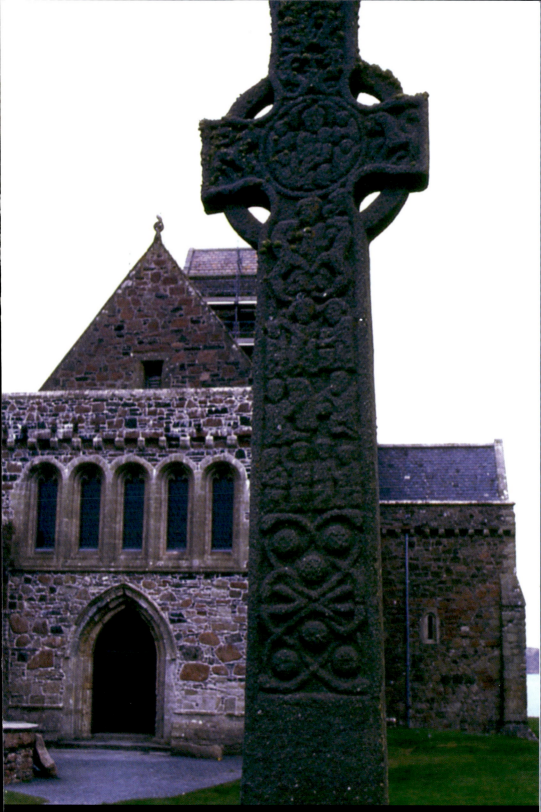

Above: Torosay Castle, Isle of Mull

Below: Colorful Tobermory, Isle of Mull

St. Magnus Cathedral, Kirkwall, Orkney

Above: Stromness, Orkney

Below: The towering Stones of Stenness, Orkney

■ West Skye: The Cuillin & Waternish

The west of Skye comprises four regions: **Minginish**, **Dunvegan**, **Duirinish** and **Waternish**. In the south, Minginish is dominated by the menacing backdrop of the **Black Cuillin**, seen clearly from the head of Loch Brittle.

Carbost is the home of world-famous **Talisker**, Skye's only distillery. Farther north is **Dunvegan Castle**, home to the chiefs of MacLeod for over 700 years. West of Dunvegan the Duirinish Peninsula is dominated by "MacLeod's Tables" – two flat-topped hills called **Healabhal Bheag** and **Healabhal Mhor** – and boasts a thriving crofting community. North of Dunvegan the road curves east back toward Portree at the base of the cliff-ringed Waternish Peninsula.

 INFORMATION SOURCES: The tourism office is at 2 Lochside, Dunvegan, Isle of Skye IV55 8WB; open year-round.

Attractions & Sights

 Dunvegan Castle (Dunvegan, Isle of Skye IV55 8WF, ☎ 1470-521 206, fax 1470-521 205, enquiry@dunvegancastle.com, www.dunvegancastle.com; open year-round, 10am-5:30pm; shorter hours in winter; adult/concession/child £6.50/£5.50/£3.50). The ancestral home of the Chiefs of MacLeod for nearly eight centuries, and still the home of the present Chief, Dunvegan has been visited by the Queen, her parents and Sir Walter Scott. The castle is steeped in the history of clan battles, legends, tragedies, murders most foul and romances. On display are fine paintings, antiques, rare books and clan treasures such as the **Fairy Flag**, believed to possess miraculous powers, the medieval **Dunvegan Cup** and the bull's horn that each male heir must still drain of claret to prove his manhood. Other displays include a lock of Bonnie Prince Charlie's hair, the glasses worn by the boatman who piloted the Prince on his hazardous sea crossings and a pincushion belonging to Flora MacDonald.

The summer boat trips through **Loch Dunvegan** are popular and get up close to the resident seal colony. You might also see herons, Arctic terns and other birds. Boats leave the castle jetty every 20 minutes subject to sea and weather conditions (☎ 1470-521 500).

Talisker Distillery (Carbost, Isle of Skye IV47 8SR, ☎ 1478-614 308, fax 1478-614 302; open year-round; Mon-Sat, 9-4:30 in season; limited opening days/times in winter months so call ahead; admission £4, including a shop voucher; children free). Having survived a disastrous fire in 1960, this remote distillery – the only one on Skye – continues to produce a single malt regarded by many as one of the finest available. The huge, long-lasting flavor of Talisker's 10-year-old malt is sweeter than Islay malts and tinged with slight pepperiness. It is a superb dram and you owe it to yourself to indulge!

Lochalsh & The Isle of Skye

Adventures

On Foot

 Cuillin Guides (Stac Lee, Glenbrittle, Isle of Skye IV47 8TA, ☎ 1478-640 289, cuillinguide@lineone.net, www.cuillin-guides.co.uk). Mountaineering courses, rock climbing and scrambling, based at the foot of the Cuillins.

Traversing the Cuillin Ridge is a tough and challenging expedition, combining walking, scrambling, climbing and abseiling. With a distance of around nine miles and an ascent of 10,000 feet, the ridge demands high levels of fitness, commitment and mountain skills.

The **Black Cuillin** is a Mecca for walkers – 11 Munros strung out along a knife-edge ridge, where climbers contend with sheer drops, frightening levels of exposure and magnetic rock that sends compass needles into a spin. Add to that Skye's famously inclement weather and the complete traverse is an undertaking for only the very experienced.

Sgurr na Banachdich is a relatively safe Munro and, although straightforward by Cuillin standards, its central position on the main ridge provides an excellent view. Park by Glen Brittle Youth Hostel and follow the good path east then northeast following the southern river bank, along the way passing some beautiful pools and waterfalls. Continue for over a mile to a junction in the river. You can now see Coire a'Ghreadaidh straight ahead and Coir' an Eich to the southeast (right). Continue following the west bank of the small stream to the grassy start to Coir' an Eich, which turns to a stony, zigzag path. Climb above a short scree section to where the flat ridge joins the main ridge. The summit (marked with a cairn) lies on the edge of a cliff a few hundred yards more to the southeast (4-5 hours; difficult).

Elgol to Loch Coruisk is a superb coastal walk around Loch Scavaig through beautiful scenery to the serene Loch Coruisk, surrounded by the jagged Cuillin peaks. Take the B8083 south of Broadford to Elgol where you can park (post buses also run from Broadford to Elgol).

From Elgol follow the path signposted Coruisk, along a steep grassy slope beneath Ben Cleat to the Bay at Camasunary. From here, the path runs above the sea and has a couple of difficult sections to negotiate, although the scenic rewards are considerable. Shortly before you reach Loch Coruisk, you encounter the "Bad Step," a huge sloping rock slab overhanging the shore. Take care with your footholds on the exposed narrow ledge and use your hands on the slanting crag for grip and balance. The final obstacle is crossing the River Coruisk, officially the shortest river in Britain, by way of two series of stepping stones, which may be difficult if the river is high after heavy rain (5-7 hours; moderate/difficult).

In & On the Water

Dive & Sea the Hebrides (Shore Park, Loch Bay, Waternish, Isle of Skye IV55 8GD, ☎ 1470-592 219, fax 1470-592 399, diveskye@dive-and-sea-the-hebrides.co.uk, www.dive-and-sea-the-hebrides.co.uk). Scenic diving from a new charter boat, including wrecks, pinnacles, tidal, reef and night dives, and the chance to see seals, porpoises dolphins and whales.

Bella Jane **Boat Trips** (Elgol, Isle of Skye IV49 9BJ; before 10 am, ☎ 1471-866 244 7:30-10am; 800-731 3089 freephone, bella@bellajane.co.uk, www.bellajane.co.uk; late March to mid-Oct). Boat trips to stunning Loch Coruisk, visiting a seal colony and glimpsing other wildlife amid magnificent scenery. The trips allow 1½ hours ashore to explore and enjoy the scenery and there is free tea, coffee and shortbread. There are also trips by the RIB *AquaXplore* to Canna, Rum and Soay and the Cuillin Mountains. Advance booking is advisable for both boats.

Wildlife Watching

Loch Scavaig: It takes some getting to, either by boat or walking from Elgol, but Loch Scavaig presents an unforgettable sight and boasts a seal colony in its sheltered waters.

Dunvegan Seal Colony: See under Dunvegan Castle, page 425.

Shopping

Edinbane Pottery (Edinbane, Isle of Skye IV51 9PW, ☎ 1470-582 234, fax 1470-582 426, stuart@edinbane-pottery.co.uk, www.edinbane-pottery.co.uk). Specialists in handmade wood-fired and salt-glazed functional pottery.

Skye Silver (The Old School, Colbost, Dunvegan, Isle of Skye IV55 8ZT, ☎ 1470-511 263, fax 1470-511 775, sales@skyesilver.com, www.skyesilver.com). Large display of original sterling silver and gold jewelry, including Celtic designs, ceramic tiles and gifts.

Skyeskyns (17 Loch Bay, Waternish, Isle of Skye IV55 8GD, ☎ 1470-592 237, clive@skyeskyns.co.uk, www.skyeskyns.co.uk). Watch leather being made on a free guided tour of Scotland's only traditional exhibition tannery, which produces hand-combed Highland fleeces, natural sheepskins and other goods.

■ Where To Stay & Eat

See the *Accommodation* and *Dining* price charts on pages 395 and 396.

South Skye

Kinloch Lodge (Sleat, Isle of Skye IV43 8QY, ☎ 1471-833 214, fax 1471-833 277, kinloch@dial.pipex.com, www.kinloch-lodge.co.uk; DB&B £££££, lunch £££, dinner ££££). Much-fêted country-house style and warm hospitality at the ancestral home of Lord and Lady Macdonald. Lady Macdonald is a celebrated cook and writer; join one of her culinary demonstrations to discover the secrets of her award-winning fare.

Lime Stone Cottage (4 Lime Park, Broadford, Isle of Skye IV49 9AE, ☎ 1471-822 142, info@limestonecottage.co.uk, www.limestonecottage.co.uk; B&B ££). Romantic, century-old crofthouse whose olde worlde charm includes exposed stone walls, beams and log fire. All rooms command views over Broadford Bay and mainland Wester Ross.

East & North Skye

Bosville Hotel (Bosville Terrace, Portree, Isle of Skye IV51 9DG, ☎ 1478-612 846, fax 1478-613 434, bosville@macleodhotels.co.uk, www.macleodhotels.co.uk/bosville; B&B £££, lunch £, dinner ££). Fine hotel overlooking Portree Harbour. The hotel's **Chandlery Seafood Restaurant** serves interesting French-style cooking using fine local produce.

Cuillin Hills Hotel (Portree, Isle of Skye IV51 9QU, ☎ 1478-612 003, fax 1478-613 092, office@cuillinhills.demon.co.uk, www.cuillinhills.demon.co.uk; B&B £££££, dinner £££). Upmarket hotel set in grounds overlooking Portree Bay and the Cuillin Mountains.

The Isles Inn (Somerled Square, Portree, Isle of Skye IV51 9EH, ☎/fax 1478-612 129, stay@theislesinn.co.uk, www.theislesinn.co.uk; B&B ££). Comfortable rooms, good food and an open fire in an atmospheric inn on Portree's main square. There is regular live traditional music.

Portree House & Garden Bistro (Home Farm Road, Portree, Isle of Skye IV51 9LX, ☎ 1478-611 171, fax 1478-611 181, enquires@portreehouse.com, www.portreehouse.com; B&B ££, lunch £, dinner ££). Elegant Georgian house providing peaceful accommodation. The bistro serves New World and traditional cuisine complemented by local and European beers, and malt whiskies to enjoy in front of the fire.

Rosedale Hotel (The Harbour, Portree, Isle of Skye IV51 9DB, ☎ 1478-613 131, fax 1478-612 531, www.rosedalehotelskye.co.uk; open April-Nov; B&B £££, dinner £££). Family-run hotel located on the Portree waterfront looking toward the Isle of Raasay.

Viewfield House Hotel (Portree, Isle of Skye IV51 9EU, ☎ 1478-612 217, fax 1478-613 517, info@viewfieldhouse.com, www.viewfieldhouse.com; open mid-Apr to mid-Oct; B&B £££, dinner ££). Fine 200-year-old house set in 20 acres of woodland, with a classic Victorian interior. The first night is available on a dinner, bed & breakfast basis only.

Skeabost Country House Hotel (Skeabost Bridge, By Portree, Isle of Skye IV51 9NP, ☎ 1470-532 202, fax 1470-532 454, reception@skeabostcountryhouse.co.uk, www.skeabostcountryhouse.co.uk; B&B £££, lunch ££, dinner £££). Victorian hunting lodge secluded in 29 acres of landscaped grounds on the shores of Loch Snizort, with log fires, fine dining and individually styled rooms.

Harbour View Seafood Restaurant (7 Bosville Terrace, Portree, Isle of Skye IV51 9DG, ☎/fax 1478-612 069, kenneth@harbourviewskye.co.uk, www.harbourviewskye.co.uk; ££-£££). Traditional cottage restaurant serving great seafood and seasonal game accompanied by a roaring peat fire, candlelight and gentle Celtic music.

The Granary (Somerled Square, Portree, Isle of Skye; £). Tasty, reasonably priced filled rolls and soup provide a great lunch on the move. Get there early or you'll end up queuing with half of Portree.

Jan & Jed's Cottage (½ of 2 Lower Ollach, Braes, Isle of Skye IV51 9LJ, ☎ 1478-650 301, jan.scott@amserve.net; B&B ££). Cozy cottage B&B enclosed within a pretty garden in a quiet location overlooking the Isle of Raasay.

Flodigarry Hotel (Staffin, Isle of Skye IV51 9HZ, ☎ 1470-552 203, fax 1470-552 301, info@flodigarry.co.uk, www.flodigarry.co.uk; B&B ££££, lunch ££, dinner £££). Impressive period country house beautifully set beneath the dramatic Quiraing pinnacles, offering lovely bedrooms, quality cuisine and daily guided walks.

Uig Hotel (Uig, Isle of Skye IV51 9YE, ☎ 1470-542 205, fax 1470-542 308, manager@uighotel.com, www.uighotel.com; B&B ££, dinner ££-£££). Former coaching inn and farmstead offering many bedrooms overlooking Uig Bay and Loch Snizort, and good bar and restaurant meals.

West Skye

Greshornish House Hotel (Edinbane, By Portree, Isle of Skye IV51 9PN, ☎ 1470-582 266, fax 1470-582 345, campbell@greshornishhotel.demon.co.uk, www.greshornishhotel.co.uk; DB&B £££-££££). Mansion house whose history dates back to 1215, with four-poster beds, open coal fires and resident piper to escort you into dinner.

Roskhill House (Roskhill, By Dunvegan, Isle of Skye IV55 8ZD, ☎ 1470-521 317, fax 1470-521 761, www.roskhillhouse.co.uk; B&B ££-£££, dinner ££). A traditional 19th-century crofthouse on Skye's northwest coast. The bedrooms are cozy cottage style and the lounge (originally the village store) maintains exposed stone walls, beams and open log fire.

Rowan Cottage (9 Glasnakille, By Elgol, Isle of Skye IV49 9BQ, ☎/fax 1471-866 287, rowan@rowancottage-skye.co.uk, www.rowancottage-skye.co.uk; open Mar-Nov; B&B ££, dinner £££). A traditional crofthouse situated off the beaten track near Elgol. Every room looks over Loch Slapin and Loch Eishort to the Sleat Peninsula. Evening meals are available by prior arrangement, and emphasize fresh local produce and locally caught seafood.

Sligachan Hotel (Sligachan, Isle of Skye IV47 8SW, ☎ 1478-650 204, fax 1478-650 207, reservations@sligachan.co.uk, www.sligachan.co.uk; B&B £££, dinner ££). With the Cuillin towering behind and Loch Sligachan at its foot, this hotel is perfect for mountaineers and walkers who also appreciate their home comforts, with good food and a wide range of real ales and malts available.

Three Chimneys (Colbost, By Dunvegan, Isle of Skye IV55 8ZT, ☎ 1470-511 258, fax 1470-511 358, eatandstay@threechimneys.co.uk, www.threechimneys.co.uk; B&B £££££, dinner ££££+). The culinary renown of this award-gobbling candlelit crofters' cottage travels far and wide, although the restaurant isn't immune from the occasional mixed review. There is a good wine cellar and stylish new accommodation rooms.

Lochalsh & The Isle of Skye

Isle of Raasay

The lovely island of Raasay (meaning "island of roe deer") measures just over 14 miles long by three wide and lies off the eastern shore of Skye. Its intensely peaceful green pastures, woodlands and heather moors provide a glimpse of Highland life in times past and hide a sad history of retribution and clearances. After the island sent Jacobite fighters to Culloden and briefly sheltered Bonnie Prince Charlie in the battle's aftermath, raiding Government troops burned 300 houses, slaughtered islanders and livestock and holed the island's boats. Local poet **Sorley MacLean** (1911-96) poignantly recorded the mid-19th-century clearance of over 100 people to make way for sheep. The village of **Hallaig**, in the southeast, is remembered not only through MacLean's verse but also by a cairn in memory of the cleared inhabitants.

To the north of the ferry pier is Inverarish, the island's only village. It comprises two rows of terraced cottages built to house workers of the island's iron ore mine, which closed in 1920. Many of Raasay's 170 inhabitants now live in these cottages.

■ Getting Here

By Ferry

Caledonian MacBrayne (☎ 1475-650 100, www.calmac.co.uk) runs a regular car-ferry service (Mon-Sat) between Sconser in Skye (on the main A87 road and bus routes to Portree) and Raasay (15 minutes).

There are no buses on Raasay. If you don't have your own car, the transport facilities of the **Outdoor Centre** (see next page) can help you to get around easily on the island.

■ Attractions & Sights

Brochel Castle (northeast coast) The stark ruin of a once-grand castle that commanded a cliff above a delightful small bay with superb views across to craggy mainland peaks from Kintail to Torridon. Dating from the 15th century, this MacLeod castle once had three stories and four towers. The last clan chief to live here died in 1671, after which the clan seat moved to Raasay House. The castle has been uninhabited since the 17th century and care needs to be taken around the ruin, as it is in many parts unstable.

The Battery (southwestern shoreline, near Raasay House). The circular fortification was originally armed with six cannons and was built in response to the threat of French invasion in 1810. The Battery is also adorned with a pair of dubiously ornate mermaids, the cost of which helped bankrupt Raasay House's MacLeod lairds.

St Moulag's Chapel (behind Raasay House). The ruined 13th-century church is dedicated to St Moulag, an Irish missionary, who it is believed visited the island in the 6th century. There may be the ruins of an even earlier church beneath the present chapel.

Dun Borrodale (Inverarish). Remains of an Iron Age broch, with traces of galleries or chambers visible within the walls.

Calum's Road (Brochel to Arnish road in the north of the island). This 1½-mile section of road was built single-handedly by the local postman over an eight-year period after his requests to the local Council were repeatedly declined.

■ Adventures

 Raasay Outdoor Centre (Raasay House, Isle of Raasay IV40 8PB, ☎ 1478-660 266, fax 1478-660 200, info@raasay-house.co.uk, www.raasayoutdoorcentre.co.uk) offers a wide range of activities and courses for groups and individuals with high-quality instruction from experienced guides. Activities include kayaking, sailing, windsurfing, rock climbing, abseiling, walking and orienteering. All-inclusive three-day multi-activity breaks cost adult/child £185/£168.

You'll be amazed by the views from the summit of **Dun Caan**, Raasay's curious, flat-topped miniature mountain and embarrassed at how little effort was required. The walk starts from Bailemeanach, about three miles north of Inverarish, where a clear path climbs gently inland to a small lochan. The path drops steeply into a valley then skirts the loch that provides most of the island's drinking water. It next climbs steadily to the small plateau on top of the steeply buttressed sides of Dun Caan. The panoramic view from the summit is one of the finest in Scotland: a huge amphitheater of majestic peaks with the majestic Skye Cuillin to the west, the jagged peaks of Wester Ross to the east and the faint outline of the Outer Hebrides to the north. Few Munro summits provide views as good as this. Take care on the summit as the way you came up is the only way down, and the other sides of the mountain are precipitous.

Instead of returning the same way, you can follow an alternate route through the middle of the island; there's a faint path beside the Inverarish burn, although this can be muddy. Heading south from Dun Caan, you soon reach a lochan, where you take the route to the right (2 hours; easy).

The **north end** of Raasay is rugged, remote and unspoiled, and offers superb walking. Picturesque bays line the west coast and the rocks glow pink-brown in the afternoon sun. To the northwest is the craggy headland of Staffin, beyond which shimmer the Outer Hebrides; to the east are excellent views of Ben Alligin and the Torridon hills. From Arnish at the end of Calum's Road you can walk north on a clear path to Kyle Fladda, a small island cut off at high tide – watch the water level. The bay is full of mussels, some containing tiny pearls. To the east, a marked path leads to the ruined township of Umachan. You can continue north as far as Kyle Rona, the northernmost point of Raasay (about three hours from Arnish).

■ Wildlife Watching

 Raasay is great for **otter** spotting. The shoreline near the ferry terminal provides good sightings as do the rocks to the north of The Battery (near Raasay House), where otters frequently swim between Raasay and the nearby islet, Goat Island. The island is also rich in other fauna, including the celebrated Raasay vole, roe deer, seals, occasional golden eagles, kestrels and snipe.

■ Where To Stay & Eat

See the *Accommodation* and *Dining* price charts on pages 395 and 396.

 Raasay Outdoor Centre (Raasay House, Isle of Raasay IV40 8PB, ☎ 1478-660 266, fax 1478-660 200, info@raasay-house.co.uk, www.raasayoutdoorcentre.co.uk; B&B ££, lunch £, dinner ££). Historic Georgian mansion enjoying a superb view over the Skye Cuillins (with binoculars you can clearly make out the serrated ridge climbing to Sgurr nan Gillean). The rooms vary from traditional doubles to modern bunkrooms. The candlelit **Dolphin Café** is superb, combining the relaxed informality of a café with the cozy ambience of a bistro and the fine cuisine of a restaurant. Get there early and expect to spend plenty of time gazing out of the windows.

Northern Highlands

North of the Great Glen, the Highlands stretch away in a huge area of towering mountains, forested glens, sweeping moorland and rugged coastline. This sparsely populated area encompasses the magnificent peaks of **Wester Ross**, the lonely beaches and sheer cliffs of **Sutherland** and **Caithness**, traditional crofting communities in northwest Sutherland, historic fishing villages and occasional bustling towns.

DON'T MISS

Drive the exhilarating hairpins up to the **Bealach na Ba**.

Walk or climb in **Torridon** and **An Teallach**.

Explore Sutherland's many fine beaches, especially **Sandwood Bay**.

Enjoy superlative **wild brown trout fishing** in the lochs of Assynt and rivers of Sutherland.

Watch seabirds at **Handa Island** and **Duncansby Head**, and dolphins at **Chanonry Point**.

Best Freebie: Drive the **Wester Ross Coastal Trail** (except it's not really free, as you'll use up a lot of film).

Wester Ross

Wester Ross stretches from **Lochcarron** in the south to **Achiltibuie** in the north. In between lies a spectacular wilderness bursting with unforgettable vistas of magnificent mountains, tranquil sea lochs and a succession of picturesque villages and fishing ports strung out along its jagged coastline. Once visited, you'll never forget Wester Ross.

■ Special Events

Walk Wester Ross Festival (May/Jun; www.walkhighland.co.uk). Daily guided walks for all levels among some of Scotland's finest mountain scenery.

■ Lochcarron & Applecross Peninsula

Facing south on the shore of **Loch Carron**, and surrounded by mountain scenery, Lochcarron is a typical coastal village and start of the nerve-jangling drive to Applecross over the **Bealach na Ba** (see *Scenic Drives*, below).

Special Events

Lochcarron Highland Games (Jul; ☎ 1520-722 554). Traditional Highland Games on the Attadale Estate.

Attractions & Sights

Attadale Gardens & Nursery (Strathcarron IV54 8YX, ☎/fax 1520-722 603, info@attadale.com, www.attadale.com, open April-Oct, Mon-Sat, 10am-5:30pm, adult/child £3/1). Water gardens, waterfalls, sculpture and rhododendron walks set around a pretty house with views over Skye and the sea. Plants include bamboo, ferns, Himalayan primulas, and trees and shrubs from Chile and the USA.

Smithy Heritage Centre (Ribhuachan, Lochcarron, Strathcarron IV54 8YS, ☎ 1520-722 722, smithy@balnacra.com, www.balnacra.com/smithy.htm; open Easter-Oct, Mon-Sat, 10:30am-5pm; admission by donation). The blacksmith's workshop dates from around 1820 and was used for farrier (horseshoeing) and agricultural ironwork until the 1950s. The smithy contains a restored forge, video with Gaelic songs and local history exhibition.

Scenic Drives

Bealach na Ba ("Pass of the Cattle") is an ear-popping, film-devouring and nerve-jangling drive from Lochcarron to Applecross over a 2,053-foot (626-m) pass (the highest road in Britain) enjoying superb views over the Isles of Skye, Raasay, Rum and Eigg. The former drove road climbs between two huge buttresses of sheer rock by a series of steep switchbacks. There can be snow on the summit even in the summer. It's a narrow single-lane road, but the forward visibility is reasonable. Allow half a day to enjoy the scenery comfortably and don't even consider driving this road in the dark! If the drive to Applecross has whetted your appetite, you can continue north.

The **Wester Ross Coastal Trail** takes you through more spectacular mountain and coastal scenery past Torridon, Loch Maree Gairloch and Ullapool, from where you can continue through progressively more remote country from Assynt to Lochinver (if you can believe it, the scenery gets even better around Lochinver). The official trail route is marked by a fish symbol.

■ Torridon

Torridon is one of the most beautiful mountain ranges in Scotland, characterized by tiered-wall summits and soaring ramparts, scoured by glaciers to leave great corries and U-shaped valleys. Glorious peaks, including the unmistakeable corries and ridges of **Beinn Eighe** (3,313 feet), **Liathach** (3,456 feet) and **Beinn Alligin** (3,232 feet) on the north side of the glen, make Torridon a paradise for hillwalkers. The trio is best viewed on the coastal road from Applecross. They rise dramatically from the waters of the loch (the appearance of snow on their summits in summer is actually glittering Cambrian quartzite on the upper slopes).

Special Events

Torridon Mountain Heritage Weekend (Oct; ☎ 1445-760 234, www.torridon-mountains.com). Weekend of events to help people appreciate Torridon's mountain environment, with walks, talks, archaeological and geographical visits and a ceilidh.

Attractions & Sights

Beinn Eighe National Nature Reserve (southeast end of Loch Maree, near Kinlochewe; ☎ 1445-760 254 reserve office, ☎ 1445-760 258 visitor center, www.snh.org.uk; visitor center open Easter-Oct, daily). Britain's oldest National Nature Reserve was established in 1951 to protect the ancient pinewood west of **Kinlochewe**, but also encompasses a huge cluster of rugged peaks, ridges and scree-covered slopes between Loch Maree and Glen Torridon. The reserve offers walking trails, picnic areas, and the opportunity to see red deer, roe deer and pine martens in the woods, and golden eagles, buzzards and other birds of prey soaring overhead.

Adventures

 The **Coire Mhic Fhearchair** walk (pronounced, approximately, "corrie-vik-erika") takes you through a majestic mountain landscape to a small lochan high in one of Scotland's finest corries – tinged by tragedy as the scene of a fatal air crash.

Start from the Glen Torridon parking area (from Torridon, the parking area is on your left just after a large knoll, four miles past the National Trust Visitor Centre). Follow the path from the parking area signposted Coire Mhic Nobuil (pronounced "corrie-vik-noble"), which climbs steadily into Coire Dubh Mor, broadly following a small stream. To your left rises **Liathach** and to your right **Beinn Eighe**. About two miles into the walk you cross the stream over a series of stepping stones. A short distance afterwards (marked by a cairn), the track splits into two. Follow the right (northern) fork that leads uphill over rockier terrain around the side of Sail Mhor, rising steeply beside a stepped waterfall and into the corrie. As you near the corrie, the view below becomes a wild landscape capped by mountains and splashed with small lochans. The corrie itself is dominated by the tiered sandstone and quartzite Triple Buttress, which soars above its boulder-strewn floor and is reflected perfectly in the lochan.

Again crossing a burn by way of stepping stones, follow a path along the left to the far side of the lochan. Here, shortly after the Second World War, a Lancaster bomber crashed when it failed to clear the mountain in bad weather. Despite the efforts of local people, there were no survivors. Remains of the bomber (including a partly embedded wheel) can still be seen in the far southwest of the corrie (4 hours; easy/moderate).

The waymarked **Beinn Eighe Mountain Trail** climbs through different zones of climate, vegetation and wildlife. The path isn't always clear, but a series of cairns marks the route. The trail starts from the parking area beside Loch Maree, around two miles northwest of Kinlochewe. The walk climbs beside a stream through natural pine woodland, some of the largest pines being over 350 years old. The path zigzags steeply up past the Tansley Bog and Trumpet Rock to the summit cairn, from where you can see 31 Munros in good visibility. To the south, the four-mile ridge of Beinn Eighe dominates the view. The path then follows cairns across the plateau to the Lunar Loch, before descending beside a steep gorge before returning through woodland to the parking area (2-3 hours; moderate).

For those who don't wish to do the Mountain Trail, an easier one-mile Woodland Trail starts from the same parking area.

■ Gairloch & Loch Maree

Gairloch is an attractive, thriving settlement that has been a popular holiday destination since Queen Victoria visited in 1877. For centuries, Gairloch was an important cod-fishing base, although its harbor now lands mainly crab, lobster and prawn. Crofting, the other traditional local pursuit, also survives, but tourism is now the single biggest influence on the local economy. East of Gairloch is Loch Maree, with its peaceful shores, wooded, historic islands and towering backdrop of Slioch – a leading contender for Scotland's most picturesque loch.

Attractions & Sights

Gairloch Heritage Museum (Achtercairn, Gairloch IV21 2BP, next to the tourism office and community center; ☎ 1445-712 287, info@gairlochheritagemuseum.org.uk, www.gairlochheritagemuseum.org.uk; open April-Sept, Mon-Sat, 10am-5pm & Oct, Mon-Fri, 10:30am-1pm, winter months by arrangement; adult/concession/child £3/£2/£0.50). Established by the local heritage society, whose members are often on hand to share their real-life experiences, the museum displays Gairloch's history from the earliest times to the present. Displays include the interior of a typical thatched crofthouse, a peat fire, village shop and school classroom. There are also working models and hands-on activities, such as corn grinding, together with a library and archive material for more detailed research.

Adventures

 Slioch (pronounced "slee-ock"), a rocky fortress rising above the northern shores of Loch Maree, marks the way to some of the finest mountain scenery in Scotland. The mountain looks impenetrable but its eastern flank hollows out enough for a path to reach the summit.

East of Kinlochewe a narrow road crosses the river north toward the few houses of Incheril and leads to a parking area. Follow the path through a gate that soon picks up the north bank of the Kinlochewe River. Cross the footbridge and climb northeast (right) up **Glen Bianasdail**. The path climbs steadily as you approach the foot of **Meall Each**, from where you can see the buttressed flank of Slioch. A grassy plateau holding two lochans (pass to the right of these) breaks the climb, above which the path weaves steeply through crags and outcrops before easing as you approach the trig point (a surveyors marker) and, immediately north, the summit cairn.

From the summit, you can look north over a great wilderness of lochs and crags. You can enjoy these views a while longer by following the ridge east toward **Sgurr an Tuill Bhain**. This narrows and provides superb views down to Lochan Fada, northeast of the summit, below you. Drop down into the broad basin of a hollow that guides you back to the path along Glen Bianasdail to the **Kinlochewe River,** from where you can retrace your steps to Incheril (4-6 hours; moderate/difficult).

Gairloch Marine Life and "Sail Gairloch" Cruises (Pier Road, Gairloch IV21 2BQ, ☎ 1445-712 636, mail@porpoise-gairloch.co.uk, www.porpoise-gairloch.co.uk, open April-Oct). Wildlife cruises and visitor center displaying photos, videos and sounds of wildlife seen on cruises – birds, seals, porpoises, whales and occasionally dolphins.

Shopping

Serendipity Crafts (Strath, Gairloch IV21 2BZ, ☎ 1445-712 397). Two floors of Scottish gifts and clothing.

The Conservatory (closed Sun) serves all-day breakfasts, light lunches and afternoon teas.

■ Poolewe to An Teallach

Loch Ewe played an important role as a naval assembly point in both world wars. It was from here that great convoys set off for Murmansk, West Africa and North America, and ships sheltered here after the Orkney fleet was attacked. Lying at its head is the sleepy village of Poolewe, which boasts the famous **Inverewe Garden** and one of Scotland's finest country hotels. From Poolewe, the road weaves north through the tiny villages of **Aultbea**, **Gruinard** and **Dundonnell** to the splendid jagged peaks of **An Teallach** – arguably Scotland's finest mountain.

Attractions & Sights

Inverewe Garden (NTS; Poolewe IV22 2LG, ☎ 1445-781 200, fax 1445-781 497, inverewe@nts.org.uk; guided tours April-Oct, 9:30am-9pm or sunset;

Nov-Mar, 9:30am-4pm; visitor center and shop open April-Oct, 9:30am-4pm; later in summer; adult/concession/family £7/£5.25/£19). This thriving garden beside Loch Ewe is the daring vision of **Osgood Mackenzie**, who was given the estate by his widowed mother in 1862. He soon built a house and began to create a garden on what had been a barren, windswept promontory. Because of its Gulf Stream-warmed climate, the garden boasts many plants that ordinarily do not flourish so far north, including giant rhododendrons from western China, soaring gum trees and daisy-bushes from Australia and New Zealand, climbers from Chile and flowering bulbs from South Africa. Additionally, there are noteworthy native species, including attractive Scots pines. Mackenzie's original garden (the **Walled Garden**) is one of the highlights. Its pretty, enclosed terraces sustain a succession of flowers and a wide variety of fruit and vegetables.

Adventures

 The **Kernsary Walk** from Poolewe follows the attractive paths beside Loch Kernsary with excellent views to **Slioch**. Start in Poolewe, just north (toward Inverewe Gardens) of a long white building beside the road. Take the inland path signposted "Kernsary," which climbs gently through open country with excellent views of Loch Kernsary. After just over an hour, you reach a white farmhouse at which you turn right, skirting the head of **Loch Maree** (turning left leads to total wilderness). Continue along the track to join a quiet road along the river that brings you back into Poolewe (3 hours; easy).

Translated as "the forge," **An Teallach** (pronounced "an-chellak") is a leading contender for Scotland's most spectacular mountain. Towering high above the head of Little Loch Broom to the south of Dundonnell, several sharp pinnacles cap the steep, weathered sandstone walls of the jagged and twisting ridges. A full traverse of the main ridge is a lengthy and in places technical undertaking that only experienced mountain walkers should attempt. Fortunately, reaching the mountain's two Munro summits requires no more than a stiff uphill walk and arguably provides the best views of the ridge and surrounding area. This is the walk described below.

Driving east through Dundonnell on the A832, park at the first layby on the left about a quarter of a mile past the Dundonnell Hotel. Walk a short distance east to a small gate on the right (south) side of the road (just before the first house) from where the walk starts. The path winds up over varied terrain in a general southwesterly direction to the north and west of **Glas Mheall Mor**, which would itself be an impressive peak were it not for what follows. The path fades in certain areas and you need to keep a lookout for several small cairns that mark the way (keep Glas Mheall Mor to your left and follow the streams uphill).

After about two hours you reach the head of the river and shortly afterwards the top of the corrie (marked by a cairn) where the serrated ridge of An Teallach first comes into menacing view. Watch here for **golden eagles**. Turn east, again following the contours of Glas Mheall Mor until you reach a large boulder on the shoulder of **Bidean a' Ghlas Thuill** (3,484 feet/1,062 m), the first of An Teallach's Munro peaks. A faint path zigzags tightly up the steep scree, taking you to the first (and highest) summit, marked by a large cairn, in around half an hour. Turn east toward the main ridge and the second Munro peak, **Sgurr Fiona** (3,480 feet/1,060 m). While crossing the comfortably broad ridge, take time to enjoy the view of the magnificent pinnacles, steep plunges and **Toll an Lochain** far below. At the end of the ridge an obvious path continues gently to the right of Sgurr Fiona, and a broad but faint path rises sharply to the left. Although steeper, the path to the left is the easier climb to the summit. The ridge beyond Sgurr Fiona narrows considerably; unless you are an experienced climber, turn back and return the way you came (4-5 hours; moderate/difficult).

 Loch Ewe Boating (Stone Ewe Croft, Midtown, Inverasdale, Poolewe IV22 2LW, ☎ 1445-781 729, fax 1445-781 727, ric@high-land-adventures.co.uk, open May-Sept). Sailing and boating on Loch Ewe, with instruction if required.

Seudraidh Books & Guides (22 Pier Road, Aultbea IV22 2JQ, ☎ 1445-731 486, fax 1445-731 553). Guides and instruction in fly fishing, and guided walking.

Shopping

Slioch Outdoor Shop (Cliffton, Poolewe IV22 2JU, ☎/fax 1445-781 412, info@slioch.co.uk, www.slioch.co.uk). Outdoor and extreme-weather clothing, as worn by the RAF and many mountain rescue teams, direct from the manufacturer.

Creative Designs at Stepping Stones ("Corriehallie," Dundonnell, Garve IV23 2QN, ☎ 1854-633 229, fax 1854-633 328). A small gallery at the foot of An Teallach that sells beautiful pottery, cards, crafts, art and soothing music.

■ Ullapool

The peaceful fishing port of Ullapool sits on the shore of **Loch Broom** and is the largest settlement in Wester Ross. The village was built in 1788 as a herring station and its whitewashed cottages retain great charm. Ullapool is the main ferry terminal for **Stornoway** in the Outer Hebrides.

 INFORMATION SOURCES: The tourism office is at Argyle Street, Ullapool IV26 2UB; open year-round.

Attractions & Sights

Ullapool Museum & Visitor Centre (7-8 West Argyle Street, Ullapool IV26 2TY, ☎ 1854-612 987, ulmuseum@waverider.co.uk; open April-Oct, Mon-Sat, 10am-5pm, Nov-Mar, Sat, 10am-4pm; adult/concession/child £3/2/0.5). Follow the story of a Highland community through a large-screen audiovisual show, artifacts, archives, photos, touch-screens and exhibitions, housed within a church designed by Thomas Telford. There is also a genealogy research facility and shop.

Adventures

Summer Queen Cruises (1 Royal Park, 1 IV26 2XT, ☎ 1854-612 472, cruises@summerqueen.co.uk, www.summerqueen .co.uk; cruises April-Oct, including Sundays in summer). Cruise to the Summer Isles, landing on

Tanera Mor, to see **seals**, **porpoises** and **seabirds**, and occasionally **whales** and **dolphins**.

 Seascape Expeditions (Dundonnell, Garve IV23 2QN, ☎ 1854-633 229). Two-hour RIB trips from Ullapool (Loch Broom Filling Station) to the Summer Isles, along the way experiencing rugged coastlines and viewing **seals** and **seabirds**.

Entertainment

 The Ceilidh Place (14 West Argyle Street, Ullapool, ☎ 1854-612 103, reception@ceilidh.demon.co.uk). Ullapool's main entertainment venue offers live music (folk, jazz, classical) most summer nights and serves light daytime snacks and evening meals (££-£££).

Shopping

Captain's Cabin (Quay Street, Ullapool IV26 2UE, ☎ 1854-612 356, fax 1854-612 596). Gifts, preserves and glassware, outdoor clothing and equipment, and books.

Strandlines (West Argyle Street, Ullapool IV26 2TY, ☎ 1854-612 439, strandlines@ecosse.net). Designer knitwear hand-framed or hand-knitted on the premises to original designs.

Sutherland & Caithness

■ Lochinver & Assynt

Lochinver is a busy fishing port in the heart of the parish of Assynt, the coastal area that stretches from **Ullapool** to **Kylesku**. Assynt is an area of striking mountain scenery and traditional crofting communities. Inland, hundreds of unspoiled hill lochs offer excellent wild brown trout fishing while superb peaks, such as **Quinag** and **Suilven**, dominate the views.

 INFORMATION SOURCES: The tourism office is at Assynt Visitor Centre, Main Street, Lochinver IV27 4LX; open Easter-Oct.

Attractions & Sights

The Hydroponicum (Achiltibuie, near Ullapool IV26 2YG, ☎ 1854-622 202, fax 1854-622 201, info@thehydroponicum.com, www.thehydroponicum.com; April-Sept, 10am-6pm, tours on the hour through 5pm; Oct, Mon-Fri, 11:30am-3pm, tours noon & 2pm; adult/concession/child/family £4.75/£3.50/£2.75/£12.50). Hydroponics is the growing of plants without soil, using water to supply nutrients. Take a tour of the "garden of the future" and discover the secrets of growing plants – even banana plants and fig trees – in small pots without soil. Growing houses display plants and produce from different climatic zones, and there is also a cottage garden, children's trails, a shop and café.

Adventures

 Assynt's 150 lochs boast some of the best **wild brown trout** fishing in Europe. The following organizations will help you get the most from your fishing in the area:

Assynt Angling Association (Loch Assynt Lodge, Assynt IV27 4HB, ☎ 1571-844 257, fax 1571-822 226, assynttrout@talk21.com, www.assynt-angling.co.uk; open 15th Mar-6th Oct). The Association sells permits for brown trout and salmon fishing. There is bank fishing on numerous hill lochs and boats available on 19 lochs (tickets for boats from The Altnacealgach Bar, Ledmore, ☎ 1854-666 260, and Ardglas Guest House, Lochinver, ☎ 1571-844 257). Permits are also available from the Lochinver tourism office and several local guest houses.

Assynt Crofters' Trust (North Assynt Estate, Stoer, Assynt IV27 4JG, ☎/fax 1571-855 298; open 15th Mar-15th Oct). Permits and boats for wild brown trout fishing on over 200 lochs. Permits are also available from the Lochinver tourism office and a number of local guest houses.

Assynt Sporting Co (School House, Drumbeg, Assynt IV27 4NW, ☎ 1571-833 269; open April-Oct). Ghillie (guide) service and lessons for wild brown trout fishing, with boat and tackle rental available.

Highland School of Fly Fishing (Resallach House, Elphin, Assynt IV27 4HH, ☎ 1854-666 334, info@flyfishing-scotland.net, www.flyfishing-scotland.net). Fly fishing instruction and guiding for salmon, brown trout and sea trout.

Statesman Cruises (Old Ferry Pier, Kylesku, ☎ 1971-502 345, fax 1571-844 446, statesmancruises@talk21.com; cruises May-Sept). Cruises to **Eas a' Chual Aluinn**, Britain's highest waterfall, passing seal colonies and possibly spotting eagles, divers and other birds.

Summer Isles Cruises (Post Office, Achiltibuie IV26 2YG, ☎ 1854-622 200; cruises May-Oct). Cruise around the Summer Isles from Badentarbet Pier, Achiltibuie, aboard the *Hectoria* to see seabirds and visit the seal colony. All-day cruises let you go ashore and there are evening deep-sea angling trips.

Shopping

Highland Stoneware Potteries (Lochinver IV27 4LP, ☎ 1571-844 376, fax 1571-844 485, potters@highlandstoneware.co.uk, www.highlandstoneware.com). Watch quality ceramics, including tableware, cookware, gifts, collectibles and tile panels, being made and painted.

Drumbeg Designs Craft Shop (Tigh-na-Bruach, Drumbeg IV27 4NW, on the B869 Assynt coastal road; ☎ 1571-833 263, www.drumbegdesigns.com; open Easter-Oct; £). This shop has a lovely selection of crafts, including pottery, candles, woolens, handmade soaps, aromatherapy oils and hand-painted silks. They also serve light meals; see below.

■ Northwest Sutherland

Northwest Sutherland is another of Scotland's untamed frontiers – a vast wilderness of mountains, moorland, heather-clad hills and precipitous sea cliffs.

Dotted around are hundreds of lochs, many containing feisty wild brown trout, and lily-filled lochans.

AUTHOR'S NOTE: *Don't be misled by the map; the "main" A838 road that runs through this crofting landscape is single-lane for most of the way until the eastern half of the north coast.*

Despite its small size, **Kinlochbervie** is one of the country's busiest fishing harbors, where you can still watch catches being landed. Farther north, a rough walking path leads from **Blairmore** to **Sandwood Bay** – one of the remotest and most beautiful beaches in Scotland, and reputedly haunted by mermaids.

In this region of the Highlands, the coastline in the form of huge Atlantic cliffs starts to take over from mountains as the most striking landscape feature, and includes the cliffs at **Clo Mor** – the highest on mainland Britain. Moving away from the coast the overwhelming sensation is one of total isolation.

INFORMATION SOURCES: The tourism office is at Durine, Durness, Sutherland IV27 4PN; open year-round.

Attractions & Sights

Cape Wrath is the most northwesterly point on the British mainland; it affords views over spectacular wild scenery and some of Britain's highest cliffs, seabirds, seals and a 523-foot lighthouse built by Robert Stevenson in 1828. Access is via the **Cape Wrath Ferry** from Durness (Balnakeil, Durness, ☎/fax 1971-511 376) and **Cape Wrath Minibus** (Heatherlea, Sangomore, Durness IV27 4PZ, ☎ 1971-511 287/511 343; operates May-Sept). The timetable varies through the season and it's best to check with either the ferryman or the Durness tourism office.

Smoo Cave (just off the A838 about two miles east of Durness). A gaping limestone cavern on Scotland's northern coast that comprises three underground chambers, an impressive waterfall and many legends. Measuring 30 meters (96 feet) wide and 15 meters (48 feet) high, this is one of the largest cave entrances in Britain. The cave formed over millions of years by the action of rain and sea on the area's soft and soluble limestone rocks. Water hollowed out caverns and widened cracks until the stream disappeared down a sinkhole, forming the almost-70-foot (21-meter) **Allt Smoo waterfall**, down which the stream tumbles into an underground chamber before finally flowing out of the mouth of the main cave.

The cave's position at the head of a narrow 800m inlet has led some to speculate that the inlet may at one time have been roofed. Recent excavations show that the cave was in use 6,000 years ago by the earliest settlers in the north.

A wooden pathway extends into the cave, which is illuminated. For those wishing to do more exploring, 20-minute boat tours of the inner chambers (following in the footsteps of Sir Walter Scott who, in 1814, was the first to enter the inner chambers) are available subject to weather conditions (April-May, 11am-4pm & June-Sept, 10am-5pm; adult/child £3/£1.50).

Adventures

 Cape Adventure International (Ardmore, Rhiconich IV27 4RB between Kylesku and Durness, ☎/fax 1971-521 006, info@capeventure.co.uk, www.capeventure.co.uk, open Easter-Oct) Outdoor activities on the shores of a remote sea loch in northwest Sutherland, including sea kayaking, climbing, abseiling, land yachting, surfing, orienteering, walking and wilderness weekends. All equipment provided.

> **DID YOU KNOW?** Loch Eriboll, east of Durness, is the deepest sea loch in Britain; Atlantic and Russian convoys gathered here during World War II before making their dangerous voyages.

Wildlife Watching

Handa Island Nature Reserve (☎ 1971-502 347; accessible by ferry from Tarbet Pier, near Scourie; open Easter-early Sep, ferry sailings, Mon-Sat, every half-hour from 9:30am-2pm, last return from Handa, 5pm). Handa Island was inhabited for many centuries by hardy islanders who survived on a diet of potatoes, fish and seabirds, and who even had their own queen and parliament. Today, Handa is a sanctuary for some of Britain's most significant breeding seabird colonies. The island's sandstone cliffs are the summer home of nearly 200,000 seabirds, including Britain's largest colony of breeding **guillemots**. Resident birds also include **puffins**, **razorbills**, **skuas**, **kittiwakes** and **terns**. The cliffs tower 400 feet above the sea on the island's north coast, from where you might also see **whales**, **dolphins**, **porpoises**, **seals** and occasionally **basking sharks**. A footpath circles the island; allow three hours for the walk. Overnight stays in the Handa bothy can be arranged through the **Scottish Wildlife Trust** (☎ 1463-714 746).

Shopping

Balnakeil Wines (Sangomore Headland, Durness IV27 4PZ, ☎ 1971-511 346, ronnie@durness.org). Handmade country wines, candles, liqueurs, cards, paintings and confectionary.

■ The North Coast

The north coast of Scotland is characterized by high sea cliffs and sandy beaches. Inland, the vast peat bogs of the "Flow Country" are an important wildlife habitat. The coastal villages of **Tongue**, **Bettyhill** and **Melvich** boast excellent beaches; nearby, a number of clearance villages – including **Achanlochy**, six miles south of Bettyhill on the B873, and **Rossal**, another 10 miles along the B873/B871 – tell a sadder story.

Tongue is one of the principal north coast villages. Crossing the causeway over the **Kyle of Tongue** there are magnificent views south to **Ben Loyal** – the "Queen of Scottish Mountains" – and north to **Tongue Bay** and the **Rabbit Islands**.

Attractions & Sights

Strathnaver Museum (Clachan, Bettyhill, near Tongue KW14 7SS, ☎ 1641-521 418, strathnavermus@ukonline.co.uk; open April-Oct, Mon-Sat, 10am-1pm & 2pm-5pm; adult/child £1.9/0.5). Housed in the former parish church, the museum tells the story of the Strathnaver Clearances, and provides information on local history showing agricultural machinery, archives and Clan Mackay memorabilia. There is a late-8th-century Pictish cross slab in the church graveyard.

Dounreay Visitor Centre (Dounreay, By Thurso KW14 7TZ, ☎ 1847-802 572, fax 1847-802 236, www.ukaea.org.uk; open May-Oct, 10am-4pm). Displays describe the operation of the no-longer-operational Dounreay Fast Reactor and the decommissioning work that will be carried out here over the next 50-60 years.

Adventures

 Ben Loyal is – with good reason – called the "Queen of Scottish Mountains," standing solitary and magnificent in northern Sutherland. The views from this climb get better with each step. From Tongue village take the A836 toward Lairg. At Lettermore, as you approach Loch Loyal on your left, look for a small crofthouse on your right with a river bridge just beyond it. Park here.

With the loch behind you walk from the bridge down the track to the right of the house. Continue through a turning circle, beyond which the path continues across grass and to the right of a small hill to ascend the small valley to the top. From here, you can see the back of Ben Loyal with a low saddle to the right. Approach to the left of the saddle, walk up the ramp-like hill rising to the right and then to a small top. Ascend the next rise with the valley now opening up to your right and continue to the next top with a small pool. Continue up the hill following it to the left. The jagged top of Ben Loyal now appears above you to the right. Walk through the rocks to descend a small valley to the right of a lochan and up the final rise. At the top, walk along to your right to see the rock formation of the summit. You are now surrounded by sheer cliffs so take care, particularly if mist comes down. Continue to the back of the rock formation and take the second, and final, left turning of the path to a windswept gap between the rocks. The path continues before you onto a small ragged top with views over Tongue, Melness, Ben Hope and the sea. Return the same way, taking care not to venture too close to the steep edges on your left (4-5 hours; moderate/difficult).

Wildlife Watching

 Forsinard Nature Reserve (24 miles north of Helmsdale on the A897, ☎ 1641-571 225, www.rspb.org.uk; visitor center open Easter-Oct, 9am-6pm). Comprising 25,000 acres of blanket bog, Forsinard's deep peatlands lie at the heart of the Flow Country of Sutherland and Caithness. **Golden plovers**, **dunlins** and **merlins** are among the birds that breed on the reserve.

■ Caithness

The history of Caithness stands out from that of the rest of the Highlands. It merges contrasting influences: Norse and Scot; seaman and clansman; Viking and Gael. Long before the Vikings arrived in the ninth century, the area already boasted a thriving culture, evidenced by a wealth of archaeological sites, including the **Grey Cairns of Camster**. Caithness was once richly endowed with castles, although many are now in ruins and difficult to locate. The unremarkable John o'Groats is the farthest point from Land's End on the British mainland (876 miles).

 INFORMATION SOURCES: The tourism office is at Riverside, Thurso KW14 8BU; open Easter-Oct.

Attractions & Sights

 Castle of Mey (Thurso KW14 8XH, ☎ 1847-851 227, fax 1847-851 473, www.castleofmey.org.uk; open mid-May through September, but closed first half of August; hours are Tues-Sat, 11am-4:30pm & Sun, 2-5pm; adult/concession/child/family £5/£4.50/£3/£15). The late Queen Mother bought the remote Castle of Mey in 1952, saved it from ruin and developed the gardens. Isolated on the northernmost coast of mainland Scotland, the castle became the home she cherished for its privacy, and was where she entertained many friends. Inside, the rooms are comfortable rather than lavish. Outside, the sheltered gardens grow fruit, vegetables and flowers.

Dunbeath Heritage Centre (The Old School, Dunbeath KW6 6ED, ☎ 1593-731 233, info@dunbeath-heritage.org.uk, www.dunbeath-heritage.org.uk; open Easter-Oct, 10am-5pm; call to check winter opening times; adult/concession £2/£1, children free). Museum exploring the mysteries of the Caithness area (Picts, Vikings, clans, crofters and fishermen), including runic stones, local archaeology, wildlife and local family histories, all set in the former classroom of writer Neil Gunn.

Caithness Glass (Airport Industrial Estate, Wick KW1 5BP, ☎ 1955-602 286, fax 1955-605 200, visitor@caithnessglass.co.uk, www.caithnessglass.co.uk; open year-round, Mon-Sat, 9am-5pm; Easter-Dec also open Sun, 11am-5pm). On weekdays you can watch the glassmaking process from spacious galleries and visit the cutting and engraving studios. There is also an exhibit and factory shop, and a licensed restaurant.

Grey Cairns of Camster (four miles northwest of Lybster on the Watten road). Two well-preserved Neolithic chambered cairns, which are over 5,000 years old.

Waterlines Visitor Centre (Lybster Harbour, Lybster KW3 6AH, ☎ 1593-721 520, fax 1593-721 325; open May-Sept, Mon-Sat, 11am-5pm, Sun noon-5pm; adult/child £2.50/£0.50). Housed in beautifully restored buildings, exhibits record Lybster's history as a herring port, show how the land evolved and describe the local birdlife. Watch nesting birds live as a camera zooms in on colonies on the Caithness cliffs. There is a coffee shop here, and facilities for yachtsmen.

Adventures

Dornoch & District Angling Association (c/o Kaitness, Poles Road, Dornoch IV25 3HP, ☎ 1862-810 589, fax 1862-811 164; open Mar-Oct). Freshwater angling for rainbow and brown trout, sea trout and salmon on local lochs.

John o'Groats Ferries (Ferry Office, John o'Groats KW1 4YR, ☎ 1955-611 353, fax 1955-611 301, office@jogferry.co.uk, www.jogferry.co.uk; trips May-Sept). Day-trips to Orkney from John o'Groats.

Northcoast Marine Adventures (Sunfield, Scarfskerry, By Thurso KW14 8XW, ☎ 1955-611 797, mobile 7867-666 273, fax 1847-851 841, info@north-coastmarine-adventures.co.uk, www.northcoast-marine-adventures.co.uk; cruises Mar-Oct). Marine wildlife-watching by jet-drive RIB from John o'Groats harbor; departures every second hour from 10am-8pm. See birds and seals, and visit caves and geos. A "whitewater adventure" ride is available by prior arrangement (you'll get a full refund if you come back dry!), with life jackets and waterproofs supplied; not suitable for children under age 12.

Wildlife Watching

 Duncansby Head (near John o'Groats). The **Old Red Sandstone cliffs** reach a height of 250 feet and are spectacular examples of coastal landforms, with carved sea arches, caves, geos (inlets) and stacks, including the famous **Stacks of Duncansby**. These "seabird city" cliffs are packed with puffins, guillemots, razorbills, kittiwakes, fulmars and shags; aggressive skuas patrol overhead and squadrons of gannets fish the waters below. The **Geo of Sclaites** is a particularly good point for viewing birds and the flora of the cliffs.

■ Mid & East Sutherland

This area stretches from the **Dornoch Firth** in the south to **Helmsdale** in the north, and inland to beyond **Lairg**. The Struie Viewpoint on the **Moray Firth Tourist Route**, on the B9176 (west of Edderton) high above the Dornoch Firth, provides a great view of the East Sutherland landscape stretching away to the north.

THE GREAT SUTHERLAND GOLD RUSH

From Helmsdale, a short drive up the Strath of Kildonan takes you to **Baille an Or** and **Suisgill** – the heart of the Great Sutherland Gold Rush of 1869. Robert Gilchrist, a local man returning home after 17 years in the Australian gold fields, made the first finds. Others soon rushed to Kildonan, which developed into a shantytown housing hundreds of prospectors. The gold rush ended within a year, although small quantities are occasionally still found.

Prosperous coastal towns such as **Dornoch**, **Golspie** and **Brora** are recognized holiday resorts. Dornoch clusters around its 13th-century cathedral. The last witch burned in Scotland went up in flames here in 1722 – an event commemorated by the **Witch's Stone**. Dornoch is internationally famous for its golf course – ranked 13th in the world. Golspie is overlooked by a historic monument to the First Duke of Sutherland, whose family has lived at nearby Dunrobin Castle since the 13th century. Brora is famous for its salmon river, whisky, fine tweeds and a great beach. Inland, Lairg lies at the heart of a significant archaeological landscape. The nearby **Ord Archaeological Trail** is a route to some of the best prehistoric sites in the area.

 INFORMATION SOURCES: The tourism office is at The Coffee Shop, The Square, Dornoch IV25 3SD; open year-round.

Attractions & Sights

Croick Church (10 miles west of Ardgay). The East Sutherland glens witnessed some of the earliest of the Highland Clearances, when many crofters were forcibly evicted from the land to make way for sheep. Croick Church is a particularly poignant reminder of these times and has become a place of pilgrimage for many visitors on account of the many names and bitter messages scratched on its east window by dispossessed crofters who sought refuge here in 1845.

Historylinks Museum (The Meadows, Dornoch IV25 3SF, ☎ 1862-811 275, historylinks@dornoch.org.uk; open May-Sept, Mon-Sat, 10am-4pm; adult/concession £2/£1.50, children free). The museum's displays recount the history and development of Dornoch with exhibits and objects illustrating the town's long and sometimes troubled past. Exhibits cover the Dornoch Light Railway, the Meikle ferry disaster, Andrew Carnegie, Skibo Castle (where Madonna got married) and the eventful history of Dornoch Cathedral.

 Dunrobin Castle & Gardens (Golspie KW10 6SF, ☎ 1408-633 177, fax 1408-634 081, info@dunrobincastle.net; open April-Oct, generally from 10:30am but days and hours vary seasonally, call ahead; adult/concession/child/family £6.50/£5.70/£4.50/£17.50). Dunrobin has been the home of Clan Sutherland since the early 14th century, and the castle is one of the oldest continuously inhabited houses in Britain. Although more a huge house with turrets rather than a true defensive fortress, Dunrobin contains impressive collections of furniture, silver, tapestries, family portraits and memorabilia, and is set in pretty, formal gardens. The summerhouse museum contains hunting trophies and other interesting objects. There are daily falconry demonstrations, a restaurant/tea room and gift shop.

Falls of Shin (Achany Glen, By Lairg IV27 4EE, ☎ 1549-402 231, info@fallsofshin.co.uk, www.fallsofshin.co.uk). A short walk takes you down to a platform where you can see wild salmon leaping spectacularly up the waterfalls (Aug-Sept are the best months; June-July are also good). There are forest walks – look for deer and otters – and an excellent restaurant. The Harrods shop seems slightly incongruous until it starts raining, when the flood of customers shows just how good a business venture it is; restaurant & shop open 9am-6pm in summer and 10am-5:30pm in winter.

Brora Heritage Centre (Coal Pit Road, Brora KW9 6NE, ☎ 1408-622 024, ☎ 1408-633 033 Oct-Apr; open May-Sept, Mon-Sat, 11am-5pm). Displays and hands-on guides to the heritage, archaeology and artifacts of this coastal village.

Clynelish Distillery (Brora KW9 6LR, ☎ 1408-623 000, fax 1408-623 004; open Easter-Sept, Mon-Fri, 10am-5pm, Oct, Mon-Fri, 11am-4pm, Nov-Easter, by appointment only, last tour one hour before closing; admission £4, including a shop voucher). The distillery enjoys great views over Brora and the North Sea and produces a malt that is fruity and slightly smoky.

Timespan Heritage Centre (Dunrobin Street, Helmsdale KW8 6JA, ☎ 1431-821 327, fax 1431-821 058, admin@timespan.org.uk, www.timespan.org.uk; open April-Oct, Mon-Sat, 9:30am-5pm & Sun, 2pm-5pm; adult/concession/child/family £4/£3/£2/£10). Excellent exhibitions on Helmsdale's heritage, from Picts and Vikings through murders at Helmsdale Castle, the last witch burning, the harrowing Highland Clearances and the Kildonan Gold Rush, to today's crofting, fishing and the neighboring oil fields. There is also an art gallery, gift shop, herb garden and café.

Golf

Royal Dornoch Championship Course (18-hole links, 6,514 yards; Golf Road, Dornoch IV25 3LW, ☎ 1862-810 219, fax 1862-810 792, rdgc@royaldornoch.com, www.royaldornoch.com; green fees £45-£76). This renowned links is one of the most popular courses in Scotland. There is plenty of room off the tee and the greens are large and undulating.

Shopping

The Jail Dornoch (Castle Street, Dornoch IV25 3SD, ☎/fax 1862-810 555, shopping@jail-dornoch.com, www.jail-dornoch.com). Large shop selling cashmere and woolens, country clothing, gifts, crafts and jewelry together with a small gallery of Highland art. There are great displays in the former cells.

Orcadian Stone Company (Main Street, Golspie KW10 6RH, ☎/fax 1408-633 483; open Easter-Oct, closed Sun). Orkney gold and silver jewelry, gemstone beads, minerals and stone lamps, as well as an exhibition of minerals, fossils and rocks unique to Scotland.

■ Where To Stay & Eat

See the *Accommodation* and *Dining* price charts on pages 395 and 396.

Lochcarron

Applecross Inn (Shore Street, Applecross IV54 8ND, ☎ 1520-744 262, fax 1520-744 400, www.applecross.net; B&B ££, lunch £, dinner £££). Charming, waterfront inn with recently refurbished rooms, excellent food, including platefuls of fresh local seafood, and a lively bar frequented by locals.

Kishorn Seafood Bar (Kishorn, Strathcarron IV54 8XA, ☎ 1520-733 240, kishornseafoodbar@supanet.com, open April-Oct, but evenings only in July-Aug; £-££). This (licensed) wooden hut serves fresh, simply cooked oysters, mussels, lobsters and scallops and other snacks, including a superb seafood platter, and single-handedly puts Kishorn on the map. The perfect way to build up your courage before driving over the Bealach na Ba!

Torridon

 Ben Damph Lodges (Torridon IV22 2EY, ☎ 1445-791 242/791 251, fax 1445-712 253, bendamph@lochtorridonhotel.com, www.bendamph.lochtorridonhotel.com; open April-Oct; B&B ££, dinner £-££). The Victorian stable and farm buildings of the former Ben Damph House (now Loch Torridon Hotel) have been converted into 14 low-cost family rooms, each sleeping up to six. The bar buzzes with walkers and climbers and the restaurant serves hearty, reasonably priced meals.

Loch Torridon Country House Hotel (Torridon IV22 2EY, ☎ 1445-791 242, fax 1445-712 253, enquiries@lochtorridonhotel.com, www.lochtorridonhotel.com; B&B ££££, lunch ££, dinner ££££). Built in 1887 as a grand shooting lodge, the hotel occupies a beautiful position on the shore of Loch Torridon in 58 acres of parkland with resident Highland cattle. The Victorian splendor includes ornate ceilings, wood paneling and magnificent bathrooms. The restaurant offers fine dining accompanied by an extensive wine list and over 300 malt whiskies. The staff ranger can organize a wide range of outdoor activities for guests.

Gairloch& Loch Maree

 The Creel Restaurant & Charleston House Restaurant (Gairloch IV21 2AH, ☎ 1445-712 497, reception@charlestonhouse.co.uk, www.charlestonhouse.co.uk; open Easter-Oct; B&B ££, dinner ££-£££). The charming John and Morag Walmsley have transformed this former fish-agent's house (dating from 1776) into a waterfront gem. The bedrooms are well-furnished and comfortable, but the highlight is the Creel Restaurant, which serves stunning food with friendly bistro informality. Morag's cooking is seriously good and the chatty John ensures good conversation while helping guests choose from a carefully selected list of wines, beers and malts. Wood beams, exposed stone walls, a real fire and atmospheric Moroccan lamps create the perfect intimate environment in which to enjoy some of the finest food in the Highlands (the rack of lamb cooked in a traditional Aga stove is the finest the author has tasted). Reserve early.

Badachro Inn (Badachro, near Gairloch IV21 2AA, ☎ 1445-741 255, www.badachroinn.com; lunch £, dinner ££). Overlooking peaceful Badachro Bay, the inn specializes in local seafood (see the "Specials of the Day" blackboard). There is a good selection of real ales and fine wines.

Rua Reidh Lighthouse (Melvaig, near Gairloch IV21 2EA, ☎ 1445-771 263, ruareidh@netcomuk.co.uk; B&B £-££, dinner ££). Guest house/hostel accommodation in the former keeper's house next to the still-operational light tower. The cozy sitting rooms have wood fires and the set menu dinners in the conservatory are excellent value. Walking holidays, climbing and multi-activity courses are available.

Old Mill Highland Lodge (Talladale, Loch Maree IV22 2HL, ☎ 1445-760 271; open Mar-Oct; B&B ££££, dinner £££). Custom-built small Highland lodge hotel occupying the site of a former grain store and horse mill, surrounded by two acres of gardens. There is good food and an extensive wine list.

Poolewe to An Teallach

Pool House Hotel (Poolewe IV22 2LD, ☎ 1445-781 272, fax 1445-781 403, enquiries@poolhousehotel.com, www.poolhousehotel.com; open Feb-Dec; B&B £££££, dinner ££££+). Nestling beneath tranquil mountains at the head of Loch Ewe, dreamy Pool House is a lavish retreat that wins awards for environmental friendliness as well as luxurious pampering. Its suites are enormous, sumptuously furnished and individually styled with huge, comfortable beds and spacious Victorian bathrooms. Fine dining overlooking the loch is unforgettable, although exquisite sunsets and otter sightings can cause guests to desert their award-winning seven courses for the photo of a lifetime. Pool House is run almost entirely by the charming Harrison family and it's worth forcing yourself out of your suite occasionally to walk their lovable dog Scampi. A stay at Pool House comes as close as anywhere to capturing the magic of the Highlands themselves.

Bridge Cottage Café (Main Street, Poolewe, ☎ 1445-781 335; £-££). A cozy café serving freshly made, wholesome snacks and home baking. The soups are excellent, as is the drinking chocolate. The café doesn't have many tables so you might have to wait a short time; if so, amuse yourself by browsing the connected gallery.

Aultbea Hotel (Aultbea IV22 2HX, ☎/fax 1445-731 201, aultbeahotel@btconnect.com, www.aultbeahotel.co.uk; B&B ££-£££, dinner ££). A late 19th-century coaching inn beautifully and quietly set on the shore of Loch Ewe, with comfortable rooms, friendly service and a restaurant enjoying gorgeous views (including sunsets) over the loch to the mountains of Torridon. The food is good (try the delicious seafood platter) and reasonably priced, too.

Dundonnell Hotel (Dundonnell, Little Loch Broom, near Ullapool IV23 2QR, ☎ 1854-633 204, fax 1854-633 366, enquiries@dundonnellhotel.co.uk, www.dundonnellhotel.com; B&B ££££, dinner ££-£££). Comfortable hotel set in a former coaching inn near the foot of An Teallach. The restaurant serves good food, which is just as well as there isn't much else in the area.

Ullapool

Royal Hotel (Garve Road, Ullapool IV26 2SY, ☎ 1854-612 181, fax 1854-612 951, info@royalhotel-ullapool.com, www.royalhotel-ullapool.com; B&B ££, dinner ££). This privately-owned hotel has recently been refurbished, and has bright and spacious bedrooms, some with balconies overlooking the loch. The **Waterfront Bar & Restaurant** offers good beer with bar and restaurant dining.

Riverside Hotel (Quay Street, Ullapool IV26 2UE, ☎/fax 1854-612 239, c.macrae@riversideullapool.com, www.riversideullapool.com; B&B £-££). Comfortable guest house with well-furnished bedrooms and a cozy lounge.

Ferry Boat Inn (Shore Street, Ullapool IV26 2UJ, ☎ 1854-612 366, fax 1854-613 266, reservations@ferryboat-inn.com, www.ferryboat-inn.com; B&B ££, dinner ££). A friendly, informal 18th-century inn situated on the shore of Loch Broom. The guests' lounge, dining room, bar and some of the pleasant bedrooms enjoy loch views. The old-fashioned bar has an open fire and serves meals year-round. Local musicians play in the summer. The intimate restaurant opens from spring to late autumn and emphasizes fresh local produce.

Caledonian Hotel (Quay Street, Ullapool IV26 2UG, ☎ 1854-612 306, fax 1854-612 679, caledonian@british-trust-hotels.com, www.british-trust-hotels.com; B&B £££, dinner ££). A large hotel with modern, comfortable bedrooms. The **Caley Inn** serves breakfast, lunch, dinner, teas, coffees and drinks, and has Internet access.

Brae Guest House (Shore Street, Ullapool IV26 2UJ, ☎ 1854-612 421; open May-Oct; B&B ££, dinner ££). A friendly, long-established B&B on the seafront overlooking Loch Broom with an optional à la carte evening meal.

Ardvreck Guest House (North Road, Morefield, near Ullapool IV26 2TH, ☎ 1854-612 028, fax 1854-613 000, ardvreck.guesthouse@btinternet.com; B&B ££). Ardvreck is situated in crofting land 1½ miles north of Ullapool and overlooks the village and Loch Broom. There are good-quality bedrooms and a lounge with great views.

The Sheiling Guesthouse (Garve Road, Ullapool IV26 2SX, ☎/fax 1854-612 947, www.guesthouseullapool.co.uk; B&B ££). An excellent modern and comfortable guest house standing peacefully beside Loch Broom. The superb breakfasts include homemade sausages and three types of locally smoked fish. Local fishing can be arranged. Cook-for-yourself accommodation is also available in Skiba Lodge.

Sutherland & Caithness

Lochinver & Assynt

 Inver Lodge Hotel (Lochinver IV27 4LU, ☎ 1571-844 496, fax 1571-844 395, enquiry@inverlodge.com, www.inverlodge.com; open April-Oct; B&B ££££, dinner £££). Modern, luxurious hotel set peacefully above the fishing village of Lochinver with the view to the rear dominated by the domed peak of Suilven. The spacious, high-quality rooms provide traditional comforts and carry the names of local lochs and mountains. The large dining room windows face westward (as do the bedrooms) and watching fishing boats returning to port under a reddening sky can make dinner a lengthy affair. There is a comfortable guest lounge, solarium, sauna and billiard room.

Inchnadamph Hotel (Assynt IV27 4HN, ☎ 1571-822 202, fax 1571-822 203, info@inchnadamphhotel.co.uk, www.inchnadamphhotel.co.uk; open Mar-Dec; B&B ££). A 200-year-old former coaching inn offering an informal atmosphere and good home cooking.

Summer Isles Hotel (Achiltibuie IV26 2YG, ☎ 1854-622 282, fax 1854-622 251, summerisleshotel@aol.com, www.summerisleshotel.co.uk, open Easter-Oct; B&B ££££, lunch ££, dinner ££££). Individually styled, family-owned hotel located at the end of a long, single-lane road. The restaurant serves mostly home produced or locally caught produce.

Drumbeg Designs Craft Shop (Tigh-na-Bruach, Drumbeg IV27 4NW, on the B869 Assynt coastal road; ☎ 1571-833 263, www.drumbegdesigns.com; open Easter-Oct; £). This welcome stop on the Assynt coastal road has a selection of home baking, cream teas, soups and sandwiches.

Northwest Sutherland

 Kylesku Hotel (Kylesku IV27 4HW, ☎ 1971-502 231, fax 1971-502 313; open Mar-Oct; B&B ££-£££, dinner ££). Small, privately owned hotel standing in beautiful Highland scenery.

Old School Hotel (Inshegra, Kinlochbervie, near Durness IV27 4RH, ☎/fax 1971-521 383; B&B ££). Newly built accommodation with spectacular views and a restaurant noted for its fresh seafood.

Balnakeil Bistro (Balnakeil Craft Village, Durness IV27 4PT, ☎ 1971-511 335; open Easter-Oct; lunch £, dinner £-££). Licensed, friendly bistro serving all-day food, including good home baking.

Loch Croispol Bookshop & Licensed Restaurant (17c Balnakeil Craft Village, Durness IV27 4PT, ☎ 1971-511 777, loch.croispol@btclick.com, www.scottish-books.org; lunch £; dinner ££). Snacks, lunches and evening meals (high season only), with a shop selling books on Scottish history and Gaelic.

Seafood Restaurant (Tigh Na Mara, Tarbet, Scourie IV27 4SS, ☎/fax 1971-502 251, pearcejjpearce@aol.com; open April-Sept; ££). House specializes include fresh local crabs, lobsters, prawns and mussels caught by local fishermen.

The North Coast

 Cloisters (Church Holme Talmine, near Tongue IV27 4YP, ☎/fax 1847-601 286, reception@cloistertal.demon.co.uk, www.cloistertal.demon.co.uk; B&B ££). Comfortable B&B accommodation in a new house built in the style of the neighboring 19th-century church in which the owners live.

Tongue Hotel (Tongue IV27 4XD, ☎ 1847-611 206, fax 1847-611 345, info@tonguehotel.co.uk, www.scottish-selection.co.uk/tongue; open April to mid-Nov; B&B £££, lunch ££, dinner £££). Originally the Victorian hunting lodge of the Duke of Sutherland, the hotel retains its historic character with period pieces, wood paneling, individually styled bedrooms and a relaxing ambience.

The Sheiling Guest House (Melvich KW14 7YJ, ☎/fax 1641-531 256, thesheiling@btinternet.com, www.b-and-b-scotland.co.uk/thesheiling.htm; open April-Oct; B&B ££). Award-winning guest house on a croft opposite Melvich beach on Scotland's north coast. Owners Joan (a former folk singer) and Hugh Campbell offer a warm welcome and maintain a mountain of information on local attractions and activities. Breakfast is a delicious banquet: the "full Scottish" will keep most people going the entire day and the wild loch trout is excellent. Not surprisingly, return visitors often fill the rooms.

Melvich Hotel (Melvich KW14 7YJ, ☎ 1641-531 206, fax 1641-531 347, info@melvichhotel.co.uk, www.melvichhotel.co.uk; B&B ££, dinner ££). Comfortable, informal country hotel set on a cliff-top overlooking Melvich Bay. The lounge bar has peat fires, views to Orkney, 100 malt whiskies and real ales brewed on the premises. The restaurant serves good food.

Caithness

 Castle Arms Hotel (Mey, Thurso KW14 8XH, ☎ 1847-851 244, info@castlearms.co.uk, www.castlearms.co.uk; B&B ££, dinner ££). A former 19th-century coaching inn set in six acres of open parkland, a short distance from the Castle of Mey.

Forss Country House Hotel (Forss, By Thurso KW14 7XY, ☎ 1847-861 201, fax 1847-861 301, jamie@forsshousehotel.co.uk, www.forsshousehotel.co.uk; B&B £££, dinner £££). A listed building dating back to 1810, with spacious bedrooms, deep cast baths and almost 300 single malt whiskies.

Le Bistro (2 Traill Street, Thurso KW14 8EJ, ☎ 1847-893 737, fax 1955-641 230, closed Sun-Mon; lunch £, dinner ££). Informal restaurant serving seafood and local produce.

Dunbeath Hotel (The Village, Dunbeath, By Wick KW6 6EG, ☎ 1593-731 208, fax 1593-731 242; B&B ££, dinner ££). Small hotel set in beautiful surroundings, with comfortable bedrooms and good food and wine.

Portland Arms Hotel (Lybster, By Wick KW3 6BS, ☎ 1593-721 721, fax 1593-721 722, info@portlandarms.co.uk, www.portlandarms.co.uk; B&B £££, lunch £, dinner £££). The hotel has newly decorated bedrooms, log fire, bistro-bar and informal dining in the farmhouse-style **Jo's Kitchen**, with its Aga stove.

Bord de l'Eau (2 Market Street, Wick KW1 4AR, ☎ 1955-604 400; closed Mon; ££). Small, family-run restaurant serving traditional French cuisine using local fish and fresh produce. The service could be friendlier.

Mid & East Sutherland

Royal Marine Hotel (Golf Road, Brora KW9 6QS, ☎ 1408-621 252, fax 1408-621 181, info@highlandescape.com, www.highlandescapehotels.com; B&B ££££, lunch ££, dinner £££). Designed by Sir Robert Lorimer after the First World War, the excellent Royal Marine oozes discreet elegance – wooden arched entrance hall, grand staircase and paneled snooker room – that suggests a much older building than its actual vintage. Facilities include formal and informal dining, bar, sitting room decorated with antique golf clubs, and leisure club, including indoor pool, steam room, solarium, gym and curling rink.

Links Hotel (Golf Road, Brora KW9 6QS, ☎ 1408-621 252, fax 1408-621 181, info@highlandescape.com, www.highlandescapehotels.com; open May-Sept; B&B ££££, dinner ££). The building was converted from a private Edwardian residence into a hotel in the 1920s, and sits above James Braid's Brora golf course with views beyond the first and 18th fairways to the sea. The bar, restaurant, lounge and many guest rooms have sea views. Guests have full use of the nearby Royal Marine Hotel's leisure facilities.

Dornoch Castle Hotel (Castle Street, Dornoch IV25 3SD, ☎ 1862-810 216, fax 1862-810 981, enquiries@dornochcastlehotel.com, www.dornochcastlehotel.com; B&B £££, dinner £££). 15th-century tower set in walled gardens overlooking the 13th-century cathedral, with roaring fires, locally sourced cuisine, interesting wines and malts, and a resident ghost.

Eagle Hotel (Castle Street, Dornoch IV25 3SR, ☎ 1862-810 008, fax 1862-811 355, info@eagledornoch.co.uk, www.eagledornoch.co.uk; B&B ££). Mid-19th-century listed property, centrally located in Dornoch. The stone building was recently refurbished throughout and provides a friendly, informal atmosphere.

2 Quail (Castle Street, Dornoch IV25 3SN, ☎ 1862-811 811, info@2quail.com, www.2quail.com; B&B £££, dinner £££). Well-furnished accommodation and an intimate Victorian dining room serving well-cooked, traditional cuisine.

Carbisdale Castle (Culrain, near Lairg IV24 3DP, ☎ 870-004 1109 castle, ☎ 870-155 3255 Scottish Youth Hostel Association, reservations@syha.org-.uk, www.carbisdale.org; B&B £). One of the most spectacular youth hostels you'll ever find, with its own statue gallery, art collection, beautifully decorated public and dining rooms and, of course, a resident ghost.

The Nip Inn (Main Street, Lairg IV27 4DB, ☎ 1549-402 243, fax 1549-402 593, info@nipinn.co.uk, www.nipinn.co.uk; B&B ££). Centrally located in Lairg, the hotel's rooms are basic but comfortable; the menus are varied and use local fish and game.

Park House (Lairg IV27 4AU, ☎ 1549-402 208, fax 1549-402 693, david-walker@park-house.freeserve.co.uk, www.fishinscotland.net/parkhouse; B&B ££, dinner ££). Victorian-style family home set in tranquil surroundings on the banks of Loch Shin. Spacious, comfortable rooms and home-cooked food. Fishing and other field sports are available.

Falls of Shin (Achany Glen, By Lairg IV27 4EE, ☎ 1549-402 231, info@fallsofshin.co.uk, www.fallsofshin.co.uk; £-££). Spacious, cabin-style restaurant serving a wide range of hot and cold dishes and snacks, including excellent carvery roasts.

Easter Ross & The Black Isle

■ Tain to Dingwall

Between Dingwall and the Dornoch Firth, the rich farmland of Easter Ross provides a backdrop for the communities of **Evanton**, **Alness**, **Invergordon** and **Tain**. Tain lays claim to being Scotland's oldest **Royal Burgh**, with a charter dating back to 1066. The world-famous **Glenmorangie Distillery** lies on the northern edge of the town.

Attractions & Sights

Glenmorangie Distillery (Tain IV19 1PZ, ☎ 1862-892 477, fax 1862-894 371, visitors@glenmorangieplc.co.uk, www.glenmorangie.com; open year-round, but opening days/times vary seasonally so call ahead or check the web site; reservations advisable; £2 admission is applied to shop purchases). On the shores of the Dornoch Firth, Glenmorangie produces one of the most popular malt whiskies, whose delicate balance and underlying smokiness make it eminently drinkable. The copper stills are the tallest in Scotland and the original still house contains historical artifacts from the distillery's past.

Tain Through Time (Tower Street, Tain IV19 1DY, ☎/fax 1862-894 089, www.tainmuseum.demon.co.uk; open April-Oct, 10am-6pm; Nov-Mar, Saturday only, noon-4pm; adult/child £3.50/£2.50). The turbulent history of the ancient burgh is presented via an audiovisual show, live acting, artifacts, photographs and documents, all in a beautiful churchyard setting. See the church as it would have appeared in pre-Reformation times. Learn the story of St Duthac's miracles and see how the sanctuary was violated in horrible circumstances. Take the personal CD tour of the town to discover who had their cheek branded with the Tolbooth key and how Andrew Carnegie upset the town council.

Tarbat Discovery Centre (Tarbatness Road, Portmahomack, By Tain IV20 1YA, ☎ 1862-871 351, fax 1862-871 361, info@tarbat-discovery.co.uk, www.tarbat-discovery.co.uk, open Mar-Apr and Oct-Dec, 2-5pm, May-Sept, 10am-5pm; closed Jan-Feb; adult/concession/child £3.50/£2/£1). Set in a historic church, the exhibition is based on an important archaeological dig and displays carved Pictish stones and a Viking silver horde. Touch-screens and videos add to the fun, and conducted tours of the dig are available July-Aug.

Adventures

 TroutQuest (West End, Glen Glass, Evanton, near Dingwall IV16 9XW, ☎/fax 1349-830 606, roger@troutquest.com, www.troutquest.com). Fly-fishing holidays in Ross-shire and excursions throughout the northern Highlands, with instruction available.

Cruises

JR Mackenzie Agri & Marine (Carn Bhren, Portmahomack, By Tain IV20 1YS, ☎ 1862-871 257, fax 1862-871 256, agrimole@aol.com, open April to mid-Nov) Sea angling (equipment supplied), dolphin watching and other nature trips from Portmahomack.

Shopping

Tain Pottery (Aldie, Tain IV19 1LZ, ☎ 1862-894 112, fax 1862-893 306, sales@tainpottery.co.uk, www.tainpottery.co.uk). Watch the transformation of raw clay into artistic, hand-painted stoneware and browse a vast range of quality gifts.

■ Strathpeffer

Strathpeffer became famous as a Victorian spa town, growing from a small hamlet in 1819 to a resort town boasting an extraordinary collection of grand hotels and fine villas by 1914, many of which can still be seen.

Attractions & Sights

 Highland Museum of Childhood (The Old Station, Strathpeffer IV14 9DH, ☎ 1997-421 031, info@hmoc.freeserve.co.uk, www.hmoc.freeserve.co.uk; open April-Oct, days/times vary seasonally; adult/concession/family £1.50/£1/£3.50). An audiovisual presentation presents the customs and traditions of childhood in the Highlands, and there are collections of childhood treasures, dolls and toys. Hands-on activities are available for children, and there is a gift shop and coffee shop.

■ The Black Isle

The Black Isle isn't black and isn't even an island. In fact it's a green peninsula, at the tip of which lies the ancient and charming town of **Cromarty**, guarded by its "Sutors" – two hills that overlook the narrow harbor entrance. The town is over 700 years old; from medieval times pilgrims passed through Cromarty on their way north to the **Shrine of St Duthac** at Tain. Pilgrims (and at least two Scottish kings: James IV and Robert the Bruce) crossed by ferry between Cromarty and Nigg – a route still operated today by a small car ferry. The present town dates largely from the 18th to 19th centuries and blends imposing mansions with humble fishermen's cottages set around narrow, picturesque lanes.

 INFORMATION SOURCES: The tourism office is at the Picnic Site, North Kessock IV1 1XB; open Easter through October.

Getting Here

 The **Cromarty-Nigg Ferry** (☎ 1381-610 269, ☎ 7768-653 674 mobile, info@cromarty-ferry.co.uk, www.cromarty-ferry.co.uk; runs June-Oct). This might be the smallest car ferry in Britain – it carries a few passengers and only two cars at a time – but it significantly reduces driving time to Cromarty from the north, which would otherwise require traveling all the way around the Cromarty Firth.

Attractions & Sights

Cromarty Courthouse Museum (Church Street, Cromarty IV11 8XA, ☎ 1381-600 418, fax 1381-600 408, courthouse@mail.cali.co.uk, www.cromarty-courthouse.org.uk; open April-Oct, 10am-5pm; Nov-Dec, noon-4pm; adult/concession/family £3.50/£2.50/£10). George Ross's 1772 courthouse has been transformed into an award-winning local history museum. The well-designed displays include a video introduction to the town; an interactive DVD, *Generations in Stone,* that incorporates 360° panoramic views from many locations around Cromarty, and animatronic recreations of a courtroom trial and the slightly spooky figure of Sir Thomas Urquhart, whose lifelike model's eyes follow you while he pronounces on a variety of subjects. There is also a one-hour audio tour of the town's principal landmarks.

Hugh Miller's Cottage (NTS; Church Street, Cromarty IV11 8XA, ☎ 1381-600 245, fax 1381-600 391, fgostwick@nts.org.uk; open Good Friday-Sept, noon-5pm; Oct, Sun-Wed, noon-5pm; adult/concession/family £2.50/£1.90/£7). Hugh Miller is one of Cromarty's most famous sons and became a stonemason, geologist, theologian, editor and writer. The atmospheric, late 17th-century cottage where he was born in 1802 is one of the oldest buildings in Cromarty and the last to retain its thatched roof. It has been a museum since 1890 and provides absorbing insights into Miller's work and 18th-century life in the area. Its tiny rooms have unbelievably small doorways and contain many artifacts and furniture belonging to generations of the Miller family. A small selection of Miller's fossil collection is on display together with file copies of his writings in *The Witness*, which he edited for 16 years. The small ground-floor bedroom in which Miller was born now contains a library of works by and about Miller and his time, together with some of his best folk tales and legends.

Black Isle Brewery (Old Allangrange, Munlochy, near Inverness IV8 8NZ, ☎ 1463-811 871, fax 1463-811 875, greatbeers@blackisle-brewery.com, www.blackislebrewery.com; open year-round, Mon-Sat, 10am-5:30pm, June-Oct also open Sun, 12:30pm-5pm). Tours show you how top-quality organic beers are produced, and you can buy your favorites from the brewery shop.

Groam House Museum (High Street, Rosemarkie IV10 8UF, ☎ 1381-620 961, fax 1381-621 730, groamhouse@ecosse.net, open May-Sept, Mon-Sat, 10am-5pm; Sun, 2pm-4:30pm; Oct-Apr, Sat-Sun, 2pm-4pm). This small museum displays the **Rosemarkie Cross Slab** and several other enigmatic Pictish stones found nearby, but disappointingly provides little information on the Picts themselves. If you want to find out about the Picts you need to visit Pictavia in Brechin (see page 300).

Adventures

 The **MacFarquhar's Bed** walk leads to a sheltered bay rich in plant life, with caves and a natural arch in the rocks. From Cromarty House, follow the south road out of Cromarty to Mains Farm. Continue over the hill, mostly by way of dirt track, and down through an avenue of trees to reach a stile at the bottom of the field. A narrow path meanders down to the old salmon fishing bothy and the view of the huge crag, called "MacFarquhar's Bed," hollowed out of the sea. The path is steep and eroded in areas so take care (3-4 hours; easy/moderate).

The popular **Cromarty's South Sutor** walk climbs to an impressive viewpoint providing excellent panoramas over the Cromarty Firth and surrounding counties. Follow the Reeds Park path running by the shore east from Cromarty, with fine views of the sea and North Sutor. Continue to the foot of the path that then climbs steadily by way of flights of steps through the woods. Information panels at the viewpoint indicate the main landmarks visible. Return by the same route or take the easy road to return to Cromarty (2 hours; easy).

Black Isle Riding Centre (Drumsmittal, North Kessock, By Inverness IV1 3XF, ☎/fax 1463-731 707). Lessons, treks and mini-rides through woodland for small groups. All abilities are welcome but advance booking is essential.

Wildlife Watching

 The sand spit at **Chanonry Point** in Rosemarkie, near Fortrose, is a great place to watch Moray Firth dolphins, which often put on playful leaping displays just feet from the beach. I've seen them that close to shore, sadly through binoculars as I was at Fort George on the other side of the firth.

Cruises

Dolphin Ecosse (Harbour Workshop, Victoria Place, Cromarty IV11 8YE, ☎ 1381-600 323, fax 1381-600 800, info@dolphinecosse.co.uk, www.dolphinecosse.co.uk). Boat trips from Cromarty to view dolphins, porpoises, whales and seabirds.

Dolphin Trips (Elmbank, Rosehaugh Drive, Avoch IV9 8RF, ☎/fax 1381-620 958, 7779-833 951 mobile, www.dolphintripsavoch.co.uk; cruises April-Oct). One-hour trips to see ospreys, otters, seals and dolphins.

Where To Stay & Eat

See the *Accommodation* and *Dining* price charts on pages 395 and 396.

Tain to Dingwall

 Glenmorangie House (Cadboll, Fearn, By Tain IV20 1XP, ☎ 1862-871 671, fax 1862-894 371, relax@glenmorangieplc.co.uk; B&B ££££, dinner £££). Traditional Highland mansion with log fires, polished wood and walls adorned with oil paintings, prints and memorabilia. And, of course, you can say you've stayed at Glenmorangie.

Morangie House Hotel (Morangie Road, Tain IV19 1PY, ☎ 1862-892 281, fax 1862-892 872, wynne@morangiehotel.com, www.morangiehotel.com; B&B £££, lunch £, dinner ££-£££). Victorian mansion with spacious rooms.

Tulloch Castle Hotel (Tulloch Castle Drive, Dingwall IV15 9ND, ☎ 1349-861 325, fax 1349-863 993, enquiries@tullochcastle.co.uk, www.tul-lochcastle.co.uk; B&B ££££). Twelfth-century castle hotel with large, elegantly furnished rooms, set on the edge of the market town of Dingwall.

Strathpeffer

Craigvar (The Square, Strathpeffer IV14 9DL, ☎/fax 1997-421 622, craigvar@talk21.com, www.craigvar.com; B&B ££). High-quality B&B in an attractive Georgian house with comfortable, sizeable rooms, original fireplaces and a good breakfast menu.

Ord House Hotel (Muir of Ord IV6 7UH, ☎/fax 1463-870 492, eliza@ord-house.com, www.ord-house.com; open May-Oct; B&B £££, dinner £££). This 17th-century house was the home of the laird of Clan McKenzie. Its 60 acres of surrounding gardens and woodland ensure tranquility. The interior is furnished with antiques, and open log fires burn in the hall, drawing room and bar. A resident ghost takes down paintings she doesn't like!

The Black Isle

Royal Hotel Cromarty (Marine Terrace, Cromarty IV11 8YN, ☎ 1381-600 217, fax 1381-600 813, info@royalcromartyhotel.co.uk, www.royalcromarty-hotel.co.uk; B&B ££, dinner ££). Rather tired seafront establishment, but it's the only hotel in Cromarty.

The Anderson (Union Street, Fortrose IV10 8TD, ☎ 1381-620 236, info@the-anderson.co.uk, www.fortrosehotel.co.uk; B&B ££, dinner ££). A striking turreted exterior, bedrooms furnished with antiques, international cuisine, and fine beers and whiskies.

Braelangwell House (Balblair, near Cromarty IV7 8LQ, ☎ 1381-610 353, fax 1381-610 467, braelangwell@btinternet.com, www.btinter-net.com/~braelangwell; open Mar-Nov; B&B ££-£££). A beautiful and grand Georgian house set in a small estate of ancient woodland and gardens. The interior is luxuriously furnished, including billiard and ballrooms, conservatory and richly decorated candlelit dining room, and there is an excellent breakfast menu.

Plough Inn (48 High St, Rosemarkie, near Fortrose, ☎ 1381-620 164, fax 1381-620 164). Charming 18th-century pub with two beer gardens that serves high-quality local produce, seafood and real ales, including beer from the local Black Isle Brewery.

Inner Hebrides

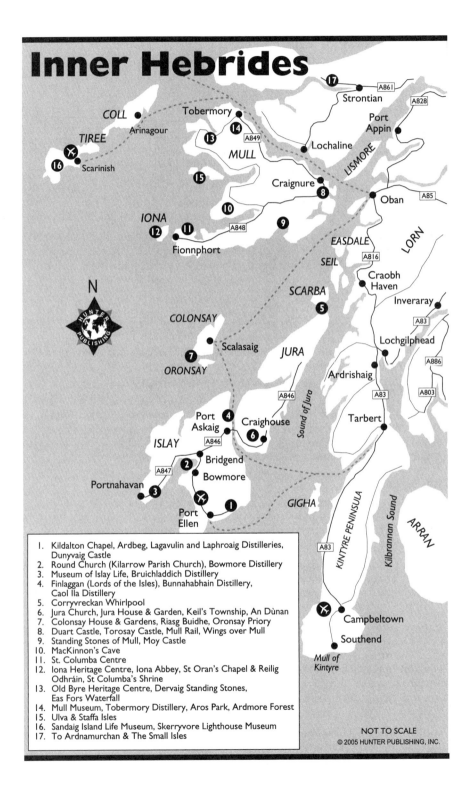

COLL

Tobermory

TIREE Arinagour

⑬ ⑭ A849

Scarinish ⑯ ✈

MULL

⑮

IONA ⑩

⑫ ⑪ A848

Fionnphort

N

COLONSAY

Scalasaig

⑦

ORONSAY

Port Askaig ④ Craighouse

ISLAY A846 ⑥

② Bridgend

A847 Bowmore

Portnahavan ③

✈

Port Ellen ①

GIGHA

⑰ A861

Strontian A828

Port Appin

Lochaline

LISMORE

Craignure ⑧

Oban A85

EASDALE

SEIL A816

Craobh Haven

Inveraray

SCARBA ⑤

LORN

JURA

Lochgilphead

A886

Ardrishaig

A846

Sound of Jura

A83 A803

Tarbert

KINTYRE PENINSULA

Kilbrannan Sound

ARRAN

A83

✈

Campbeltown

Southend

Mull of Kintyre

1. Kildalton Chapel, Ardbeg, Lagavulin and Laphroaig Distilleries, Dunyvaig Castle
2. Round Church (Kilarrow Parish Church), Bowmore Distillery
3. Museum of Islay Life, Bruichladdich Distillery
4. Finlaggan (Lords of the Isles), Bunnahabhain Distillery, Caol Ila Distillery
5. Corryvreckan Whirlpool
6. Jura Church, Jura House & Garden, Keil's Township, An Dùnan
7. Colonsay House & Gardens, Riasg Buidhe, Oronsay Priory
8. Duart Castle, Torosay Castle, Mull Rail, Wings over Mull
9. Standing Stones of Mull, Moy Castle
10. MacKinnon's Cave
11. St. Columba Centre
12. Iona Heritage Centre, Iona Abbey, St Oran's Chapel & Reilig Odhráin, St Columba's Shrine
13. Old Byre Heritage Centre, Dervaig Standing Stones, Eas Fors Waterfall
14. Mull Museum, Tobermory Distillery, Aros Park, Ardmore Forest
15. Ulva & Staffa Isles
16. Sandaig Island Life Museum, Skerryvore Lighthouse Museum
17. To Ardnamurchan & The Small Isles

NOT TO SCALE
© 2005 HUNTER PUBLISHING, INC.

The Hebrides

The Hebrides are a magical archipelago of hauntingly beautiful, wildly romantic islands that you will never forget. There are some 500 islands and islets in total, divided into the **Inner Hebrides** and **Outer Hebrides**, of which fewer than 100

are inhabited. The islands together cover an area of 2,900 square miles (7,510 square km) and their terrain is rocky, with many moors, lakes and valleys.

The **Vikings** invaded the Hebrides in the eighth century and retained control until 1266. Scottish chieftains, primarily clans MacDougall and MacDonald, ruled the islands over the next few centuries. The Crown gradually reduced the chieftans' influence, a process continued and accelerated after union with England in 1707, and gained full control over the Hebrides by 1748.

The Inner Hebrides

The islands known as the Inner Hebrides are located along the west coast of Scotland, to the north and south of the Western Highlands. The largest of these islands is **Skye**, which is covered in the *Highlands* chapter as it is connected by road bridge to the mainland (see pages 412-432). The other major islands of the Inner Hebrides are **Islay, Jura, Colonsay, Mull, Coll** and **Tiree**.

DON'T MISS

Experience the intense spirituality of **Iona**, birthplace of Scottish Christianity.

Tour Islay's superlative whisky distilleries, starting with **Ardbeg**, **Lagavulin** and **Laphroaig**.

Walk wild on **Jura** for magical scenery and solitude, and marvel at the awesome spectacle of the **Corryvreckan whirlpool**.

Explore the whispering ruins of **Finlaggan**, former power base of the Lords of the Isles.

Unwind on sleepy **Colonsay** and walk at low tide to neighboring **Oronsay**.

Enjoy **Tobermory**, Mull's colorful capital.

Sail to the **Small Isles** and climb the remote **Hebridean Cuillin** on Rum.

Best Freebie: **Oronsay Priory** and **High Cross**.

Isle of Islay

Islay (pronounced "eye-la"), the southernmost of the Hebridean islands, is a rich and fertile land with a windswept landscape of flat, exposed, peaty moorland, sheltered woodland, high cliffs and wide sandy beaches. Scattered around are several interesting villages, mostly dating from after the 18th-century Highland Clearances. Lying directly in the path of the Gulf Stream, the island enjoys a mild, if often wet, climate.

Islay has a long history stretching from Neolithic times. Over thousands of years, its settlers have left a rich archaeological heritage, ranging from Stone Age chambered cairns, Bronze Age standing stones and Iron Age forts, to the more recent ruins at Finlaggan, the former power base of the MacDonald Lords of the Isles, and the poignant townships deserted after the Highland Clearances.

■ Special Events

The Islay Festival (May/Jun; Islay festival Office, Geirhilda, Back Road, Port Ellen, Isle of Islay PA42 7DR, ☎ 1496-302 413, fax 1496-302 112, islayfestival@lineone.net, www.islayfestival.org) A celebration of the best of Islay malt and music with distillery open-days, tastings, ceilidhs, concerts, dancing, golf and fishing competitions.

Islay Jazz Festival (Sep; Columba Centre, Bowmore, Islay, PA43 7LN, ☎ 1496-810 044) A weekend of concerts spread over many venues, including distilleries, bird sanctuaries, stately homes, village halls and a Gaelic college.

INFORMATION SOURCES: The tourism office is at The Square, Bowmore, Isle of Islay PA43 7JP, ☎ 870-720 0617, fax 1496-810 363, info@islay.visitscotland.com; open year-round.

■ Getting Here

By Air

Loganair (☎ 845-773 3377) flies to Islay (Islay Airport ☎ 1496-302 022) from Glasgow (daily except Sunday).

By Ferry

Caledonian MacBrayne (☎ 1475-650 100, www.calmac.co.uk) operates car-ferry services from Kennacraig on the Kintyre Peninsula to Port Ellen and Port Askaig on Islay (2 hours).

■ Getting Around

By Car

It is well worth exploring the island by road, if for no other reason than to witness the charming habit Islay drivers have of waving to each other, even to total strangers. Rental cars are available from **D&N McKenzie** (Glenegedale, near the airport, ☎ 1496-302 300, fax 1496-302 324). The road across central Islay is invitingly straight, but be careful, as it's far from level (it largely floats on a bed of water-logged peat).

DID YOU KNOW? *Peat forms when persistent rain clogs soil, preventing bacteria from breaking down dead vegetation. Islay is largely covered in peaty moorland. A newcomer to the island (and large parts of the Highlands and other islands, as the author can testify on his first visit years ago) will turn on a tap and wait for the yellow coloration in the water to clear. It never does!*

By Taxi

Carol's Cabs (☎ 1496-302 155, ☎ 7775-782 155 mobile, taxi@carols-cabs.co.uk) provides round-the-clock taxis and minibuses.

■ Port Ellen & South Islay

Port Ellen is Islay's main ferry port and has a long row of whitewashed houses strung around the bay of Loch Leodamais. The island's three most famous whisky distilleries – Laphroaig, Lagavulin and Ardbeg – are a short drive along the northeastern shore. There was once a distillery in the town itself, but that is now the malting factory supplying the other distilleries. To the west, Kilnaughton Bay has a fine beach, behind which rises the rugged Oa peninsula with its rocky cliffs, once the home of smugglers and illicit stills. Running the length of Laggan Bay stretches the Big Strand – seven miles of dune-backed sandy beach – accessed from Kintra or from a track beside the airport.

Attractions & Sights

Kildalton Chapel (six miles northeast of Port Ellen, take the road signposted Ardbeg) The chapel at Kildalton dates from the 13th century and was known as the Church of St John of Jerusalem. The chapel has a stone font at its west door and tradition has it that the font never dries up. In the churchyard stand many sculptured stones and interesting memorials. The most outstanding of these is the beautiful nine-foot **Kildalton Cross**, the only surviving complete Celtic high cross in Scotland. The cross was carved from a solid slab of Islay grey-green epidiorite containing numerous granules of feldspar, which has been closely matched to outcrops at nearby Port na Cille. The Kildalton Cross is closely related to the group of major crosses – St Oran's, St John's and St Martin's – at Iona, and like them probably dates from around 800. The cross is decorated with biblical scenes on one side, including the virgin and child and David and the lion, and beautiful interlacing designs on the other. The interlacing designs, having neither beginning nor end, are thought to represent eternity.

Ardbeg Distillery (Port Ellen, Isle of Islay PA42 7EA, ☎ 1496-302 244, fax 1496-302 040, www.ardbeg.com; open year-round; June-Aug, 10am-5pm, Sept-May, Mon-Fri, 10am-4pm; admission £2, includes a shop voucher; reservations recommended for tours) Established in 1815, Ardbeg was once a noted haunt for whisky smugglers and illicit distilling. A difficult past saw the distillery close for many years until restoration began in 1997. Fresh Ardbeg is once again flowing, and it's considered one of the finest malts available (particularly the 17-year-old) for its robust, powerful and smoky character. There is an excellent visitor center and beautiful café converted from the original kiln and malt barn.

Lagavulin Distillery (Port Ellen, Isle of Islay PA42 7DZ, ☎ 1496-302 400, fax 1496-302 733; open year-round, Mon-Fri, tours by appointment only; admission £4, including a shop voucher) Lagavulin Bay (pronounced "lagga-voolin"), commanded by the ruins of Dunyvaig Castle, was once the haunt of smugglers. Richly peaty water running down from the Solan Lochs, a long distillation in distinctive pear-shaped stills and long maturation in sea-pounded warehouses give Lagavulin its rich, peaty character smoothed by soft, mellow edges, and a reputation as one of Scotland's finest malts. The 16-year-old is one of the author's favorite drams. Go to nearby Dunyvaig Castle for the best distillery photos.

CLASSIC MALTS CRUISE

Every summer, around 100 yachts take part in the Classic Malts Cruise, celebrating Scotland's most famous export with a regatta through 200 miles of the most scenic waters of the Inner Hebrides. After a party at Oban Distillery on the west coast of Argyll, the yachts sail their own routes to two of the most famous names in Scotch whisky: **Talisker** on Skye and **Lagavulin** on Islay.

The cruise takes place in the second two weeks of July and brings together classic and new yachts from around the world, united in a passion for sailing, camaraderie, breathtaking scenery and the finest malt whisky. The three distilleries provide the social focus for the fortnight, throwing open their hallowed halls and welcoming crews to private tours and tastings, buffets, music and dancing (the buffet and ceilidh at Lagavulin, which marks the end of the cruise, is legendary).

Yes, it's a bit of a marketing ruse by Diageo, which owns the participating distilleries. Yes, it's liver-threatening. But, it's also wonderfully enjoyable and a unique and indescribably stylish way of bringing together so much of what makes Scotland, and the Hebrides in particular, such a magical destination.

For more information, contact the **World Cruising Club** (120 High Street, Cowes, Isle of Wight PO31 7AX, ☎ 1983-296 060, fax 1983-295 959, classicmaltscruise@worldcruising.com, www.worldcruising.com) Book early – the cruise is limited to 100 boats and often fills up within four to five weeks of applications opening in January. If you need to charter a boat, **Sail Scotland** (☎ 1309-676 757, www.sailscotland.co.uk) has details of charter boats.

Laphroaig Distillery (Port Ellen, Isle of Islay PA42 7DU, ☎ 1496-302 418, fax 1496-302 496, www.laphroaig.com; open year-round, tours Mon-Fri, 10:15am & 2:15pm, advance booking required; admission and tours free) Laphroaig (pronounced "la-froyg") is Gaelic for "beautiful hollow by the broad bay." Its malt whisky, first distilled in 1815, is the most idiosyncratic of the characteristic peaty malts of southeastern Islay with a unique, complex, medicinal quality that connoisseurs either love or hate. Laphroaig is an acquired taste – don't try this as your first single malt or you'll probably never drink whisky again. Become a Friend of Laphroaig to own your own plot of distillery land on which you collect rent (a dram!), take part in auctions and receive special offers.

ISLAY'S MALT WHISKY DISTILLERIES

Islay is heaven for lovers of single malt whisky – as evocative for the whisky connoisseur as Bordeaux is for the wine buff. Endowed with the fertile soils, peaty water and exuberant sea breezes essential for the distillation of superlative whiskies, Islay was once the home of 21 distilleries, of which seven survive today. Islay malts are characterized above all else by peat. Miles and miles of peat bog in the west of the island have for centuries provided islanders with household fuel and provide the raw material that so distinguishes the island's famous whiskies.

Three of the most revered names in malt whisky – Ardbeg, Lagavulin and Laphroaig – are virtually neighbors on the island's rugged southeastern shores, their mesmerizing whitewashed buildings, pagoda roofs and large-painted distillery names (visible from quite a distance out at sea) adding to the drama of the coastal landscape. These three, along with Bowmore, are the island's grandest malts. Even if one of these is your idea of the perfect malt whisky, don't ignore the others: Caol Ila, Bruichladdich and Bunnahabhain. Each of the seven is worthy of a visit.

Dunyvaig Castle (Lagavulin Bay, accessed via a track just north of Lagavulin Distillery) Situated on the eastern side of Lagavulin Bay, opposite the famous distillery, the castle ruins (pronounced "dun-oo-vig") probably date from the 16th century, although the Vikings may well have built a fortification on this site as early as 1200. Somerled's grandson built a fort here to protect the fleet crucial for his control of the Hebrides. It was from here in 1314 that 1,800 Islay men departed to help Robert the Bruce trounce the English at Bannockburn. The massing of warships on this occasion earned the fortress its name "Dunyvaig," Gaelic for "fort of the little ships."

In 1545, the castle was granted back to its former owners the MacDonalds of Dunyvaig. During the 17th century, Dunyvaig was an active military and political base. In 1615, royal troops under the command of Sir Oliver Lambert laid siege to and badly damaged the castle.

Lurabus Township (see Mull of Oa walk under *Adventures*, below, for directions) These lonely and evocative clusters of ruined buildings scattered along a ridge overlooking the sea are the largest and best preserved of numerous deserted townships on the east coast of the Oa Peninsula. The buildings are rubble-built and gable-ended, constructed of locally extracted stone. The township was abandoned following the Highland Clearances at the end of the 18th century yet several ruins preserve internal details such as fireplaces and even shelving.

Adventures

On Foot

 From Port Ellen follow the signpost for **Mull of Oa**. Just before reaching the conifer forest on your left, turn left toward the hilltop radio mast. Park anywhere along this track up to the mast, but take care not to block the road (you can drive farther, although it's more enjoyable to walk from here).

The road forks a short distance up the stony track. Your route follows the right-hand fork, although you might first need to detour up the hill to avoid walking through a herd of Highland cattle. Pass the green-painted agricultural building and continue along the track. You pass through rolling heather-clad moorland and occasional hills, enjoying excellent views over the sea and fabulous vistas of Port Ellen. Most interestingly, your route passes several townships of ruined stone houses.

After walking for about an hour and a half, you pass a particularly impressive set of ruins that includes houses, with clearly visible shelving and fireplaces, and the low walls of a large public building. Shortly afterwards, the track deteriorates rapidly and soon disappears altogether. Continue for a short distance to a steep cliff and a winding path down to an enclosed, south-facing sandy cove – wonderful on a sunny afternoon. (3-4 hours; easy)

This fascinating walk to **Kintra** through remote country passes abandoned crofting townships and reaches a dramatic cliff-top viewpoint high above Laggan Bay and Loch Indaal. Start from Kintra Farm, three miles northwest of Port Ellen. Head west along the rough track parallel to the shore. Follow the path as it turns left (south), passing through a gate and across a footbridge. Continue uphill to the first former township at Frachdale with its ruined houses, byres and small circular corn-drying kiln. Turn right (west), through a gate and over the hill toward Grasdale. This is the largest of the former townships and comprises three groups of buildings spread over about a quarter-mile. Look for the standing stone amid the ruins and the large corn-drying kiln on the hillside just before the first of the ruins. From Grasdale cross the stream near the old stone wall below Tockmal, the neighboring township across the valley. The line of the main street is still visible running along the fronts of the houses and there are the ruins of a chapel.

The path from Tockmal chapel is indistinct and you need to take care when it reaches the sea cliffs that fringe the headland. The coast has many natural arches and caves, and An Saighdear – an impressive sea stack. Turning right (east) along the cliffs, a faint path leads uphill from the Rudha Mor headland past two ruined walls. Follow the sheep tracks and contour around the hill above Laggan Bay, staying high on the hillside. Cross under the fence above Alt Fada and take the path above the birch woods. The way ahead joins a track eventually leading back to the footbridge and Kintra. (2-3 hours; easy/moderate)

Cultoon Farm (contact Jim or Lynn Wilson at Cultoon Farm, Portnahaven, Isle of Islay PA47 7SZ, ☎ 1496-860 323) offers clay pigeon and live shoots on 1,800 acres in the Rhinns of Islay. Shoot woodcock, snipe, pheasant, partridge, rabbits and hares, guided by keepers and their dogs. A large loch provides duck, mallard, teal and widgeon, and evening duck shoots can be arranged. Guns and cartridges are supplied and visitors can stay at the farm. Beginners are welcome.

Machrie Golf Course (18-hole links, 6,226 yards; Port Ellen, Isle of Islay PA42 7AN, ☎ 1496-302 310, fax 1496-302 404, machrie@machrie.com, www.machrie.com; green fees £35) A beautiful course overlooking the bay with sand dunes, blind holes and blind shots presenting a considerable challenge.

On Horseback

Ballivicar Farm (Port Ellen, Isle of Islay PA42 7AW, ☎ 1496-302 251) offers riding over hills and sandy beaches for beginners and advanced riders. Longer rides for experienced riders can include a stop at a suitable hostelry.

In the Water

Islay Dive Centre (10 Charlotte Street, Port Ellen, Isle of Islay PA42 7DF, ☎ 1496-302 441, ann@islaydivecentre.co.uk, www.islaydivecentre.co.uk) offers scuba diving (wreck dives, cave dives, drift dives, rockface dives, scenic dives and wreck dives) and seal-watching boat trips.

Where To Stay & Eat

Glenmachrie Guest House (Port Ellen, Isle of Islay PA42 7AW, ☎/fax 1496-302 560, glenmachrie@lineone.net, www.glenmachrie.com; B&B £££, dinner £££) The warmth of proprietor Rachel Whyte's welcome and her boundless energy and good humor take only seconds to make guests feel totally at home and turn fellow guests into good friends. Based on a working 450-acre farm, Glenmachrie operates on environmentally friendly principles and Rachel takes particular care to ensure guests don't starve: afternoon tea with cakes, shortbread and a dram of Islay's finest is followed by sherry and canapés; then an award-winning evening meal using delicious organic produce from the farm.

HOTEL PRICE CHART	
Per person, per night, based on double occupancy in high season. B&B rate includes breakfast; DB&B includes dinner and breakfast.	
£	Under £20
££	£21-£35
£££	£36-£50
££££	£51-£80
£££££	Over £80

The Inner Hebrides

Rachel's knowledge of Islay is matched only by her enthusiasm to share it with her guests. An absolute gem!

Machrie Hotel & Golf Links (Port of Ellen, Isle of Islay PA42 7AN, ☎ 1496-302 310, fax 1496-302 404, machrie@machrie.com, www.machrie.com; B&B £££-££££, dinner £££) Originally an 18th-century farmhouse, the Machrie Hotel's whitewashed buildings glisten beside an attractive 18-hole links course, close to the miles of white sand beach of the Big Strand. The bedrooms are spacious and comfortable. The restaurant, formerly the farm byre (cowshed), serves excellent local produce and the hotel even has its own whisky. A number of angle-roofed lodges complete with kitchens are also available.

Glenegedale House (Port Ellen, Isle of Islay PA42 7AS, ☎ 1496-302 147; B&B £££) 17th-century house enjoying uninterrupted views over Laggan Bay, with a charming sitting room warmed by an open fire. The restaurant specializes in local beef, lamb, game and seafood and there are daily "Introduction to Whisky" seminars (booking essential). No credit cards.

Ardbeg Distillery (Port Ellen, Isle of Islay PA42 7EA, ☎ 1496-302 244, fax 1496-302 040, www.ardbeg.com; lunch £-££) The wonderfully atmospheric café (placemats made from laminated checks, distilling schedules, etc), converted from the original kiln and malt barn, serves a good range of home cooking and baking, including a famous "Clootie Dumpling" and delicious homemade soup.

DINING PRICE CHART	
Indicates the price per person for a full meal, excluding drinks. Generally three courses, though fixed menus of five or more courses may be available.	
£	Under £10
££	£11-£20
£££	£21-£30
££££	£31-£40

■ Bowmore & Bridgend

Bowmore on Loch Indaal was built in 1768 as the capital of Islay and has the most shops and services on the island (although Port Ellen has a larger population). Islay's most famous building, the **Round Church**, stands at the top of Bowmore High Street.

Attractions & Sights

Kilarrow Parish Church – the Round Church – is at the top of Main Street, Bowmore. This eye-catching 18th-century church is remarkable for its circular structure and occupies a striking position at the head of Main Street, overlooking the village of Bowmore. Built by Daniel Campbell in 1767, the church is one of only two round churches in Scotland. The round structure is supposed to leave no corners in which the devil can hide.

Bowmore Distillery (Bowmore, Isle of Islay PA43 7JS, ☎/fax 1496-810 671, www.morrisonbowmore.com; open year-round, Mon-Fri; also open Saturday morning in summer; adult/concession £2/£1, including a shop voucher) The oldest distillery on Islay, Bowmore has stood on the shores of Loch Indaal since 1779. It's one of a dwindling number that still produces its own floor-malted barley (laboriously hand-turned using traditional wooden malt shovels). Bowmore's water, drawn from the Laggan River, takes on the flavor of rich Islay peat while percolating through rocks in the hills. The maturing whisky is held in damp cellars below sea level where it gathers further rich, mellow flavors from Spanish and American oak casks.

Adventures

 Islay Estates (Head Gamekeeper, Islay Estates, Newton House, Bridgend, Isle of Islay PA44 7PD, ☎ 1496-810 293 or Islay Estate Office at ☎ 1496-810 221) manages a large number of freshwater lochs in which brown trout can be caught, the best months being May-July. The main lochs are Gorm, Skerrols and Finlaggan and these fish well throughout the season. There are also good trout in Loch Ardnave, although this is not recommended after July because of weed growth. Loch Ardnahoe is very deep and noted for large trout from June onwards. Lochs Laingeadail, Drolsay and Leathan are less accessible but offer a great day out for people wishing to combine fishing with a walk into beautiful, remote scenery.

Shopping

Celtic Craft Shop (High Street, Bowmore, Isle of Islay, ☎ 1496-810 262) Handmade leather goods, original paintings by local artists, local art/craft items, silver Celtic jewelry and local pottery.

The Celtic House (Shore Street, Bowmore, Isle of Islay PA43 7LD, ☎ 1496-810 304, sales@roysceltichouse.com, www.roysceltichouse.com) Scottish gifts, including Celtic jewelry and leather items stamped with the Seal of Islay, clothing, prints, Highland stoneware, crystal pottery, Celtic watches and books.

The Islay Woollen Mill Company (Bridgend, Isle of Islay PA44 7PG, ☎ 1496-810 563, fax 1496-810 677) This century-old mill maintains the traditions of 18th-century weaving and produced tweeds used in the films *Braveheart*, *Rob Roy* and *Forrest Gump*. The mill also contains a unique collection of antique weaving machinery, including the only remaining example of the "Slubbing Billy."

Where To Stay & Eat

See *Accommodation* and *Dining* price charts on pages 465 and 466.

 Harbour Inn (The Square, Bowmore, Isle of Islay PA43 7JR, ☎ 1496-810 330, fax 1496-810 990, info@harbour-inn.com, www.harbour-inn.com; B&B £££, dinner ££-£££) Mid-range hotel in the heart of Bowmore, with a restaurant serving local seafood, beef, lamb and game. Reservations are recommended, even for residents.

Lochside Hotel (Shore Street, Bowmore, Isle of Islay PA43 7LB, ☎ 1496-810 244, fax 1496-810 390, bookings@lochsidehotel.co.uk, www.lochsidehotel.co.uk; B&B £££, dinner ££) Family-run hotel in the heart of Bowmore, with reasonably priced dining and a bar boasting 400 single malts.

Cottage Restaurant (45 Main Street, Bowmore, Isle of Islay PA43 7JJ, ☎ 1496-810 422; £-££) Family-owned restaurant and coffee shop with takeout service.

■ Port Charlotte & West Islay

Port Charlotte is a charming village on the Rhinns of Islay looking east over Loch Indaal. The village grew up around the fishing industry and has rows of well-kept whitewashed cottages. The Museum of Islay Life and Bruichladdich Distillery are both well worth a visit.

Attractions & Sights

Museum of Islay Life (Port Charlotte, Isle of Islay PA48 7UA, ☎ 1496-850 358; open Easter-Oct, Mon-Sat, 10am-5pm & Sun, 2pm-5pm; Nov-Easter, Mon & Sat, 10am-4pm; adult/concession/child/family £2/£1.20/£1/£5) This award-winning museum is housed in the former Free Church and illustrates life on Islay from prehistoric times to the early 20th century. Despite the museum's modest size, the displays provide a fascinating insight into Islay's history. Exhibits include the clockwork mechanism from the **Rhinns lighthouse**, an illicit whisky still, leather-working hand tools, the making of Islay malt whisky, and the many shipwrecks that line the island's coasts. Rc-creations of a Victorian bedroom and kitchen illustrate vividly how Islay's residents once lived. There are also displays on Islay's numerous ancient monuments and excavations. The **Gordon Booth Library**, also in the church, provides reference material, including books, photographs and archive material, for those wishing to delve even deeper into island life.

Bruichladdich Distillery (Bruichladdich, By Port Charlotte, Isle of Islay PA49 7UN, ☎ 1496-850 221, fax 1496-850 477, www.bruichladdich.com; open year-round, tours Mon-Fri, 10:30am, 11:30am & 2:30pm; Sat, 10:30am; admission £3.50, including a shop voucher) Recently re-opened after several years' inactivity, Bruichladdich (pronounced "brook-laddie") is the only independent Islay distillery and retains much of its original 19th-century machinery, including a beautiful, old-fashioned still room with exposed beam ceiling. There is a great tour and you can fill, seal and label your own bottle directly from casks personally chosen by Master Distiller Jim McEwan. Those with a real thirst for whisky knowledge can attend a six-day residential course at the Bruichladdich Academy.

Where To Stay & Eat

See *Accommodation* and *Dining* price charts on pages 465 and 466.

Port Charlotte Hotel (Main Street, Port Charlotte, Isle of Islay PA48 7TU, ☎ 1496-850 360, fax 1496-850 361, info@portcharlotte-hotel.co.uk, www.portcharlottehotel.co.uk; B&B £££) Restored Victorian hotel set on the shore of Loch Indaal with a conservatory and gardens opening directly onto a sandy beach; the entire resort has great sea views. The excellent restaurant's specialties include local seafood, beef and lamb. You won't be able to stop eating the local oysters.

Croft Kitchen (Port Charlotte, Isle of Islay PA48 7UD, ☎/fax 1496-850 230, douglas@croftkitchen.demon.co.uk; open April-Oct, early closing Wed; lunch £, dinner ££) This bistro-style café-restaurant is an Islay institution and opens all day from morning coffee to dinner. Specialties include local shellfish and game and the ever-popular lunchtime soup is delicious and great value.

■ Port Askaig & North Islay

The north of Islay is wild and rugged, dominated by glorious views over the **Sound of Islay** to the shapely tops of the **Paps of Jura** beyond. The road plunges down to the hamlet of **Port Askaig**, from where ferries depart for Jura and Colonsay. A single-lane road continues for a short distance, ending after the distilleries at **Caol Ila** and **Bunnahabhain**.

SOMERLED & THE LORDS OF THE ISLES

Twelfth-century Scotland was under constant threat of Viking invasion and the Norwegians held the western seaboard from Lewis in the Outer Hebrides to the Isle of Man. Natives beseeched Somerled (a warrior king of Gaelic-Norse descent) to rid them of the invaders, and in a battle in the Sound of Islay in 1156 Somerled wrested control of the southern Hebrides and much of mainland Argyll from the Norsemen.

For three centuries Somerled's dynasty, the "Sons of Somerled" (mainly clan Donald), enjoyed huge power and influence across the area. From the mid-14th century, they began to style themselves "Lords of the Isles," a title eventually recognized by the Crown, and ruled their kingdom from Finlaggan on Islay. The power of the Lordship peaked under John, 4th Earl of Ross, in the late 15th century. However, the Crown was becoming suspicious of the Lordship's political machinations and alliance with Edward IV of England. In 1493, James IV decided to break the power of the Lords and forfeited all John's lands and destroyed many of the buildings at Finlaggan. In the early 16th century, unsuccessful attempts were made to revive the Lordship of the Isles. The title itself survives and is currently held by Prince Charles.

Attractions & Sights

Finlaggan, Powerbase of the Lords of the Isles (The Finlaggan Trust, The Cottage, Ballygrant, Isle of Islay PA45 7QL, ☎ 1496-810 629, fax 1496-810 856; site open at all times, interpretation center open May-Sept, 1-4:30pm; Apr & Oct, Tues, Thurs & Sun only, 1-4pm). Finlaggan was the base of the MacDonald Lords of the Isles for three hundred years. From here, the Lords ruled the Atlantic seaboard from Kintyre to the Isle of Lewis in the Outer Hebrides. Two of the three islands in Loch Finlaggan – Eilean Mor (Large Island) and the smaller, circular Eilean na Comhairle (Council Island) – contain the ruins of buildings where the Lords were installed and lived. Eilean Mor is accessible by a wooden walkway over the reed-lined loch shallows. The ruins include the turf dyke on which stood the protective timber palisade, the great hall, extensive living quarters, chapel, a stone jetty and paved roads, providing evidence that the island's inhabitants were wealthy and sophisticated. Council Island was reached from Large Island by a stone causeway and was the meeting place for the Lordship's Council. Excavations on Council Island have uncovered massive lime-mortared walls, thought to be the remains of a medieval castle.

Bunnahabhain Distillery (Port Askaig, Isle of Islay PA46 7RP, ☎ 1496-840 646, fax 1496-840 248; open year-round, tours April-Oct, Mon-Fri, and by appointment, Nov-Mar) Unusually for an Islay malt, Bunnahabhain (pronounced "boona-harven," meaning "mouth of the river") is lightly peated and accessible even to Scotch whisky novices (it's an excellent malt), although the distillery now also produces more traditional, peated whiskies. There is a small, informal visitor center and shop.

Caol Ila Distillery (Port Askaig, Isle of Islay PA46 7RL, ☎ 1496-840 207; open Mar-Oct, Mon-Thurs, tours by appointment; admission £3, including a shop voucher) Located on Islay's northeast coast, the huge windows of the Caol Ila (pronounced "cull-eela") still room frame magnificent views over the Sound of Islay toward the Paps of Jura. The view is so astounding it's almost surprising that the malt whisky is of equal quality. The author's favorite is the powerfully-flavored but unbelievably smooth and drinkable 12-year-old, although the 18-year-old boasts even more followers. An undiscovered gem!

Adventures

 A seaside walk to **Ardnave Point** on the northern coast of Islay offers a good chance to see seabirds and seals and, on clear days, the Isle of Colonsay eight miles to the northwest. Ardnave Point is 10 miles north of Bowmore, on the western side of Loch Gruinart.

Park at Loch Ardnave and walk west along the northern shore of the loch toward Ardnave Farm. Follow the track between the farm buildings and through a gate on the left in the direction of the sea. The path turns northeast following the coastline and soon disappears. Continue to follow the coast on the short springy turf away from the sand dunes. The terrain switches between rocky shore, beach and grassy dunes. Ardnave Point, the northernmost point of the walk, is a peninsula of sand dunes and lush machair (seaside flower meadow) where the soil and climate combine to create good grazing for sheep and cattle.

Turn back southward along the western shore of Loch Gruinart, one of the best places on Islay to view geese and wading birds in winter. At low tide look for seals basking on the sands. You eventually join a coastal path that leads back to the farm. On your way back toward Bowmore, look for Kilnave Cross, a richly carved early Christian cross. It stands beside the ruins of Kilnave Chapel, a mile south of Ardnave Loch overlooking Loch Gruinart (1-1½ hours; easy).

Wildlife Watching

Islay is famous among birdwatchers, particularly between early October and early April, when it hosts huge concentrations of wintering geese, ducks and waders. The island is the non-breeding home for much of the Greenland population of barnacle geese (around 35,000 birds) and the distinctive sub-species of Greenland white-fronted geese (around 15,000 birds). Other wintering waterbirds include greylag geese, whooper swans and occasional pink-footed and brent geese. Huge concentrations of ducks occupy the wet marshes, freshwater lochs and sheltered sea inlets. Birds of prey are abundant and include golden eagle, buzzard, sparrowhawk, merlin, kestrel, peregrine and hen harrier. Islay is also the Scottish stronghold of the rare chough (an endangered member of the crow family).

In the summer months, resident species such as shelduck, chough, oystercatcher, redshank, curlew, lapwing, snipe, greylag geese, yellowhammer, pied wagtail, stonechat, the birds of prey, black guillemot and red-throated diver are joined by seabirds such as arctic and little terns, fulmar, kittiwake, gannet, razorbill and guillemot.

Mammals commonly seen year-round on Islay include hares, red and roe deer, common and grey seals and, more elusively, otters.

Islay Marine Charters (Erasaid, Bridgend, Isle of Islay PA44 7PL, ☎/fax 1496-850 436, info@islaymarine.co.uk, www.islaymarine.co.uk) offers wildlife cruises, private charter and sea angling (rod rental available). The two-hour wildlife cruise sails from Port Askaig and passes Caol Ila and Bunnahabhain distilleries. The viewable wildlife almost always includes common seals, guillemots, herons and shags, along with gulls and possibly birds of prey, and roe deer. Otters and, occasionally, golden eagles have also been seen. A longer cruise is available to the wild and remote Loch Tarbert on the western side of the Isle of Jura.

Where To Stay & Eat

See *Accommodation* and *Dining* price charts on pages 465 and 466.

Port Askaig Hotel (Port Askaig, Isle of Islay PA46 7RD, ☎ 1496-840 245, fax 1496-840 295, hotel@portaskaig.co.uk, www.portaskaig.co.uk; B&B £££, dinner ££) A picturesque, 400-year-old inn on the shores of the Sound of Islay overlooking the ferry pier with views across to the Paps of Jura. There is a restaurant and all-day bar meals. An apartment with kitchen is also available.

Isle of Jura

Jura is a wildly beautiful, rugged and mountainous island dominated by three distinctive peaks – the Paps of Jura – visible from miles around. Its human population of under 200 compares with around 6,000 deer (Jura means "deer island"). Jura is little developed – there is only one village, one hotel, one distillery and one road, single-lane of course (which only covers a small proportion of the island). There is no direct ferry access from the mainland, which restricts visitor numbers and preserves the island as a paradise

The Inner Hebrides

for walkers and those wanting to escape from it all. Visitors who make the effort to reach Jura, and particularly those who venture to its remote and untamed west coast, are rewarded by some of the most spectacular, wild scenery in Scotland, including 115 miles of coastline with caves, cliffs, raised beaches and long stretches of deserted white sand.

West Loch Tarbert carves a dramatic inroad into the heart of Jura and nearly cuts the island in two. Exploring the area by boat lets you see the coastal caves, some of which contain rudimentary altars. Islanders would rest here while transporting their dead to Iona or Oronsay for burial. From where the road/track peters out toward the northeast of the island, you can continue north by foot or cycle to view the famous Corryvreckan whirlpool.

> **DID YOU KNOW?** George Orwell wrote his classic novel *1984* in a cottage in Barnhill, on Jura's northeast coast, from 1946-48. The house still exists and can be rented by the week (see page 475).

■ Special Events

Jura Fell Race (May; contact organizer Andy Curtis on arj.curtis@talk21.com) This challenging race takes in seven mountain summits (including the Paps) within its 16-mile span.

■ Getting Here & Getting Around

By Ferry

Serco Denholm (☎ 1496-840 681) operates a car ferry from Port Askaig on Islay to Feolin on Jura, the journey taking five minutes. Ferries run regularly throughout the day and no advance booking is required.

The Colonsay boat, ***Lady Jayne*** (Homefield, Isle of Colonsay PA61 7YR, ☎ 1951-200 320, fax 1951-200 242, byrne@colonsay.org.uk), takes foot passengers (no vehicles) to the head of Loch Tarbert in Jura; from there it is a one-kilometer walk to the road.

By Bus

The local bus is run by **Alex Dunnichie** (☎ 1496-820 314).

■ Attractions & Sights

Corryvreckan Whirlpool (Gulf of Corryvreckan, between the north of Jura and the Isle of Scarba) The awe-inspiring whirlpool between the isles of Jura and Scarba has been classed by the Royal Navy as "unnavigable." Here, in the narrow strait, the Irish Sea meets the incoming Atlantic tide head on. The effects are most evident when a flood tide is accompanied by a strong westerly wind – when the channel transforms into a whirling maelstrom with roaring water columns leaping over 20 feet above the raging vortex.

Countless sailors have died in the whirlpool. The cauldron is attributed to a tall underwater rock pinnacle off the shore of Scarba, the top of which is only

Above: Italian Chapel, Lamb Holm, Orkney

Below: Crofthouse Museum, Shetland

Above: Kitchener Memorial, Marwick Head, Orkney

Below: Waterfront Cottages, Stromness, Orkney

Eshaness Cliffs, Shetland

Above: Mussel Farming, Lower Voe, Shetland

Below: A Shetland traffic jam

15 fathoms below the surface (the Gulf itself can be as deep as 150 fathoms). At flood and ebb tides, a tremendous volume of fast-running water strikes the pinnacle, creating the characteristic whirling motion. The whirlpool is best seen from a boat, although it can also be viewed from the north of Jura (or Scarba). Drive north to the end of the Jura road just beyond Lealt, from where it is an eight-mile walk to the Corryvreckan viewpoint.

LEGEND OF THE CORRYVRECKAN WHIRLPOOL

Legend has it that in order to win the hand of a chieftan's daughter on Jura, Breacken, the Scandinavian prince who gave his name to the Corryvreckan Whirlpool, had to pass a test of courage by anchoring himself in the whirlpool for three days. He returned to Norway and had three ropes made, one of hemp, one of wool and one of the hair of virgins. Unfortunately, all the ropes snapped, including the one made of the virgins' hair – because one of the maidens had been unfaithful – and the prince drowned. Breacken's body was dragged ashore by his faithful dog and he was buried in a cave on the northwestern shore of Jura.

Isle of Jura Distillery (Craighouse, Isle of Jura PA60 7XT, ☎ 1496-820 240, fax 1496-820 344, www.isleofjura.com; tours by appointment only; admission free) Drawing its water from the Bhaille Mharghaidh spring, Jura's only distillery was established in 1810, although there is evidence illicit distilling took place in a nearby cave long before that. The distillery produces a smooth, subtle and very drinkable malt that's full of island character.

Jura Church (north end of Craighouse; open year-round; admission free) The church is visually unspectacular but is over 200 years old. An exhibition of old photographs of Jura life is displayed in a room behind the church.

Jura House Walled Garden (Ardfin, Isle of Jura, ☎ 1496-820 315, www.jurahouseandgardens.co.uk; open year-round; admission £2, children free) Walled gardens surrounded by woodland, fields and beach. The organic garden contains a large selection of unusual plants, including perennial borders, an exotic Australasian corner and a burn (stream) stepping down to a wildflower meadow with a tea-tent and plants for sale.

■ Adventures

Jura is superb walking country, although you need to take into account the seasonal deerstalking activities. The annual cull takes place between July and mid-February, with most estates starting in mid-August. If you are planning to walk during this period follow the marked routes and check with the individual estates if uncertain whether a particular route is likely to cause disturbance (or risk you getting shot!).

Keils Township is a short walk easily accessible from Craighouse; it passes one of Jura's oldest settlements and an ancient burial ground. Start from Craighouse and follow the shore northwards (with the sea on your right) for about half a mile. Turn left along the track signposted "Keils" and follow this to the village. Keils lies in a fold in the land and is not visible from the main road. The village is now almost deserted, but it is still possible to see the houses, barns and enclosure walls of a once-extensive township.

Follow the track to the right and through the village. After passing a large barn on your right, turn west (left) at the next junction. Continue uphill through a deer fence gate (don't forget to close it) to the burial ground at Cill Earnadail (be careful if the bull is there). Cill Earnadail may once have been the site of a monastery, dedicated to St Earnan, who is believed to be buried here. The burial ground also contains a mausoleum of the Campbells of Jura together with some ancient flat grave slabs. Return the same way to the track junction, this time continuing straight ahead along a path leading back to the road and Craighouse (1 hour; easy).

The **An Dùnan** walk follows an old hill track to one of Jura's best-preserved Iron Age hill forts, perched on top of a natural rock outcrop overlooking the Sound of Jura. Start from Knockrome, three miles north of Craighouse (turn off the main road at the three-arched bridge). From Knockrome follow the track northwards through a gate behind the cluster of houses. Pass through a second gate above the old school and continue down toward the shore. Pass over a footbridge and go through the gate beside the wooded stream. Turn right toward the bay and follow the shore, taking care on the mud, sand and spongy turf as there is no clear path here. Just past the next wood (Garbh Achadh) bear left to join a rough track that leads out to An Dùnan on the peninsula. Faint traces of the building and pathways survive, although its exact structure will never be known. The rocks here are steep and the fort is best approached from the northeast.

The three **Paps of Jura** dominate the southern half of the island, their beautiful conical peaks of quartzite rising 2,400-2,500 feet. The highest peak is Beinn an Oir, at 2,571 feet ("Mountain of Gold"); the other two are Beinn Shiantaidh ("Holy Mountain," 2,476 feet) and Beinn a'Chaolais ("Mountain of the Kyle," 2,408 feet). The Paps are not that easy to get to or climb; the upper slopes are steep and consist mainly of scree and quartzite lumps (4-5 hours to climb one Pap; difficult).

There is no definitive path to the Paps. The most popular route starts at the three-arched bridge about five miles north of Craighouse. Park there and follow the Corran river to the foot of Loch an t'Siob. Stay on the southern bank of the river; the northern bank tends to be muddy and requires several stream crossings. Cross the river at the foot of the loch and head northwest up the slope to the saddle between Beinn an Oir and Beinn Shiantaidh, from where you can decide which of the Paps to climb (2 hours; moderate).

■ Wildlife Watching

 Jura's wild and unspoiled landscape is prime wildlife viewing country. Appropriately for an island named "Deer Island" Jura is one of the best places to view red deer – Britain's largest native mammal. Majestic stags and graceful hinds can readily be seen, often from the car. Seals are numerous and readily seen at various sites along the coast. Otters are common around the coast and freshwater lochs and rivers, and can sometimes be seen playing in family groups.

Jura is well known for its raptors: white-tailed sea eagles visit regularly and residents include golden eagles, buzzards, peregrine falcons, hen harriers, kestrels, merlins and sparrow hawks. The short-eared owl lives in the hills and hunts by day; tawny owls and barn owls enliven the woodlands after dark.

■ Where To Stay & Eat

See *Accommodation* and *Dining* price charts on pages 465 and 466.

 Jura Hotel (Craighouse, Isle of Jura PA60 7XU, ☎ 1496-820 243, fax 1496-820 249, jurahotel@aol.com, www.jurahotel.co.uk; B&B ££-£££, dinner ££) Located opposite Jura's distillery, this is the island's only hotel and focal point of island life. The rooms aren't large and some of the bathrooms are positively cramped, but the views over the bay are excellent. The hotel serves good bar meals, which is just as well, since this is about the only place on the island to eat out. The hotel also has a field with areas for camping.

Gwen Boardman (7 Woodside, Craighouse, Isle of Jura PA60 7YA, ☎ 1496-820 379; open April-Sept; B&B £) provides B&B accommodation in Craighouse.

 Barnhill (Contact Mrs D. Fletcher, ☎ 1786-850 274, lennieston@aol.com; from £400 per week) This remote cottage on the northeast coast of Jura is where George Orwell wrote *1984*; it now provides accommodation for seven.

Colonsay & Oronsay

Colonsay is one of the loveliest of the Inner Hebridean islands with its rich archaeology, pristine sandy beaches and unhurried pace of life. The Argyll mainland lies 25 miles away to the east, and to the west only the Dhu Hirteach lighthouse stands between the island and Canada. The annual rainfall is only half that of mainland Argyll – Colonsay's sun record is similar to that of Tiree, Scotland's record holder. Gaelic remains a living language on Colonsay and occasional courses are run at the island's hotel.

Oronsay is a virtually uninhabited tidal island reached by crossing the Strand from Colonsay at low tide. Legend has it that St Columba made his first landfall on Oronsay on his way to Iona. A monastery was founded on Oronsay, which flourished, collapsed and was rebuilt as an Augustinian Priory by the Lords of the Isles in the 14th century. The priory's school of stonecarvers left the great cross and about 30 magnificent grave slabs.

■ Getting Here & Getting Around

By Ferry

 Caledonian MacBrayne (☎ 1475-650 100, www.calmac.co.uk) operates a car ferry between Oban and Colonsay. The journey takes 2¼ hours, and it's a beautiful one, passing between the mainland and the islands of Kererra and Mull before sailing south and west past the islands of Seil, Luing, Scarba and Jura. In the summer a Wednesday sailing from Kennacraig on the Kintyre Peninsula calls at Islay and then Colonsay, then retraces its route. The Wednesday sailing from Oban also does an extended run to Port Askaig on Islay. This allows passengers from Kintyre and Islay to spend about six hours on Colonsay, and passengers from Colonsay to have six hours on Islay.

In fair weather, the *Lady Jayne*, operated by Kevin and Christa Byrne (Homefield, Isle of Colonsay PA61 7YR, ☎ 1951-200 320, fax 1951-200 242, byrne@colonsay.org.uk), takes foot-passengers only to Colonsay, from Mull, Islay and Jura.

By Car

Note that, because the island is so small, touring caravans, trailers and motor-homes are not permitted.

■ Attractions & Sights

Colonsay House & Gardens (Isle of Colonsay PA61 7YU, ☎ 1951-200 211, fax 1951-200 369, colonsay@dial.pipex.com, www.colonsay.org.uk/gardens.html; woodland gardens open year-round, admission free; walled gardens open Easter-Sept, Wed noon-5pm & Fri 3-5pm, adult/child/family £2/£1/£5). Considered one of the finest rhododendron gardens in Scotland, Colonsay's 20-acre woodland gardens were mostly planted in the 1930s and have great variety, not only of rhododendrons but also of trees and shrubs, including some exotic southern hemisphere species.

The walled gardens surround Colonsay House, occupied by the Howard family. These have rolling lawns and a more formal feel. They are filled with colorful mixed borders, climbing roses and clematis, and, unusually, agapanthus. Produce from the organic kitchen garden is available for sale. The café serves lunches and teas with home-baked local produce.

Riasg Buidhe (pronounced "risk-boowie") was a fishing village; it was abandoned in 1918. The houses stand at a surprising distance from the shore and require a bit of a hike to reach. Head up the eastern road past the shop and port for about a mile. You will see a small loch on your left and an unsightly rubbish dump to your right. Follow a rough track past the dump in the direction of the coast, taking care on the uneven and often boggy ground. There are occasional sections of stone path, but the going can be heavy through the clumps of heather. You will reach the abandoned village in about 30 minutes.

Oronsay Priory (Isle of Oronsay, at the far end of the road from the Strand; open at all times). The present Oronsay Priory was established by John I,

Lord of the Isles, sometime between 1325, when he became head of Clan Donald, and 1353, the date of the earliest surviving document relating to the priory. The ruined priory stands within a stone wall enclosure and the remains of the cloister and high altar are well preserved. Legend links the priory to St Columba, who made his first landfall on Oronsay after leaving Ireland on his journey to Iona. At that time, there was a strong link between Oronsay and Iona. Celtic carved stones can be seen, including effigies and grave slabs, some with beautiful and detailed designs. Most impressive is the Oronsay Cross standing within the priory grounds, one of the finest of its kind. It has Romano-Celtic interlacing, with a carving of Christ on the front, and intricate interlacing spirals on the back. The great cross and effigies date from the 14th/15th centuries and are thought to have been brought to the island rather than carved here.

CROSSING THE STRAND TO ORONSAY

Oronsay is joined to Colonsay at low water by the Strand, a mile-wide stretch of flat sands bordered by mussel-strewn rocks. You can drive a car (ideally a 4WD) across the Strand, but the track is very rough on the Oronsay side and walking is the better, and more interesting, option.

Find out the time of low tide from the hotel or local residents. You have two hours on either side of this to get across to Oronsay and back. From the parking area at the southernmost end of the Colonsay road, head out over the sand in a south-southwesterly direction (continue in the direction of the road bearing slightly right). There will usually be vehicle tracks to follow. About half-way across you will see a short section of road on Oronsay, rising left to right over a low hill. Head for this – it's the rough road that eventually leads to the priory.

Once over the Strand it's another 30- to 45-minutes walk to Oronsay Priory, the island's main attraction, so it pays to chase the tide out rather than wait for low tide before setting out. Wearing wellies or taking off your shoes and splashing across the shallows will give you even more time on Oronsay.

■ Adventures

On Foot

 The **Kiloran Bay walk** leads from the island's main settlement to one of its most beautiful bays and a wonderful expanse of golden sand. Start from Scalasaig, walking east away from the ferry terminal and passing the shop. Follow the road over the hill toward Loch Fada. Turn right at the road junction toward Colonsay House, and turn left at the gates. Continue along the road until just after a sharp bend to the left. Turn right over a footbridge onto a track, which you follow over machair until you reach a second stream. Turn left toward the bay and its sweep of golden sand ("Tràigh Bàn," meaning "white beach"). A Viking boat burial, the traditional laying to rest of noble warriors, was discovered on the beach in the late 19th century. At the end of the beach cross another stream to regain the road you followed from Colonsay House (3-4 hours; moderate).

Colonsay Gun Club (☎ 1951-200 312) organizes regular shoots, which are advertised in the shop and hotel. There is no need to bring a gun, but do bring your license.

On the Water

 Fishing is available in all the lochs; the season runs from 17th March to 30th September. The lochs are managed to conserve the native brown trout population (there are no rainbows or imported fish). There are very few restrictions, but adult visitors are asked to confine themselves to fly-fishing only. Up to four good-sized fish per day may be kept for the table, all others are to be returned. There are no restrictions on island residents or their bona fide private guests, but all others are requested to join the Colonsay Fly Fishing Association (either at the hotel, or at the office of Colonsay Estate, ☎ 1951-200 211, fax 1951-200 369, colonsay@dial.pipex.com, www.colonsay.org.uk/gardens.html). Members will receive access to the fishing log, and will also be able to use the boats provided.

■ Golf

 Colonsay Golf Course (18-hole links, 4,775 yards; Isle of Colonsay PA61 7YP, ☎ 1951-200 364, fax 1951-200 312; membership £10) The remote 18-hole links course is on natural machair and is reputedly over 200 years old. Play is restricted to members only, but full membership costs only £10 per year (no green fees). Membership is available at the hotel or at the office of Colonsay Estate.

■ Wildlife Watching

 Colonsay offers up to 150 resident and migrant birds. The island is an important habitat for corncrakes and waders and is a stronghold of the chough, an endangered member of the crow family. The western cliffs are home to enormous colonies of seabirds, notably fulmars, guillemots, razorbills, kittiwakes, shags and all types of gull. The beaches and rocky inlets support colonies of ringed plovers, terns, oystercatchers and eiders among others. Seals are easily seen around the coastline and otters can also be sighted. Feral goats roam across the island, especially at Balnahard at the rugged north end of the island.

Oronsay and the **Oronsay Nature Reserve** are home to an abundance of wildlife, including the rare corncrake and chough. The corncrakes arrive at the beginning of May and their strange cry (echoed in their scientific name *Crex crex*) can best be heard on warm evenings between May and July. Now rare in England, the chough is found here year-round.

Grey seals, otters and dolphins may be seen along the coast all year. There are also gannets, guillemots, cormorants and shags, three species of diver, mergansers and shelducks.

Spring sees the passage of waders such as dunlins, turnstones and greenshanks, and Oronsay is also a nesting ground for lapwings, redshanks, snipes, skylarks, oystercatchers, terns and eiders. Summer brings many attractive butterflies, including the dark green fritillary and rare marsh fritillary. During the autumn and winter months, barnacle and white-fronted geese from Greenland shelter on Oronsay, and flocks of twites feed on seeds left where the cows have been fed.

■ Entertainment

Ceilidhs are held in the village hall during the summer months. Ask locally for dates and times.

■ Shopping

 Colonsay Bookshop (Isle of Colonsay PA61 7YP, 1951-200 232, bookshop@colonsay.org.uk) The island's tiny bookshop carries a large selection, specializing in titles with a Colonsay, Scottish or Hebridean flavor, as well as an antiquarian section for rarer sources. If the owner is busy elsewhere you might be given the key and invited to browse on your own!

The Colonsay publisher, **House of Lochar** (Isle of Colonsay, ☎/fax 1951-200 232, lochar@colonsay.org.uk, www.houseoflochar.com), sells specialist books, many with a Gaelic or Hebridean theme.

■ Where To Stay & Eat

See *Accommodation* and *Dining* price charts on pages 465 and 466.

 Isle of Colonsay Hotel (Isle of Colonsay, Argyll PA61 7YP, ☎ 1951-200 316, fax 1951-200 353, colonsay.hotel@pipemedia.co.uk, www.colonsay.org.uk/hotel.html; B&B ££££, dinner ££) Originally a hunting lodge for Colonsay House, the excellent hotel provides tranquil and refined accommodation. The bedrooms are stylishly furnished in earthy shades and sensuous fabrics that tempt inactivity. Many images of old Colonsay life evoke the island's long history. The restaurant serves delicious specialties, including local lamb and beef, Colonsay's renowned oysters, and a good selection of daily specials. As the island's only hotel, its cozy public bar is a great place to meet locals, or challenge them at the popular weekly quizzes (Thurs, 9:30pm – get there early in the summer when it gets very crowded).

Seaview Farmhouse (Isle of Colonsay PA61 7YR, ☎ 1951-200 315; B&B ££) Comfortable en-suite accommodation on a working croft, with superb views and good home cooking.

Colonsay Backpackers' Lodge (Isle of Colonsay, ☎ 1951-200 312; £ excluding breakfast) Spacious former gamekeeper's house with excellent loch views provides twin and family rooms.

Isle of Mull

Mull is the second-largest island in the Inner Hebrides and in Ben More boasts Scotland's only island Munro (mountain above 3,000 feet) outside Skye. The island's plant-covered, glacier-scoured landscape varies from woodland gorges and windswept mountaintops to turbulent rocky shores, broad bays and beautiful beaches.

Man's occupation of Mull dates back over 6,000 years to when the first hunter-gatherers lived in sea caves and hunted with bone and flint tools. The first farmers arrived 5,000 years ago in the New Stone Age and built cairns, standing stones and stone circles. The Celts invaded around 700 BC and in the ensuing Iron Age built hill forts, crannogs and brochs, the remains of which are still visible today.

Mull is excellent for walking, both for the unspoiled variety of its terrain and its multifarious wildlife. High-level walks are concentrated in the center and south of the island with coastal walks more prevalent to the north.

■ Special Events

Mull Traditional Music Festival (April; ☎ 1688-302 009/302 350). A weekend of traditional music, with local bars reverberating to the sounds of accordions, penny-whistles and pipes.

Mendelssohn on Mull Festival (June; 1 Atholl Place, Edinburgh EH3 8HP, ☎ 131-228 7979, fax 131-229 1966, www.mullfest.org.uk) A week of concerts, recitals and art celebrating the composer's visit in 1829.

Tobermory Highland Games (July; ☎ 1688-302 270/302 009/302 350) Traditional Highland Games followed by an evening dance.

Mull Car Rally (Oct; Walkers Castle, Hurst Green, Clitheroe BB7 9QJ, ☎ 1254-826 564, fax 1254-878 188, info@2300club.org, www.2300club.org) Popular car rally attracting enthusiasts from all over the UK to compete on the island's tricky roads.

■ Getting Here & Getting Around

By Ferry

Caledonian MacBrayne (☎ 1475-650 100, www.calmac.co.uk) operates three car-ferrys to Mull with several trips daily: Oban to Craignure, Lochaline (Morvern) to Fishnish and Kilchoan (Ardnamurchan) to Tobermory (Tobermory ferry runs Mon-Sat year-round, on Sundays in June-Aug only).

By Bus

Bowmans Buses (☎ 1680-812 313) operates a regular route on Mull from the ferry terminal at Craignure to Tobermory.

■ Craignure & South Mull

Craignure is Mull's main ferry port and lies in the east of the island, guarded by Duart and Torosay castles. Craignure is a tiny village with a friendly population. The center and south of Mull is rugged and mountainous – a haven for walkers and wildlife. Mull boasts one of the highest concentrations of golden eagles in Europe and sea eagles have recently returned to its sea cliffs. The southwestern peninsula is known as the "Ross of Mull" and extends from Pennyghael to Fionnphort, from where you catch the ferry to Iona, and boats to Staffa and the Treshnish isles.

 INFORMATION SOURCES: The tourism office is at **The Pier, Craignure**, Isle of Mull PA65 6AY, ☎ 870-720 0610, fax 1680-812 497, info@mull.visitscotland.com; open year-round.

Attractions & Sights

 **Duart Castle** (Craignure, Isle of Mull PA64 6AP, ☎/fax 1680-812 309, duartguide@isle-of-mull.demon.co.uk, www.duartcastle.com; open April to mid-Oct, days/hours vary seasonally; adult/concession/child/family £4.50/£4/£2.25/£11.25). Standing on a cliff-top guarding the Sound of Mull, 13th-century Duart Castle has been the home of the Chief of Clan Maclean for over 600 years. Recently restored, excellent displays show prisoners in dark and damp dungeons, the kitchen and scullery and the impressive banqueting hall. Upstairs, the state bedrooms give you an idea of just how dark and cold life must have been like in a medieval castle. The panoramic views from the battlements are excellent. If you're lucky Lady Maclean, mother of the present Chief, will be bustling around the Sea Room and giving visitors her unique insight into life and times at the castle.

Torosay Castle & Gardens (By Craignure, Isle of Mull PA65 6AY, ☎ 1680-812 421, fax 1680- 812 470, torosay@aol.com; castle and gardens open April-Oct, 10:30am-5pm, gardens open 9am-7pm in summer & daylight hours in winter; adult/concession/child/family £5/£4/£2/£12). Completed in 1858, Torosay is more of a grand house than a castle and is surrounded by 12 acres of impressive gardens interwoven by several attractive paths. Wander round the principal rooms, which include the front hall dominated by a tiger's head and a collection of red stag antlers, the central hall, dining room, library, nursery, bedroom and drawing room with excellent views of the garden. The rooms contain a wide range of antique furniture and, unusually, you are encouraged to sit on many of the chairs and sofas. The tea room terrace enjoys great views across the bay to Duart Castle.

Mull Rail (Old Pier Station, Craignure, Isle of Mull PA65 6AY, ☎ 1680-812 494, fax 1680-300 595, railway@dee-emm.co.uk, www.mullrail.co.uk; open April-Oct, 11am-5pm; single/return £3/£4, child £2/£3, family £7.50/£10.75) Scotland's first island passenger railway operates a picturesque route between Craignure and Torosay Castle. Run by rail enthusiasts, both steam and diesel locomotives haul the narrow-gauge carriages. Two trains run a busy timetable, with hourly departures from Craignure and Torosay in the early and late season, and half-hourly in high season.

Wings Over Mull (Auchnacroish House, Torosay, Craignure, Isle of Mull PA65 6AY, ☎/fax 1680-812 594, dewars@wingsovermull.com, www.wingsover-mull.com; open Easter-Oct, 10:30am-5:30pm, last admission 5pm; adult/concession/child/family £4.50/£3.50/£1.50/£10) A collection of birds of prey, including hawks, falcons, eagle, kites and vultures. Apart from flying displays at noon, 2pm and 4pm, the birds are tethered to low stumps, which isn't ideal for either birds or visitors. Pre-book for hawk-handling sessions; therey also offer hawking holidays from November to March.

Standing Stones & Moy Castle: Lochbuie, on the southern coast, is one of Mull's smallest communities, but is well worth a visit for its historic attractions and empty, rugged coastline. The drive from the Craignure-Iona road is stunning, particularly its lochside sections. However, the road is in places uneven and challenging; be wary of narrow, twisting stretches and often blind corners. The trip is best avoided if you are hurrying for a day-trip to Iona.

Shortly before arriving at Lochbuie, you pass a small bridge (Auchimor) with a signpost to the stone circle (the sign is only visible when driving south toward Lochbuie). Park just before the bridge and follow the white-painted stones through a couple of fields – about five minutes' walk. The stone circle is the most impressive on Mull and consists of eight standing stones (with a smaller stone positioned where one is missing), and a solitary stone standing a short distance away. As with most of the stone circles in the Hebrides, nobody understands its true significance, although the mystery adds to its charm.

Back at the Auchimor bridge, drive to the end of the road, park and walk left (east) across a short section of beach to the ruined tower of **Moy Castle**. The impressive outline of Ben Buie dominates the skyline to the north. The castle, built by the MacLaines of Lochbuie in the 15th century, is now locked because of its unsound structure. To the right of the castle is a galley slip where boats were pulled to shore. Continuing east you reach the lonely **Laggan Sands**. Situated in the trees is the MacLaines' mausoleum and just to the south is a dun – an ancient fort built on a cliff.

MacKinnons Cave (near Balmeanach in western Mull, off the B8035) This cave is named after the abbots and monks from Iona who would seek quiet retreats in isolated caves such as this. Check the tide times at the tourism office and get to the cave before half-tide on a dropping tide. This is one of the deepest caves on Mull and it gets very dark inside, so a flashlight (and possibly a spare) is essential. James Boswell and Doctor Samuel Johnson are thought to have estimated the cave's depth at 165 yards during a visit in 1773.

St Columba Centre (HS; Fionnphort, Isle of Mull PA66 6BN, ☎ 1681-700 660; open summer, 11am-1pm & 2-5pm, other times by arrangement with Iona Abbey) Exhibition and interpretation center focusing on the Celtic world and the life and work of St Columba, who founded the religious community on Iona in 563 AD. The exhibition helps put Iona into context.

Adventures

 Mull has numerous rivers, lochs and lochans where it is possible to catch wild brown trout, sea trout and salmon. **Loch Frisa** to the north is Mull's largest loch and offers brown trout throughout the season, and salmon and sea trout from July onwards. The **Mishnish Lochs** (regularly stocked with brown trout) and **Loch Torr** (mainly brown trout with occasional sea trout, fish usually small but numerous) are both situated close to the Tobermory-Dervaig road. The **River Lussa** runs from Loch Sguabain in Glen More to the sea at Loch Spelve and, while not the most accessible river, has some great pools. The **River Bellart** runs to the sea in Dervaig and is narrow with steep peat banks. It fishes well from late June for sea trout and from late July for salmon.

Guy Bolton (Dalriada Kennels, Ulva Ferry, Isle of Mull PA74 6NH, ☎/fax 1688-500 249), a local guide specializing in lure fishing, takes guests out on half-day (from £35) and full-day (from £60) fishing trips, boat rental and permits not included.

Ben More, Mull's only Munro (peak above 3,000 feet), is also the only island Munro outside Skye and rare in that every inch is climbed from sea level. Most people climb up and down by the direct route from Dhiseig off the B8035 beside the shores of Loch na Keal (seven miles southwest of Salen). This route now has a path (bearing southeast) for most of the way. (4-5 hours; moderate/difficult)

Wildlife Watching

 Common seals are frequently seen around Mull's shores and if you take a boat trip you are likely to spot grey seals as well. Minke whales, dolphins, harbor porpoises and bottlenose dolphins are also commonly seen in these waters.

Polecats, stoats, feral mink and cats are now the main predators on Mull. Red deer can be seen throughout the island and shy fallow deer inhabit the woodlands at Knock. Wild goats make their home on lonely coastal cliffs. Otters can also be seen on rocky shores.

Golden eagles and white-tailed sea eagles are frequently seen around mountains and hills, particularly around the central, hilly core of Mull, in early spring when they make display flights to mark their territories. With patience they can often be seen from the roadside. Mull's other birds of prey include the hen harrier, buzzard, kestrel, short-eared owl, merlin, peregrine falcon and osprey.

The great northern diver and Slavonian grebes winter on Mull's western sea lochs. Barnacle and white-fronted geese from Greenland winter on grasslands and bogs, and other wildfowl and waders can be seen around the island's muddier shores.

Where To Stay & Eat

See *Accommodation* and *Dining* price charts on pages 465 and 466.

 Craignure Inn (Craignure, Isle of Mull PA65 6AY, ☎ 1680-812 305, fax 1680-812 306, janice@craignureinn.freeserve.co.uk, www.craignure-inn.co.uk; B&B ££, dinner ££) A traditional white-washed inn close to the ferry terminal, with comfortable accommodation and excellent sea views. A highlight is the atmospheric bar, which is the village's only public bar and a great place to meet the friendly regulars. The bar meals are good too.

Old Mill Cottage (Lochdonhead, Isle of Mull PA64 6AP, ☎/fax 1680-812 442, oldmill@mull.com, www.oldmill.mull.com; B&B ££, dinner ££) A short drive from the Craignure ferry terminal, the delightful Jim and Jenny Smith run a welcoming guest house in an 1835 miller's cottage. Set in 25 tranquil acres, on which Jenny also operates a small croft of sheep and cattle, the cottage faces Loch Don with its array of waterfowl; otters inhabit the burn that once pow-ered the mill. The bedrooms are relaxing and pleasantly scented. The excel-lent evening meals incorporate fresh local produce, including lamb and beef from the croft. Another option is to stay in the original mill building, now a superb accommodation, with a kitchen for those who prefer to prepare their own meals, and its own bath.

■ Tobermory

Enchanting Tobermory, the capital of Mull, was built as a fishing port in the late 18th century. Surrounded by high wooded hills, its pristine, colorful sea-front buildings are pure picture-postcard. The village has a good variety of shops, restaurants and accommodation and the harbor is busy with fishing boats, yachts and, in summer, the Kilchoan ferry. Although tourism now out-weighs the traditional occupations of fishing and sailing, Tobermory doesn't feel at all artificial and its relaxed, lively atmosphere is sure to delight.

A gold-laden Spanish galleon is believed to lie somewhere in the mud at the bottom of Tobermory bay. Part of the defeated Armada of 1588, the ship anchored at Tobermory while fleeing the English fleet but sank when a fire caused her gunpowder to explode.

 INFORMATION SOURCES: The tourism office is at **Main Street, Tobermory**, Isle of Mull PA75 6NU, ☎ 870-720 0625, info@tobermory.visitscotland.com; open April-Oct.

Attractions & Sights

Mull Museum (Main Street, Tobermory, Isle of Mull PA75 5NY, ☎ 1688-302 493; open Easter to mid-Oct, Mon-Fri, 10am-4pm & Sat, 10am-1pm; admis-sion £1). Well-set-out little museum with photographs, illustrations, objects and explanations covering topics such as the creation of Mull, its crannogs, Armada relics and parts from a wartime plane crash.

Tobermory Distillery (Tobermory, Isle of Mull PA75 6NR, ☎ 1688-302 645, fax 1688-302 643, tobermory@mull.com, www.burnstewartdistillers.com;

open Easter-Oct, Mon-Sat, 10am-5pm with tours every hour, Oct-Easter, by appointment; admission £2.50). Founded in 1798, this small distillery is the only one on Mull; it reopened in 1990 after a decade's "silence." It markets two products – a malt and a blend – and though not the most famous name in whisky, its town location makes it one of the easier distilleries to tour.

Adventures

Edge of the World RIB Rides (The Car Park, Tobermory, ☎ 1688-302 808, us@edge-ofthe-world.co.uk). Wildlife tours, fishing trips and whale watching cruises on fast, exciting RIBs from Tobermory and Oban.

Sea Life Surveys (Ledaig, Tobermory, Isle of Mull PA75 6NU, ☎ 1688-400 223, fax 1688-302 916, enquiries@sealifesurveys.com, www.sealifesurveys-.com; open Easter-Oct; £45 for an all-day trip). Whale- and dolphin-watching trips departing from Tobermory.

Golf

 Tobermory Golf Course (9-hole inland, 4,893 yards; Isle of Mull PA75 6PR, ☎ 1688-302 338, fax 1688-302 140, tobgolf@fsbusiness.co.uk, www.golf.mull.com; green fees £13) Hilly, cliff-top course enjoying excellent views over the Sound of Mull to the Scottish mainland.

Shopping

The Gallery (Main Street, Tobermory, Isle of Mull PA75 6NT, ☎ 1688-302 772, fax 1688-302 699, shopping@thegallery-tobermory.com). Family-owned shop selling a variety of products from the islands and Scottish mainland, including Scottish and island books, and giftware ranging from travel rugs to soaps and horn craft.

Isle of Mull Cheese (Sgriob-Ruadh Farm, Tobermory, Isle of Mull PA75 6QD, ☎ 1688-302 235, fax 1688-302 546, mull.cheese@btinternet.com, www.mull.cheese.btinternet.co.uk). Makers of excellent traditional cheese from milk produced on the small family farm. The delicious cheeses have won British and French awards and are well worth trying, as is lunch or a cream tea in the "glass barn."

Isle of Mull Silver & Goldsmiths (Main Street, Tobermory, Isle of Mull PA75 6NT, ☎/fax 1688-302 345, mullsilver@btinternet.com, www.mullsilver.co.uk). Manufactures and sells silver and gold jewelry, including christening spoons, metal mirrors and candleholders.

Mull Pottery (Baliscate Estate, Salen Road, Tobermory, Isle of Mull PA75 6QA, a 10-minute walk from the town center, ☎/fax 1688-302 347, orders@mullpottery.com, www.mullpottery.com). The ceramics designed and produced here reflect a strong west-coast influence, as in the "Seashore" and "Iona" tableware ranges. There is also a gallery, workshop (check the Bargain Bins) and café.

Tobermory Chocolate (Tobermory, Isle of Mull PA75 6NU, ☎ 1688-302 526, fax 1688-302 595, info@tobchoc.co.uk, www.tobchoc.co.uk; shop openyear-round, Mon-Sat, 9:30am-5pm; in summer also open Sun, noon-4pm). Hand-made chocolates direct from a small factory. Children will love the 30-minute workshops (for under-12s – reservations essential) where they make chocolates to take home; a mail-order service is also available.

Where To Stay & Eat

See *Accommodation* and *Dining* price charts on pages 465 and 466.

 Harbour Heights (Western Road, Tobermory, Isle of Mull PA75 6PR, ☎/fax 1688-302 430, harbourheights@mull.com, www.harbourheights.mull.com; B&B ££) Recently refurbished B&B with log fires, Persian rugs and tartan-themed rooms. Guests have free use of bikes, canoes and fishing rods.

Highland Cottage (Breadalbane Street, Tobermory, Isle of Mull PH75 6PD, ☎ 1688-302 030, fax 1688-302 727, david&jo@highlandcottage.co.uk, www.highlandcottage.co.uk; closed mid-Oct to mid-Nov; B&B ££££, dinner £££) Small hotel overlooking Tobermory Bay with pleasant rooms and a cozy restaurant and conservatory lounge.

Tobermory Hotel (53 Main Street, Tobermory, Isle of Mull PA75 6NT, ☎ 1688-302 091, fax 1688-302 254, tobhotel@tinyworld.co.uk, www.thetober-moryhotel.com; B&B £££, dinner £££) Waterfront hotel set in a row of former fishermen's cottages with a seafood restaurant.

The Mishnish (Main Street, Tobermory, Isle of Mull PA75 6NU, ☎ 1688-302 009, fax 1688-302 462, www.mishnish.co.uk; £-££) Bustling seafront pub that serves good bar meals and has regular live music.

 MacGochan's (Ledaig, Tobermory, Isle of Mull PA75 6NR, ☎ 1688-302 350, macgochans@aol.com; £-££) Lively pub overlooking the harbor that serves good food all day.

Sagar Balti House (Main Street, Tobermory, Isle of Mull, ☎ 1688-302 422; ££) Reasonable Indian restaurant that also provides a takeaway service.

■ North Mull

The north end of the island is lower-lying and less rugged than the south and boasts some notable standing stones at Glengorm and Dervaig. The sheltered sandy beach at Calgary Bay is ever-popular.

Attractions & Sights

Old Byre Heritage Centre (Dervaig, Isle of Mull PA75 6QR, ☎ 1688-400 229, theoldbyre@lineone.net; open mid-April through Oct, 10:30am-6:30pm, programs including a 30-minute video are shown hourly from 10:30am-5:30pm; adult/concession/child £3/£2/£1.50). Explore the history of Mull through an exhibition gallery and video. A showcase of six habitats from seashore to mountain crag examines the island's ecology. The café is known for its "Crofter's Soup" and "Clootie Dumpling."

Dervaig Standing Stones: A short distance outside Dervaig, the Tobermory road climbs a number of steep switchbacks. Near the summit of the pass a viewpoint provides excellent panoramas over northwest Mull and a great view down to Dervaig village, with its distinctive pencil-spire church. From the small parking area, a signpost points to the forest where, just into the trees, there is a cluster of five standing stones (of which only two actually remain standing). Such stones are in such abundance in the Hebrides that they become almost part of the landscape; you will see them frequently in sheep and cattle pastures. There are four additional stones near the new cemetery; one of these has been incorporated into a wall and a second acts as a gatepost.

Eas Fors Waterfall (beside the B8073 on the west coast, facing the Isle of Ulva). Mull boasts a large number of waterfalls, of which Eas Fors is one of the most accessible and most spectacular, plunging straight into the sea. Take care if viewing the falls from the cliff above, especially on a wet or windy day, as the ground can be slippery. In addition to the main coastal falls, Eas Fors has several smaller falls on either side of the road that can also be quite picturesque.

Adventures

Aros Park, situated in the outskirts of Tobermory, formed the estate woodland of Aros House (which has now been demolished), and contains a number of waymarked Forest Enterprise walks. Start by Tobermory Distillery close to the large parking area. Walk south along the shore path and into the park with its superb views over Tobermory Bay. Scattered through the park are a small number of cottages and waterfalls. After a mile you reach a lochan (Lochan a'Ghurrabain), which has a one-mile path around it. Trout fishing is available in the lochan (permits from Browns in Tobermory). Return to Tobermory via the coastal path (2-2½ hours; easy).

 AUTHOR'S NOTE: *If you prefer not to walk the whole distance, it is possible to drive to the lochan and walk around it or to the waterfalls from there.*

Ardmore Forest lies at the northern tip of Mull, three miles northeast of Tobermory. The waymarked trail through the forest passes the ruined villages of Penalbanach and Ardmore and has spectacular views across Ardmore Bay to the Ardnamurchan Peninsula. Start from the parking area about a mile outside Tobermory on the road to Glengorm. Follow the waymarkers to the wild and unspoiled rocky coastline that is home to many seabirds. Seals are also regularly seen in the bay and otters may also be glimpsed along the shoreline (2 hours; easy).

Inter-Island Cruises (Garadh Mor, Dervaig, Isle of Mull PA75 6QW, ☎/fax 1688-400 264, jenny@mull.com, www.whalewatchingtrips.co.uk; sailings at 10am April-Oct, £45) Wildlife-watching (look for whales, dolphins and porpoises) and sightseeing boat trips departing from Croig, three miles west of Dervaig on the northwest coast of Mull.

Turus Mara (Penmore Mill, Dervaig, Isle of Mull PA75 6QS, ☎ 1688-400 242 and 800-085 8786 freephone, info@turusmara.com, www.turusmara.com; sailings April-Oct; £30-£40) Wildlife- and seabird-spotting cruises from Ulva

Ferry on Mull to the Treshnish Isles, Staffa, Iona and Fingal's Cave; watch for wildlife such as puffins and seals; occasionally whales and dolphins will be seen.

Entertainment

Mull Little Theatre (Dervaig, Isle of Mull PA75 6QW, ☎ 1688-302 828, mulltheatre@aol.com, www.mulltheatre.com; performances from April to Sept, matinees and evenings; adult/concession £12/£9). Mull Theatre's Dervaig venue is the smallest professional theater in Britain, seating just 43 in an atmospheric converted byre. The company performs plays, puppet shows, storytelling, music, comedy and drama at Dervaig and at Tobermory and other touring venues. All the venues are small, so make reservations early.

Where To Stay & Eat

See *Accommodation* and *Dining* price charts on pages 465 and 466.

Druimnacroish Hotel (Dervaig, Isle of Mull PA75 6QW, ☎/fax 1688-400 274, hotel@druimnacroish.co.uk, www.druimnacroish.co.uk; open Mar-Nov; B&B £££, dinner ££) To stay at Druimnacroish (named after the community that once occupied the site) is to experience total and intense tranquility. Recently refurbished in rich Mediterranean shades, the rooms overlook forested hills grazed by cattle and deer. The spacious conservatory, fire-warmed lounge and extensive library of local maps and books make inactivity an attractive option. The Aga-cooked meals are excellent.

Glengorm Castle (near Tobermory, Isle of Mull PA75 6QE, ☎ 1688-302 321, fax 1688-302 738, enquiries@glengormcastle.co.uk, www.glengormcastle.co.uk; B&B £££-££££) It's odd to think of this imposing 19th-century baronial castle as a B&B. Set in a 5,000-acre estate, and occupied by the owners, who raise Highland cattle and sheep, the castle oozes class and character from its enormous bedrooms and period public rooms. The views over the cliffs to the Atlantic are sensational and an intriguing trio of standing stones dominates a pasture a short distance away. A stay at Glengorm is quite an experience. Units with kitchens are available.

Bellachroy Hotel (Dervaig, Isle of Mull, ☎ 1688-400 314; B&B ££, dinner £-££) This early 17th-century droving inn is said to be the longest continuously inhabited building on Mull. There is comfortable accommodation, reasonably priced home cooking and the chance to meet locals in the bars (where there is regular live music).

Calgary Hotel (By Dervaig, Isle of Mull PA75 6QW, ☎/fax 1688-400 256, www.calgary.co.uk; open Mar-Nov; B&B £££, dinner ££-£££) Converted farm building retaining an original dovecote in the restaurant. The restaurant serves local and Scottish produce, including excellent Mull cheeses, in an informal atmosphere.

Isle of Iona

Of all the many sacred sites in Scotland, tiny and beautiful Iona, cradle of Scottish Christianity, is the most enduring and enchanting. Though only three miles (4.8 km) north to south and 1½ miles (2.4 km) east to west, people have been visiting Iona for centuries. St Columba arrived here with 12 companions in 563 to found a monastic settlement that was to become a beacon of civilization, contemplation and learning in a world benighted in the Dark Ages. Columba's monastery became the heart of the Scottish Church and has attracted pilgrims to Iona ever since the 7th century. Surviving waves of Viking raids, the abbey became one of the most important monasteries in early medieval Europe, and a renowned center of learning and artistic excellence. The gravestones of early monks can still be seen, along with several magnificent high crosses.

The bodies of kings from Scotland and Ireland, abbots and clan chiefs were all interred on Iona, carried along the Street of the Dead. It is believed that 48 Scottish kings lie in the graveyard of Reilig Odhráin, from Fergus II to Macbeth.

Around 1200, Somerled's son Reginald replaced the Columban monastery with a Benedictine abbey and built an Augustinian nunnery at a discreet distance. Close to the nunnery, the small chapel of St Ronan's was rebuilt as the parish church at around the same time. The Reformation of 1560 ended monastic life on Iona and the abbey and nunnery gradually fell into picturesque decline. The nunnery remains an attractive ruin but the abbey was restored (completed in 1965) and today once more supports a thriving Christian community.

■ Getting Here & Getting Around

By Ferry

Caledonian MacBrayne (☎ 1475-650 100, www.calmac.co.uk) operates a regular passenger ferry between Fionnphort (Mull) and Iona (5 minutes). The ferry can take cars but this is normally reserved for Iona residents (visitors may use the free parking at the St Columba Centre in Fionnphort). Bicycles are carried free of charge.

By Bicycle

Cycling is an excellent way to travel on Iona's peaceful roads. You can rent bikes from Finlay Ross (Martyr's Bay, Isle of Iona PA76 6SP, ☎ 1681-700 357, fax 1681-700 562).

■ Attractions & Sights

Iona Abbey (HS; Isle of Iona, ☎ 1681-700 512; open year-round, officially April-Sept, 9:30am-6:30pm; Oct-Mar, 9:30am-4:30am, although the abbey remains open at all times; adult/concession/child £3.30/£2.50/£1.20). Founded by St Columba in 563, the abbey houses superb collections of carved stones and high crosses, was the ancient burial ground of kings from Scotland, Norway, Ireland and France, and retains a deeply spiritual atmosphere. Visitors are welcome to join the daily services; check at the abbey entrance for times.

St Oran's Chapel & Reilig Odhráin: The 12th-century St Oran's Chapel is the oldest of Iona's surviving ecclesiastical buildings. Restored in 1957, it was probably built as a family burial chapel by Somerled or his son Reginald. It is believed that 48 Scottish kings lie in the Reilig Odhráin graveyard that surrounds the chapel. Fine medieval effigies and grave slabs once marked important burial sites, although many of these slabs were removed to the abbey cloisters to avoid further weathering and the exact location of burial sites is no longer known. The Labour Party leader John Smith, who died in 1994, also lies here.

IONA BURIALS

According to legend, Odhráin (St Oran) was buried alive as a sacrifice to prevent the walls of the first church from falling down. Dedicated to his memory, the Reilig Odhráin is the cemetery adjacent to Iona Abbey.

It was during the 9th to 11th centuries that the Reilig Odhráin cemetery became a royal burial ground. A 16th-century inventory recorded 48 Scottish, eight Norwegian and four Irish kings. Unfortunately, none of these graves is now identifiable, their inscriptions having already worn away by the end of the 17th century.

Street of the Dead: The cobbled remains of a medieval track, which connects the abbey with its burial ground and beyond to the monks' landing place at Martyrs' Bay, are still visible. The exposed section of the street leads to the low ruin of the bakehouse (where bread and ale would have been made). Another section of the street, no longer visible, would have led directly to the abbey.

The High Crosses: Four high crosses once stood before the abbey, marking the pilgrims' route. The magnificent 8th-century St Martin's Cross is the sole intact survivor and stands on the same site it has occupied for over 1,000 years. Carved from a single slab of grey epidiorite, the east side is richly carved with bosses and serpents; the west face is carved with Biblical scenes, including the Virgin and child, David and the lions, David and Goliath and Abraham with his sword raised to sacrifice Isaac.

Between St Martin's Cross and the abbey is the solid granite base of St Matthew's Cross. Closer to the abbey stands a replica of St John's Cross. The surviving fragments of the original cross, which have been blown down repeatedly, have been re-erected in the Infirmary Museum. A fourth cross, St Oran's, once stood in Reilig Odhráin.

St Columba's Shrine: Close behind the replica of St John's Cross stands the tiny stone shrine that may mark the original resting place of the saint himself.

The Abbey: Although the abbey has been much altered and restored, it preserves the formal layout of a medieval abbey – church and an adjoining cloister, around which are arranged domestic buildings. The nave is a simple rectangular shape with three processional doorways in the north wall leading to the cloister. The massive two-story tower is accessed via a precipitous spiral stair at the southwestern corner of the crossing. The upper story is inaccessible but is lit by elaborate windows and contains the belfry with a medieval pigeon loft above.

The communion table at the eastern end of the choir is of Iona marble and occupies the site of the medieval high altar. The north wall of the choir is dominated by a large double arch supported on a circular column. On the south side of the choir an arcade of three pointed arches opens into the south choir-aisle.

The covered cloister linked the church and the domestic rooms and served as a place for quiet contemplation. The east range of the cloister contained the most important offices, including the chapter house where the monks met daily to hear a chapter from the Rule of St Benedict and discuss abbey affairs. The monks' dormitory was on the upper floor of the east range. The spacious refectory is accessed by the dormitory day-stair and is lit by four original windows to the north and a modern window in the west gable. Around the cloister walls stand part of Iona's impressive collection of grave slabs, most of which were removed from Reilig Odhráin to protect the carvings from further weathering.

The Infirmary Museum: The infirmary served both as a hospital and a home for old and infirm monks. It has been restored as a museum displaying an extraordinary collection of carved stonework discovered on Iona, including early Christian gravestones, the reconstructed St John's Cross and fragments of St Oran's and St Matthew's crosses.

MacLean's Cross: The tracks between the abbey, nunnery and St Ronan's Chapel were well trodden in medieval times by locals and pilgrims alike and a prayer cross, MacLean's Cross, was erected in the late 15th century at the point where these paths meet. Carved from a single stone slab more than 3m high, the cross is decorated with tightly packed plaitwork and foliage, with a weathered carving of a crucifixion scene on its west face.

The Nunnery: The nunnery is dedicated to St Mary the Virgin and resembles a smaller version of the abbey. It was founded in around 1200 by Reginald, son of Somerled, who installed his sister Beatrice (or Bethoc) as the first prioress. Though ruined, it is one of the best-preserved nunneries in Britain and one of only two Augustinian nunneries in Scotland (the other being at Perth). The Gaelic name *An Eaglais Dhubh* means "black church," in reference to the color of the robes the nuns wore. Like the abbey monks, the nuns followed a life of contemplation and prayer. It remained occupied until the Reformation when it passed into the hands of the MacLeans of Duart. It is open at all times.

The Inner Hebrides

AUTHOR'S TIP: *Stay at least a night on Iona to enjoy the abbey and nunnery away from the day-tripper crowds. Both stay open at all times. Sit in the abbey's deserted choir or walk through its silent cloister in the early morning or late evening to fully experience the peace and tranquility the abbey offers, and begin to grasp the true significance of this intensely spiritual island.*

Iona Heritage Centre (Isle of Iona, Argyll PA76 6SJ, ☎ 1681-700 576, fax 1681-700 328; open April-Oct, Mon-Sat, 10:30am-4:30pm; admission £1.50) Set in a simple 1828 manse designed by Thomas Telford, this exhibition contains fascinating displays on Iona's local history and also has a small shop and lunchtime tea room.

THE IONA COMMUNITY

The Iona Community is an ecumenical Christian community founded in 1938 by the Rev George MacLeod. Its central commitment, enacted through its work on Iona and beyond, remains to seek "new ways to touch the hearts of all." The Community welcomes guests to week-long programs on Iona – at the abbey and nearby MacLeod Centre – from March-October and over Christmas. These programs provide opportunities for fellowship, study, discussion and relaxation. These are not "retreats"; the emphasis is on engagement with staff and other guests rather than solitary meditation.

To attend a program on Iona or volunteer (six weeks to three months), contact The Iona Community, Isle of Iona PA76 6SN, ☎ 1681-700 404, fax 1681-700 460, ionacomm@iona.org.uk, www.iona.org.uk.

■ Adventures

 Alternative Boat Hire (Lovedale Cottage, Isle of Iona PA76 6SJ, ☎ 1681-700 537, www.boattripsiona.com; sailings mid-April to late Sept). Flexible wildlife, fishing or other (you decide) trips aboard *Freya*, a traditional wooden sailboat.

 Staffa trips (Tigh-na-Traigh, Isle of Iona PA76 6SJ, ☎ 1681-700 358, dk@staffatrips.f9.co.uk, www.staffatrips.f9.co.uk; Mar-Oct; adult/child £14/£7). Boat trips to Staffa to see Fingal's Cave, with time included to explore ashore. Reservations advisable. Departures are from Iona at 9:45am & 1:45pm or from Fionnphort at 10am & 2pm.

Iona's 18-hole course lies on the western side of the island on the machair of the crofters' common grazing land. There's not a tree to be seen and the course is unique – not least for the grazing livestock and testing obstacles created by their deposits! The course is free with no green fees or reservations required.

■ Where To Stay & Eat

See *Accommodation* and *Dining* price charts on pages 465 and 466.

 Argyll Hotel (Isle of Iona PA76 6SJ, ☎ 1681-700 334, fax 1681-700 510, reception@argyllhoteliona.co.uk, www.argyllhoteliona.co.uk; open Feb-Nov; B&B ££-£££, dinner ££). The Argyll has developed from an 1850s inn into a delightful haven styled with unfussy chic and operated by charming staff on environmentally-friendly principles. Most rooms and the superb suite enjoy lovely views over the Sound of Iona and guests can relax in one of three lounges or the bright sun lounge overlooking the sea. The elegant, buzzy restaurant delivers an excellent menu in classy surroundings using local produce and vegetables from the hotel's organic garden.

Shore Cottage (Isle of Iona PA76 6SP, ☎ 1681-700 744, enquiries@shorecottage.co.uk, www.shorecottage.co.uk; closed Nov & Christmas; B&B ££). Modern, specially-built B&B accommodation facing the Sound of Iona and within a short walk of the ferry pier. The cozy rooms are thoughtfully furnished and spacious; breakfast is served in the bright sunroom.

 Iona Hostel (Lagandorain, Isle of Iona PA76 6SW, ☎ 1681-700 781, info@ionahostel.co.uk, www.ionahostel.co.uk; £ excluding breakfast). Newly built hostel situated on a working croft at the north of the island, with bedrooms sleeping two to six people. There is a well-equipped open-plan kitchen, living area with wood-burning stove and superb views.

Isle of Ulva

Ulva is a private island (owned by the Howard family) whose population of around 16 is involved in traditional sheep and cattle farming, fish farming, oyster farming and tourism. There are no paved roads or cars – just the four-wheel cross-country bikes used by the inhabitants.

Flint artifacts and bone fragments found in Livingston's Cave indicate that people lived on Ulva as early as 5650 BC. Standing stones survive as a mysterious legacy of the pre-Celtic people who lived on Ulva around 1500 BC and vanished before the Vikings arrived in 800.

Seaweed (for making glass and soap) has played an important role in Ulva's history. It was burned to produce kelp, a product in great demand in the early 19th century. The booming kelp industry allowed Ulva's population to expand to over 600 people living in 16 villages, and the ruins of those homes can still be seen today. After the kelp market collapsed and the potato blight struck, Ulva ceased to be a crofting estate; the era of Clearances followed. The abandoned villages are a sad sight, and the saddest of all is the row of small, low houses at Starvation Terrace on Ardglass point – home of the last evicted crofters for whom no place could be found.

■ Getting Here

The **Ulva ferry** (☎ 1688-500 226, foot passengers and bicycles only) sails, on demand, Mon-Fri, to the island from Mull. The ferry also sails Sundays, June-Aug, but there are no Saturday sailings.

■ Attractions & Sights

Heritage Centre (☎ 1688-500 241, fax 1688-500 100, ulva@mull.com; open Easter-Oct, Mon-Fri, 9am-5pm, June-Aug, also Sun; adult/child £4.50/£2). Talk to Ulva residents and find out all you need to know to make the most of your visit, including details of walks, archaeology and wildlife viewing.

Sheila's Cottage (☎ 1688-500 264). This is a faithful reconstruction of a traditional thatched crofthouse that was last occupied by Sheila MacFadyen early in the 20th century. The room is complete with the stick Sheila kept with one end in the fire and the other on her box bed! The cottage also contains a display on the island's history from Mesolithic times to the present day.

The Boathouse (☎ 1688-500 241, ulva@mull.com; open 9am-4:30pm; £-££). Licensed tearoom serving teas and home-cooked specialties, such as home-grown oysters with Guinness and marinated salmon.

Isle of Staffa

Staffa, an uninhabited island and National Nature Reserve half a mile long by a quarter wide, is famous for its basaltic formations – distinctive stepped columns left when lava from volcanic eruptions cooled millions of years ago. These columns form the cathedral-like structure known as **Fingal's Cave**, immortalized by Felix Mendelssohn in his celebrated *Hebrides Overture*. Other famous visitors include Queen Victoria and Prince Albert, artist JMW Turner and poets and writers Keats, Wordsworth, Tennyson and Sir Walter Scott. Staffa is home to important seabird populations and is a popular destination for viewing puffins.

■ Getting Here

By Ferry

Gordon Grant Tours (Achavaich, Isle of Iona, ☎ 1681-700 338, ☎ 1631-562 842 Oban, fingal@staffatours.com, www.staffatours.com) offers cruises from Fionnphort (Mull) to Staffa and the Treshnish Isles, plus coach and boat trips from Oban to Mull, Iona, Staffa and the Treshnish Isles.

Caledonian MacBrayne (☎ 1475-650 100), in conjunction with local operators, runs day-tours to Staffa from Oban in the summer.

Staffa trips (Tigh-na-Traigh, Isle of Iona PA76 6SJ, ☎ 1681-700 358, dk@staffatrips.f9.co.uk, www.staffatrips.f9.co.uk; Mar-Oct; adult/child £14/£7). Boat trips to Staffa to see Fingal's Cave, with time included to explore ashore. Reservations advisable. Departures are from Iona at 9:45am & 1:45pm or from Fionnphort at 10am & 2pm.

Treshnish Isles

The Treshnish Isles comprise an archipelago of uninhabited islands to the west of Mull, varying in size from 10 to 150 acres. Under the silent watch of a medieval castle, the islands are home to large colonies of breeding seabirds and, in the autumn, breeding grey seals. At Harp Rock on the island of Lunga, a vast colony of guillemots can be viewed across a narrow, precipitous ravine. Among the fallen rocks on the fossil beaches are important concentrations of breeding storm petrels. During the winter, the islands provide valuable grazing for barnacle geese.

There is ample evidence of human occupation over the centuries until the village on Lunga was abandoned early in the 19th century. Ruins include *shielings* (stone shelters used by herdsmen in summer) on Bac Mor (Dutchman's Cap), a possible early Christian chapel on Fladda and a corn kiln and possible whisky still near the abandoned village on Lunga.

■ Getting Here

Gordon Grant Tours (Achavaich, Isle of Iona, ☎ 1681-700 338, 1631-562 842 Oban, fingal@staffatours.com, www.staffatours.com) offers cruises from Fionnphort to Staffa and the Treshnish Isles, plus combined coach and boat trips from Oban to Mull, Iona, Staffa and Treshnish Isles.

Isle of Coll

Nine miles west of Ardnamurchan Point, the most westerly point of the Scottish mainland, the attractive Isle of Coll is renowned for its quietness and unspoiled beaches. Although only 13 miles long by three miles wide, the island has a varied landscape ranging from wide sandy beaches and dunes to peat bogs, inland lochs and rocky outcrops.

Coll has a rich archaeology, including two magnificent ruined brochs (towers), the remains of chambered cairns, several Iron Age forts and an abandoned crofting settlement at Sorisdale. Breachacha Castle is a fine example of a 15th-century west coast castle. The home of Clan Maclean until 1750, the castle has now been restored as a private home.

With its RSPB bird reserve, Coll is a stronghold of the endangered corncrake and is also home to many other bird species. Its scattered lochans are home to many rare water plants. The coastal waters, like the land, teem with wildlife – seals are a common sight, and dolphins and basking sharks come close enough to be spotted from the shore.

■ Getting Here

By Air

It's possible to fly to neighboring Tiree, where there are ferry connections to Coll.

By Ferry

 Caledonian MacBrayne (☎ 1475-650 100, www.calmac.co.uk) runs a car ferry from Oban five times a week in the summer and three times a week in the winter, the journey taking around 2½ hours. There are less-frequent sailings to Coll from Tiree.

■ Adventures

There is varied fishing on Coll, including numerous small trout lochs and sea fishing from the rocks or the big pier – where the ferry berths. For the best action get offshore. Good numbers of pollack – known locally as "lithe" – can be caught just a few hundred yards out. Even more fun can be the mackerel shoals. You don't even need a rod – a handline with some feathered hooks will do perfectly.

■ Wildlife Watching

 In summer, the Coll RSPB reserve is of prime importance for the corncrake, one of the rarest and fastest declining birds in Britain. They arrive on Coll in May after wintering in southeast Africa, and hide in tall vegetation such as irises and nettles before moving out to the meadows of tall grass to nest. Because they nest late and on the ground, hidden in vegetation, they are destroyed by early cutting of hay and silage. Only in the Hebrides, where hay is traditionally cut late, can they survive.

Large numbers of waders – including lapwings, snipe, redshanks and dunlins, which are declining in much of the UK – nest and feed on the damp machair. In winter, flocks of barnacle and white-fronted geese seek refuge on the reserve.

There are guided walks on the reserve every Wednesday at 2pm (RSPB Warden, ☎ 1879-230 301).

The sand dunes are designated Sites of Special Scientific Interest for their incredible richness of flowers, including many species of orchid. On the machair, several hundred species of flowering plants have been identified. The surrounding sea has a wide range of seabirds, including puffins and other auks, shearwaters, divers, terns and gannets. Patient watchers may spot otters, seals, dolphins and whales.

■ Where To Stay & Eat

See *Accommodation* and *Dining* price charts on pages 465 and 466.

Achamore Guest House (Isle of Coll PA78 6TE, ☎ 1879-230 430; B&B ££, dinner £) A comfortable guest house in the center of Coll, surrounded by beautiful scenery and within easy walking distance of excellent beaches. Bikes are available for rent together with scuba equipment run by a BSAC-qualified instructor for beginning and experienced divers.

Caolas (Isle of Coll PA78 6TB, ☎ 1879-230 438, rhumcan@aol.com, www.caolas.net; DB&B £££) A lovely old house standing in acres of unspoiled land at the extreme southwest of the island, in the center of the RSPB reserve and within walking distance of beaches. In addition to the birds in the reserve, there are plenty of farm animals, including shire horses, sheep, ducks and pigeons. The meals use organic ingredients, many of them home-grown.

Coll Hotel (Isle of Coll PA78 6SZ, ☎ 1879-230 334, fax 1879-230 317, collhotel@aol.com, www.collhotel.com; B&B ££, dinner ££) Small, family-run hotel with most rooms enjoying views across the bay. There is a candlelit restaurant with bar meals also available.

First Port of Coll (Arinagour, Isle of Coll PA78 6SY, ☎ 1879-230 262, firstportofcoll@another.com, www.firstportofcoll.com; B&B ££; dinner ££) B&B accommodation and licensed café-restaurant serving local seafood and locally raised beef and lamb. B&B accommodation might not be available in the height of summer, when the property is often rented out.

Isle of Tiree

Low-lying Tiree (few places on the island rise more than 50 feet (15 m) above sea level) is known as the sunniest place in Britain, particularly in the early summer. It boasts beautiful white sand beaches, the largest of which is Gott Bay, which arches for 2½ miles. The island's machair is one of the finest in the Hebrides, its many varieties of wild flowers displaying a host of color in the spring and summer. Gaelic is often heard on the island.

Its exposed position in the Atlantic helps Tiree's sunshine record, but makes it one of the windiest places too, creating rolling waves popular with surfers and windsurfers. Every October the island hosts a world championship windsurfing event.

Archaeological remains include a 30-foot-diameter broch (tower) at Vaul Bay, with walls 12 feet thick. In the west at Kilkenneth stands the ruined Chapel of Saint Kenneth, one of St Columba's followers. There are also four crannogs (ancient loch dwellings). Another Tiree curiosity lies between Vaul and Balephetrish. A mysterious boulder, known locally as the "Ringing Stone" because of the metallic sound it makes when hit, features over 50 Bronze Age cup marks and probably dates back to the Ice Age.

■ Getting Here

By Air

Tiree has a small airport with frequent service from Glasgow.

The Inner Hebrides

By Ferry

 Caledonian MacBrayne (☎ 1475-650 100, www.calmac.co.uk) runs a vehicle ferry from Oban to Tiree, usually via Coll (Oban to Coll is 2¾ hours, then it's almost another hour to Tiree), except on Thursdays when the boat sails directly from Oban to Tiree (3½ hours).

■ Attractions & Sights

Sandaig Island Life Museum (c/o The Hebridean Trust, 75A Banbury Road, Oxford OX2 6PE, ☎ 1865-311 468, fax 1865-311 593, info@hebrideantrust.org; open June-Sept, Mon-Fri, 2-4pm). Museum exploring Tiree life through the ages, housed in a restored terrace of thatched cottages. Displays include a unique collection of local items illustrating life in the late 19th century.

Skerryvore Lighthouse Museum (Hynish Signal Tower, Hynish, Isle of Tiree, c/o The Hebridean Trust, 75A Banbury Road, Oxford OX2 6PE, ☎ 1865-311 468, fax 1865-311 593, info@hebrideantrust.org; open during daylight hours year-round). You can climb the old signal tower and discover the story behind one of Scotland's most isolated lighthouses. The small museum records the story of the design and construction of the Skerryvore Lighthouse by Alan Stevenson (uncle of Robert Louis Stevenson).

■ Adventures

Tiree on Horseback (The Bungalow, The Reef, Kenovay, Isle of Tiree PA77 6UU, ☎ 1879-220 881, enquiries@tireeonhorseback.co.uk, www.tireeonhorseback.co.uk) offers trekking holidays on Icelandic horses.

■ Where To Stay & Eat

See *Accommodation* and *Dining* price charts on pages 465 and 466.

 The Glassary (Sandaig, Isle of Tiree PA77 6XQ, ☎/fax 1879-220 684, www.theglassary.co.uk; B&B ££, dinner ££) Refurbished hotel, converted from a byre (small barn), with a large conservatory enjoying views over machair and the Atlantic, decent bedrooms and good meals.

Kirkapol Guest House (Gott Bay, Isle of Tiree PA77 6TW, ☎/fax 1879-220 729, enquiries@kirkapoltiree.co.uk, www.kirkapoltiree.co.uk; B&B ££, dinner ££). A converted Victorian church with a great setting overlooking Gott Bay, which serves good home cooking.

Scarinish Hotel (Scarinish, Isle of Tiree PA77 6UH, ☎ 1879-220 308, fax 1879-220 410, info@tireescarinishhotel.com, www.tireescarinishhotel.com; B&B ££) A small hotel on Scarinish Harbour with panoramic views to the Treshnish Isles, Mull and Iona.

The Small Isles

The Small Isles lie between Ardnamurchan on the mainland and the Isle of Skye, and comprise the islands of **Rum**, **Eigg**, **Muck** and **Canna**.

■ Getting Here

By Ferry

Caledonian MacBrayne (☎ 1475-650 100, www.calmac.co.uk) runs a regular passenger-only ferry service from Mallaig to the Small Isles with varying daily schedules.

Arisaig Marine (☎ 1687-450 224, fax 1687-450 678, info@arisaig.co.uk, www.arisaig.co.uk; May-Sept) operates boat trips to Eigg, Muck and Rum from Arisaig Harbour.

■ Isle of Rum

Rum is the largest and most mountainous of the Small Isles. Measuring eight miles by nine, its name derives from the Norse for "wide island." Sixty-five million years ago a huge volcano erupted where Rum now stands, the core of which forms the mountains visible today in the south of the island.

A National Nature Reserve since 1957, the island is run by Scottish Natural Heritage as a wildlife and habitat sanctuary. With sea cliffs, mountains, perfect sandy beaches, colorful puffins, red deer and Rum ponies, the island is a paradise for walkers, birdwatchers and wildlife enthusiasts. The resident population numbers around 30.

DID YOU KNOW? *Farm Fields in Kinloch on the island of Rum (just behind the village shop and work buildings) is one of the earliest known human settlements in Scotland, where hunters made their homes over 8,000 years ago.*

Attractions & Sights

Kinloch Castle (Kinloch, Isle of Rum, ☎ 1687-462 037; guided tours most days; adult/child £3/£1.50) Built of red Arran sandstone, Kinloch Castle was built by the Bullough family in the latter half of the 19th century as a luxurious residence with a grand ballroom and elaborate great hall. Preserved as it was when the family left, the castle encapsulates Edwardian life and includes superb furniture and fittings, a Steinway piano and one of the few working orchestrions (a.k.a. "nickelodeons," automated organs operated by perforated paper rolls) in the world.

Adventures

Rum's wild open spaces include several low-level walks that are either waymarked or follow pony paths. For the experienced hillwalker, the Rum Cuillin offers a superb, lengthy ridge walk. Nature Reserve staff lead weekend day-walks into the heart of the island throughout the summer (Reserve Office, ☎ 1687-462 026, rumnnr@snh.gov.uk).

The Inner Hebrides

Kinloch Glen: Heading inland from Kinloch village, this circular, waymarked path leads you up above the farm fields and into the young woodlands planted here during the past 50 years. There are excellent views of the Rum mountains and the hills of remote Knoydart on the mainland. A leaflet is available from the Reserve Office (1 hour; easy).

South Side Trail: Starting from Kinloch village, this is a rugged, occasionally scrambly waymarked trail along the southern shore of Loch Scresort to Port nan Carannan. Along the way look for the well-preserved ruins of long-abandoned blackhouses; you may also spot otters (2 hours; moderate).

Kilmory boasts a beautiful, secluded beach on the north of the island with superb views over to the Skye mountains. Follow the main track leading west (inland) from Kinloch village. At the two-mile fork, follow the track to the right (north), passing an area of woodland and leading all the way to Kilmory. Along the way look for the red deer that can be very tame. The ruined ancient settlement at Kilmory lies in the shelter of the dunes. Around the evocative remains of the 19th-century settlement are 3,000-year-old mounds, a 2,000-year-old Iron Age fort and a 7th-century Christian cross. Check with the Reserve Office before setting off so as not to disturb red deer research activities in the area (5-6 hours; easy/moderate).

Harris used to be Rum's largest township and is reached by following the left (southwest) fork at the two-mile fork on the track west from Kinloch. This track takes you through central Rum, with dramatic views into the heart of the Cuillin. You can explore the old ruins of the township, the well-preserved field systems and visit the Bullough family mausoleum (6-8 hours; moderate).

Wildlife Watching

Manx shearwaters spend most of their lives at sea and winter in the waters off Brazil, but in March migrate north to breed in burrows on the upper slopes of Rum's highest hills. Rum's population of over 70,000 pairs is one of the largest breeding Manx shearwater colonies in the world. The **white-tailed sea eagle** has been successfully reintroduced to Rum after being hunted to extinction in the early 20th century and pairs are now breeding successfully in the wild. **Golden eagles** can also be seen over high ground.

■ Isle of Eigg

Taking its name from the Gaelic "eige," meaning "hollow," Eigg has a distinctive profile marked by the Sgurr – a distinctive ridge reaching 1,290 feet – in the south of the island. The Sgurr is an ancient valley; it was originally filled with pitchstone lava that erupted from a volcano on Rum some 50 million years ago. Rapid cooling of the lava led to the remarkable columnar formation exposed by erosion of the surrounding softer rock.

In the northwest, the geology is different with strange sandstone rock formations and the Bay of Laig, famous for its "singing sands," which creak musically when trodden on. In 1577 around 400 MacDonald men, women and children were massacred by the MacLeods of Skye in a beach cave (the "Massacre Cave") near the base of the Sgurr.

After a high-profile campaign, the local community succeeded in purchasing the island in 1997, which seems to have secured the island's future. Eigg's summer ceilidhs are legendary.

Attractions & Sights

The Massacre Cave: Eigg has a number of caves dotted around its craggy coast. The Massacre Cave and its sister cave, the Cathedral Cave, are a half-hour's walk from the pier.

Adventures

An Sgurr: This walk climbs steeply to the distinctive summit of Eigg (1,290 feet/393 m). There are spectacular views in all directions. From the pier, follow the road straight ahead (not the "main" road that leads around the bay). Continue beyond Galmisdale House to join the Sgurr path running over the moor and below the "nose" of the Sgurr, then along the north side until it reaches the climbing point. From here it is easy to scramble up onto the ridge top and then follow the rough path back to the summit (4 hours; moderate).

■ Isle of Muck

Muck is a small (less than two miles by one mile) and extremely fertile island owned by the MacEwan family for 100 years. It boasts a thriving, close-knit community of around 30, including a tiny school and small visitor center. Despite being close to land, it feels remote and winter storms can isolate the island for long periods.

Adventures

Ben Aerean: At the 451-foot summit of this peak, you will see the whole island laid out around you, with good views to neighboring islands and the mainland as well. Below is the summit is **Camus Mor**, a Site of Special Scientific Interest.

Lawrence MacEwen runs island tours by tractor and trailer every Wednesday in summer at 1:30pm. No reservations required; cost £1.

Craft Shop (contact Jenny at ☎ 1687-462 362) runs craft courses, including basket weaving, furniture "first aid," etc, and holds occasional ceilidhs and quiz nights.

Wildlife Watching

The island has one of the biggest and best protected bird and wildlife populations in Scotland, including strong **puffin** and **seal** colonies.

■ Isle of Canna

Long and low, Canna resembles a giant ship on the horizon. Crofts, cattle and fertile fields define the tiny island, the westernmost of the Small Isles. An established center for Gaelic culture, Canna's population of around 16 preserves generations-old traditions of island life. The island is now owned and farmed by the Scottish National Trust, which works to preserve its position as the "Garden of the Hebrides." The island has been a bird sanctuary since 1938 and 157 different species of birds have been monitored here. Archaeological evidence shows that people lived here long before the pyramids were built in Egypt. In addition to Neolithic remains, Canna also has links to the Columban and Viking eras.

Attractions & Sights

A leaflet on Canna is available from the National Trust for Scotland, 5 Charlotte Square, Edinburgh EH2 4OU, ☎ 131-226 5922. An archaeological map of the island is also available from the Royal Commission for Historical and Ancient Monuments, Bernard Terrace, Edinburgh EH8 9NU.

Adventures

Pony trekking holidays with full board can be arranged through **Hebridean Trekking Holidays** (Burnside, Isle of Canna PH44 4RS, ☎ 1687-462 829).

■ Where To Stay & Eat

See *Accommodation* and *Dining* price charts on pages 465 and 466.

Isle of Rum

Kinloch Castle (Kinloch, Isle of Rum, ☎ 1687-462 037; open Mar-Oct; B&B £, dinner £) The castle operates as a hostel in the summer but make reservations prior to arrival. Evening meals are available (also open to non-residents, reservations recommended) and packed lunches are available by arrangement.

Lea Cottage (☎ 1687-462 036; B&B £, dinner £) offers B&B accommodation on an occasional basis, with evening meals and packed lunches available on request.

Camping (SNH Reserve Office, ☎ 1687-462 026) There is a basic camping area, with toilets and running water, by the shore of Loch Scresort in Kinloch, within 10 minutes' walk of all facilities. Be warned: the site can be full of small biting insects when there is no wind!

Café-teashop (Reserve Office, ☎ 1687-462 026; £) operates in the village hall several afternoons a week during the summer and serves tea, coffee, cake, soup and other homemade food. Check opening times for the teashop with the Reserve Office (the village hall is always open for people to use).

Isle of Eigg

Kildonan House (☎ 1687-482 446; DB&B £££) is the only guest house on Eigg.

Glebe Barn (☎ 1687-482 417, www.glebebarn.co.uk; £ excluding breakfast) Comfortable hostel accommodation (twin rooms and bunkrooms) in a converted 19th-century barn.

Eigg Tea Room (☎ 1687-482 468; open daily in summer; during boat hours in winter; £) The licensed tearoom offers light lunches and cakes with stunning views of Ardnamurchan. Evening meals are available on request.

Isle of Muck

Port Mor House (near the pier, Isle of Muck, ☎ 1687-462 365; open late May through Aug; DB&B ££) Situated near the pier, Port Mor has eight bedrooms and serves good evening meals (also available to non-residents by prior arrangement).

Godag House (☎ 1687-462 371; DB&B ££) Full-board or B&B accommodation half a mile north of the harbor.

The Bunk House (☎ 1687-462 042; £ excluding breakfast) Basic, comfortable hostel accommodation with a Rayburn-warmed living room.

Camping on Muck is free of charge; check at the Craft Shop for good sites.

Vacation rentals: The island has a small number of properties with kitchens (contact Jenny MacEwen, ☎ 1687-462 362, jenny@isleofmuck.fsnet.co.uk), a couple of which are powered by the island's wind plant. For the more adventurous, a canvas replica of a Mongolian Yurt, with a wooden floor and a central stove, has been erected on the north side of the island. Close by is an American Indian Tipi.

Craft Shop (☎ 1687-462 362; open May-Sept, ££) Serves lunches, teas and, by arrangement, dinner. There are also pub nights featuring a wide range of bottled beers and crafts for sale.

Isle of Canna

Harbour View Tearoom (£), a licensed tearoom, is open daily for lunches and dinners during the summer, and also has a craft shop.

The National Trust for Scotland (Holidays Secretary, The National Trust for Scotland, 5 Charlotte Square, Edinburgh EH2 4OU, ☎ 131-226 5922) rents out a large house for groups of up to 10, with kitchen facilities (you'll need to purchase and prepare all your own meals).

The Outer Hebrides

Remote, peaceful and unspoiled, this 130-mile-long arc of islands stands majestically at Scotland's northwestern edge. Although most of the **Western Isles** rise no more than a few hundred feet above sea level, the scenery is varied and often staggeringly beautiful: from the moonscapes of east Harris, to the lowland peat of north Lewis, to South Uist's seemingly endless stretch of pristine, white sand beach.

Numerous prehistoric remains record over 6,000 years of human habitation. More recently, the islands reflect a strong Norse influence. The Vikings ruled here from the 9th century until 1280 and many place names, particularly in the north, have Norse origins.

The islands are home to a diverse range of flora and fauna and most islands have at least one nature reserve. Rare species include golden eagles, sea eagles, dolphins, whales and porpoises. The expanses of wide, open landscapes provide an unbounded haven for outdoor activities, as well as offering the perfect place to relax and unwind.

The Outer Hebrides are the home of a unique, spiritual culture – the true heartland of the Gaels and the Gaelic language. Communities are close-knit, in tune with nature and the rhythm of life. Outer Hebridean folk have a gentle, melodic lilt in their accent – one of the most beautiful of all British accents. Christianity maintains a strong hold over day-to-day life and Sunday remains a day of rest and worship. Traditional music and crafts live on in a lively and modern culture of annual festivals, music schools and local mods (events featuring choirs, musicians, storytellers, poets and actors).

DON'T MISS

Listen to the beautiful, gentle cadence of the **Western Isles accent**.

Marvel at the wondrous 4,500-year-old **Callanish Standing Stones**.

Relax on the empty **white sand beaches** of west coast Harris and the miles of even emptier white beach lining the west coast of South Uist.

Enjoy live traditional **Celtic music** in the heartland of the Gaelic culture.

Fish for **wild brown trout** in North Uist's pristine lochs.

Sail to remote **St Kilda** with its massive **seabird colonies**.

Cycle or drive the entire length of the Outer Hebrides.

Best Freebie: **Stornoway Museum**.

 INFORMATION SOURCES: Western Isles Tourist Board and Lewis Tourist Information Centre are at 26 Cromwell Street, Stornoway, Isle of Lewis HS1 2DD, ☎ 1851-703 088, fax 1851-705 244, www.visithebrides.com.

Getting Here & Getting Around

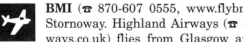

■ By Air

BMI (☎ 870-607 0555, www.flybmi.com) flies from Edinburgh to Stornoway. Highland Airways (☎ 845-450 2245, www.highlandairways.co.uk) flies from Glasgow and Inverness to Stornoway and Benbecula. Loganair (☎ 845-773 3377, www.loganair.co.uk) operating as British Airways flies to Stornoway from Glasgow, Edinburgh and Inverness, and from Glasgow to Benbecula and Barra.

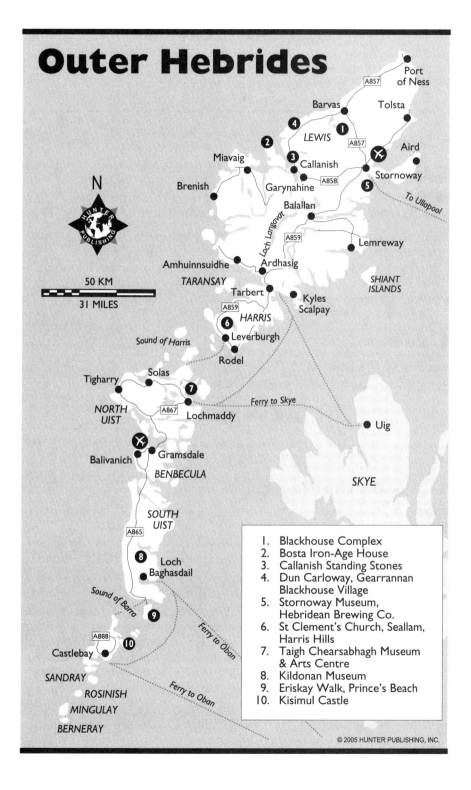

Outer Hebrides

Port of Ness

A857

Barvas

Tolsta

4

1

LEWIS

2

A857

Aird

Miavaig

3

Callanish

Stornoway

Brenish

Garynahine

A858

5

N

Balallan

To Ullapool

A859

Lemreway

Amhuinnsuidhe

Ardhasig

SHIANT ISLANDS

50 KM

TARANSAY

Tarbert

Kyles Scalpay

31 MILES

A859

HARRIS

6

Leverburgh

Sound of Harris

Rodel

Tigharry

Solas

7

NORTH UIST

A867

Lochmaddy

Ferry to Skye

Uig

Balivanich

Gramsdale

BENBECULA

SKYE

SOUTH UIST

A865

8

Loch Baghasdail

Sound of Barra

9

Ferry to Oban

A888

10

Castlebay

SANDRAY

Ferry to Oban

ROSINISH

MINGULAY

BERNERAY

1. Blackhouse Complex
2. Bosta Iron-Age House
3. Callanish Standing Stones
4. Dun Carloway, Gearrannan Blackhouse Village
5. Stornoway Museum, Hebridean Brewing Co.
6. St Clement's Church, Seallam, Harris Hills
7. Taigh Chearsabhagh Museum & Arts Centre
8. Kildonan Museum
9. Eriskay Walk, Prince's Beach
10. Kisimul Castle

© 2005 HUNTER PUBLISHING, INC.

The Outer Hebrides

BEACH LANDING ON BARRA

Flying to Barra involves landing on Traigh Mhor, the two-mile cockle-shell strand that serves as the island's runway. Flight timings need to be flexible as the runway disappears twice a day under the incoming tide!

■ By Ferry

 Caledonian MacBrayne (☎ 1475-650 100, www.calmac.co.uk) sails car ferries to the islands year-round: Ullapool to Stornoway (Lewis); Uig (Skye) to Tarbert (Harris) and Lochmaddy (North Uist); Oban to Castlebay (Barra) and Lochboisdale (South Uist).

Within the Outer Hebrides, Caledonian MacBrayne ferries also run between: Castlebay (Barra) and Lochboisdale (South Uist); Barra and Eriskay; and Berneray (North Uist) and Leverburgh (Harris). For all ferries, it's advisable to book vehicles in advance, particularly in high season, although this isn't necessary for passengers. CalMac offers reasonably priced "Hopscotch" tickets for several routes to and between the islands.

■ By Bus

Stornoway Bus Station (☎ 1851-704 327) can provide timetables and information on getting around the islands by bus.

Adventures

The vast, pristine, empty spaces of the Outer Hebrides are a dream of an outdoor playground.

■ In & On the Water

 The Hebridean coastline is a complex and dramatic labyrinth of bays, inlets, cliffs, secret coves, sandy beaches and offshore islands – a sea paddler's paradise. **Canoe or kayak** beneath cliffs and crags, navigate sea stacks and arches, enter caves and sea lochs, or paddle along some of the most beautiful and cleanest beaches you'll find anywhere.

The waters here provide a huge variety of **diving** from sandy bays, kelp forests and reefs, to numerous wrecks and fantastic wildlife. Vertical drop-offs, pinnacles, slopes and waters full of marine life, including lobster, crayfish, cuttlefish and octopus, wait to be explored. The clear water is warmed by the Gulf Stream and can provide visibility up to 160 feet (50m). St Kilda has excellent, scenic dives, along with the Flannan Isles, the west coast of Lewis, Scarp and Gasker, with its seal colony. Diving contacts are listed for each island.

With over 70 empty beaches, year-round Atlantic swells and an abundance of reefs, bays and coves to catch them, the Outer Hebrides have some of the most consistent **surf** in Europe. The waves are generally smaller and more manageable in the summer but really start to pound from September. Beware, though, that some beaches have strong currents and rips in certain swells; if you're not experienced you should check with the local surf shops or coast-guard on potential dangers. The surf shop in Stornoway (www.hebrideansurf.co.uk) offers transport and supervision.

With their miles and miles of unspoiled coastline exposed to the Atlantic bluster, the Outer Hebrides are a fantastic location for **windsurfing**. However, few people know about this so be prepared to windsurf on your own (two people in the water is a crowd!). Bring a flare-pack, spare ropes and a bag to hold them in. There might be someone on the beach to see you if you get into trouble, but there will probably just be sheep – so make sure you know all the self-rescue techniques.

Representing only 1.3% of the UK's land mass but containing 15% of its freshwater surface area, the 6,000 lochs of the Outer Hebrides offer some of the best **salmon and trout fishing** in Europe. The fishing seasons are: brown trout: 15th March-5th October; salmon and sea trout: 11th February-15th/30th October, with slight regional variations. Sea angling also offers great sport in the clear, fertile waters around the islands.

■ On Wheels

The islands of the Outer Hebrides are perfect for exploring by **bike**. The roads are quiet, the hills gentle and the views unobstructed. A great way to spend a week is to cycle from Barra in the south to Lewis in the north (so as to have the prevailing southwesterly wind behind you).

Isle of Lewis (Eilean Leòdhais)

Lewis is the largest and most populous island in the Outer Hebrides, with a population of over 6,000 in the main port of Stornoway alone. The island has some of the most extensive peat moors in Britain – splashes of small, shallow pools peppered with drier hummocks. The hue of the heather dictates the changing mood of the moor – deep russet and ochre beneath spring skies blur by late summer into carpets of purple, pink and blue. Lewis boasts world-famous archaeological sites in the Neolithic Callanish Stones, Pictish Carloway Broch and Bosta Iron Age House.

Stornoway has a vibrant social scene, including a host of restaurants, pubs and bars, organized events and ceilidhs. Common seals can often be seen in the harbor and you may spot dolphins, whales and sharks if you venture onto the water. Fans of the pipes can hear the Lewis Pipe Band as it parades through Stornoway every Saturday evening in summer.

■ Special Events

Hebridean Celtic Festival (July; PO Box 9909, Stornoway, Isle of Lewis HS2 0DH, ☎ 7001-878 787, fax 1851-621 470, info@hebceltfest.com, www.hebceltfest.com). Internationally acclaimed four-day music festival featuring some of the best traditional music, song and dance performed by Celtic artists. The shows, workshops, concerts and events draw a diverse audience and play a crucial role in preserving and developing Celtic music and culture.

Lewis Highland Games (July; info@lewishighlandgames.co.uk, www.lewishighlandgames.co.uk). Traditional heavy and strongman events and a grand parade of massed pipers and Highland dancers.

Ceòl Nis – Ness Music Festival (July; Taigh Dhonnchaidh, 44 Habost, Ness, Isle of Lewis, HS2 0TG, ☎ 1851-810 166, oifis@taighdhonnchaidh.com, www.taighdhonnchaidh.com) Five-day festival of traditional Gaelic-Celtic music in Ness, Lewis.

■ Sunday In The Highlands & Western Isles

The people of the Western Isles (Lewis and Harris in particular and, to a lesser extent, Skye, Raasay and areas of the northwest Highlands) are deeply religious. Most shops, gas stations and other services close on Sundays, and there is no scheduled public transport. Many hotel bars, pubs and restaurants also close and some B&B and guest house proprietors prefer guests not to arrive or depart on Sundays. Check in advance to avoid causing offense.

 INFORMATION SOURCES: The tourism office is at 26 Cromwell Street, Stornoway, Isle of Lewis HS1 2DD, ☎ 1851-703 088, fax 1851-705 244; open year-round.

■ Attractions & Sights

Blackhouse Complex (HS; Arnol village, Isle of Lewis, 11 miles northwest of Stornoway on the A858, ☎ 1851-710 395; open April-Sept, Mon-Sat, 9:30am-6:30pm; Oct-Mar, Mon-Sat, 9:30am-4:30pm; adult/concession/child £3/£2.30/£1). A traditional Lewis thatched house, with a byre (barn) and stackyard, 1920s whitehouse (a traditional house with mortared stone walls), complete and furnished, and consolidated ruin of a blackhouse.

Bosta Iron Age House (Bernera, Isle of Lewis HS2 9LT, ☎ 1851-612 285, ☎/fax 1851-612 331, cesb@zoom.co.uk; open Tues-Sat, noon-4pm; adult/concession/child £2/£1/£0.5). A genuine, restored late Iron Age/Pictish house revealed when a severe storm tore away the top of a sand dune. The house is shaped like a figure eight and only the roof protrudes above ground. Stone walls support sturdy wood beams. The main room has a central hearth with a ladder leading to an upper level. The second room is slightly lower and might have been used for storage. Pottery, bones, antlers and combs were discovered at the site. The resident guide is very knowledgeable and continues to excavate.

 **Callanish** (Calanais) **Standing Stones** (HS; Callanish, Isle of Lewis HS2 9DY 12 miles west of Stornoway off the A859, ☎ 1851-621 422; site open at all times, visitor centre open April-Sept, Mon-Sat, 10am-7pm & Oct-Mar, Mon-Sat, 10am-4pm; admission to the site is free, for exhibitions £1.75/£0.75). Lewis's famous Neolithic stand-

ing stones date from 2900-2600 BC and predate both Stonehenge and Egypt's pyramids. Although standing stones are common in Scotland, those at Callanish are unique in their configuration. The circle, with its tall central stone and four radiating stone "arms," resembles a Celtic cross, although the ancient site predates Christianity. The northern "arm" of stones is laid out in a double row, forming a ceremonial avenue toward the center, which contains a small chambered tomb.

The stones are of local Lewisian gneiss, the oldest rocks in Britain and some of the oldest in the world. Archaeology has revealed the history of the site. More than 5,000 years ago a circular ditched enclosure was dug; later, cultivation ridges were made for growing crops. The first standing stones – the ring and possibly the southern row – were erected about 5,000 years ago. The chambered tomb was added and eventually the remaining arms and northern avenue. Inside the cairn, vertical slabs divided the chamber that was used for communal burial for several centuries. Peat began to develop over the site around 800 BC and had built up to a depth of five feet, hiding all but the tallest stones, when it was cleared away in 1857.

No one knows the significance of the Callanish stones. One theory is that they were essential to early farming people to indicate the cycle of seasonal rituals and agricultural seasons. An unusual feature of the Callanish stones is that they are aligned with the movements of the moon rather than the sun. When viewed from the end of the northern avenue, at the extremes of the lunar cycle every 18.6 years, the moon rises within the circle at the foot of the central monolith.

More stone circles, stone rows and individual standing stones – some 20 sites in total – lie within a few miles of the main Callanish stones. Two satellite stone circles lie about a mile away, along the A858.

Stornoway Museum – Museum nan Eilean (Francis Street, Stornoway, Isle of Lewis HS1 2NF, ☎ 1851-709 266, fax 1851-706 318, rlanghorne @cne-siar.gov.uk, www.cne-siar.gov.uk; open April-Sept, Mon-Sat, 10am-5:30pm; Oct-Mar, Tues-Fri, 10am-5pm & Sat, 10am-1pm). The museum traces the history and everyday lives of Lewis and Harris communities from the time of the first settlers – perhaps as early as 9,000 years ago – to modern times. Exhibits include original objects, many from recent excavations, reconstruction drawings, photographs and a replica of the famous Lewis Chess Set (the original is in Edinburgh). The exhibition explores the breakup of the old clan-based society and the establishment of crofting at the beginning of the 17th century, people's homes and blackhouses, the domestic economy, land working, fishing and history of Stornoway.

Dun Carloway (HS; 1½ miles south of Carloway, Isle of Lewis, 16 miles northwest of Stornoway on the A858, ☎ 1851-643 338; open at all times) is one of the best preserved brochs (towers) in Scotland. Drystone brochs are found in northern and western Scotland; they date from the last few centuries BC when life in Atlantic Europe was particularly unsettled. Although brochs served as defenses against hostile neighbors and persistent raiders they were primarily dwelling places, occupied by the principal landowning families. The striking size of the broch at Carloway suggests prestige as much as practicality. As well as being one of the best preserved broch towers, Dun Carloway is possibly also one of the last to be built, perhaps sometime in the 1st century BC. The broch was entered through a single narrow passage enclosed by a stout wooden door. Its hollow wall construction helped keep out the winter cold and summer heat, with stairs within the walls for access to upper levels.

SIEGE OF THE MORRISONS & MACAULAYS

The most famous siege of Dun Carloway was in the late 16th century when the Morrisons of Ness sheltered in the broch after being caught red-handed trying to steal cattle from the MacAulays of Uig. The Morrisons holed up inside the tower and blocked the entrance. Undeterred, Donald Cam MacAulay climbed the broch and threw down burning heather, smoking the Morrisons out to face their retribution.

Gearrannan Blackhouse Village (Carloway, Isle of Lewis HS2 9AL, ☎ 1851-643 416, fax 1851-643 488, info@gearrannan.com, www.gearrannan.com). Restored blackhouse village, enjoying a wonderful coastal location, with a museum, café, gift shop and live interpretation.

Hebridean Brewing Company (18 Bells Road, Stornoway, Isle of Lewis HS1 2RA, ☎ 1851-700 123, 1851-700 234, info@hebridean-brewery.co.uk, www.hebridean-brewery.co.uk). The only brewery in the Outer Hebrides produces two fine ales: "Clansman," a light bitter with a golden color, brewed with Scottish malts; and the deep-ruby colored "Islander," brewed with specially-colored Scottish malt. Tours are available by appointment.

■ Adventures

On Foot

Tolsta to Ness: This is an exhilarating walk combining the beauty and solitude of open, rolling moorland with stunning coastal scenery. The route passes typical Lewis landscapes of heather moor and wet peatland, interspersed with small lochans and edged by sheer sea cliffs. On clear days you can see right across the Minch to Cape Wrath on the mainland. This is a linear walk; if you are only walking one way you'll need transportation at the end (4-6 hours one-way; difficult).

The walk starts at **Traigh Gheardha** (Garry Beach), one of the most attractive beaches on Lewis. Large rock stacks jut out of the sand, hiding small caves and tunnels, and a mantle of machair surrounds a freshwater lochan. The remains of **Mormaer's Castle** perch atop the largest of the stacks.

From the parking area at Traigh Gheardha head north, crossing a handsome bridge spanning the Garry River. (The road was intended to go to Ness, but was never completed.) Continue to the waterfall and then follow the green and yellow waymarkers across the moor, continuing northward. A lonely sea stack, Dun Othail, stands almost severed from the mainland by a deep ravine – Macnicol's Leap. A rock ledge on the stack conceals the foundation of a building, thought to be a small chapel.

About two miles north of Dun Othail you arrive at Cuilatotar, where the shell of a solitary house overlooks the shore. The main route turns inland to avoid a deep ravine; an alternate route marked by red-topped posts descends to Cladach Dhiobidail. At the bottom, you can cross the river (if not in spate) and follow the stream to a secluded sandy beach. Continue along the coast and rejoin the main route above the cliffs on the north side of the ravine. The walk continues past the remains of shielings (stone huts) at Filiscleitir and Cuisi-adar – temporary homes of people who spent the summer tending animals – to Ness.

Golden eagles, peregrines, herring gulls, slender necked cormorants and kittiwakes nest along the cliff-tops and you will see fulmar gliding by. You can spot common and grey seals around the base of the cliffs, plus occasional dolphins.

You can take a leisurely walk and visit the magnificent **Callanish Standing Stones** together with a couple of neighboring stone circles. Callanish is today a crofting township of around 150 people who mainly raise sheep. In the village you can see the remains of traditional blackhouses, some still preserved.

From the Callanish Visitor Centre follow the coast road east (left) turning southeast (right) at the junction with the A858. After a short distance divert south (right) along a lane to the first satellite stone circle – Callanish II (Cnoc Ceann a'Ghàrraidh). At the end of the lane the route passes some fine examples of lazybeds (parallel trenches with soil piled in between to provide a greater planting depth) once cultivated by crofters. Callanish II is an oval ring of five standing stones and at least two fallen ones. Look back west for a dramatic view of the main Callanish I site and Loch Roag.

From Callanish II turn east (left) and head inland to Callanish III (Cnoc Fhillibhir Bheag). Callanish III consists of 12 stones – a flattened ring with four stones inside it. From Callanish III pass through the gate, continue along the path to regain the A858 and return west (left) toward the parking area. In the distance on your right you can see vertical faces of outcropping Lewisian gneiss, which may have been the source of the stones in these circles. Before reaching the parking area, detour up the steep lane on the right for the main Callanish Standing Stones (2 hours; easy).

On Wheels

 Trail of the Vikings – Garynahine to Uig: This superb route passes some of the most stunning and peaceful vistas in the Hebrides: incredible white beaches, offshore islands, dramatic cliffs and glens. From the Callanish Visitor Centre follow the A858 until Garynahine. Turn right onto the B8011 and pass Crowlista and Timsgarry, until you reach Ardroil with its heritage center, café, shop and beautiful beach. Continue past Islivig and Brenish to Mealista where you turn round. On the return journey you can detour to an excellent reef beach at Valtos with its views to Pabbay and Bernera (23 miles one way).

You can rent cycles in Lewis at **Alex Dan's Cycle Centre** (67 Kenneth Street, Stornoway, Isle of Lewis HS1 2DS, ☎ 1851-704 025, sales@hebrideancycles.co.uk, www.hebrideancycles.co.uk).

The Outer Hebrides

On Water

 Stornoway Angling Association (c/o Keith Street, Stornoway, Isle of Lewis HS1 2QU, ☎ 1851-705 015, fax 1851-703 718) sells fishing permits for seven lochs containing trout, sea trout and salmon, and has boats for rent.

Stornoway Sea Angling Club (South Beach Street, Stornoway, ☎ 1851-702 021, www.stornowaysac.co.uk) organizes sea angling trips most weekends – the club has a 36-foot boat and is happy to take visitors on excursions. Temporary membership is available to visitors. The club has an excellent clubhouse with social facilities and regular events and organizes the Western Isles Open Championship in July and the Western Isles Cod Championship in August.

The **Stornoway Canoe Club** (www.stornowaycanoes.org.uk) welcomes visitors and organizes adventure trips.

Loch Mor Barvas: Excellent, largely waist-deep, sand bottomed loch with one or two rocks at the edges but visible or marked by buoys. This is where the **Windsurfing Club** is based (☎ 1851-840 316, meetings Tuesday nights May-Sept).

Island Cruising (1 Erista, Uig, Isle of Lewis HS2 9JG, ☎ 1851-672 381, fax 1851-672 212, www.island-cruising.com). Four- or six-day wildlife, diving and birdwatching cruises living in comfortable twin cabins. St Kilda is a specialty, as is diving for scallops for breakfast.

Seatrek (16 Uigean, Isle of Lewis HS2 9HX, ☎/fax 1851-672 464, webmaster@seatrek.co.uk, www.seatrek.co.uk). Short trips, day-trips and expeditions (by RIB) to locations rich in wildlife, uninhabited islands and secret lagoons. Trips offer access to stack climbing all over the Outer Hebrides, including expeditions to unclimbed stacks at Mingulay south of Barra.

VisitHebrides Engebret (Sandwick Road, Stornoway, Isle of Lewis HS1 2SL, ☎ 1851-702 303/702 304, charles@visithebrides.co.uk, www.visithebrides.co.uk). Sightseeing, fishing, birdwatching and diving RIB trips from Stornoway to the eastern coastline of Lewis and the Shiant Islands.

Multi-Activity Operators

Sgor (20a Coll, Back, Isle of Lewis HS2 0JR, ☎ 1851-820 726, tim@sgor.co.uk, www.sgor.co.uk) will arrange climbing, abseiling hillwalking and canoeing.

■ Shopping

Breanish Tweed (1A Melbost, By Stornoway, Isle of Lewis HS2 0BD, ☎/fax 1851-701 524, iansutherland@breanishtweed.co.uk, www.breanish-tweed.co.uk). Lightweight hand-woven tweed, cashmere and lambswool and bespoke (made-to-measure) tailoring of jackets, suits and skirts.

Carloway Craft (c/o 11 Upper Carloway, ☎/fax 1851-643 225, carlowaycraft@yahoo.co.uk). Celtic jewelry and other local gifts; the shop is at the entrance to Dun Carloway.

Gisla Woodcraft (Gisla, Uig, Isle of Lewis HS2 9EW, ☎/fax 1851-672 371, gisla.woodcraft@virgin.net). Hand-turned wooden gifts and other craft items.

Hebridean Replicas (15A Arnol, Isle of Lewis HS2 9DB, ☎/fax 1851-710 562, coleen@hebreplicas.demon.co.uk). Replica Lewis chess sets and Celtic tile boards, made of local stone.

Mosaic (21 North Beach, Stornoway, Isle of Lewis HS1 2XQ, ☎/fax 1851-700 155, mosaichebrides@aol.com). High-quality Scottish and international crafts and jewelry sold by Gaelic-speaking staff.

■ Where To Stay & Eat

See *Accommodation* and *Dining* price charts on pages 465 and 466.

Stornoway

 Park Guest House & Restaurant (30 James Street, Stornoway, Isle of Lewis HS1 2QN, ☎ 1851-702 485, fax 1851-703 482; B&B ££, dinner ££). Listed Victorian stone house and licensed restaurant serving island and Scottish specialties.

Royal Hotel (Cromwell Street, Stornoway, Isle of Lewis HS1 2DG, ☎ 1851-702 109, fax 1851-702 142, royal@calahotels.com, www.calahotels.com; B&B ££-£££, dinner ££). Centrally located hotel enjoying good views of the harbor and castle.

Digby Chick Restaurant (11 James Street, Stornoway, Isle of Lewis HS1 2QN, ☎ 1851-706 600, fax 1851-703 900; lunch £, dinner £££). Small friendly restaurant that serves lunchtime favorites (lasagne, deep-fried haddock, etc) with a wider evening selection such as tuna, fresh sardines and steaks.

Callanish & Westside

Eshcol Guest House (21 Breasclete, Callanish, Isle of Lewis HS2 9ED, ☎/fax 1851-621 357, neil@eshcol.com, www.eshcol.com; B&B ££). Popular guest house located on a small croft in a weaving village three miles from the Callanish Stones. Run by Neil (who was born and bred in the village) and Isobel MacArthur for over 10 years.

Loch Roag Guest House (22a Breasclete, Callanish, Isle of Lewis HS2 9EF, ☎/fax 1851-621 357, donald@lochroag.com, www.lochroag.com; B&B ££, dinner ££). Run by Donald MacArthur, the son of Neil and Isobel MacArthur of the Eshcol Guest House next-door.

Tigh Mealros (Garynahine, By Callanish, Isle of Lewis HS2 9DS, ☎/fax 1851-621 333; dinner ££). Friendly, family-run restaurant offering a cozy, relaxed atmosphere and à la carte and set menus, including local seafood.

Shawbost Inn (Raebhat Restaurant, North Shawbost, Isle of Lewis HS2 9BD, ☎/fax 1851-710 632; open May-Sept, by reservation at other times; £-££). Local produce, snacks and daily specials.

Uig

Baile-Na-Cille Guest House (Timsgarry, near Uig, Isle of Lewis HS2 9JD, ☎ 1851-672 242, fax 1851-672 241, randjgollin@compuserve.com; open Easter-Oct; B&B ££, dinner £££). Established 25 years ago, the guest house is superbly located on the remote west coast of Lewis. Dinner is available for residents and non-residents.

Bonaventure (Aird, Uig, Timsgarry, near Uig, Isle of Lewis HS2 9JA, ☎/fax 1851-672 474, jo@bonaventurelewis.co.uk, www.bonaventurelewis.co.uk; closed Nov & Feb & Sun-Mon; B&B £, lunch £, dinner ££). Stay and dine in splendid isolation on Lewis's remote west coast, enjoying the Breton and Irish charm of Richard and Jo-Ann Leparoux. There is a cozy bar, wood-burning stove and superb views over Loch Roag. No credit cards.

Ness

Galson Farm Guest House (South Galson, Ness, Isle of Lewis HS2 0SH, ☎/fax 1851-850 492, roberts@galsonfarm.co.uk, www.galsonfarm.free-serve.co.uk; B&B ££, dinner ££). Restored 18th-century farmhouse set on an 18-acre working croft on Lewis's north Atlantic coast, offering open peat fires and candlelit dinners using home-grown and local produce.

Isle of Harris (Na Hearadh)

Harris, deriving its name from the old Norse meaning "high land," is the most rugged of the Outer Hebridean islands. The exposed bedrock jutting from the North Atlantic has been shaped by wind and waves into an other-worldly landscape. The island has been described as the "high heart of the Hebrides" and offers huge diversity in its terrain. The east coast is stark and rocky, and it's hard to imagine how people ever managed to scrape together an existence. The **Harris Hills** (the highest is the Clisham at 2,623 feet/799 m) host golden eagles, grouse, red deer and Hebridean black-faced sheep. Fashioned from Lewisian gneiss – the oldest rock in the world – they resemble a strange lunar landscape. By contrast, the west coast has idyllic white sand beaches, fertile machair soil and unforgettable mountainous backdrops.

 INFORMATION SOURCES: The tourism office is at Pier Road, Tarbert, Isle of Harris, ☎/fax 1859-502 011; open year-round.

■ Attractions & Sights

 **St Clement's Church** (HS; Rodel, Isle of Harris on the A859). A fine 16th-century church built by Alexander MacLeod, 8th Chief MacLeod of Dunvegan and Harris, and containing his richly carved tomb. The timber-roofed church also contains a fine collection of late medieval sculpture. It's possible to climb a staircase and two steep ladders to the top of the tower.

Seallam! (Northton, Isle of Harris HS3 3JA, ☎/fax 1859-520 258, seallam@aol.com, www.seallam.com; open year-round, Mon-Sat, 9am-5pm; adult/concession £2.50/£2). Exhibitions on the history and natural environment of the Hebrides, with detailed information sources for the more serious student. There is a crafts shop and coffee bar.

■ Adventures

On Foot

 Rhenigidale: This is one of the most spectacular walks on Harris and rewards intrepid walkers with some of the island's best panoramas. The village of Rhenigidale was the last village in Britain to have a road built to it and was previously reached only by boat or track.

Start from the parking area on the east side of the bridge across the Lacadale Lochs, on the road from Tarbert to Kyles Scalpay. The track climbs steeply eastwards to a pass that provides excellent views back across East Loch Tarbert. From the pass, descend gently through deep peat. Just beyond the summit, a path leads off to the right to the now-deserted village of Molinginis. The ruined village stands amid elder trees above the stony beach from which it takes its name.

Return to the main track, which now starts to drop steeply, providing magnificent open views toward the headland of Rhenigidale and across Loch Seaforth to Lewis's empty hills and valleys. Well out to sea lie the Shiant Islands, once occupied by resident shepherds but now only visited occasionally by crofters.

The path zigzags down a rocky cliff-face (the Sgriob) to the head of Loch Trollamaraig. Be careful on the steep descent, particularly when the grass is wet, as it can be slippery. The lower slopes become increasingly lush and several waterfalls tumble down nearby. The path reaches the shore at the head of Loch Trollamaraig, near a bridge across a stream. The path climbs steeply inland and crosses the headland of Sron Mor. Look back for a great view of the cliff path you just descended.

The path drops sharply once more to the sea and crosses a stream, a bridge over a second stream and a gate. You now approach the long-deserted but picturesque houses at the west of the township. The track climbs again, high above the ruined houses. Pass through another gate and join the new road into Rhenigidale village (3-4 hours one-way; moderate).

On Wheels

 Castles & Heather Trail – Bunavoneader to Huishinish: A superb route through one of the most remote parts of Harris. Start at Bunavoneader where you turn west off the main A859 spinal road onto the B887. This twisting road skirts the west coast of the island and cars are few and far between. Continue past Amhuinsuidhe Castle until the end of the road at Huishinish, where you can see some of the finest beaches in Harris with views over to the Isle of Scarp (10 miles one way).

DID YOU KNOW?

DID YOU KNOW? *The island of Scarp off the west coast of Harris was the scene of a bizarre experiment in 1934 to deliver mail by rocket. Unfortunately, the rocket blew up and scattered burning mail all over the beach.*

Lunar Landscape & Atlantic Sands – Rodel circuit: A circular route highlighting the superb but contrasting coastal scenery on Harris's east and west coasts. From St Clement's Church in Rodel take the single-lane road northwards. The road bends and winds its way through beautiful coastal sea inlets and many tiny villages set in a rocky lunar landscape with marvelous views east to the Inner Hebrides. Pass Finsbay, Flodabay, Manish and many others until you reach the T-junction with the A859. Turn northwest (left) and follow the road as it turns south down the west coast of the island. The landscape here is one of low machair lands and beautiful white sand beaches. You cycle just feet from the Atlantic shores of some huge expanses of sand, such as Luskentyre and Scarista, eventually reaching Leverburgh or returning once more to Rodel (30 miles one way).

You can rent cycles in Harris at **Harris Cycle Hire** (Sorrel Cottage, 2 Glen Kyles, Leverburgh, Isle of Harris HS5 3TY, ☎ 1859 520 319, sorrel.cottage@virgin.net).

On the Water

Scenic Cruises (Flodabay, Isle of Harris HS3 3HA, ☎ 1859-530 310, fax 1859-530 289, hamish@scenic-cruises.co.uk, www.scenic-cruises.co.uk). Tailored boat trips (maximum six people) to fish and explore wildlife, natural history and local history.

Strond Wildlife Charters (1 Strond, Isle of Harris HS5 3UD, ☎ 1859-520 204, aj@erica.demon.co.uk). Day-cruises in the Sound of Harris to view wildlife, particularly seals, seabirds and otters.

The beach beyond Horgabost on the west coast of Harris is a good place for **windsurfing** in a southwesterly wind, particularly enjoyable at low tide. This is hard to beat for cruising among spectacular scenery.

Obbe Fishings (3 Lever Terrace, Leverburgh, Isle of Harris HS5 3TU, ☎ 1859-520 466, enquiry@obbefishings.co.uk, www.obbefishings.com). Wild fishing for salmon, sea trout and brown trout on an extensive fishing system covering 10 square miles. Equipment rental, ghillies (guides), boats and sea fishing are also available.

Harris Sea Angling Club (☎ 1859-530 310) arranges fishing trips and competitions.

Isle of Taransay (Tarasaigh)

Taransay lies about two miles off the west coast of Harris and was made famous in 2000 as the remote setting for the BBC's pointless production *Castaway 2000*, in which a group of people were brought to live on the island for a year. Thankfully, it is now once again deserted, with the last "real" villagers having left in the 1970s. Taransay is an island of great beauty, with a natural arch, numerous sandy beaches, machair lands and wildlife. It's also a haven for the stressed where you can enjoy your own castaway experience. The schoolhouse and Mackay house where the BBC castaways stayed have been renovated into holiday cottages (meals not included, but there are kitchen facilities; plan to bring your own supplies).

John Mackay (☎ 1859-550 260/550 257, info@visit-taransay.com, www.visit-taransay.com) offers day-trips to Taransay, April-Oct, Mon-Fri, leaving 9:30am from Horgabost beach on Harris and returning at 5pm.

■ Shopping

Isle of Harris Knitwear Company (Grosebay, Isle of Harris HS3 3EF, ☎ 1859-511 240, fax 1859-511 297). Traditional knitwear handmade on Harris using babysoft wool.

Scalpay Linen (Rover Cottage, Isle of Scalpay HS4 3XU, ☎ 7867-752 448, fax 1859-540 298, www.scalpaylinen.com). Beautiful linen products woven and hand-finished locally, including tea towels, cushions and scented sachets.

Tweeds & Knitwear (4 Plockropool, Drinishader, Isle of Harris HS3 3EB, ☎ 1859-511 217, www.harristweedproducts.co.uk). Harris Tweed, wool and knit garments, and weaving demonstrations.

HARRIS TWEED

Lady Dunmore popularized Harris Tweed in the 19th century when she had the Murray tartan copied by Harris weavers. This became so successful she began marketing the tweed to her friends. Since then Harris Tweed has become renowned the world over. Only pure new wool is used in its production, which involves many stages; raw wool is washed, scoured, carded, spun and warped before finally being woven. Only then can tweed carry the "ORB" Certification Mark to show it is a genuine Harris Tweed.

Over the decades, Stornoway has emerged as the hub of the Harris Tweed industry with the bulk of the cloth being woven by Lewis crofter-weavers. Although the initial and finishing processes are nowadays carried out by mills, every single web of cloth is still woven by weavers in their own homes.

■ Where To Stay & Eat

See *Accommodation* and *Dining* price charts on pages 465 and 466.

 Harris Hotel (Tarbert, Isle of Harris HS3 3DL, ☎ 1859-502 154, fax 1859-502 281, harrishotel@btopenworld.com, www.harrishotel.com; B&B £££, dinner ££-£££). Family-owned hotel dating from 1865, with bright, modern rooms.

Leachin House (Tarbert, Isle of Harris HS3 3AH, ☎/fax 1859-502 157, enquiries@leachin-house.com, www.leachin-house.com; B&B £££, dinner £££). Built in 1892 by Norman MacLeod, reputedly the "father" of the Harris Tweed industry, Leachin stands alone in a landscaped garden overlooking the sea, and offers tranquility and high-quality cooking.

First Fruits Tearoom (Pier Road Cottage, Tarbert, Isle of Harris HS3 3DJ, ☎ 1859-502 439/502 469; £). Cozy, traditional tearoom.

Rodel Hotel (Rodel, Isle of Harris HS5 3TW, ☎ 1859-520 210, fax 1859-520 219, reservations@rodelhotel.co.uk, www.rodelhotel.co.uk; B&B ££££, dinner £££). Refurbished, historic hotel located in south Harris, with comfortable rooms and good food.

Scarista House (Scarista, Westside, Isle of Harris HS3 3HX, ☎ 1859-550 238, fax 1859-550 277, timandpatricia@scaristahouse.com, www.scarista-house.com; B&B ££££, dinner ££££). Georgian house, formerly the manse, enjoying great views over the ocean, three mile-long shell sand beach and heather-clad mountains. There are also cottages with kitchens available. The excellent dining room (open to non-residents) serves organic produce, including herbs from the garden, and specializes in seafood, a favorite being whole lobster. Reservations essential.

Am Bothan Bunkhouse (Ferry Road, Leverburgh, Isle of Harris HS5 3UA, ☎/fax 1859-520 251, ruari@ambothan.com, www.ambothan.com; £ excluding breakfast). A superb hostel with cabins and dormitories. The wonderfully decorated communal sitting room has a high ceiling, pool table, peat fire and modern kitchen.

An Clachan (Leverburgh, Isle of Harris HS5 3TS, ☎/fax 1859-520 370; open April-Oct; £). Tearoom serving home baking, homemade soup and filled rolls. There is also a craft shop and St Kilda exhibition.

Isle of North Uist (Uibhist a Tuath)

North Uist is 13 miles of stunning beaches, machair and freshwater lochs interrupted by dark, rolling moorland hills. From the air, the island looks like a waterlogged sponge, with spines of glaciated stone flooded by meltwater from the last Ice Age. The west coast looks out to the small Isle of Vallay, which can be reached at low tide and is home to a deserted mansion house. To the north is the pretty island of Berneray, home to an active, friendly community and reputedly Prince Charles's favorite island. This is where the Harris ferry arrives, and is now linked to North Uist by causeway.

North Uist is a haven for wildlife watchers and perfect for walking, kayaking and fishing. To the west lie the **Monach Islands** where around 9,000 grey seal pups are born every year.

 INFORMATION SOURCES: The tourism office is at Pier Road, Lochmaddy, Isle of North Uist, ☎ 1876-500 321; closed in winter.

■ Attractions & Sights

Taigh Chearsabhagh Museum & Arts Centre (Lochmaddy, Isle of North Uist HS6 5AA, ☎ 1876-500 293, fax 1876-500 240, admin@taigh-chearsabhagh.org, www.taigh-chearsabhagh.org). Award-winning museum and arts center standing close to the high-tide mark in the village of Lochmaddy. The center is a focus for life in North Uist, and welcomes countless visitors each year to experience its arts, culture and heritage. There are two galleries, a museum, an arts workshop, a shop and a café.

■ Adventures

Uist Outdoor Centre (Cearn Dusgaidh, Lochmaddy, Isle of North Uist HS6 5AE, ☎/fax 1876-500 480, info@uistoutdoorcentre.co.uk, www.uistoutdoor-centre.co.uk) Kayaking, navigation, boat handling and diving from the Centre's 5.8m powerboat *Sea Fury*. Other activities include rock climbing and abseiling from sea cliffs/crags, overnight expeditions and offshore island survival skills, with lots of opportunities to view wildlife. Full board, or accommodation in four-person bunkrooms with kitchens.

With an incredible ratio of water to land, North Uist is famous for its **sea trout** fishing – some of the best in Europe. With so many lochs to choose from, you can always find a loch teeming with healthy wild fish all to yourself.

■ Wildlife Watching

The **RSPB Balranald** nature reserve on the west coast bursts with coastal waders and divers. **Lochmaddy Bay** is a marine conservation area and its lagoons form the most extensive and diverse saline lagoon system in the UK – home to one of the densest otter populations in northwest Europe.

■ Where To Stay & Eat

See *Accommodation* and *Dining* price charts on pages 465 and 466.

Lochmaddy

Lochmaddy Hotel (Lochmaddy, Isle of North Uist HS6 5AA, ☎ 1876-500 331, fax 1876-500 210, info@lochmaddyhotel.co.uk, www.lochmaddyhotel.co.uk; B&B £££, dinner ££). Traditional whitewashed Highland building, close to the ferry terminal. The bedrooms are individually furnished and many have views of Lochmaddy Bay. The restaurant serves the best in local seafood and game; the lounges have real fires, sea views and serve bar meals. There is also a separate house with kitchen facilities for those who prefer to prepare their own meals.

Old Courthouse (Lochmaddy, Isle of North Uist HS6 5AE, ☎/fax 1876-500 358, mjohnson@oldcourthouse.fsnet.co.uk; B&B ££). Reasonably priced B&B accommodation in an imposing Georgian villa.

Locheport

Langass Lodge (Locheport, Isle of North Uist HS6 5HA, ☎ 1876-580 285, fax 1876-580 385, langasslodge@btconnect.com, www.langasslodge.co.uk; B&B £££, dinner £££). Isolated near a stone circle and overlooking a sea loch, this charming small hotel offers spectacular views and good country-house cooking specializing in local seafood and game.

Carinish Inn (Carinish, Isle of North Uist HS6 5EJ, ☎ 1876-580 673, fax 1876-580 665, carinishinn@btconnect.com; B&B £££, dinner ££). Comfortable hotel refurbished in 1999, with à la carte and bar menus incorporating the finest local ingredients.

Temple View Hotel (Carinish, Isle of North Uist HS6 5EJ, ☎ 1876-580 676, fax 1876-580 682, templeviewhotel@aol.com, www.templeviewhotel.com; B&B £££, dinner £££). Family hotel with extensive views of the island of Baleshare, the 13th-century ruin of Trinity Temple, moorland and distant hills. The sun lounge is a great place to watch the sun set over the lochs.

Claddach Kirkibost Centre (Isle of North Uist HS6 5EP, ☎/fax 1876-580 390, urachadh@aol.com; open in summer only; £). Conservatory café with views to Kirkibost Island; serves local produce and home baking, and holds cultural events throughout the season. Internet facilities are available.

Isle of Berneray

 Lobster Pot Tearoom (5a Borve, Berneray, Isle of North Uist HS6 5BJ, ☎/fax 1876-540 288; £). Enjoy homemade soup, sandwiches, toasties, cakes and pastries while enjoying the views across the Sound of Harris.

Isle of Benbecula (Beinn Na Faoghla)

Benbecula, the "island of fords," is sandwiched between North and South Uist (and connected to both by bridges and causeways). The island is characterized by small islands and islets, historic remains, extensive, low-lying machair plains and expanses of shallow, sandy bays. With its airport, college, hotels and cafés, Benbecula is the administrative center of the Southern Isles and is the most built-up area of the Outer Hebrides outside Stornoway.

■ Adventures

Uist Community Riding School (The Stables, Balivanich, Isle of Benbecula HS7 5LA, ☎ 1870-604 283, ucrs@hotmail.com) offers road, beach and picnic rides and hacks (cross-country rides) for all ages and abilities. Beach riding is the highlight.

Uist Sea Angling Club (14/16 Balivanich, Isle of Benbecula, ☎ 1870-602 109) can provide information on sea angling, boat and equipment rental.

■ Shopping

D MacGillivray & Co (Balivanich, Isle of Benbecula HS7 5LA, ☎ 1870-602 525, fax 1870-602 981, macgillivraysfloor.furnishings@virgin.net). Harris Tweed jackets, hand-knitted "oily" Harris wool sweaters, tartan rugs, Hebridean jewelry, local pottery, souvenirs, Highland dress, bagpipes and more. A mail-order service is available.

■ Where To Stay & Eat

See *Accommodation* and *Dining* price charts on pages 465 and 466.

 Creagorry Hotel (Creagorry, Isle of Benbecula HS7 5PG, ☎ 1870-602 024, fax 1870-603 108, reception@creagorryhotel.co.uk; B&B ££££, dinner ££). Recently renovated hotel dating to 1885, with Gaelic-speaking staff.

Dark Island Hotel (Liniclate, Isle of Benbecula HS7 5PJ, ☎ 1870-603 030, fax 1870-602 347, darkislandhotel@msn.com; B&B £££, dinner £-££). Modern, medium-sized hotel offering a choice of economy, standard and VIP rooms. Local crab and peat-smoked salmon are house specialties.

Stepping Stone Restaurant (Balivanich, Isle of Benbecula HS7 5LA, ☎ 1870-603 377, fax 1870-603 121; lunch £, dinner ££-£££). A wide range of seafood and Scottish specialties, ranging from sandwiches, rolls, takeaways and home baking to three-course evening menus.

Isle of South Uist (Uibhist a Deas)

South Uist has a superb white shell beach stretching continuously for over 20 miles down its western coast. The incredible machair and dunes alongside the beach brim with flowers and wildlife such as corncrakes and otters. The jagged east coast is broken by fjord-like inlets and bays. South Uist people preserve their Hebridean traditions – community crofting activities like peat cutting, wool dyeing and seaweed gathering remain part of everyday life.

■ Special Events

Ceòlas Summer Music School (Jul; ☎/fax 1878-700 154, info@ceolas.co.uk, www.ceolas.co.uk) Music and dance summer school with expert instruction in piping, fiddling, singing, dancing and the Gaelic language, combined with concerts, ceilidhs and informal sessions in local pubs.

 INFORMATION SOURCES: The tourism office is at Pier Road, Lochboisdale, Isle of South Uist, ☎ 1878-700 286; closed in winter.

■ Attractions & Sights

Kildonan Museum (Kildonan, Isle of South Uist HS8 5SQ, ☎ 1878-710 343/700 279; open April-Sept, Mon-Sat, 10am-5pm & Sun, 2pm-5pm)

Museum describing the history, archaeology, crafts and culture of South Uist, with local crafts and a bright café.

■ Adventures

A great cycling route is the **Frisky Whisky Trail** from Loch Bee to Eriskay, a trip of some 30 miles down the entire length of South Uist and over the causeway to Eriskay. From Loch Bee in South Uist, follow the A865 south, with rocky gneiss hills to your left and flat machair leading to the sea on your right. Along the way you pass the Loch Druidibeg Nature Reserve and Kildonan Museum. Allow plenty of time for this route as it's well worth diverting along any of the single-lane roads to the west to see the vast stretch of uninterrupted beach running down the west coast.

You can rent cycles at **Rothan Cycles** (9 Howmore, Isle of South Uist HS8 5SH, ☎ 1870-620 283, www.rothan.com).

The waters of **Loch Bee** on South Uist provide perfect flat-water windsurfing conditions: the water is only waist- to chest-deep with a solid, sandy bottom. The small parking space just off the A865 is the ideal place to rig and launch.

■ Where To Stay & Eat

See *Accommodation* and *Dining* price charts on pages 465 and 466.

North End

Orasay Inn (Lochcarnan, Isle of South Uist HS8 5PD, ☎ 1870-610 298, fax 1870-610 267, orasayinn@btinternet.com; B&B ££, lunch £, dinner ££). Small, family-run hotel that serves some of the finest food in the Outer Hebrides, including local seafood, game and superb desserts.

South End

Borrodale Hotel (Daliburgh, Isle of South Uist HS8 5SS, ☎ 1878-700 444, fax 1878-700 446, reception@borrodalehotel.co.uk; B&B ££-£££, dinner ££). Small family-run hotel with a cozy interior of wood and exposed stone, and an extensive menu.

Lochboisdale Hotel (Lochboisdale, Isle of South Uist HS8 5TH, ☎ 1878-700 332, fax 1878-700 367, hotel@lochboisdale.com; B&B £££, dinner ££). Fishing hotel situated by the shore at the ferry terminal.

Polochar Inn (Pollochar, Isle of South Uist HS8 5TT, ☎ 1878-700 215, fax 1878-700 768, polocharinn@btconnect.com; B&B ££-£££; dinner ££). Traditional inn enjoying outstanding panoramic views toward Barra and Eriskay. The à la carte and bar menus incorporate local produce.

Isle of Eriskay (Eiriosgaigh)

Tiny but beautiful Eriskay is romantically remembered as the site where Bonnie Prince Charlie first landed on Scottish soil in his doomed quest to gain the English crown. Its second claim to fame is the sunken wreck of the SS *Politician*, the whisky-laden cargo ship that sank off the island in the 1940s and inspired Sir Compton McKenzie's novel *Whisky Galore*. The island is now linked to South Uist by causeway.

■ Adventures

 Eriskay Walk: From the ferry terminal, follow the main road to the right. Continue up the hill, past the crossroads and down past Am Politician (see below), and on to the old cemetery. Continue along the track until you reach **Coilleag a' Phrionnsa** ("Prince's Beach"), the beach where Bonnie Prince Charlie first stepped ashore in Scotland. Walk about three-quarters of the way along the beach and then along the sand dune and up to regain the main road.

Turn right and continue along the main road until you reach the letterbox. Stay right toward **Acarsaid** (harbor). On reaching the trees follow the rock face uphill for a panoramic view of the islands of Skye, Soay, Canna, Rum, Eigg and Muck.

Retrace your steps to the trees and continue along the track to the right. At the end of the track, follow the waymarkers across a stile, along the shore and up the hill fence until you see a lily-splashed loch hidden in a small dip. Nearby at the end of the walk is a secluded little bay where you might catch sight of otters.

Return to the main track, along to the letterbox and to your left along the road. Turn right and follow the waymarkers on the short climb up to **Loch Crakavaig**, past the water station.

Head north from the loch and regain the road. On your approach enjoy a spectacular view of Eriskay and the archipelagos to the north and south. Return along the main road, on your way passing the **Statue of Our Lady of Fatima**, erected on the site of the original Catholic church of Eriskay (3 hours; moderate).

■ Where To Eat

See *Accommodation* and *Dining* price charts on pages 465 and 466.

 Am Politician (Baile, Isle of Eriskay HS8 2JL, ☎/fax 1878-720 246; £-££). The only bar on the Isle of Eriskay serves popular seafood meals. Reservations are required for dinner.

Isle of Barra (Eilean Barraigh)

The smallest of the main islands, Barra measures only five by eight miles, but captures the charm of the Hebrides with its beaches, tranquility and strong Gaelic culture. With a single ring road all the way around the island, Barra is a compact playground for cycling on quiet roads, walking and heritage. The secluded bay in Barra's main harbor town, **Castlebay**, shelters the impressive **Kisimul Castle**, ancient seat of Clan Macneil. The ceilidh dances held by its close-knit community are renowned and welcome visitors.

Barra boasts over 1,000 species of **wildflowers** as well as varied fauna, and its waters are home to **dolphins**. Linked by causeway to Barra are the white sands of the nearby **Isle of Vatersay**, which can be seen from Castlebay.

 INFORMATION SOURCES: The tourism office is at Main Street, Castlebay, Isle of Barra, ☎ 1871-810 336; closed in winter.

■ Attractions & Sights

 **Kisimul Castle** (HS; Castlebay, Isle of Barra, ☎ 1871-810 313; open April-Sept, 9:30am-6:30pm; adult/concession/child £3.30/£2.50/£1, includes boat crossing). Kisimul is only surviving medieval castle in the Outer Hebrides. It has been the seat of the Chiefs of Clan Macneil for centuries. The castle was extensively restored in the 20th century, complete with great hall, kitchen, chapel, dungeon and 60-foot tower.

■ Adventures

 Vatersay Walk: From the parking area at the south of Vatersay, cross the road, walk through the gate and head across the sandy machair to the monument to the Annie Jane shipwreck. Descend through the dunes onto West Beach and continue to its southern end. The hilltop site of Dun Vatersay is ahead of you. Walk a short distance to the right, above the rocky shoreline, then strike up left on an old fence-line to the top of the dun.

Descend southeast from the dun. Go through a gate and follow the waymarkers across the open, rocky ground. You reach the remains of an old wall, now overgrown. Follow this wall south, southwest until you see a standing stone ahead. From the stone, descend east toward the sea along a small valley, keeping to its northern side.

Follow the shore round to the beautiful sandy beach of South Bay. Take care to avoid a small but very steep inlet along this part of the shore. At the far end of the beach climb up and head northeast across open, grassy land. The ruins of Eorisdale can be seen to your right. Keep north of the stream that flows toward Eorisdale and head north toward Vatersay Bay. Follow the shoreline west and walk north along the beach. Cut back through the dunes near the north end to return to the parking area (4-5 hours; moderate).

You can rent cycles at **Barra Cycle Hire** (29 St Brendan's Road, Isle of Barra HS9 5XJ, ☎ 1871-810 284).

 Clearwater Paddling (Castlebay, Barra, ☎ 1871-810 443, info@clearwaterpaddling.com, www.clearwaterpaddling.com) offers guided sea kayaking – day-trips and longer expeditions – and walking trips in Barra.

The magnificent shell beach of **Traigh Mhor**, home to Barra's airstrip, is an ideal flat-water windsurfing location (but take note of the restrictions due to the aircraft!).

Barra Fishing Charters (Oiteag na Mara, Bruernish, Isle of Barra HS9 5UY, ☎/fax 1871-890 384) offers trips to uninhabited islands, sea angling and wildlife excursions, and will collect you from Barra or Eriskay.

■ Where To Stay & Eat

See *Accommodation* and *Dining* price charts on pages 465 and 466.

 Castlebay Hotel (Castlebay, Isle of Barra HS9 5XD, ☎ 1871-810 223, fax 1871-810 455, castlebayhotel@aol.com, www.castle-bay-hotel.co.uk; B&B £££, dinner ££) Family hotel overlooking the castle and Kisimul Castle. The bedrooms are comfortable and the pretty dining room serves local seafood and fish landed by local boats.

Isle of Barra Hotel (Isle of Barra HS9 5XW, ☎ 1871-810 383, fax 1871-810 385, barrahotel@aol.com; open end-Mar to early Oct & New Year; B&B ££-£££, dinner ££) Modern family-run hotel enjoying a spectacular location, with most rooms and the restaurant overlooking the wide sandy crescent of Halaman Bay.

Northbay House (Bolnabodach, Isle of Barra HS9 5UT, ☎/fax 1871-890 255, northbayhouse@isleofbarra.com; B&B ££) Comfortable and spacious B&B accommodation in an attractive former school situated beside a quiet loch. There is good home baking.

Islands of St Kilda (Hiort)

 These volcanic islands lie 40 miles to the west of the main Outer Hebrides archipelago and form the last outcrop of Europe's northwest ridge. With their dramatic, foreboding landscape and position as the remotest community in Britain, these islands have long held a special affection – for their poignant history, spectacular seabirds and lonely isolation.

Owned by the National Trust for Scotland, St Kilda was once populated by the hardy Kildians, who due to poverty and starvation were forced to leave the islands in 1930. There is an abandoned village on the island, where the houses remain relatively intact. St Kilda became Scotland's first **World Heritage Site** in 1986.

St Kilda is famous for hosting the most important seabird colony in northwest Europe, with over one million birds, including the largest **gannet** colony in the world on Boreray and adjacent stacks (around 60,000 pairs – a quarter of the world's gannet population); the largest **fulmar** colony in Britain (around 62,000 pairs); and the largest **puffin** colony in Britain (around 140,000 pairs).

The extreme isolation of St Kilda allows only a limited number of species to flourish, although those that do have often evolved unique characteristics. A flock of primitive sheep, found nowhere else in the world, survived on the isolated island of Soay. After the human population was evacuated, some of these sheep were transferred to Hirta, where they now survive completely unmanaged. An unusual form of blackface sheep also survives marooned on Boreray.

The **National Trust for Scotland** (Highlands and Islands Office, ☎ 1463-232 034, fax 1463-732 620, www.kilda.org.uk) takes parties to St Kilda from Oban between mid-May and August to work on restoration and archaeology projects. A two-week project with full board in the restored cottages costs around £500. Apply early (applications close on the 31st of January each year) as demand is high. You can also stay independently on the NTS campsite, which has a wash block but no other facilities; you must take your own food.

Orkney & Shetland

Viking invaders swamped the northern Scottish outposts of Orkney and Shetland and it's the Norse rather than Gaelic influence that dominates here. Orkney and Shetland only became part of Scotland in 1471 after King Christian of Denmark pledged the islands as a dowry on the marriage of his daughter Princess Margaret to Scotland's James III.

Orcadians and Shetlanders aren't pressing for independence but neither do they consider themselves Scottish. Anyone overdoing the traditional "Tartanalia" would probably get laughed all the way back to the ferry, although the northern islanders are happy to help sustain the Gaelic whisky tradition!

High cliffs and massive seabird colonies characterize these island groups. Lochs teem with wild brown trout. Humans have settled these islands for many millennia, as evidenced by the countless ancient monuments. Orkney is lush and fertile; Shetland is more a barren remoteness. Both are outstandingly beautiful and unspoiled. Both maintain vibrant traditions of folk music.

The midsummer sun sets very late at such latitudes and even then, it barely dips below the horizon. There are no real hours of darkness in midsummer – just an extended twilight.

The Orkney Isles

 The Orkney Islands lie off the northern tip of Scotland where the North Sea meets the Atlantic Ocean. Orkney comprises around 70 islands (the exact number is uncertain as many are little more than skerries – small uninhabited islets), of which only 17 are inhabited. The islands are very fertile and, with the exception of Hoy and Rousay, low-lying.

Orkney's largest island is known as **Mainland** and is divided into two areas – northwest and southeast – at the isthmus between Kirkwall and Scapa Bay. The road south over the Churchill Barriers connects Mainland with the islands of Burray and South Ronaldsay.

The Vikings settled Orkney from the 8th century and the Norsemen brought with them their own language – Old Norse – that replaced the indigenous Pictish language. Old Norse developed over the years into Norn, which remained the language of many rural Orcadians until it finally died out in the 18th century.

Orkney boasts an exceptional concentration of archaeological treasures, dramatic coastal scenery, a friendly population and some of the finest local produce in Europe. Orkney has a vibrant cultural scene, exemplified by a full calendar of annual festivals.

Orkney Isles

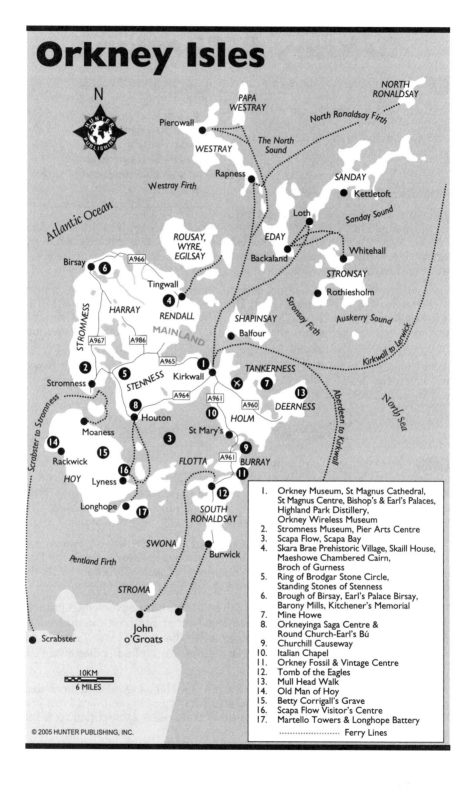

N

PAPA
WESTRAY

NORTH
RONALDSAY

Pierowall

North Ronaldsay Firth

The North
Sound

WESTRAY

Rapness

SANDAY

Kettletoft

Westray Firth

Loth

Sanday Sound

Atlantic Ocean

ROUSAY,
WYRE,
EGILSAY

EDAY

Whitehall

Birsay

A966

Backaland

STRONSAY

Tingwall

Rothiesholm

HARRAY

RENDALL

SHAPINSAY

Auskerry Sound

STROMNESS

A967

A986

MAINLAND

Balfour

Stronsay Firth

Kirkwall to Lerwick

A965

Stromness

STENNESS

Kirkwall

TANKERNESS

A964

A961

A960

DEERNESS

Aberdeen to Kirkwall

North Sea

Houton

A961

HOLM

Moaness

St Mary's

Rackwick

FLOTTA

A961

BURRAY

HOY

Lyness

SOUTH
RONALDSAY

Longhope

SWONA

Burwick

Pentland Firth

STROMA

Scrabster

John
o'Groats

10KM
6 MILES

Scrabster to Stromness

© 2005 HUNTER PUBLISHING, INC.

1. Orkney Museum, St Magnus Cathedral,
   St Magnus Centre, Bishop's & Earl's Palaces,
   Highland Park Distillery,
   Orkney Wireless Museum
2. Stromness Museum, Pier Arts Centre
3. Scapa Flow, Scapa Bay
4. Skara Brae Prehistoric Village, Skaill House,
   Maeshowe Chambered Cairn,
   Broch of Gurness
5. Ring of Brodgar Stone Circle,
   Standing Stones of Stenness
6. Brough of Birsay, Earl's Palace Birsay,
   Barony Mills, Kitchener's Memorial
7. Mine Howe
8. Orkneyinga Saga Centre &
   Round Church-Earl's Bú
9. Churchill Causeway
10. Italian Chapel
11. Orkney Fossil & Vintage Centre
12. Tomb of the Eagles
13. Mull Head Walk
14. Old Man of Hoy
15. Betty Corrigall's Grave
16. Scapa Flow Visitor's Centre
17. Martello Towers & Longhope Battery
    ·················· Ferry Lines

DON'T MISS

Explore Orkney's astonishing **Neolithic sites**: Skara Brae village; the standing stones at Brodgar and Stenness; Maeshowe chambered cairn; and Knap of Howar on Papa Westray, possibly Europe's oldest stone house.

Enjoy quiet contemplation in the atmospheric **Italian Chapel**.

Listen to traditional **folk music** at the annual festival and at informal venues throughout the year.

Feast on Orkney's outstanding **food and drink**, particularly its seafood, lamb, whisky, beer and ice cream.

Visit Kirkwall's striking 12th-century **St Magnus Cathedral**.

Dive in **Scapa Flow** to the sunken wrecks of the German First World War fleet.

Island-hop and walk to **The Old Man of Hoy** and visit the stark ruin of **St Magnus Church** on Egilsay.

Best Freebie: Fishing for **wild brown trout** in Orkney's teeming lochs.

Special Events & Activities

 Orkney Folk Festival (last weekend May; Festival Office, Town House Annex, Stromness, Orkney KW16 3AA, ☎ 1856-851 331, fax 1856-851 636, www.orkneyfolkfestival.com). Enduringly popular programs of traditional and contemporary folk music, including ceilidhs, workshops, talks, concerts and impromptu music, based in Stromness.

Orkney Jazz Festival (April; ☎ 1856-850 298, www.stromnesshotel.com). A program of mainly traditional jazz played by local and guest performers.

St Magnus Festival (June; 60 Victoria Street, Kirkwall, Orkney KW15 1DN, ☎ 1856-871 445, fax 1856-871 170, info@stmagnusfestival.com, www.stmagnusfestival.com). Orkney's long-established midsummer festival of music, art and drama, attracting performers and artists from far and wide.

Orkney Beer Festival (Aug; ☎ 1856-850 298, www.stromnesshotel.com). Try a wide range of cask-conditioned ales, including Orkney's fine local ales and guest beers, at the Stromness Hotel.

Orkney Science Festival (Sept; ☎ 1856-876 214, howie.firth@moray.uhi-.ac.uk, www.oisf.org.uk). Science demonstrations, hands-on activities and debates on topics ranging from astronomy to zoology explore science's links with everyday life. Entertainment includes tours, traditional music, dancing and several ceilidhs. Festival locations include Kirkwall, Stromness and elsewhere in Orkney.

The Ba' (Christmas Day & New Year's Day; ☎ 1856-872 838/872 849, www.bagame.com). Traditional street rugby played by Kirkwall residents divided into "Uppies" and "Doonies," with games raging up and down the town after starting outside St Magnus Cathedral.

The Orkney Isles

Orkney provides superb brown trout fishing in its many lochs (Harray is easily the most famous), which are varied, generally accessible and free. The season runs from 15th March to 6th October. The **Orkney Trout Fishing Association** (☎ 1856-761 586, editorial@orkneytroutfishing.co.uk, www.orkneytroutfishing.co.uk) provides information on where to fish and the best lures and flies to use.

Orkney also provides excellent sport for the sea angler. **Orkney Islands Sea Angling Association** (☎ 1856-811 311, comps@anglingorkney.co.uk, www.anglingorkney.co.uk) organizes trips and rents equipment throughout the year.

 INFORMATION SOURCES: Orkney Tourist Board is at 6 Broad Street, Kirkwall, Orkney KW15 1NX, ☎ 1856-872 856, fax 1856-875 056, info@visitorkney.com, www.visitorkney.com.

Getting Here & Getting Around

■ By Air

 British Airways (☎ 870-850 9850, www.ba.com) operates flights to Kirkwall from Edinburgh, Glasgow, Aberdeen, Inverness and Shetland.

Loganair (☎ 1856-872 494/873 457, www.loganair.co.uk) operates spectacular inter-island flights between Kirkwall and six of Orkney's Northern Isles (Stronsay, Eday, Westray, Papa Westray, Sanday and North Ronaldsay).

■ By Coach & Bus

Scottish Citylink (☎ 870-550 5050, www.citylink.co.uk) operates daily coaches from Inverness to Scrabster connecting with the 7:30pm ferry to Stromness and the 4:15 and 9am ferries from Stromness.

Orkney Coaches (☎ 1856-870 555, www.rapsons.com) operates a bus network from Mainland to South Ronaldsay, most routes not operating on Sunday.

■ By Ferry

Orkney Ferries (☎ 1856-872 044, www.orkneyferries.co.uk) operates services between many of the Orkney islands.

NorthLink Ferries (☎ 845-600 0449, www.northlinkferries.co.uk) operates several services on its luxurious modern car ferries:

Between **Scrabster** and **Stromness** there are three services a day each way Mon-Fri, and two each way Sat-Sun.

There are four **Aberdeen to Kirkwall** sailings a week (Tues, Thurs, Sat & Sun) and three **Kirkwall to Aberdeen** sailings a week (Mon, Wed & Fri).

There are three **Lerwick to Kirkwall** sailings a week (Mon, Wed & Fri) and four **Kirkwall to Lerwick** sailings a week (Tues, Thurs, Sat & Sun).

AUTHOR'S NOTE: A minibus transfer service is available to and from Stromness and Kirkwall to meet with evening arrivals and departures (☎ 845-600 0449 for details).

Pentland Ferries (☎ 1856-831 226, www.pentlandferries.com) operates daily car-ferry services between Gills Bay, about three miles west of John o'Groats, and St Margaret's Hope.

John o'Groats Ferries (☎ 1955-611 353, www.jogferry.co.uk; sailings May-Sept) operates a daily passenger-only ferry between John o'Groats and Burwick. There are four sailings a day from June to the beginning of September and two a day in May and through mid-September. Each sailing connects with a coach service to Kirkwall.

John o'Groats Ferries (orkneybus@jogferry.co.uk; May-Aug) also operates a daily bus and ferry service in summer from Inverness to Kirkwall; the ticket (single/return £28/£40, children half price) includes bus travel from Inverness to John o'Groats, the ferry from John o'Groats to Burwick and bus from Burwick to Kirkwall. There is one service a day during May and two a day from June-Aug.

■ By Car

James D Peace (Junction Road, Kirkwall KW15 1JY, ☎ 1856-872 866, fax 1856-875 300, info@orkneycarhire.co.uk, www.orkneycarhire.co.uk)

John G Shearer (Ayre Service Station, Kirkwall, ☎ 1856-872 950, fax 1856-875 460, jgshearerandsons@talk21.com)

WR Tullock (Castle Street, Kirkwall KW15 1HD, ☎ 1856-876 262, fax 1856-874 458, info@wr-tullock.co.uk, www.orkneycarrental.co.uk)

Norman Brass (Blue Star Filling Station, North End Road, Stromness KW16 3AG, ☎ 1856-850 850, fax 1856-850 985, normanbrass@btconnect.com, www.orkney.org/normanbrass)

Stromness Car Hire (16 John Street, Stromness KW16 3AD, ☎ 1856-850 973, fax 1856-851 777).

Food & Drink

It's a wonder that Orcadians aren't all the size of grizzly bears, such is the quality of the produce caught, reared and harvested on their doorstep. The top-quality seafood doesn't come as a surprise and the local beef and lamb (including the distinctively flavored North Ronaldsay lamb) are as good as you'll find anywhere. The delicious local ice cream and cheese are difficult to stop eating. Orkney Brewery produces excellent beers, especially "Dark Island," but do take care with the appropriately named 8.5% strength "Skull Splitter"! Orkney doesn't have much in common with the Gaelic Highlands, but Highland Park Distillery produces one of the finest single malt whiskies. Don't hold back on eating and drinking while in Orkney – you'll only regret it later.

The Orkney Isles

Kirkwall

Orkney's capital is a busy market town founded in around 1035 by Earl Rognvald Brusason. Its name derives from the Old Norse for "church bay," referring to the town's setting around an attractive bay and a much older church than the present cathedral.

Until the early 20th century, Kirkwall was little more than a single street that wound its way south from the shore, past the cathedral into what is now Victoria Street. This area remains Kirkwall's main commercial district and is known to locals as "up the street" or "doon the toon" depending on where they live. This split of the old town is believed to lie at the root of Kirkwall's famous Ba' street rugby competitions, still played between "Uppies" and "Doonies."

Although Kirkwall has a Castle Street, nothing now remains of the castle (built in the 14th century by the Sinclair Earls) apart from a commemorative plaque. The castle stood at the junction of Albert Street, Castle Street and Broad Street but was destroyed in 1615 after the Earl and his son rebelled against James IV. The surviving ruins were finally demolished in the 19th century.

 INFORMATION SOURCES: The tourism office is at 6 Broad Street, Kirkwall, Orkney KW15 1NX, ☎ 1856-872 856, fax 1856-875 056; open year-round.

■ Attractions & Sights

 **St Magnus Cathedral** (Palace Road, Kirkwall, Orkney, ☎ 1856-874 894; open April-Sept, Mon-Sat, 9am-6pm & Sun, 2-6pm; Oct-Mar, Mon-Sat, 9am-1pm & Sun, 2-5pm; services weekly; donations welcome; guided tours £5, summer only). Earl Rognvald, nephew of the martyred Earl Magnus, founded the cathedral in 1137 as a memorial to his slain uncle. The magnificent building is constructed of red sandstone from just outside Kirkwall and yellow sandstone from Eday; its architecture blends Norman and early Gothic styles. The oldest work is in the choir area, the transepts and the eastern nave.

The remains of St Magnus (southeast choir) and St Rognvald (northeast choir) lie in massive rectangular stone piers, probably placed there in the early 13th century, re-discovered during renovation work in 1919 and re-interred in 1923. Massive Norman pillars dominate the nave, and both nave aisles are lined with many dramatic 17th-century grave slabs, containing many reminders of mortality – coffins, hourglasses, skulls and other bones. Many inscriptions finish with the chilling decree Memento Mori – Remember Death.

St Magnus Centre (Palace Road, Kirkwall, Orkney KW15 1PA, ☎ 1856-878 326; open April-Sept, Mon-Sat, 9:30am-5:30pm & Sun, 1:30-5:30pm, Oct-Mar, Mon-Sat, 12:30-2pm) The recently opened center, adjacent to the cathedral, contains a study and interpretation center for the cathedral, including a 15-minute multilingual film *The Saga of St Magnus*, which celebrates the cathedral and its martyred saint. There is also a bright café overlooking the cathedral grounds.

ST MAGNUS

In the early 12th century, Orkney was ruled jointly by two earls – Earl Magnus and his cousin Earl Haakon. The cousins fought and, in an attempt to make peace, they agreed to meet on the island of Egilsay around 1116 (the exact year isn't known). The jealous Haakon ordered a cook to murder Magnus and seized power. Tales of the sanctity of Magnus soon grew and when Rognvald won the Earldom of Orkney from the son of Haakon in the 1120s, he promised to build a great stone church as a memorial and final resting place for his martyred uncle. Both Magnus and Rognvald were canonized and their remains lie within stone pillars in the cathedral's choir.

Bishop's & Earl's Palaces (HS; Palace Road, Kirkwall, Orkney, opposite St Magnus Cathedral; ☎ 1856-871 918; open April-Sept, 9:30am-6:30pm; adult/concession/child £2.20/£1.60/£0.75). The Bishop's Palace is a 12th-century hall house built by Earl Rognvald at around the same time that he began building the great cathedral of St Magnus. The original palace comprised a stone hall built over a timber-floored basement. Bishop Robert Reid completely rebuilt the great hall in the 16th century, to improve security and upgrade accommodation. The principal addition was the high circular tower dominating the approach from the town and containing the bishop's apartment. Climb the tower for a superb view over the cathedral.

The notorious Patrick Stewart ("Black Pattie") inherited the Earldom of Orkney in 1593 from his father Robert Stewart, an illegitimate son of James V. In around 1600, he began construction of the new Earl's Palace to replace the neighboring Bishop's Palace. The Earl's Palace was built in extravagant Renaissance style with fine turret rooms, and completed in around 1606. Unfortunately, by 1608 Earl Patrick's mounting debts forced him to hand over the barely completed palace to Bishop James Law. In the following year, Patrick was imprisoned in Edinburgh Castle. His son Robert briefly seized the palace in 1614 although it was soon re-taken. Black Pattie and his son were executed for treason in 1615 (Patrick's execution was the last public beheading in Scotland).

Highland Park Distillery (Holm Road, Kirkwall, Orkney KW15 1SU, ☎ 1856-874 619, distillery@highlandpark.co.uk, www.highlandpark.co.uk; open April & Sept-Oct, Mon-Fri, 10am-5pm; May-Aug, Mon-Sat, 10am-5pm & Sun, noon-5pm; Nov-Mar, Mon-Fri, 1pm-5pm; tour and film, adult/concession/child £4/£3/£2.25; film only, £1). Highland Park is the home of Orkney's superb and justifiably popular single malt (one of the author's favorite drams!) which delivers its huge flavor with a smoothness that even whisky novices can enjoy from their first sip. The 12-year-old is fine enough but, if finances permit, try the 18-year-old, the favorite of many distillery workers. Highland Park is one of the few distilleries that still malts its barley (spread out on the floor and periodically turned), which makes a tour worthwhile even for veterans of other distillery tours. The award-winning visitor center includes an excellent video, *The Spirit of Orkney* (which you can watch enjoying a dram), and a cozy café. Regular tours April-Oct, every half-hour, 10am-4pm; and Nov-Mar, Mon-Fri, 2pm only; in-depth tours are available for real enthusiasts – call for details.

The Orkney Isles

Orkney Wireless Museum (Kiln Corner, Junction Road, Kirkwall, Orkney KW15 1LB, ☎ 1856-871 400, sfirth@owm.org.uk, www.owm.org.uk; open April-Sept, Mon-Sat, 10am-4:30pm & Sun, 2-4:30pm; adult/child £2/£1) Displays of historic wartime communications equipment, especially relating to the Scapa Flow naval base, including a spy radio.

Orkney Museum (Tankerness House, Broad Street, Kirkwall, Orkney, ☎ 1856-873 191; open April-Sept, Mon-Sat, 10:30am-5pm; May-Sept also open Sun, 2-5pm; Oct-Mar, Mon-Sat, 10:30am-12:30pm & 1:30-5pm) Housed in one of Kirkwall's finest townhouses, this excellent and surprisingly large museum introduces Orkney's rich history and archaeology. Starting from the early settlements of the Stone, Bronze and Iron Ages, the museum takes you through the Picts, Vikings and Middle Ages, through to the rule of the Earls of Orkney and the present day.

■ Adventures & Tours

 Sail Orkney (20 George Street, Kirkwall, Orkney KW15 1PW, ☎/fax 1856-871 100, www.sailorkney.co.uk). Bareboat yacht charters to explore Orkney's two main cruising areas: the 40 islands and skerries to the north of Mainland, with excellent cruising never far from a safe haven; and Scapa Flow to the south, also surrounded by numerous islands. Charters normally start and finish in Kirkwall, although boats can be delivered to Stromness.

Discover Orkney Tours (44 Clay Loan, Kirkwall, Orkney KW15 1QG, ☎/fax 1856-872 865, john@discoverorkney.com). Guided tours and walks with a local guide.

Wildabout Tours Orkney (5 Clouston Corner, Stenness, Orkney KW16 3LB, ☎/fax 1856-851 011, wildabout@orkney.com; tours Mar-Oct). Full-day and half-day archaeology, history and wildlife tours with varying itineraries; pick-up and drop-off from Stromness and Kirkwall. Tour fees vary but are typically adult/concession £23/£20, plus admission fees.

■ Golf

 Kirkwall Golf Course (18-hole parkland, 5,411 yards; Grainbank, Kirkwall, Orkney KW15 1RD, ☎ 1856-872 457, www.orkneygolfclub.co.uk; green fees £15). An interesting and well situated course on the outskirts of Kirkwall, with marvelous views over the bay, the adjacent islands and lush green fields.

■ Entertainment

Several venues in Kirkwall offer live traditional music during the year. Schedules occasionally vary so call first to confirm.

Albert Hotel (Mounthoolie Lane, ☎ 1856-876 000) has traditional music throughout the year in its Bothy Bar, on Sunday evenings from 8:30pm.

Kirkwall Hotel (Harbour Street, ☎ 1856 872 232) has live traditional music from early June to the end of August, on Wednesday evenings from 9pm.

There are summer Saturday lunchtime (1-2pm) concerts of traditional music in and around **St Magnus Cathedral** (☎ 1856-874 894).

■ Where To Stay & Eat

See *Accommodation* and *Dining* price charts on pages 465 and 466.

 Albert Hotel (Mounthoolie Lane, Kirkwall, Orkney KW15 1JZ, ☎ 1856-876 000, fax 1856-875 397, enquiries@alberthotel.co.uk, www.alberthotel.co.uk; B&B ££-£££, dinner ££). A friendly, cozy hotel in the heart of Kirkwall with attractive bedrooms and a range of dining options. The **Stables Restaurant** offers excellent fine dining; the atmospheric **Bothy** is a traditional bar that serves bar lunches and suppers and has traditional music on Sunday evenings; **Matchmakers** is a modern lounge bar that also serves lunches and suppers.

Kirkwall Hotel (Harbour Street, Kirkwall, Orkney KW15 1LF, ☎ 1856-872 232, fax 1856-872 812, enquiries@kirkwallhotel.com, www.kirkwallhotel.com; B&B ££-£££). Large traditional Victorian hotel prominent on the harbor, with some sea-view rooms. The bar and restaurant serve fresh local produce.

Ayre Hotel (Kirkwall, Orkney KW15 1QX, ☎ 1856-873 001, fax 1856-876 289, ayre.hotel@orkney.com, www.ayrehotel.co.uk; B&B £££, dinner ££-£££). A pretty family-run hotel on Kirkwall's harbor with some sea-view rooms and fresh local produce in the restaurant and bar.

Lav'rockha Guest House (Inganess Road, Kirkwall, Orkney KW15 1SP, ☎/fax 1856-876 103, lavrockha@orkney.com, www.lavrockha.co.uk; B&B ££, dinner ££). Comfortable accommodation and reasonably priced evening meals, close to the Highland Park Distillery.

Foveran Hotel (St Ola, By Kirkwall, Orkney KW15 1SF, ☎ 1856-872 389, fax 1856-876 430, foveranhotel@aol.com, www.foveranhotel.co.uk; B&B £££, dinner ££-£££). Small, family-run hotel and restaurant quietly located overlooking Scapa Flow. The bedrooms are comfortable and well-equipped and the restaurant wins awards.

The Chimes (Blackhill Road, Sunnybank, St Ola, By Kirkwall, Orkney, ☎ 1856-877 623, pettitt@thechimes.fslife.co.uk; B&B ££, dinner ££). Quietly set B&B accommodation two miles from Kirkwall, with views of the harbor, Kirkwall and Scapa Flow. Evening meals are available.

Busters Diner (1 Mounthoolie Place, Kirkwall, Orkney, ☎ 1856-876 717, fax 1856-872 477, bustersdiner@netscapeonline.co.uk; £-££). A large selection of pizzas and other American, Italian, Mexican and vegetarian meals to eat in, take away or for delivery.

Mustard Seed Coffee Shop (86 Victoria Street, Kirkwall, Orkney, ☎ 1856-871 596; £) serves reasonably priced, hearty lunches. Across the road, **Mustard Seed Café** (65 Victoria Street, Kirkwall, ☎ 1856-879 015) serves lighter snacks, including delicious home baking and "fair trade" (a movement promoting better wages and employment opportunities to artisans and farmers worldwide) teas and coffees.

Stromness

Stromness is Orkney's second-largest town and the main port for ferries from Scrabster. The town is architecturally distinctive, with neat rows of stone houses, many with their own small piers and slipways, and twisting paved

The Orkney Isles

streets. Because of its compactness, it's a nicer place to stay than Kirkwall and, despite the transient nature of many visitors, the locals are easy to befriend in the excellent local bars.

 INFORMATION SOURCES: The tourism office is at Ferry Terminal, Stromness, ☎ 1856-850 716, fax 1856-850 777; open year-round, hours follow ferry schedule in winter.

■ Attractions & Sights

Stromness Museum (52 Alfred Street, Stromness, Orkney KW16 3DF, ☎ 1856-850 025; open April-Sept, 10am-5pm; Oct-Mar, Mon-Sat, 11am-3:30pm; adult/concession/child £2.50/£2/£0.50). The museum tells the story of the town from its early days as a safe haven for trading ships, its prosperous war years, large-scale herring fishing and through to the present. Not surprisingly, there is a strong nautical theme, including **The Pilot's House**, which incorporates a recreated captain's parlor and an exhibition on Arctic whaling.

One of the most fascinating displays relates the history of the German First World War fleet sunk in Scapa Flow, together with the stories behind the losses of HMS *Hampshire*, *Vanguard* and *Royal Oak* in Orkney waters. Ship's bells, propellers, sinks and even a toilet, together with crockery and personal items such as caps, pipes and medals bring home the human side of warfare. A separate natural history exhibition displays the diverse wildlife and geology of Orkney.

SINKING OF THE GERMAN FLEET

Germany was forced to surrender its navy as part of the Armistice that ended the First World War. 74 German ships were interned in Scapa Flow while negotiations continued. With most of his sailors sent home and thinking that peace talks had broken down, Admiral von Reuter ordered the scuttling of the German fleet on 21st June 1919. SMS *Friedrich der Grosse* was the first to sink at around noon. By 5pm that afternoon, 52 ships had sunk and the remainder were beached. Most of the ships were salvaged for scrap during the 20s and 30s. The remaining three battleships and four light cruisers now provide a favorite attraction for divers from around the world.

Pier Arts Centre (28-30 Victoria Street, Stromness KW16 3AA, ☎ 1856-850 209, fax 1856-851 462, info@pierartscentre.com; open year-round, Tues-Sat, 10:30am-12:30pm & 1:30-5pm). Contemporary exhibitions and arts events plus a collection of 20th-century British art, located in two attractive waterfront buildings.

■ Adventures

 Scapa Flow, Northern Europe's deepest natural harbor, is ringed by islands and blessed with Orkney's clear waters, which creates the perfect environment for diving. The expanse of almost-land-locked sea in Scapa Flow has served as a harbor since Viking longboats first invaded these waters, and provided a safe anchorage for the Royal Navy during both world wars.

The wrecks of the sunken German First World War fleet provide some of the best wreck-diving in the world, mostly in deep water. For less experienced divers, the ships sunk to block the entrances to Scapa Flow (now more effectively blocked by the Churchill Barriers) provide equally fascinating diving in shallower water. In all cases, there is the opportunity to view teeming underwater life around the wrecks.

The Diving Cellar (4 Victoria Street, Stromness, Orkney KW16 3AA, ☎ 1856-850 055, fax 1856-850 395, leigh@divescapaflow.co.uk, www.divescapaflow.co.uk). Fully equipped dive center offering equipment rental, boat charters and diving packages.

Halton Charters (3 Ness Road, Stromness, Orkney KW16 3DL, ☎ 1856-851 532, bob@mvhalton.co.uk, www.mvhalton.co.uk). Day-boat and live-aboard diving charters in Scapa Flow aboard the 76-foot MV *Halton*.

Scapa Flow Charters (5 Church Road, Stromness, Orkney KW16 3BA, ☎/fax 1856-850 879, www.scapacharters.co.uk). Day-boat and live-aboard diving charters in Scapa Flow and Orkney's North Isles, plus sea fishing and wildlife tours.

Scapa Scuba (Lifeboat House, Dundas Street, Stromness, Orkney KW16 3DA, ☎/fax 1856-851 218, diving@scapascuba.co.uk, www.scapascuba.co.uk). Diving courses and guided dives in Scapa Flow, boat charter, equipment rental and half-day trial dives for complete beginners.

■ Golf

Stromness Golf Course (18-hole links, 4,762 yards; Ness Road, Stromness, Orkney KW16 3DL, ☎ 1856-850 772, www.stromnessgc.co.uk; green fees £15). A challenging course set against the backdrop of the Hoy hills.

■ Entertainment

A couple of Stromness venues offer live traditional music during the year. Schedules vary so call first to confirm.

Ferry Inn (John Street, ☎ 1856-850 280) has traditional and contemporary folk music in its lively bar on Wednesday evenings, starting 9pm, from May to September, and once monthly during the winter.

Stromness Hotel (Victoria Street, ☎ 1856-850 298) has traditional music on Thursday evenings, starting 9pm, from May to September, and regularly throughout the rest of the year.

■ Where To Stay & Eat

See *Accommodation* and *Dining* price charts on pages 465 and 466.

Ferry Inn (John Street, Stromness, Orkney KW16 3AA, ☎ 1856-850 280, fax 1856-851 332, adrian@ferryinn.com, www.ferryinn.com; B&B ££, lunch £, dinner ££-£££). Historic inn with comfortable rooms set by the ferry terminal. The atmospheric bar is decorated with nautical charts, noted for its real ales and vibrant atmosphere, and is regularly acclaimed as one of Scotland's finest pubs. The restaurant menu highlights fine local produce, including Orkney steaks, North Ronaldsay lamb and fresh seafood. The inn is the best place to meet friendly, colorful Orcadians (some of whom take advantage of the all-day license and might be enjoying a pint while you are still having breakfast!). Wednesday folk evenings and other live music complete the inn's impressive credentials.

Stromness Hotel (Victoria Street, Stromness, Orkney KW16 3AA, ☎ 1856-850 298, fax 1856-850 610, info@stromnesshotel.com, www.stromnesshotel.com; B&B £££, dinner ££). Imposing Victorian hotel with bright and spacious rooms, set in the heart of Stromness. The restaurant overlooks the harbor and serves quality local produce. There is a choice of the lounge bar, **Still Room** (a whisky bar, with over 100 malt whiskies) or cozy **Flattie Bar** with its open fire and Orkney ales on tap. The hotel has an attractive rear garden and – a rare luxury in Stromness – a private parking area. The hotel has traditional music on Thursday evenings from May-Sept.

Ferry Bank (2 North End Road, Stromness, Orkney KW16 3AG, ☎ 1856-851 250; B&B £-££). Traditional B&B with views over the harbor and good breakfasts.

Hamnavoe Restaurant (35 Graham Place, Stromness, ☎ 1856-850 606; open April-Sept; dinner only, ££-£££). Atmospheric dining room with an open fire and excellent à la carte menu, with daily specials from local fishing boats.

Julia's Café & Bistro (20 Ferry Road, Stromness, ☎ 1856-850 904; £-££). Good-quality all-day food, including tasty home baking, cappuccinos and more formal evening meals. There is also a cyber café.

Orkney Hamper Company (78 Victoria Street, Stromness, Orkney KW16 3BS, ☎/fax 1856-850 551, enquiries@orkneyhampers.co.uk, www.orkneyhampers.co.uk; £). Superb hampers filled with Orkney's finest produce as well as freshly made sandwiches, rolls and soups, and delicious Orkney ice cream.

Argo's Bakery (50 Victoria Street, Stromness, Orkney KW16 3BS, ☎ 1856-850 245, fax 1856-851 264, sales@argosbakery.co.uk, www.argosbakery.co.uk; £). The bakery produces fine bread, cakes and biscuits, made daily using traditional techniques. The bakery's proprietors also own **The Café** (22 Victoria Street, Stromness, Orkney, ☎ 1856-850 368; £), which offers a selection of snacks, including toasties, pizzas and baked potatoes, to eat on its harbor-view patio or take away.

West & North Mainland

The area of Mainland to the west of Kirkwall contains an astonishing array of prehistoric sites. The extraordinary excavation at Skara Brae Prehistoric Village provides a unique insight into the life of Orcadians 5,000 years ago. The Maeshowe Chambered Cairn, Stones of Stenness and Ring of Brodgar Stone Circle were the greatest monuments of their age in northern Scotland and the northern isles, and stand in testimony to the cultural achievements of the Neolithic peoples of northern Europe. These are considered the **Heart of Neolithic Orkney World Heritage Site**.

AUTHOR'S TIP: *If you plan on visiting several of Orkney's Neolithic monuments, you can save money with an **Orkney Pass** from Historic Scotland (☎ 131-668 8600, www.historic-scotland.gov.uk), which manages many of these properties: adult / concession / child / family £12 / £9 / £3.50 / £24 (less when the Broch of Birsay is closed). The pass remains valid until you have visited all of the sites.*

■ Attractions & Sights

Skara Brae Prehistoric Village (HS; 19 miles northwest of Kirkwall on the B9056, ☎ 1856-841 815; open April-Sept, 9:30am-6:30pm; Oct-Mar, Mon-Sat, 9:30am-4:30pm & Sun, 2-4:30pm; adult/concession/child £4/£3/£1.20; joint ticket with neighboring Skaill House, adult/concession/child £5/£3.75/£1.30). Northern Europe's best-preserved Neolithic village contains houses and a workshop connected by low passageways. They retain their original stone furnishings, and provide an extraordinary insight into ancient life on Orkney. The site was first uncovered in the winter of 1850 when a wild storm lashed the Bay of Skaill and tore grass and sand from a high dune, revealing the 5,000-year-old farming village below.

Skara Brae is remarkable because it is so well preserved. Many houses (and their contents) survived largely intact because they were made of stone. A reconstructed house forms an entrance to the village, although the original site is so well preserved it requires little imagination to picture what life must have been like all those millennia ago. Each house has the same internal structure comprising a single spacious room with a hearth in the middle, box beds to the side and a large dresser opposite the door. Small cells possibly served as storage or were used as toilets.

It's not known where the Skara Brae villagers originated from, but it's clear they settled here because of the region's rich fertile soil. They grazed cattle, grew crops and gathered wild berries and herbs. Deer and boar roamed the land, the lochs and sea were filled with fish, and nesting seabirds provided meat and eggs. To help bring home the overwhelming antiquity of the site, a useful time-line connects the reconstructed house to the original village. Stonehenge (2100 BC) and even the Giza Pyramids (2500 BC) are positively recent compared with Skara Brae's 3100 BC vintage. Skara Brae was inhabited for around 600 years, from 3100 BC to 2500 BC. Just as nobody knows where the settlers came from, nobody knows why the site was abandoned – a mystery that adds to the site's fascination. The visitor center provides a helpful audiovisual presentation and displays original artifacts.

Skaill House (HS; 19 miles northwest of Kirkwall on the B9056, ☎ 1856-841 815, open April-Sept, 9:30am-6:30pm, entrance by joint ticket with neighboring Skara Brae Prehistoric Village: adult/concession/child £5/£3.75/£1.30). Skaill House is most famous as being the home of William Graham Watt, 7th Laird of Breckness, who was the first to discover traces of his long-lost neighbors at nearby Skara Brae and exhibited findings from the site in his dining

The Orkney Isles

room. Skaill was built in 1620 for Bishop George Graham, though the house is presented in its 1950s state when the Scarth family lived here.

Ring of Brodgar Stone Circle (HS; five miles northeast of Stromness on the B9055, ☎ 1856-841 815; open at all times). The Ring of Brodgar is a magnificent circular late-Neolithic or early-Bronze-Age stone ring. It comprises a huge circle of upright stones with an enclosing ditch spanned by causeways, constructed sometime between 2500 and 2000 BC.

The circle is 340 feet (104 m) wide and originally had 60 tall stones erected on it, of which 36 still stand as stones or stumps. Archaeologists believe that the builders of Brodgar were the descendants of those who constructed the Stones of Stenness, disposed of their dead in Maeshowe Chambered Cairn and lived in settlements like Skara Brae.

Little excavation has taken place at Brodgar and there is little direct evidence indicating its use. It is believed that ancient community ceremonies took place here. It has also been suggested that the site was used for lunar observations, although again there is little evidence to support this. One of the stones was struck by lightning on 5th June 1980 causing it to shatter. Similar lightning strikes might also account for the damaged state of several other stones in the ring.

Maeshowe Chambered Cairn (HS; nine miles west of Kirkwall on the A965, ☎ 1856-761 606; entrance by guided tour, open April-Sept, 9:30am-6:30pm; Oct-Mar, Mon-Sat, 9:30am-4:30pm & Sun, 2pm-4:30pm; adult/concession/child £3/£2.30/£1). Maeshowe is the finest chambered tomb in Britain, comprising a huge mound covering a stone passage and large burial chamber with cells recessed in the walls. The Neolithic cairn is estimated to be 5,000 years old and was constructed with amazing precision from huge sandstone slabs. The burial mound measures 115 feet (35 m) across and 23 feet (7 m) high. Around it is a ditch nearly 46 feet (14 m) wide and 7 feet (2 m) deep. In the 12th century, Vikings broke into the cairn and inscribed the interior walls with Viking graffiti – 24 groups of stone-carved runes forming the best such collection in the world.

Excavations only revealed small pieces of a skull and some horse bones, although evidence from similar structures suggests Maeshowe's use as a burial site (the original bones may have been removed when the Vikings broke in). Archaeologists also believe the site may have had uses beyond burial, for instance to make offerings to gods or ancestors.

The passage aligns with the mid-winter sunset; at the end of the shortest day of the year, the setting sun shines into the chamber. A live webcam of the sun shining into the chamber can be viewed at www.maeshowe.co.uk during a two-month period from early December.

Standing Stones of Stenness (HS; five miles northeast of Stromness on the B9055, ☎ 1856-841 815; open at all times). The ruin of a ring of huge stones surrounded by the remains of a circular earthen bank. Sometime between 3000 and 2000 BC people set up these 12 great stones, the tallest being 19 feet (5.7 m) high, in an ellipse pointing a little west of north. Around the stones, they dug a ditch 20 feet (6 m) wide and about 7.5 feet (2.3 m) deep. Archaeologists found pottery, cremated bone (animal or human) and evidence of fire in the small, central slab setting – possibly offerings or burial ceremonies. Near the stones are signs of much later activity. Pits were dug and in their fill was pottery similar to the jars found in nearby Iron Age settlements of 3,000 years later.

A short distance east of the Standing Stones of Stenness are the remains of **Barnhouse**, a partly-reconstructed Stone Age village of 3000 BC, thought to be the homes of the builders of Maeshowe and the Stenness Stones.

Broch of Gurness (HS; Aikerness, 14 miles northwest of Kirkwall on the A966, ☎ 1856-751 414; open April-Sept, 9:30am-6:30pm, closed 12:30-1:30pm; adult/concession/child £3/£2.30/£1). Brochs – tall, dry-stone towers, each with surrounding villages and encircling defenses – dominated the Orcadian landscape during the last centuries BC. Although some 500 examples have been found in northern and western Scotland, brochs with sizeable villages like Gurness are particular to Orkney and northern Caithness on the Scottish mainland.

Around 2,000 years ago, Gurness was a busy farming village and probably one of the most important settlements in Orkney. The impressive remains of the broch include not only the tower and surrounding houses but also a later Pictish farm and Viking burial site. At the heart of the complex stands the tower, with walls perhaps originally over 30 feet (10 m) tall, surrounded by a deep ditch and stone-faced wall. Between the wall and tower stand the remains of as many as 14 houses. The houses had no windows and were entered from a shared passage. Inside each was a hearth, large floor-standing tank, store cupboards, cubicles and sleeping chambers, separated by screens of upright flagstones. The houses are well preserved and it's not difficult to imagine the dark, smoky conditions their inhabitants must have endured here.

During excavations in the 1930s, archaeologists discovered several collapsed buildings around the central broch, dating from the Iron Age or Pictish (5th-8th century) era. The best preserved of these is nicknamed the "shamrock" because of its distinctive shape. The building has a single low entrance leading into a small room with a central hearth, from which four chambers radiate. Long after the broch was abandoned, the area was re-used by the Vikings as a cemetery; a stone-lined grave of a pagan woman who was buried with jewelry and some metal tools is still visible.

Brough of Birsay (HS; on a tidal island at Birsay, 20 miles northwest of Kirkwall off the A966, ☎ 1856-721 205, Earl's Palace, Birsay; open 11th June to 30th Sept, 9:30am-6:30pm, subject to tides; adult/concession/child £1.80/£1.30/£0.50). Picts were already farming the Birsay area before the Norse settlers arrived. The Brough of Birsay was a Pictish and Norse power base and contains a Pictish well, replica carving, extensive remains of Norse houses and the ruins of a 12th-century church. The island can be accessed by a concrete causeway for approximately two hours on either side of low tide (no boat access is available). Check tide tables at Skara Brae (☎ 1856-841 815) and take care in windy conditions.

Earl's Palace Birsay (HS; Birsay on the A966, ☎ 1856-721 205/841 815; open at all times). These are the remains of a residence constructed by Robert Stewart (1533-93), Earl of Orkney, in the 16th century and completed by his son. The compound comprises four ranges of buildings set around an open courtyard with projecting towers at three of the four corners. The palace stood as a monument to Robert's royal pretensions and the tyrannical way in which he administered his estate (although his son, Earl Patrick, proved even more of a despot). The palace was used only occasionally by later earls and by the 18th century had fallen into disrepair.

Kitchener's Memorial (Marwick Head, Birsay). Field Marshal Earl Kitchener of Khartoum, the British Minister of War, was on board HMS *Hampshire* in June 1916 on his way to make a morale-boosting visit to troops in Russia when the ship hit a mine and exploded. Most of the men aboard perished and Kitchener's body, like those of many others on board, was never recovered. This memorial to Kitchener was raised by the people of Orkney on a high cliff at Marwick Head.

Barony Mills (Boardhouse Loch, Birsay, Orkney, ☎ 1856-721 439/771 276; open April-Sept, 10am-1pm & 2-5pm; adult/concession/family £1.50/£1/£4). This is the last working water-powered meal mill in Orkney and dates from 1873. There have been mills on this site since Viking times and the names of millers have been written on the wall.

■ Adventures

The superb **Marwick Head** walk takes you high above breathtaking cliffs overlooking crashing Atlantic waves and thousands of seabirds, and passes Kitchener's Memorial. Start from the parking area at the end of the track to Mar Wick, about eight miles north of Stromness, off the B9056 between Birsay and the Bay of Skaill.

Walk north (with the sea on your left) along the bay, through a pair of kissing gates (cleverly designed to allow people to go through easily, while blocking livestock) and onto a grassy coastal path. The path soon begins to ascend onto increasingly higher cliffs. Take care near the cliff edges as they aren't protected and it's a very long way down! The cliff-top path is alive with color in late spring when the wild flowers are at their best; look for the many rabbits that scurry about here.

After passing the Kitchener Memorial continue along the cliff-top until you reach a gate where you follow a path to your right (inland). This leads down to a parking area at a road where you again turn right to return to Mar Wick, the two kissing gates and the starting point; 2 hours; easy.

East & South Mainland

Southeast of Kirkwall, Mainland is largely agricultural and is connected to the islands of Burray and South Ronaldsay by the road over the Churchill Barriers.

■ Attractions & Sights

Mine Howe (Tankerness, Orkney, ☎ 1856-861 234/861 209, www.mine-howe.com; open May, Sun & Wed, 11am-3pm; June-Aug, 11am-5pm; early Sept, daily, 11am-4pm; late Sept, Sun & Wed, 11am-2pm; adult/child £2.50/£1.25). A mysterious structure comprising three sunken chambers 20 feet below ground. Access is by two steep, ladder-like staircases. At the bottom of the first are two long, low chambers, from which a second flight of steps leads to a drop of about five feet into the lower chamber. The purpose of the structure is unknown, although it is possible it was associated with ritual or religion – entry into the underworld perhaps? An investigation in 2000 by the

Channel 4 series *Time Team* concluded it probably had a ritual significance – possibly as a shrine.

Orkneyinga Saga Centre, Round Church & Earl's Bú (Orphir, just off the A964 east of Houton; open year-round, 9am-5pm). This is the scene of the *Orkneyinga Saga* – the stories of successive Earls of Orkney, many of whom were as powerful as kings. The *Saga* was written in Old Norse (similar to modern Icelandic) around 1200. Written mainly for entertainment, the *Saga* tells stirring tales of heroism, women and fearless seafaring, and is explained in the audiovisual presentation, *An Orkney Saga*.

The ruined round church is almost certainly the church mentioned in the *Orkneyinga Saga*. Its circular shape is unique among surviving Scottish medieval churches and may have been inspired by the rotunda of the church of the Holy Sepulchre in Jerusalem. The church remained in use until 1705 when it was replaced by a new building. The original church was used for storage until 1756 when two-thirds of the rotunda was pulled down to provide stone to repair the new church.

The nearby 12th-century ruins of the Earl's Bú manor house of the Norse Earls of Orkney comprise a group of farm buildings, a drinking hall, storerooms and chambers.

 **Churchill Causeways** (along the A961 south of Mainland, connecting it with the islands of Burray and South Ronaldsay). During both World Wars, ships were sunk to block the narrow channels that lead into Scapa Flow between the southern islands (some of the sunken ships are still visible). After a U47 submarine evaded the defenses to sink HMS *Royal Oak* in October 1939 with the loss of 833 lives, British Prime Minister Winston Churchill ordered that the Eastern approaches should be permanently closed to protect the fleet. It was a considerable feat of engineering to link the five islands and required causeways 9,150 feet long and up to 70 feet deep. Wire cages filled with rock ("bolsters") were fixed to the seabed to prevent them from being washed away by fast and powerful currents. Layers of large concrete blocks capped the structures. The causeways took four years to complete (built with the help of Italian POWs) and were opened in May 1945. The causeways today form part of the road network connecting South Ronaldsay and Burray to the Orkney Mainland.

Italian Chapel (Lamb Holm on the A961; open April-Sept, 9am-10pm; Oct-Mar, 9am-4:30pm). This jewel of trompe l'oeil painting and sculpture, disguised within an unassuming exterior, is an outstanding testament to human artistry and resourcefulness, crafted as it was by Italian prisoners of war from a couple of Nissen huts, barbed wire, bully beef cans and other assorted junk and debris. The chapel is the only surviving building from Camp 60 on Lamb Holm, which housed Italian POWs brought in to help build the Churchill Causeways.

The artistic genius behind the chapel was Domenico Chiocchetti, who placed the huts end-to-end and transformed the interior into a magnificent place of worship, incorporating pictorial and decorative work, altar, tabernacle, candlesticks, lamps, colored glass and ornamental woodwork. Above the altar is Chiocchetti's masterpiece based on Nicolo Barabino's *Madonna of the Olives*.

The chapel was only used for a short time as the prisoners were moved away for repatriation in May 1945 (Chiocchetti remained to finish the font). The Lord Lieutenant of Orkney promised the prisoners that Orcadians would cherish and maintain their chapel, and it remains a special and moving place.

Orkney Fossil & Vintage Centre (Viewforth, Burray, Orkney KW17 2SX, ☎ 1856-731 255; open April-Sept, 10am-6pm; adult/concession £2/£1). The museum houses a collection of fossils, many dating from the Devonian period 300-350 million years ago. Fossils are displayed from Orkney and Caithness (mainly of fish) and from around the world. Ultraviolet light shows off a small display of minerals to good effect. Upstairs is a rather unfocused museum. The archive room contains evocative old photographs and books and is well worth a browse. However, the "vintage" displays appear somewhat haphazard, including domestic, agricultural and war-related items, together with a curious collection of box cameras. There is a small gift shop and good café serving hot and cold snacks, lunches and high teas.

Tomb of the Eagles (Liddle, South Ronaldsay, Orkney KW17 2RW, seven miles south of St Margaret's Hope, ☎ 1856-831 339, info@tomboftheeagles-.co.uk, www.tomboftheeagles.co.uk; open April-Oct, 9:30am-6pm & Nov-Mar, 10am-noon, other times by arrangement; adult/concession/child £3.50/£3/£1.50). Family-run museum exhibiting finds from a 5,000-year-old cliff-top Stone Age tomb (entered by pulling yourself through a low tunnel lying on a skateboard). Sea-eagle talons found in the tomb are believed to be the emblem of these people – hence the name. Visitors have the unique and slightly strange opportunity to handle some of the original Neolithic artifacts, such as skulls and other bones, during the talks.

■ Adventures

On Foot

The circular walk to **Mull Head** (near Deerness) on the East Mainland follows a dramatic coastline ringed by towering cliffs and offering some fine viewpoints out to sea. Start from The Gloup parking area, signposted beyond the end of the B9050, near Skaill, about 13 miles southeast of Kirkwall on the A960.

The Gloup is a partially collapsed sea cave and from its viewing platforms you can sea and hear the surf as it crashes into the precipitous chasm below. Follow the path toward the sea (east) and follow the coastline left (north). Just before a mile, you reach the ruins of the **Brough of Deerness**, believed to be an old Norse settlement. The ruins are only accessible by a steep and narrow rocky path. You can make out the outlines of several buildings on its grassy summit, including a small stone chapel.

Take care on the cliff path as it narrows in places. Rounding a headland, you reach Mull Head, standing at 155 feet, which provides a great cliff-top viewpoint. Continuing along the cliffs, the path turns south. Turn left uphill (southeast) along a fence and pass through a pair of kissing gates. Follow the path downhill and back to the parking area (time 2½-3 hours, grade: easy).

In & On the Water

Scapa Flow Diving Centre (Cara 3, Grimness, South Ronaldsay, Orkney, ☎/fax 1856-831 821, dave@scapaflowdivingcentre.co.uk). Diving from South Ronaldsay, as well as sea fishing and wildlife tours.

Roving Eye Boat Trips (Houton Pier, Westrow Lodge, Orphir, Orkney KW17 2RD, ☎ 1856-811 360, weather updates 1856-811 309, fax 1856-811 737, k2bichan@aol.com, www.orknet.co.uk/rov; Easter-Sept, daily at 1:20pm, weather permitting; adult/child £25/£12.50). View underwater wildlife and the sunken wrecks of the German WWI fleet without having to dive. Three-hour cruises visit the site of the SMS *Dresden*, SMS *Köln* and *Escort F2*; a remote-operated vehicle maneuvers to one of the wrecks and sends back high-quality video images viewed on monitors. On the way back you'll pass seal colonies.

■ Entertainment

Sands Hotel (Burray, Orkney, ☎ 1856-731 298) has traditional music on the last Saturday of each month, starting at 9pm. Call ahead for details.

Hoy

Hoy means "High Island" in Old Norse. This is the second-largest island in Orkney; the north and west of Hoy are hilly and "Highland" in character, whereas the south and east are low-lying and more typical of Orkney.

The north has some spectacular sea cliff scenery, including Orkney's most famous landmark – the sea stack the **Old Man of Hoy**. A short distance north of the Old Man rises **St John's Head**, the highest vertical cliff in Britain. The summits of **Ward Hill** (the highest point in the Orkney Isles at 1,570 feet/479 m) and the neighboring Cuilags have a sub-Arctic glaciated environment. From the summit of Ward Hill you can see every Orkney island except Rysa Little, which – ironically – is the nearest.

 Orkney Ferries (☎ 1856-872 044, www.orkneyferries.co.uk) operates a car-ferry service between Houton Terminal on Mainland (Orphir, ☎ 1856-811 397) and Lyness in south Hoy, with several sailings a day during the week and a reduced weekend schedule.

There is also a passenger- and cycle-only service between Stromness and Moaness Pier in north Hoy (via Graemsay). The service operates several times a day during the week and twice a day on weekends.

North Hoy Transport (☎ 1856-791 315/791 261), **Bu Farm** (☎ 1856-791 263) and **Glen Rackwick** (☎ 1856-791 262) run minibus and taxi services.

You can rent **bicycles** at Moaness Pier (☎ 1856-791 225).

■ Attractions & Sights

Old Man of Hoy (Rora Head, near Rackwick), the famous 450-foot (280-m) sea stack, is Orkney's most recognized landmark and is clearly visible from the ScrabsterStromness ferry. The Old Man is the remains of a collapsed natural arch carved by the sea through a narrow promontory; it was first climbed in 1966 in a televised ascent and remains a Mecca for visitors, although in time it too will erode and collapse. The Old Man and all the surrounding cliffs swarm with nesting seabirds (kittiwakes, fulmars, guillemots, razorbills, shags, puffins and skuas) during spring and early summer.

Scapa Flow Visitor Centre & Museum (Lyness, Hoy, ☎ 1856-791 300; open year-round, Mon-Fri, 9am-4:30pm; and Sat-Sun, 10:30am-4pm, mid-May to Sept; donations requested). This small but interesting museum occupies what was once the pump house of the Royal Navy's **Lyness Naval Base**. The fascinating story of Scapa Flow is told through an audiovisual presentation, photographs and many original artifacts retrieved from wrecks. A short distance inland is the **Lyness Naval Cemetery**, in which lie many heroes from famous naval tragedies, including the Battle of Jutland (1916), the sinking of the *Hampshire* by a mine off Birsay (1916), blowing up of the *Vanguard* off Flotta (1917) and the torpedoing of the *Royal Oak* in Scapa Flow (1939).

Martello Towers & Longhope Battery (Longhope Bay, southeast end of Hoy). Only the Hackness (south) Tower is open to the public (HS; ☎ 1856-841 815; April-Sept, 9:30am-6:30pm; adult/concession/child £3/£2.30/£1). The towers were built in 1813-15 on either side of Longhope Bay to protect Baltic convoys assembling in the Sound of Longhope against French and American privateers. Renovated in 1866, they were also used during the First World War.

Dwarfie Stane (HS; two miles southwest of Moaness in the north of Hoy, ☎ 1856-841 815). A huge block of sandstone, in which a Neolithic burial chamber has been cut, and which it is possible to access.

Betty Corrigall's Grave (midway between Moaness and Lyness in the east of Hoy) is the grave of a young Lyness girl who took her own life after being abandoned pregnant by a visiting sailor. She was buried in this lonely spot away from hallowed ground on the parish boundary.

■ Adventures

The long walk to the **Old Man of Hoy** (13 miles round-trip) passes through the pretty township of Rackwick before arriving at some of Britain's highest sea cliffs and one of Orkney's best known landmarks. For a shorter walk, take the bus or a taxi to Rackwick, from where it is a round-trip of five miles (around three hours) to the Old Man.

Start from Moaness Pier, where the Stromness ferry docks. Follow the road directly inland and then uphill. Continue straight on at the "No Mountain Bikes on Path" sign (where the road turns sharply right), and skirt along the base of Ward Hill, Orkney's highest hill at 1,565 feet.

You reach **Berriedale Wood** (the northernmost native woodland in Britain) on your right after about three miles. Continue along a rough moorland path to eventually rejoin the road to Rackwick, a remote crofting township, which until recently was largely abandoned. Take some time to appreciate the splendor of the Rackwick valley, set beside a sand and boulder beach and bounded by high cliffs and steep heathery hills.

Continue through Rackwick along the faint path behind the hostel. The path climbs steeply around the peak of Moor Fea on your right before descending gradually toward the cliffs opposite the Old Man; take care near the cliff edge. Return by the same way (5-8 hours; moderate).

Louise Budge (Stoneyquoy Farm, Lyness, Hoy, Orkney KW16 3NY, ☎ 1856-791 234, visithoy@talk21.com, www.visithoy.com) offers tours of Hoy in a six-passenger people carrier, meeting the morning ferry from Houton, serving lunch on her 200-acre farm and returning you for the afternoon ferry from Lyness. Booking is essential.

Hills of Hoy (Lyness, Hoy, Orkney KW16 3NY, ☎ 1856-791 240, fax 1856-791 027). Island tours by arrangement in seven- or eight-seater mini buses. Taxi services are also available.

■ Wildlife Watching

 The Hoy Ranger (Ley House, Hoy, Orkney KW16 3NJ, ☎/fax 1856-791 298, chris.rodger@rspb.co.uk) provides free, guided walks by arrangement through areas such as Rackwick, Ward Hill and Berriedale.

Shapinsay

Shapinsay (pronounced "shaping-see") is a low-lying, green and fertile island whose calm bays were used by King Haakon's Viking fleet in 1263 on the way to the Battle of Largs. The island has a number of storm beaches or "ayres" – areas of saltwater cut off from the sea by narrow strips of land. There are examples at Vasa Loch on the west coast and Lairo Water in the middle of Veantro Bay on the north coast. The island is home to impressive Balfour Castle and Balfour village was built in the late 18th century to house estate workers.

Orkney Ferries (☎ 1856-872 044, www.orkneyferries.co.uk) operates regular daily car-ferry sailings between Kirkwall and Shapinsay.

■ Attractions & Sights

Balfour Castle (Shapinsay, Orkney KW17 2DY, ☎ 1856-711 282, fax 1856-711 283, balfourcastle@btinternet.com, www.balfourcastle.co.uk; adult/child £17/£8.50, including ferry, tour and afternoon tea). The turreted Victorian castle and its gardens is open for tours on Sundays in summer, guided by a family member; you'll also enjoy afternoon tea in the Servants' Hall with home baking, local cheese and homemade jams.

Burroughston Broch (south of the northeastern point of Shapinsay). Iron Age broch with a cell and well, excavated in the 1860s. The site is a good point from which to view seals.

Shapinsay Heritage Centre (The Smithy Café & Craft Shop, Balfour Village, Shapinsay, ☎ 1856-711 722; open Mar-Dec, lunch £, dinner £). Displays of photographs, documents and artifacts from the island's past, in a building that originally housed the village smithy, with a sail loft above.

■ Adventures

The RSPB has built an observation hide overlooking the **Mill Dam Wetland Reserve**, half a mile north of Balfour Village. The reserve is home to many breeding birds, including pintails and other ducks, waders, black-headed gulls and water rails. Whooper swans and greylag geese winter here.

Groat's Charters (Houseby, Shapinsay, ☎/fax 1856-711 254, enquiries@orkneyangling.co.uk, www.orkneyangling.co.uk). Fishing trips, island trips and fishing holidays throughout the year.

Rousay

Rousay (pronounced "roe-see") is an unusually hilly and glaciater-scoured island containing some of the richest and best-preserved prehistoric monuments in Orkney. Much of the island is designated a **Site of Special Scientific Interest**. In particular, the northwest coast has a range of exciting cliff formations as well as a rich variety of wildflowers.

Quandale and **Westness** in Rousay are the only townships in Orkney to have suffered major clearances. The wild and open landscape of Quandale includes relics of turf dykes and ruined crofts. In the mid-19th century, the laird evicted 210 people from Westness in an attempt to modernize his estate.

Orkney Ferries (☎ 1856-872 044, www.orkneyferries.co.uk) operates regular daily car-ferry services between Tingwall Terminal on Mainland (Evie, ☎/fax 1856-751 360), Rousay and the neighboring islands of Wyre and Egilsay.

A **Postbus** operates (Mon-Sat) on the island's circular road; its schedule coincides with ferry arrivals.

■ Attractions & Sights

Trumland Visitor Centre (ferry terminal, Rousay, ☎ 1856-821 398). Exhibition on the islands of Rousay, Wyre and Egilsay, including detailed information and interpretation of the islands' many ancient sites.

Knowe of Yarso Chambered Cairn (HS; three miles west from the pier, Rousay, ☎ 1856-841 815). An oval cairn with concentric walls enclosing a Neolithic chambered tomb, which was divided into three compartments and which once contained the remains of 29 bodies. This is the highest of the Orkney tombs and has great views over Eynhallow Sound and south toward Mainland and Hoy.

Midhowe Broch & Cairn (HS; near Scabra Head, five miles northwest from the pier, Rousay, ☎ 1856-841 815). The best-preserved broch in Orkney, dating from the Bronze/Iron Age, with the remains of later buildings around it. Three brochs were built at different stages, originally as defensive dwellings. Much evidence survives of the internal appearance of the houses. The adjacent huge and impressive Stone Age cairn (the "Great Ship of Death") has 25 stalls within an oval mound (now protected by a barn). It contained the remains of 25 people and is the largest known cairn of its kind. Access is very steep; follow the black-and-white poles.

Taversöe Tuick Chambered Cairn (HS; half a mile west from the pier, Rousay, ☎ 1856-841 815; admission free). A Neolithic chambered cairn with the unusual arrangement of two burial chambers, one above the other (the only other example in Orkney is on Eday). Access to the chambers can be muddy.

■ Adventures

 The **Westness Walk** of just over a mile heads north from Westness House, a historic 17th-century laird's house on the west coast. It spans a rich area of archaeological monuments, including settlements from the first Stone Age settlers, Pictish Iron Age, Viking invaders, the period of the Earls and the troubled crofting times (1 hour; easy).

Faraclett Head is a circular coastal path high above hidden cliffs with excellent views over neighboring Egilsay. The walk starts from the parking area at the end of the road to Faraclett in northeast Rousay. Walk uphill and turn left before the house on your right. Follow the faint waymarked path and cross a stile and cairn on your left. Follow the path to your right to Faraclett Head, which has distinctive terraces created by glaciation. Don't venture close to the cliffs on the northwest side of the headland as these overhang. The path crosses two stiles and returns to Faraclett. Look for the massive Yetnasteen standing stone below the path shortly before you arrive back at Faraclett (1-2 hours; easy).

Rousay Traveller History Tours (Bellona, Rousay, Orkney KW17 2PU, ☎/fax 1856-821 234; adult/concession/child £15/£10/£6, excluding ferry; tours June-Aug, Tues-Fri). A minibus meets the 10:40 am ferry from Tingwall and takes you on an exploration of Rousay's archaeology, history, wildlife and folklore. Picnics are available at additional cost. Depart Rousay 5:30pm, earlier if desired.

Wyre

Wyre (meaning "Spearhead" on account of its angular shape) is only two miles long but is steeped in Viking history.

 Orkney Ferries (☎ 1856-872 044, www.orkneyferries.co.uk) operates regular daily car-ferry services between Tingwall Terminal on Mainland (Evie, ☎/fax 1856-751 360), Wyre, and the neighboring islands of Rousay and Egilsay.

■ Attractions & Sights

Cubbie Roo's Castle & St Mary's Chapel (HS; half-mile from the Wyre pier). This is one of the earliest stone castles in Scotland, built in about 1145 by the Norseman Kolbein Hruga (the giant Cubbie Roo of *Orkneyinga Saga* legend), and is a small rectangular tower enclosed within a circular ditch. The well-preserved ruined chapel dates from the late 12th century and is in Romanesque style. It was founded by either Cubbie Roo or his son Bjarni, Bishop of Orkney.

Wyre Heritage Centre (midway along the Wyre road). Photos and memories of Wyre life in times past and a special section on Cubbie Roo.

Egilsay

Egilsay (pronounced "aye-gul-see") etched its place in history as the site of the peace meeting in around 1116 between Earl Magnus and his cousin Earl Haakon. Haakon murdered Magnus at a spot now marked by a cenotaph. Magnus was later canonized and Kirkwall's magnificent cathedral built in his memory. St Magnus Church was built for the many pilgrims who visited the site and its dramatic ruin serves as a continuing reminder of the Viking heritage of these islands.

Orkney Ferries (☎ 1856-872 044, www.orkneyferries.co.uk) operates regular daily car-ferry services between Tingwall Terminal on Mainland (Evie,

☎/fax 1856-751 360), Egilsay and the neighboring islands of Wyre and Rousay.

■ Attractions & Sights

 St Magnus Church (HS; half a mile from the pier, Egilsay, ☎ 1856-841 815; admission free). The dramatically sited ruin of a complete but roofless 12th-century Norse church with a round tower. It's one of only two remaining examples of Viking round-towered churches.

Stronsay

Stronsay (pronounced "stroan-see") is a low-lying island about seven miles long, fringed by a number of lovely sandy beaches. Deeply indented by three large bays, the island is often described as being "all arms and legs." The southeastern coast between Odiness Point and Lamb Head has magnificent cliff scenery, including the Vat of Kirbuster, a gaping hole in the cliff (known as a *gloup*) spanned by the finest natural arch in Orkney.

Kelp production was Stronsay's major industry during the 18th century. In the 19th century, Whitehall village became one of Scotland's major herring ports. Its harbor was a forest of 300 boat masts and its several curing stations employed hundreds. Unfortunately, the herring disappeared and the industry declined in the 1930s.

Loganair (☎ 1856-872 494/873 457, www.loganair.co.uk) operates twice-daily flights (Mon-Sat) between Kirkwall and Stronsay.

Orkney Ferries (☎ 1856-872 044, www.orkneyferries.co.uk) operates daily car-ferry services between Kirkwall and Whitehall on Stronsay (via Eday).

DS Pearce (Samson's Lane, Stronsay, ☎ 1857-616 335) has rental vehicles and provides a taxi service.

■ Attractions & Sights

Stronsay Fish Mart (Whitehall, Stronsay, ☎ 1857-616 386; open year-round, hours vary – call ahead). The renovated fish market houses information on the herring industry, a café and hostel.

Lamb Ness & Lamb Head (at the southeastern point of Stronsay, six miles from Whitehall). A beautiful promontory dotted with interesting archaeological sites, including "Pict Houses," and home to myriad seabirds. At the neck of the isthmus is **Danes Pier**, a natural rock structure said to be once the site of a Norse harbor but now a haven for seals.

Vat of Kirbuster (between Odiness Point and Lamb Head on the southeastern coast of Stronsay, five miles from Whitehall). A superb example of a *gloup* – a hole in the rock spanned by a natural arch. The coastal scenery is superb but take care on the high cliffs.

Papa Stronsay, a small island off the northeastern coast, is home to Orkney's monks and has many historic sites and plenty of wildlife. The **Mound of the Celtic Cross** is a memorial to the monks and hermits who made their homes on Orkney's islands. The island was bought by a monastic order in

1999. The monks offer free boat rides to the mound and around Papa Stronsay by arrangement and subject to weather (☎ 1857-616 389).

■ Wildlife Watching

 Grey seals come ashore to breed in the autumn and can be seen in large numbers on **Linga Holm** and the **Holm of Huip**. **Common seals** can be seen on Papa Stronsay, Linga Holm, in the Bay of Holland and the north of Mill Bay. The **Torness Camping Barn** (☎ 1857-616 314) in the south of the island has a hide that is also worth visiting if you want to view seals.

Eday

Known as the "Isthmus Isle" on account of it being pinched in its middle between the bays of Doomy and London, Eday (pronounced "aye-dee") differs from the rest of Orkney's Northern Isles in being cloaked by peat moorland. Eday's red sandstone is displayed magnificently at the cliffs of Red Head. The quality of this stone has long been recognized and much of the stone for Kirkwall's St Magnus Cathedral was quarried at Fersness on Eday.

The first farming settlers arrived in Eday some 5,000 years ago and their chambered tombs are the most notable archaeological monuments on the island. Islanders still carry out traditional fishing and shell fishing. Peat was once exported as far as Edinburgh and remains the island's principal fuel, cut in early summer using the traditional "tuskar."

Loganair (☎ 1856-872 494/873 457, www.loganair.co.uk) flies two return trips to Eday from Kirkwall on Wednesdays, although the schedule is liable to change – call to check times.

Orkney Ferries (☎ 1856-872 044, www.orkneyferries.co.uk) operates daily car-ferry services between Kirkwall and Eday (also calling at the neighboring islands of Stronsay and Sanday). Routes and schedules vary through the week.

Mr A Stewart (Stackald, Eday KW17 2AA, ☎ 1857-622 206, alan.stewart@btclick.com) provides rental cars, taxi service and minibus tours (see below).

You can rent bikes from **Mr Burkett** (☎ 1857-622 331).

■ Attractions & Sights

Cliffs of Red Head (northern tip of Eday). The magnificent red sandstone cliffs rise sheer above the strong tidal races of Calf Sound and offer sweeping views of the Northern Isles and Fair Isle. Nesting seabirds include guillemots, razorbills and puffins. These cliffs are very colorful with wildflowers in early summer.

Prehistoric site (west of Noup Hill in the north of Eday). Some finely preserved field boundaries sweep around a large unexcavated prehistoric house, which contains a saddle quern (saddle-shaped stone for grinding grain). Two prominent standing stones and the remains of a stalled (chambered) tomb can be seen on the hill above.

Stone of Setter (north of Mill Loch in the north of Eday) is one of the finest single prehistoric standing stones in Orkney. Though weathered, it still stands over 15 feet high.

The path from the road to the Stone of Setter continues north beyond the stone to a line of burial cairns. The roof of the **Braeside Chambered Tomb** has been removed and its center dug out, but the internal layout can still be made out. **Huntersquoy Chambered Tomb** has two chambers, one above the other, reached by separate passages (the only other example on Orkney is Taversöe Tuick on Rousay). **Vinquoy Hill Chambered Cairn** is a tomb consisting of a central chamber with four small compartments.

On the **Calf of Eday** (small island to the northeast of Eday) stand several important archaeological structures, such as Iron Age houses (including a large roundhouse with radial internal divisions), a long-stalled cairn with two internal chambers, two chambered tombs and a ruined 17th-century salt works. The Calf of Eday supports over 32 bird species, particularly around Grey Head, its northern point.

Carrick House (Bay of Carrick, in the northeast of Eday; open mid-June to mid-Sept, Sun, from 2pm; opening days vary, call to check; conducted tours £2). Standing on the shore of the bay, the house was built in the early 17th century by John Stewart, Earl of Carrick and younger brother of Patrick Stewart, Earl of Orkney ("Black Pattie"). John Gow the pirate was imprisoned here in 1725.

■ Tours

Eday Minibus Tours (☎ 1857-622 206, alan.stewart@btclick.com; tours early May through Aug, Mon, Wed & Fri). Two-hour minibus tours followed by bird-watching at Mill Loch and visits to the nearby archaeological sites before being taken back to the ferry terminal. Packed lunches are available.

■ Wildlife Watching

Grey and **common seals** can be seen all around Eday. Common seals are often visible at low tide along the east side of **Calf Sound** (facing Calf of Eday in the northeast of the island).

Westray

Westray (meaning "West Island" and pronounced "west-ree") is one of Orkney's most prosperous isles. It is known for its farming – particularly beef cattle – and fishing fleet, and has a population of around 580.

Loganair (☎ 1856-872 494/873 457, www.loganair.co.uk) operates two flights a day (Mon-Sat) between Kirkwall, Westray and Papa Westray.

Orkney Ferries (☎ 1856-872 044, www.orkneyferries.co.uk) operates daily car-ferry services between Kirkwall and Westray. The ferry docks at Rapness in the south; from here a bus takes passengers to Gill Pier to meet the ferry for Papa Westray.

Rental cars are available from **D. Groat** (Sand o'Gill, ☎ 1857-677 374).

M & J Harcus (Pierowall, ☎ 1857-677 450) provides bus rental and runs bus tours.

T Logie (☎ 1857-677 218) sells gas and runs a taxi service (closed Sun).

You can rent bikes from **May Bain** (Twiness, Rapness, Westray, ☎ 1857-677 319) and **D. Groat** (Sand o'Gill, ☎ 1857-677 374).

Tom Rendall, the Harbourmaster (Gill Pier, Pierowall, Westray, ☎ 1857-677 216), provides boat trips to Papa Westray, daily and as required.

■ Attractions & Sights

 The Gentlemen's Cave (northwest coast of Westray – ask an islander to show you). The cave provided refuge for Orkney lairds who supported the Jacobites in 1745-46, and is said to be linked by an underground passage to Noltland Castle.

Westray Heritage Centre (next to Pierowall Hotel, Westray, ☎ 1857-677 414; open mid-May to mid-Sept, Tues-Sat, 10am-noon & 2pm-5pm; also Sun-Mon, 11:30am-5pm; adult/concession/child £2/£1.50/£0.50). Housed in the town's 19th-century school are permanent displays of Westray's history, flora and fauna, plus temporary exhibitions on local topics. In addition, there are local crafts and a coffee shop.

Noltland Castle (HS; one mile west of Pierowall village, Westray, ☎ 1856-841 815; open mid-June through Sept, 9:30am-6:30pm). A fine, ruined three-stepped or Z-plan tower house. The structure, dating from 1560-73 but never completed, provides complete all-round visibility against attack and is notable for the large number of gun loops and its impressive staircase.

St Mary's Medieval Parish Church (HS; Pierowall village, Westray, ☎ 1856-841 815). Ruined medieval church with some finely lettered tomb-stones. Most of the structure dates from the 17th century, although the south wall is a remnant of the original 13th-century building.

Cross Kirk Medieval Parish Church & Norse Settlement (HS; Tuquoy, three miles south of Pierowall, Westray, ☎ 1856-841 815). Small but elegant 12th-century church comprising a nave and chancel. The church is one of the best constructed in Orkney; it was built by a wealthy Norse chieftain, the remains of whose farm can be seen to the west where massive walls are being exposed in the shoreline. The church was used as the local parish church but is now roofless.

Castle o'Burrian & Stanger Head (southeast of Westray, near Rackwick Bay). The precipitous rock stack was an early Christian hermitage and is a great place to watch puffins. Take care on the cliff-top and don't try to climb the stack. You can view all of Orkney's seabirds at Stanger Head.

■ Adventures

West Westray is a long cliff-top walk high above the sea, passing dramatic landscapes and huge numbers of seabirds, and enjoying panoramic views south to Rousay. Start from the parking area at Noup Head, four miles west of Pierowall, and follow the cliff path south, taking care near the cliffs. For a shorter circular walk take the inland path just before two miles, which returns you to the road to Noup Head.

The Orkney Isles

All along this stretch of coast are natural arches, caves and geos (narrow inlets), many of which can be seen from the path. These have been carved by thousands of years of marine erosion. There is another parking area at Kirbist, at the southern end of the walk, about four miles from Pierowall (3-4 hours; moderate).

The **Westray sailing club** (☎ 1857-677 406; June-Aug, Tues & Thurs, 7pm) meets twice weekly for points racing (weather permitting) and holds a regatta on the last Saturday in July.

■ Wildlife Watching

 Birdwatchers should head directly to the Noup Head cliffs in the northwest of the island, where huge numbers of nesting seabirds can be seen between April and July. Only St Kilda is reckoned to host more breeding seabirds each year. **Peregrine falcons** also inhabit the cliffs.

Puffins are a special attraction in Westray. They arrive to nest in late April and usually leave at the end of July. Greatest numbers can be seen mid-afternoon and evening at Noup Head and the Castle o'Burrian.

Papa Westray

Measuring just four miles by a mile, Papa Westray's scenery ranges from impressive cliffs at its northern tip, through wide sandy bays to rolling agricultural land. It is known locally as "Papay," meaning "Island of the priests" and pronounced "pa-pee." The island was home to farmers long before the pyramids were built in Egypt and is the site of the oldest house in northwestern Europe – the Knap of Howar. In the Dark Ages, the island was an important place of pilgrimage; St Boniface Kirk is one of the earliest Christian sites in northern Scotland. Pictish brochs have been found at several sites, notably at Munkerhoose and St Tredwell's Chapel.

 Orkney Ferries (☎ 1856-872 044, www.orkneyferries.co.uk) operates car-ferry services between Kirkwall and Papa Westray (via Westray) Tues & Fri. There are additional sailings to Papa Westray on Sundays in summer – call to check schedule.

A **passenger ferry service** (☎ 1857-677 216) operates between Westray and Papa Westray with several crossings daily (by request Oct-Apr). The ferry is free if connecting directly with the Rapness ferry in southern Westray.

Car rental and local **taxis** are available from Sue Jeffrey (☎ 1857-644 202).

Loganair (☎ 1856-872 494/873 457, www.loganair.co.uk) operates two flights daily (Mon-Sat) between Kirkwall, Westray and Papa Westray.

> **DID YOU KNOW?** At less than two minutes (it's been done in one), the flight between Westray and Papa Westray is the world's shortest scheduled flight and covers a distance shorter than the length of the main runway at London's Heathrow Airport.

■ Attractions & Sights

St Bonifice Kirk (midway along the west coast of Papa Westray, near the airport). One of the earliest Christian sites in northern Scotland, the old kirk, with its 12th-century stonework, has recently been restored.

St Tredwell's Chapel (on the eastern shore of Loch of Saint Tredwell, south Papa Westray). On a small peninsula can be seen the traces of an Iron Age fortification and the walls of a medieval chapel and beehive cells. This was a place of pilgrimage until the 18th century.

Knap of Howar (HS; quarter-mile west of Holland Farm, Papa Westray, ☎ 1856-841 815; admission free). Possibly the oldest stone house still standing in northwest Europe, dating to before 3500 BC in the early Neolithic period. There are two houses, roughly rectangular, with stone cupboards and stalls. These houses are contemporary with Orkney's chambered tombs.

The Water Mill (northeast corner of Loch of Saint Tredwell, south Papa Westray). Standing on an isolated headland, this mill last ground oats a century ago and the remains of the undershot wheel and millstones can still be seen.

Holland Farm (in the heart of Papa Westray, near the shop, ☎ 1857-644 251). This was the seat of the Traill lairds of Papay for three centuries and the farm is one of the most extensive traditional steadings in Orkney. On display are a dovecote, corn-drying kiln, mill tramp powered by horses, museum created in a farm workers' bothy and an interesting array of island artifacts, including the parish handcuffs.

Holm of Papa Westray Chambered Cairn (HS; on the island of Holm of Papa Westray, ☎ 1856-841 815; admission free). One of the most impressive chambered cairns in Orkney, comprising a massive tomb with a long, narrow chamber divided into three, with 14 beehive cells opening into the walls. Jim Davidson operates boats to the Holm of Papa Westray (☎ 1857-644 259).

■ Wildlife Watching

Puffins, skuas, arctic terns and many other seabirds can be seen on **North Hill**, a wild and windswept nature reserve at the north of the island. The RSPB Warden (☎ 1857-644 240) provides guided tours in summer on Tues, Thurs & Sat afternoons.

Sanday

Sanday (meaning "Sand Island" and pronounced "san-dee") is an attractive island that easily lives up to its name, with stunning beaches lining the island's sweeping bays and inlets. At low tide, great areas of sand flats and rocks are exposed and provide rich feeding grounds for thousands of wintering wading birds and haul-out areas for seals. The extensive dune systems are rare outside the Hebrides.

Farmers attracted to the island's light, sandy soils first settled Sanday in 4000 BC. They erected great stone tombs, Quoyness being among the finest. The hundreds of prehistoric mounds at Tofts Ness form one of the most important funerary landscapes in Britain.

The Orkney Isles

Orkney Ferries (☎ 1856-872 044, www.orkneyferries.co.uk) operates daily car-ferry services between Kirkwall and Sanday (docking at Loth in the southwest), with certain sailings via Eday.

Loganair (☎ 1856-872 494/873 457, www.loganair.co.uk) operates twice-daily flights (Mon-Sat) between Kirkwall and Sanday.

You can **rent a car** in Kettletoft (☎ 1857-600 321) and from Marygarth Manse (☎/fax 1857-600 467), which also rents **bicycles**.

■ Attractions & Sights

Quoyness Chambered Cairn (HS; on the southern point of Els Ness, 2½ miles from Kettletoft village, Sanday, ☎ 1856-841 815; admission free). A Neolithic chambered tomb, dating from around 2900 BC, which once served a whole community. The cairn has triple retaining walls containing a passage, a main chamber and six subsidiary cells.

Tofts Ness Prehistoric Funerary Complex (north of North Loch at the northeastern point of Sanday). The site comprises 500 burial mounds, representing thousands of years of human life, and is one of the most important prehistoric sites in Britain.

Ortie Abandoned Village (south of Whitemill Bay in the north-central part of Sanday). The remains of a 19th-century village that once housed more than 60 people.

■ Tours

Sanday Package Tour (Motor Hirer, Marygarth, Sanday, ☎ 1857-600 467; early May-late Sep, Wed & Fri; adult/concession £30.50/£25.50 including ferry). Inclusive tours of Sanday from Kirkwall (for a minimum of four), departing Kirkwall at 10:10am and arriving back at 7:40pm. The tour incorporates many historic and scenic sights and includes a packed lunch.

■ Adventures

The short **Backaskaill Bay** walk visits one of Sanday's stunning sand beaches. It starts from Kettletoft, about seven miles northeast from the Loth ferry terminal. Follow the road through the village and continue north, turning left after just over a mile. Continue along the road as it turns back toward Backaskaill Bay, which is typical of many bays on Sanday. These bays make ideal spots for watching **birds** (especially waders) and basking **seals** on low tide rocks and skerries. Behind the beach the machair supports a number of maritime flowers and plants.

Look for the ruined **Cross Kirk** where the path rejoins the road. The church is 16th century, although it probably stands on the site of an earlier Viking settlement. The graveyard is surrounded by a high stone wall. Take care near the building.

Nearby is the ruin of a **corn mill**. Although only a low wall marks the outline of the structure, if you look from the bridge over the old mill stream you can still see where the mill wheel once turned. Continuing beyond the mill you reach the road back to Kettletoft (2-3 hours; easy).

■ Wildlife Watching

Despite its small size, Sanday supports about 5% of Britain's total seal population. The low-lying rocks of **Tres Ness**, **Els Ness** and **Kettletoft**, the three promontories extending south from the center of the island, are favorite spots to view seals, as is **Otterswick** in the north-center. The **Holms of Spurness** at the southwestern tip of the island is a favorite breeding site for grey seals, which pup in October.

■ Shopping

Orkney Angora (Sanday, Orkney KW17 2AZ, ☎/fax 1857-600 421, info@orkneyangora.co.uk, www.orkneyangora.co.uk). Established family mail-order business that produces thermal clothing from Angora rabbit wool.

North Ronaldsay

Although this island – the remotest of Orkney's Northern Isles – is farther north than the southern tip of Norway, the climate of North Ronaldsay (pronounced "ronald-see") is far less severe, warmed as it is by the Gulf Stream. Being so remote, it differs from many of Orkney's other islands: old traditions survive, Orcadian surnames predominate, and the ancient custom of communal sheep-grazing on the seashore is still pursued.

SEAWEED-EATING SHEEP

North Ronaldsay's isolation and scarcity of natural resources taught its inhabitants the value of its abundant seaweed. The island's sheep live on a narrow strip of beach outside a 13-mile stone dyke surrounding the island. This prevents the sheep from grazing the grassland and forces them to live on this seaweed, which gives their meat a unique flavor. The sheep are brought inside the wall only at lambing and are herded into stone "punds" for clipping and dipping by the collective efforts of the island's sheep farmers – possibly the last example of communal farming in Orkney.

Loganair (☎ 1856-872 494/873 457, www.loganair.co.uk) operates two flights daily (Mon-Sat, three on Wed) between Kirkwall and North Ronaldsay and one flight on Sundays in summer. The schedule is subject to change – call to confirm times.

Orkney Ferries (☎ 1856-872 044, www.orkneyferries.co.uk) operates car-ferry sailings from Kirkwall to North Ronaldsay each Friday, May-Sept, with fortnightly Sunday sailings May-Aug.

Garso No 1 (☎ 1857-633 244) provides an island taxi service, rents cars and minibuses and operates tours.

■ Attractions & Sights

Broch of Burrian (Stromness Point, at the southern tip). The broch (tower) lies at the heart of an extensive Iron Age settlement that stood on the shore at Stromness Point. On the landward side of the broch are the buried remains of a village, beyond which are two deep fortification ditches. The settlement was

The Orkney Isles

occupied into the Pictish period (to 800 AD), evidenced by the discovery of distinctively Christian relics. Among these are the "Burrian Cross," found inscribed on a flat piece of stone, which has been adopted as a motif in modern Orcadian jewelry.

 Standing Stone (quarter of a mile northeast of Gretchen Loch in the southwest of North Ronaldsay). This lone standing stone rising over 13 feet high is unlike most in Orkney in that it has a hole through its upper part, leading some to believe it was an out-marker for a stone circle that stood on Tor Ness in the north of the island.

The Old Lighthouse (Dennis Head at the northeastern point). The beacon was first lit in 1789 and was necessitated by the high number of shipwrecks – as many as 16 between 1773-88. However, the lighthouse proved unsatisfactory and the light was moved in 1806 to Start Point in Sanday.

 The New Lighthouse (to the north of the Old Lighthouse at Dennis Head) was lit in 1854 and, measuring 109 feet, is the tallest land-based lighthouse in Britain. Tours of the New Lighthouse are available (☎ 1857-633 257; open May-Sept, Sun, noon-5:30pm).

Where To Stay & Eat

See *Accommodation* and *Dining* price charts on pages 465 and 466.

West & North Mainland

 Standing Stones Hotel (Stenness, Orkney KW16 3JX, ☎ 1856-850 449, fax 1856-851 262, www.standingstoneshotel.com; B&B ££). A pleasant hotel with comfortable rooms and a restaurant looking across Stenness Loch toward the Stenness Standing Stones and Ring of Brodgar.

Mill of Eyrland (Stenness, Orkney KW16 3HA, ☎ 1856-850 136, fax 1856-851 633, kenandmorag@millofeyrland.demon.co.uk, www.millofeyrland.com; B&B ££, dinner ££-£££). Delightful B&B accommodation in a converted mill with visible workings. There is a pretty garden with a mill stream; evening meals are available.

East & South Mainland

Quoyburray Inn (Tankerness, Orkney, ☎ 1856-861 255, info@quoyburray.co.uk; £-££). Good bar food and à la carte evening meals in the Kiln Bar and beamed Rafters Restaurant.

Sands Hotel (Burray, Orkney KW17 2SS, ☎ 1856-731 298, info@thesandshotel.co.uk, www.thesandshotel.co.uk; B&B £££, dinner ££). Modernized hotel set in a 19th-century herring station on the harbor front overlooking Scapa Flow. The bedrooms are bright and all have sea views. The excellent restaurant offers a full à la carte menu with fine local produce, including fish bought directly from the fishing boats opposite.

Vestlaybanks (Burray, Orkney KW17 2SX, ☎ 1856-731 305, fax 1856-731 400, vestlaybanks@btinternet.com, www.vestlaybanks.co.uk; B&B ££, dinner ££). Spacious B&B accommodation in a house overlooking Scapa Flow and surrounded by the sea on three sides. Evening meals are available and feature local produce and seasonal organic vegetables.

Roeberry House (St Margaret's Hope, South Ronaldsay, Orkney KW17 2TW, ☎ 1856-831 228, fax 1856-831 838, susan.trueman@btopenworld.com; B&B ££). Referred to locally as Roeberry "Castle," this finely decorated country mansion dates from 1861 and is one of Orkney's grandest houses. Roeberry stands in grounds a short distance outside St Margaret's Hope and enjoys excellent sea views. Stay on a Wednesday or Sunday and you can enjoy afternoon tea and home-baked cakes in the seaview conservatory.

Creel Restaurant & Rooms (Front Road, St Margaret's Hope, South Ronaldsay, Orkney KW17 2SL, ☎ 1856-831 311, alan@thecreel.freeserve-.co.uk, www.thecreel.co.uk; B&B ££, lunch £, dinner £££). Seafront accommodation in one of three individually furnished bedrooms, with a restaurant that serves fresh local produce.

Murray Arms Hotel (Back Road, St Margaret's Hope, South Ronaldsay, Orkney KW17 2SP, ☎ 1856-831 205, info@murrayarmshotel.com, www.murrayarmshotel.com; B&B ££, dinner ££). Small, traditional hotel in the heart of St Margaret's Hope with a public bar and decent food.

Hoy

Stromabank Hotel (Longhope, Hoy, Orkney KW16 3PA, ☎ 1856-701 494, mail@stromabank.co.uk, www.stromabank.co.uk; B&B ££, lunch & dinner £). Basic but comfortable accommodation with a pleasant dining room (open to the public daily except Thursdays).

Stoneyquoy Farm (Lyness, Hoy, Orkney KW16 3NY, ☎ 1856-791 234, visithoy@talk21.com, www.visithoy.com; B&B £, dinner ££). Comfortable B&B on a 200-acre working farm. The breakfasts are good and evening meals are also available.

St John's Manse (Lyness, Hoy, ☎ 1856-791 240, fax 1856-791 027; B&B £). Comfortable B&B in a converted manse with sea views and a secluded garden.

Hoy Inn (south of Moaness Pier in north Hoy, ☎ 1856-791 313; £) opens seasonally, on an irregular basis depending on staff availability, serving lunches, evening meals and bar suppers. Call ahead.

Scapa Flow Visitor Centre & Museum Café (Lyness, Hoy, ☎ 1856-791 300; open April-Sept; £). Lunches, snacks, drinks, soup and sandwiches to order.

Shapinsay

Balfour Castle (Shapinsay, Orkney KW17 2DY, ☎ 1856-711 282, fax 1856-711 283, balfourcastle@btinternet.com, www.balfourcastle.co.uk; open Mar-Dec; B&B ££££, dinner £££). Beautiful, spacious accommodation in an elegantly furnished Victorian baronial mansion set in 70 acres of wooded grounds. The original walled kitchen garden provides fruit and vegetables picked daily to enhance the dining experience.

Girnigoe (Shapinsay, Orkney KW17 2EB, ☎ 1856-711 256, jean@girnigoe.f9.co.uk; B&B £, dinner ££). Comfortable farmhouse B&B that serves good home baking at breakfast with evening meals also available.

Smithy Café & Craft Shop (Balfour Village, Shapinsay, ☎ 1856-711 722; open Mar-Dec; lunch £, dinner ££). Open daily for home baking, soups,

The Orkney Isles

toasted sandwiches and filled rolls, à la carte evening dining and a takeout service.

Rousay

Taversöe Hotel (Rousay, Orkney KW17 2PT, ☎ 1856-821 325, fax 1856-821 274, taversoehotel@aol.com; B&B ££). A bleak-looking inn with good sea views and decent home cooking.

Bellona (Rousay, Orkney KW17 2PU, ☎/fax 1856-821 234; B&B ££). B&B at the home of the Rousay Traveller History Tours, with a lounge and private sauna available.

Trumland Farm Hostel (Rousay, Orkney KW17 2PU, ☎ 1856-821 252, fax 1856-821 314, trumland@btopenworld.com; £). Two dormitories, a single room and campsite are available.

Pier Restaurant & Public House (☎ 1856-821 359; £-££). Bar snacks and lunches are served, as are evening meals on request. Bike rental and Internet access are also available.

Stronsay

Stronsay Hotel (Whitehall, Stronsay KW17 2AR, ☎/fax 1857-616 213, info@stronsayhotel.com; B&B ££, dinner ££). Refurbished small hotel with four bedrooms and evening meals specializing in seafood, with vegetarian and vegan menus also available.

Bird Reserve (Mill Bay, Stronsay, ☎ 1857-616 363; DB&B ££). The owners of the Bird Reserve offer B&B, full-board and camping accommodation.

Eday

Sui Generis (Redbanks, Eday, Orkney KW17 2AA, near the ferry terminal in the southeast of the island; ☎/fax 1857-622 219, enquiries@suigenerisfurniture.co.uk, www.suigenerisfurniture.co.uk; B&B ££, dinner £). Charming B&B accommodation in the beautifully designed house of the local crafters of fine furniture and other wood crafts.

Mrs Popplewell (Blett, Carrick Bay, Eday KW17 2AB, ☎ 1857-622 248; DB&B ££). B&B accommodation, packed lunches and evening meals.

Mrs Cockram (Skaill, Eday KW17 2AA, ☎ 1857-622 271; closed during lambing April-May; DB&B ££) B&B accommodation, packed lunches and evening meals, as well as information on local birds and wildlife.

Westray & Papa Westray

Cleaton House Hotel (Westray, Orkney KW17 2DB, ☎ 1857-677 508, fax 1857-677 442, cleaton@orkney.com, www.cleatonhouse.co.uk; B&B ££-£££, lunch £, dinner ££). Refurbished Victorian mansion occupying an isolated promontory looking toward Papa Westray. The interior retains many period features, the bedrooms are beautifully comfortable and the food is superb. You can meet locals in the bar and join the annual Midsummer's Night trek up Fitty Hill to toast the midnight sun.

Pierowall Hotel (Pierowall, Westray, Orkney KW17 2BZ, ☎ 1857-677 472, fax 1857-677 707, pierowall@orknet.co.uk, www.orknet.co.uk/pierowall; B&B ££). Family-run village hotel with comfortable rooms, which is renowned for its seafood, including some of the best fish and chips in Orkney (also available to take away) and freshly grown vegetables.

Dorothy Groat (Sand o'Gill, Westray, ☎ 1857-677 374; B&B £, dinner £) provides B&B accommodation, with evening meals available, and has cycles for rent.

Beltane House (Papa Westray, ☎ 1857-644 267, fax 1857-644 295; B&B ££, dinner ££, hostel accommodation £). Small family-run guest house and hostel that serves coffees, snacks and evening meals.

Daybreak (Papa Westray, ☎ 1857-644 275; DB&B ££). B&B and full-board accommodation are available in the island Post Office, which also offers crafts for sale.

Sanday

Orkney Retreat (Belsair Guest House, Kettletoft, Sanday, Orkney KW17 2BJ, ☎ 1857-600 206, joy.sanday@quista.net; B&B £-££, dinner £-££). Small retreat center offering relaxed accommodation in peaceful surroundings, tasty home cooking and healing appointments. Meals are available for non-residents by arrangement.

Kettletoft Hotel (Kettletoft, Sanday, Orkney KW17 2BJ, ☎/fax 1857-600 217, contact@kettletofthotel.co.uk, www.kettletofthotel.co.uk; B&B ££, dinner ££). A small family-run hotel situated by the harbor in Kettletoft with excellent views over the pier toward Backaskaill Bay. The home cooking uses local produce where possible, they serve real ales, and there is a fish and chips takeout service on Wednesday and Saturday evenings. The hotel also has bikes for rent.

North Ronaldsay

The Observatory Guest House (North Ronaldsay, Orkney KW17 2BE, ☎ 1857-633 200, fax 1857-633 207, alison@nrbo.prestel.co.uk, www.nrbo-.f2s.com; DB&B ££). Solar- and wind-powered accommodation, forming part of an international chain of stations recording bird migration. The licensed café and restaurant is open to non-residents.

Garso Guest House (North Ronaldsay, ☎/fax 1857-633 244; DB&B ££). B&B accommodation, lunches and evening meals are available at the remote north of the island.

Burrian Inn & Restaurant (near North Ronaldsay airport, ☎ 1857-633 221; full board – DB&B plus light lunch – £; lunch/dinner, £). Orkney's northernmost pub serves teas and snacks.

The Shetland Isles

As close to Norway as it is to Scotland, Shetland is remote, bleak and rugged – far more so than Orkney – and comprises about 100 windswept islands, of which only 15 are continuously inhabited. Its outstanding beauty remains unspoiled and blessed with peace and solitude.

DON'T MISS

Discover traditional Shetland lifestyles at the **Islesburgh Centre** demonstrations.

Walk the towering high cliffs at **Eshaness**.

Explore centuries of human settlement at **Jarlshof** and nearby **Old Scatness**.

Sail to **Mousa**, with its seal colonies and remarkably well preserved broch.

Enjoy traditional Shetland music at informal **Simmer 'n Sessions** held at pubs throughout the islands.

Watch the huge seabird colonies at **Hermaness**, from where you can see Muckle Flugga, Britain's northernmost outpost. For easier seabird viewing, head south to **Sumburgh Head**, where you can almost watch puffins from your car, or take a boat trip to Bressay.

Shop for distinctive **Fair Isle** knitwear.

Best Freebie: **Crofthouse Museum**.

The islands are bordered by jagged cliffs teeming with seabirds, white sand beaches and sea inlets, and are virtually treeless. You are never more than three miles from the sea. The human population is vastly outnumbered by over 330,000 sheep and massive seabird colonies, including some 20,000 gannets, 160,000 guillemots, 200,000 puffins and 600,000 fulmars.

People took a long time to reach Shetland. The first settlers had arrived in Scotland by 6500 BC and Orkney soon afterwards, but there is no evidence of people in Shetland before 3500 BC, probably arriving from Orkney. Neolithic settlers built oval stone-walled houses. There are many remnants from the Bronze Age and even more from the Iron Age. The extraordinarily well-preserved **Mousa Broch** and superb archaeological site at **Jarlshof** are the highlights of Shetland's prehistory.

Shetland's position at the heart of north European sea routes has for centuries contributed to the development of a rich and diverse economy and distinctive culture steeped in legends and myths. The greatest abiding influence on Shetland has been that of the Vikings, who arrived not to rape and pillage but to farm and settle. Indeed Shetland (and Orkney) only became part of Scotland in 1471, after King Christian of Denmark pledged the islands as a dowry on the marriage of his daughter to Scotland's James III. Shetlanders are immensely proud of their Viking ancestry and express this most vividly through annual fire festivals (the most famous being Lerwick's *Up Helly Aa*) that re-enact the traditional ceremonial burning of a Viking longship.

Shetland also lies at the heart of the North Sea oil fields, which feed Europe's largest oil refinery at Sullom Voe. This oil prosperity has bequeathed the islands modern amenities and a good infrastructure, most evident in the excellent local roads. Still, apart from Lerwick, Scalloway and, at a push, Brae, Shetland's towns are little more than loosely scattered hamlets.

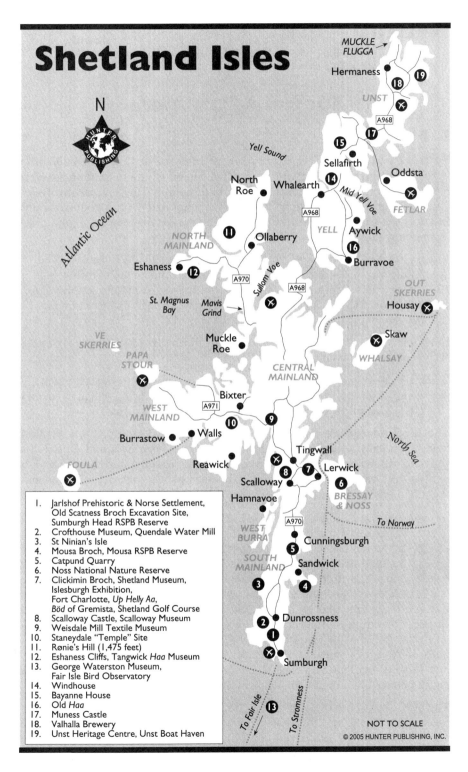

Shetland Isles

N

The Shetland Isles

MUCKLE FLUGGA

Hermaness

⑱ ⑲

UNST

✈ A968

⑰

Yell Sound

⑮

Sellafirth

Oddsta

North Roe   Whalearth   ⑭   Mid Yell Voe   ✈

FETLAR

A968

Atlantic Ocean

NORTH MAINLAND   ⑪   Ollaberry   YELL   Aywick

Eshaness ⑫   ⑯

Burravoe

St. Magnus Bay   Mavis Grind   A970   Sullom Voe   A968

OUT SKERRIES

Housay ✈

VE SKERRIES   Muckle Roe

Skaw ✈

PAPA STOUR ✈   WHALSAY

CENTRAL MAINLAND

Bixter   A971

WEST MAINLAND   ⑩   ⑨

North Sea

Burrastow   Walls

Reawick   Tingwall

FOULA ✈   ⑧ ⑦ Lerwick

✈   Scalloway   ⑥

Hamnavoe   BRESSAY & NOSS

To Norway

WEST BURRA   A970   Cunningsburgh

⑤   Sandwick

SOUTH MAINLAND   ③   ④

② Dunrossness

①

✈ Sumburgh

⑬

To Fair Isle   To Stromness

NOT TO SCALE

© 2005 HUNTER PUBLISHING, INC.

1. Jarlshof Prehistoric & Norse Settlement, Old Scatness Broch Excavation Site, Sumburgh Head RSPB Reserve
2. Crofthouse Museum, Quendale Water Mill
3. St Ninian's Isle
4. Mousa Broch, Mousa RSPB Reserve
5. Catpund Quarry
6. Noss National Nature Reserve
7. Clickimin Broch, Shetland Museum, Islesburgh Exhibition, Fort Charlotte, *Up Helly Aa*, *Böd* of Gremista, Shetland Golf Course
8. Scalloway Castle, Scalloway Museum
9. Weisdale Mill Textile Museum
10. Staneydale "Temple" Site
11. Rønie's Hill (1,475 feet)
12. Eshaness Cliffs, Tangwick *Haa* Museum
13. George Waterston Museum, Fair Isle Bird Observatory
14. Windhouse
15. Bayanne House
16. Old *Haa*
17. Muness Castle
18. Valhalla Brewery
19. Unst Heritage Centre, Unst Boat Haven

DID YOU KNOW? Shetland's midsummer sun stays above the horizon for almost 19 hours. From mid-May to mid-July, it doesn't really get dark, and the all-night twilight is called the "simmer dim."

Special Attractions

■ Events

 Up Helly Aa (last Tues in Jan; ☎ 1595-693 434, fax 1595-695 807). Annual traditional Viking fire festival, in tribute to Shetland's Norse heritage and celebrating the end of winter. The festival involves a flaming torch parade, burning a replica longship and drinking, dancing and feasting the night away in a dozen halls. Smaller fire festivals take place throughout Shetland from January to March.

Shetland Folk Festival (Apr-May; ☎ 1595-694 757, info@sffs.shetland.co.uk, www.sffs.shetland.co.uk). Traditional music festival first held in 1981 with workshops and concerts by local and guest artists. Concerts and dances are held throughout Shetland and there are also informal music sessions at the festival club in Lerwick.

Lerwick Music Week (June; Shetland Arts Trust, ☎ 1595-694 001). A week of live music in Lerwick.

Walking Festival (Sep; ☎ 1595-693 434, www.visitshetland.com). A week-long exploration of the islands through a fascinating range of history, wildlife, geology and archaeology walks, guided by local experts.

Shetland Accordian & Fiddle Festival (Oct; ☎ 1595-693 162, www.shetland-music.com). The highly acclaimed festival of concerts and dances has run since 1988 and swings to the sound of reels, jigs and marches. The highlight is the Grand Dance, where up to a dozen bands play virtually non-stop accordion and fiddle music.

■ Birdwatching

 Shetland is a birdwatcher's paradise. A million seabirds nest in spectacular colonies on the islands' rugged sea cliffs and feed in the rich offshore waters. The largest colonies at Hermaness in Unst and the island of Noss can be viewed by land or sea. The famous Bird Observatory on Fair Isle has recorded over 350 species, including many rare migrants. 90% of Britain's breeding population of the rare red-necked phalarope can be viewed on Fetlar. Sumburgh Head boasts the most accessible viewing of breeding puffins (known in Shetland as "tammy nories"), guillemots, razorbills, shags and kittiwakes. The island of Mousa is also popular for night trips to see storm petrels breeding in the walls of the Iron Age broch.

The best time to see most breeding birds is between late May and late July. Peak migrant season is from early May to early June and again from mid-September to early October. Even non-birdwatchers can't fail to marvel at the sight, sound and even smell of tens of thousands of birds nesting on towering cliffs above the crashing sea. It's worth carrying a pair of binoculars with you whether you think you're a birdwatcher or not.

LOW-FLYING SKUAS: If you plan to walk across Shetland's dramatic cliff-tops during the summer nesting season, you are likely to encounter swooping skuas, trying to chase you away from their nests. They rarely make contact, but holding a stick above your head will keep them from coming too close. Alternatively, simply enjoy the close encounters with nature!

■ Shetland Ponies

Charming and instantly recognizable by their low, stocky build and flowing mane and tail, Shetland ponies stand anywhere between 28-42 inches high. For over 12 centuries, these fascinating small horses have roamed the exposed hills and moors of Shetland. Ponies can be seen grazing by the road at many locations in Shetland, such as Dunrossness (south mainland), Tingwall (just north of Lerwick), Walls (west mainland) and the island of Unst.

■ Fishing

Shetland offers superb wild brown trout fishing, with over 300 well-stocked lochs. The **Shetland Anglers' Association** (www.troutfishing.shetland.co.uk) owns or rents most trout fishing rights, and you can buy a £20 permit that entitles you to almost unlimited fishing on mainland lochs. The brown trout season runs 15th March-6th October. Visit the Association Clubrooms in Burns Lane, Lerwick, for up-to-date information on how the lochs are fishing and what tactics to use.

Shetland also enjoys rich sea angling grounds offering good sport and large catches, including skate, shark, cod, halibut, haddock, mackerel, catfish and tusk. Boats and tackle can be rented locally.

INFORMATION SOURCES: Shetland Islands Tourism is at Market Cross, Lerwick, Shetland ZE1 0LU, ☎ 1595-693 434, fax 1595-695 807, info@visitshetland.com, www.visitshetland.com. It provides information and advice, books accommodation, sells maps, guides and timetables, arranges tours and changes currency.

Getting Here

■ By Air

Kept busy by the oil industry, Shetland's **Sumburgh Airport** is Scotland's fourth busiest. British Airways (☎ 870-850 9850, www.ba.com) operates regular services to Sumburgh from Kirkwall, Inverness, Aberdeen, Glasgow and Edinburgh, as well as London and several other British cities.

Loganair (☎ 1595-840 246, www.loganair.co.uk) operates regular scheduled inter-island services from **Tingwall** (Lerwick) Airport to the islands of Foula, Papa Stour, Out Skerries and Fair Isle. There is also a regular service to Fair Isle from Sumburgh Airport.

■ By Ferry

NorthLink Ferries (☎ 845-600 0449, www.northlinkferries.co.uk) operates two routes to Lerwick on its luxury car ferries.

- **Aberdeen-Lerwick**: There is one overnight service every day, arriving in Lerwick and Aberdeen at 7am the following morning (crossing time 12-14 hours). To enjoy the journey to the full, it's worth booking a cabin. Tucking into an early breakfast while the ferry sails past the cliffs of Sumburgh Head is an experience you won't forget in a hurry.

- **Orkney-Lerwick**: There are four Kirkwall to Lerwick sailings a week (Tues, Thurs, Sat & Sun) and three Lerwick to Kirkwall sailings a week (Mon, Wed & Fri).

Smyril Line (☎ 1595-690 845, www.smyril-line.com) operates a luxury cruise ferry between Norway, the Faroe Islands, Denmark, and Iceland, which calls into Lerwick on a regular basis

Shetland Islands Council (www.shetland.gov.uk) operates ferry services linking the larger islands with the Shetland mainland. **Car ferries** operate to the islands of Bressay, Whalsay, Yell, Unst, Fetlar and Skerries. **Passenger-only services** operate to Papa Stour, Foula and Fair Isle.

Getting Around

■ By Car

 Driving in Shetland can be a pleasure. The roads are wide, particularly if you've just arrived from Orkney's narrow lanes, well-maintained (a sign of Shetland's oil wealth) and refreshingly quiet.

You can rent cars in Lerwick from **Bolts Car Hire** (26 North Road, Lerwick, Shetland ZE1 0PE, ☎ 1595-693 636, fax 1595-694 646, info@boltscarhire-.co.uk, www.boltscarhire.co.uk); **Star Rent-A-Car** (22 Commercial Road, Lerwick, Shetland ZE1 0LX, ☎ 1595-692 075, fax 1595-693 964, info@star-car.co.uk, www.starcar.co.uk), which also has an office at Sumburgh Airport (☎ 1950-460 444); and **John Leask** (The Esplanade, Lerwick, Shetland ZE1 0LL, ☎ 1595-693 162, fax 1595-693 171, leasks@zetnet.co.uk, www.leasks-travel.co.uk).

■ Tours & Cruises

Elma Johnson's Island Trails (☎ 1950-422 408, info@islandtrails.co.uk) Elma, a true Shetlander, dresses in traditional costume as she guides you around fascinating Shetland sites – including the Crofthouse Museum and old Lerwick – and regales you with tales of romance and mystery (the crofthouse tour also includes traditional fiddle music and dancing).

See Shetland Tours (☎ 1595-690 777, sarah@seeshetland.co.uk, www.see-shetland.co.uk) Half-day and full-day tours – including the mainland, archaeology and Unst/Yell – with the first customer of the day choosing the itinerary. From £30 for a half-day sightseeing tour.

Bressaboats (Bressay, Shetland ZE2 9ER, ☎ 1595-693 434, ☎ 7831-217 042 mobile, dunter@seabirds-and-seals.com, www.seabirds-and-seals.com). Cruise with knowledgeable guides from Lerwick to the island of Bressay and the Noss Nature Reserve; or from Yell to Fetlar and Unst, including the Hermaness reserve and Muckle Flugga lighthouse. Underwater cameras add an extra dimension to these highly recommended excursions. Sailings from May to August.

For the 3½-hour **Bressay & Noss** cruise depart Victoria Pier, Lerwick, daily except Wednesday at 9:30am & 2pm; adult/child £30/£20. For the 7-hour **Unst & Fetlar** cruise depart Mid Yell Pier Wednesday at 10am; £70 per person.

Lerwick

Shetland's lively capital bustles around its busy harbor, where fishing boats and oil-industry vessels rub fenders with recreational yachts and cruisers. The town is a mixture of old and new that grew from humble beginnings as a scattered shoreline of fishing huts looking across to the island of Bressay.

The stone-flagged **Commercial Street** winds between tall stone buildings through the heart of the town with its pretty shops, cafés and restaurants. South of the harbor is Lodberries, with its historic boat-loading jetties and warehouses, a throwback to old Lerwick's days as a smuggling hotbed.

 INFORMATION SOURCES: The tourism office is at Market Cross, Lerwick, Shetland ZE1 0LU, ☎ 1595-693 434, fax 1595-695 807, info@visitshetland.com, www.visitshetland-.com; open year-round.

■ Attractions & Sights

Clickimin Broch (HS; a mile southwest of Lerwick on the A970; ☎ 1466-793 191). An Iron Age broch with associated secondary buildings, standing on a promontory on a small loch. The broch has a typical circular layout, with galleries and stairway within the wall thickness. Although it may originally have stood up to 30 feet (10 m) tall, the broch has lost most of its upper portion. The promontory was inhabited from 1000 BC to 500 AD. Over these 15 centuries the site was extensively built and rebuilt, with structures ranging from an oval Bronze Age farmhouse to an Iron Age ring fort, "blockhouse" and finally the broch and wheelhouse settlement. The site was abandoned before the Vikings arrived in the 9th century. To get here, follow the signs for

Clickimin Campsite and Leisure Centre and the broch stands at the far side of a lochan beside the parking area.

Shetland Museum (Lower Hillhead, Lerwick, Shetland ZE1 0EL, ☎ 1595-695 057, fax 1595-696 729, museum@sic.shetland.gov.uk, www.shetland-museum.org.uk; open Mon, Wed & Fri, 10am-7pm; Tues, Thurs & Sat, 10am-5pm). An excellent museum exploring 5,000 years of Shetland life. Artifacts include a unique collection of 5,000-year-old "Shetland knives" made from attractively patterned stones; replicas of St Ninian's Isle treasure, a collection of 28 silver objects found buried in a pre-Norse church site; and remains of 18 people from a 5,000-year-old burial site discovered in Sumburgh. More recent objects (from the 18th- to 20th-century) include displays on maritime heritage, crofting, fishing, whaling and the islands' famous Fair Isle knitwear. The museum also houses a contemporary art gallery and a huge photographic archive.

Islesburgh Exhibition (Islesburgh Community Centre, King Harald Street, Lerwick, Shetland ZE1 0EQ, ☎ 1595-692 114, fax 1595-696 470, enquiries@islesburgh.org.uk, www.islesburgh.org.uk; open mid-June to early Sept, Mon & Wed, 7pm-9:30pm; adult/concession £3/£2). These live demonstrations of local crafts and culture are an excellent and enjoyable introduction to Shetland life. Old images present a pictorial history of the islands. Watch demonstrations of hand spinning and knitting then browse through a large collection of Shetland knitwear. Listen to live Shetland music and watch traditional folk dances. You can even try out some of the easier steps for yourself. A craft shop showcases local offerings, although these are limited to small jewelry items and lots of puffin souvenirs. The knitting and music demonstrations are great but the highlight is the recreated crofthouse depicting life in the 1920s. Sitting down on an old chair and chatting to the charming volunteers as they knit cheerfully is the easiest and most pleasant way to learn about Shetland life through the ages.

Fort Charlotte (HS; between Market Street and Charlotte Street in central Lerwick, ☎ 1466-793 191) is a five-sided coastal artillery fort with cannons and bastions overlooking Lerwick harbor. The fort was built in 1665 to protect the Sound of Bressay during the second Dutch war. Named after King George III's queen, the fort was reconstructed in 1781-82 during the American War of Independence. In its heyday, the fort garrisoned 270 soldiers, but it didn't remain in service for long and may not have been completed before peace was declared. The 18th-century defenses and buildings all survive, with some superficial Victorian alterations.

***Up Helly Aa* Summer Exhibition** (The Galley Shed, St Sunniva Street, Lerwick; open mid-May to mid-Sept, Tues & Sat, 2pm-4pm; Tues & Fri, 7pm-9pm; adult/concession £3/£1). The exhibition presents the history of the celebrated Lerwick fire festival held each January and includes a replica galley, costumes, shields, paintings, photographs, memorabilia and a video.

Böd of Gremista (Gremista, a short distance north of the Lerwick ferry terminal, signposted from the A970, ☎ 1595-694 386/695 057, www.shetland-museum.org.uk; open June to mid-Sept, Wed-Sun, 10am-1pm &

2pm-5pm). A böd was a small store for boat and fishing equipment, sometimes also with fish drying and fish oil storage facilities. A few böds, like the one at Gremista, also had upstairs living accommodation for the fishing station manager. A familiar landmark on the road to Lerwick since the late 18th century, the Böd of Gremista (birthplace of Arthur Anderson, co-founder of P&O Ferries) has been restored to show how it once looked. The upstairs accommodation seems almost over-restored and might appear modern were it not for the antiquated furniture, in particular the box bed and spinning wheel. In contrast, the atmospheric downstairs salt store is packed with salt barrels, animal skin buoys and all manner of other equipment used for catching, drying and processing fish. The kitchen with its open fire, old wooden furniture and drying fish is equally evocative. Knowledgeable guides help you make the most of your visit.

■ Golf

 Shetland Golf Course (18-hole parkland, 5,776 yards; Dale, Shetland ZE2 9SB, three miles north of Lerwick, ☎/fax 1595-840 369, clubmanager@shetlandgolfclub.co.uk, www.shetlandgolfclub.co.uk; green fees £15). Undulating moorland course with wide fairways but some hard walking. A stream running the full length of the course provides a natural hazard.

■ Entertainment

Islesburgh Exhibition (Islesburgh Community Centre, King Harald Street, Lerwick, Shetland ZE1 0EQ, ☎ 1595-692 114, fax 1595-696 470, enquiries@islesburgh.org.uk, www.islesburgh.org.uk; open mid-June to early Sept, Mon & Wed, 7pm-9:30pm; adult/concession £3/£2). Excellent demonstrations of local crafts and culture, including live Shetland music and dancing. See page 568 for more information.

The Lounge (Mounthooly Street, Lerwick) is a lively bar, popular with locals and visitors, with live traditional music on Wednesday and Friday evenings.

■ Shopping

Jamieson & Smith Wool Brokers (90 North Road, Lerwick, Shetland ZE1 0PQ, ☎ 1595-693 579, fax 1595-695 009, shetland.wool.brokers@zetnet.co.uk, www.shetland-wool-brokers.zetnet.co.uk). offers the most extensive range of Shetland knitting yarns, spun directly from fleece, including some real bargains.

Jamieson's Knitwear (93-95 Commercial Street, Lerwick, ☎ 1595-693 114) has a spinning mill in Sandness in the west mainland (☎ 1595-870 285) and sells a good range of pure Shetland knitwear.

Loose Ends (96 Commercial Street, Lerwick, Shetland ZE1 0EX, ☎ 1595-694 004, fax 1595-694 253, info@loose-ends.shetland.co.uk; closed Wed) has a wide range of knitting and needlework products for the craft enthusiast.

Shetland Soap Company (111 Commercial Street, Lerwick, Shetland ZE1 0DL, ☎/fax 1595-690 096, manager@shetlandsoap.co.uk). Unique range of handmade soaps, creams and bath products produced locally by a community business.

SHETLAND & FAIR ISLE KNITWEAR

Shetland and Fair Isle knitwear is world-famous. Its exceptional quality derives from the very fine wool of the small Shetland sheep, which creates garments that are soft and warm. The Shetland tradition of making patterned woolen garments goes back many centuries, and would have been part of the daily household routine from very early times. Shetland knitting remains a cottage industry despite the knitters now producing half a million garments a year. In 1921, the then Prince of Wales (later King Edward VIII) put Shetland knitwear firmly on the fashion map when he wore a Shetland-knitted Fair Isle sweater while golfing at St Andrews.

Bressay & Noss

Just east of Lerwick is the island of Bressay, and beyond that the island of Noss, a National Nature Reserve. Bressay shields Lerwick from the full force of the sea, and the sheltered waters of Bressay Sound have provided a safe anchorage since Viking times and enabled Lerwick to develop as an important port.

Both islands have exhilarating coastal scenery and good walks. Gentle grassy slopes grazed by sheep and rabbits give way to dramatic sheer cliffs. Boat trips around the two islands take you right up to the cliffs and their spectacular seabird colonies. Grey seals are also commonplace.

A regular **car-ferry** service runs throughout the day to Bressay from the dock beneath Fort Charlotte in Lerwick. If you are continuing to Noss from here, follow the single-lane road for three miles across the island; the Scottish Natural Heritage warden (☎ 1595-693 345; open mid-May to mid-Aug, 10am-5pm, closed Mon & Thurs) will take you across to Noss in an inflatable boat.

■ Wildlife Watching

 Noss National Nature Reserve (☎ 1595-693 345; open mid-May to mid-Aug, 10am-5pm, closed Mon & Thurs; adult/concession £3/£1.50). The 876-acre island of Noss is one of the most famous seabird reserves in the UK. Sandstone cliffs soar to 592 feet (181 m), with a honeycomb of nesting ledges for huge numbers of birds, including 20,000 gannets, 10,000 fulmars, 45,000 guillemots, 5,000 kittiwakes and 4,000 puffins. Late May to mid-July is the best time to see breeding seabirds on Noss. The walk around the island takes about three hours and covers moderate terrain.

South Mainland

The narrow peninsula that runs 25 miles south from Lerwick boasts several valuable archaeological sites and many opportunities to view wildlife. A ridge of hills forms the spine of the south mainland, around which spread green fertile land, rocky coves and extensive sand dunes, including the tombolo (an offshore island connected to the mainland by a sandbar, created by the tides) that joins St Ninian's Isle to the mainland at Bigton.

■ Attractions & Sights

Crofthouse Museum (Dunrossness, four miles north of Sumburgh Airport, signposted from the A970, ☎ 1950-460 557/1595-695 057, www.shetland-museum.org.uk; open May-Sept, 10am-1pm & 2-5pm). A wonderfully evocative restored crofthouse and steading presented as it would have been occupied in the 1870s-80s. Constructed in typical "but-and-ben" style (the "but" was the combined kitchen, living and working area and the "ben" was the main sleeping room), the attached byre and barn were accessible without having to venture outside – very useful in the biting Shetland winter. Low ceilings, low doorways and tiny windows helped keep out the cold and wind but made for cramped living conditions. A peat fire provided heat and light, supplemented by small, smelly fish-oil lamps. The box beds and other wooden furniture were made of driftwood, Shetland being essentially treeless. A short distance away beside a brook is a diminutive water mill, where farmers ground grain. Knowledgeable guides help you really imagine what life must have been like in the crofthouse in the 19th century.

Mousa Broch (Mousa boat trips sail from Leebitton, Sandwick, Shetland, ☎/fax 1950-431 367, info@mousaboattrips.co.uk, www.mousaboattrips.co.uk; daily sailings mid-April to mid-Sept, to/from Mousa, 2pm/5pm; additional sailings Fri & Sun, 12:30pm/3pm; adult/child £8/£4). The broch at Mousa is the tallest and best-preserved example of such fortified dwellings, whose ancient walls still tower to a staggering 42 feet (13 m) high. These massive, dry-stone circular towers are unique to northern and western Scotland and date mainly from about 2,000 years ago. It is possible to enter inside Mousa Broch, view various galleries, storerooms and living chambers, and climb the staircase within the outer wall to the open parapet. You can't help but marvel at how Iron Age farmers built such a structure two millennia ago, and at how it has survived so well over the years.

Quendale Water Mill (Dunrossness, Shetland ZE2 9JD, ☎ 1950-460 969, info@quendalemill.shetland.co.uk, www.quendalemill.shetland.co.uk; open May-Sept, 10am-5pm; adult/concession/child £2/£1/£0.50). A restored overshot watermill displaying agricultural machinery, old photographs, video of the working mill and displays on butter making and rabbit catching. There is a café and the shop sells crafts, knitwear and souvenirs.

Warp and Weft Visitor Centre (Hoswick Visitor Centre, Sandwick, Shetland, ☎ 1950-431 406; open May-Sept). A curious exhibition of photographs, weaving looms and antique radio equipment. The excellent café serves great home baking and light meals and is a much more compelling reason to visit.

St Ninian's Isle, a small island joined to the mainland by a tombolo at Bigton, became famous in 1958 when a schoolboy discovered a hoard of silver bowls and ornaments at the island's tiny Celtic chapel. The treasure, believed to date from around 800, is kept in Edinburgh, although the Shetland Museum in Lerwick displays replicas. The island is now only inhabited by sheep but is a good spot for picnics, swimming and walking.

Sculptured rock surfaces at the **Catpund Quarry** beside the Catpund Burn (above the A970 between Sandwick and Cunningsburgh) reveal a remarkable Viking quarry where bowls, urns and other utensils were fashioned from the soft rock.

Jarlshof Prehistoric & Norse Settlement (HS; Sumburgh, next to the Sumburgh Hotel, 22 miles south of Lerwick on the A970, ☎ 1950-460 112; open April-Sept, 9:30am-6:30pm, closed 12:30-1:30pm; adult/concession/child £3.30/£2.50/£1). The well-preserved remains of an ancient settlement, whose ruins are most notable for spanning an extensive timeline, from Bronze and Iron Age houses, Iron Age broch, late Iron Age wheelhouse, Viking longhouse and medieval towerhouse.

The site was probably settled long before 2000 BC, the first settlers farming the sandy flats by the shore. Among the sand dunes, Bronze Age farmers built a cluster of a half-dozen oval stone houses with thick buttresses creating cells. Fragmentary ruins of several of these houses survive. Early-Iron-Age settlers built their circular houses on top of those of their Bronze Age predecessors. Middle-Iron-Age people built a great stone tower (broch), one of hundreds constructed around Scotland's northern coasts and islands between 200 BC and 200 AD. The smooth circular wall of stone slabs fitted together without mortar and rose perhaps 15-30 feet (5-10 m) high, demonstrating a mastery of dry-stone building. When the tower fell into disrepair it was plundered for the construction of four or five wheelhouses (one inside the broch) and only the base survives today. The wheelhouses are very well preserved (the buttresses, the "spokes" of the "wheels," are almost intact) and walking inside them is one of the highlights of the Jarlshof site. The Vikings arrived here about 800 and built a 68-foot (21-m) longhouse of traditional Norse design. Earl Patrick, perhaps the worst of the Scottish lairds who followed the end of Norse rule, built a house on the site in the late 16th century, with a great hall and other ranges of buildings. The complex was sacked in 1608 and was a ruin by the end of the 17th century.

Old Scatness Broch Excavation Site (Sumburgh, Shetland, off the A970, just south of Sumburgh Airport, ☎ 1595-694 688 Shetland Amenity Trust; open July, Mon-Thurs, 10am-5pm; Sat-Sun, 10:30am-5:30pm; adult/child £2.50/£1.50). Old Scatness is an ongoing excavation of a thriving Iron Age village with a broch at its heart. The multi-period settlement also includes an aisled roundhouse and wheelhouses, together with Pictish, Norse and post-medieval settlement enclosed within a ditch. The exciting discovery of the site was made by chance in 1975 during construction of a new airport road. Bradford University archaeologists began excavating in 1995. An informative video provides background on the excavation and guided tours let you watch from viewing platforms as the team continues to excavate. A reconstructed wheelhouse and roundhouse allow you to experience life within these structures and there are also living history demonstrations (such as ale brewing) and occasional archaeological experiments. The site is developing from an excavation site into an ongoing visitor attraction, with correspondingly higher entrance charges – call to check.

■ Wildlife Watching

Sumburgh Head RSPB Reserve (at the southern point of the Shetland mainland, ☎ 1950-460 800; open at all times). Sumburgh Head has the UK's most easily accessible puffin colony, best viewed in the afternoon/evening from May to mid-August. Park here, walk up to the lighthouse (Shetland's first), look over the wall and there they are, along with a supporting cast of guillemots, kittiwakes and shags. You don't even need binoculars. Walls and fences make this a much safer viewing spot than many cliff-tops. Seals often lie on the rocks below and Sumburgh Head is also a good spot for whale-watching, particularly in June and July when humpback, minke and killer whales, and the more common harbor porpoises, feed in the swirling tides around the head. The RSPB offers free guided tours.

The boat trip to **Mousa RSPB Reserve** (see page 571) allows plenty of time not just to examine the broch but also to walk around the island and view its **seabird** and **seal** colonies. Also available are evening trips to Mousa to see **storm petrels** and wildlife or local history cruises around Mousa Sound (☎ 1950-431 367).

■ Where To Stay

Lerwick, Bressay & Noss

Grand Hotel (149 Commercial Street, Lerwick, Shetland ZE1 0EX, ☎ 1595-692 826, fax 1595-694 048, www.kgqhotels.co.uk; B&B £££). An appropriately grand, traditional building whose turrets and gables impose themselves over Lerwick's skyline. Rooms are large and comfortable and its location in the heart of Lerwick couldn't be more convenient. There are bars, a restaurant and the nearest thing to a nightclub in Shetland.

Queen's Hotel (24 Commercial Street, Lerwick, Shetland ZE1 0AB, ☎ 1595-692 826, fax 1595-694 048, www.kgqhotels.co.uk; B&B £££). Picturesque and old-fashioned looking hotel with good facilities and a quiet location at the southern end of Lerwick harbor.

Glen Orchy House (20 Knab Road, Lerwick, Shetland ZE1 0AX, ☎/fax 1595-692 031, www.guesthouselerwick.com; B&B ££, dinner ££). Formerly a convent and rectory, the refurbished Glen

HOTEL PRICE CHART	
Per person, per night, based on double occupancy in high season. B&B rate includes breakfast; DB&B includes dinner and breakfast.	
£	Under £20
££	£21-£35
£££	£36-£50
££££	£51-£80
£££££	Over £80

Orchy enjoys a quiet location, just a few minutes' walk out of central Lerwick, opposite the (free) Knab golf course. Bedrooms are comfortable and well equipped and dinner is available by arrangement.

Fort Charlotte Guest House (1 Charlotte Street, Lerwick, Shetland ZE1 0JL, ☎ 1595-692 140, fortcharlotte@btopenworld.com; B&B ££). Modern accommodation situated in the heart of Lerwick.

Solheim Guest House (34 King Harald Street, Lerwick, Shetland ZE1 0EQ, ☎/fax 1595-695 275; B&B ££, dinner £-££). Friendly guest house well located for the town. Evening meals are available by arrangement.

Carradale Guest House (36 King Harald Street, Lerwick, Shetland ZE1 0EQ, ☎ 1595-692 251; B&B ££, dinner ££). Neighbor of the Solheim, this guest house also provides evening meals on request.

Maryfield Hotel (Bressay, Shetland ZE2 9EL, ☎ 1595-820 207, fax 1595-820 745, wooddh@lineone.net; B&B ££, dinner £££). Small, family-run hotel a short ferry ride from Lerwick serving gourmet seafood meals and platters served in the dining room and hearty bar meals.

South Mainland

Sumburgh Hotel (Sumburgh, Shetland ZE3 9JN, ☎ 1950-460 201, fax 1950-460 394, sumburgh.hotel@zetnet.co.uk, www.sumburgh-hotel-.zetnet.co.uk; B&B ££, dinner ££). This former home of the Laird of Sumburgh is beautifully situated on Shetland's southernmost peninsula, close to the towering cliffs of Sumburgh Head and the archaeological sites of Jarlshof and Old Scatness. The staff are friendly and the rooms comfortable. The **West Voe** restaurant serves fresh local produce with views over Jarlshof. The lively and well-stocked bar also serves good food and is a great place to meet locals.

Spiggie Hotel (Scousburgh, Shetland ZE2 9JE (near Sumburgh), ☎/fax 1950-460 40; B&B ££). Small family-run hotel a short distance north of Sumburgh. There is home cooking using local produce, a public bar and good views.

St Ninian's Isle Café (Brake, Bigton, Shetland ZE2 9JA, ☎ 1950-422 417; open May-Sept, closed Tues; £). Snacks, hot and cold drinks and Shetland crafts.

■ Where To Eat

See *Dining* price chart page 466.

Lerwick, Bressay & Noss

 Great Wall (Viking Bus Station, Commercial Road, Lerwick, Shetland, ☎ 1595-693 988; ££). Excellent Chinese and Thai cooking; eat in the attractively designed restaurant or take away.

Monty's Bistro (5 Mounthooly Street, Lerwick, Shetland ZE1 0BJ, ☎ 1595-696 555, fax 1595-696 955; lunch £, dinner ££). Intimate bistro serving well-prepared modern cuisine, including daily specials that showcase local produce; closed Sun-Mon.

Islesburgh House Cafeteria (King Harald Street, Lerwick, Shetland ZE1 0EQ, ☎ 1595-692 114, fax 1595-696 470, www.islesburgh.org.uk; £). Hot and cold meals, whole food and healthy options in a nicely decorated café; closed Sunday.

Havly (9 Charlotte Street, Lerwick, ☎ 1595-692 100, ravetvik@lineone-.net.uk; closed Sun; £). Norwegian café serving home baking, soup, pizzas and burgers.

There are a couple of good fish and chips shops in Lerwick, particularly **Ian's** on the Esplanade facing the harbor and **Fort Café & Takeaway** beneath Fort Charlotte.

Central & West Mainland

The busy fishing port of **Scalloway** was the capital of Shetland in the 17th century. A ruined castle dominates the town and the rugged isles of **Trondra** and **Burra** protect it from the full force of Atlantic gales. Scalloway was an important fishing port whose harbor became the headquarters for the Second World War "Shetland Bus" operations to rescue refugees from occupied Norway.

To the east of Mavis Grind lies **Sullom Voe**, Shetland's largest sea inlet, famous for its oil terminal and otters! The west mainland has barely been affected by the oil industry of the past few decades and remains unspoiled and steeped in the crofting tradition. A web of side-roads leads to dozens of beautiful quiet corners offering miles of hill and coastal walks, excellent wildlife watching and some great angling.

Beneath the village of Voe nestles the pretty hamlet of **Lower Voe**, at the head of Olna Firth with its calm water and mussel farming. There isn't much to do here, but the view and excellent bar-restaurant are more than enough reason to linger.

■ Attractions & Sights

Scalloway Castle (HS; Scalloway, Shetland, ☎ 1466-793 191; the key to the castle is available from Shetland Knitwear Shop & Sun, from Scalloway Hotel, Mon-Sat, 9:30am-5pm). The castle was built in 1600 by Patrick Stewart, Earl of Orkney and Lord of Shetland, as his principal Shetland residence. Scalloway's bristling silhouette of steep gables, tall chimneys, enriched dormers and conically roofed turrets perfectly characterizes the architectural elaboration of the time.

The castle comprises a four-story rectangular main block with an additional wing at one corner. The well-preserved ruins of the great hall on the first floor provide a good impression of life in the 17th-century castle. Earl Patrick was executed for treason in 1615, after which the castle changed hands a number of times before finally falling into disrepair.

Scalloway Museum (Main Street, Scalloway, ☎ 1595-880 642/880 666; open May-Sept, Mon, 9:30-11:30am & 2-4:30pm; Tues-Fri, 10am-noon & 2-4:30pm; Sat, 10am-12:30pm & 2-4:30pm; Sun by arrangement). This small museum houses a variety of local artifacts such as old furniture, including chairs and baby cots; cooking pots and utensils; sewing machines; costumes; typewriters; and musical instruments. There is a fascinating display on the covert exploits of the Norwegian resistance during the Second World War and Scalloway's role in these operations, known as the **Shetland Bus**. Other exhibits recall Scalloway's seafaring past with displays on fishing, fish processing and whaling. Knitted woolens are available for sale.

> **DID YOU KNOW?** The "Shetland Bus" was the name given to the hazardous boat trips made between Shetland and Norway to assist the Norwegian resistance movement during World War II. The "bus" operated during the German occupation of Norway, beginning in 1940 until the end of the war. The base was initially in Lunna before moving to Scalloway in 1942. The two bases launched more than 200 trips to Norway, landing agents and arms; carrying out sabotage, including blowing up bridges and enemy headquarters, and sinking ships; and returning with refugees. Pupils from Scalloway School have produced a web site on the Shetland Bus: www.shetland-heritage.co.uk/shetlandbus.

Weisdale Mill Textile Museum (Weisdale, Shetland ZE2 9LW, 14 miles north of Lerwick, ☎ 1595-830 419; open Tues-Sat, 10:30am-4:30pm; Sun, noon-4:30pm; adult/child £1/free). Housed in a restored water mill and run by the Shetland Guild of Spinners, Weavers & Dyers, this is the place to find out everything you wanted to know about knitting fibers in general and Shetland's most famous product in particular (Shetland's knitters produce about a half-million garments a year).

An introductory video provides the background, and a number of showcases display fine examples of Shetland knitting, including Fair Isle sweaters and intricate lacework. You can get an up-close look at the unusual four-needle knitting technique that allows garments to be created without seams. A helpful book of samples lets you feel the differences between the major knitting fibers. The mill setting is purely coincidental (the building was a grain mill rather than textile mill), although the excellent **café** makes great use of the view down the stream. Upstairs is the **Bonhoga Gallery**, which exhibits work by local and other artists.

Staneydale "Temple" (HS; three miles southwest of Bixter off the A971, ☎ 1466-793 191). The heel-shaped ruin of a Neolithic hall, thought to be almost 4,000 years old, and containing a large oval chamber. Surrounding the hall are the remains of field walls, several oval-shaped houses and cairns of the same period.

■ Adventures

Thordale Equestrian Centre (Mid Walls, Shetland ZE2 9PE, ☎ 1595-809 799, info@thordale.co.uk, www.thordale.co.uk; closed Monday). Accompanied hacks and treks to the beach and across open moorland, experiencing the unique gait of pint-sized Icelandic horses. Advance booking required.

■ Wildlife Watching

Sullom Voe (which translates to "place in the sun") is the site of Europe's largest oil terminal, although incredibly, its rocky shoreline is also one of the best places for spotting otters, if you don't mind the constant blare of the flare stack while you're waiting.

■ Where To Stay

See *Accommodation* and *Dining* price charts on pages 465 and 466.

Burrastow House (Walls, Shetland ZE2 9PD, ☎ 1595-809 307, fax 1595-809 213, burr.hs@zetnet.co.uk, www.users.zetnet.co.uk/burrastow-house; open April-Oct; B&B ££-£££, dinner £££). Secluded on a promontory on the remote west of Shetland, 18th-century Burrastow House offers elegant accommodation and the utmost tranquility with superb views over the island of Vaila. Charming hosts, peat fires, a cozy library, airy conservatory and paneled dining room make for a comfortable stay. The delicious evening meals highlight homegrown and home-reared produce. Otters and seals can occasionally be seen from the house and guests may fish in one of three private lochs.

Busta House Hotel (Busta, Brae, Shetland ZE2 9QN, ☎ 1806-522 506, fax 1806-522 588, reservations@bustahouse.com, www.bustahouse.com; B&B ££££, dinner ££-£££). A romantic 16th-century laird's home tinged by a tragic family history, Busta House offers charm, elegance and tranquility beside the peaceful shore of Busta Voe. Spacious public rooms, peat fires, wood beams, extensive lists of wines and malts, and a friendly ghost complete the country-house picture; the cozy restaurant serves fresh local produce.

Inn on the Hill (The Westings, Whiteness, Shetland ZE2 9LJ, ☎ 1595-840 242, fax 1595-840 500, www.westings.shetland.co.uk; B&B £££). Situated close to the summit of Wormadale Hill, the inn is surrounded by the moors of the Whiteness Valley and offers great sea views from all of its comfortable bedrooms. The bar serves cask-conditioned ales.

Westayre (Muckle Roe, By Brae, Shetland ZE2 9QW, ☎ 1806-522 368, westayre@ukonline.co.uk, www.westayre.shetland.co.uk; B&B ££, dinner ££). Peaceful B&B accommodation on a working croft close to sandy beaches and high cliffs. There is good home cooking and baking, and evening meals are available.

■ Where To Eat

See *Accommodation* and *Dining* price charts on pages 465 and 466.

 Da Haaf Restaurant (North Atlantic Fisheries College, Port Arthur, Scalloway, Shetland ZE1 0UN, ☎ 1595-880 747, fax 1595-772 001; open Mon-Fri; £-££). A wide choice of the freshest fish served in an excellent setting overlooking the harbor. Meat and vegetarian dishes are also available.

Weisdale Mill Café (Weisdale, Shetland ZE2 9LW, 14 miles north of Lerwick, ☎ 1595-830 400; closed Mon; £). Delightful café overlooking the former mill stream and serving excellent home baking, lunches and delectable light snacks.

Pierhead Restaurant & Bar (Lower Voe, Shetland ZE2 9PX, ☎/fax 1806-588 332; £-££). Wonderfully atmospheric bar-restaurant enjoying a picturesque location in the peaceful hamlet of Lower Voe. You'll rub shoulders with local fishermen while enjoying an excellent menu.

North Mainland

The north mainland, known as "Northmavine," is all but an island itself, joined to the rest of Shetland mainland by the narrow isthmus at Mavis Grind. Here, it's possible (just) to throw a stone from the shore of the North Sea into the Atlantic Ocean. The area to the north of Mavis Grind is gloriously wild and boasts some of the finest scenery in Shetland. Northmavine is capped by the dramatic cone of **Rønies Hill** (at 1,475 feet/450 m) Shetland's highest peak), at the summit of which is a well-preserved chambered cairn. From here on a clear day, you can see all of Shetland, from Fair Isle in the south to Muckle Flugga in the north. At the head of Rønies Voe are the remains of two Norwegian whaling stations. The cliffs around Eshaness provide great walking in spectacular scenery.

■ Attractions & Sights

Tangwick Haa Museum (Eshaness, Shetland ZE2 9RS, ☎ 1806-503 389; open May-Sept, Mon-Fri, 1-5pm, Sat-Sun, 11am-7pm). The Haa, built in the late 17th century as a laird's house, now houses a museum illustrating aspects of life in the north mainland through artifacts and photographs.

■ Adventures

 Eshaness Cliffs is a stunning cliff walk starting from the lighthouse at Eshaness (most lighthouses are circular to minimize the impact of strong waves but the one at Eshaness is square to avoid the expense of curved furniture!). Exposed to the full force of Atlantic storms, continual pounding by waves has carved dramatic cliff scenery at Eshaness, including some of the best stacks, arches and caves in Britain. In places the ancient lava flows have been cut away at different rates to form a series of steps in the cliffs. Over the centuries, severe storms have dislodged and thrown rocks high into the air; the scattered blocks can be seen all along the cliff-top.

Take the B9078 road to Eshaness. As you approach you can see **Dore Holm**, Shetland's most famous natural arch that resembles a drinking horse when viewed from the north. Park at the lighthouse and set off north (with the sea to your left). Watch where you walk, as the cliff is high and sheer, and cuts sharply inland at several spots. To emphasize the point, a short distance from the lighthouse is **Calders Geo**, a huge, rock-strewn inlet carved by the sea along a line of weakness in the cliffs. Two insignificant holes in the north side open into a vast cave running through the headland to a third, much larger entrance 330 feet (100 m) to the north.

An additional 20 minutes north, the **Holes of Scraada** is a partly collapsed cave forming a long gaping hole in the cliff-top. At the bottom of its sheer walls is the strange spectacle of the tide lapping beneath a massive cliff. Inland from the Holes of Scraada stands the **Broch of Houlland**, occupying a strong defensive position beside a bleak lochan. Two causeways (one now under water) link the broch to the adjacent island and the remains of later settlement can be seen built on the mound left by the fallen tower (1-2 hours; easy).

■ Where To Stay & Eat

See *Accommodation* and *Dining* price charts on pages 465 and 466.

 St Magnus Hotel (Hillswick, Shetland ZE2 9RW, ☎ 1806-503 372, fax 1806-503 373; B&B ££, dinner ££). Attractive Norwegian mansion providing well-equipped bedrooms, acclaimed restaurant, bistro-bar and sauna. The Sunday carvery is reasonably priced at £6.95.

Almara (Urafirth, Hillswick, Shetland ZE2 9RH, ☎/fax 1806-503 261, almara@zetnet.co.uk, www.almara.shetland.co.uk; B&B ££, dinner ££). B&B accommodation in a friendly family home near Hillswick; you may also opt to cook for yourself. Evening meals are available.

The Booth (Hillswick, Shetland ZE2 9RW, ☎ 1806-503 348, thebooth@freeuk.com; open May-Sept, limited availability at other times; £-££). One of many Hanseatic trading posts built by German merchants in the Middle Ages, The Booth is a wonderfully cozy and atmospheric cottage warmed by an open fire. It was a center of trade for over three centuries, and is now a delightful vegetarian café-restaurant that serves hot meals, snacks and delicious home baking, with occasional live music. There are no prices and you won't be given a bill after your meal. You are simply invited to leave a donation (in the wooden box by the door) to support the attached **Hillswick Wildlife Sanctuary**.

Yell

Yell is the second largest island in Shetland and has a coastline that is long and varied. It is the least fertile of the inhabited islands, with much of it blanketed with heather and peat moor. The island is roughly rectangular, almost rent in two in the middle by the voes of Whalefirth and Mid Yell.

High on a hill in the heart of the island stands the stark ruin of **Windhouse**, reputedly Shetland's most haunted house (skeletons were found walled up and beneath the floorboards). This site has been occupied for over 5,000 years, the oldest remains being the 2,000-year-old broch.

A daily **car-ferry service** (☎ 1957-722 259) operates between Toft, on north mainland, and Ulsta in the southwest of Yell. There are regular sailings throughout the day, but in summer it's advisable to book in advance as these can be busy.

John Leask & Son (☎ 1595-693 162, www.leaskstravel.co.uk) runs a summer bus service to Yell from the **Viking Bus Station** in Lerwick, departing Wednesdays, 8am.

■ Attractions & Sights

Bayanne House (Sellafirth, Yell, Shetland ZE2 9DG, ☎ 1957-744 219, www.bayanne.co.uk). A working croft with a craft workshop where you can watch knitting; an archaeological site; and a genealogy facility to help you trace your ancestry and research Shetland family history.

Old Haa (Burravoe, Yell, Shetland ZE2 9AY, ☎ 1957-722 339; open late April through Sept, Tues-Thurs & Sat, 10am-4pm; Sun, 2-5pm; donations welcome). Dating from 1672, the former laird's house is the oldest building in Yell. It now houses an exhibition of local flora, fauna, arts and social history, and has a craft shop and a tearoom serving excellent baked treats.

■ Wildlife Watching

 Yell is one of the best places in Europe to see otters; they are attracted by the rich food supplies in the offshore shallows and the low peaty coastline that is ideal for excavating their holts. Good otter viewing spots include **Ulsta**, where the ferry from the mainland docks; **Whalefirth** in the west center; and the northern shore of **Basta Voe** in the northeast. These spots are also good for viewing grey and common seals basking on rocks at low tide.

Unst

Unst is the island of northern superlatives: Britain's northernmost inhabited island; Britain's northernmost castle, etc. Compressed into an area of just 12 miles by five are towering cliffs, jagged sea stacks, sheltered inlets, sandy beaches, heather-clad hills, peat bogs and fertile farmland.

Walking as far north as you can in Britain takes you to a point overlooking **Muckle Flugga** rock, whose charming name is matched by its dramatic **Stevenson lighthouse**. Despite the height of the lighthouse, such can be the fury of the sea here that keepers would occasionally find fish in the courtyard after a gale. Britain ends beyond Muckle Flugga at the lonely **Out Stack**.

Baltasound harbor once challenged Lerwick as Shetland's main herring port in the late 19th- and early 20th-century boom years. The resident population swelled to 10,000 with the influx of gutters and coopers housed in timber huts to support some 600 boats.

A daily car-ferry service (☎ 1957-722 259/722 268) operates between Gutcher (on Yell) and Belmont (on Unst). There are several sailings a day but summer sailings can be very busy and reservations are strongly advised. Gutcher is about 40 minutes by car from Ulsta, where the ferry arrives from the mainland.

Loganair (☎ 1595-840 246, www.loganair.co.uk) operates flights between Sumburgh/Tingwall on the mainland and Unst on Mondays and Wednesdays to Fridays.

John Leask & Son (☎ 1595-693 162, www.leaskstravel.co.uk) runs a summer bus service to Unst, departing on Wednesdays at 8am from the Viking Bus Station in Lerwick.

■ Attractions & Sights

Muness Castle (HS; four miles northeast from the pier at Belmont, ☎ 1466-793 191). The northernmost castle in Britain, Muness was built in 1598 by Laurence Bruce, and designed by the same architect as Scalloway Castle. The castle fell into disuse after being sacked by Danish pirates after about 50 years. The house has circular towers at diagonally opposite corners and retains some fine architectural details.

Unst Heritage Centre (Haroldswick, Unst, Shetland ZE2 9ED, ☎ 1957-711 528; open May-Sept, 2-5pm; adult/child £2/free). Museum depicting the history of Unst through displays of crofting, fishing, geology and examples of spinning and fine lace knitting. There is also information on genealogy.

Unst Boat Haven (Haroldswick, Unst, Shetland, ☎ 1957-711 528; open May-Sept, 2-5pm; adult/child £2/free). Unique collection of traditional small fishing and sailing boats, fishing artifacts, and photos of all aspects of maritime heritage.

Valhalla Brewery (Baltasound, Unst, Shetland ZE2 9DX, ☎/fax 1957-711 658, sonnyandsylvia@valhallabrewery.co.uk, www.valhallabrewery.co.uk). Britain's northernmost brewery provides guided tours, free tastings and the chance to buy these excellent ales at their source.

■ Adventures

Hermaness Circuit is a superb walk over a typically magnificent Shetland coastline of cliffs, arches and offshore sea stacks. Start from the Scottish National Heritage Visitor Centre, reached by road from Haroldswick in the northwest. The walk initially heads south and west across the moor (where you are quite likely to be bombarded by skuas – wear a hat or carry a stick over your head!) and gives no indication of the high cliffs to come. The walk along the cliff-tops is enlivened by thousands of puffins and other seabirds; gannets can be seen fishing offshore or just sitting in great colonies.

Continuing as far north as you can walk in Britain takes you to a vantage point overlooking Muckle Flugga and its lonely lighthouse. Return south to your starting point along the western shore of Burra Firth (4 hours; easy).

■ Wildlife Watching

Hermaness Natural Nature Reserve (northwest corner of Unst, reached from Haroldswick, ☎ 1595-693 345; Visitor Centre open mid-April through Sept, daily, 9am-5pm). Hermaness, the northernmost headland in Britain, is home to one of Europe's most important seabird colonies, best viewed between May and August. In summer the west coast of the reserve is alive with thousands of puffins and guillemots, with kittiwakes, razorbills and shags also present in smaller numbers; 16,000 raucous pairs of gannets nest on the cliffs and stacks.

■ Shopping

Spindra Pottery (Uyeasound, Unst, Shetland, ☎ 1957-755 250/711 232). Unst pottery for sale in Britain's northernmost working pottery. Courses let you make your own clay souvenir.

Fetlar

Fetlar, dubbed "The Garden of Shetland," is a green, fertile island of rich farming pastures that once supported a population of 900, although the present population is only a tenth of that. It boasts 300 species of flowering plants and excellent birdlife. The coastline varies from low sand beaches to high rugged cliffs and sea stacks. Fetlar has more natural arches per mile of coastline than anywhere else in Shetland.

A daily **car-ferry service** (☎ 1957-722 259) operates to **Oddsta** on Fetlar from Gutcher (in Yell) and Belmont (in Unst). There are several sailings a day but summer sailings can be very busy and advance bookings are strongly advised. Gutcher is about 40 minutes by car from Ulsta on Yell, where the ferry arrives from the mainland. There is no public transportation and no gas or diesel on Fetlar.

■ Attractions & Sights

Fetlar Interpretive Centre (Beach of Houbie, Fetlar, Shetland ZE2 9DJ, ☎ 1957-733 206, info@fetlar.com, www.fetlar.com; open May-Sept, Tues-Sun, 12:30-5:30pm). Museum of local history and wildlife, story-telling recordings, 1930s film and interactive multimedia displays.

■ Wildlife Watching

The **red-necked phalarope**, one of Britain's rarest birds, can be seen at very close quarters in Fetlar. The island's 30-40 pairs represent approximately 90% of the entire UK population. During June and July these remarkably tame and brightly colored birds feed along the shores of the Loch of Funzie (pronounced "finnie"), which is part of the RSPB reserve, and can be viewed from the society's hide (rspb.scotland@rspb.org.uk, www.rspb.org.uk).

Where To Stay & Eat

See *Accommodation* and *Dining* price charts on pages 465 and 466.

Yell

 Pinewood Guest House (South Aywick, East Yell, Shetland ZE2 9AX, ☎ 1957-702 427; B&B £-££, dinner ££). Peaceful B&B accommodation with beautiful sea views overlooking Fetlar, Unst and the Skerries; traditional home cooking with evening meals available.

Mrs G Leask (Hillhead, Burravoe, Yell, Shetland ZE2 9BA, ☎ 1957-722 274, rita.leask@btopenworld.com; B&B £, dinner £). Comfortable B&B accommodation with an attractive garden, open peat fire and good home cooking (including evening meals).

Mrs M Tulloch (Post Office, Gutcher, Yell, Shetland ZE2 9DF, ☎ 1957-744 201, fax 1957-744 366; B&B £, dinner £). B&B accommodation in the local Post Office beside the Unst/Fetlar ferry, with good home cooking (including evening meals).

Hilltop Bar (Mid Yell, Shetland, ☎ 1957-702 333; £-££). Tea, coffee, bar lunches and suppers.

Unst

Baltasound Hotel (Baltasound, Unst, Shetland ZE2 9DS, ☎ 1957-711 334, fax 1957-711 358, balta.hotel@zetnet.co.uk, www.baltasound-hotel.shetland.co.uk; B&B ££, dinner ££). Britain's northernmost hotel has accommodation in either the main building or pine-log chalets. Lunch and evening menus feature fresh local produce, including local organic salmon. The bars stock a fine selection of beers, wines, spirits and malt whiskies as well as the locally brewed ales.

Buness Country House (Baltasound, Unst, Shetland ZE2 9DS, ☎ 1957-711 315, fax 1957-711 815, buness-house@zetnet.co.uk, www.users.zetnet.co.uk-/buness-house; B&B £££, dinner £££). Beautiful 16th-century family house set by the north shore, with four comfortable bedrooms overlooking the bay. The sea-facing conservatory is a great room in which to enjoy the locally sourced menus, and there is also a guest lounge and well-stocked library. Lunches and cream teas are available by arrangement.

Mrs SJ Firmin (Prestegaard, Uyeasound, Unst, Shetland, ☎ 1957-755 234, prestegaard@postmaster.co.uk; DB&B ££). B&B in a striking Victorian manse, five minutes' drive from the ferry. There is good home cooking, including reasonably priced evening meals.

Mrs J Ritch (Gerratoun, Haroldswick, Unst, Shetland, ☎ 1957-711 323; B&B £, dinner £). B&B accommodation in a modernized traditional crofthouse with evening meals available. This is the closest accommodation to Hermaness (within walking distance).

Fetlar

Mrs Lyn Boxall (Gord, Houbie, Fetlar, Shetland ZE2 9DJ, ☎ 1957-733 227, lynboxall@zetnet.co.uk; DB&B £££) provides comfortable accommodation and good home cooking.

Fair Isle

Lying midway between Orkney and Shetland, this tiny jewel is one of the most remote of Britain's inhabited islands. Fair Isle is famous for its world-class birdwatching (recording over 350 species) and the intricate, colorful knitwear that bears its name. Magnificent cliffs surround the island, which is dotted with traditional crofts and the remains of ancient civilization.

For centuries islanders traded with passing ships, bartering their hand-knitted garments for goods they couldn't produce, and Fair Isle knitwear was prized for its ability to beat the bitter cold of the Antarctic and Himalayas. Purists maintain that the island is the only source of "Fair Isle" knitwear, although nowadays Shetland-produced garments also carry the Fair Isle label.

■ Getting Here

By Ferry

The mailboat ferry **Good Shepherd IV** (☎ 1595-760 222) carries 12 passengers from Grutness, near Sumburgh, to Fair Isle on Tuesdays and alternate Thursdays and Saturdays. In summer, there is an additional fortnightly sailing from Lerwick. Re-confirm bookings before 9:30am on the intended day of travel (crossing time 2½ hours).

By Air

Loganair (☎ 1595-840 246, www.loganair.co.uk) flies to Fair Isle from **Tingwall** (near Lerwick) on Mondays, Wednesdays and Fridays, with an additional Saturday flight in summer. In the summer there is also a Saturday flight from **Sumburgh**.

■ Attractions & Sights

George Waterston Museum (Fair Isle, ☎ 1595-760 244). Housed in the former Fair Isle School, the museum displays the island's history from prehistoric times to the present and is dedicated to the former Scottish director of the RSPB, whose work had a major influence on the island. Exhibits include artifacts, photos, displays on crofting and fishing, knitwear, archaeology and natural history, and there is a reconstructed crofthouse kitchen.

■ Wildlife Watching

Fair Isle is an internationally important breeding site for seabirds and offers some of Europe's best puffin viewing. From April to August the cliffs swarm with thousands of fulmars, kittiwakes, razorbills, guillemots, black guillemots, gannets, shags and puffins, while skuas and terns nest on the moorland. Grey and common seals are frequently seen around the island, and porpoises are often sighted in summer.

■ Shopping

Fair Isle Crafts (fairislecrafts@fairisle.org.uk, www.fairisle.org.uk/fairisle-crafts). The island's knitting co-operative is the only producer of Fair Isle knitwear on Fair Isle and still uses hand-frame machines. It sells traditional knitwear world-wide, with garments costing from £20-£180.

■ Where To Stay & Eat

See *Accommodation* and *Dining* price charts on pages 465 and 466.

Fair Isle Bird Observatory (Fair Isle, Shetland ZE2 9JU, ☎/fax 1595-760 258, fairisle.birdobs@zetnet.co.uk, www.fairislebirdobs.co.uk; open late April through Oct; DB&B ££). Single, twin and dormitory rooms overlooking the scenic coastline. Accommodation is on a full-board basis with meals taken together with staff and other guests. Book early if you want to stay during the May and September migrations.

Index

Index